CRIMINAL [IN] JUSTICE

*This book is dedicated to all the students who have
taught me over the last 20 years.*

Sara Miller McCune founded SAGE Publishing in 1965 to support the dissemination of usable knowledge and educate a global community. SAGE publishes more than 1000 journals and over 800 new books each year, spanning a wide range of subject areas. Our growing selection of library products includes archives, data, case studies and video. SAGE remains majority owned by our founder and after her lifetime will become owned by a charitable trust that secures the company's continued independence.

Los Angeles | London | New Delhi | Singapore | Washington DC | Melbourne

CRIMINAL [IN]JUSTICE

A CRITICAL INTRODUCTION

AARON FICHTELBERG

University of Delaware

Los Angeles | London | New Delhi
Singapore | Washington DC | Melbourne

⑤SAGE

FOR INFORMATION:

SAGE Publications, Inc.
2455 Teller Road
Thousand Oaks, California 91320
E-mail: order@sagepub.com

SAGE Publications Ltd.
1 Oliver's Yard
55 City Road
London, EC1Y 1SP
United Kingdom

SAGE Publications India Pvt. Ltd.
B 1/I 1 Mohan Cooperative Industrial Area
Mathura Road, New Delhi 110 044
India

SAGE Publications Asia-Pacific Pte. Ltd.
18 Cross Street #10-10/11/12
China Square Central
Singapore 048423

Acquisitions Editor: Jessica Miller
Editorial Assistant: Sarah Manheim
Content Development Editor: Adeline Grout
Production Editor: Tracy Buyan
Copy Editor: Cate Huisman
Typesetter: Hurix Digital
Proofreader: Eleni Maria Georgiou
Indexer: Scott Smiley
Cover Designer: Gail Buschman
Marketing Manager: Jillian Ragusa

Library of Congress Cataloging-in-Publication Data

Names: Fichtelberg, Aaron, author.

Title: Criminal (in)justice : a critical introduction / Aaron Micah Fichtelberg, University of Delaware.

Description: Thousand Oaks, California : SAGE, [2020] | Includes bibliographical references and index.

Identifiers: LCCN 2019006426 | ISBN 9781544307930 (pbk.)

Subjects: LCSH: Criminal justice, Administration of—United States. | Discrimination in criminal justice administration—United States.

Classification: LCC HV9950 .F53 2020 | DDC 364.973—dc23
LC record available at https://lccn.loc.gov/2019006426

19 20 21 22 23 10 9 8 7 6 5 4 3 2 1

BRIEF CONTENTS

DETAILED CONTENTS

ABOUT THE AUTHOR

Aaron Fichtelberg was in school a long time. He received his BA from the University of California at San Diego, a master's degree from DePaul University, an LLM from Utrecht University in the Netherlands, and a PhD from Emory University. He is currently an associate professor at the Department of Sociology and Criminal Justice at the University of Delaware, where he has taught criminal law and criminal justice for 15 years. This is his fourth book. His earlier works are *Crime Without Borders: An Introduction to International Criminal Justice* (Pearson, 2007), *Law at the Vanishing Point* (Routledge, 2008), and *Hybrid Tribunals: A Comparative Examination* (Springer, 2015). He has also published in journals such as *The Journal of International Criminal Justice*, *Criminal Justice Ethics*, the *Journal of Science and Engineering Ethics*, and the *Journal of Theoretical and Philosophical Criminology*. His work generally combines the study of criminal justice with a critical perspective provided by the humanities.

He lives in Kennett Square, Pennsylvania, with his wife and two sons, and he is bad at writing about himself.

ACKNOWLEDGMENTS

There are so many people who have helped me write this book that it would be impossible to mention everybody here. Some of those who have been most helpful include everybody at SAGE, especially Jessica Miller, Adeline Grout, Cate Huisman, and Neda Dallal. My colleagues at the University of Delaware, especially Aaron Kupchik, Benjamin Fleury-Steiner, Karen Parker, Ronet Bachman, Susan Miller, Robin Andreasen, Ivan Sun, and Eric Rise have all been invaluable to me for their intellectual, personal, and professional support. Amy Schullery has also been a great source of personal and professional guidance during the writing of this book. The anonymous reviewers have been incredibly helpful; even when their comments were tough and critical, it was immensely valuable, and I am grateful for all their feedback (even the ones that stung to read). I am especially grateful to Connie Koski for going through earlier drafts with a fine-tooth comb.

Reviewers of the draft manuscript throughout the development of this book were as follows:

Avi Brisman, Eastern Kentucky University

Beverly Crank, Kennesaw State University

Jeffery P. Dennis, Minnesota State University, Mankato

Amy Baumann Grau, Shawnee State University

Janet A. Heuer, Bemidji State University

Milton C. Hill, Stephen F. Austin State University

Caron Jacobson, Governors State University

Connie M. Koski, Longwood University

Scott R. Maggard, Old Dominion University

Favian Martin, Arcadia University

Rosie Miller, Coahoma Community College

Karin Tusinski Miofsky, Lakeland University

Patricia Marek O'Neill, Hudson Valley Community College

Jennifer M. Ortiz, Indiana University Southeast

Rebecca Pfeffer, University of Houston—Downtown

Selena M. Respass, Miami Dade College

Melinda R. Roberts, University of Southern Indiana

Norman Rose, Kent State University

Ginger Silvera, Zayed University

Martha Sherman, The Pennsylvania State University

Carol L. S. Trent, Saint Francis University

Mercedes Valadez, California State University, Sacramento

Sheryl L. Van Horne, Eastern University

Monica Williams, Weber State University

Scott M. Walfield, East Carolina University

Dominic D. Yin, City College of San Francisco

Of course, none of this would matter to me if it weren't for my wonderful wife, Renée Bowers, and my two amazing children, Oliver and Theodore. I hope we leave you a better world.

This book has changed a great deal since I started writing it nearly a decade ago. It will change in the future. If you as a student or professor have any feedback you'd like to give about it, I'd happily receive it. I can be reached at *afichte@udel.edu*. Even your critical comments can help make future editions better.

I wanted to write a brief preface to explain a few things about this book that might help you better use it in your classes. In writing it, I was trying to achieve something both very specific and, I believe, unique. On one hand, I wanted to provide a critical take on criminal justice, one that didn't treat deeply troubling aspects of the American criminal justice system as though they were accidental to the overall functioning of the system. Protecting an unjust social order is an essential function of American criminal justice at every level, and I wanted this book to reflect that reality.

On the other hand, this book is intended as an introductory textbook and is meant to serve as a gateway to understanding a very complex set of interlocking institutions. Toward this end, a lot of this book discusses criminal justice in a more traditional fashion. While I wanted students to comprehend the role that racial profiling plays in policing and the historic role that the police played in maintaining social and economic inequalities, I also wanted them to understand more routine things, such as the difference between municipal police departments and sheriff's departments, or general aspects of the Uniform Crime Report. While it's important to see the way that the courtroom work group and plea bargains funnel poor people into guilty pleas, it's equally important to understand voir dire procedures or how the appellate system is structured. Even if students are completely closed off to the critical approach presented here, they can still learn a lot about how the system works, though undoubtedly it will be diminished without this critical edge.

I've been teaching a long time, and I've learned that imposing one's views on students is not an effective or even an ethical teaching strategy. It is not effective because many students, particularly those from privileged or conservative backgrounds, are deeply committed to the traditional values of criminal justice and are often very reluctant to abandon them. They believe that the police are almost always a force of law and order and that the criminal justice system generally does what's right when it comes to the "bad guys." Abandoning that worldview is uncomfortable and difficult for many students. Being a dogmatic or overbearing teacher doesn't help. Usually it only closes students' minds and puts them in a defensive crouch.

I have struck a conversational tone throughout this book because I believe that engaging with students is a much more persuasive way to get a point across. Equally important, these students are human beings and deserve to be respected as such. Engaging with them rather than imposing one's views on them embodies this. In my experience some of my best students are often those who are my ideological opposites. Once they understand that they will be treated with respect by their professor, I find that they open and are far more willing to consider other views in the long run. This book was written with this in mind, raising questions and issues for the student to think through rather than forcing a perspective on them. I have tried to use the boxed sections such as "What Would You Do?" to get students to think critically without forcing them to adopt any particular worldview.

Finally, I've worked with SAGE to find ways to keep down the cost of this book. One of the challenges that underprivileged students face is the high price of textbooks, and the publisher agreed with me to strip down some parts of the book to keep the prices low. It may not always be as flashy as other criminal justice books, but I hope this means that more students can afford it. An expensive book that many students can't buy doesn't do a lot of good.

I hope that this will be the first of many editions of this book, and I'm hoping that a second edition will be improved with feedback from instructors and students who have used it in the trenches. Please feel free to provide me with any feedback so that I can try to make it better in the future.

DIGITAL RESOURCES

⑤SAGE edge™

edge.sagepub.com/fichtelberg

SAGE edge for instructors supports your teaching by making it easy to integrate quality content and create a rich learning environment for students with

- A **password-protected website** for complete and protected access to all text-specific instructor resources.

- **Test banks** that provide a diverse range of ready-to-use options that save you time. You can also easily edit any question and/or insert your own personalized questions.

- **Editable, chapter-specific PowerPoint slides** that offer complete flexibility for creating a multimedia presentation for your course.

- **Lecture notes** that summarize key concepts by chapter to help you prepare for lectures and class discussions.

- **Carefully selected video and multimedia links** that embrace classroom-based exploration of key topics.

- **Sample course syllabi** for semester and quarter courses that provide suggested models for structuring your courses.

- **A course cartridge** for easy LMS integration.

SAGE edge for students enhances learning, it's easy to use, and it offers

- An **open-access website** that makes it easy for students to maximize their study time, anywhere, anytime.

- **eFlashcards** that strengthen understanding of key terms and concepts.

- **eQuizzes** that allow students to practice and assess how much they've learned and where they need to focus their attention.

- **Carefully selected video and multimedia links** that embrace classroom-based exploration of key topics.

GENERAL INTRODUCTION

There are a lot of reasons why students take an introductory criminal justice course. Some pick it because they're starting a major in criminal justice and figure it's the first step in their education. Others pick it because they're shopping for a major that they can use to get a secure and interesting career in the future and think that criminal justice might fit the bill. Some take it because they have some electives to fill and this one sounds more interesting than the others that are offered at their school (or perhaps, because the time when the course is scheduled allows them to sleep in or focus on things like sports, partying, or their "real classes"). Some take it because, at many colleges, criminal justice has a reputation as an "easy *A*," a course that a student can sail through without much effort. Still others just take it because they're interested in the subject. Students enroll in a criminal justice course for a host of reasons, many of which have nothing to do with the subject of the course itself, and any professor worth the title knows this when she walks into the class on the first day.

Why mention this at the beginning of this book? Because I hope to start with a somewhat different perspective than most criminal justice books, one that will address all kinds of students in different ways, and hopefully engage those students who aren't interested in the subject at the outset. For example, if you're considering starting a career as a criminal justice major, I want to show you some of the realities lying behind the myths about the field so that you can make an informed decision about your future. Many unscrupulous universities weave fantastical stories about working in the criminal justice field as detectives, forensic investigators, or criminal profilers, hoping to lure students into their department. (For example, even though there are almost no jobs in forensic science, biology departments have developed courses and majors on the subject to get "butts in seats" and the tuition money that accompanies them.) If you're just looking for an easy *A* or a chance to sleep in, I hope to make the subject interesting enough that at a minimum, you don't mind coming to class and reading this book. You just might find something useful and valuable on these pages.

If you're going to major in criminal justice, a good introductory course can be valuable for your future. If it is well structured, it should lay the foundations for what lies ahead in your studies—providing a rough outline of many of the subjects that you are going to study in future classes. In most criminal justice programs, each of the subjects discussed in this book will be the topic of at least one entire course that will further develop the information that is offered here. Law, courts, policing, and criminology are all basic elements of the criminal justice program in most universities, so this course should help lay the groundwork for each of these subjects. You'll know what some of your future classes are going to look like if I've provided a decent guide.

There may be other reasons to study criminal justice that aren't so obvious. American society is obsessed with crime. Not only is it a staple of prime-time drama (more on this later), but over the last half century it has been a big feature of American politics. Anybody running for office either locally or nationally must address crime and justice issues, and almost without exception they do so with a "get tough on crime" mentality. Prison and police, courts, and executions are commonplace subjects for political debate, and even issues that seem unconnected to crime, such as immigration, have been framed as crime problems through a fear of gangs and drugs. As the criminologist Jonathan Simon put it, over the last five decades, "Americans have built a new civil and political order structured around the problem of violent crime. In this new order, values like freedom and equality have been revised in ways that would have been shocking . . . in the late 1960s . . . all in the name of repressing seemingly endless waves of violent crime" (Simon, 2007). Crime is so central to our politics that every citizen should have a realistic understanding of crime and justice so that she may be an informed voter. Politicians and policymakers often count on the fact that most people are ignorant about the facts of crime and justice issues when they hit the campaign trail seeking votes.

The odds are pretty good that you will have an encounter with the criminal justice system sometime in your life if you haven't already. You may be victimized by a criminal and turn to the police for help. You may be a suspect who is arrested or interrogated by the police. The police may stop by your house when you're hosting a party to ask you to turn the noise down, or they may pull you over for speeding or running a red light. Regardless of whether you're a victim, a suspect, or just an innocent bystander, it is important that you know how the system works so that you can protect yourself and your interests. When an officer stops a driver, she will often ask the driver, "Do you know why I stopped you?" The driver may innocently respond with some explanation of her infraction ("Because I failed to signal when I changed lanes?"), but what may seem like innocent cooperation is in fact an admission of guilt that can be used in court later on. A simple question from an officer such as, "May I look around your car?" is a request to search your car (one that can be lawfully refused) and can be an easy way for police officers to get evidence against you. When a person is arrested and interrogated by the police, there is often a subtle game being played in which interrogators manipulate an unknowing suspect into saying or doing something that can get her into trouble. In short, the system sometimes exploits the ignorance of citizens, and so knowing your rights and understanding the mechanics of the criminal justice system can be crucial to getting through the system and maybe avoiding prison.

Most students have some idea about what criminal justice is, and what police officers, courts, and the other criminal justice professionals do. But these ideas are usually shaped by movies and television. These shows are entertainment, not reality, and they often play fast and loose with the facts of crime and criminal justice. Few officers engage in high-speed chases through crowded city streets like they do in movies and TV, and serial killers are extremely rare. Gun play almost never happens. As one New York City prosecutor put it, "[The film] *Dirty Harry* has more shootings in a movie's half-hour than the New York City Police Department cop with the most shootings in his entire career" (Sexton, 1998). No attorney would dare pound his fist on the desk and shout at a judge, "This whole courtroom is out of order!" as Al Pacino famously did in . . . *And Justice for All*. Most trials are bureaucratic and at times boring affairs, and most police officers spend most of their time on far more mundane activities than catching bad guys. Criminal justice is fascinating for a lot of reasons, but they're probably not the ones that you think. Rather than flashy crimes and daring detectives, American criminal justice is more about who we are as a society, who is going to have power over us, and how we are going to be controlled by those in power.

WHY A "CRITICAL" INTRODUCTION?

This text is described as a *critical* introduction to criminal justice. What does this mean? How is it different from a normal introductory textbook? Simply put, most criminal justice textbooks provide a more or less straightforward analysis of how the criminal justice system operates. According to this approach, criminals are people who violate the law (thieves, drug dealers, and murderers), and the purpose of the criminal justice system is to apprehend these people and either put them on the path to a law-abiding life or punish them for their misdeeds. Different books may criticize parts of this picture and try to give it nuance, usually with a small set of discussion questions at the end of a reading that allow students to critically evaluate the topics discussed in the chapter. For the most part, almost all introductory textbooks stick to this conventional approach. Crime, justice, law, and order are taken for granted as the best categories for understanding the workings of the criminal justice system.

While some textbooks may challenge parts of the conventional approach to criminal justice in places, popular media—film, television, books, et cetera—rarely if ever challenge it. Almost all crooks are seen as *bad guys*—enemies of decency and threats to the innocent—and the police are almost always *good guys*—defenders of the innocent and protector of the broader social order. Because as we all know, law and order are inherently good things. The police investigate criminals, apprehend them, and throw them in jail, or when absolutely necessary, kill them. On the whole, the system is aimed at stopping injustice and protecting order against those who threaten it.

Even when movies or television present a more complicated view regarding good guys and bad guys (sometimes, the fugitive is accused of a crime she didn't commit or is being pursued by corrupt officers), almost all crime-based television shows and movies still neatly break the world into tidy moral categories. When the corrupt officers are exposed at the end of the movie or the fugitive is redeemed, the world is returned to the way that it's supposed to be—police are good; crooks are bad. When the story is over, our moral view of the universe is largely unshaken. Some movies and television programs (such as *The Wire*, for example) provide a more complicated view about good guys and bad guys, but these are usually the ones that almost nobody goes to see: We want our crime films to come with neat moral messages, and filmmakers know this. We want to know who the good guys are—the people we should root for, and we want to know who the bad guys are—the people we should despise. Not only do we want this, we also want to know ahead of time that the bad guys will be arrested or, more likely, dead, before we reach the bottom of our overpriced popcorn. On our screens, we expect our criminal justice to be heavy on the Justice.

But what if the world doesn't neatly break down into good guys and bad guys anywhere? What if criminal justice is only partially about justice but is also about a great deal of other things? It is undoubtedly true that most criminal justice professionals (police, judges, lawyers, etc.) see themselves as catching bad guys and sincerely believe that they are helping others. In many cases, they are. They do tremendous good in protecting people from crooks and other predators who want to harm them.

But these criminal justice professionals are not fighting crime purely out of the goodness of their hearts—they do it for a paycheck. They may want to help society and fight crime, but if crime were too low, paradoxically, they would no longer need to exist. Thus, while the police fight crime, they have a financial interest in crime existing and therefore have an economic interest in society needing them around. There's nothing shocking about this: Police officers are people too, and as such they live by the same laws of supply and demand as everybody else does. If crime disappeared, so would their jobs.

Politicians are the same way. They usually want to make their communities better places in which to live, but to do this, they need to keep their jobs as lawmakers, which in turn means getting votes in elections. The public often thinks that the criminal justice system is too soft on crime, independent of whether it in fact is, and the public tends to fear criminals even where there is little crime to be afraid of. One of the things we will see is that the public's fear of crime is often high when crime rates are relatively low. Politicians sometimes fan these fears when they need to get votes. It's usually far better strategy for a politician to be too tough on criminals than risk being too kind to them. During the 1988 presidential election campaign, for example, a furlough program in Massachusetts overseen by then-governor Michael Dukakis allowed an offender out of prison named Willie Horton who later raped a woman. Many observers believe that relentless political commercials on the subject cost the governor the presidency—a lesson that all politicians remember. Thus, while the system is about fighting crime, in some ways it is also about politicians trying to maintain their popularity and keep their jobs.

Our society is full of economic and social inequalities. Wealthy people have more influence than poor people. Whites are in the majority and are usually at the top of the social order. Men have a great deal of social and economic influence when compared to women and others. As a result, the wealthy, the white, and the male have an outsized influence on the laws and policies pushed by the government. Criminal laws and policing practices reflect these inequalities in a host of ways that we will examine here. They also subtly influence the way that we think about crime, law, government, and even each other, often creating fear, prejudice, and distrust between different groups. Politicians and criminal justice professionals work in a society where everybody isn't equal, but the law is meant to apply equally to everyone. It is only natural that criminal justice in America would reflect these deeper inequalities. This is the line taken in this book.

This approach is part of the tradition known as *critical theory*, which has a long history in social sciences, psychology, economics, and philosophy. To be critical in the academic sense (and not, say, the guy who doesn't like a movie or your new haircut) is to look at a society as *fractured*. By this I mean that society is shot through with all kinds of injustices and inequalities, and these injustices shape how we live on a daily basis. Racial inequalities, gender inequalities, and economic inequalities run through our society, shape it on every level, and they do so in ways that are often invisible to us. The term that sociologists use to describe these problems is that they are *structural*: Problems that are rooted in the foundations of our society and our social, cultural, and political institutions are built upon them. Structural problems are nobody's fault: They are part of a social system that nobody chose but that we all participate in. Some people benefit from these structural inequalities, but many don't. Critical theorists believe that our society is deeply unjust, and that this injustice shapes our society on every level.

To really understand the criminal justice system from a critical perspective then, you need to understand the society that it is designed to protect. Crime in many ways reflects structural inequalities, and the criminal justice system can only do so much to stop it. Poverty and inequality create crime much more than do "greed" or "evil." To fight crime without addressing the deeper, structural problems in our society is to cure a symptom while ignoring the underlying disease. Protecting order in an unequal society is always going to be problematic. The analysis of criminal justice here will often examine the role that the law, the police, and other criminal justice actors play in protecting the deeper inequalities that shape American life in the first half of the 21st century. The criminal justice system is a tool for maintaining an unequal, unjust social order.

This doesn't mean that the criminal justice system is entirely bad. The police, the courts, and other aspects of criminal justice provide many important and valuable services. The police often protect people who live in fear of crime and help those who are in danger. We're better off with police forces and laws that protect the public. But they don't protect everyone in the same way or to the same degree. As we will see, there are vast differences in how the criminal justice system works and who it benefits, and these differences often reflect these deeper social inequalities.

A critical approach to criminal justice is certainly a far cry from the movies, prime-time TV, or adolescent fantasies about heroes and villains. It is not a straightforward idea and doesn't provide simple answers regarding how to improve the criminal justice system or how to reduce crime. But to have a sophisticated, college-level understanding of modern criminal justice and to understand why it is so important and so controversial in contemporary society, it is vital to "put away childish things" (1 Corinthians 13) and see the criminal justice system as it really is, in the full light of day. Even if that can sometimes make you uncomfortable.

THEMES OF THE BOOK

Throughout the text there will be several different themes that will recur. I want to bring them to your attention now so that you will notice them in future chapters. They're important aspects of the entire American criminal justice system, including policing, courts, and corrections. These themes are *conservatism*, *race*, and *discretion*. These three factors have a tremendous influence on American justice on every level. I'll briefly explain what I mean by each of these here:

When I say that the American criminal justice system is *conservative*, I mean that the system is set up to protect the current state of things, the *status quo*. The criminal justice system is not designed to change the world. It is designed to maintain the existing order. This is good in many ways, but if you are unhappy with the way things are and want to change them, the criminal justice system will not help you. Most people who have tried to change the world in important ways—those opposed to the Vietnam War, those opposed to slavery, and those opposed to segregation—were labelled as criminals by many of their contemporaries. They were often arrested and sometimes beaten by the police because of their efforts. These activists were not punished because their causes were unjust, but because the criminal justice system is not sympathetic to those who want to change the status quo, particularly if they believe they must break the law to do it.

The importance of *race* in American criminal justice cannot be overstated. Since the United States was founded, we've had a race problem. This country was built upon principles of individual liberty and equality, but the founding fathers had no problem enslaving tens of thousands of their fellow human beings. (The Constitution itself only counted slaves as 3/5 of a person, after declaring in the Declaration of Independence that "all men are created equal.") After the Civil War, millions of African Americans were oppressed by racist segregation laws abetted by a lack of sympathy and at times hostility from white

Americans. Now, racial issues are significantly more complicated than they were in the 19th or early 20th century, but there remains a great deal of dissatisfaction with the state of American society among a great deal of African Americans.

Criminal justice has historically been one of the primary tools for keeping black Americans marginalized. Through aggressive policing, racially biased laws, and the large-scale incarceration of blacks in the United States, African Americans have been kept in a subordinate position in American life. As a result, most black Americans have very different kinds of interactions with the police than do most white Americans. Organizations like #blacklivesmatter have brought this to the public in a dramatic way over the last few years, and this movement has gone a long way toward exposing the racial divisions in American perceptions of criminal justice. *One simply cannot understand American criminal justice without understanding its historical role in keeping black people down and the role that it still plays in maintaining racial inequality.* We will discuss the racial elements of criminal justice throughout this book, and I will make the case that the racial inequalities we see in the criminal justice system are historically connected to slavery.

Finally, *discretion* is an extremely important aspect of criminal justice. The image of a criminal justice *system* implies that everything in the system happens more or less automatically. Many of the actors in the criminal justice system—police, prosecutors, judges, et cetera—have a freedom of action known as *discretion* that allows them to decide how they will deal with an individual suspect. Thus, a cop that pulls over a speeding driver may decide to give the driver a ticket or let her go with a warning. (This could depend on a lot of things: the seriousness of the infraction, the attitude of the driver, etc.) A prosecutor may charge an offender with first- or second-degree murder depending on whether she thinks she can get a conviction for the more serious offense, or she may accept a plea bargain— not wanting to risk a trial. Finally, a judge has a wide range of options in how to punish an offender (prison, rehabilitation, probation, etc.), all of which are almost totally at her discretion. All these actors—police officers, prosecutors, prison guards, et cetera—have a great deal of leeway in how they handle any individual that comes through the system. The system has a great deal of built-in flexibility: Not all laws need to be enforced, and not all lawbreakers are prosecuted.

TRUMP

I have taught criminal justice for more than 15 years, but I never found a book that suited my critical approach to the subject. As a result, I began writing this book to use it in my own classes several years ago. Since I began writing it, criminal justice has become a significantly more important part of public discussions. Police-officer killings of African Americans like Tamir Rice, Eric Garner, Freddie Gray, Walter Scott, and Michael Brown, among others, pushed the issue of criminal justice reform to the front of public debate. Groups like #blacklivesmatter became a major force in pushing for reforms in policing and in the criminal justice system more generally, and this movement led to a ferocious response from the largely white #bluelivesmatter movement. Equally important, the federal government under President Obama began to slowly reform some parts of the criminal justice system at the federal level, influencing how the system worked across the country.

Many of these changes came to a screeching halt with the inauguration of Donald Trump as president in 2017. President Trump had made his unflinching support for the police a major part of his campaign and had attacked #blacklivesmatter on the stump. He described poor black neighborhoods as war zones and portrayed immigrants as thugs, drug traffickers, and terrorists. Under his watch, he declared, "Safety would be restored." Equally important, he appointed former Alabama senator Jeff Sessions as his first attorney general, the federal government's top law enforcer. Throughout his career, Sessions has steadfastly opposed reforming criminal justice, and as attorney general he has rolled back many of the policies that the Obama administration had championed to make the system less harsh on offenders. Clearly, Trump and Sessions marked a dramatic shift backward for criminal justice that will have a great deal of impact on this system over the coming years.

That said, this edition of the book is being written halfway into the Trump administration, and it has proven extremely difficult to predict what will happen next for the president. He has already been accused of acts that could get him removed from office and is facing an independent investigation for his administration's ties to a foreign power. Ironically, many conservatives who have pushed for a more aggressive criminal justice system have expressed concerns that prosecutors have too much power to investigate the president and that federal investigators must be constrained. This means that this administration's more severe criminal justice policies could be reversed by his successor if Trump does not serve his full term in office or after he has departed. For this reason, although I will certainly discuss the policies of the Trump administration and the Sessions (now Barr) Justice Department, I will not dwell too heavily on them, as they may change dramatically over the next few years. The world has become too volatile to assume that things will continue along a predictable path.

One final word of caution. As you can probably already tell, this textbook will probably put forward some ideas that you will disagree with. You should feel free to disagree with this book. Too many textbooks pass off their opinions as a neutral, impartial analysis by deploying the bland tone of an encyclopedia article. On issues like crime and justice, there is very little neutral ground, and there is very little consensus about what the facts truly are. What you will have in this book is an analysis rooted in facts, but one that is open to debate and differences of opinion. The point of this book is *not* to indoctrinate you into thinking about criminal justice in a critical way (because critical scholarship valorizes different perspectives, this would be a self-contradiction), but to open you up to seeing the criminal justice system in a lot of different lights, some positive, others negative. You may choose your own way to look at things and your own perspective. The point here is to help you develop an *informed* perspective on criminal justice, one that doesn't take conventional assumptions about law and order for granted. That, in my view, is the essence of education.

Thus, this book will strive to be controversial, to say things that might get your blood pumping, particularly if you see yourself as a strong proponent of law and order. If you believe that criminals are bad people who choose to commit crimes, you will probably not agree with a lot of what I say here. Again, this is fine. Rather than rejecting the analysis here as nonsense because it doesn't fit with your worldview, a better approach is to try to refute it. Research, read, discuss the subject with your friends, and arrive at a different conclusion, rather than doing what most of us do when we encounter facts or analyses that differ with our views—dismiss them out of hand and turn to those with whom we agree. In most cases, higher education should not be about being *told stuff*, but being guided to thinking about our world in a different light.

THE STRUCTURE OF THIS BOOK

This text will be structured into several sections. In the first section, we will be discussing "crime." Here we will look first at the concept of crime by asking a number of related questions. What is crime? How does crime as a category relate to law? To morality? To society? Here we will also discuss public perceptions of crime, including commonly believed myths about crime. Then we will turn explicitly to criminal law as one way of understanding crime, examining basic aspects of the legal system and the legal construction of crime. After this, we will look at social scientific approaches to measuring and explaining crime, focusing largely on sociological approaches, but also looking at economic, biological, and psychological explanations of criminal behavior. Then we will turn to the critical tradition, the approach that grounds much of the rest of this book. This approach seeks to see crime and the criminal justice system as reflecting the deeper structural inequalities that shape our society.

After having discussed crime as such, we will then turn to the criminal justice system, that is, the public and private institutions that deal with criminals. Here we will follow the course that an individual offender follows: We will start with arrest and look at policing, police procedures (including searches and seizures), and police institutions. Then, we will go to court and see how the different actors in the courtroom interact with each other and with the criminal defendant. If the convicted criminal's appeal is unsuccessful, she will be placed in what we call the correctional system (though as we will see, "correcting" convicted criminals is not a high priority in most prisons), including potentially the death penalty—the fourth section of the book. Finally, at the end we will discuss a unique exception—the case of juvenile justice, exploring how our thinking about kids changes how we view their responsibility for breaking the law.

Keep in mind that when we get to the criminal justice system, we will only be able to speak in generalities. The United States is a federal system in which almost all criminal justice issues are handled at the state level. Each state has its own laws, its own procedures, and its own criminal justice institutions. That means that there is a great deal of variety among the states regarding how the police are organized, how a trial is run, and how offenders are punished. Focusing on one state would be too limited and not very helpful if you live outside of that state, and discussing every variation among the states would take too long. As a result, I have chosen to speak only in broad terms about many aspects of criminal justice, providing a few specific examples of how criminal justice is carried out in different states. If you are interested, you can research criminal justice practices in your own state to notice the differences.

A COMMENT ABOUT TERMINOLOGY

I want to say a few things about the words I have chosen to use in this book. Part of taking a critical perspective involves understanding how the words we use shape how we look at reality. *Crime* and *criminal* are just words, but when they are used to describe a person, they can be very harmful. I have tried to be somewhat careful in how I describe people and things in this text to avoid being misleading. One example of this is my decision to use the feminine pronoun as the "generic" pronoun, when it is common to use the masculine pronoun. This is a bit weird, because the clear majority of people arrested and prosecuted for crimes are men, as are police officers, judges, and prosecutors. It is particularly glaring in terms of imprisonment: Men are approximately 14 times more likely to go to prison than women.

Nonetheless, using the feminine pronoun to describe victims, offenders, and criminal justice professionals seems fair. If this makes readers uncomfortable, think of it as a challenge to how we think: When we see *he* used generically, we unconsciously think of a man and only later qualify our thinking to include women. Men and male conduct become the norm and women the exception. Here, we are doing the opposite, speaking as though the ordinary person were a woman and then qualifying our thinking to apply to a man. Nonetheless, keep in mind that these are meant to be generic terms—*she* can be a man, a woman, or a person who doesn't fit onto either side of the gender binary.

Further, throughout this book I have used different words to describe people. When a person hasn't been accused of a crime, I have referred to her as a "citizen." When she has been stopped by the police, she becomes a "suspect." When she has been charged with a crime, she is a "defendant," and when she has been convicted she has become an "offender." If she is incarcerated, she is a "prisoner." If she is on death row, she is "the condemned." Each change of terminology points to a change in the legal and social status the person has both in and outside of the criminal justice system: As we will see, a prisoner has significantly fewer rights than a suspect, and a citizen who is suspected of nothing has more rights than a person about whom the officer has a reasonable suspicion. This is just to give you a warning that I'm going to change my terminology as the book goes on, and these changes have some significance. Keep in mind that beneath each of these labels is a human being with thoughts, feelings, hopes, and fears, just like you or me. In a system that often dehumanizes people who break the law, this in itself can be a critical act.

Sarah Yeh

Our image of who is a criminal is shaped by the media and by culture. What does a criminal look like to you?

CRIME

In the first part of the book, we will be discussing "crime." The word is between quotation marks here, because one of the things we need to keep in mind is that the concept of crime is not an exact one. It is not static, it is not unchanging, and it is certainly not uncontroversial. Moreover, our notion of a "criminal" is often the creation of our imagination, stoked by popular stories and myths—not by reality. When you imagine a criminal, you probably think of a mugger, rapist, bank robber, et cetera—perhaps a guy in a ski mask with a gun lurking in a dark alleyway. You probably don't think of the guy from your dorm who smokes pot or your friend who buys beer for the college party where some of the drinkers are under age. (She might be a hero in your mind.) The mattresses that we sleep on come with a tag that warns us of criminal penalties if they are removed. Until a few years ago, people in certain states were criminals if they engaged in gay sex. On the other hand, people like Martin Luther King and Mohandas Gandhi were arrested and prosecuted as criminals for violating unjust laws, and few people would describe them as criminals today.

The media, be it the news, drama, or the internet, feeds us crime stories on a 24-hour cycle, and this is where most of us learn about it. Every day, local and national news programs feature stories about crime with grainy security cam footage or shaky phone videos. These news programs are then followed by either a crime-related TV drama or a documentary on crime (*Cops, America's Most Wanted, To Catch a Predator, Law & Order, Bones,* etc.) showing police officers chasing crooks through crowded city streets or slamming a "perp" onto their car hood as they read him his rights and declare that he's going behind bars "for a long, long time." Given the fact that crime is almost always on TV or in the news in one way or another, it's probably safe to say that the American media is obsessed with the subject.

However, television and the news media are only obsessed with a certain type of crime: crimes that will attract viewers and will get these viewers to sit through their advertisements. Ordinary everyday crime and crime that doesn't have an interesting "hook" is ignored. Often this hook is violence or sex in one form or another—"if it bleeds, it leads," as the journalistic cliché goes. And when crimes are reported, the bigger picture is often ignored in favor of the gory, erotic, or otherwise sensationalist elements of the offense. This in turn leads the uninformed viewer to develop a skewed perspective of the nature and reality of crime in America today, which can lead many people to fear things that they need not fear, and to overlook criminal activities that produce real social harm.

Let me provide a few examples of misleading media representations of crime. Every year thousands of people go missing, and news programs frequently feature stories on some of these unfortunate people. But not every person who goes missing gets attention, and it is telling who the media choose to focus on. Young, white girls often gather far more media attention than any other type of person, and noticeably, minority victims are frequently ignored. A pretty blonde girl is sure to get attention, while a poor minority girl from the inner city is likely to be overlooked. People like Elizabeth Smart and Natalee Holloway are featured for weeks on the news, while others are completely ignored. Once it was pointed out, it became so obvious that observers began to label the phenomenon as *missing white woman syndrome* (Liebler, 2010). If you got all your news from the TV, you'd sincerely (and falsely) believe that kidnapping was common, and that pretty young white girls were the primary victims of such crimes.

Another example of media misrepresenting crime is its obsession with serial killers. Though we have no real hard numbers on the subject, there have been very few genuine serial killers in history, and dying at the hands of such a killer is very unlikely. According to FBI statistics, about 150 people are killed a year by serial killers, half the number killed by slipping in the bathtub. (Serial killers are simply people who have killed more than one person over an extended period; they need not be Hannibal Lecter–type slashers.) But if you watched news shows as well as crime dramas, you would believe that America was packed with brutal but colorful murderers who stalk and kill at random. Each year, Hollywood churns out dramas about vicious serial killers either in the horror genre (*Halloween*, *Friday the 13th*, etc.) or in the crime genre (*Seven*, *The Silence of the Lambs*). The public is fascinated with people like John Wayne Gacy, Richard Ramirez, and Jack the Ripper, who are regularly the subjects of documentaries, books, and movies, even though these figures are barely a ripple in the world of homicide.

The media will often ignore crimes that are either too technical or too complex to make a good story. White collar crimes such as insider trading or securities fraud can cause massive damage, robbing people of their savings and their homes, leaving innocent people destitute and their lives ruined. Environmental crimes like illegal dumping of dangerous materials can kill thousands. The problem with these crimes is that they often don't make good television: We get lost in the details, and the technical aspects of business or environmental law are confusing and often boring. They don't come wrapped up in a tidy story about good guys and bad guys. This means that few people know of Jeffrey Skilling (the president of Enron, a bankrupt energy corporation, who was convicted in a massive fraud and insider trading case) or Bernard Madoff (who was convicted of running a massive scam known as a *Ponzi scheme* that cost investors billions), while famous killers like Scott Peterson and O. J. Simpson are national celebrities. White collar crime is pervasive and destructive but largely ignored by both the news and by television drama, unless it can be tied into something juicier.

Sometimes the media will be briefly consumed by one type of crime that will seem to sweep the nation. Out of nowhere, crimes that nobody ever heard of seem to appear in epidemic proportions. For example, in the 1980s, there was a great fear that heavy metal music was linked to crimes such as murder and suicide, and that it encouraged the practice of Satanism, even though there was scant evidence that the millions who listen to heavy metal were more prone to crime than anybody else. Similarly, youth crime has been blown out of proportion by a society that is understandably afraid of crime in schools; extreme cases like the shooting at Columbine High School haunted everybody's views about what high school students were like (again, despite the fact that high school is not a particularly violent place, particularly in affluent suburbs). In each case, an understandable fear, sometimes prompted by one or two extreme cases, was taken by the news media and blown way out of proportion, creating widespread public fear. In the face of a frightened public, politicians and policymakers are obliged to respond with new policies that are meant to placate the public.

Sociologists call these phenomena *moral panics*. A moral panic is an intense public response to a perceived problem that is way out of proportion to its reality. Whether it is freeway shootings, Satanism, child abduction, or teen sex, public fear and outrage is fostered by a media seeking to give the public what they want. Even crimes like terrorism can be seen as a moral panic, as the number of Americans killed by terrorists is miniscule compared to the number killed by other types of homicide. "Experts" appear on talk shows, lending these fears a veneer of legitimacy, and a few, admittedly awful cases become focal points for public discussion. Few of these experts, however, point out the boring reality that very few kids are abducted, teen sex rates are lower than they were a generation ago, and Satanic cults that conduct human sacrifices are largely a myth. As we will see, the reality of crime is a complex thing, and its causes are a continuing point of debate, but chasing the latest moral panic is not an effective way to prevent crime, much less study it.

The point of all of this is to say that our everyday understanding of crime is shaped by a media that has no interest in portraying crime as it really is. Instead they are interested in attracting viewers or readers to generate clicks and sell advertising space. This means that the portrayal of crime on television and the movies usually says more about our society, the things that we care about as a people, than it does about crime itself. So why is the public so fascinated with certain types of crime, and why does it ignore other, more damaging sorts of crimes, the crimes that are far more likely to affect our lives? Our fear of losing control of our children in a world where they are increasingly targeted by advertisers turns into a fear that our children are being led to a life of crime or may be a victim of a child predator. Our sometimes-strict understanding of what a "good girl" ought to do turns into an obsession with women who kill or teens who have sex. Our anxiety about our inability to be completely secure in our lives turns into an obsession with serial killers. Public attitudes toward crime say more about the public than they do about crime.

I should note that this brief discussion is a great oversimplification of a vast array of studies about the media and its portrayal of crime. Many scholars have examined how race, violence, sex, and other issues have been used by the media to boost their ratings, and how a prolonged exposure to these stories can affect a viewer's perception of crime and justice. Moreover, other scholars have examined how a single newspaper will depict similar crimes in very different ways depending on factors such as the race of the victim or the race of the offender. Stories are not simply there to be reported in a neutral and objective way, but rather the reporters frame the story in a particular way, picking out certain facts as important while downplaying others. These framing choices are often the result of unconscious assumptions and prejudices on the part of the reporters and, in turn, they are seen by an audience that similarly has their own set of unconscious prejudices. Thus, the media's portrayal of crime is not simply an effort to get viewers, but is also the result of a great deal of filtering and shaping during the reporting process.

In this section, we will look past the media's construction of crime, as well as the public obsession with comparatively trivial types of crime, and look at the reality of crime. We will look at it on the conceptual level (looking at the concept of "crime"), the legal level (examining basic aspects of criminal law), the empirical level (looking at the way that crime data is gathered), and the theoretical level (looking at theories about what causes crime). Once we have explored the concept of crime across these various dimensions, we will then turn to society's response to crime, that is, the **criminal justice system**, in the later parts of the book.

Criminal justice system: The various organizations that respond to criminal behavior: courts, judges, police, et cetera, whose purpose is to fight crime.

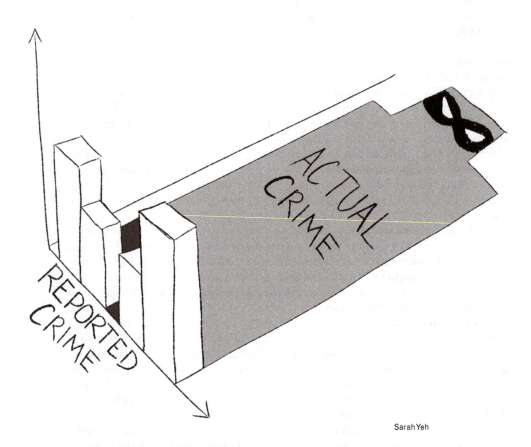

Sarah Yeh

A lot of crime does not show up in official crime data. How significant do you think this is for understanding the causes of crime?

CHAPTER ONE

DEFINING, CLASSIFYING, AND MEASURING CRIME

While we all can probably easily conjure up an image of what a criminal looks like without much effort, the word itself is not as simple as it may first appear and can mean a lot of different things in different contexts. "Criminal" is *not* necessarily synonymous with a lawbreaker or with a "bad guy." What is a crime and what is a criminal is in many ways very complicated both legally and socially.

It is also helpful to remember that the terms *crime* and *criminal* are not merely descriptive, they are also *normative*. Calling an action a crime or calling a person a criminal does not simply describe what she is or the act she does, it is also making a judgment about the act or the person.[1] We are not just describing them, we are also saying that they are bad and deserve to be condemned by decent people. In this way, *crime* and *criminal* are a lot like the term *evil* or the term *ugly*: When you use these words to describe something, you're also rendering a verdict on it and casting it in a negative light. That is, when you call somebody a criminal, you are saying something derogatory about her.

It is because of this normative quality that the term *criminal* has so much power. The term draws a moral line and puts a person, group, idea, or party on the wrong side of that line. This is why many different political groups try to use these terms to their advantage in public debate. Antiabortion activists want to label doctors who provide abortions as criminals, leftists want to describe the actions of President Trump as criminal, and animal rights activists claim that "meat is murder." Each of these groups is using the language of crime rhetorically to try to get people to think about abortion providers, the president, or carnivores in the way that they think about murderers, rapists, and serial killers. They are using the terms of crime and justice to win a war of ideas, usually without having to prove that their own ideas are the best ones. (The term *rhetoric* refers to the skillful manipulation of language to convince another to see the world the way you do.)

Of course, the rhetoric of crime is not just for antiabortion protestors or radical leftists. It is used by and against all kinds of people trying to push all sorts of political agendas. Sometimes the language has been used so effectively that public opinion has been changed, and acts that were once perfectly legal became criminal. Similarly, acts that were once criminal became legitimate because of similar rhetorical techniques—people convinced others that acts that were considered criminal weren't really so bad. Some things we are glad to see

---

[1] As I mentioned in the introduction, I will use the feminine pronoun as the generic pronoun throughout the book.

criminalized have only been criminalized because groups were able to convince others that they should be criminalized. Dog fighting, for example, was criminalized because people were convinced that cruelty toward animals should be criminalized, despite the fact that millions of animals are raised in miserable conditions and killed for food every day and that dog fighting was once a cherished tradition in the West (Villavicencio, 2007). Homosexuality was once considered criminal (and in some cases punishable by death) but is now considered socially acceptable by much of American society. Crime shifts over time as different groups have effectively changed public opinion about what behaviors we should accept and what we should condemn.

All of this is to say that we should use a critical eye when looking at the concept of crime. It's not a neutral term and means different things in different contexts. *Crime* is what linguists call a *contested concept*—it is never a simple matter to determine what is or what should be a crime and who should be considered a criminal, and the uses of this term are almost always open to debate. A lot of people who use the term are pretending that they're describing an act as a crime, when really what they're saying is that these acts are bad and should be punished. They are further saying that the government should intervene to forcibly prevent people from engaging in these acts. Therefore, we need to carefully, skeptically examine the terms *crime* and *criminal* in their different contexts before reaching any sort of conclusion about the best way to define them.

In some ways, this chapter will be the most philosophical chapter in the book, as we explore ways to define and measure crime. In the first part, we will examine different approaches to analyzing the concept of crime itself. They are all "definitions" of crime, but unlike definitions found in a dictionary, each provides a different framework for thinking about crime as a subject of study, essentially treating crime in a very different way. Here, we will look at *legal*, *moral*, and *sociological* approaches to thinking about the nature of crime. Each of these takes on crime will have its own strengths and weaknesses, but none of them will be "the right one." In some contexts, a moral approach will look stupid, while in other contexts it will make a great deal of sense. Sociological definitions of crime are great if you're a practicing sociologist, but if you're a lawyer, you probably don't care what Durkheim said about crime. There is no need to come to a final answer about the best definition of crime, because it is such a complex phenomenon that it can be helpful to use a variety of lenses to examine it. Once we have described these different ways to define the subject, we will turn to some of the different ways that we can classify various types of criminal activity.

DEFINING CRIME

Learning Objective 1.1—Identify different approaches to defining crime.

Legal Definitions of Crime

The simplest approach to defining a crime is saying that a crime is a violation of the law. These laws are passed by governments and set out on paper, and all we need to do is consult them to figure out which acts are criminal and which aren't. After all, police officers won't arrest someone for doing something that doesn't violate the law (in theory), and (again, in theory) they will probably arrest you if you do something that violates the law. Thus, a crime is any act that violates criminal law, and individuals that commit such acts are criminals. Enough said.

Of course, there's obviously something compelling about this approach, and if you asked somebody who hadn't thought very carefully about it, she would probably give this as her answer. It makes sense: In many ways, the law is a useful guide for understanding the contours of the criminal justice system as a whole. Usually a person cannot be arrested unless she violates a criminal law, so an illegal act is usually an individual's entry point into the criminal justice system. The courts apply criminal law when they determine whether or not a person is guilty, and the law usually spells out the appropriate punishment for an individual. This means, obviously, that the law has a great deal to say about crime and criminal justice more generally.

However, there are some important problems with such a narrow way of understanding crime, and there are a lot of important aspects of crime that are overlooked if we focus solely on law. For example, the odds are that you have *never* actually looked at your state's criminal code or the federal criminal code. You may not even know what these are, much less where to find them. We all know that murder and robbery are crimes, but could you give the definition of murder in your state, or explain the difference between murder in the first degree, murder in the second degree, and manslaughter in your state? That, of course, is assuming that your state makes these distinctions, as not every state has different degrees of murder in its criminal code. While we may think that we know what the law says, legal definitions ("constructions" to be more precise) of individual crimes are often strange—they are the products of legislative processes that can be confusing to somebody who doesn't closely follow them.

In addition to the fact that we usually don't know our local criminal laws, the law varies dramatically from state to state. There are fifty different criminal codes in different states, along with a federal code, and each state's constructions of crime are reflections of local politics, local history, and local values. Some acts might be a crime in Virginia but not in California (such as the use of marijuana—which is still a federal crime but is legal in several states). The same crime might have very different definitions in different states. This means that, technically speaking, one could commit the same act in one state and it would be a crime, and yet it would be perfectly legal in another. While this doesn't disqualify this legal definition, it does show that it is limited: It is difficult to study crime across the various legal jurisdictions that make up the United States.

Finally, just because a person violated a criminal law doesn't mean that the state will enforce that law. The police, prosecutors, and judges may choose to ignore lawbreaking behavior for a whole host of reasons. The offense might be too small to be worth their time, they might have other priorities, or the offender may not be somebody who criminal justice professionals are interested in pursuing. This means that in some cases, determining whether an act violated the law is not a good guide to determining whether a person will be arrested or punished. Sometimes, the police will ignore your conduct or let you off with a warning. Other times, the officer may choose to intervene in behavior that is not really criminal. For example, being a nuisance may not always be a crime, but the police will intervene if they wish. The police don't strictly enforce many laws—they are just too busy to do that. Rather they will usually enforce laws only when the laws that are broken are serious ones (robbery, murder) or when they have a good reason to want to enforce the law.

As was already mentioned, there are many cases where there is a big difference between our beliefs about crime and what the law tells us is criminal. Martin Luther King Jr. was arrested and imprisoned for breaking laws in the South during his fight against segregation. So was Gandhi in his fight against British colonialism in India (and Jesus, for that matter). Few of us would leap to call them criminals. Hitler's genocidal murder of Jews, the Roma, homosexuals, and others was perfectly legal under German law at the time he ordered them. History is full of cases where good people trying to fight clear injustice are arrested and imprisoned, and people who commit great evils are shielded by the law. The law is clearly an important lens through which to look at crime, but it cannot be the only one. The legal definition of crime is technically accurate, but it is only technically accurate, which is its biggest weakness.

Moral Definitions of Crime

The reality is that the law has very little to do with our everyday thinking about crime or our interest in the subject. We don't find crime fascinating or upsetting because we care about what the law says. Often, we're angry about something deeper than mere lawbreaking when we get worked up about crime—something that makes our blood boil when we see somebody do something horribly wrong, regardless of what the law says. We consider crimes to be acts that are profoundly wrong, and we believe that criminals are bad people. Killers, rapists, and robbers are not just people who violate a rule—they are people who commit evil. We could go so far as to say that a moral definition of crime is something like, "Crime is an act of great immorality."

Criminal justice scholars distinguish between acts that are *malum prohibitum* and those that are *malum in se*. These Latin terms refer to two types of crimes that we can commit. *Malum prohibitum* describes acts that are wrong because they are prohibited, while *malum in se* refers to acts that are bad in themselves. Some acts may be prohibited and thus criminalized without necessarily being wrong. For example, it is illegal to drive the wrong way down a one-way street, and you can get in big trouble for doing it. However, it is not inherently wrong to drive this way—if nobody is harmed or inconvenienced, it doesn't make a difference where you drive. Acts that are *malum in se* are more classical crimes like murder and rape—murder is never okay, and a murder clearly hurts its victim and those around her. These terms point to the basic insight of the moral approach to crime—we believe that criminal acts are *wrong* because they are *wrong*, not because they are against the law.

This sense of wrongness explains why we get so worked up about crime in a way that we don't about other types of lawbreaking. It offends us to see somebody hurt an innocent person or steal money, and it gives us a great deal of satisfaction to see these people brought to justice. When we see a criminal "get away with it," that is, commit a crime without being caught or paying any price for it, many people are outraged and upset. The satisfaction we feel when we see justice done, the offender caught and punished, is one of the reasons why we are glued to many TV crime dramas and the resolution where the bad guy is inevitably caught. (There's a whole genre of self-described "justice porn" videos that are meant to provoke pleasure by seeing bad people get their just deserts.) The resolution gives us a certain kind of satisfaction—we can't wait to see the criminal get what is coming to her.

Some have even gone so far as to claim that morals are superior to laws and our moral principles constitute a "higher law" that we should obey, even if it means violating the actual laws that are on the books. Theologians call this *natural law*, and this idea has been used to justify all kinds of acts of *civil disobedience*—deliberate lawbreaking based on a moral objection to the law. As the Catholic philosopher St. Augustine put it, "An unjust law is no law at all." In American history, Martin Luther King used natural law to justify his protests against segregation. In his famous "Letter From Birmingham Jail," King argued that any law that doesn't uphold human dignity isn't really law and should be ignored by all decent people, regardless of whether or not a legislature passed it.

Thus, the moral approach has some advantages over the legal definition of crime: It feels more like what we mean when we talk about crime. It gets to the core of crime in a way that mere lawbreaking doesn't—violating the law by itself doesn't usually rile people up; hurting innocent people does. However, it shouldn't surprise you to learn that moral definitions of crime have problems, too. While we might agree that crimes can be defined as serious moral wrongs, this doesn't mean that we can agree on what these "serious wrongs" are. The world is full of vastly different moral codes with their own lists of right and wrong conduct, and people who live under these codes subscribe to very different moral views. This view is known as *moral relativism*—people have different views about right or wrong, and judging between them is often very difficult.

Even if we could find a few basic moral principles that we could agree upon, something like "murder is wrong" or "stealing is wrong," we still run into problems. While we can agree on a principle, when we try to apply it to actual cases, we often run into difficulties. Some people would find abortion to be completely acceptable, while others would call it murder. They might even disagree about whether abortion is "killing" in the first place. Many of you illegally download movies from the internet but may not consider it stealing. We can all agree that Martin Luther King was correct to oppose segregation laws, but we might find other uses of natural law somewhat more objectionable. (It's been used by people who murdered abortion doctors, for example.) Many cultures have very different ideas about killing: "Honor killings" (the killing of a family member who has shamed the rest of the family) are considered noble by many people who live in some societies, but they would surely be considered murder elsewhere. The belief that some things are just plain wrong is fine, but that only leads to a whole new series of problems.

None of this is to say that relativism is right, and that morality is simply a matter of opinion or a product of one's culture. (Philosophers have been debating this question for thousands of years.) Rather, it's just to point out that there are a lot of problems with simply accepting the moral definition of crime at face value. Thinking about the moral aspect of crime requires thinking about the nature of morality and its relation to culture, history, and the broader society. While theft may be immoral, stealing to feed one's family is clearly different from stealing purely out of greed. In addition, many acts of stealing are legal, but perhaps shouldn't be. As the folk singer Woody Guthrie once sang, "Yes, as through this world I've wandered, I've seen lots of funny men. Some will rob you with a six-gun, and some with a fountain pen." Some of the biggest crimes can be committed with the blessing of the government, and the worst of all (the Holocaust, the genocide of the Native Americans, the killing of millions of Africans by the King of Belgium in the 19th century) have been committed by governments themselves.

Sociological Definitions of Crime

Emile Durkheim, one of the founders of modern sociology, was fascinated with how people reacted to crime in their societies. Durkheim observed that crime and punishment are features of every society, even in places where there is no formal law or government, such as in the remote corners of the world. However, he noticed that acts that were considered "criminal" in one society would not necessarily be crimes in another—they might even be considered honorable. Within a single society, an act that would be considered a horrible crime in one context could be considered noble in another—killing a stranger in a bar fight is murder; killing him on a battlefield can be heroism. In addition, acts that cause a great deal of harm can be perfectly legal (such as certain banking practices), and acts that produce no harm whatsoever can be a crime. An infraction may seem trivial in our society but in another could be a shocking violation of social norms requiring serious punishment. Crime is everywhere, but criminal acts are dramatically different from place to place, and even within the same society.

From these insights about crime, Durkheim reached two primary conclusions: (1) Because they are universal phenomena, crime and punishment must serve a purpose for society beyond simply protecting the public from evildoers, and (2) any real understanding of crime cannot be found in the acts that a society believes to be criminal—they are just too varied to fall under a single definition. Relativists are right in that there is no single notion of crime, and moralists are right in believing that crime produces an emotional reaction from the public. However, neither definition looks at the question in the right way according to Durkheim.

Durkheim believed that the key to understanding crime is not to look at the criminal act itself, but instead to look at a society's response to that act. What defines a crime is that society determines an act should be punished, regardless of whether the act is harmful in itself. The primary element of *all* crime is that people in a society think that these acts deserve punishment. Law is secondary. The criminal law only follows a society's beliefs about what acts should be punished but does not really define criminality. When an outrageous act occurs that is not yet illegal, governments will race to follow popular opinion and quickly amend the criminal code so that it better matches society's values. If a government failed to criminalize acts that the public thought should be criminalized, it would quickly lose popular support. Similarly, if an act was considered a crime by the law but not considered something that should be punished by society, the law would be ignored by the public and thus be ineffective. Neither the nature of the act nor the law matter in defining crime for Durkheim: It is the response by the larger society, and sociologists, as people who study the society, can help understand this phenomenon.

In Durkheim's view, the fact that crime exists in some form or another in all societies shows that society *needs* crime—that crime serves a function for the broader social order. He believed that a society must develop a very strong set of rules to maintain its social bonds. When somebody breaches these rules, these social bonds (what Durkheim calls its "collective consciousness") are threatened, and our connection to others in our community is harmed. The way to deal with this weakness is to punish the individual who broke the rules, not because she "deserves it," but because this punishment serves to reinforce the community's bonds. As Durkheim puts it, "Punishment constitutes essentially a reaction of passionate feeling . . . which society exerts through the mediation of an organized body [the government] over those of its members who have violated certain rules of conduct" (Durkheim & Halls, 1997, p. 52). The point of punishment for Durkheim is not to stop bad things from happening, but rather to reinforce a community's values and its sense of solidarity. This allows the society to remain intact, and if there were no crimes, it is likely that society would disintegrate.

These three approaches to defining crime, the legal, the moral, and the sociological are all very useful for understanding crime in different contexts, and each has its own uses. The point is not to say that one is "correct" but rather to understand that each definition highlights one aspect of a very complex phenomenon. There are other ways we could also define crime if we were so inclined: We could also discuss religious conceptions of crime (most religious texts have a set of activities that should be punished, for example), economic definitions of crime (that define crime in terms of its harm on economic activity), or other approaches. All of these are useful, and none is absolutely correct: They each provide different insights into what crime is and suggest ways to study it.

CRIMINAL (IN)JUSTICE

Marijuana Laws

No drug illustrates the changing nature of crime better than marijuana. Originally criminalized at the beginning of the 20th century, it is now listed as a "Schedule I" drug alongside heroin, methamphetamine, and cocaine under federal law, meaning that it has a high abuse potential and no medical use. When Bill Clinton ran for president in 1990, he admitted that he has smoked marijuana but claimed that he did not inhale it. The use of marijuana and its criminality was linked closely to race: In earlier generations, it was considered a "ghetto drug" and a danger to white Americans. Harry Anslinger, head of the Federal Bureau of Narcotics in the 1930s, linked cannabis to Mexican immigrants popularizing the term "marijuana" to make the drug sound like a foreign import. Anslinger also mercilessly targeted black jazz musicians, most notably singer Billie Holiday, for their recreational use of the drug (Hari, 2015). Behind these attacks was a fear of the corruption of white America, and in particular white women, but they were largely small-time efforts compared to the later "war on drugs."

Now marijuana is mainstream. According to the Gallup polling company, 13% of Americans use marijuana regularly, and 43% of Americans have tried it (McCarthy, 2016). Many states have legalized the drug, either for medicinal uses or, in the case of nine states, recreational use. Even though it remains illegal under federal law, Congress passed the Rohrabacher-Farr Amendment in 2003 that prevents the FBI or other federal law enforcement bodies from enforcing federal marijuana laws in states where it is legal for medical use. It's likely that the walls of at least one dorm room at your college have posters glorifying the use of marijuana. It's barely even cool to smoke pot in a lot of places.

There is still an active antimarijuana movement in the United States that has sought to get rid of the Rohrabacher-Farr Amendment and push the United States back on the path of criminalization. According to the American Civil Liberties Union, marijuana still counts for 52% of all arrests in the United States. Marijuana arrests are also still linked to race: Despite the fact that blacks and whites use marijuana in roughly the same numbers, blacks were four times more likely to be arrested for possession of the drug ("Marijuana Arrests," 2017). Even though many people use the drug, with few serious side effects stemming from casual usage, it remains heavily policed, mostly for minorities.

Should marijuana be criminalized in your view? Why or why not? How could law enforcement prevent the uneven enforcement of marijuana laws?

CLASSIFYING CRIME

Learning Objective 1.2—List different criteria for classifying crime.

We can break down the concept of crime into different categories in different ways. Not all crime is the same, and we should distinguish between crimes so that we don't treat things that are fundamentally different as though they were the same. Both football and bowling are sports, but beyond this, they don't share a lot in common. If we tried to find connections between these two sports, we would find some (they both use teams, for example), but we'll probably get in trouble if we make too many connections or treat them too similarly. The same goes for crime. And just as for sports, we can break crimes down in different ways (pro sports versus amateur sports, sports that use a ball versus those that don't, sports that are competitive versus sports that are recreational, etc.). We can do the same thing with crime. Here are a few ways to break down crime:

Severity of the Offense

One way that crimes are divided up, for example, is based on the severity of the offense—how much harm is done by the crime. For example, most states in the United States distinguish between misdemeanors (relatively minor infractions) and felonies (major infractions that can lead to imprisonment for one year or more). Some legal systems, however, don't use this system or have more fine-grained distinctions, such as Class A, B, and C felonies (each with different punishments) and a similar structure for misdemeanors.

Classification Based on the Victim

More useful than distinctions based on the severity of the criminal act are classifications based on the type of victim. This can be useful because different types of crime may have different features. In many cases, different kinds of crimes are committed by different kinds of people for different kinds of reasons, and they should probably be separated. For example, a robber who steals property but hurts nobody is probably going to be a different type than a person who commits cold-blooded murder. A drug dealer is probably different from a drunk harassing people on a street corner. This means that distinctions need to be made. While there are a lot of different ways to break down crime, the most commonly used categories are: crimes against persons, crimes against property, crimes against public order, and crimes against the state.

Crimes Against the Person

This is probably the most serious category of crimes, but it is also the easiest to define. Crimes against persons are crimes that directly target individuals, usually by causing them bodily harm. These are crimes like rape, murder, and assault. (They are usually described as crimes against "the person" and not "against people" because it is only specific harms done to specific people that count.)

Misdemeanors: Relatively minor infractions, often punished by under one year of imprisonment.

Felony: Serious offenses, usually punished by over one year of incarceration.

Crimes against persons: Crimes where a victim is physically harmed (examples: murder, assault, rape).

Crimes against property: Crimes that cause financial or economic harm (examples: theft, embezzlement).

Crimes against public order: Crimes that undermine society's stability and make it a less pleasant place to live (examples: loitering, public drunkenness).

Crimes against the state: Crimes that hurt a government (examples: espionage, treason).

Crimes Against Property

These are crimes where individuals are not bodily harmed by criminal activity, but their possessions or finances are affected. These can include burglary, arson, embezzlement, et cetera. Of course, these crimes could lead an individual to be harmed (a person could be killed in a fire, or a person whose medications are stolen by a burglar could die), but then, if the prosecutor believed that the crime caused bodily harm, the person could be convicted for murder, and hence a crime against property would become a crime against the person.

Crimes Against Public Order

These are acts where nobody specific is hurt and property is not damaged or taken, but the behavior is nonetheless considered harmful to society. These offenses typically make a place a less pleasant place to live even if there is no single victim that one can point to. For example, public drunkenness, loitering, or panhandling (asking strangers for change) are behaviors where no individual person is often harmed, but they still affect everyone's quality of life.

Crimes against public order raise difficult questions about the role of criminal justice in a society. While it is obvious that the police should protect people, and almost as obvious that they should protect private property, it is not quite as clear why they should protect public order. Sometimes loitering laws are used to harass people who are considered undesirable by society at large. A group of young men hanging out on a corner are often considered to be loitering, while a group of professionally dressed people engaged in the same activity would probably not. Antirioting laws have been used to suppress lawful forms of protest, and antinuisance legislation can be used to harass innocent people. What might seem like loitering to one person might be socializing to somebody else, and a group of young people, particularly people of color hanging out on a corner, is apt to be seen very differently from a group of white people. While we all like public order, enlisting the police in protecting *our* definition of such order is tricky business and can lead to the mistreatment of people who are doing nothing worse than being "the wrong kind of person."

Crimes Against the State

There is only one crime specifically defined in the U.S. Constitution: treason. Article III, Section 3, reads,

> Treason against the United States, shall consist only in levying War against them, or in adhering to their Enemies, giving them Aid and Comfort. No Person shall be convicted of Treason unless on the Testimony of two Witnesses to the same overt Act, or on Confession in open Court.

In such cases, the victim is the government (or more technically "the state") itself. Other crimes that often fall under this category are *espionage* (spying), sedition (attempting to stir up rebellion against the government), counterfeiting, and tax evasion. In each of these cases, the offense undermines the power and authority of the government to run public affairs.

The founding fathers cared a great deal about this, because they themselves were considered traitors by Great Britain. The Declaration of Independence was, to the British at least, an act of treason, and were an American group to declare independence now, they would be prosecuted as criminals if they acted on it. Nonetheless, other countries define treason much more broadly and use crimes against the state as the basis for arresting and punishing critics of the government. The term *treason* is often thrown around in political debate, and the line between legitimate dissent and treason is a tough one to draw in a country with passionate political disagreements like ours. Dissent, essential to democracy, is often seen by critics as a form of criminal insubordination.

Even though America has a long tradition of tolerating criticism, at different times, the government has criminalized public disagreement with the government. Under the Adams administration, Congress passed the Alien and Sedition Acts in 1798. These laws made it a crime (essentially) to criticize the government, and these were used to arrest numerous critics of his administration. The government passed similar laws in 1918 during the First World War, and used them to target critics of American participation in the war. When countries get swept away by events, their citizens can often consider dissent to be a form of treason and wish to use the organs of the state to stifle people who disagree with the strongly held views of the majority. Even in a country that cherishes its freedom, there are always those who want to suppress dissenting opinions, particularly radical ones.

Other Ways to Classify Crime

There are a lot of other ways to distinguish between different types of crime. For example, we can distinguish between *street crime* and white collar crime. Street crime is crime that happens in a public place and usually is done for financial gain, such as mugging, but could also include so-called "stranger rape" (where a man attacks a woman whom he doesn't know) or even murder. White collar crimes are crimes committed in a business context, such as insider trading, price fixing, or embezzlement. When they're being clever, criminologists describe the split between the two types as one between "street crime" and "suite crime." Again, it's not too difficult to imagine that different kinds of people do these different kinds of crimes, and they probably shouldn't be examined in the same ways.

The concept of white collar crime is a relatively new one. The term was invented by the criminologist Edwin Sutherland, who stirred up controversy when he coined the term (Sutherland, 1983). According to Sutherland, criminologists have overlooked white collar criminality because the people who commit corporate fraud and other types of corporate criminal activity don't look or act like criminals. They are often considered upstanding members of society and are given a great deal of respect by judges, politicians, and police officers. Simply because white collar criminals are usually not physically dangerous does not mean that they are not criminals capable of causing great harm. By focusing on street crime and violent crime, we often miss out on a category of crime that can hurt millions of people.

White collar crime: Crime that occurs in a professional context (example: stealing from your employer).

Corporate crimes: Crimes committed for a company's profits (example: price fixing).

There are also several other types of crime that should be mentioned. *Environmental crimes* are offenses that are committed against nature directly and secondarily against people. These include things like dumping toxic waste, destruction of natural resources, illegal poaching of endangered animals, et cetera. Corporate crimes are crimes committed by corporations. Corporate crimes are like white collar crimes insofar as they both take place in a business setting, but corporate crimes are done for the benefit of the corporation and not for private, personal gain. Corporate crime can include issues such as misrepresenting a company's fiscal status or bribing a public official to secure a lucrative contract. Hate crimes are crimes that are committed against a person because of the victim's race, religion, gender, sexual orientation, or disability. Racist attacks are hate crimes, as are attacks on gays and lesbians, and the perpetrators can face very stiff prison sentences under federal law. *Sex crimes* are crimes of a sexual nature. *War crimes* are crimes committed during armed conflicts, such as killing unarmed civilians, torturing prisoners, or using banned weapons like poison gas and biological weapons. *Cybercrimes* such as identity theft, fraud, or distributing child pornography take place over the internet. Each of these crimes has its own characteristics, including its own type of offender, and criminologists usually study them separately. There are a vast number of overlapping categories of offenses, and one criminal act could be a combination of any number of them.

Hate crimes: Crimes motivated by antipathy toward a group (example: gay bashing).

REALITY CHECK

Crime Versus Fear of Crime

Violent crime has dropped substantially over the last two decades. However, you may be surprised to learn that the American public's fear of crime has *increased* over this same period. Studies suggest that the public either does not know or does not believe the numbers, as Figure 1.1 shows.

The *General Social Survey* (GSS), a nationwide survey of public attitudes (including attitudes about crime) supports these numbers. Despite being safer than ever, the American public is more anxious than ever about crime—a fear that politicians have been eager to exploit for their own benefits.

Figure 1.1 Public Perception About Violent Crime, 1993–2015

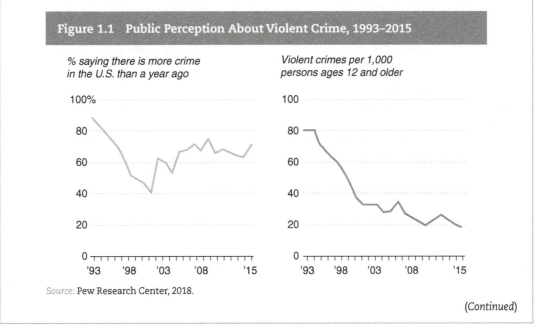

% saying there is more crime in the U.S. than a year ago

Violent crimes per 1,000 persons ages 12 and older

Source: Pew Research Center, 2018.

(Continued)

(Continued)

The fear of crime varies among different sectors of the population in ways that are particularly telling. As one social scientist observed, "There is seemingly no identifiable statistical relationship between those who are the most at risk of becoming victims of crime and those who report being the most fearful" (Lee, 2007, p. 3). For example, elderly Americans are more often afraid of criminal behavior but are less likely to be victimized by violent crime than are younger people. While white people are less afraid of crime than African Americans, social scientists have discovered that living near African Americans increases the fear of crime among whites (Skogan, 1995). The fear of crime, then, is the product of a complex network of social factors, only some of which are linked to the actual chance that a person will be a victim of a crime.

There are many possible explanations for this disconnect between crime and the fear of crime. Politicians and private security companies have a lot to gain by you believing that your safety is in danger at all times. Politicians can get tough on criminals (always a convenient tactic in a political campaign) and target them with tougher laws, and security companies can sell you an array of home and personal security equipment to keep you safe—but only if you're first scared. Of course, the news media can increase their viewership by highlighting the most sensational crimes and concocting bogus crime trends (Romer, Jamieson, & Aday, 2003). Finally, many of us don't think about crime until it impacts our lives, that is, when we or people we know are victimized, meaning that we are inclined to focus on our negative experiences rather than on our relative safety. Our fear of crime is stoked and manipulated by a number of different groups and factors, each of which has its own interest in making sure we feel unsafe. In his inaugural address, President Trump bemoaned "the crime and gangs and drugs that have stolen too many lives and robbed our country of so much unrealized potential" and declared it an era of "American carnage."

Given these realities, it is unsurprising that criminal justice policies, that is, the government's approaches to fighting crime, are often driven by a public that is unaware of the facts about crime in America. Voters often cast their ballots based upon what they think is going on, independent of facts. This means that, for politicians, "getting tough on crime" is almost always a safe bet when campaigning, regardless of whether or not getting tough actually reduces crime. In many parts of the criminal justice system, the influence of the fear of crime and the need to "get tough" has sometimes led to policies that are counterproductive but are profitable for businesses that work in the criminal justice field, such as private security companies or prison construction companies. While it is too simplistic to describe manipulation of fear of crime by the media and the proposal of "solutions" provided by the various businesses in the criminal justice world (prison construction, private security, etc.) as a conspiracy, it can often feel that way.

Why do you think young people underestimate their likelihood of being victimized? Why do older people overestimate their chance of being victimized? How often do you think about being victimized?

MEASURING CRIME

Criminal justice policies: Ways that societies seek to prevent crime through laws, policing, and other programs.

Learning Objective 1.3—Compare and contrast different ways of measuring crime.

Newspapers, TV, and radio often talk about the *crime rate*: It's going up, it's going down, it's leveled off, it's remained steady, et cetera. But what do we mean by "the crime rate"? Where do we get these numbers from? Since so much crime happens in the shadows and a lot of crime goes unreported, how can we know whether crime is increasing or decreasing?

There isn't a "crime rate" in the sense of a single definitive measure of how much crime has occurred or whether crime is increasing or decreasing. There are many reasons for this, one of which we've already discussed: There is no consensus on how to define it. Additionally, it is often difficult to determine how to measure a crime. For example, a thief breaks into a house carrying a sack full of cocaine, steals some money, and then punches one of the homeowners when she tries to stop the thief. Did four crimes happen here or just one? If we count all four separately, then it looks like there's a massive, sudden crime spree going on in the poor woman's living room. If we count only one or two of these as significant, then we are overlooking important crimes that might affect how people think of their neighborhood. If a person is initially charged with attempted murder but then accepts a plea bargain for a lesser crime, which offense actually took place on the night in question? There are different measures of crime, that is, different ways of determining the crime rate, each of which has its strengths and weaknesses and its own blind spots, that is, crimes that it is likely to miss. Each measurement of the crime rate provides only a partial view of what is happening in American society today. We can add them together and develop a rough picture of what is happening, but we will never really know with complete accuracy what is happening in the world of crime at any moment.

Further, there are many different crime studies. Some are done at the national level, some at the state level, and some at the local level. There are even international crime surveys taken by the United Nations. You could do a crime analysis of your own by polling your classmates, seeing who had been a crime victim in the last year, or if you're bolder, ask them who has committed a crime in the last year. All of these are useful, and all tell us different things about what crimes are happening and what people are doing and not doing about it. Typically, however, crime is measured in three ways: police reports, victimization surveys, and perpetrator surveys. In the section that follows, we will discuss each means for measuring crime, covering their respective strengths and weaknesses.

Police Reports

The simplest way to get crime data is to consult the people who most often deal with the criminal element: the police. Police reports tap into data that officers collect at the time of arrest to give us an idea of the crime rate. The two most well-known of these are the Uniform Crime Report (UCR) and the National Incident-Based Reporting Service (NIBRS). This data is gathered by officers on site and then sent to the FBI, where it is compared with other arrest data around the country to give Americans a sense of the crime rate.

The UCR was originally developed in the 1920s by the International Association of Chiefs of Police in order to have a single, nationwide resource for understanding and studying criminality in America. Material from the UCR is collected by the Justice Department and released in a series of publications, culminating in an annual study titled *Crime in the United States*. In this report, the department breaks crime down into seven major categories: felonious homicide, rape, robbery, aggravated assault, burglary (breaking or entering), larceny-theft, and auto theft. The NIBRS was created in the 1970s and goes into more detail about the crimes that police respond to. In both systems, however, when

Uniform Crime Report (UCR): A federally run measure of crime based largely on police reports.

the individual is arrested, the police enter the appropriate data into a database, and the data is then sent on to federal officials. However, not every crime is treated the same: The UCR uses what it calls the hierarchy rule—only the most serious crimes are recorded in the report, while lesser offenses are not. Thus if an individual assaults another person and steals her car, the police will not report both crimes to the UCR; rather, only the more serious offense (assault) will appear. A lot of lesser offenses will not show up in the crime data reported to the FBI.

Hierarchy rule:
The practice of the Uniform Crime Report of only counting the most serious crime in its measures.

Table 1.1   Crime Reported by UCR

The UCR only studies a selection of crimes and breaks them down into two different categories (or "Parts"). They are listed below:

Part I Offenses	
1. Criminal Homicide	5. Burglary
2. Forcible Rape	6. Larceny-Theft (except motor vehicle theft)
3. Robbery	7. Motor Vehicle Theft
4. Aggravated Assault	8. Arson

Part II Offenses	
9. Other Assaults	20. Offenses Against the Family and Children
10. Forgery and Counterfeiting	21. Driving Under the Influence
11. Fraud	22. Liquor Laws
12. Embezzlement	23. Drunkenness
13. Stolen Property: Buying, Receiving, Possessing	24. Disorderly Conduct
14. Vandalism	25. Vagrancy
15. Weapons: Carrying, Possessing, etc.	26. All Other Offenses
16. Prostitution and Commercialized Vice	27. Suspicion
17. Sex Offenses	28. Curfew and Loitering Laws (Persons under 18)
18. Drug Abuse Violations	29. Runaways (Persons under 18)
19. Gambling	

The NIBRS was created in part to avoid the problem created by the reporting of multiple crimes. By focusing on "incidents" rather than "crimes," the NIBRS gives a more accurate understanding of criminality. Beyond the fact that a particular incident occurred, the NIBRS includes information regarding victims, known offenders, any relationships between offenders and their victims, and arrestees, as well as information on any property involved in the crime. Most of this information does not appear in the UCR. This provides a more nuanced and thorough understanding of a particular criminal incident. While this provides researchers with a better understanding of the reality of crime, fewer police departments participate in the NIBRS, leaving significant gaps in the data that it provides.

Of course, there are some pretty significant problems with using police reports to determine the crime rate. For one thing, not every crime is reported to the police, and unreported crimes would rarely appear in either the UCR or the NIBRS. Many victims are criminals themselves or have other reasons to be wary of the police, and thus are disinclined to call 911 when they are victimized. Prostitutes, drug dealers, and illegal immigrants all tend to avoid calling the police, as would people who were already wanted for other crimes. (This makes people living outside the law, such as sex workers and undocumented aliens, particularly vulnerable to criminals who can rip them off with little danger of being caught.) Also, some victims do not call the police because they think it would be futile to do so or would lead to other negative consequences. A great number of domestic violence cases go unreported because victims fear revenge from their abusive spouse or losing the family's primary breadwinner to prison. Further, many crimes go *unnoticed* by their victims: If your wallet is stolen, you may mistakenly believe that you simply left it somewhere and think nothing further of it. In the perfect crime, the victim doesn't even know that she has been victimized. This means that there are a number of offenses that go unnoticed by the police and therefore do not appear on the UCR or NIBRS.

Victimization Surveys

The second way to learn about crime rates is to study crime victims. Victimization surveys do this through numerous methods, including anonymous surveys, phone interviews, and visiting households to ask people if they have been a victim of a crime over the last year or so. The most well-known victimization survey is the National Crime Victimization Survey (NCVS). Created in 1972 by the Department of Justice as a supplement to the UCR, the NCVS is meant to provide a second window into crime in America. A random selection of homes is contacted every six months and asked about their experiences with crime. If an interviewee reports being victimized, then the interviewer asks follow-up questions about the crime itself, determining different aspects of the crime, the victim, and the perpetrator. The NCVS only focuses on more serious crimes like rape, assault, and theft, ignoring lesser offenses. This allows researchers to develop crime data alongside the UCR and figure out which crimes are underreported to the police and what factors make it more likely that a victim will turn to the police after a crime.

Like police reports, victimization surveys have weaknesses that may distort their findings. Of course, some crimes are perceived as "victimless," such as prostitution, buying

Victimization surveys: A means of measuring crime by asking people whether they have been the victim of a crime.

National Crime Victim Survey (NCVS): A survey of crime that involves calling a random selection of homes and asking about crimes that they have experienced..

and selling drugs, et cetera, and these would probably not be reported by those involved in them. Not only does the NCVS ignore these and other minor crimes, it is also limited in its research to people who are the heads of their households, meaning that the homeless are ignored, and minors are not interviewed. This can lead to the underreporting of domestic violence and other household crimes. In addition, respondents may misinterpret what happened, believing that they simply lost their MP3 player, when in fact it was stolen (or vice versa). Likewise, victims who do not own a phone, such as many homeless people, will not appear in the NCVS.

Perpetrator Self-Report Studies

The final means by which we can learn about crime data is through what are known as perpetrator self-report studies. In these cases, people voluntarily, though anonymously, report the crimes that they have committed. This can be done via a written or phone survey or through interviews where subjects are guaranteed anonymity. For example, many states conduct surveys in their schools about drug use among teens and preteens in order to understand the scope of the drug problem in their own states. These studies can create ethical grey areas, as researchers may have knowledge about illegal behavior that the police do not know about. Many of these studies are *longitudinal*, meaning that they examine behavior over time to determine which periods of a person's life are most vulnerable to criminal activity. Others can test how widespread a certain criminal activity is; thus we can learn about stealing from a workplace, a minor crime that is probably very widespread in the working world. Self-report studies can provide another important way to understand the prevalence of crime and criminality, particularly in its most minor but widespread forms.

Obviously, self-report studies function on the honor system and, as a result, they can easily be misleading. A person may not trust her interviewer and not admit her crimes. A person may want to exaggerate her criminal behavior in order to impress somebody, or just because it's fun to make things up. It's not difficult to imagine a bunch of teenagers in a class making up wild stories about sex and drugs when they're filling out a survey, and it's also not hard to imagine earnest crime researchers and the media falling for outlandish tales of teen misbehavior—just as they've done many times in the past. Nonetheless, despite their weaknesses, self-report studies can provide information that victimization surveys or police reports can't: For example, small-time white collar crimes such as stealing from work would probably not appear in other crime studies. Small-scale drug abuse is similar: Many crimes are undiscovered by the police, and victims sometimes won't come forward about the crimes that they have endured, but might own up to them in a situation of anonymity.

Perpetrator Self-Report Studies: A means of measuring crime where individuals are (usually anonymously) asked about the crimes they have committed.

The Crime Rate

Added together, these different ways of measuring crime provide a series of accounts of crime in the United States and, in some cases, around the world. While each approach only provides a partial understanding of the frequency of crime and the types of offenses that are committed, we can arrive at a few conclusions about the overall crime rate. For example, if the UCR and the NCVS both show an increase in crime over a certain period, we can conclude that there probably really was an increase in crime over that time. Though it is not a certainty, overlapping data can be a reliable guide to what is going on out there in terms of crime. Nonetheless, there is still what social scientists refer to as the **dark figure of crime,** that is, crime that does not appear in any of these data collection methods. This dark figure lurks behind all talk of crime rates. We can never know the true crime rate and can only make informed, educated guesses about it with the data from these various sources.

Dark figure of crime: Crime that does not show up in traditional crime research.

SOME STATISTICS…

The Crime Drop

According to virtually all measures (the UCR, the NCVS, etc.), violent crime has significantly decreased throughout the country as murders, rapes, robberies, and other behaviors have decreased almost universally (see Figure 1.2).

These numbers are reflected in the homicide rate in particular (see Figure 1.3).

We can further compare these crime trends with trends for property crime where, again, the decline is similar. Theft, burglary, and car theft follow remarkably similar paths (see Figure 1.4).

It is also interesting to note that the crime drop is not only an American experience. In most of the industrialized world, crime

Figure 1.2   Rate of Violent Victimization, 1993–2017

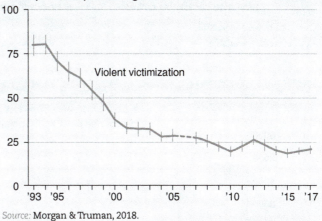

Rate per 1,000 persons age 12 or older

Source: Morgan & Truman, 2018.

has decreased. Though the numbers are hard to measure, as each country measures its crime rate in different ways using different standards and measuring tools, "There has been a significant and prolonged 'crime drop' in many industrialized nations" (Farrell, Tilley, & Tseloni, 2014, p. 436). While homicide rates have often been lower in Canada than in the United States, there remains a similar *trend* in homicide in both countries: It increased dramatically, and then sharply dropped in the 1990s (see Figure 1.5).

Figure 1.5 is misleading—keep in mind that the two countries didn't have the same number of homicides; rather the crimes followed similar *patterns* over time.

Despite the fact that many Americans still consider crime to be a serious problem, for the most part Americans are safer than they have ever been.

(Continued)

(Continued)

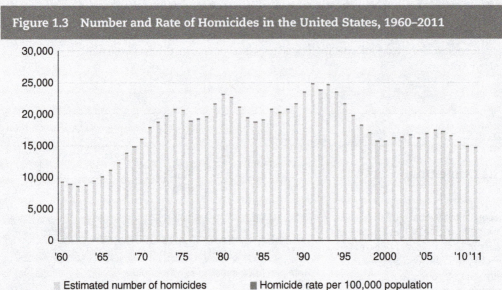

Figure 1.3   Number and Rate of Homicides in the United States, 1960–2011

Estimated number of homicides   Homicide rate per 100,000 population

Source: Smith & Cooper, 2013.

Note: Latest data available.

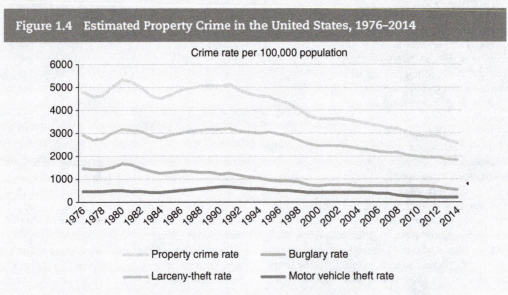

Figure 1.4   Estimated Property Crime in the United States, 1976–2014

Crime rate per 100,000 population

Property crime rate   Burglary rate

Larceny-theft rate   Motor vehicle theft rate

Source: FBI, Uniform Crime Reports, prepared by the National Archive of Criminal Justice Data, January 10, 2019.

Note: Latest data available.

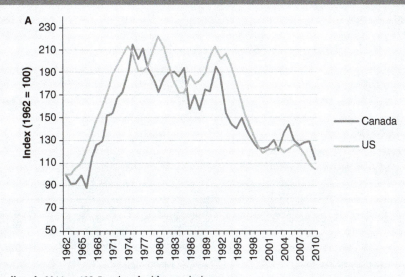

Figure 1.5   Homicide Trends in the United States and Canada, 1962–2010

Source: Farrell et al., 2014, p. 428. Reprinted with permission.

Note: Latest data available.

As we have seen so far, there is good reason to be skeptical about our ability to have a completely accurate picture of the crime rate in the United States. There are a lot of unknowns about the world of crime, and any generalizations about it must be carefully qualified. Nonetheless, there are some things we can say about crime rates in the United States with some confidence. Most notably, there has been a marked decrease in violent crime over the last two decades according to almost all measurements. This *crime drop* as it is known among social scientists seems to be a reliable phenomenon, and it follows a steep rise in the crime rate in the several decades that preceded it (see Figure 1.6).

The crime drop has presented a challenge for criminologists who seek to discover the causes of crime and explain variations in the crime rate. Essentially, none of the commonly available theories predicted such precipitous decline in criminality and, as a result, novel theories have been proposed to address the issue.

The Politics of Crime Data

While resources like the UCR and the NCVS seem to provide a neutral way to determine what's going on in the world of criminality, crime data is very political. Police officials and politicians often distort or misrepresent their crime data for a variety of reasons. Obviously, a low crime rate could reflect well on a police force—showing that they have crime under control in their jurisdiction. It could also help politicians, real estate developers, and others who want to portray a city or neighborhood as a safe place to do business, live, and raise a family. Surprisingly, however, there can also be a strong incentive to *inflate* crime statistics,

Figure 1.6 Estimated Violent Crime Rate in the United States, 1960–2014

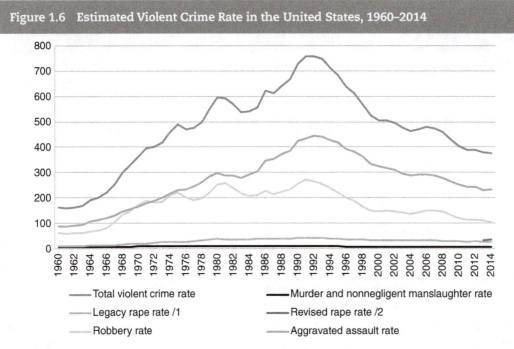

- Total violent crime rate
- Legacy rape rate /1
- Robbery rate
- Murder and nonnegligent manslaughter rate
- Revised rape rate /2
- Aggravated assault rate

Source: FBI, Uniform Crime Reports, prepared by the National Archive of Criminal Justice Data, January 10, 2019.

Note: Latest data available.

that is, to make crime seem worse than it probably is. If crime rates are low, there isn't a pressing demand for additional funds for police officers, vehicles, training, weapons, and other tools of policing. A high crime rate can provide justification for additional funding and provides politicians with a chance to talk tough.

There are many examples of crime statistics being manipulated for financial gain or for good public relations. In 2014, Dekalb County, Georgia, was found to have inflated its crime rates in order to secure $2.3 million in federal funding ("DeKalb County," 2014). The police department in Phoenix, Arizona, was investigated in 2011 for misreporting kidnapping statistics in order to get over a million dollars in federal stimulus money (Hermann, 2011). In 2011, the 77th Precinct in New York City was accused of manipulating its crime statistics by falsely stating that a crime had not happened (Yakas, 2011). A study by the magazine *Chicago* showed that a series of murders were classified as less serious crimes by the police or converted into noncriminal cases in 2013 (Bernstein & Isackson, 2014). A former police chief in Biscayne Park, Florida, was sentenced to three years in prison for ordering officers to arrest innocent black people in order to give the impression that his department was solving crimes (Hauser, 2018). Similar cases have occurred in many other cities in the United States as police departments and politicians manipulate the data to serve their own political or financial interests.

Hate crimes are particularly difficult to measure, because they are widely underreported by local law enforcement officials (see Figure 1.7). A hate crime is a crime where the victim is targeted because of her race, religion, gender, et cetera. The Department of Justice collects information submitted by local law enforcement regarding hate crimes, but

Figure 1.7   Violent Hate Crime Victimizations Reported and Not Reported to Police, 2004–2015

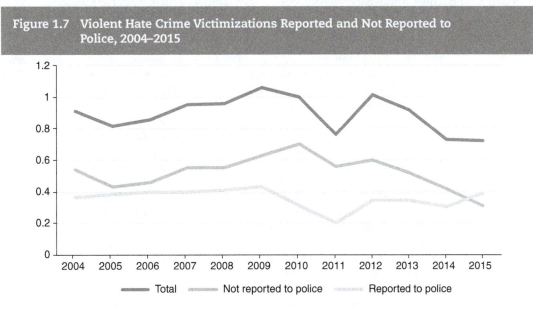

Source: Masucci & Langton, 2017.

Note: Latest data available.

the data that local law enforcement provides has been terrible in many cases. Simply put, no local government wants its area to be associated with hate crimes, and so these jurisdictions do not provide accurate information to federal officials about it (Bjork-James, 2019).

You are a crime statistician responsible for developing crime data for a city that has long struggled. For many years there has been a high crime rate, and the city's reputation as a dangerous place has affected the property values in the city and made the problem worse, as wealthier residents have fled and businesses have been reluctant to invest there. Despite public perceptions, the crime statistics are misleading—crime is only bad in a few neighborhoods, and the rest of the city is generally safe. When you've tried to point out these differences in your data, nobody outside the city seems to care; all they see is a high crime rate in town.

In response to this problem, the city government and the police department have developed a plan to weigh crime in different neighborhoods differently. Crime in these few high-crime neighborhoods would count less in the overall crime rate than crimes in other neighborhoods. In part, this would come from the police, who would record offenses in these neighborhoods less often or as lesser offenses than those in other neighborhoods. In part, they have asked you to count each crime in these neighborhoods as only half of a crime. (Thus for every two crimes there, you only count one.) This, the officials believe, would provide a more accurate picture of crime in the city and would help boost investment, something that would benefit everybody.

Would you be willing to participate in this project? Do you think such an approach to measuring crime in the city would be fairer or more accurate than taking all crime in the city as a whole?

Officers are not likely to record some offenses as hate crimes, but victimization studies can provide a different perspective. Being associated with bigotry is not a "good look" for local officials, and therefore they do not report these offenses, and the public is left with a distorted view of hate in America.

Another thing to keep in mind when looking at crime statistics, particularly in relation to arrest rates, is that a net increase in crime does not necessarily mean that more crime has occurred, and a net decrease in crime doesn't mean that there is less crime. An increase in crime may simply mean that more officers are being diligent in their job and arresting more people. A decrease in crime could mean that the police are slacking off or finding other ways to artificially lower their crime rate. Finally, just because a large number of people are arrested does not mean that these suspects are being convicted of any crimes—convictions or acquittals usually do not show up in crime data. Offenders may be released because there is not enough evidence to hold them, they may be acquitted, or they may be convicted, but of a significantly lesser offense than the one that the officers arrested them for. Statistics are easily misleading and are often distorted for a whole array of reasons.

In the next chapter, we will turn away from crime as a social phenomenon and turn to one particular way of understanding crime, the legal one. Obviously criminal law has a great deal to say about what crime is and is in many ways the most important way to classify crime. However, keep in mind the discussion in this chapter about law—seeing criminals as lawbreakers is only *one* way to look at crime. In further chapters in this section we will examine psychological, sociological, and economic approaches to studying crime.

CHAPTER SUMMARY

The concept of "crime" is not a straightforward one. There are different ways to define the term, including legal (crimes are violations of the law), moral (crimes are actions that are seriously immoral), and sociological (crimes are actions that society believes deserve punishment) approaches, each of which has its own strengths and weaknesses. Similarly, there are numerous ways to classify crime; it can be classified based on the type of victim (persons, property, public order, the state), the seriousness of the offense (misdemeanors, felonies), where the crime happens (white collar crime, domestic crime, street crime). Crime is measured either through the examination of arrest rates, the surveying of crime victims, or from the self-reports of those who perpetrate crimes. These can be brought together to come up with some sense of the overall crime rate, though no measure is perfect.

REVIEW/DISCUSSION QUESTIONS

1. Can you think of issues other than abortion where different groups use the rhetoric of crime to advance their cause?

2. The different ways of defining crime all have their own strengths and weaknesses. Which do you think is best? Why?

3. Which form of measuring crime do you think is the best? If you were moving into a neighborhood and could research crime data about it, which type of crime data would mean the most to you?

4. Should communities be required to publicize their crime rates? Do you think this could lead to more governments fudging their crime data?

5. Why do you think groups that are least likely to be affected by violent crime (namely, the elderly) are most afraid of crime, while those most likely to be a victim (young people) are less likely?

KEY TERMS

Corporate crimes 14
Crimes against persons 12
Crimes against property 12
Crimes against public order 12
Crimes against the state 12
Criminal justice policies 16

Criminal justice system 3
Dark figure of crime 21
Felony 12
Hate crimes 15
Hierarchy rule 18
Misdemeanors 12

National Crime Victim Survey (NCVS) 19
Perpetrator Self-Report Studies 20
Uniform Crime Report 17
Victimization surveys 19
White collar crime 14

$SAGE edge™

Get the tools you need to sharpen your study skills. SAGE edge offers a robust online environment featuring an impressive array of free tools and resources.

Access practice quizzes, eFlashcards, video, and multimedia at edge.sagepub.com/fichtelberg

Sarah Yeh

Lady justice is blindfolded to symbolize fairness. Is criminal justice really fair?

CHAPTER TWO

CRIMINAL LAW

When you think of the word *law*, what comes into your mind? Perhaps images of heavy, leather-bound books sitting on a dark wooden bookshelf. Perhaps the famous "Lady Justice" statue, standing blindfolded, holding a sword in one hand and a scale in the other. Maybe it's a robed judge banging her[1] gavel surrounded by expensively dressed lawyers and court officers in an oak-lined room as some unfortunate defendant glumly looks on. Images of law are everywhere in our culture and, as an institution, the law has an exalted position: Being a lawyer is usually taken to be a prestigious career, and knowledge of the law is considered a powerful weapon. Of course, practicing law can also be a way to make a lot of money. . . .

These pictures are not "the law," of course. They are symbols of law—images that convey the power it has over our lives. Many aspects of this image are cultivated by lawyers and other legal professionals to enhance the status of legal professionals and to make them seem important and deserving of a big paycheck. Some of these images are there to show that law deserves deference—the law is serious business and must be treated with respect. In the modern computer age, there is little need for leather-bound law books, and most of them are purely decorative. Judicial robes serve no practical purpose either. Gavels are fun, but there are better ways to silence a room. The law is draped with ancient symbolism— much of which is irrelevant to modern society but nonetheless persists in order to convince the public that the law matters a great deal.

Given the obsession that our culture has with all things criminal, it is unsurprising that many people think of law first and foremost as criminal law and believe that most lawyers deal with criminals in one way or another. Criminal law is only one part of a much larger legal system, however. In fact, criminal law is a relatively small part of the legal profession, and among lawyers it tends to be less prestigious than other fields. Students who go to law school will take courses in criminal law, but will also take courses in corporate law, tax law, torts, constitutional law, and real estate law, among many others. In addition, there is a distinction between criminal law (sometimes called "crim" by law students) and criminal procedure (often referred to as "crim pro"). Criminal law, usually referred to as *substantive criminal law*, deals with the legal definitions of crimes, while criminal procedure

---

[1] As of 2018 there are 5,947 women judges out of 17,840 total judges in state courts, composing 33% of all judges. In the federal courts, 428 out of 870 federal judges are women (National Association of Women Judges, 2018).

deals with things like the conduct of trials and the limitations on the police's ability to search a person's property, et cetera, all of which will be discussed in later chapters. Substantive criminal law is only a small sliver of the legal world, but it is a very important one for many reasons.

THE RULE OF LAW

Learning Objective 2.1—Describe the concept of the rule of law and its importance in American society.

One useful thing to understand about the law is that different parts of the law serve different functions. Constitutional law determines how the American people organize their government. Tort law deals with private injuries (when one person hurts another person) and only allows for monetary compensation for victims. Family law determines issues of marriage, divorce, and children. Criminal law, on the other hand, can be understood as a set of lines that, if you cross them, the state will intervene and deny you your freedom through the police, the courts, and the prisons, et cetera. Only a few other domains of law authorize the government to hold an individual against her will (laws regarding the institutionalization of the mentally ill or laws regarding immigration are other examples), and criminal law is the only portion of the law that allows the government to kill its own citizens (through execution) when we're not at war.

This unique power to deprive people of their freedom makes criminal law an important part, if not the most important part, of government. Bad criminal laws can be easily abused by powerful individual or groups who want to crush dissent or target unwanted minorities. Almost every dictatorship in the world uses criminal laws as a weapon against its opponents, and the prisons of the world are full of people who were sent to prison for simply disagreeing with those in charge. China can arrest a person for "creating a disturbance" (Press, 2014), and countries like Egypt and Turkey use vague antiterrorism and public safety laws to arrest journalists and other people who shine an unflattering light on their governments. Criminal laws are necessary to ensure law and order in a society, but they are also very dangerous things to people who love their freedom.

Because it is so dangerous, almost democratic societies place limits on criminal law through the principles composing *the rule of law*. The rule of law is meant to prevent criminal law from becoming a tool of would-be dictators. Some of these principles are a ban on *ex post facto* laws, a ban on unclear laws (*"void for vagueness"*), and *strict construction* in legal interpretation. *Ex post facto* laws are laws that attempt to criminalize behavior that occurred before the laws were passed. For example, a law that was passed on Tuesday criminalizing the wearing of baseball hats could not be used to punish a student who wore one on Monday. This sounds obvious, but some laws are so unclear that a new interpretation of a law can function in an *ex post facto* way. For example, in one California case, a man kicked his estranged, pregnant wife in the belly, causing her to miscarry (*Keeler v. Superior Court*, 1970). At the time, the California penal code said that it was murder to kill a "human being." Whether or not you personally believe that an unborn child is a human being, there is probably no way that the defendant could have known with certainty that he was committing murder at the time of the attack. There was no clear determination as to whether a fetus was considered a "human being" under the law at the time. (In this case, the court ruled that it wasn't.) Without clear guidance in a case like this, it's easy to see how *ex post facto* laws can exist and be problematic.

The *vagueness doctrine* states that valid laws must clearly describe which acts are prohibited. Of course, all criminal laws prohibit certain activities, but there is often an issue about how broad the law must be to be effective. They must use language broad enough to apply to a variety of different situations, but not so broad that you don't know when you've violated them. Think of all the different ways that you can "assault" somebody: with a rock, with your fists, with your car; all of these are captured under the term *assault*, but what about assaulting people by yelling at them with a loudspeaker turned up so high that it makes their ears bleed? Or flinging water at them in a way that is annoying? All laws must be somewhat general to cover a bunch of different situations, but the more general they get, the more they run the risk of being too vague. The most notorious of these are loitering and public morals laws, which try to regulate something like "standing around doing nothing," which is very hard to precisely define. People should have a fair warning about when they're about to break the law, so they can make a choice about what to do.

Vague laws invite themselves to be enforced selectively by police officers, who can pick which acts violate the law and which don't. To use one famous case, in *Papachristou v. City of Jacksonville* (1972), a group of defendants challenged a city ordinance banning "wandering or strolling around from place to place without any lawful purpose or object." While some of the defendants in the case *may* have been engaged in suspicious activity, what this means isn't really clear. It is interesting to note that four of the defendants who had been cited together were black men in the company of white women. Other cases have produced similar results. Vague laws are used by officers selectively to target people they considered undesirable: A group of middle-class white people drinking wine in front of their house is having a pleasant conversation, a group of black men drinking beer in front of their house is loitering (Roberts, 1998). Poorly written laws can easily be applied in an unfair or biased way.

The final element of the rule of law is *strict construction*. This rule means that judges should interpret criminal laws as narrowly as possible. Whenever there are two equally plausible interpretations of a law, judges should apply the one that is more limited in scope. This prevents judges or the police from unfairly prosecuting people for violating a law that they had every reason to believe they were obeying.

Criminal Law and Common Law

America is a "common law" country, and common law principles are used in federal law as well as in laws in all but one state.[2] Common law is a legal tradition that dates to medieval England. There are many important features of common law that distinguish it from the *civil law* tradition used in much of the rest of the world. Most important for now, however, is the role that judges play in interpreting the law. Judges have a lot of power in telling us what the law means: They interpret the law, and sometimes in doing so effectively create new laws. For this reason, the common law system is sometimes described as "judge made law." Judges create new laws by writing down the reasons that they give for their interpretation and, by doing so, the judges create a binding *precedent* that the next judge must follow.

Common law: The legal tradition in England and the United States where courts determine the meanings of laws through a series of opinions or precedents that are binding.

---

[2] Louisiana is the only state to not use common law, because of its history as a French colony.

(Judges are very hesitant to break with existing precedent.) The legal term for this is *stare decisis*, which translates roughly as "to stand by things decided." Therefore, when we talk about the law in America, we refer to cases like *Marbury v. Madison*, *Miranda v. Arizona*, or *Roe v. Wade*, rather than pieces of legislation or to legal codes. In these cases, judges made influential decisions that created precedents. Effectively they made the law. It is also one of the reasons why politicians fight so viciously about who gets to serve on the different courts, as judges have a huge role in shaping the law.

The common law tradition shapes many aspects of our criminal justice system beyond simply how the courts render their decisions. It shapes how crimes are organized under the law, how crimes are defined, and most importantly, how trials are conducted. Almost all modern crimes were originally common law crimes, and how the common law defined crimes like rape, murder, and arson has shaped how we think of them now. The way our legal system is structured is in many ways an accident of history. Other societies have legal systems that are very different, and in some ways, much better.

Federalism and Law

As was already mentioned, there is not one American criminal law. There are (at least) 54 distinct legal systems in the United States, and many more depending on how you count them. There is federal criminal law, a series of laws passed by Congress and signed into law by the president. Federal laws apply all over the country and can be found in Title 18 of the United States Code. There are also the legal codes of the 50 individual states, each of which was drafted by its respective state legislature. If we want to count it, we can include the common law, which still functions as a body of law standing in the background, as it were, providing judges with guides on how to interpret state and federal laws when they face ambiguities. A 53rd legal system would be the Uniform Code of Military Justice (UCMJ), which technically is a part of federal law but doesn't apply to people outside of the military. (It is in Title 10 of the US Code.) There are also the legal codes of the various territories under the control of the U.S. government, such as Eastern Samoa and the Mariana Islands.

Alongside these is the *Model Penal Code* (MPC). This is not law per se, but it has an important influence on criminal law around the country. The MPC was created by a group of lawyers who were a part of an influential organization known as the American Law Institute (ALI), which sought to provide order and uniformity to American law. Essentially, these lawyers looked through the different legal systems around the United States and developed a legal code that they believed made more sense than the haphazard laws that existed in many states. These laws became the MPC. These rules have been used by the states to change or reform the existing legal codes so that they can be more rational and fairer. The MPC has never been adopted whole by the states, but it nonetheless has had a profound influence on American criminal law in many states, and judges sometimes refer to it in their decisions.

All of this means that there are different crimes in different states and that the same crime may be defined very differently in two different states. To make things more complicated, even if an offense is defined the same way in two different states, the courts in each one may interpret the statute differently based on their own precedents and the preferences of the judges there. Because there are so many different sources for criminal law, it can be very difficult to determine what the law is in any given case. All of this makes American law a very complex set of rules that requires highly trained professionals to interpret and apply. This is one of the reasons why lawyers get paid so much money; the law is complex, and *nothing* is straightforward in it. It's also the reason why I cannot simply tell you what the law is in this chapter. It's simply too diverse, and there are too many different legal codes. We must account for these different factors when examining the law, and the law will look different depending on the state you're in and even depending on the judge you are assigned.

THE "INGREDIENTS" (ELEMENTS) OF CRIME

Learning Objective 2.2—List and describe the three elements of crimes.

Despite the complications in American criminal law, the laws in every state have a similar structure, and (almost) all crimes have the same basic elements. With only a few exceptions, all criminal offenses have two fundamental components: an *actus reus* (a guilty act) and a *mens rea* (a guilty mind), and some crimes have a third factor: *causation*. Therefore, in most cases we can break crime down, legally speaking, into a simple equation:

$$\text{ACTUS REUS} + \text{MENS REA} + (\text{CAUSATION}) = \text{CRIME}$$

As we will see, there are some important exceptions to this formula, but for the moment we can stick with it. We will discuss each of these aspects of the legal construction of crime in turn.

Actus Reus

The first requirement of a crime is that there must be a "guilty act." A criminal must *do something* to commit a crime. Usually this means that a criminal must move her body of her own free will and do some sort of harm. If an individual passes out and is then moved onto private property, then she hasn't trespassed. Similarly, if I only contemplate killing a person but don't act on it, I haven't committed a crime. We don't punish somebody for doing something against her will and we don't punish people who simply think about committing a crime. As silly as it sounds, to be a criminal, one must *act* in an unlawful way.

Beyond these simple examples, there are many crimes where the *actus reus* is somewhat more ambiguous, and pinning down the criminal act is a matter of interpretation. The *actus reus* of murder is usually easy to determine, as it is for other more straightforward sorts of offenses. **Inchoate crimes** are crimes where a person has not actually hurt somebody but will probably do so in the future. These crimes include solicitation, conspiracy, and attempt. For these offenses, the *actus reus* can be simply saying certain words to another person, such as asking a prostitute to exchange money for sex. Making an agreement with somebody else to commit an offense with another person can be the *actus reus* of conspiracy. However, the acts that compose many other crimes are unclear. For example, when has one committed the crime of *attempted murder*? While aiming a gun at another, pulling the trigger, and missing your target (what is sometimes called a "completed attempt") is clear, other acts that might be attempted murder are not so clear. For example, if I earnestly write in my diary that I want to kill another person, describing my plan in detail, have I attempted to murder somebody? What about if I buy a gun with

Actus reus: "The bad act." The action that constitutes the offense.

Mens rea: "The bad mind." The psychological state that must accompany the *actus reus* of the offense.

Inchoate crimes: Crimes that have yet to lead to any real harm, such as attempt, solicitation, and conspiracy.

the idea that I want to kill somebody but have yet to do anything else? Have I committed attempted murder? The lines of what constitutes a criminal act can sometimes be less clear than we imagine.

In the 2002 science fiction movie *Minority Report*, the police, aided by the power of psychics, are authorized to arrest somebody for "future crimes," crimes that this person will carry out in the future but has yet to commit. Inchoate crimes are reminiscent of this film. These criminals have yet to hurt anybody when they are arrested, but they are probably going to do so in the future. The *actus rei* of solicitation, attempt, and conspiracy are harmless on their own. After all, agreeing with another person to murder a third person is not the same as murdering her, and it's possible that one or both conspirators will back out of their plan before anybody is hurt. A man who solicits a prostitute has not "done the deed," though he probably will. A person who buys a gun and drives to her ex-lover's house may kill the lover, or she may decide to go home instead. When the police are allowed to arrest an individual for an inchoate crime, they can stop a crime before anybody is hurt, but this also raises the likelihood that a person who is ultimately harmless will be punished.

The law punishes actions, not failures to act. That is, in most cases we do *not* punish an individual for not helping another person in need, no matter how easy it might be to do so. The law doesn't require that we help others, only that we don't hurt them. In 1997, Jeremy Strohmeyer, a 20-year-old from Long Beach, California, murdered a 7-year-old girl, Sherrice Iverson, in the women's restroom in a Nevada casino. His friend, David Cash Jr. observed the attack from the next stall but did nothing to stop it. Instead of rescuing the girl, Cash left the bathroom and went for a walk. After the body was discovered and Strohmeyer was arrested, Cash was unmoved. As he put it, "I'm not going to get upset over somebody else's life. I just worry about myself first. I'm not going to lose sleep over somebody else's problems" (Zamichow, 1998). Despite demands from Iverson's family that Cash be prosecuted, there were no grounds for charging him, as the law did not criminalize doing nothing. Unless you have a legal duty to act, for example if you were a cop or a lifeguard, a failure to act is not an *actus reus*. In response to cases like these, some states have passed "good Samaritan" laws (including Nevada, which passed a law after Iverson's murder), which are meant to encourage people to help others if they can do it safely. But the general rule remains that it is not a crime to do nothing when one could have prevented a crime from happening (Dressler & Garvey, 2015).

Mens Rea

The other main element of a crime is the *mens rea* or culpable mental state. Most, though not all, criminal statutes spell out the required mental state that must accompany the *actus reus*. The most common form of *mens rea* is *intent* (as in "intentional homicide"), but there are many others: recklessness, negligence, et cetera. One thing to keep in mind, however, is that each of these terms has a special legal meaning that is often very different from the way we use these terms in everyday life.

There could be any number of different *mentes reae*, and some laws don't even include an explicit *mens rea* when they define an offense. Some statutes are very specific, such as Texas's kidnapping law, which states "A person commits an offense if he intentionally or knowingly abducts another person," while others are quite vague or use terms that we *never* use in our ordinary life. Massachusetts describes malicious damage in this way: "Whoever destroys or injures the personal property, dwelling house or building of another in any manner or by any means not particularly described or mentioned in this chapter shall, if such destruction or injury is willful and malicious," be guilty of malicious damage.

The following are some of the most common ones, *mentes reae* that are found in American criminal law.

Intent

To do something intentionally is to knowingly and willingly do it. The criminal wants to produce a certain outcome and acts to bring that result. A person who sees another standing in front of her, pulls out a gun, aims it, and pulls the trigger is almost always acting intentionally, unless there are some very strange circumstances surrounding the shooting, such as a mistaken belief that the gun is only a toy. Unless the court has compelling reasons to think otherwise, we usually intend the normal consequences of our actions.

Recklessness

This second form of *mens rea* refers to a crime where an individual did not want to cause harm but acted so dangerously that she made it very likely that something bad would happen. The technical legal language describes reckless behavior as a "*gross deviation* from the standard of conduct that a law-abiding person would observe in the actor's situation" (Hall, 2008, p. 63, italics added). An individual who fires her gun into the air in celebration is being reckless, as the bullet will eventually come down and could hurt someone. The shooter knew this was a possible result of her action—even if she did not wish to hurt anyone when she pulled the trigger. It is reckless to drive drunk, to speed, and to throw rocks from an overpass onto a busy freeway. While people who are reckless are not usually punished as severely as people who intentionally commit crimes, crimes of recklessness are usually considered serious.

Negligence

It is often difficult to distinguish negligence from recklessness, and it's sometimes a bit of a guess as to which applies to a case. When a person has acted negligently, she did not know that she was doing something wrong or dangerous but *should have known* that she was. In fact, any reasonable person would have known that the actions were risky. As Oregon's criminal code defines it, criminal negligence occurs when

> a person fails to be aware of a substantial and unjustifiable risk that the result will occur or that the circumstance exists. The risk must be of such nature and degree that the failure to be aware of it constitutes a gross deviation from the standard of care that a reasonable person would observe in the situation. (ORS § 161.085, 2017)

A person who *genuinely* believes that there is nobody below her window and drops a brick without looking is negligent. If she thought somebody could be there but did not check, she was reckless. It is perhaps fair to describe negligence as a form of "criminal stupidity"—negligent persons aren't bad, they are simply behaving in a way that is so thoughtless and so dumb that they ought to be punished.

Often the difference between recklessness and negligence is unclear and hinges on the beliefs of the offender at the time that she acts—something that is extremely difficult to know. To be reckless requires not only that the individual be aware of the risks in her behavior but also that she does not wish to hurt anybody, while to be negligent requires that she be unaware of the risk. A person who truly believes that the house is empty before setting it on fire is negligent if somebody is killed, but a person who suspects that there *may* be somebody in the house when she strikes the match is reckless when her victim perishes. This may sound like splitting hairs, but in cases where an accident causes another to be hurt or killed, the accused's awareness can mean the difference between a lengthy prison term and a relatively short one. Moreover, if the prosecutor cannot prove in court that the defendant was aware of the dangers of her actions, the jury may elect to convict the defendant, but only for a lesser crime with a *mens rea* of negligence.

Other Mentes Reae

While intent, reckless, and negligence are the most common forms of *mens rea*, criminal statutes can specify any number of different *mentes reae* with greater or lesser specificity. For example, a statute can use the term *malicious* as a *mens rea*. Other legal codes might use antiquated terms like *wicked, fraudulently,* or *wantonly* for their offenses, leaving judges to figure out what they mean in a modern context. As a rough guide, the portion of the statute that refers to the mental state of the alleged offender is usually the *mens rea* of the offense. Some *mens rea* terms may sound strange or use out-of-date language (such as *depraved heart murder*), and it is usually up to the courts to determine what they mean and how to apply them in a modern context.

Strict Liability

Most criminal offenses have an *actus reus* and a *mens rea* that are explicitly stated in the legal statute. However, this is not always the case. Some laws fail to mention a *mens rea* and leave it up to the courts to figure out what is appropriate for the crime. Others, however, do not require any *mens rea* for the individual to be prosecuted. To use one example from the South Carolina criminal code ("Carrying fire on lands of another without permit"),

> It shall be unlawful for any person to carry a lighted torch, chunk or coals of fire in or under any mill or wooden building or over and across any of the enclosed or unenclosed lands of another person at any time without the special permit of the owner of such lands, mill or wooden building, whether any damage result therefrom or not. (SC Code § 16-11-160, 2012)

Notice that the law does not say anything about intent, negligence, et cetera—all that matters is that you were carrying a lighted torch. Laws like this, laws without a *mens rea* component to them, create a different form of criminal liability, known as strict liability. Other examples of strict liability offenses are statutory rape laws (that is, the crime of having consensual sex with a minor) as well as many laws regulating the sale of alcohol to minors. Under strict liability, individuals can be punished for violating the law independent of whether they were reckless, negligent, or acting intentionally. All that matters is that they committed the *actus reus* of the crime.

Strict liability offenses: Crimes that do not require a *mens rea.*

The rationale behind strict liability offenses is that individuals who participate in risky sorts of activities accept a higher level of responsibility for their conduct than those who don't. That is, if you want to sell alcohol, mess around with explosives, use torches, or engage in extramarital sex, you understand that the state won't accept any excuse for your behavior if you accidentally violate the law. The lawmakers believe that saying "I didn't know that the girl was underage, and she looked like a grownup to me" is a cop-out in these circumstances—and it gives the statutory rapist an easy excuse later when he gets caught. People who run liquor stores have an economic interest in not knowing the age of their customers and would probably consciously decide to remain ignorant about it if they thought that they could get away with it. While most strict liability offenses are misdemeanors, some, like statutory rape, are felonies, and offenders can end up being imprisoned for a long time independent of whether they knew they were breaking the law at the time.

Causation

The final element of a crime is *causation*. The individual's act must have caused actual harm. For example, an attacker's bullet must have caused the death of the victim for the suspect to be charged with murder. If the victim was already dead, then it is obviously not murder. Not every crime requires causation (for example, possession of a controlled substance does not), but for those that do require a specific result, such as homicide, there must be a causal link between the *actus reus* and the outcome. While this may sound obvious, determining the cause of death can be difficult, and despite what you've seen on TV, forensic medicine is not an exact science.

Not only must the criminal act cause the outcome, is must also have been the *proximate cause* of the outcome. If a man strikes another with a baseball bat, and the person he struck dies in the hospital a few days later, he caused the victim's death. However, if in fact the cause of death was gross malpractice on the part of the hospital staff, which failed to adequately treat the wound and left it open to infection, then it is not so clear that the attacker is truly responsible for his victim's death. In criminal law, proximate causes are those actions that make a person criminally responsible for the outcome, usually the death of a victim. In some cases, there are many different causes for a result, but the prosecutors must determine who is responsible. One helpful way to think about it is to say that every proximate cause is a cause, but not every cause is a proximate cause.

A good example of the difference between cause and proximate cause is to be found in *Kibbe v. Henderson* (1976). In this case, the two defendants met a third, named George Stafford, at a bar, and after getting him drunk, started to drive him home. Rather than taking him home, however, the two men robbed Stafford and left him by the side of a rural, two-lane highway. In his drunken state, Stafford wandered into the road and sat down. He was then hit by a driver going 10 miles per hour above the speed limit. While the two defendants caused Stafford's death, insofar as he would not have been by the side of the road if they had not robbed him, the court ruled that the defendants were not the proximate cause of the victim's death and therefore they could not be prosecuted for killing him. There were too many other intervening factors—Stafford's own drunkenness, his decision to wander into the road, the driver's speeding—to hold the defendants responsible for his death. A person can cause a death without being legally responsible for it.

Homicide

One crime that has undergone a great deal of change in American legal history is criminal *homicide*. There is a big difference in how homicides are treated under the law, and homicide law varies a great deal from state to state. To use the example we discussed earlier, some states distinguish between first- and second-degree murder in their penal codes, but others don't. Some states distinguish between murder and manslaughter, while others don't. There is no single way to distinguish between types of homicide, and the different legal approaches to murder in different states have a long history. They reflect broader changes in American law and politics, but they also reflect our views about the morality of human behavior: Which homicides are the worst, and which killings are a little more understandable (though still criminal)?

Modern homicide law developed out of the common law—the laws created by English judges and passed on to America during the colonial period. Under the common law, murder was described as "the unlawful killing of another being with malice aforethought." *Malice aforethought* (the *mens rea* of murder) meant many different things, but for simplicity's sake, we can say that the term was a lot like the modern notion of intent (Dressler & Garvey, 2015, p. 253). Thus, accidental killings were not considered murder, even if they were the result of negligence. In traditional common law, a person convicted of murder was automatically given the death penalty, unless there were extraordinary circumstances.

Murder was not the only form of homicide that developed out of the common law, however. An exception was carved out for *manslaughter*, often described as intentionally killing "in the heat of passion." While still intentional homicide, manslaughter was not considered as bad as traditional murder and did not merit the death penalty. Manslaughter referred to killings such as the murder of a cheating spouse or other situations where a person was presented with an immediate, highly emotional situation that caused her to kill another person. These killings weren't considered lawful but were not punished as severely as murder. Hence, the key distinction in homicide law under common law was between the killers who should be executed (murder) and those who should be allowed to live (manslaughter).

What we now know as degrees of murder, such as first- or second-degree murder, came later in the United States. In 1793, the Commonwealth of Pennsylvania

> resolved that all murder perpetrated by poison or by lying in wait, or by any kind of willful, premeditated and deliberate killings, shall be deemed murder in the first degree, and all other kinds of murder shall be murder in the second degree. (Keedy, 1949, p. 771)

A conviction for first-degree murder meant execution (Keedy, 1949). Neither second-degree murder nor manslaughter was considered a capital offense, that is, an offense that merited execution. This led to greater diversity in the law and restricted execution to the "worst" forms of homicide.

While many states followed Pennsylvania's lead in distinguishing between degrees of murder, not every state agreed with Pennsylvania's way of formulating this distinction. There are several different ways that states have sought to distinguish between degrees of murder. Some states distinguish between first-degree murder and second-degree murder by describing first-degree murder as intentional homicide and second-degree murder as

Capital offenses: Offenses that merit the death penalty.

reckless homicide. Others distinguish them in different ways based upon what sorts of killings they deem to be worse than others. The point is that first-degree and second-degree murder are legal terms with different meanings in different states.

One final element of homicide law is the *felony-murder rule*. This rule, inherited from the common law, says that a person can be convicted of murder if, in the act of committing a felony, she kills another person. This killing does not need to be malicious, intentional, or reckless for it to be murder. For example, if, in the middle of a robbery, a victim has a heart attack and dies, the robber could be convicted of murder, even though in many senses she did not kill the victim. If a person commits a felony and somebody dies as a result, it's usually murder, regardless of whether or not killing the victim was a part of the original plan.

DEFENSES

Learning Objective 2.3—List the three major categories of criminal defenses and the five specific defenses.

A *defense* in the law is anything that the accused uses to either get herself acquitted or to have her punishment reduced by the court. There are three general categories of defenses, and under these are several different specific defenses. The first form of defense is known as a *failure of proof* defense. This defense simply means that the prosecution has failed to prove that the defendant committed the crime. The second category of defense is called a *justification*. This defense acknowledges that the defendant committed the crime but argues that she shouldn't be punished, because it was the right thing to do at the time. This would include *self-defense* and *necessity*. A third category of defense, *excuses*, acknowledges that the defendant committed the crime, but she should not be punished because she is not really to blame for her actions. An example of this is *insanity*.

CRIMINAL (IN)JUSTICE

Life in Prison for Loaning Keys

Ryan Holle, a Florida man, was sentenced to life in prison without parole as an accomplice to murder, because he loaned his keys to friends who used his car to commit a burglary in 2003. When a woman was killed in the burglary, Holle was charged as an accomplice. Since the victim was killed during the commission of the robbery, Holle was charged with first-degree murder under the felony murder rule, despite being miles from the killing. The prosecutor argued that Holle knew his friends were using his car to commit the robbery, and thus Holle bore responsibility for the girl's death. (As the prosecutor put it, "No car, no crime") (Liptak, 2007). Before his trial, Holle rejected a plea bargain that would have given him a 10-year sentence, because he did not believe he was guilty of any wrongdoing. Holle's sentence was reduced to 25 years, and he is scheduled to be released in 2024.

Do you believe that it is fair to punish Holle so severely? If not, how much punishment would be appropriate in this case? Why? If he thought that there could be trouble during the burglary but still loaned the keys, would that affect your decision?

Failure of Proof

The failure of proof defense simply states that the defendant is not guilty because the prosecutor failed to show beyond a reasonable doubt that the defendant committed the crime. To be more specific however, the defendant argues that the prosecution did not show that she committed the *actus reus* with the required *mens rea*. The burden of proof is on the prosecution in a criminal trial. That means that the defendant is considered innocent until the prosecution has proven that she is guilty beyond a reasonable doubt. The defendant does not need to prove that she is innocent, merely that the prosecution did not show that she is guilty—which is why an acquitted defendant is found "not guilty" rather than "innocent" at trial.

Justifications

A justification defense asserts that the individual committed the crime, technically speaking, but should not be punished for her actions because, given the circumstances, they were the right thing to do. The most common examples of this are *self-defense* and *necessity*.

Self-Defense

Though it is usually the government's job to protect the innocent and get the "bad guys," the law understands that the police cannot protect everybody all the time, and people sometimes need to act on their own when their safety is threatened. Hence the law allows for individuals to use force to protect themselves in certain situations.

However, just because an individual believes that she has been threatened by somebody, this does not mean that she may automatically resort to force: There are some strict limitations on our right to self-defense. We do not live in the Wild West, where anybody can take the law into her own hands. Like all laws, the laws of self-defense vary from state to state, but here are a few common limitations placed on our right to self-defense:

1. *Last resort*. In most cases, you cannot use force in self-defense unless you've tried every other option. This means retreating when necessary. In most cases, if someone acts aggressively against you, you do not have the right to stand up to her in self-defense. You are obliged to be a grown-up and walk away from the conflict if it is possible. Only if that doesn't work and all other options are exhausted (you have "retreated to the wall" as the saying goes) are you allowed to use force in self-defense.

   The exception to this rule is the *castle doctrine*. This doctrine says that persons need not retreat from their own home or similar locations if they are threatened.

2. *Proportionality*. A second limitation on the use of force in self-defense law regards the amount of force a person may use in self-defense. Deadly force may only be used when there is a reasonable fear that an individual will either be killed or seriously harmed by an attacker. A fistfight, for example, does not usually justify using a gun in self-defense, unless the defender fears for her life.

3. *Reasonable belief.* Individuals must reasonably believe that they are in immediate danger when they act in self-defense. A mere suspicion or fear that a person could hurt them is insufficient for self-defense.

4. *Nonaggressor.* Individuals may not claim self-defense if they themselves were aggressors in the encounter. If an individual initiated the violent encounter of her own free will, for example, if she attacked another person or mutually agreed to fight (so-called mutual combat), she cannot then claim to have acted in self-defense if she used force to protect herself against another.

Many states, particularly states that are more politically conservative, have begun to expand the right of self-defense. Stand-your-ground laws are laws that have been created to make it easier for a defendant to claim that she acted in self-defense. The common element of stand-your-ground laws is that they expand the traditional castle doctrine beyond the confines of your home to any place where a person is lawfully allowed to be. Essentially, individuals are no longer required to retreat from any public place if they are threatened. If you can be there lawfully and somebody confronts you, you are not required to retreat and may legally use force against an aggressor. Among the biggest proponents of these laws is the National Rifle Association, which aggressively seeks to expand the scope of gun rights in the United States (Dionne, 2012).

On one level, stand-your-ground laws make sense: It seems weird that a person can threaten you in public, and you have a legal obligation to flee. However, these laws also make conflicts much more likely to become violent—a refusal to back down means that the situation can easily escalate, particularly if either individual is armed. Critics charge that these laws are a recipe for unnecessarily violent confrontations under the guise of self-defense. Others point out that the culturally entrenched fear of African Americans means that they are more likely to be killed by people acting in self-defense if the restrictions on it are relaxed—one study of stand-your-ground laws showed a "quantifiable racial bias" in these laws (Ackermann, Goodman, Gilbert, Arroyo-Johnson, & Pagano, 2015). Further, it is usually possible to call the police and ask for their assistance in exercising your rights rather than using force against a person who is threatening you, especially in an era of cell phones. Like many aspects of criminal law, your views about individual rights, politics, and gun ownership are likely to shape your views about the importance of stand-your-ground laws.

Necessity

The second major form of justification is *necessity.* A necessity claim means that the defendant was forced to break the law in order to prevent something worse. For example, if an individual is lost in the woods during a snowstorm and must break into a locked cabin to survive the cold, she can use this defense against a charge of breaking and entering (Schwartz, 2008). The difference between self-defense and necessity is that only property is damaged or taken in a case of necessity, while in self-defense, individuals are using force against another person to protect themselves. Also, in necessity, the harm prevented by breaking the law must be greater than the harm done by breaking the law, whereas in self-defense, if we are legitimately acting in self-defense, we could kill many people to save ourselves.

Stand-your-ground-laws: Laws that make it easier for individuals to use force in self-defense.

WHAT WOULD YOU DO?

Self-Defense and Joe Horn

Joe Horn was a 61-year-old (white) retiree living with his daughter in Pasadena, Texas, when he spotted two men robbing the house next door in November 2007. His neighbors were on vacation at the time of the incident. Horn picked up the phone and called 911 to report the incident. Here is the transcript of his conversation with the 911 dispatcher (iyarah, 2007):

Horn: He's coming out the window right now, I gotta go, buddy. I'm sorry, but he's coming out the window.

Dispatcher: Don't, don't—don't go out the door. Mr. Horn? Mr. Horn?

Horn: They just stole something. I'm going after them, I'm sorry.

Dispatcher: Don't go outside.

Horn: I ain't letting them get away with this shit. They stole something. They got a bag of something.

Dispatcher: Don't go outside the house.

Horn: I'm doing this.

Dispatcher: Mr. Horn, do not go outside the house.

Horn: I'm sorry. This ain't right, buddy.

Dispatcher: You're going to get yourself shot if you go outside that house with a gun, I don't care what you think.

Horn: You want to make a bet?

Dispatcher: OK? Stay in the house.

Horn: They're getting away!

Dispatcher: That's all right. Property's not worth killing someone over, OK?

Horn: [curses]

Dispatcher: Don't go out the house. Don't be shooting nobody. I know you're pissed and you're frustrated, but don't do it.

Horn: They got a bag of loot.

Dispatcher: OK. How big is the bag . . . which way are they going?

Horn: I'm going outside. I'll find out.

Dispatcher: I don't want you going outside, Mr. Horn.

Horn: Well, here it goes, buddy. You hear the shotgun clicking and I'm going.

Dispatcher: Don't go outside.

Horn: [yelling] Move, you're dead!

[Gunshots]

When an officer arrived on the scene, he saw Horn shoot the burglars in Horn's own front yard and that both burglars "had received gunfire from the rear." Both burglars were undocumented aliens with criminal records, neither carried guns (though one apparently had a sharp metal tool in his pocket), and both had died from gunshots in the back delivered by Horn.

What would you do if you were in Horn's position? Would you use your weapon to protect your neighbor's property? Should there be limits regarding your ability to use lethal force in self-defense? What should these limits be?

Source: https://www.youtube.com/watch?v=LLtKCC7z0yc.

Excuses

When she uses an excuse defense, a defendant is saying that her acts were wrong, but for some reason, she shouldn't be punished. Given her situation, she isn't really to blame for her actions, because she isn't responsible for her behavior. The most common excuse defenses are *insanity* and *duress*.

Insanity

The term *insanity* is often misunderstood. Even though we associate insanity with mental illness, the term itself is not used by professional psychologists. Insanity is a legal concept designed for criminal trials, not a term used by professional psychologists to diagnose their patients. (If you use the word *insane* in your psychology class to describe a person, you will probably get dirty looks from your professor.) The two terms are meant to do different things. A person who is mentally ill needs treatment for her condition, whatever that may be. A person who is declared insane by a court of law is determined to not be responsible for her actions. You can be both mentally ill and insane, but you can also be mentally ill, even severely mentally ill, but not be considered insane by a court of law. This means that, for the most part, courts and legal experts (not psychologists) have developed the insanity defense.

There are several different versions of the insanity defense in criminal law, and they vary state by state (and have changed over time). The most common version of the insanity defense is called the *M'Naughten Rule*, which was the very first one used in a court. (It was formulated during the trial of Daniel M'Naughten, a British man who murdered a civil servant in 1843.) The M'Naughten rule states that a person is *not guilty by reason of insanity* (sometimes abbreviated as NGRI) if

> at the time of the committing of the act, the party accused was laboring under such a defect of reason, from disease of mind, and not to know the nature and quality of the act he was doing; or if he did know it, that he did not know he was doing what was wrong.

Thus, to be declared insane under this rule, a defendant must be unaware of the fact that she should not have committed the crime. This means that a person who suffers delusions, believing that her roommate is in fact an alien monster and attacks her, is probably insane under this definition. However, if a person who is mentally ill murders an ex-lover out of a paranoid and delusional jealousy and then flees the scene of the crime, she is most likely *not* insane under this definition, because she knew that her acts were wrong. (Otherwise, she would not have fled.) The fact that it requires the defendant to believe that she was right makes the M'Naughten rule the most difficult form of the insanity defense to prove in a court of law.

The M'Naughten Rule is not the only version of the insanity defense in criminal law, however. A second formulation of the insanity defense, the so-called *irresistible impulse* test, states that, alongside the M'Naughten Rule, a defendant can claim insanity if she is unable to control herself because of her mental illness. Thus, a person could *know* an act is wrong, but nonetheless be unable to stop herself from acting out. Finally, the broadest definition of insanity is the so-called *Durham Test*, which says that a defendant is not guilty by reason of insanity if the defense can show that the defendant's actions were "a product of mental disease or defect." (Dressler & Garvey, 2015). Different versions of each of these rules appear in different state penal codes around the country, although with somewhat different language in each state.

The insanity defense is not the only way that a court can consider a defendant's mental health in a trial—it is just the only way that a defendant can be acquitted because of her mental illness. If a defendant's condition is bad enough, a court can conclude that she is not competent for trial, meaning that the trial cannot go forward because the defendant cannot understand the charges against her. Other times, the defendant can claim to suffer from *diminished capacity*, claiming that her mental illness was so severe that she could not formulate the *mens rea* of an offense. For example, if a defendant believed that a police officer was in fact an alien, she could not form the *mens rea* required for the crime of intentionally killing a police officer (*Clark v. Arizona*, 2006). In other cases, the trial can go forward, and the defendant is declared *guilty but mentally ill*, referred to as GBMI. This means that the defendant will undergo psychiatric treatment along with punishment but is still guilty of the crime. Finally, a mentally ill person can be civilly committed, meaning that she is placed in a mental hospital for mental health care without having been convicted of a crime. (See Chapter 12 for more on this.) While many consider these options to be easier or preferable to normal imprisonment, involuntary commitment can be more restricting and last longer than would a traditional prison sentence.

Duress

In December 2004, a gang invaded the homes of two executives of the Northern Bank in Belfast, Northern Ireland, and held their families hostage. The gangsters demanded that the executives assist them in robbing their employers, or they would kill their families (Caollai, 2010). The men obliged their captors, walking into the bank, essentially filling duffel bags with cash and then presenting them to the gang. Then, after the bank closed, the executives held the doors open for the robbers and allowed them to ransack the bank, clearing out as much cash and other forms of currency as they could get their hands on. After the robbers took the money, they fled the area while their accomplices released the hostages. Later, members of the terrorist organization known as the Irish Republican Army (IRA) were arrested for what is now known as one of the biggest robberies in that region's history—with a take of over $33 million.

The executives essentially robbed the bank, but they weren't prosecuted because they acted under *duress*. Provided that the threat is both real and serious, a person cannot be prosecuted for criminal acts committed under duress. The law does not expect you to risk your life or the lives of others to avoid breaking the law. When you act under duress, you commit a crime against your will—you have no realistic choice in the matter.

There is one important limitation to the defense of duress, however. A defendant cannot use it as a defense for murder. Were a gun put to an individual's head and she were ordered to kill an innocent person, she could not then claim that she was forced to do it. This means that, practically speaking, the law requires you to die or face prosecution for murder in these cases. The fear is that, were duress accepted in such cases, people would too easily give in and commit the most horrible of crimes, figuring that they would not pay any price for their unwillingness to escape. In addition, in many killings committed under duress, the killer put herself in the situation, such as by joining a gang. As one judge put it,

SOME STATISTICS…

Mental Illness in the Criminal Justice System

Very few defendants use the insanity defense, and even fewer use it successfully. The legal bar is just too high for many defendants to meet, even when they have serious mental illnesses. According to one study, *the insanity defense is invoked in less than 1% of all criminal cases and is only successful in about 26% of these cases* (Callahan, Steadman, McGreevy, & Robbins, 1991). Research among the different insanity cases shows that those diagnosed with schizophrenia (60%) are most likely to get an insanity acquittal (Lymburner & Roesch, 1999). In one study of Georgia criminal courts, after the state created a "guilty but mentally ill" defense in 1981, there was an increase in the number of people convicted of crimes and a decrease in the number of offenders found not guilty by reason of insanity (see Figure 2.1).

Georgia juries, when given the options of either finding a defendant not guilty or guilty but mentally ill, were more likely to choose the latter, everything else being equal.

This low rate of insanity defense claims means that there are a lot of offenders who are mentally ill but not legally insane (see Table 2.1). The Bureau of Justice Statistics points out that about half of all people incarcerated have some kind of mental health issue, either in their past or in recent history.

Some of these offenders receive counseling or medication while incarcerated, but many go undiagnosed and untreated. Mental health and criminal justice are often closely connected in the modern world, and imprisonment can often be an inadequate and expensive substitute for mental health care.

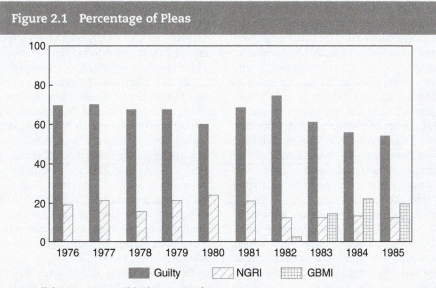

Figure 2.1   Percentage of Pleas

Guilty · NGRI · GBMI

Source: Callahan, McGreevy, Cirincione, & Steadman, 1992.

(Continued)

(Continued)

Table 2.1 Mental Health of Inmates in Prison and Jail			
	Percentage of Inmates in . . .		
Mental Health Problem	**State Prison**	**Federal Prison**	**Local Jail**
Any Mental Problem	56	45	64
Recent History	24	14	21
Symptoms	49	40	60

Source: **Doris & Glaze, 2006.**

REALITY CHECK

The Insanity Defense

Several high-profile cases involving defendants who claimed such a defense have given the insanity defense a bad reputation. Perhaps the two most famous are John Hinckley Jr., who attempted to assassinate Ronald Reagan in 1981, and Dan White, a San Francisco politician who killed two colleagues in 1978. Both successfully used the insanity defense in their cases. White notoriously used his intake of sugary foods as evidence of his insanity, a defense that was widely mocked as "the Twinkie defense." Because of these cases, there was a great deal of backlash against the insanity defense, and many states either abolished it outright or highly restricted its use.

However, both of these cases are more complicated than they might first appear. Hinckley had claimed that his obsession with the actress Jodie Foster led him to try to kill the president. While he was acquitted of the charges against him, he was not set free. He was institutionalized in a mental hospital for 35 years as he underwent treatment, probably a longer term than he would have served had he been convicted of attempted murder. He was finally let out on supervised released in 2016 but forbidden to have contact with any of his victims, including Foster.

White's Twinkie defense was harshly attacked in the media, and many reported a false story that he had claimed that the sugary snacks caused him to kill. In truth, White's lawyers had argued that he suffered from mental illness, and as part of this illness, his diet had changed. They did not claim that junk food made him into a killer. White was not acquitted of the killings but was convicted of the lesser offense of manslaughter rather than murder because of his mental illness. He spent five years in prison and committed suicide in 1985, two years after his release.

Our views about the insanity defense are closely connected to our beliefs about mental illness more generally. If you are skeptical about mental illness—if you believe it is just a lot of self-indulgent whining for example, you are unlikely to take the defense seriously. However, the more you take mental illness issues seriously, the more likely you are to take the insanity defense seriously. Despite our attitudes toward mental health issues, legal barriers are high for the insanity defense, and it is only rarely used—it is a difficult case to make in court, and juries as well as the general public are often skeptical about it (Hans & Slater, 1983).

If duress is recognized as a defense to the killing of innocents, then a street or prison gang need only create an internal reign of terror and murder can be justified, at least by the actual killer. Persons who know they can claim duress will be more likely to follow a gang order to kill instead of resisting than would those who know they must face the consequences of their acts. (*People v. Anderson*, Supreme Court of California, 28 Cal. 4th)

While most criminal laws don't expect people to be particularly heroic, the law says that in cases like these, it's up to the individual to find a way out, and no excuses will be accepted for failing to do so.

WHERE DO I FIT IN?

ARMED STUDENTS

Along with laws making it easier to use lethal force in self-defense, gun rights groups have aggressively promoted laws allowing college students to be armed and even to carry concealed weapons on campus. Proponents of "campus carry" laws argue that armed students would be better able to protect themselves from attacks such as the 2007 Virginia Tech shooting, when senior Seung-Hui Cho murdered 32 people and wounded 17. Rather than relying on campus security, an armed student body could better protect itself in an immediate and dire emergency, they argue. Different states have different laws on the issue. Some have state laws allowing armed students, including students armed with concealed weapons, but many states have no laws on the subject. Many public and private universities have campus rules banning armed students.

Critics argue that more guns on campus will not make them any safer and may make violence more likely, as armed students may draw their guns in a fit of anger. Critics also argue that the presence of armed students in a classroom could intimidate their peers and instructors, disrupting the learning environment, particularly when discussing controversial subjects. As one professor put it,

Many of us entered the profession without knowing that we would have to consider whether a student who is upset about his grade, uncomfortable with a lecture on black queer sexuality, or disagrees with our placing slavery and white supremacy at the center of American

(Continued)

(Continued)

history might have a gun holstered on his waist (Makalani, 2016). They argue that guns have no place in a learning environment.

This will surely continue to be an issue, as campus shootings are on the rise in the United States. According to one report, the number of shootings in the 2015–2016 school year was 243% higher than in 2001–2002. Leaving out the massacres at Virginia Tech and a mass shooting in Northern Illinois University in 2008, there has been a consistent increase in campus shootings over the last 15 years (Cannon, 2016). While these shootings are largely centered on states in the South, surprisingly more than half of the shooters were not students or employees of the college or university where they attacked, though most of the victims were students.

Do you support allowing students to carry concealed weapons on campus? Do you think this will increase violence on campus or decrease it? Would you feel differently about your classroom if you knew that one or more of your peers was carrying a gun? If so, how would it change your perception of the class?

CHAPTER SUMMARY

In this chapter, we have discussed various elements of substantive criminal law, but, except for the analysis of murder, we have largely stuck to the general features of the law. We haven't gone into the details of what constitutes assault, robbery, possession of a controlled substance, et cetera. Each of these offenses could have its own section in this chapter, as each type of crime has a history, shows a remarkable variation from state to state, and raises important questions about law, order, and justice in the modern world. When looked at closely, each individual offense in modern criminal law is fascinating and raises unique questions about the contours of right and wrong.

Rather than going into these specific crimes, however I have tried to give you the tools to look at these various laws and understand how to read them. That means that you should be able to examine a statute, separate its *actus reus* from the *mens rea*, and understand how to interpret these aspects of a statute. Because there is such a variety among the criminal laws in the different states, it would be too time consuming to do more than this. If you want to know more about your own state's criminal code, you can probably find it online without much effort. But without understanding the broader legal context of these statutes, that is, the way that lawyers interpret and apply them, by themselves they are not very useful.

In this chapter, we have looked at the legal construction of crime: how law is seen by lawyers and legislatures. In the next chapter, we will begin to examine crime as seen by scientists of various forms. There we will look at how biologists, psychologists, anthropologists, and sociologists examine criminal behavior, rather than lawyers. *Criminology* encompasses these scientific approaches to crime, though as we will see, criminology is a widely diverse field with many different perspectives on the nature and causes of criminal behavior.

REVIEW/DISCUSSION QUESTIONS

1. Go online and find your own state's criminal code. Pick one criminal offense and find the *mens rea* and *actus reus*. How did you know where they were in the law?

2. What are the main kinds of defenses? Do you think that each defense should be allowed in criminal law? Which ones might you want to get rid of?

3. Critics of the Trump administration have charged that some of his actions are a threat to the rule of law. Do you see actions by Trump that do this? If so, which actions? If not, why not?

EXERCISE: *ACTUS REUS* AND *MENS REAS*

Can you find the *actus reus* and *mens reas* of the crime?

Texas:

§ 28.03. Criminal Mischief.

(a) A person commits an offense if, without the effective consent of the owner:
   (1) he intentionally or knowingly damages or destroys the tangible property of the owner;
   (2) he intentionally or knowingly tampers with the tangible property of the owner and causes pecuniary loss or substantial inconvenience to the owner or a third person; or
   (3) he intentionally or knowingly makes markings, including inscriptions, slogans, drawings, or paintings, on the tangible property of the owner.

Vermont

§ 1101. Bribing public officers or employees

(a) A person shall not, directly or indirectly, corruptly, give, offer or promise to an executive, legislative or judicial officer, or to any employee, appointee or designee of any executive, legislative or judicial officer, or to a person who is a candidate or applicant for an executive, legislative or judicial office, a gift or gratuity
   (1) with intent to influence his or her finding, decision, report or opinion in any matter within his or her official capacity or employment . . .

Alaska

§ 11.41.270. Stalking in the second degree.

(a) A person commits the crime of stalking in the second degree if the person knowingly engages in a course of conduct that recklessly places another person in fear of death or physical injury, or in fear of the death or physical injury of a family member.

KEY TERMS

Actus reus 33
Capital offenses 38
Common law 31

Inchoate crimes 33
Mens rea 33
Stand-your-ground-laws 41

Strict liability offenses 36

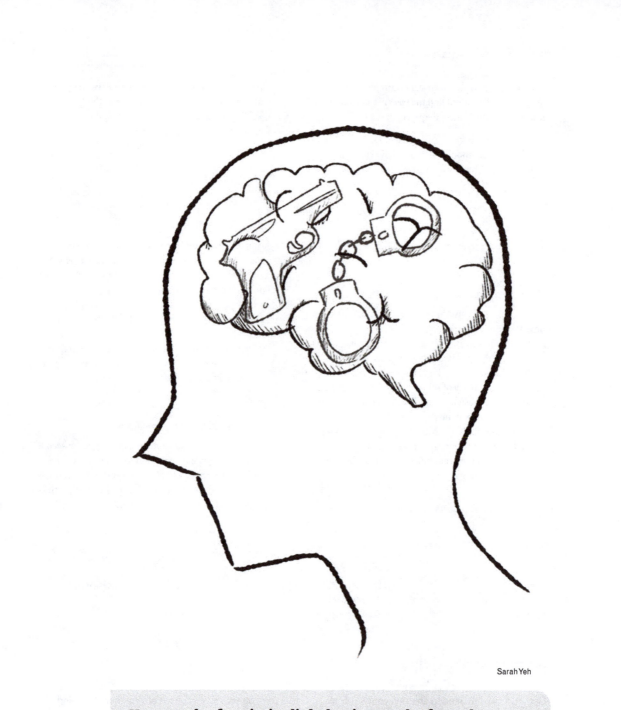

Sarah Yeh

How much of a criminal's behavior results from the criminal and how much of it is a product of society?

CHAPTER THREE

CRIMINOLOGY

Criminology is the scientific study of criminal behavior. Although the term was coined at the end of the 19th century, people have studied crime in one way or another throughout the history of civilization. Most criminologists seek to explain *why* people commit a crime by finding the root causes of criminal behavior—either in the makeup of the individual criminal or in the composition of her social group. This ties it closely to *criminal justice policy*: how societies seek to prevent crime through laws and other institutions. Simply put, once the true causes of crime are discovered by criminologists, these causes can be addressed by the criminal justice system and crime rates can be lowered. While such a straightforward approach oversimplifies how criminal justice policy is formulated, it nonetheless is true that criminologists are often helpful in determining how government officials address crime problems.

The famous historian of science, Thomas Kuhn, described the development of science as passing through a series of paradigms, that is, a series of different assumptions about the nature of the world (Kuhn, 1996). These paradigms structure scientific research, determining what to study and how to study it. Criminology has followed this pattern. There are different paradigms of criminology—different ways that criminologists have sought to explain criminal behavior—each with its own assumptions. Each paradigm contains numerous different criminological theories, but each shares a set of beliefs about the root causes of criminal behavior and views regarding how crime should be studied and explained. Some of these criminologists (who we will describe as *classical criminologists*) have focused on individual choice to explain criminal behavior. Others (*psychological criminologists*) have looked at the unique psychological makeup of the offender, trying to understand what makes the criminal different from law-abiding citizens. Finally, others (*sociological criminologists*) have placed crime in a broader context, seeing criminal behavior as a complex by-product of social forces that are beyond any individual. We will look briefly at key aspects of each of these approaches to studying criminal behavior in this chapter.

Each of these paradigms contains within it many different theories, and we will discuss only the most important of them here. In addition, while each has important contributions to make to our understanding of crime, just like the definitions of crime discussed in the previous chapter, none of them is completely right. They all have strengths and weaknesses, and none works in every case. Some of these approaches are better than others for explaining a particular type of crime, but none of them is a silver bullet that explains every type of criminal behavior or every kind of criminal. Theories that explain the behavior of

Paradigms: Underlying assumptions about the nature of reality that shape scientific theories.

solitary serial killers probably won't be as helpful in understanding the acts of white collar criminals, drug dealers on the street, or computer hackers. Theories that explain how the crime rate in a city goes up and down probably won't help us much in understanding the actions of violent terrorists. All these approaches are still used by criminologists today to study criminal behavior, and all of them are still relevant. As long as "crime" remains a broad and varied concept, consisting of a lot of different kinds of crime and different sorts of criminals, there will probably not be a single, unified criminological theory.

Moreover, except for some sociological theories, all the criminological theories that we will discuss here assume that *crime is a problem* and that the criminal's failure to obey the law is what needs to be explained. This is to say that all the criminologists we will be looking at believe that the normal thing to do is to obey the law and that there must be something wrong with anybody who can't or won't do so. Offenders may have emotional issues, have grown up in desperate poverty, or suffer from some other disorder that makes them blameless for their actions, but nonetheless they need some kind of help so that they can "lead a normal life." Society is assumed to be akin to a healthy body, and crime is a disease within that body that needs to be diagnosed and hopefully cured.

While you might share that view, keep in mind that in the next chapter, we will look at a different paradigm of criminology: the *critical* tradition. For critical criminology, crime is not a disease in need of a cure but is in many ways a perfectly understandable response to a society that itself is "sick" from injustice and inequality. According to critical criminologists, researchers do not need to explain criminal behavior, but rather should examine how society misperceives responses to inequality as deviant and study how the criminal justice system works to protect these inequalities. While we will discuss these theories in greater depth in the next chapter, keep in mind that the criminological theories we will discuss here are almost all laboring under the uncritical assumption that crime is bad, and that law and order are good—not every criminologist agrees with this assumption.

RELIGIOUS APPROACHES TO CRIME

Learning Objective 3.1—Examine the relationship between religion and criminal behavior in the premodern world.

Before we delve into modern criminology, it's worth taking some time to look at older ways of thinking about criminal behavior, ways that predate science but still shape the way a great number of people think about crime. Before modern science was developed, people's lives were primarily shaped by their religious beliefs, and all the world was explained by reference to God's (or gods') relations with humans. Floods, fires, famines were all explained as divine punishment for human sin, an angry God (or gods) exacting revenge for the sins of the people. Society had failed to act in the right way, and this had angered the divine authorities. On the other hand, economic prosperity and victory on the battlefield were taken as signs of God's favor. Religion defined a society's moral code, determined its form of government, and shaped its sense of place in the world. It makes sense that their understanding of criminal behavior would be linked to their religious beliefs. (Before we begin to feel too superior about these things, remember that evangelical ministers in America today routinely blame natural disasters like hurricanes on God's wrath.) The belief that crime has supernatural causes makes a great deal of sense if you see the world in terms of God and the Devil.

While religious views about crime and morality predate modern religion, the Christian era brought in some novel elements—criminal behavior has sometimes been seen to be a result of demonic possession or witchcraft. There have been numerous witchcraft trials over the centuries in both Europe and the United States, many of which were incited by diseases, famines, or other misfortunes that were ascribed to supernatural causes. During the Salem witch trials in Massachusetts in 1692 and 1693, 19 people were executed by the colonial government because they were accused of being witches. While this sounds silly to the ears of modern people who use the words *witch hunt* to refer to a fake trial, recent attempts to link Satanic practices to more contemporary crimes have been used in questionable cases like those of the West Memphis Three (a group of "goth" teenagers who were falsely convicted of murdering three boys) and the McMartin Preschool Molestations (a series of disproven allegations of Satanic abuse in a California child care facility in the early 1980s), among others. There have always been fears that criminals are in league with Satan and that they are doing the bidding of evil forces in the world. Even some criminals have bought into this worldview: While on death row, Sean Sellars, a man convicted of murdering his mother and stepfather, converted to Christianity and blamed his crimes on demons that had inhabited his body. (He was executed in 1999.) While there is little fear of witchcraft among serious minds in the contemporary world, many still understand crime in terms of spiritual warfare.

Further, it is worth noting that religion often has a positive influence on criminal behavior. Criminologists have seen that people who are more religious are less likely to engage in criminal behavior. In their famous "hellfire" theory, two criminologists argued that a fear of consequences in the afterlife can keep people on the straight and narrow (Hirschi & Stark, 1969). Studies have further shown that religious belief can also help victims recover from traumatic violent crime (Bradley, Schwartz, & Kaslow, 2005). Former criminals are also less likely to reoffend after they've been incarcerated if they are more religious and are involved with religious programs (Johnson, Larson, & Pitts, 1997). It is undeniable that, for many believers, religion plays a positive role in helping avoid crime and in recovering from its most damaging effects.

The appeal of religious approaches to explaining criminal behavior is that they resemble the moral views about crime that we discussed in Chapter 1. Because we cannot help but see crime as bad or evil, and Christians personify this evil in Satan, religious views about crime make sense for many. To fit criminal behavior in the moral framework of sin, redemption, God, and the Devil is to put it into a context that is deeply rooted in the beliefs of many and that, in some ways, makes more sense than scientific explanations of it. This is why this approach to crime is both ancient and modern and is not likely to disappear no matter how secular societies become. As long as there is crime and there are people with religious beliefs, there will be parts of our society that blame crime on human sin and see criminal conduct in a spiritual and religious light.

CLASSICAL CRIMINOLOGY

Learning Objective 3.2—Describe the role of the Enlightenment in explaining crime and the idea that crime can be viewed as rational behavior.

While religious explanations of criminal behavior are always going to be with us, they have been eclipsed in the last 300 or so years by other, more modern approaches to the subject. Remember, in earlier periods of Western history, religion was used not only to explain crime, but also storms, earthquakes, fires, famines, and floods. Similarly, wealth, health, and all other good things in life were often taken as signs of God's blessing. That meant that religious beliefs were not seeking merely to explain human behavior but also shaped how people saw the natural world. Since the fall of the Roman Empire, much of the West was ruled by religious authorities, and it was religious beliefs, including theology and Scripture, that controlled how people saw their world and shaped how they lived. They learned about good and evil from the same people that they learned about disease and the seasons: the clergy.

That began to change in the middle of the 17th century, as religious beliefs began to be eclipsed by newly developed notions of science and reason. We now call this period, where western civilization turned away from superstition and toward science, the *Enlightenment*. Ancient scholars whose writings were lost to the West (but preserved by a few monks and by scholars in the Muslim world) were rediscovered, and researchers began to experiment with early forms of the scientific method. Religious explanations for the world were put aside (though few Enlightenment writers would openly denounce religious authorities), and scientific explanations were put in their place. Physics, philosophy, math, chemistry, and biology began to be studied free of superstition, and theories were developed without looking at Scripture for confirmation or proof. Reason and evidence, not faith, became the primary tool for making sense of the world around us.

The new Enlightenment ideals of reason and science were not only used to make sense of the natural world, but Enlightenment thinkers also began to study human society, using these tools to analyze and guide human behavior. If scientists can cure diseases of the body through science, why not use science to cure social diseases like war, poverty, inequality, and crime? Philosophers like Thomas Hobbes, Adam Smith, John Locke, Jeremy Bentham, and Jean-Jacques Rousseau began to develop what they saw as scientific laws of economics, politics, and society more generally that could be used to tackle practical problems in human civilization. Modern social science began out of this attempt to turn the power of reason onto the practical problems faced by humanity, and it is out of this effort that the earliest forms of scientific criminology, which are commonly described as classical criminology, developed.

The two most well-known classical criminologists are Jeremy Bentham and Cesare Beccaria. An Italian philosopher, Beccaria sought to develop a set of rational principles of social control that could be used to reduce crime. In his influential treatise, *An Essay on Crimes and Punishments* (1764/1872), Beccaria specifically warned against thinking about justice in a religious sense when crafting laws: "We should be cautious how we associate with the word justice, an idea of anything real, such as a physical power, or a being that actually exists" (p. 19). Rather than thinking of justice in a religious fashion, Beccaria argued that we should think of justice as "nothing more than that bond, which is necessary to keep the interest of individuals united; without which, men would return to the original state of barbarity" (p. 18). And therefore, "All punishments, which exceed the necessity of preserving this bond, are in their nature unjust" (p. 18). Punishment should not be about revenge or about pleasing God, but rather it should be conceived as a tool for maintaining social harmony and treated accordingly: "Crimes are only to be measured by the injury done to society" (pp. 18–19). The purpose of punishing criminals is to maintain social order. Nothing more, nothing less.

Classical criminology: Criminological theories of the enlightenment era that sought to use reason to explain and prevent criminal behavior.

Bentham was well known as a philosopher and legal reformer in 18th-century England. Bentham used a theory of rational egoism as a guide to explain human behavior. Rational egoism begins with a basic assumption about human nature: human beings are hardwired to seek their own pleasure and to avoid feeling pain whenever possible. As Bentham put it,

> Nature has placed mankind under the governance of two sovereign masters, *pain* and *pleasure*. It is for them alone to point out what we ought to do, as well as to determine what we shall do. . . . They govern us in all we do, in all we say, in all we think: every effort we can make to throw off our subjection, will serve but to demonstrate and confirm it. (1823/1879, p. 1)

Even when we look like we're acting from purely noble motives (say, we give money to a homeless person), we are actually doing it for selfish reasons—such as feeling good about ourselves or impressing the people around us. There is no such thing as selflessness for Bentham—we are always in some ways in it for ourselves. From this single assumption about human beings, one that he believed to be irrefutable, he developed an entire theory of law, government, politics, and criminal justice.

Despite his somewhat cynical view of human nature, Bentham was a reformer who wanted to rid the world of superstition and irrationality—including what he believed to be irrational approaches to crime and justice. Crime, he argued, was not a product of "evil," "immorality," or "sin," but was simply the acts of a normal person behaving in a completely rational manner. Criminals are just pursuing their self-interests in the way that any of us would in those circumstances. That is, if it were possible to steal something you desired with little risk involved, it would not only not be "evil" to take it, it would be irrational to do otherwise. To try to convince the criminal that it was wrong in some vague, religious sense of the term would be pointless and a little stupid. Criminals are not "immoral" or "evil" but are rational beings making a rational calculation about the potential risks and rewards of their actions. For Bentham then, crime is a rational response to a situation, a belief on the part of the criminal that the risk is worth the potential rewards of the crime.

It follows for Bentham that the criminal justice system should adapt to human nature. Rather than seeing criminals as sinful and punishment as a form of moral judgment, punishments should be designed so that they prevent future crime. This means that punishments should *deter* future criminal behavior—giving potential criminals good reasons to avoid criminal activity. For example, if the punishment for being caught is worse than the potential rewards that one would get from committing the crime, or if it is likely that you will be caught, you are probably not going to commit the crime if you are behaving rationally. This means that punishments should be worse than the rewards that come from breaking the law, and the likelihood of punishment should be high enough that breaking the law isn't worth the risk. If we can just figure out the right set of policies and punishments, we can stop a lot of crime before it happens by simply appealing to the criminal's rational self-interest.

It's clear that these classical criminologists represent an important development in the understanding of crime. They do not rely on superstition and instead seek to fashion crime control policies around some set of rational principles. Despite the appealing simplicity of rational egoism, there are some serious problems with applying it to criminal behavior.

Rational egoism: The theory that individuals rationally seek to promote their own interests.

Much crime is in fact irrational. For example, many homicides occur in intensely emotional moments, where an individual has neither the time nor the inclination to reflect on the consequences of her actions. Similarly, many criminals are young people or the mentally ill, and they are unable to fully gauge the consequences of their actions. Such offenders do not think about their activities in the ways that Bentham and Beccaria think they should and are probably not going to be deterred by the threat of punishment. While for a select group of individuals, Bentham's rational egoism makes sense (for example bank robbers or white collar criminals), the classical model does not fit many potential criminals who are not acting rationally when they engage in criminal activity.

Modern Variations

Despite its weaknesses in explaining many forms of criminal behavior, classical criminology remains influential today. Rational egoism, the central tenet of classical criminology, still stands at the core of much modern economics, and many economic approaches to studying crime argue that we can see criminal behavior as a product of rational action. Economic models of crime see criminal activities as economic transactions like buying a car or opening a bank account. Drug traffickers, for example, are engaged in economic transactions like other business persons, only they have extra expenses and risks involved with their line of work. The fact that the police can arrest and confiscate your product is simply another cost associated with drug commerce, and a rational drug trafficker simply calculates this into her decisions about pricing. The more studies of crime look like economics, the more they are indebted to Bentham's and Beccaria's rational egoism.

Classical criminology is in many ways closer to mathematics than it is to science: It starts with an axiom (rational egoism) and deduces conclusions about human behavior, including criminal behavior, from it. That axiom isn't so much proven by researching how people act as it is assumed at the beginning. Aside from economics, where a mathematical approach still has influence, a great deal of criminology has turned away from this deductive approach and has become empiricist in orientation. By *empiricist*, I mean that these criminologists link their theories to observations and studies of actual human beings, making these theories much more scientific and less philosophical than those of Bentham and Beccaria. The remainder of the theories that we will discuss in this chapter are much more scientifically minded than those of the classical criminologists, though they all share the assumption that criminality should be examined and studied without the intrusion of moral judgments about sinfulness or evil.

BIOLOGICAL CRIMINOLOGY

Learning Objective 3.3—Summarize the influence of evolutionary theory on crime.

Many influential theories over the years have sought to link an individual's criminal behavior to her physical or biological makeup. Much of this research has been conducted with a great deal of care, while some has merely been an excuse for pseudoscientific racism—blaming the inferior genes of less advantaged ethnic groups (black people, Jews, etc.) for their poor social situation and their criminal conduct. Discredited movements such as *eugenics* sought to show that the genetic makeup of certain groups made them better suited for survival, while those with "weaker genes" should be weeded out of the human race.

While such movements (and the work of many pseudoscientists who have sought to show the genetic inferiority of African Americans and other nonwhites) have left many very skeptical about biological explanations for complex social behaviors like crime, they have nonetheless played an important role in the development of criminology.

Two early movements in biological criminology are *phrenology* and Cesare Lombroso's *atavism* theory. Phrenology was a field of research, now debunked, that claimed that an individual's character and personality could be determined by studying the shape of her skull. Phrenologists believed that different aspects of our personality and our faculties were associated with sections of the brain, and that these, in turn, shaped the skull that surrounded them. Individuals could show criminal traits like greed, secretiveness, and destructiveness marked on the head in ways that could be measured and analyzed by an expert. Phrenologists like Félix Voisin (1794–1872) believed that, using phrenology, a criminal mind could be "rearranged" so that the offender was transformed into a law-abiding citizen. While linked in some remote way to modern neuroscience, phrenology was dismissed as pseudoscience and abandoned by the end of the 19th century.

Lombroso (1835–1909) was an Italian criminologist who developed a biological theory of criminal behavior rooted in Darwin's evolutionary theory. According to Lombroso, all human beings can fit into certain "types" and possessed certain traits, called atavisms, that are passed down over generations. Under certain conditions humans can even revert to the traits of earlier, more primitive generations. A criminal, along with the insane and other forms of social deviants, is imbued with atavisms that represent a less-evolved type of human. For these people, criminality is inherited from their ancestors, and their thinking and behavioral patterns have failed to fit with those of evolved human society. Criminals have not evolved as completely as law-abiding citizens. Their primitive character makes them ill-suited for the modern world.

While these theories probably seem crude to those of you who are studying biology, psychology, or evolutionary theory, there remain a wide array of more sophisticated efforts to link evolutionary biology to criminality. Sociobiology is the field of research that links social behavior to human evolution, maintaining that most social institutions (be it religion, war, the family, etc.) can be explained as a product of the evolutionary process, helping the species survive to pass their genes on to their ancestors. Many criminologists believe that violence correlates to high levels of testosterone, though the evidence for this is mixed (Archer, 1994). Biocriminology and neurocriminology are newer fields that have developed to try to understand the complicated connections between the body, the brain, and an individual's criminal behavior. While we will not dwell on these topics much in future chapters, many people who study crime have begun to return to the theories of Lombroso and others, only with an updated scientific understanding of the workings of the human brain and (hopefully) less racial bigotry.

PSYCHOLOGICAL CRIMINOLOGY

Learning Objective 3.4—Describe the three main psychological theories and their influence on criminology.

Over the last century, psychology has had an enormous influence over every aspect of human society. It has shaped how we talk about ourselves as terms like *neurotic*, *psychopath*, and *narcissistic*, all of which originated in psychology, have filtered into modern culture.

Phrenology: The (now debunked) theory that a person's personality and propensity for crime can be determined by studying the shape of her skull.

Atavism theory: The criminological theory that sees criminal behavior as a result of holdovers from earlier, primitive forms of human life.

Sociobiology: The belief that much of our social behavior is determined by our biological makeup.

Moreover, psychology affects how we think about ourselves: We are constantly analyzing our own behavior, looking for some deeper explanation for our actions, some deep need that we are seeking to fulfill, some hidden pain in our lives that we are constantly trying to escape. In many ways, we live in a world constructed by psychologists: We are all amateur "shrinks," using what we know about the science to study ourselves and those around us. Clearly, then, it is no surprise that psychology has a lot to say about criminals and criminal behavior.

Here we will discuss a few basic psychological theories and how they can help explain some kinds of criminal behavior:

Freud and Psychoanalysis

One of the best known and most controversial psychological theories developed from the work of Austrian psychiatrist Sigmund Freud. Freud is so influential in the history of psychology that his image—that of a bearded man that asks probing, sexual questions in a thick, Austrian accent—has become a caricature for all psychologists. Freud posited that we human beings are only dimly aware of what's going on in our own minds, and we are often ignorant of the true feelings and motives that shape our behavior. This is because there is a vast unperceived level of thought called the *unconscious* lying beneath our conscious mind. It is where all our darkest desires lurk, unknown even to ourselves, and are struggling to be fulfilled, and it is the real driver of our actions. Our desires bubble up into our conscious life in various forms, such as in dreams and in so-called Freudian slips, where we accidentally express our unconscious desires. For the most part we can control these desires, but for some individuals they are so powerful that they can cause irrational or delusional behavior, which can be criminal in nature.

In his later works, Freud spelled out his view by describing the mind as consisting of three parts: the *ego*, the *superego*, and the *id*. The id embodied the deep desires of a person, many of which are forged in infancy and most of which would be socially unacceptable to fulfill. (Among other things, Freud posited that we want to sexually possess our mothers from an early age.) The superego is the "conscience" of the mind, constantly demanding that we repress our urges and act in a socially and morally appropriate manner. The ego lies between them, trying to meet the demands of the id while dealing with the guilt-inducing superego. In most people, the ego can maintain the balance between the demands of the id and the superego, but when this balance breaks down, when the id becomes too demanding or the Superego too strict, abnormal behavior results.

The central claim of psychoanalysis is that our abnormal behavior is a product of our unconscious desires and that we can understand "crazy," "abnormal," or just plain "weird" behavior by unpacking our experiences, particularly those that took place during early childhood. Freud believed that these experiences—the traumas and frustrations of childhood—have lasting effects on a person's unconsciousness and manifest themselves in behavior that is either self-destructive or harmful to others. But because these experiences are largely repressed, we don't realize how they are affecting us. By getting to the root of these early experiences, a psychologist (or technically, a psychoanalyst) can help her patient understand her problems, find their sources, and thereby overcome them. Thus, psychoanalysis consists in an individual speaking about herself and her experiences until the analyst can find the hidden, unconscious meanings of her behavior. Eventually, the subject

Psychoanalysis: The psychological theory that people are motivated by unconscious drives or desires.

will give indications of how she feels unconsciously, which the analyst can use to help her patient solve her psychological problems. This approach is costly and time consuming, but analysts believe it is the only way to get to the root of an individual's psychological problems and fix them.

For the psychoanalyst then, criminal behavior is rooted in unconscious desires that cannot be controlled by the individual's conscious mind. We all must repress our urges to make our way through the world, but some people are better than others at repressing them or channeling our sexual energy into activities that are socially acceptable. Criminals cannot do this, and as a result their behavior is antisocial and at times violent. A person who murders women may be acting out his deep-seated anger at his parents by picking victims who (unconsciously) remind him of his parents and thereby allowing him to express his rage. A man who is prone to fighting could be searching for a release for his repressed homosexual desires, using violence to express his same-sex attractions in a way that is socially acceptable. A criminal who sells drugs or robs banks may be unconsciously searching for the parental approval that she never received as a child. Criminal behavior according to psychoanalysts is often the result of an individual's unconscious desires finding a way to manifest themselves—but unlike law abiding citizens, these people's drives come out in ways that are detrimental to society at large.

As an explanation of criminal behavior, this certainly seems useful when we look at the strange behavior of some criminals. The idea that there may be some deep psychological longing that serial killers and other bizarre criminals are seeking to satisfy can make sense. When an otherwise normal person is revealed to have a dark, sinister secret, it makes sense to wonder why she would resort to such strange behavior and to search for some deep hidden reason. For example, the "BTK Killer" was a serial killer named Dennis Rader who tortured and brutally murdered 10 people, including children, in Wichita, Kansas, over the course of 15 years while living an otherwise normal life as a father, husband, and church volunteer. He reportedly had a fetish for women's underwear, which may have been linked to his killings—though certainly most people with a fetish like this are in no way dangerous. (He was caught and is now serving 10 life sentences in Kansas state prison.) Clearly there is something deeply troubled about many people who engage in criminal activity, particularly crimes that are bizarre, illogical, or self-destructive. Whether you find Freud's account of the unconscious or the power of our sexual drives over our lives compelling, the belief that criminals who engage in bizarre sorts of behavior are doing so for motivations that they themselves may not ultimately understand and are unable to control makes a good deal of sense in many cases.

Behavioral Theory

The primary competitor to psychoanalysis at the dawn of modern psychology was B. F. Skinner's behavioral theory. Rather than suggesting that our actions were the result of unconscious forces within the mind, as Freud had maintained, Skinner believed that our behavior was learned throughout our lives by our interactions with the environment. We are conditioned to behave in certain ways because of our experiences in the past—we are shaped through learning. Just as we train our pets by giving them treats when they do what we want (and punish them when they misbehave), people are trained by the world around them to behave in certain ways based on a system of rewards and punishments. (Skinner's

Behavioral theory: The psychological theory that argues that criminal behavior is learned through a series of rewards and punishments.

view is called *operant conditioning*, which distinguished it from earlier forms of behavioral psychology known as *classical conditioning*.) All behavior is a response to stimulations in the environment and can be manipulated by changing these stimulations.

The overall theme of behavioral theory is that our thoughts and actions are shaped by our experiences and the consequences of our actions. Behaviors and their rewards or punishments become fused in the individual to the point where they are automatically linked in a way that is beyond the conscious will of the individual. Society rewards behaviors, and in some cases, can reward criminal behaviors such that the individual effectively becomes programmed for a life of crime. On the other hand, criminal behavior can be prevented by changing the internal wiring of the criminal: punishing (or ceasing to reward) behavior that is criminal and rewarding (or ceasing to punish) behavior that is not. It simply becomes a matter of reprogramming the criminal and turning her into a law-abiding person.

According to behavioral theory, criminals are simply responding to the rewards that they have received over the course of their lives. If criminal behavior is rewarded (say, by praise or by money), it will be adopted by the individual. If it is punished, it will disappear. (This is similar in some ways to classical criminology, but the key difference is that classical criminologists thought that this system of punishments and sanctions was part of the conscious, rational calculation of the criminal, whereas behaviorists don't assume that individuals think about the rewards and punishments of their behavior and that learned behavior is hardwired into the individual's brain.) If criminals learn to be criminal by being rewarded for their behavior, they can also unlearn these behaviors by changing the system of rewards and punishments that they face in their environment. By punishing criminal behavior, or at a minimum ceasing to reward it, the individual should unlearn these behaviors over time in a process known as *extinction*.

CRIMINAL (IN)JUSTICE

Life Course Criminology and Young Offenders

On February 13, 2017, Jamie Garnett was found dead by the police in her home in Gary, Indiana. Her daughter Chastinea Reeves, 15, was missing, and an Amber Alert (a missing child notice) was sent out in the area. She had shown up at a relative's house early in the morning stating that somebody had broken into their house, but ran out the back door shortly thereafter, prompting the alert. After nearly 12 hours of panic, she was discovered safe the next day by police, wandering the streets of Gary.

But the relief at finding Reeves safe changed soon after when she became a suspect in the killing. She was charged with the murder along with a 16-year-old accomplice who helped her get rid of Garnett's car and dispose of some items used in the murder. The unique nature of the case led the prosecutor to ask that Reeves be charged as an adult. The fact that "the offense charged is of heinous or aggravated nature" and was part of a pattern of illegal behavior by Reeves that she was not suitable for the juvenile justice system (Jacobs, 2017). In June 2017 the court granted the motion, and Reeves's case was sent to an adult court for trial, concluding that "it would not be in the best interests of the child and of the safety and welfare of the community for the child to remain within the juvenile justice system."

While the U.S. Supreme Court ruled in 2005 that defendants cannot be executed if they were under the age of 18 when they committed their crimes, nonetheless juveniles can be prosecuted and sentenced as adults in many states. Juveniles tried as adults are not given many of the same protections as others their age and can face much stiffer sentences, including the possibility of life imprisonment without parole in some states.

Life course criminology tracks criminal behavior over time, examining the social, psychological, and physiological changes that mark an individual's life and how these impact a person's criminal behavior. Persons are far more likely to engage in criminal activity in their teens through their mid-20s than later in life; most likely the criminal behavior will cease by the end of their 20s, when they will have probably settled down to a career and a family. Moreover, there is ample psychological evidence that young people lack the cognitive ability to understand the consequences of their actions, a deficit that can easily lead to criminal behavior. As such, a person who commits a crime when she is young, such as Reeves, is likely to be a very different person when she is older. In short, committing crimes as a juvenile does not necessarily mean that the individual will commit crimes as an adult.

Further, criminological research shows that there is a racial imbalance in which juveniles get charged as adults. A number of studies have shown that minorities in general, and African Americans in particular, are more likely to be tried as adults than their white counterparts (Lehmann, Chiricos, & Bales, 2017). Psychological research has shown that subjects are more inclined to be punitive when they consider an African American juvenile as opposed to a white one. Determining who gets to be a child, and who gets treated as a child by the criminal justice system, is not a colorblind process.

While we may recoil in horror at the gruesome murder that Reeves is accused of, it is highly doubtful that a 25-year-old Reeves would have committed this crime. It is also highly likely that if she is found guilty (her trial is pending as of this writing), she will look upon her behavior very differently when she is older. This case is extreme, but many young people, even most young people, engage in behavior that is dangerous and harmful. Only some get the chance to move on with their lives after paying their dues.

In your view, should juveniles be charged as adults in some cases? What age would you consider to be a cutoff point where an offender is too young to be charged as an adult? What changes do people undergo in their 20s that make them less likely to engage in criminal conduct?

Learning Theory

A third psychological approach to understanding individual criminality focuses on the offender's exposure to criminal behavior. Learning theory posits that individuals are inclined to copy those around them and thereby mimic their behavior. A person who is exposed to a great deal of violence when she is young (say, through an abusive parent) will be violent and abusive herself. The most famous proponent of social learning theory, Albert Bandura (1925–), conducted a series of experiments known as the "Bobo Doll" experiments, wherein children observed an adult being violent to a doll. Then, the child was placed in a room with the same doll and, in many cases, she imitated what she saw the adult do. Clearly, then, exposure to violence can be linked with later violent behavior.

Learning theory: The belief that our behavior is learned from observing others.

WHAT WOULD YOU DO?

Criminal Behavior

Your younger brother is 14 years old. He has recently been running around with a different crowd than when he was younger. Some of these kids are "stoners," and many of them smoke cigarettes and engage in petty crime such as shoplifting or selling marijuana.

You are worried about what might happen if he spends too much time with these kids. You had similar friends when you were younger, and some of them stopped their criminal behaviors. Others didn't. When you left for college, you made a clean break with that crowd, but you're worried that your kid brother won't make the same

choices you did. But when you discuss it with him, he tells you that he's fine, his friends are just goofing around, and to mind your own business. But you've noticed that his grades are slipping.

You've begun to research more about your brother and his friends by asking around and using social media.

What behaviors would you look for in this group? How would this information help you determine whether your brother is correct about them? If, after research, you truly were concerned about things, how would you respond and try to convince your brother to change his social circle?

Learning theory is like behavioral theory—both believe that criminal behavior is learned from interacting with those around us. The significant difference between the two is that behaviorists see criminal behavior as a product of rewards and punishments, whereas learning theory sees it as a consequence of modeling our behavior on the behavior of others.

Differential Association Theory/Social Learning Theory

The basics of social learning theory and behavioral theory were adopted by criminologists primarily through an approach known as differential association theory, which was developed by Edwin Sutherland and his colleagues. In his book *Principles of Criminology*, Sutherland proposed several basic principles that explain the development of criminal behavior in individuals. This list is adapted from Sutherland, Cressey, and Luckenbill (1992, pp. 89–90):

Differential association theory: The criminological theory that argues that criminal behaviors and outlooks are determined by those that we spend time with.

1. *Criminal behavior is learned.* People are not inherently criminal, but rather pick it up from their environment.

2. *Criminal behavior is learned in interaction with other people through communication.* Crime is picked up through communication, not mere observation.

3. *Individuals learn criminal behavior in intimate groups.* They do not adopt criminal behavior through the media (music, movies, television), but rather through close acquaintances.

4. *Individuals learn techniques of crime as well as attitudes toward criminal activity.* Learning to become a criminal involves learning special skills for committing a crime (say for example, how to sell drugs without getting caught or ripped off) as well as the appropriate way to think about the criminal activity. This can include rationalizations (explanations why drug trafficking is okay) as well as motives (someone can develop a desire to be a drug kingpin by associating with other drug dealers).

5. *Individual attitudes and motivations toward law and order are shaped by the attitudes of those around us.* Some groups express a positive attitude toward authority, and others do not. These differing attitudes rub off on us and shape our future behaviors.

6. *Individuals become criminals because of differential associations.* This means that a person becomes criminal when she picks up negative attitudes toward the law and toward authority that are stronger than those that are positive toward these institutions. These negative attitudes are what are called *differential associations*. We are all exposed to a certain amount of contempt for law and authority—but when these attitudes outweigh affirmative ones, we are likely to become criminals.

7. *These differential associations can have different effects depending on their frequency, their duration, their priority, and their intensity.* It's not just who we encounter that shapes our attitudes and behaviors, but also when we encounter them (that is, at what stage in our lives). In addition, the precise nature of our encounters with these "bad influences" affects individuals. People who have long-term exposure, especially at a young age, to people with contempt for law and who valorize criminal behavior are more likely to become professional criminals in the future.

8. *While criminal behavior is an expression of general human needs and human values, it cannot be explained by these needs or values.* Everybody needs food and other basic goods to survive—but crime cannot simply be understood as an expression of this need to survive. While lawbreakers and law-abiding people both have these needs, only some of them seek to meet them by breaking the law. So, the answer to the question "Why do people commit crime?" is not "because they need to survive," because that explains both lawful and criminal behavior. Criminal behavior must be a product of something more—people commit crimes not because they need to survive, but because they have been taught to commit crime.

Thus, differential association theory expands and develops social learning theory in a way that is explicitly meant to explain why and how individuals become criminals: Criminal behavior is the product of a complicated set of social interactions that shape our attitudes toward the law as well as our justifications for our own behavior. If we associate with people who are criminally minded, it is likely that their behavior will shape us, and we will follow our peers into criminality.

REALITY CHECK

Criminal Profilers

Criminal profilers use the tools of modern psychology to determine the identity of a criminal based on her choice of targets, the clues she leaves behind, and the methods she used. They are renowned for reaching startling conclusions about a criminal: age, ethnic background, hobbies, work, marital state, et cetera, based on the criminal's *modus operandi*, that is, her choice of victims and her chosen means for attacking them. Small clues are used to unearth important details that help the police track down criminals. It is unsurprising then that profilers are featured on television (*Profiler* and *Criminal Minds,* to name two) and in movies (*The Silence of the Lambs*) as celebrated heroes of modern criminal justice, and self-described criminal profilers such as Pat Brown and Dayle Hinman make frequent appearances on CNN and Fox News to discuss whatever crime stokes the public imagination. Many students go into criminal justice or abnormal psychology with the hope of someday becoming a criminal profiler and unlocking the secrets of a mysterious serial killer or kidnapper.

Unfortunately, the realities of criminal profiling do not live up to the hype. While there are some people in law enforcement who do work that resembles criminal profiling, there are in fact very few. The FBI does have a Behavioral Sciences Unit that employs a small number of people (about 20) who do "profiling." Most police departments are too small to afford personnel that would engage in such specific tasks, and the few that work in private industry often do it as a side job that accompanies their regular work. Very few criminals are apprehended by profiling techniques but are instead found through more traditional methods such as eyewitnesses or DNA evidence. This, of course, does not mean that many university criminal justice programs don't eagerly promote the idea that students can become profilers if they take their courses; the programs are doing this, of course, primarily to boost their enrollments.

There are few reasons to take criminal profiling seriously as a method for uncovering the identity of criminals. Scientific studies of the reliability of profiling as a means for detecting criminals have shown that "profilers do not seriously outperform other groups when predicting the characteristics of an unknown criminal," and that "profiling appears at this juncture to be an extraneous and redundant technique for use in criminal investigations" (Snook, Eastwood, Gendreau, Goggin, & Cullen, 2007, p. 448). The journalist and author Malcolm Gladwell investigated the claims of criminal profilers and found them to be akin to the predictions of psychics and similar con artists, providing descriptions that were vague and contradictory and therefore could be "correct" no matter who the killer turned out to be. As Gladwell, discussing a prominent profiling debunker who had criticized efforts to identify a killer, put it,

> The answer [to why profilers look successful], he suspected, lay in the way the profiles were written, and, sure enough, when he broke down the rooftop-killer analysis, sentence by sentence, he found that it was so full of unverifiable and contradictory and ambiguous language that it could support virtually any interpretation. (2007, p. 43)

In short, much profiling is in fact an elaborate ruse used by so-called experts to reach broad conclusions that could never be disproven. It may be good entertainment, but rarely is profiling good policing.[1]

If profilers do so little, why are so many people inclined to believe that criminal behavior can be interpreted so cleverly? Why has the myth of the profiler endured if there is no factual basis for it?

---

[1] For a defense of criminal profiling, see Dern, Dern, Horn, & Horn, 2009.

SOCIOLOGICAL CRIMINOLOGY

Learning Objective 3.5—List the three most influential sociological theories of criminal behavior.

For sociological criminologists, crime is best understood not by looking at individual criminals, but by examining what they describe as the *social structure*. By *structure*, sociologists mean broad "invisible" forces that shape our lives: These can include our socioeconomic class (that is, where we fit within a society's economy), our race, and our gender as well as an array of broader forces that affect us. Sociologists do not necessarily seek to explain why any individual committed a specific crime (such as why Susan sells drugs or why Mike robbed a liquor store), but instead seek to explain things in a much larger way. (Why do some women enter the drug trade? Why do some people commit robberies?) This makes sociological explanations less useful in understanding any individual criminal act, but instead can help explain why crime falls or rises at any given time, as well as how big social changes affect crime. In scientific terms, we would say that psychological theories of crime are *micro* explanations (focusing on the individual), whereas sociological criminologists provide *macro* explanations (focused on the group as a whole). Sociological and psychological approaches aren't necessarily incompatible, they are simply working through different paradigms and therefore making different assumptions about behavior.

Émile Durkheim and Strain Theory

One of the founders of modern sociology was Émile Durkheim, a French scholar who wrote widely on sociological issues and developed some of the basic concepts of the discipline. One of Durkheim's claims was that "crime" was not an objective part of social life, that is, crime and what is criminal depends to a large degree on how society as a whole feels about a particular activity. For example, homosexuality was criminalized for a long time in the United States and to be gay was to be a criminal, whereas now it is common and acceptable in much (but certainly not all) of the country. Killing another person is considered wrong but is praiseworthy in some contexts (such as killing a terrorist). Although all societies have a concept of "crime," criminal acts vary so widely from place to place that it is pointless to find a common theme. As Durkheim put it,

> The only common characteristic of all crimes is that they consist . . . in acts universally disapproved of by members of each society . . . crime shocks sentiments, which, for a given social system, are found in all healthy consciences. (1973/1893, p. 82)

Durkheim's point is that, to understand crime, we should not look for anything in the act itself, but rather look to how society responds to the act. If a society thinks that an action ought to be punished, then it is a crime in that society; if a society does not feel that actor should be punished, then it is not a crime.

Along with seeing "crime" as relative to a society, Durkheim made a further contribution to criminology that influenced many later criminologists. In his study *Suicide* (1897/1997), Durkheim sought to show how an act that seems the most intimate and personal (what could be a more personal choice than taking one's own life?) is in fact shaped by large social forces, and that if a society changes its structure, the number of people who commit suicide would probably change. Poverty, religion, and social instability can all affect the choices of individuals to commit suicide. One of the features of a society that Durkheim claimed shaped suicide was what he called *anomie*. Anomie is a state where individuals feel that there is no structure or there are rules to life and that, as a result, nothing really matters. It occurs when there is a breakdown in the community in which the individual lives, and values lose their place in our lives. When societies change rapidly and old ways of life disappear, individuals experience anomie and may prove more likely to commit suicide.

While Durkheim's analysis of anomie was largely focused on suicide and what he called "anomic suicide," later sociological criminologists used the concept for studying criminal behavior. The most famous of these was Robert K. Merton. Merton, a sociologist at Columbia University, argued that social structures could be understood to be shaped by two factors. On one hand, there are the socially prescribed goals, things that we are told that we ought to pursue in our lives. On the other are the socially permissible means ("institutionalized means") to achieve these goals (Merton, 1938). For example, you are probably going to school to better your life. And by "bettering your life," you (probably) mean something like making money, having social status, and being happy. You figure that getting a college education is probably a good way to get money and happiness, or at least your parents and teachers have told you that this is the way to do this.

Many of us follow this pattern in our lives: Society tells us what goals are best in life, and it also tells us the appropriate means for achieving these goals. Almost everybody in 21st-century America wants to be economically and socially successful in life and believes that education and hard work are the means to get there. If an individual is "blocked" from this track by circumstances, she can often resort to criminal behavior in some form in order to achieve these goals. Anomie is the result of this conflict. Thus, for strain theorists, much criminal behavior is a result of the problems that develop when an individual can't or won't adapt to the rules prescribed by society.

Strain theory categorizes five possible responses to these social expectations (see Figure 3.1). Some responses can lead to different forms of criminal behavior, but they need not. These responses go under the following headings: *conformity*, *innovation*, *retreatism*, *ritualism*, and *rebellion*. We will address each in turn.

Conformity. Although we often consider conformity to be a bad thing in American society, in strain theory, conformists are simply law-abiding citizens who have accepted the goals prescribed by society and have also accepted the means to achieve these goals. If you are currently in school because you believe that an education is a way to get ahead in life (and by "ahead in life" you mean financial success and social status), you are a conformist according to strain theory.

Strain theory: Criminological theory that believes that crime often results from the inability of people to realize socially prescribed goals by socially prescribed means.

Innovation. An innovator is an individual who ascribes to the goals that society prescribes for us (money, respect) but can't or won't use the socially acceptable means to achieve them. Poorer people and people with less social status may be unable to go to college, for example, and thus find it very difficult to get a decent job and make enough money to be successful. Instead of seeking money through education and hard work in a lawful profession, an innovator will seek wealth and success by another route—sometimes one

Figure 3.1 Robert K. Merton's Deviance Typology

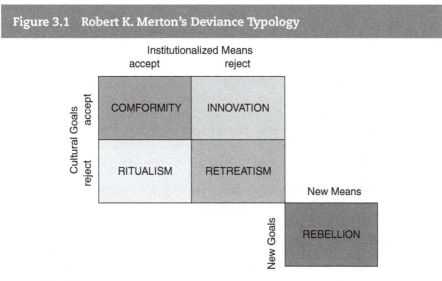

Source: Wikimedia Commons.

that is illegal. Drug dealers often want the same things that law-abiding citizens want; they have simply chosen to get these things in a different way than those deemed acceptable by the broader society. Many traditional criminals who are engaged in criminal activity for economic and/or social benefit are innovators; their motives are the same as ours, but their means are different.

Retreatism. Retreatists reject both the goals of society and the socially acceptable means to achieve these goals. This individual is often considered to be a dropout—a person who has checked out of society and has little to live for. Drug addicts, alcoholics, and drifters might in many cases be good examples of people who are retreatists. Noncriminal retreatists might be hermits.

Ritualism. A ritualist accepts the means society prescribes to achieve success but rejects the goals of success. Admittedly this is a rare category, but an individual who is going through the motions in her life without any ambition, drive, or sense of a goal might be a ritualist. For a ritualist, life is nothing but an empty routine.

Rebellion. Rebels are like retreatists insofar as they both reject society's goals and equally reject the means to achieve these goals. The primary difference between the two categories is that the rebel replaces society's goals with alternative goals and develops her own alternative means to achieve these goals. The best example of this type of social deviant might be a radical terrorist. Most terrorists believe in a set of values very deeply, but these values are incompatible with those of mainstream society. On the other hand, they also have a set of means to achieve these goals: terrorist violence. Thus, rebels often live and die by a strongly felt code, but that code is incompatible with the rest of the society that they are in.

Social Disorganization Theory and the Chicago School

The Chicago School is named after a group of researchers who studied crime at the University of Chicago in the early part of the 20th century and focused their analysis on the changing nature of the modern city. Their theory examined the social characteristics of different parts of the city and how these shaped criminal behavior—which is why their approach is sometimes referred to as the "social ecology." In short, they argued that the characteristics of a community shaped criminal behavior there, and that as traditional values broke down in these areas, the residents, particularly young people, became susceptible to criminal activity. The term *social disorganization* refers to this breakdown of values in these neighborhoods, and so the Chicago School's view was often called social disorganization theory.

It was commonly held at the time that inner-city crime was a product of the groups that lived there, usually immigrants. Many observers believed that the ethnic groups that lived in these areas (such as Italians, the Irish, etc.) were more prone to crime than others and, as a result, immigrant neighborhoods had a higher crime rate. These views were typically tied to anti-immigrant racism, which saw certain ethnic and racial groups (white, Anglo-Saxon Protestants) as superior to others. Social disorganization theory effectively flipped this argument on its head and maintained that it was not the type of people who occupied the neighborhood that led to a rise in crime rates, but rather the area itself that shaped the community that lived there. The fact that many high-crime neighborhoods remained dangerous even as different ethnic groups cycled in and out of them suggested that the ethnic makeup of the area's population was not the deciding factor in the amount of crime there.

The Chicago School divided the social life of cities into several concentric circles stretching out from the downtown business districts (see Figure 3.2). Each circle denoted a type of community that lived there and suggested a set of challenges for its residents. They argued that certain neighborhoods served as transitional neighborhoods and were prone

Social disorganization theory: The belief that crime is often a result of a lack of certain social factors, such as stable families.

Transitional neighborhoods: Neighborhoods with a large number of immigrants.

Figure 3.2   The Concentric Zone Model

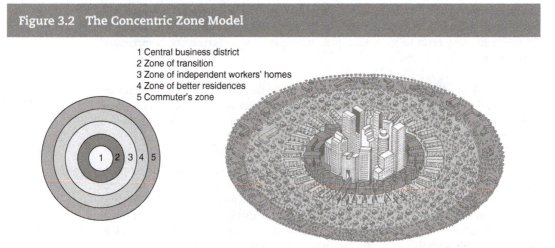

1 Central business district
2 Zone of transition
3 Zone of independent workers' homes
4 Zone of better residences
5 Commuter's zone

Source: Rubenstein, James M., *Contemporary Human Geography*, 3rd ed. Copyright © 2016. Printed and electronically reproduced by permission of Pearson Education, Inc., New York, New York.

to high crime rates. These are poor neighborhoods that face a high degree of population turnover. Groups came into these areas, usually from overseas, and many left as soon as possible, indicating that few had any lasting commitment to the community. This meant that they made little effort to protect and improve it.

When groups moved into these transitional neighborhoods, they underwent dramatic changes in the face of their surroundings: Poverty and stress, alongside a breakdown of their native cultures, became widespread. As traditional values and ways of life were swept away by the economic demands of their new, urban, American lifestyle, the old sources of social order (such as family and religion) become difficult to sustain. These challenges led to an increase in crime, as younger generations adapted to American values, while their parents struggled to keep up. As a result, parents were no longer able to keep their children on the straight and narrow path. If individuals were economically successful, they quickly left the transitional area for a more stable environment, dooming its remaining residents to poverty and crime. Given the economic and social realities of these areas, it is natural that crime would remain high here, regardless of the ethnic makeup of the population living there.

The point of social disorganization theory is that crime is not the result of individual choices or the ethnic makeup of a community, but rather depends on the social environment in which one lives. As different immigrant groups transitioned into American society in the 19th and 20th centuries (Irish, Italian, Polish, etc.), they were put through the process of social disorganization in these transitional neighborhoods. If they could find stability, often through blending in with mainstream society, they left, and others in similarly dire circumstances moved in to repeat the cycle. Essentially, social disorganization argues that it is the social environment that makes crime, not the individuals who live there.

Since the Chicago School developed social disorganization theory, there have been numerous refinements and modifications to the theory. Criminologists have sought to enrich our understanding of the nature of the social ties that can reduce crime rates. For example, the criminologist Mary Pattillo examined black neighborhoods in Chicago and found there a class of criminals who were considered a part of the community, and that "the incorporation of gang members and drug dealers into the networks of law-abiding kin and neighbors thwarts efforts to completely rid the neighborhood of its criminal element" (Pattillo, 1998, p. 747). Others have sought to reframe the emphasis on social ties as "social efficacy" or "social capital" to provide a more nuanced understanding regarding how social order, or the lack thereof, can affect crime rates in a city (Kubrin & Weitzer, 2003).

Labeling Theory

As much as we all wish to see ourselves as unique beings and are told that we should "just be ourselves," the reality is that we all try either consciously or unconsciously to fit into a prescribed social role most of the time. That role may be "good student," "nerd," "rebel," or "professor"—regardless, we all seek to fit into some sorts of existing social categories and adjust our behavior accordingly. We dress a certain way based on the image we want to project to others about ourselves. We talk in a certain way based on how we hope to be perceived. We even walk in a certain way based on how we want others to think of us—usually based on some socially defined role. (A slow, stooping walk communicates very different things than a brisk walk with one's head held high.) These self-conscious behaviors are necessary because these categories or labels help us to shape our own behavior as well as to understand the behavior of others—it's too hard to approach every person and every social interaction without a set of labels or assumptions to guide us. Labels are how we navigate our social world, helping us shape our own behavior and understand the behavior of others.

If, like many college students, you recently graduated from high school, you are intimately familiar with the social power of labels. The lives of most American high school students are packed with labels that further help define their place within the various social cliques on campus. A "jock" and a "nerd" are likely not going to be friends at most schools, and a "goth" and a "good kid" will probably not hang out either. It is no shock that many jocks look similar, and that nearly all "stoners" look alike and congregate together: The students themselves are shaping their behavior based on the labels, and consequently the individuals are labeled. (Even being "unique" is a kind of label, as people who are labeled unique must constantly struggle to show others just how unique they are.) As much as we

SOME STATISTICS . . .

Weather and Crime

There was a desert wind blowing that night. It was one of those hot dry Santa Anas that come down through the mountain passes and curl your hair and make your nerves jump and your skin itch. On nights like that every booze party ends in a fight. Meek little wives feel the edge of the carving knife and study their husbands' necks.

—Raymond Chandler (1946)

While criminologists point to a lot of different factors that are *criminogenic*, that is, they are likely to lead to criminal behavior, a surprisingly strong one is the weather. Independent of other social factors, the climate shapes crime. For example, numerous studies have shown that hot weather increases crime (particularly violent crime) and that rain decreases it overall. Particularly on weekends, there is a marked increase in crime with an increase in the temperature. Consider the data from Cleveland, Ohio, shown in Figure 3.3.

On the other hand, large amounts of rain often lead to a decrease in crime. According to one study, *a one-inch increase in average weekly precipitation correlates to a 10% reduction in violent crime.* On the other hand, it is sometimes linked to an increase in property crime such as burglary (Jacob, Lefgren, & Moretti, 2007).

There are a lot of possible explanations for these weather-based fluctuations in the overall crime rate. Psychologically, heat is often correlated with aggressive behavior—people are more violent when the temperature rises (Baron & Bell, 1976). You've probably experienced this in your own life: People get irritable and cranky when the mercury rises. On the other hand, there are also several sociological factors that can help explain this effect. People tend to be outdoors more when the temperature rises and therefore are more likely to run into other people. These encounters can sometimes lead to violence when things get tense. More people interacting means a greater likelihood of conflict. Either way, as global temperatures rise over the next decades because of climate change, we can expect these changes to affect crime, and pretty much everything else in our lives.

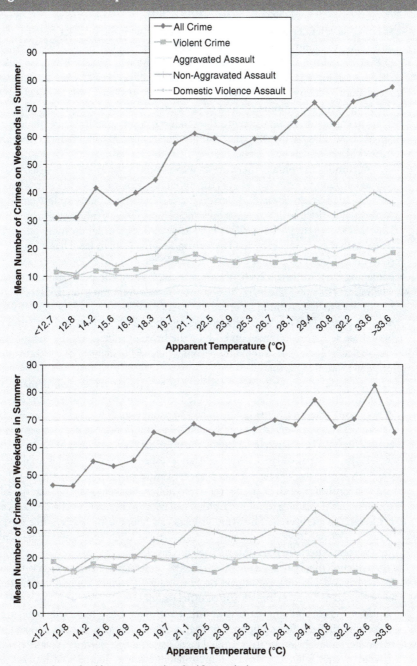

Figure 3.3 The Temperature-Crime Correlation

Source: Butke & Sheridan, 2010. Reprinted with permission.

all like to think of ourselves as above the opinions of our peers, we all see ourselves through the reflections of others and, at the same time, actively seek to shape how others see us.

Labeling theory studies the connection between the terms that we use to make sense of ourselves and our behavior—particularly how the labels given to us can affect our future as either an offender or a nonoffender. It is linked with the broader field of *symbolic interactionism*—the field of sociology developed by Erving Goffman (1959), Edwin Lemert (1951), and Howard Becker (1997) that studies how humans use symbols like labels to shape social interactions and to determine who is "like us" and who is an "outsider." The idea behind labeling theory is that if a person is given a label with criminal connotations —"thug," "crook," "scumbag," "junky," "gangster"—and she accepts this label, she is more likely to engage in criminal activity. If offenders can successfully shake off or escape harmful labels, it is less likely that they will become criminals and less likely that they will be treated like criminals by society.

According to Lemert, there are two elements to the labeling process that point the way to becoming a criminal. First is the initial breaking of social rules, in what criminologists call the *primary deviance*. A person is arrested for an offense or is accused of a crime. At this point, the labeling process takes place, and the individual can be given a negative label that shapes later behavior. *Secondary deviance* occurs when the individual acts in accordance with the label that she has been given, and the deviant label has been taken into her self-conception. The primary deviance is only meaningful if society chooses to attach a damaging label to the individual who perpetrates it; if the perpetrator isn't labeled, for whatever reason, then she is free to continue on as before. But a deviant label can shape the rest of her life by becoming a permanent part of her identity, creating what is known as a *deviance career*. This is what interests labeling theorists: not criminal activities per se, but how these activities are taken up both by the broader society and by the individuals who are labeled by society. If criminality becomes part of the identity of the individual, it helps shape her future behavior.

Say a young person is arrested for a relatively minor crime: selling marijuana. There are many different labels that can be applied to her when this happens. She could be labeled a "good kid" who simply made a mistake and should not "have her life ruined" by a criminal record. Alternatively, she could be labeled a "thug" or a "dealer"—meaning that she is far less likely to be treated leniently by the criminal justice system or those in the broader society. If the negative label is applied to her (especially if this label is applied in a public way by a court), she will have a much harder time making it in the world—jobs, housing, and relationships will all be harder for her to obtain. She may even take up the label herself and embrace it, leading to more criminal behavior on her part as she fashions an identity for herself as a criminal. The same process can happen for many other deviant labels: "criminal," "loser," "pervert," "rapist," "freak"—these labels can have terrible consequences for a person, especially if she internalizes this label.

Labeling theory has not only been used to understand the causes of criminal behavior, it also has had a significant impact on how many offenders are handled by the criminal justice system. Many criminal justice officials understand that criminal convictions can be life changing and stigmatizing and that such labels can have a long-term impact on those who they are forced upon. For that reason, many courts have allowed individuals to escape being labeled by the criminal justice system by offering either *diversion programs* (that is, programs like drug and alcohol rehabilitation in lieu of punishment) or a chance

Labeling theory: The theory that says that criminal behavior is often a result of society labelling individuals as criminals.

to expunge an offender's criminal record, that is, to have the offender's crime "wiped" from her record, removing any of the stigma remaining for her transgressions.

Since its inception, labeling theory has had many critics (Paternoster & Iovanni, 1989). Skeptics have argued that labeling theory overestimates the impact that labels have on human behavior and that other factors have significantly more influence. Others have argued that empirical support for labeling theory is weak and that crime data does not back up the claim that social labels influence future criminal behavior. Defenders argue that these critics oversimplify the views of labeling theory when they formulate and test their hypotheses about the relation between labels and criminal conduct (Farrington & Murray, 2013).

Hirschi's Social Control Theory

In the 1969 book *Causes of Delinquency*, the criminologist Travis Hirschi "flipped the script" on the study of criminal behavior (Hirschi, 1969/2001). Rather than starting with the view that most people are law-abiding citizens and then trying to explain why criminals are different, Hirschi believed that everybody can become a criminal under the right conditions. Therefore, instead of asking why some people commit crimes, Hirschi asked, why don't most people commit them? That is, he tried to understand why people obey the law, not why they break it. This led to the development of a school of criminology known as social control theory, an approach that sought out the roots of law-abiding behavior, rather than the sources of criminal behavior.

According to Hirschi, what keeps most people from participating in criminal behavior are the *bonds of attachment* that we form with others. These bonds keep us on the right path in several ways; they are the social glue that prevents lawbreaking. People are more likely to become criminals if they fail to develop these bonds and more likely to obey the law if these bonds are strong.

According to Hirschi, there are four major forms of attachment that help maintain a society: attachment, commitment, involvement, and belief.

1. *Attachment*: This refers to our psychological connection to others. How much do we care about others? How much do the feelings of others affect us? Psychopaths, for example, feel no attachments to others, and therefore are more likely to commit crimes.

2. *Commitment*: How much effort has an individual put into obeying social norms? How much do persons have to lose if they break the law? If you've invested a lot of time and effort into a traditional, successful life, you are less likely to risk it all in criminal activity.

3. *Involvement*: People who are busy in their lives with work, family, church, et cetera are less likely to commit crimes. "Idle hands are the devil's workshop." If we're bored or have too much free time, we're more likely to commit a crime.

4. *Belief*: Does a person believe in the values and laws of a society? As we discussed earlier, people who are more religious believe that laws should be obeyed and are less likely to break them.

Social control theory: An approach that seeks out the roots of law-abiding behavior, rather than the sources of criminal behavior.

Hirschi used this social bond theory to study high school students in California and found that young people who maintained strong bonds with their family and their community, as well as those involved in school and community activities, were significantly less likely to become criminals. Those who didn't were more likely. Keeping busy, keeping involved, and believing in the value of the social order all reduce the likelihood that a person will commit a crime.

WHERE DO I FIT IN?

EXPUNGEMENT

As labeling theory suggests, having a criminal record can have a lasting impact on how a person is treated by others. Prospective employers can use your criminal history as a basis for denying you a job. It can ruin your credit rating and your chances of getting into graduate school or law school. So, having a clean criminal record can be essential to leaving some significant mistakes in your rearview mirror and moving forward in life. Fortunately, for minor offenses, many states are aware of this problem and have allowed a route for a convicted offender to clean her criminal record in a process known as *expungement*. If you have a criminal record and want to leave your misdeeds behind you, here are some of the basic facts you need to know about getting your criminal record expunged. Bear in mind that expungement rules and procedures vary a great deal from state to state, so you should look closely at how your state handles expungement before proceeding:

To get your record expunged, there are usually several steps you must take:

1. You must establish that your offense is expungable. Many states have a list of offenses that cannot be removed from your record, and often only a select few offenses are candidates for expungement. (These usually include crimes committed while the individual was a minor, minor drug offenses, and first offenses.)

2. You must establish that you've completed all the requirements of your sentence (community service, probation, drug testing, etc.).

3. You must submit a certified criminal history report (usually available from the state government).

4. You must submit a notarized petition to the court requesting that your conviction be expunged.

5. The state attorney general's office will then inform the court as to whether it accepts the petition and agrees to have the crime expunged from the record. If this office approves, your record can be expunged by the court. If your request isn't approved by the attorney general, then you often must go to court to convince a judge to expunge your record.

Once your record is expunged, you no longer need to disclose your conviction in job interviews or rental applications, though for certain types of jobs (for example, in schools), or for certain types of licenses (for example, those pertaining to firearms), you may be required to mention your previous criminal record.

The Crime Drop: Applied Criminology?

As was discussed in Chapter 1, violent crime has dropped dramatically over the last several decades. The causes of this crime drop are a mystery, but it has still provided some important insights about the nature of criminal behavior and its causes. One thing we know about the drop is that it does not seem to correlate either to poverty or to unemployment. While the drop began in relatively prosperous times, the mid-1990s, it has continued despite economic turbulence. In the late 2000s, during the so-called great recession, unemployment was higher than it had been for decades, and the crime drop continued. Many people thought that this economic crash would lead to a return to the higher crime rates of the three preceding decades, but to the best of our knowledge, this has not happened. This means that economic explanations of criminal behavior, that violent crime is a response to poverty, do not work here. (We should be careful about overgeneralizing and mistakenly assuming that there is *no* link between economics and crime.)

There have been several attempts to explain the crime drop. One theory points to the rise in incarceration rates over the last 30 years. Essentially, these criminologists argue that everybody who would be committing crimes today is already in prison and therefore is not out breaking laws. Because the criminal justice system has been so harsh over the last several decades, small-time offenders and repeat offenders have been sentenced to very long periods in prison, meaning that they can't reoffend. Others have shown that states with higher incarceration rates do not necessarily see lower crime rates. A study by The Sentencing Project, a group that advocates criminal justice reform, showed that in three states that reduced their prison populations (New York, New Jersey, and California), violent crime rates fell at a greater rate than in other states where the incarceration rates increased (The Sentencing Project, 2014). While, again, there may be a real connection between incarceration and crime rates, the link between mass imprisonment and the crime drop is more complicated than it might initially seem.

A highly controversial explanation offered by the famous *Freakonomics* author Stephen Levitt points to an unsuspected cause of the drop: abortion (Levitt & Dubner, 2009). Abortion became legal throughout the country in 1972 with the *Roe v. Wade* decision of the U.S. Supreme Court. Levitt argues that the rise of legalized abortion meant that many children who might have turned to violent crime were aborted. That is, children born into poverty or to parents who can't take care of them are more likely to commit crime than are other kids, and these are the exact children who are likely to be aborted. Because they are never born, they never commit crime. Obviously, this explanation is controversial, as to liberals it smacks of social engineering (killing off the poor to make society better), and to conservatives it sounds like a claim that legalized abortions benefit society. Other, similar theories have looked at the reduction of lead in the environment (such as from car exhaust and paint) as a cause for the crime drop (Drum, 2016).

Some criminologists have attributed the crime drop to an aging baby boom population, better health standards (including medications for at-risk youth and the reduction of lead in the water supply), the development of computer technology (to distract young people from criminal behavior) and changing police tactics. (For a very brief survey of some of these explanations, see "10 [Not Entirely Crazy] Theories Explaining the Great Crime Decline," Goldstein, 2014.) There are problems with all these explanations. One fact that many explanations overlook is that the crime drop was not just an American phenomenon—it happened in many other countries around the world where the incarceration boom didn't happen and where abortion laws did not change in the 1970s (Dijk, Van Kesteren, & Smit, 2007). Regardless of what the ultimate explanation for the crime drop is (if there is a single explanation), the phenomenon is a mystifying but ultimately positive development.

CHAPTER SUMMARY

This has only been a very short tour of some of the fundamentals of criminological theory. We have examined classical theories of crime rooted in individual rational interest, biological theories rooted in our natural makeup, and psychological and sociological theories. Keep in mind that all the theories that we have discussed here have many different interpretations and subtheories that take the basic ideas outlined in this chapter and develop them in a variety of different directions. As new crime problems have developed (crack in the 1980s, terrorism in the 2000s), the theories have been changed as criminologists have sought to keep their theories relevant in changing circumstances. Criminology is a diverse and growing field that provides important insights into the overall nature of the phenomenon of crime. If you are a criminal justice major, there's a decent chance you'll be taking a course on criminology somewhere during your studies, and you'll see just how much more complex some of these theories can become.

The main point of this chapter has been to introduce you not only to some of the main criminological theories, but also to the main *types* of theories. Crime is a complicated phenomenon with a lot of different elements, and it makes sense that there would be a lot of different ways to approach it. At the beginning of the chapter, we saw that different criminological theories are using different paradigms to ask different questions. Psychological theories ask, "What makes this person commit a crime?" Sociological theories ask, "Why do people commit crimes?" Different questions result in very different kinds of answers. In any individual situation, crime researchers will have to decide not only what caused a crime, but also what kinds of questions they want to ask about the subject. That is, they will have to ask which paradigm they wish to use to interpret, understand, and explain criminal behavior. If a person is developing a policy for crime control in a city, it is probably best that she stick to sociological theories. If she is looking to determine how best to help an individual criminal who has been sentenced to prison, it is probably best that she use psychological theories. There is no simple answer to how criminal justice professionals and criminal justice policymakers should seek to explain or understand criminal behavior, and all the theories have their place.

In the next chapter, we will turn to yet more paradigms of criminology. These rely on some of the work that we've studied here—but take them in a radically different direction. What distinguishes these latter criminological theories is that they try to upend much of our thinking about what crime is. That is, they want to change our thinking about who the bad guys and who the good guys are in crime and criminal justice.

REVIEW/DISCUSSION QUESTIONS

1. Which criminological paradigm do you find most compelling for examining crime? What do you think their key similarities and differences are?

2. How might different criminological theories shape criminal justice policy? That is, if you used one of these theories as a tool for preventing crime, how would you do it?

3. Think of one crime or criminal that you've read about. How might different criminological theories explain the offender's behavior?

KEY TERMS

Atavism theory 57
Behavioral theory 59
Classical criminology 54
Differential association theory 62
Labeling theory 72

Learning theory 61
Paradigms 51
Phrenology 57
Psychoanalysis 58
Rational egoism 55

Social control theory 73
Social disorganization theory 68
Sociobiology 57
Strain theory 66
Transitional neighborhoods 68

Sarah Yeh

Foucault believed that schools, prisons, and other institutions are all obsessed with controlling our lives. How is school like prison?

CHAPTER FOUR

CRIME AND INEQUALITY

Critical approaches to criminology question a great number of common assumptions about crime and justice. Most important, they seek to challenge the traditional split between "good guys" and "bad guys" that often shapes our thinking about law and order. While critical criminologists all share this goal, there is a wide array of different schools of critical criminology, each of which takes its analyses in different directions, focusing on different aspects of social inequality and criminal justice. They don't necessarily disagree with each other, they just emphasize different aspects of social inequality or different ways to explain it. In this chapter, we will explore some of the different streams of critical criminology, all of which start from a shared set of assumptions, but each of which takes these assumptions in very different directions.

We will start our discussion of critical criminology with the father of the subject: Karl Marx. Although Marxism is now associated with the disastrous communist governments of the 20th century, his views are still relevant and influential in the modern world, and his theories have shaped a great deal of contemporary criminology. Then we will turn to a few later versions of critical criminology: critical race theory and feminist criminology. At the end of the chapter, we will discuss other branches of critical criminology, including postmodern theory and ecological criminology. While these theories are very different from each other, each in its own way seeks to get beyond the conventional perspective that criminals are bad and that the police and the criminal justice system are good.

ECONOMIC INEQUALITY AND CRIME

Learning Objective 4.1—Explain how economic inequalities shape conceptions of crime, law, and justice.

Karl Marx (1818–1883) was a German economist, sociologist, philosopher, and social activist who was interested in the ways that economic systems have shaped society in human history. According to Marx, society is composed of different economic classes (such as workers and business owners) who have differing and ultimately conflicting interests. For Marx, in all societies there is a struggle for power among these different classes, each of which is seeking to advance its own interests—usually at the expense of the other classes. The business owner wants to make profits, and employees want to make a salary and provide a decent life to their families. To an extent, of course,

Marxism: The social theory formulated by Karl Marx that views society as structured by conflicts between economic groups or classes.

their interests coincide—a profitable company can pay its workers—but if the business owner has a choice between making more money and paying the workers more, the owner will usually choose to make more money if she can get away with it. According to Marx, all human history is a conflict between different classes, each of which seeks to advance its own interests in the face of opposing interests of other classes. Marx called this conflict class struggle. In the medieval period, the peasants, the nobility, and the church were different classes with different interests who often fought each other for domination. In the Roman world, the elites, the peasants, and the slaves all sought a path to dominance. All history consists of some form of class struggle, according to Marx.

While Marx argued that society is composed of classes in conflict with each other, what shapes this conflict is the economy. As new discoveries are made, and new technologies are invented, they change the way that the economy functions and thereby alter the dynamics of class conflict. Changes in how we produce goods change how society is organized, as these new developments pick out winners and losers. Some classes lose ground if they can't adequately adapt to new economic realities, some gain power, and still others may be eliminated entirely. For example, once steam power and factories came into existence during the Industrial Revolution of the late 18th century, the traditional nobility, whose power was based on the control of land and farming, was no longer the only group with economic power. New groups (factory owners) harnessed the new technologies for their own ends and began to challenge the old nobility's dominance—eventually overthrowing the old aristocracies. To use a more contemporary example, with the rise of computers, new groups (techies) have gained power, challenging others who once controlled how products are made and information is disseminated. The old economy of "brick and mortar" stores and the profits of record companies and entertainers are now under threat by online stores and streaming music sites. Each of these changes in the economy marks a stage in the class conflicts that define human history. Ultimately whoever can generate the most economic power, what Marx calls capital, wins in the class conflict, until later economic developments change, and a new class rises.[1]

While they are fighting each other for control of society, both sides of the conflict believe that they are morally right and can usually provide reasons for why they deserve to be on top. That is, the wealthy people of the world justify their wealth, and they try to convince people in other classes that they are right to be dominant. (Poor people are lazy, or poor people are naturally inferior to the rich, or rich people have been chosen by God to be successful; these are some common reasons that rich people have used to justify their wealth and privilege.) Marx used the term ideology to describe these beliefs: Classes create and promote ideologies that justify their advantages and try to convince the other classes that their ideology is the correct one. For example, Marx famously described religion as "the opiate of the masses." By this he means that religious beliefs are often used to keep poor people in line, resigned to their fate, and unwilling to question the status quo. For Marx, the class conflict that is at the

Class struggle: The Marxist theory that human history is shaped by the fight for power between different economic groups (classes).

Ideology: In Marxism, the view that the beliefs and values of a society reflect the interests of the dominant class.

---

[1] Here I am ignoring the part of Marx's theory that claims that one class, the proletariat, will rise and become the dominant class for all time (his theory of socialism), as this is not relevant to the study of crime. Moreover, it's the part of his theory that is most demonstrably false.

heart of human society is one that is often a conflict of ideas. Ideologies are intellectual weapons that groups use to seek to control of the minds of peoples occupying the lower classes and to justify their power.

While religion is one of the most obvious forms of ideology, there are many others, some of which are intimately connected with criminal justice. Political theories such as liberalism and conservativism are ideologies that shape American life—each of which serves the interests of a different group. One of the most important aspects of American ideology is the concept of *private property*: the belief that we own certain objects and that, as a result, we have the absolute right to do with them what we wish. This idea has not always been with us, and its modern form was only created in England in the 18th century by philosophers like John Locke. Jean-Jacques Rousseau, the French philosopher, was skeptical of this idea and thought it was harmful for humanity. As he famously said,

> The first person who, having enclosed a plot of land, took it into his head to say *this is mine* and found people simple enough to believe him, that man was the true founder of civil society. What crimes, wars, murders, what miseries and horrors would the human race have been spared, had someone pulled up the stakes or filled in the ditch and cried out to his fellow men: "Do not listen to this imposter. You are lost if you forget that the fruits of the earth belong to all and the earth to no one!" (Rousseau, 1755/1992, p. 44)

Private property, the bedrock of modern capitalism, is an ideology according to Marx (and Rousseau), and it is an ideology that serves the interests of the rich. It allows them to believe that they have a right to own as many homes and cars and have as much money as they wish, and those without property have the right to starve.

Of course, the notion of private property is closely linked to the notion of theft. Taking other peoples' property is not only considered morally wrong but is considered to be a serious crime in almost all societies. But if Marx is right and private property is part of capitalist ideology, then we should be skeptical about this belief. A Marxist would argue that property is not truly owned by any individual, the wealthy do not have a right to everything they own, and therefore it is not necessarily wrong for a person who needs something badly to take it from somebody who has but doesn't need it. In the novel *Les Miserables* by the French writer Victor Hugo, the protagonist Jean Valjean is arrested and sentenced to five years in prison for stealing bread to feed his starving sister. While we might agree that private property is important, it's hard to say that it was wrong for Valjean to steal the bread. Many might say that it was a bigger wrong for Valjean to be arrested and punished for doing something that was ultimately good. Many "Robin Hoods" who steal from the rich and give to the poor are considered heroes, even if they live by a code that does not respect private property.

Les Miserables is, of course, an extreme example of the excesses of private property, but a Marxist would point out the massive economic inequalities in our society and the role that the ideology of private property plays in upholding it. One percent of the earth's population owns more than the other 99% combined—and many of the poor die from diseases that would be easily treatable if they had more resources (Oxfam International, 2015).

Americans deeply believe in the concept of private property and that one should work hard to earn her own fortune, but from a Marxist perspective, this belief serves primarily to keep the poor in their poverty and allow the wealthy to justify their privileges. The fact that very few people who are born in poverty in the United States are successful in escaping their condition and face so many additional challenges in life shows that often hard work is insufficient for success. Equally important, the wealthy have the power to influence the government to get it to create laws that reflect their interest in protecting their property—and hence the criminal justice system becomes a tool of the wealthy classes, according to a Marxist criminologist.

For a Marxist criminologist, criminal laws reflect the ideology of the ruling class and ultimately promote its interests. Criminals are often just those people who refuse to play by society's accepted rules—people who are seeking to advance themselves in a system that is stacked against them. Marxists can even go further and argue that many people who society finds admirable (corporate CEOs, politicians, church leaders) are in fact the *real* criminals, because they help support and promote a social system that is fundamentally unjust. Society would be better served if much of their wealth were confiscated and used to benefit the poor. As it stands, Marxists see a direct link between criminality and social inequality. In capitalist society, the criminal justice system is complicit in maintaining inequality: It arrests people who try to change the system, and it protects the private property of those few who are lucky enough to possess it.

Equally important for the Marxist is the belief that crime does not exist because criminals are "bad people" with no respect for the law. Rather a great deal of criminal activity is an understandable response to an unjust and unequal society. Rapists and pedophiles are surely criminals, but other so-called criminals like drug dealers and thieves are simply trying to succeed in a system that is designed to keep them down. Like the innovators of strain theory from the last chapter, criminals in a capitalist society are simply following capitalist values to their extreme—the only difference is that wealthy and powerful people can influence the politicians who make the laws that protect their interests, and the criminal element can't. The capitalists can influence government to keep their businesses legal. Thus Marxists change the equation regarding who are considered the bad guys and the good guys in capitalist society: The police and the criminal justice system are (often) the bad guys, and the criminals are (often) the good guys.

Marx was the first critical sociologist, but many criminologists have been influenced by his ideas since. Sometimes, these people are called *conflict criminologists*, because they see society as a struggle between different groups, and they argue that crime and criminal justice policy reflect this struggle. Here, we will primarily refer to these scholars as *critical criminologists*. As a critical researcher, Marx was fundamentally interested in how economic differences, that is, class conflict, shaped society. But later critical criminologists focus on other ways that the criminal justice system is unfair: most often in terms of race or gender. In the following sections, we will examine these schools of critical criminology, seeing how they develop Marx's ideas, and take them in different directions.

There was one other feature of Marx's work that was taken up by later critical criminologists. For Marx, research was not simply a way to shed light on how society works. Rather, criminology and other types of social analysis are supposed to be tools for making the world a better place. As he famously put it in relation to philosophy, "Up until now, philosophers have only interpreted the world; the point however is to change it" (1888/1978, p. 109). Marx was actively trying to change society so that it would be more equal and saw his work as part of this struggle—he was a devout communist, and throughout his life he worked to organize workers to overthrow capitalism. Research should not just sit there in books but should be a tool for making society better—researchers should be engaged in changing the institutions that they find so unjust and unfair. If a theory did not help liberate the poor, it was useless for Marx. Following Marx's lead, almost all critical criminologists see themselves as activists in part, working to change the criminal justice system in ways that they believe will make it fairer for those who are on society's bottom rung. They are not simply studying crime and society's response to it, they usually see themselves as activists trying to change the system for the better.

RACIAL INEQUALITY AND CRIME

Learning Objective 4.2—Demonstrate the different ways that the criminal justice system reflects society's racial inequalities.

Marx was primarily interested in how the conflict between different economic classes shapes a society, and Marxist criminologists study how class struggle plays out in the worlds of crime and criminal justice. But there are other ways to look at the impact of social conflict on the criminal justice system. One of the most important of these, particularly in the United States, is through the lens of *race*.

America has been a racially polarized society since its formation, and we have been shockingly hypocritical about racial issues for a very long time. The Declaration of Independence, the founding document of the United States, declared that "all men are created equal, that they are endowed by their Creator with certain unalienable Rights, that among these are Life, Liberty and the pursuit of Happiness." At the same time as this document was being written, Americans held nearly a million people in slavery, subjected to brutal and dehumanizing treatment. After the Civil War, Jim Crow laws and segregation laws in the South kept many black Americans in circumstances that were in many ways indistinguishable from slavery—even as the nation was fighting wars to spread democratic values and human rights abroad (Blackmon, 2009). The United States fought two world wars abroad to protect democratic societies while denying the right to vote to huge sections of its own population. The civil rights movement gave many African Americans political equality and the right to vote, but many remain mired in poverty and subject to all kinds of barriers limiting their ability to succeed and participate in American life. Many white (and other nonblack) Americans remain suspicious and fearful of African Americans and largely unsympathetic to their situation. Many black Americans feel distrusted and marginalized by the rest of society.

Critical race theory looks at how society in general, and the criminal justice system in particular, keeps African Americans subordinate. Clearly the over-policing and over-incarceration of black Americans, particularly young, male blacks, plays a large role in keeping African Americans poor and marginalized. African Americans are far more likely to be stopped by the police than white people are (Meehan & Ponder, 2002).

Critical race theory: The view that American society is structurally unequal and that minorities are targeted by the government in general and by the criminal justice system in particular.

If they are stopped, they are more likely to be searched (Knowles, Persico, & Todd, 1999). And they are more likely to be arrested by the police (Kochel, Wilson, & Mastrofski, 2011). The incarceration rate for black men is significantly higher than the rate for any other group, even though they commit crime in no greater proportion than any other group. When convicted of similar offenses, African Americans get longer sentences than other offenders (Kansal & Mauer, 2005). Native Americans fare even worse (Franklin, 2013). Although the causes of this inequality are complicated and debatable, it is a demonstrable fact that African Americans and other minorities are dispropor-tionately targeted by American criminal justice.

As we discussed in the introduction to this book, American criminal justice is closely bound up with racial issues, and the criminal justice system has played a signif-icant role in perpetuating racial inequalities in America. As we will see in more depth

CRIMINAL (IN)JUSTICE

The Convict Lease System

The Thirteenth Amendment officially abol-ished slavery in the United States in 1865. This amendment, coupled with a set of laws and political reforms, was intended to protect the formerly enslaved population of the American South and help them become full members of a new American society in the aftermath of the Civil War. While the amendment declares that "neither slavery nor involuntary servitude . . . shall exist within the United States, or any place subject to their jurisdiction," it left one crucial exception. Slavery was abandoned "except as a punishment for crime whereof the party shall have been duly convicted." In some parts of the South, this exception became a tool to re-enslave the people who had just been liberated. These policies became one of several important ways that American crimi-nal justice has been turned against its black citizens.

The end of slavery led to a labor shortage in the South as few of the freed blacks wished to return to the work that they had previously been forced to perform. To obtain the labor needed, southern states passed a series of new laws that were designed to enable the arrest of the

newly freed former slaves. Laws were passed, known as the "Black Codes," which crimi-nalized harmless behavior such as vagrancy among southern blacks, and these laws were then used as an excuse to arrest the "offend-ers." Once they were detained, these African Americans could be leased by the government to local plantations and other industries —often the same places where they had been enslaved before the Civil War. These laws were often designed with loopholes for white vagrants to avoid a similar fate.

Critical race theorists often point out that the convict-lease system represents one of a set of ways that the Civil War did not truly lead to the emancipation of the black population. Instead, the war marked a change in how blacks were kept in servitude, but they remained enslaved. Rather than enslaving blacks directly, the post-war criminal justice system became a tool of the former slave owners, allowing them to keep African Americans politically marginalized and forced into a new but very familiar form of bonded labor. These laws continued in different forms in the South through the 20th century, and their legacy persists today.

in later chapters, many aspects of American criminal justice, particularly policing and prisons, but also laws and courts, have been shaped by the racial dynamics of American society. After the Civil War, African American prisoners were used as labor in private businesses in a situation not that different from antebellum slavery. During the struggle against segregation in the South in the 1960s, the police were often used to harass, abuse, and even kill civil rights activists. "Bull" Connor, head of the Birmingham, Alabama, Police Department, used his officers to viciously beat activists who sought legal equality for blacks, as did many other local law enforcement officials. In contemporary America, many African Americans blame the police for using excessive force against black youth—and almost weekly a new report appears about police officers attacking and sometimes killing unarmed black men. The distrust between the police and African Americans runs deep and has a long history, and this distrust is the basis for the research of many critical race theorists.

One theme discussed among critical race theorists that we will discuss more in later chapters relates to laws that look racially neutral on paper, but that have a very different influence on blacks and other minority groups than on white people. No criminal laws dictate that different racial groups are to be punished differently (this would be unconstitutional), but in practice, seemingly race-neutral laws may lead to wildly disproportionate consequences for different races. To use one example, until recently the possession of crack cocaine was punished significantly more severely than was the possession of powdered cocaine (Sklansky, 1994). While this does not mean that black people are to be treated worse than whites, the reality is that crack cocaine was and remains a drug that is sold and used by African Americans. There is very little chemical difference between the two drugs—they are effectively the same except that one is often consumed by wealthier white people and the other by poor black people. (This disparity was reduced by the Fair Sentencing Act of 2010, but it still exists.) Other cases include loitering laws, which are often used to justify the police harassment of minorities and other people considered to be socially undesirable, an issue we discussed in Chapter 2. Some laws that seem race neutral (that is, they don't explicitly treat the races differently) nonetheless are profoundly racist in their impact.

Another aspect of critical race theory is racial threat theory. Developed by the sociologist H. M. Blalock (1967), this theory argues that black Americans are perceived as a threat to white Americans' power, wealth, and security, and as such must be controlled by white dominated society. According to Blalock, racial minorities represent three different sorts of threats to white Americans: economic threat, political threat, and symbolic threat. "Symbolic threat" occurs when whites perceive minorities as deviant and a threat to culture (such as when white people complain about the way that young black men allow their pants to "sag" below their waistline) (Dollar, 2014). According to Blalock, the feeling of insecurity or threat among white people causes them to use the power of the state, primarily through the criminal justice system, to maintain their domination over other groups. According to this model, the state is a tool of white *hegemony*, that is, the dominance of white people over other minorities politically, economically, and ideologically. By marginalizing minorities and enforcing the values that are associated with white culture, the state ensures that white ideals and white people remain the dominant force in society.

Racial threat theory: The theory that white Americans see African Americans as a threat to their power, wealth, and security, and as such must be controlled.

SOME STATISTICS ...

Race in the Criminal Justice System

There are a lot of statistics—some collected by criminologists, some by state and federal governments—that show just how differently the criminal justice system treats minorities. As with every other important topic, the data does not lend itself to a simplistic analysis, but a lot of it nonetheless backs up the assertion of critical race theorists that the criminal justice system targets African Americans for excessive policing and excessive punishment. The criminal justice system looks very different if you are black or brown than if you are white. Keep in mind that statistics can be misleading, but they can still help us get an understanding of how the criminal justice system supports and promotes racial inequalities.

Here are a few pieces of data to help as a foundation.

As you can see in Figure 4.1, blacks are about 13% of the population, whites are 61%, and Hispanics are 18%. But African Americans (and Hispanics) are much more likely to be poor: The percentage of whites who live in poverty is 11.6%, while the percentage of African Americans who live in poverty is 25.8% (Macartney & Bishaw, 2013), and the median income for white Americans is $71,000.00 per year, while the median income for African Americans is $43,000 per year (Pew Research Center, 2016). Finally, the incarceration rate of African Americans is significantly higher than those for other races (see Figure 4.2).

Though they are a relatively small percentage of the U.S. population, African Americans are disproportionately imprisoned, and they are disproportionately poor.

Of course, these statistics by themselves do not definitely show that the United States oppresses African Americans. Conservative critics can always charge that blacks commit more crimes than do white people and are therefore more likely to be arrested and imprisoned. It's

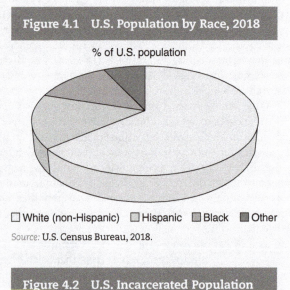

Figure 4.1   U.S. Population by Race, 2018

% of U.S. population

☐ White (non-Hispanic)   ☐ Hispanic   ■ Black   ■ Other

Source: U.S. Census Bureau, 2018.

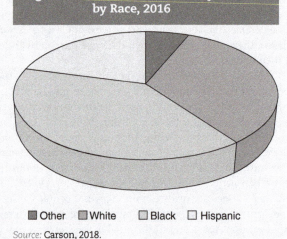

Figure 4.2   U.S. Incarcerated Population by Race, 2016

■ Other   ■ White   ☐ Black   ☐ Hispanic

Source: Carson, 2018.

undeniably true that most crime data show that violent crimes are disproportionately committed by African Americans. The homicide rates from the Bureau of Justice Statistics show that over half of all homicides are committed by African Americans (Figure 4.3).

The same report shows that a nearly identical percentage of African Americans (47%) are victims and that most of the homicides committed by blacks are on other blacks. (When it comes to nonviolent crime, the data is a little fuzzier.)

If we adjust crime data based on income and compare poor blacks to poor whites, the crime data looks quite different (Figure 4.4). Poor people of all races are more likely to be victimized by violent crime and are more likely to commit violent crimes, and poor blacks and poor whites are victimized at roughly the same levels (Harrell, Langton, Berzofsky, Couzens, & Smiley-McDonald, 2014).

Moreover, even though blacks do not report use of illegal drugs more than whites, they are much more likely to be arrested for drug use. In Beckett's study of the drug trade in Seattle (Beckett, Nyrop, & Pfingst, 2006), to use one example, researchers discovered that "African Americans constituted 16% of observed drug dealers for the five most dangerous drugs but 64% of drug dealing arrests for those drugs" (The Sentencing Project, 2013, p. 11).

Black offenders tend to get harsher sentences than white offenders when they commit

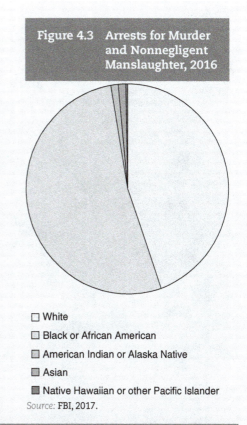

Figure 4.3   Arrests for Murder and Nonnegligent Manslaughter, 2016

☐ White

☐ Black or African American

▨ American Indian or Alaska Native

▨ Asian

▧ Native Hawaiian or other Pacific Islander

Source: FBI, 2017.

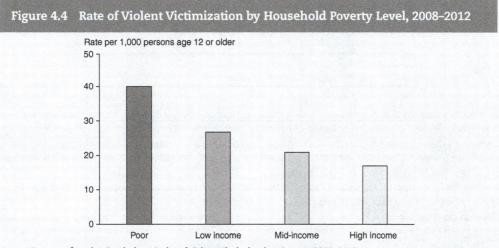

Figure 4.4   Rate of Violent Victimization by Household Poverty Level, 2008–2012

Rate per 1,000 persons age 12 or older

Source: Bureau of Justice Statistics, National Crime Victimization Survey, 2008–2012.

Note: Poor refers to households at 0% to 100% of the Federal Poverty Level (FPL). Low income refers to households at 101% to 200% of the FPL. Mid-income refers to households at 201% to 400% of the FPL. High income refers to households at 401% or higher than the FPL.

(Continued)

(Continued)

BLACK/WHITE DISPARITY

These data show the racial disparity in incarceration rates for black and white U.S. residents in each state.

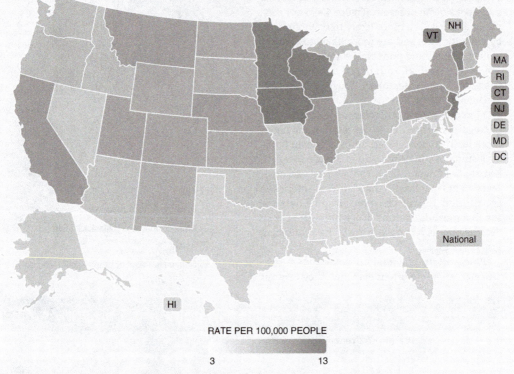

RATE PER 100,000 PEOPLE

3   13

Source: The Sentencing Project, 2016. Reprinted with Permission.

identical crimes. In a study of over 77,000 federal criminal cases, criminologist David Mustard discovered that African Americans received sentences that were 5.5 months longer than those of white offenders (Hispanics received sentences 4.5 months longer), even when you factor in the severity of the crime and other related issues. There is no state where a higher percentage of white people are incarcerated than black people.

The map in Figure 4.5, compiled by the Sentencing Project (sentencingproject.org), shows that in every state in the United States, there are higher percentages of the black population incarcerated than the white population— it is only a matter of how many more African Americans are imprisoned.

It is important to keep in mind that, from a critical perspective, this kind of data can only tell us so much about inequality in America, and it probably wouldn't convince a hardcore skeptic regardless. More important, crime statistics and incarceration rates only provide a picture of the world as it is. Critical race theorists argue that the crime rate and the economic inequalities in America reflect deeper injustices that go back centuries. It is understandable if black people commit more crimes—after all, they are often denied traditional routes to success and must overcome deep prejudices in American society to get a fair shot at success. In one famous study, job applicants with black-sounding names like Lakeisha or Jamal were 33% less likely to get a call back for an interview than were identical applicants with white-sounding names like Emily or Greg (Bertrand & Mullainathan, 2004). Also, the data presented here has all of the problems that we discussed in the first chapter: It can be biased and inaccurate in a host of ways. Unfortunately, we cannot know what the racial makeup of prisons would look like in a society that never had segregation or slavery, we can only study the world as it is with all its imperfections.

GENDER INEQUALITY AND CRIME

Learning Objective 4.3—Describe the role that gender inequality plays in the study of crime and criminal justice.

While feminism as a label still has negative connotations to some, the principles behind it remain important, even if they are often misunderstood by critics. Given that it is trying to promote the interests of nearly half of humanity, it is no surprise that feminism is a complicated and conflicted movement. What holds all feminists together is the idea that men and women ought to be treated equally in society, and that for the most part, they are not. What distinguishes different forms of feminism is what is meant by *equality* and how much society needs to change for men and women to truly be equal. Some are moderate and believe that, with some relatively minor changes, society can be equalized—we just need to remove barriers for women to succeed and make changes that consider the fact that women are physically and psychologically different from men. Others, called radical feminists, are closer to Marx and maintain that society would have to be completely transformed from top to bottom, including dismantling institutions like the family and marriage, for true gender equality to be realized.

Feminists all agree that most of the power in America is currently possessed by men, the gender that has controlled society, government, and culture since the beginnings of civilization. Feminists call this male-centered social order the patriarchy and seek to overcome it through various forms of political action. According to feminist scholars, for millennia, society has been shaped according to the perspectives, desires, and needs of men, and many women have been fooled into accepting these male standards as the obviously right ones—similar to Marx's views about the ideologies of different classes. Any woman who has wanted power or success in life has had to get it on the terms that men have set down. Whether it is standards of what it is to be beautiful (young, skinny, large breasts) or what it means for a woman to be fulfilling her "natural role" in life (taking care of the home, raising kids, caring for her husband), men have defined women's roles in society. We live in a society dominated by men and male perspectives on right and wrong, good and bad, and the proper conduct for the different genders.

Feminist criminologists take the assertion that society is male dominated and uses it to analyze crime and critique the criminal justice system in a variety of different ways. As

Patriarchy: The feminist view of society that argues that social power is in the hands of men and serves male interests.

Daly describes it, "The central questions asked by feminist scholars concern the place of sex/gender relations in the shaping of crime, justice, and criminology" (Daly, 2005). Like other feminists, feminist criminologists are involved in a wide array of different forms of research and hold different views about the nature of gender inequality. Here I will focus on a few of the most significant streams of feminist criminology.

Some feminist criminologists argue that crimes that impact women are studied less than those that affect men, simply because women's concerns are not taken seriously by society more generally. For example, homicide is a crime that affects women in ways that are very different from the ways that it affects men, but women as victims are not researched in significant depth. As one researcher points out, "Women are more likely to be victimized by intimates (e.g., spouses or boyfriends), whereas men are typically killed by strangers or acquaintances," but "the empirical research is extremely limited with regard to gender inequality and female homicide victimization" (Vieraitis & Williams, 2002, pp. 35–36). Other crimes affect women almost exclusively, such as rape, and these need to be studied with an eye specifically toward how women experience rape without assuming that men and women would respond to unwanted sexual advances in the same way. Rape is rarely a means for male sexual gratification but is more often a crime of violence—a way for a man to terrorize and control a woman, meaning that it is a tool of male dominance. By putting the victimization of women in the center of the study of victims of crime, feminists can enlighten us about the unique ways that women are mistreated in a patriarchal society. One in six women has been the victim of an attempted or completed rape, and the majority of rapes are committed by someone known to the victim (Figure 4.6).

Feminist criminology: The criminological theory rooted in the view that women are treated unjustly in society and that these inequalities are reflected in criminal justice.

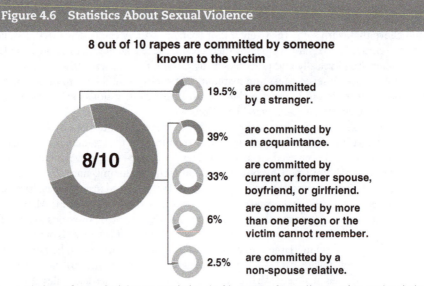

Figure 4.6   Statistics About Sexual Violence

8 out of 10 rapes are committed by someone known to the victim

8/10

19.5%   are committed by a stranger.

39%   are committed by an acquaintance.

33%   are committed by current or former spouse, boyfriend, or girlfriend.

6%   are committed by more than one person or the victim cannot remember.

2.5%   are committed by a non-spouse relative.

Source: Victims of Sexual Violence: Statistics. (n.d.). RAINN. https://www.rainn.org/statistics/victims-sexual-violence.

Other feminist criminologists focus on crimes where women are perpetrators, and in their research, they seek to understand why women resort to criminal behavior. Traditionally, most criminologists have studied male offenders for many reasons but primarily because there are far more of these than there are female offenders. Why women are less likely to engage in criminal behavior was unquestioned as was the unique nature of the female criminal. An examination of female offenders reveals that many women engage in criminal behavior for reasons that reflect women's unequal position in society. For example, some women commit crimes such as theft and drug dealing because they are the sole caretakers of their children and must find a way to feed their families without another wage earner in the home (Chesney-Lind & Pasko, 2013; Grundetjern, 2018). As one convicted crack dealer put it, "I don't regret it because without the extra income, my kids wouldn't be fed every day. Even though I do have a good job when I work and stuff like that, it's hard raising two kids by yourself" (Ferraro & Moe, 2003, p. 20). Others may do so for different, less noble reasons, but regardless, they have motivations that can't adequately be understood by using theories that are designed to explain the criminal behavior of men. Putting female offenders at the center of a study of criminal behavior reveals many important facts that are overlooked if we treat such offenders as a mere afterthought.

Still others examine the roles played by women within the criminal justice system, focusing on the unique challenges faced by female police officers, female court workers, and female correctional officers. As women have moved into traditionally male fields, they have affected an important shift in how the criminal justice system operates. Female criminal justice professionals face challenges that men rarely do—sexual harassment, for example —and also bring unique skills to the field of criminal justice. Female criminal justice professionals may take approaches to their work that are different from those of men, some of which may be better suited to the job. By studying how the presence of women in the criminal justice system changes the way it operates, criminologists can learn how to improve the criminal justice system overall.

Recently feminists have been debating carceral feminism. Carceral feminists believe that the best response to rape and other crimes against women is to aggressively push for harsher punishments against those who commit these crimes. When Brock Turner, a Stanford University student who was convicted of rape and several related offenses stemming from a January 15 attack on a woman outside of a fraternity house, was given a six-month sentence by a male judge, some feminist critics charged that the sentence was far too light. In response, they led a successful recall campaign against the judge who gave the sentence, hoping to send a message that those who assault women will face serious consequences. Skeptics, including many feminists, have charged that carceral feminists ultimately hurt the poor and minorities and don't solve the problem of patriarchy. Wealthy accused rapists can use money to hire lawyers to defend themselves and avoid the harshest punishments, while poor defendants cannot. Instead, these critics argue that feminist criminologists should seek to change the beliefs of people about women rather than "excessively" punish men who hurt women. "The underlying logic of carceral feminism relies on increased policing, legal frameworks, and arrest, as opposed to political, social, and economic changes that would alter power relationships between men and women" (Sweet, 2016, p. 203).

Carceral feminism: The feminist theory that the best response to crimes against women is to aggressively push for harsher punishments against those who commit these crimes.

REALITY CHECK

False Accusations of Rape

The fear that a woman would falsely accuse a man of rape is common among men. Men often fear that a woman could accuse a partner of rape after the fact out of a desire for revenge for some reason, and her alleged attacker would be unable to defend himself because the encounter happened in private. In the 17th century, the English jurist Lord Hale put it succinctly, arguing that rape "is an accusation easily to be made and hard to be proved, and harder to be defended by the party accused, tho never so innocent" (1736/1847, p. 634). Because of the unique context where rape occurs, men are said to be particularly vulnerable. The alleged attacker could be forced into a "he said, she said" situation, and his life could be ruined.

It is undeniable that there are false accusations of rape, but they are relatively few. One study of 136 alleged rapes over 10 years found 8—about 5.9%—that were false accusations (Lisak, Gardinier, Nicksa, & Cote, 2010). Extrapolating from other research on the subject, the researchers estimate that about 2%–10% of all rape allegations are false. Going beyond accusations, many of which are dismissed by investigators before they get to the point of prosecution, determining the number of people convicted for rapes that they did not commit gets more complicated. One study of the 345 exonerations from 1989 to 2003 found 121 (36%) of these were for rape. None of this is definitive, but it does suggest that accusations are uncommon and convictions even less so.

On the other hand, there are good reasons to believe that rape is an underreported crime. According to the Justice Department, nearly 77% of rapes were not reported to the police in 2016; this figure is much higher than the rate of unreported assaults (56%) (Morgan & Kena, 2018). There are good reasons for this: Women who report being raped can face retaliation from their attacker or from broader society, which often harshly judges women's sexual behavior, even when it is nonconsensual. When Christine Blasey Ford came forward and accused Supreme Court Justice Brett Kavanaugh of assaulting her in high school, she was publicly ridiculed in the media and by President Trump himself—an extreme example of what is a common experience for rape victims. Some fear the stigma of being labelled a rape victim by those around them. Still others think that they won't be believed or even blame themselves for the attack (Williams, 1984).

False accusations of rape are terrible, but they are relatively rare compared to the massive number of rapes and sexual assaults that go unreported in America. Over the last few years, some women have responded to the election of Donald Trump (who once bragged about sexually assaulting women and "grabbing them by the pussy") and public accusations against celebrities like Harvey Weinstein and Bill Cosby by coming forward with their own stories of sexual harassment, sexual abuse, and rape. Many feminists hope that the stigma surrounding rape will lift in the #MeToo era, and more women will come forward to share their stories no only on social media, but also with the police.

Are there ways to prevent false accusations of rape? Are there good ways to encourage rape victims to come forward? What are they in your view?

There is no single feminist perspective on crime and criminal justice, and there is no single subject studied by feminist criminologists. There is widespread disagreement among feminists about what feminism means and what are the best ways to talk about gender inequality in America today. This should not be surprising, given the fact that, according to feminists, women face challenges from the patriarchy on many different fronts. Because women's inequality is such a complicated issue, it makes sense that feminists who try to study and understand this inequality would be complicated, too.

Feminism and Rape

One important example of the influence of feminism is in how the criminal justice system handles the crime of rape. We're used to thinking about rape as numbering among the most horrifying and brutal crimes one could commit, but it wasn't always this way. Historically, rape was considered a relatively nonserious offense by the public, and only a generation ago, rape jokes were a common staple for comedians. The crime was even defined in such a way that it was legally impossible for a husband to rape his wife. (Rape was defined as "carnal knowledge of a woman by a man *other than her husband*, by force and against her will" in the common law [Dressler & Garvey, 2017, p. 403].) Rape wasn't taken very seriously by American culture and, as a result, wasn't taken seriously by the criminal justice system.

There are many aspects of rape that make it a unique crime, but the thing that matters most for us is what it reveals about gender relations in our society. It is commonly believed that men always want sex and will pursue it whenever it is available. Women are expected to be "pure" and not invite unwanted male sexual advances—to do otherwise is to somehow be immoral. If a woman dresses provocatively or flirts with men, she must "want it," and it's her fault if a man attacks her. We don't look at any other crime and ask what victims did to "deserve" what they got. As feminists have pointed out, none of these views about sexual relations are natural, but rather reflect patriarchal views about the appropriate roles for men and women. Women are supposed to guard their own virtue and be on guard against sexually aggressive men, who "naturally" pursue sexual gratification whenever it is available to them.

Rape is the one crime that, historically at least, was defined by men, committed by men, and prosecuted by men, but men were almost never its victims. As a result, the law has generally reflected the views of men about sex and the fear that men could be falsely accused of rape by a woman seeking revenge. Whether these fears are founded (they're not—most experts believe that rape is underreported as a crime—see "Reality Check: False Accusations of Rape"), they have historically been used, alongside the aforementioned assumptions about women's sexual conduct, to limit the prosecution of rape and affected how the law was constructed.

How has rape law reflected the perspective of men? Perhaps the most significant way is through the so-called *resistance requirement*. Often, criminal law has required that women resist their attacker to establish that they were raped. If a woman failed to resist, even if the sex was nonconsensual (for example, if the woman said "no" to her attacker but did not fight back), there was usually no rape, legally speaking. Of course, if a woman resists her attacker, it will often do absolutely no good, as men are usually much stronger, and few women have been taught basic self-defense techniques. In addition, if a woman resists, it is highly likely that she will be beaten by her attacker, only worsening her condition. Even if

REALITY CHECK

What if Robbery Were Treated Like Rape?

This script is an excerpt from "The Rape of Mr. Smith" an article by Connie Borkenhagen (1975).

In the following situation, a holdup victim is asked questions by a lawyer.

"Mr. Smith, you were held up at gunpoint on the corner of First and Main?"

"Yes"

"Did you struggle with the robber?"

"No."

"Why not?"

"He was armed."

"Then you made a conscious decision to comply with his demands rather than resist?"

"Yes."

"Did you scream? Cry out?"

"No, I was afraid."

"I see. Have you ever been held up before?"

"No."

"Have you ever GIVEN money away?"

"Yes, of course."

"And you did so willingly?"

"What are you getting at?"

"Well, let's put it like this, Mr. Smith. You've given money away in the past. In fact, you have quite a reputation for philanthropy. How can we be sure that you weren't CONTRIVING to have your money taken from you by force?"

"Listen, if I wanted—"

"Never mind. What time did this holdup take place, Mr. Smith?"

"About 11:00 P.M."

"You were out on the street at 11:00 P.M.? Doing what?"

"Just walking."

"Just walking? You know that it's dangerous being out on the street that late at night. Weren't you aware that you could have been held up?"

"I hadn't thought about it."

"What were you wearing at the time, Mr. Smith?"

"Let's see . . . a suit. Yes, a suit."

"An EXPENSIVE suit?"

"Well—yes. I'm a successful lawyer, you know."

"In other words, Mr. Smith, you were walking around the streets late at night in a suit that practically advertised the fact that you might be a good target for some easy money, isn't that so? I mean, if we didn't know better, Mr. Smith, we might even think that you were ASKING for this to happen, mightn't we?"

How is Mr. Smith's experience different from how you think an ordinary crime victim would be treated by the police? Why does this interrogation feel wrong? Does this strike you as similar to how young women are criticized for their sexual behavior by our society? Why or why not?

Source: Borkenhagen, C. (1975). Reprinted with permission.

resisting would make a difference, many women report freezing up during the attack and feel that they are having an out-of-body experience that prevents them from resisting their attacker (Hopper, 2018). Requiring that a rape victim resist her attacker is both pointless and dangerous, but, from a male perspective, it makes perfect sense: If a man did not resist his attacker, we would find something odd about it.

Rape law has changed a great deal over the last four decades, and many of these sexist assumptions have disappeared from our criminal codes. The reason for this is, quite simply, that women have begun to play a significantly larger role in the legal profession, and their views about rape have begun to be incorporated into the law. Women began attending law school, becoming lawyers, judges, and law professors, and were thereby able to change the laws in a way that reflected women's views about rape. For example, the resistance requirement has largely been eliminated from the books in most states, and it has become easier to prove that a man committed rape. In addition, the "marital rape" exception was removed from the law. To an extent at least, modern rape law has begun to reflect a woman's perspective.

Beyond changing the law, feminists have changed how rape is investigated and how rape victims are treated by the criminal justice system. One example of this is rape shields. Under these laws, it is unlawful to ask about a rape victim's sexual history, that is, details about her sex life, during a trial. This prevents defense lawyers from turning the prosecution of the rapist into an interrogation of the victim's behavior or her sexual morality—issues that are irrelevant to whether she was raped. In addition, it prevents crafty defense lawyers from intimidating rape victims by threatening to disclose embarrassing personal details regarding their sexual history in open court. By preventing the defense from bringing up distracting issues about the rape victim's "virtue" (to use an antiquated term), rape shield laws protect the victim while keeping the trial's focus on the relevant issue: Did the defendant commit the crime?

In the past, the law did not reflect the experience of women, because they had very little power to influence a system that was controlled by men and reflected men's point of view. The law did not change because men became more sensitive to women's experiences —it changed because women gained influence in our political and legal system and used this power to change the law. While there is still a great deal of work to do to prevent rape and to ensure that this crime is treated appropriately by the criminal justice system (many rape kits that hold evidence about the identity of rapists are untested around the United States; see "Evidence of Rape Ignored," 2013), feminist lawyers and criminologists have dramatically improved the way that rape is handled by criminal justice professionals. As women play an increasingly influential role in the American legal community, graduating from law schools and police academies in increasing numbers, and as feminist criminologists continue to work for change in the criminal justice system, it will be interesting to see what other laws and policies begin to reflect a feminist perspective.

INTERSECTIONALITY

Learning Objective 4.4—Identify the ways that race, sex, and class overlap in American inequality.

As Marxist, feminist, and critical race scholars developed their theories, some researchers were dissatisfied with all of them. While each perspective provided important insights, none of them alone felt sufficient. Often advocates of the different critical theories ignored the contributions of the others, as though theirs was the only key to understanding inequality in America and in the rest of the world. The different theories were all a part of the story of American inequality, but none of them alone was adequate to truly grasp it in all its complexity. As the sociologist Patricia Hill Collins put it in relation to black women, "Regardless of social class and other differences among U.S. Black women, all were in some way affected by intersecting oppression of race, gender, and class" (Collins, 2008, p. 15).

Rape shields: Laws that prevent defense lawyers from interrogating the sexual history of rape victims.

Intersectionality theory tries to understand how different factors shape criminal behavior and criminal justice without assuming that it is all about one of them. As Daly and Stephens put it, intersectional criminologists study

> how class, gender, and race (and age and sexuality) construct the normal and deviant . . . how these inequalities put some societal members at risk to be rendered deviant or to engage in law-breaking, and . . . how law and state institutions both challenge and reproduce these inequalities. (Daly & Stephens, 1995, p. 193)

Intersectionality: The critical approach that seeks to understand how different inequalities (race, class, gender) interact.

Thus, to use one example, violence against black women cannot be understood adequately without understanding how "the experiences of women of color are frequently the product of intersecting patterns of racism and sexism, and how these experiences tend not to be represented within the discourses of either feminism or antiracism" (Crenshaw, 1991, pp. 1243–1244). By examining how different forms of oppression interact, we can get a better understanding of the complex experiences of marginalized groups. In many ways, intersectionality is at the heart of a great deal of modern critical criminology, and it has been tremendously influential over the last two decades.

WHAT WOULD YOU DO?

When Your Friend Is Raped

You've hung out with your friend, Shannon, since freshman year, and since then, you've also known her on-again-off-again boyfriend Lewis. They've gotten together and broken up more times than you can count, and each time you've been there for her. Every time they would break up, and after you've helped her work through the pain, you'd turn around and they had reconciled.

On Monday, after your chemistry class, you get a text from Shannon to meet up. You head over to the cafeteria, and she is sitting at a table with a blank look on her face. She tells you that she met up with Lewis last night at his apartment to "talk things through." After a few drinks, they began kissing but shortly after, Shannon decided that she couldn't go through with it—she was done with him.

As Shannon described it, Lewis didn't get the message. "I told him 'no,' but he kept going. I was unsure of what was going on. It was like it was happening to somebody else. I just . . . froze." She said that she was frightened and confused as it was happening. Afterward, Shannon woke up in the middle of the night in Lewis's bed and walked back to her apartment. After hearing Shannon's description, you realize she was raped.

Shannon doesn't know what she should do. She doesn't want to go to the police, because "Lewis is a good guy and shouldn't have his life ruined." She also isn't sure anybody would believe her, because she was drinking with Lewis and spent the night in Lewis's apartment, and (as she put it), "Who would sleep next to her rapist?" You, Lewis, and Shannon are all in a pretty tight group of friends, and you know that many of them would probably side with Lewis, because he's popular and well liked in your group. On the other hand, it's clear to you that Lewis raped Shannon.

What would you counsel Shannon to do and why? Would you inform the campus police against Shannon's wishes? Why or why not? What resources other than the police are available on your campus for rape and sexual assault survivors?

GREEN CRIMINOLOGY, QUEER CRIMINOLOGY, AND POSTMODERNISM

Learning Objective 4.5—Examine the environmental, postmodern, and queer criminology movements.

Green Criminology

Green criminology is the field that uses criminological methods to examine the harm done to the environment through human activity. Many types of criminal activity have a profound impact on the natural world, including things like illegal polluting (dumping toxic waste in unlawful or unsafe ways), unlicensed hunting (called "poaching"), the trade of endangered animals, and the environmentally damaging extraction of natural resources, such as through mountain top removal mining. Green criminologists combine the goals of the environmental movement and the methods of criminology to understand how governments, private companies, and explicitly criminal groups harm the environment through their activities. Green criminologists examine how corporate and personal greed conspire against the environmental interests of the rest of the planet. Some green criminologists go further and argue that some activities that are technically legal but harmful to the environment should nonetheless be thought of as crimes and studied by criminologists as if they were.

Postmodernism

Postmodernism is a catchall term that refers to a wide variety of different theories that are used in sociology, literary studies, and philosophy. What all of them hold in common is a skepticism toward the idea that human beings are making progress toward a better world and that there is a single right way to organize society. Among the influential criminologists who could be labeled "postmodern" are Michel Foucault and Jonathan Simon, though there are many others. They are both concerned about the way that criminal justice policies, and even the study of criminal behavior, creates tools for human beings to be controlled and manipulated in ways that we don't realize. Even if we haven't committed a crime, we are constantly monitored in a wide variety of ways as though we were criminals. Without even using force or violence, our everyday activities are controlled by a network of social systems that constantly track, monitor, and evaluate us. This means that the old means of controlling people (the police) are less important than the "postmodern" controls that take over our lives in a million big and small ways.

Probably the most important postmodern criminologist was Foucault, whose work has influenced almost every field of social science. A French philosopher and historian, Foucault's most influential book, *Discipline and Punish* (Foucault & Sheridan, 1995), studied the history of prisons and other institutions, such as schools and the military, over the past 400 years. Foucault's perspective on this history is unique: He argues that while prisons *seem* to have become more humane over time as they abandoned physical torture, bloody executions, and other gruesome punishments in favor of incarceration and rehabilitation, in reality these institutions have become more controlling and more dominating, as every aspect of prisoners is studied, analyzed, examined, and controlled for the sake of maintaining discipline and order in the prison. The prison is no longer about stopping crime; it has become about controlling the offenders' "souls," for lack of a better term. Rather than a

Green criminology: The field of criminology that studies environmental crimes.

Postmodernism: A collection of social theories that question both conservative and leftist criminology theories and reject the idea that there is a right way to organize a society.

place where bodily injury is inflicted, the modern prison becomes a place where the actions and even the thoughts of the prisoner are controlled and manipulated by the prison's disciplinary system.

Foucault argues further that the prison is just one example of an institution that is obsessed with both ordering and controlling human behavior—in business, government, and even sexuality, both liberals and conservatives are fixed on directing and monitoring what we do, how we live, and how we think. Schools, prisons, hospitals, and other institutions begin to look very similar as they become obsessed with controlling and shaping human behavior. We are monitored and molded by a vast number of public (police, prisons) and private (insurance companies, doctors) groups, who also monitor each other and themselves, in a society based entirely on subtly controlling everybody's behavior. The prison is only the most obvious example of a society set on total control of all aspects of human behavior, what Foucault calls a disciplinary society.

Foucault's ideas have been very influential in almost every field of social science and the humanities, and his views about crime control have been taken up by many prominent criminologists in England and the United States. The most notable of these perhaps is Simon. In his book *Governing Through Crime* (2009), he argues that in the United States, crime control has become a major tool by which the government has expanded its power over its citizens. The dangers of crime have become a convenient excuse for the government to expand its power with little protest from the populace, who are understandably concerned about public safety.

> Crime has provided a precious wedge for government. Because the power of the state to criminalize conduct and severely punish violations was one unquestioned in the Constitution, the ability of the state to take drastic action against convicted wrongdoers provides an unparalleled constitutional avenue of action. It was an avenue which both conservatives and liberals would take with vigor. (Simon, 2009, p. 29)

Like Foucault, Simon argues that the overreach of the government through the criminal justice system is not simply a tool of the powerful over the weak, as Marx or most other critical criminologists would maintain, but rather is a universal tool used by all sides. Liberals use the criminal justice system to attack conservatives (say, by criminalizing corporal punishment for children) as much as conservatives do it to liberals. Simon's fear is not that conservatives will use the criminal justice system to perpetuate social injustice, but rather that government control over people will increase beyond what is appropriate for a free society.

Two major features distinguish the postmodernists from other critical criminologists. First, according to postmodernists, the problems that they see in contemporary criminal justice are not simply the result of power struggles among different groups, but rather are the result of the actions of all different sides. Progressives and conservatives both share blame for the overcontrolling criminal justice system that we currently have. The problem for Simon and Foucault is not who oversees criminal justice in the United States, but rather the way that power monitors and controls more and more of our lives. Second, they do not suggest that there is a simple way to fix this problem that they diagnose: Empowering the weak will not necessarily stop the problem of excessive control over our lives. In fact, it could make it worse—simply changing who controls the levers of power only lulls people into a false sense of security.

Queer Criminology

Crime and criminal justice have been at the center of the gay experience in America for a long time. People whose sexuality does not fit the traditional heterosexual model have often been treated as criminals, and those people whose gender identities don't match up with their anatomy have often been targets of violent crime. It is fitting then that many historians believe that the modern LGBTQ rights movement (LGBTQ stands for "lesbian, gay, bisexual, transgender, and queer") began with a police raid at the Stonewall Inn, a gay bar in Manhattan in 1969. Queer criminologists take this point up and seek to understand how crime and the criminal justice system impact the lives of these sexual and gender minorities.

There is a lot of complex terminology in queer studies, and it can sometimes be difficult for those who are not part of the queer community to completely grasp it nuances. Most queer scholars argue that there is a difference between our *sex*, that is, our biological makeup as male or female, and our *gender*, that is, the social characteristics that we attribute to men and women. Our sex is relatively fixed, but gender is a social construction that changes over time. Long hair and the color pink, for example, were once associated with masculinity, but now in the 21st century they're considered feminine. In America, crying in public is not considered manly, but in much of the world straight men cry (and hold hands, and tell each other that they love each other). The way men and women dress, act, and love are all social constructs for the most part. They change over time and are very different in different parts of the world, and not everybody feels completely comfortable in the gender that they've been told is theirs.

Queer criminology: The field of criminology that examines crime and justice issues that impact lesbian, gay, transgendered, bisexual, and queer people.

Perhaps it is because our genders are so important to our identity, but are ultimately so fragile, that society often rigorously punishes many people who step out of the normal gender roles. Men who love men and women who love women have been punished in Western societies for a long time. Biological males who see themselves as women are degraded and are subject to violence and even murder when their trans identity is discovered. Young people who are gay are sometimes sent to camps where church leaders and pseudo-psychologists try to turn them into heterosexuals, though there is no evidence that such conversions are successful. Queer people can be subject to blackmail, abuse, and violence of all kinds. In 2016, a Florida man motivated by a hatred of gays murdered 49 people at the Pulse Nightclub, a prominent gay club in Orlando, Florida, before killing himself. Murder and suicide rates for LGBTQ Americans are significantly higher than for others, and rates are increasing even as the people in this community get more rights from the government.

Queer criminologists study the different ways that crime and justice issues affect the LGBTQ population (Panfil, 2018). They can do this in several different ways. Some queer criminologists study the unique issues that queer people face in the world of crime, including antigay violence and similar hate crimes and crime within the LGBTQ community, such as intimate partner violence in gay couples. Others outline some of the unique challenges that LGBTQ crime victims face in dealing with a criminal justice system that is often either ignorant of their situation or unsympathetic to their concerns. For example, many gay men are hesitant to call the police when they experience violence from their intimate partners because of their previous experiences with police homophobia (Finneran & Stephenson, 2013). Finally, some queer criminologists criticize mainstream criminologists (and other critical criminologists) for inadequately understanding the social construction of gender and sexuality in their examinations of crime and justice. By challenging the assumptions and stereotypes of sexuality and gender, queer criminology provides new ways to think about how social inequalities shape criminal justice.

CHAPTER SUMMARY

This chapter has been a study of the different forms of critical criminology. Starting with the Marxist view that crime and criminal justice reflect the dominant interests of class struggle, we have seen how this idea developed and adapted to changing times. Critical race theory uses this assumption to examine how crime and justice play a role in the oppression of racial minorities in the United States. Feminists see criminal justice as deeply gendered and biased against women. Intersectionality seeks to combine these different insights to place crime in a much more nuanced light. All believe that society is deeply flawed and see these flaws reflected in our criminal justice system and the ways that we think about crime.

The important thing you should take away from these critical approaches is that while they are different, they each start with the same basic claim: There is something

deeply wrong with our society today, be it racism, sexism, economic inequality, or something else. Further, these deeper problems are reflected in crime and in the criminal justice system in America. The poor commit more crime because society has made them poor. Minorities commit crime because they have been marginalized. Finally, the criminal justice system serves as a tool for protecting the privileges of those on top (the wealthy, whites, men) by controlling those on the bottom to prevent them from becoming a threat. Criminal justice can only be fixed according to these theories if the deeper problems in society are addressed—anything short of that is simply a bandage placed on a gaping wound.

While the approach in this book is a critical one and is heavily influenced by these types of critical criminology, they will not be the only theories we will use going forward. We will also refer to the more traditional criminological theories examined in the previous chapter, as they also have important insights about policing, courts, and corrections. In the next section, we will turn away from the analysis of crime and criminal behavior and toward the other side of the equation: how society responds to crime. This means turning away from crime itself and toward the criminal justice system, including policing, courts, and the system of punishment and corrections. Of course, criminology and criminal justice are linked insofar as our beliefs regarding the causes of crime shape criminal justice policy. Further, critical criminologies are focused as much on studying and critiquing criminal justice as they are on crime itself. For critical criminologists, crime is not the problem, society is. So, while the focus of this book is now shifting, the material we have covered so far will remain relevant.

REVIEW/DISCUSSION QUESTIONS

1. Which social inequalities discussed by critical criminologists do you find to be the most significant (if any)? Why?

2. How can society begin to address some of these deeper social inequalities through changing the way that we deal with crime?

3. Intersectionality theory says that race, gender, and class overlap in different ways in criminal justice.

   Look at a crime discussed in your newspaper. How might the crime have been different had the offender (or victim) been a different age, race, or gender?

4. In the last chapter, we discussed more conventional criminological theories. How are the theories we've discussed in this chapter like, or different from, those in the last chapter?

KEY TERMS

Carceral feminism 91
Class struggle 80
Critical race theory 83
Feminist criminology 90
Green criminology 97

Ideology 80
Intersectionality 96
Marxism 79
Patriarchy 89
Postmodernism 97

Queer criminology 99
Racial threat theory 85
Rape shields 95

Sarah Yeh

America is presently undergoing a bitter debate about police and violence. How do you feel about the #blacklivesmatter movement? Is it helpful?

POLICING

The police stand at the core of modern society for many reasons. They are sometimes described as the "thin blue line" that stands between civilization and barbarism—brave men and women who risk their lives to keep civilization from sliding into chaos. They are the heroes who keep us safe from predators, rapists, and others who seek to do us great harm. Many young children idolize the police and play "cops and robbers" at an early age. No television crime show would be compelling if it did not include police at the center of the story, and police work has been a large part of modern entertainment for well over a century. As much as our culture is obsessed with crime, it is also fascinated with the police. Many, if not most, enthusiastically embrace a romantic view of what they do and how they "protect and serve" the American people.

Police officers are also, understandably, at the center of the study of criminal justice. If you are a criminal justice major, there is a good chance that you are seriously considering working in law enforcement. Whether it is at the federal level in the FBI, the Department of Homeland Security, or the Secret Service; or at the domestic level as a municipal officer, county police officer, or state trooper; many young people hope for a career in law enforcement in some form or another. They want to fight crime for a living, because it seems both noble and exciting. Along with the military, the medical professions, and firefighting, policing stand as one of the most admired professions in America today (McCarthy, 2016).

On the other hand, in some parts of American culture, the police are highly denigrated, distrusted, and even hated. Previous generations referred to the police as "pigs," and the slogan "fuck the police" remains popular among some American youth. Cooperating with the police, "snitching," is considered by some to be collaborating with an enemy. Fooling, escaping from, and even harming police officers are consistent themes in American culture, from films like *Scarface* to rap lyrics and YouTube videos. Evading the police is a sport for many young people. It might be fair to say that the police are hated as much as they are loved. As the 2016 election showed, police brutality is a flashpoint—some chant "black lives matter" and assert that police officers are violent, racist bullies, while others quickly rush to their defense, chanting "blue lives matter."

In the introduction to this section of the book, we will be looking at the police through several different lenses, keeping in mind the public's ambivalence about this institution. At first, we will discuss some of the basic means for conceptualizing the police, talking about how the police fit in with our views about government as well as how to think about the various activities that the police carry out. The police are involved in a great number of different tasks, and policing is a very complicated phenomenon—it goes far beyond simple law enforcement. Once we have addressed these larger, more abstract issues with regard to policing, we will delve into its history and its current forms. Finally, we will examine some of the problems involved with police misconduct in the final chapter of this section.

THE POLICE AND AMERICAN GOVERNMENT

One thing to keep in mind about policing in America is that the police are closely bound up with the state, that is, with the government. The police are, for the most part, in the service of the state—but in a unique fashion that separates them from the postal worker, the mailman, or even the soldier. The German sociologist Max Weber observed that the thing that makes the modern state distinct from other social institutions (such as the church, or private companies) is that the state has a monopoly on the legitimate use of force. In the modern world, the government is the only institution that can harm people and get away with it, legally speaking. If you hit your neighbor, you have broken the law. If a cop does it, it is usually legal. In fact, when the state uses force against its own people, it is almost always done through the police. The police are the hammer of the state; deploying police is how the government imposes force on its own people.

This, then, is the first clue as to why there is such a strong public ambivalence about the police in America: One's feelings about the government are likely to affect one's views about the police. If you think that the government isn't on your side, that is, if you think that the government doesn't serve your interests, or it is even out to get you, then you are likely to bear some measure of hostility toward the officers who represent it. You are likely to hate the police. If you support the government, then it is likely that you will feel more positive toward them: You are likely to respect and admire the police. Conservatives tend to support the government's authority and therefore support the police, while leftists oppose the government and therefore are more likely to oppose the police.

There is also a deeper source of the ambivalence toward the police. Democracies like America are premised on the idea that to, quote Abraham Lincoln, the government is "of the people, by the people, for the people." However, the police, by their very nature, are imposed *on* the people and against their will. While the police are clearly necessary to maintain law and order, they do not fit comfortably within our view of our society: When the police assert their authority over us, they represent a government that is forcing itself on an ostensibly free people. There was a great amount of unhappiness in the United States and in England when the first permanent police forces were proposed in the 19th century—the police were viewed as a step toward totalitarianism and unsuited for a free people. Americans value freedom, and one of the primary functions of the police is to restrict our freedom. This might help you understand why feelings toward the police are so mixed. Freedom and policing are in some ways incompatible.

POLICING AS A VERB VERSUS POLICE AS A NOUN

The terms *police*, *law enforcement officer*, and even *cop* are often considered synonymous. The modern idea of a *police officer* is that of a trained professional, usually in a uniform, involved in various activities from arresting lawbreakers to directing traffic to maintaining order in times of social unrest. But the police do a lot more than this.

Keep in mind that *policing* is first and foremost a verb and not a noun. By this, I mean that it is activities that define police forces, and not vice versa. There are a lot of organizations that police parts of our lives that we do not recognize as police organizations. Park rangers, restaurant inspectors, and IRS accountants police aspects of our lives, but we don't necessarily recognize accountants or restaurant inspectors as police officers. The earliest appearances of the term *police* (in the early 17th century) refer to efforts "to maintain civil order in (a state or country); to organize or regulate" (*Oxford English Dictionary*, n.d.). It is only in the late 17th and early 18th centuries that the term began to refer to law enforcement and related activities. As we will soon see, the notion of police and the tasks that we assign to the police in the 21th century are relatively new. A lot of policing is done by people we wouldn't consider to be part of the police, and this has always been the case.

Policing, then, refers to a variety of different activities, tasks that are completed by a variety of different organizations and individuals both inside and outside of government. Roughly speaking, we can break these tasks down into three different categories: *controlling deviance*, *maintaining order*, and *providing public assistance*. Though there is a good deal of overlap among these three tasks (and there are probably some activities that would not fit into these categories), they define many of the tasks that are associated with modern policing.

Controlling Deviance. The set of tasks most associated with policing are those involved with handling lawbreakers and other "bad guys" who threaten public safety. *Deviance* is a broad, sociological term that refers to actions that violate social norms. Some deviants are lawbreakers, but deviant behavior can be all manner of activity that is not expressly illegal. At one time, homosexuals were considered deviant, as were drug addicts and people who were just "weird." A person can be disruptive or otherwise threatening to public order without breaking a law, and it is often the police who usually must find a way to deal with these people.

When deviant people break laws, the police control them through *law enforcement*. Often this involves arresting and processing serious lawbreakers, or alternatively citing (or ticketing) individuals who break less significant laws or municipal codes. Other times, controlling deviance and enforcing the law does not require arresting people. It can involve stopping a person, giving her a warning or a citation of some kind, and then sending her on her way. Sometimes deviance can lead to an "off the books" beating. In many cases the police have a great amount of discretion in handling people who violate the law or other social norms, and enforcing the law by arresting people is only one weapon in their arsenal.

Maintaining Order. Another aspect of policing consists in ensuring that a society runs smoothly and helping resolve the problem when things break down. When there is an accident on a highway, the police are there to make sure that the injured are taken care of and traffic is not disrupted. When there are large crowds at a rock concert or a protest, the police are around to make sure that things don't get out of hand. They will arrest lawbreakers in these protests, but they're also directing people to exits, helping anybody who is injured, and providing instructions for those people who don't know what they're supposed to be doing. Maybe you've been to a party that has gotten too loud, and the police have shown up to get you to turn the noise down and make sure that there is no underage drinking going on. The authority and respect that police command often gives them the ability to control crowds or traffic without much pushback from the public. A great deal of a police officer's time is simply spent keeping the gears of society running smoothly.

Providing Public Assistance. Along with controlling deviance and maintaining order, police officers also serve the public in a variety of great and small ways. Many times, the police are the first on the scene at an accident, fire, or other emergency and will help whoever needs assistance. A lost child may need assistance finding her parents, and the police will help her out. They are first responders, meaning that they are trained to deal with a variety of noncriminal emergencies alongside paramedics and firefighters. A domestic quarrel may not rise to the level of criminality, but the police will often intervene to prevent the situation from escalating and to make sure that the noise is kept down so as not to disturb the neighbors. The officers are there just to help others, not as law enforcers but rather as trained professionals who can aid in a tough situation.

The police do a lot more than simple law enforcement. Their daily responsibilities run the gamut of the very dangerous to the highly mundane—and at any moment the mundane can become dangerous or vice versa. It might be useful to break down the notion of policing in a variety of different ways to have a better understanding of the wide variety of policing that happens in the United States.

ACTIVE VERSUS PASSIVE POLICING

One way to think about the various roles that the police play in contemporary society is to understand police activities on a spectrum between *passive* and *active* policing. By *passive policing*, I mean policing activities that are in response to crimes that have already happened or disorder that has already occurred. A crime has been committed, and the police are simply trying to figure out what happened and who is responsible for the act. Criminal investigations are a clear example of passive policing: By the time the police are involved, the harm has already been done, and all that matters from a policing perspective is to find out what happened, to determine who is responsible, and to arrest the guilty party. The offender may harm others in the future, but there is no guarantee that it will happen again, and this isn't really relevant to their investigation—they are searching for the person because of what already happened. What can happen in the future is only a secondary concern. Passive policing is responsive policing, reacting to a crime that has already happened.

A great deal of policing goes beyond waiting for crime to happen. Some forms of policing seek to deal with offenders before anybody gets hurt. At the other end of the spectrum from passive policing is *active policing*: activities where police officers seek to catch would-be criminals before they can cause any harm. In active policing, officers are policing the public regardless of whether a crime has been committed. Active policing can be very mundane: A police officer patrolling the streets on foot is a form of active policing. Regardless of whether a crime has been committed, an officer is nearby. In these cases, the police are not investigating crime, they are *preventing* crime.

Sting operations are a good example of active policing. In a sting operation, police officers seek to entice would-be offenders to break the law in a controlled situation so that officers can arrest them with limited risk and minimal effort. Some police departments use so-called *bait cars*–cars that are secretly controlled remotely by officers who can cut the engine after the thief starts to drive away with the car—to catch car thieves in the act. In other sting operations, officers dress up as prostitutes and walk the streets, hoping to arrest "Johns," men who are seeking to buy sex. Video cameras posted around a city can help spot criminals, but they also keep the innocent under surveillance. Catching a car thief is a good thing, and arresting Johns might be good, but the officers themselves have created the situation where the theft would occur: If there is no bait car, there is no crime.

Less dramatically, community outreach can be a form of active policing. Meeting with people in a neighborhood can make it easier to get information about criminal activities in the area and build up trust between the population and the police more generally. As we learned from social control theory in Chapter 2, a faith in criminal justice institutions and a respect for law and order can make it more likely that a person obeys the law down the road. By helping generate support for law enforcement, policing can stop crime before it even happens.

Active policing can sometimes skirt the line of *entrapment*. Entrapment is "a law-enforcement officer's or government agent's inducement of a person to commit a crime, by means of fraud or undue persuasion, in an attempt to later bring a criminal prosecution against that person" (Garner, 2009, p. 573). If a police officer tricks an individual into breaking the law, it is entrapment and is illegal, but if the officer creates a situation where a person chooses to break the law on her own, then the officer has not committed entrapment, and the lawbreaker is a criminal. Otherwise good people, people who may not have chosen to break the law on their own, can be induced into breaking the law through active sorts of police activities. It is sometimes a thin line between active policing and entrapment. The more active policing is, the closer it gets to that line.

The distinction between active and passive policing is not a hard and fast one, but it is important for several reasons. First, the more active the police are, the more they intrude into the lives of ordinary people. If we are not planning to break the law, having an officer around looking over our shoulders can still be intrusive and affect how we behave. Cameras capturing all manner of behavior, criminal or otherwise, can affect how we live and how we interact with each other in any number of ways. While we do not live in a *police state*, that is, a society where our lives are completely controlled by the police, the more active the police are, the more American society looks like such a state. In active policing, we trade our privacy for security to some extent: We accept that the police are intruding into our lives regardless of whether we are committing crimes so that they may be better able to catch criminals before the criminals can cause harm.

FORMAL VERSUS INFORMAL POLICING

A further distinction to keep in mind is between formal and informal policing (Lundman, 1980). The sociologist Albert Hunter distinguishes between different forms of social control: The private (the controls between friends and family), the parochial (neighbors and communities), and the public (governmental and legal institutions) all serve to keep us in line but in different ways (Hunter, 1985). A great deal of the social controls that we experience are *informal*: Your peers, your professors and teachers, your R.A. if you're living in the dorms, and a host of other people all help control your behavior in some way or another, that is to say, they police you. Usually these do not require strict rules or procedures, and very rarely do they invoke formal organizations or bureaucracy. If your minister catches you breaking a law, she may decide to let you off with a lecture and a warning about proper conduct. If your parents catch you, they can ground you. If you start acting like a jerk, your friends may shun you. These are all ways that we police each others' behavior, but none involve the intervention of government officials or bureaucracy. Just as important, they rarely come backed with a threat of violence.

On the other end of the spectrum is *formal social control*. This type of policing is closer to what we often recognize as policing when we don't think too carefully about it. Unlike our friends, family, or church, it is highly unlikely that any of the people who control us formally know us personally. Formal policing involves government officials, often with uniforms and badges, and usually includes paperwork and other types of official record-keeping. It often comes with the implied threat that failure to comply will lead to violence. When you are arrested, you usually undergo a very formal process involving paperwork, meetings with government officials, and formalized hearings. These records can then become publicly available, making it difficult for you to escape whatever charges you have faced. A criminal record can destroy some careers and follow you for the rest of your life. On the other hand, formal records allow officials to keep tabs on repeat offenders and to address serious problems before they get out of control.

Again, as with active and passive policing, practices can be anywhere on a spectrum between formal and informal controls. If you are stopped for speeding, an officer can opt to handle the situation informally and let you go with a warning. If you're a kid out after curfew, the officer can drive you home to your parents and let them deal with you. Or the officer might choose to become more formal and arrest you or cite you for a criminal offense. Usually, in smaller cases, formal policing only happens after informal approaches have failed. The police only become involved in a situation when other institutions like the church or the family have not brought an individual to heel. In many cultures, there is a strong expectation that misbehavior will be handled within the family, tribe, or village, and it is the family's fault if one of their members misbehaves and more formal policing procedures must be implemented.

As we will see in the next chapter, much of the history of American policing is a movement toward more active and more formalized types of policing. Early policing (such as vigilante groups and night watchmen) were not very formal, and most deviance was dealt with through community organizations like the church or within the family. A person had to step pretty far out of line before government officials became involved. Similarly, there were few resources to engage in active sorts of policing before the 20th century: There simply wasn't the technology and money to spend keeping tabs on people who had not broken the law. Further, many people would have resented the intrusions of active policing. Understanding these distinctions can help us see how dramatically policing has changed over the years, moving in directions that have been nearly invisible but that have had a profound impact on American lives.

POLICING FROM A CRITICAL PERSPECTIVE

The role of the police is essentially a conservative one. It is the primary job of police officers to protect the existing social order. Police usually protect this order without concern as to whether the order itself should be maintained. If social critics are right, and society is deeply unjust, then the role of the police becomes troubling. The stability that the police protect is maintained at the cost of a great deal of social injustice. There is often a lot to be gained by shaking up the system and allowing for some social instability. Many great movements such as the civil rights movement and the LGBTQ movement engaged in activities that were both disruptive and illegal, and those who participated in them were arrested while fighting for legitimate causes. Similarly, those engaged in other forms of mass disobedience have had legitimate grievances against the status quo but have been harassed and arrested by the police—who are usually only doing their job and maintaining stability. This doesn't mean that the police officers were wrong (or that they were right) to arrest civil rights activists; rather it means that they have played a role in preserving a social order that critics find deeply unjust.

One example of the police serving a conservative function is the way police help preserve racial inequalities in America. We can understand why many African Americans fear and distrust the police if we look at the role of the police in supporting racial inequalities (Drake, 2015). Many black Americans feel alienated from broader American society and believe that the society doesn't offer them a genuine chance to succeed. According to one poll,

> Half or more of African Americans say they have personally been discriminated against because they are Black when interacting with police (50%), when applying to jobs (56%), and when it comes to being paid equally or considered for promotion (57%). (NPR/Robert Wood Johnson Foundation/Harvard T. H. Chan School of Public Health, 2017, p. 1)

What they see is a white society offering economic success and respectability to white people, while they are denied such things. Standing beside this is a police force that is responsible for protecting this racially unjust society. Insofar as police officers are seen as supporting the (white) institutions that are preventing black Americans from succeeding, it stands to reason that many African Americans would resent them.

The data shows that different races of Americans hold very different perceptions of the police. A 2016 Pew Research poll found that three quarters of white Americans believed that the police are doing an excellent or good job, while only one third of African

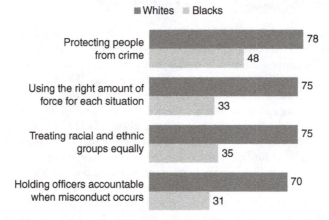

Figure II.1 Confidence in Police by Race, 2016

Blacks are about half as likely as whites to have a positive view of police treatment of racial and ethnic groups or officers' use of force

% saying the police in their community do an excellent or good job when it comes to . . .

■ Whites ■ Blacks

	Whites	Blacks
Protecting people from crime	78	48
Using the right amount of force for each situation	75	33
Treating racial and ethnic groups equally	75	35
Holding officers accountable when misconduct occurs	70	31

Source: **Pew Research Center, September 2016, "The Racial Confidence Gap in Police Performance."**
Note: Whites and blacks include only non-Hispanics.

Americans did (Morin & Stepler, 2016). This means that blacks are about half as likely as whites to support the police. Similarly, they are half as likely to believe that officers treat different racial groups equally or use force in an appropriate way.

If you believe that society is deeply unfair and unjust, you are far more likely to see the police as a barrier to change and a defender of inequality.

Of course, this doesn't mean that we would like police officers to enforce only the laws that we personally think are good laws and ignore the ones we disapprove of. Rather, the point is that the police should not be seen as an unquestionably good thing for a society. To the extent that a society and its laws are unjust or unfair, their police will be unjust or unfair. If the society is unjust, then the police are a tool of those injustices. The police reflect the society that they are protecting, and that is their greatest strength as well as their greatest weakness.

This frustration with the police has recently found a voice in the #blacklivesmatter movement. Inspired initially by the acquittal of George Zimmerman for the killing of Trayvon Martin in 2012, the movement has sought to highlight the abuse that the black public faces from the police on an almost daily basis. While much of the emphasis has been on police violence against unarmed African Americans, leaders of the movement have expanded their targets to include bail, trials, and incarceration—all of these are institutions that, they charge, mistreat black Americans. Their complaints have a great deal of merit—as we will see in future chapters, all levels of the criminal justice system are stacked against African Americans and the poor. Because they are usually the first point of contact

#blacklivesmatter: The movement that seeks to criticize the excessive use of force against African Americans.

between the criminal justice system and the public, and because they sometimes use violence against the public, the police are subject to the greatest amount of criticism by this new and growing movement.

In the first chapter of this section, we will examine the history of policing in Europe and the United States—seeing how the policing that we now see as completely normal was considered very abnormal at its inception. Then we will discuss the various activities that the police engage in (including the use of force) as well as some aspects of modern professional policing, such as the organization of policing, police training, and police searches. This will set us up for a discussion of police deviance, that is, what happens when the police misbehave.

Sarah Yeh

A uniformed police force was once considered a danger to liberty. Why has it become accepted today?

CHAPTER FIVE

THE HISTORY OF POLICING

In this chapter, we will follow the history of American policing from its origins in England up to the present day. As I mentioned in the introduction to this section, the term *policing* denotes a complex set of activities, and only a few of these have remained consistent over time. During some periods, the police did very little; in other eras they were involved in activities that are very different from what we recognize now as legitimate police work. In some periods, the police were involved in feeding the poor and fighting fires, for example. We may not even recognize some of these different historical forms as police, but they all made important contributions to the history of law enforcement and have in their own way shaped what we now recognize as modern policing. History has a great way of showing how much things that seem eternal to us have changed over time, and that much of what we take for granted as normal is in fact a consequence of a bunch of peculiar historical accidents.

Despite some dramatic changes, there is a pattern to the history of American policing. Relying on the categories that we discussed in the previous chapter, we can say that the police, particularly in the United States, have consistently become more *active* and more *formalized* over time, particularly over the last 100 years. This is to say that, over the decades, the police have become more involved in our daily activities in a way that they never would have before—the police are a part of our lives whether or not we are lawbreakers or crime victims. They patrol the streets, they monitor traffic, and they engage in a wide variety of activities that have very little to do with catching lawbreakers, and many people are quick to call the police when they have a problem. The presence of armed police officers has become a routine part of American life. We don't bat an eye when we see the police on our streets, a situation that earlier generations of Americans would have most likely found intolerable.

Law enforcement has changed for a host of reasons. In part, this has been the result of a learning curve in policing: Society has sought to improve policing over time and heeded lessons from its successes and failures. More deeply, policing has changed because the police have been shaped by the social, political, and economic developments that have also influenced the broader society. In small societies where everybody knew the people they interacted with, there was simply no need for a large, bureaucratic police force. Informal social controls largely worked to maintain order. In places with a lot of people, crime may be more tempting, and formal policing more necessary. Similarly, when there is a great deal of economic inequality in a single space, crime is likely to go up, and when new forms of criminality appear, such as is the case with the war on drugs or the threat of terrorism, new forms of policing are developed to address them. Like everything else in this world, the police have responded to social change by changing the way that they are organized and by changing the way that they operate.

THE RISE OF THE LONDON METROPOLITAN POLICE

Learning Objective 5.1—Recognize the historical context that created modern policing.

In much of European history since the fall of the Roman Empire, there was little need for a formal police force. There were few cities—most of the small population on the continent was consigned to rural life or in small villages, and most social control was done informally or through the feudal system. *Feudalism* was a system whereby a nobleman or lord was responsible for people who lived on his lands, often referred to as his manor. He received a portion of their income (usually crops) and in return protected them from harm. The lord in these situations was for the most part both police and judge, resolving disputes and handling criminal charges, though other figures such as the representative of the king or the church had some role to play in maintaining order. The feudal system placed almost all crime control in the hands of the landed nobility, not in any government in the way we think of it now.

Beyond the feudal system, much of the law enforcement that took place in England prior to the 18th century was very informal. In rural England, order was usually maintained by the frankpledge system. Essentially, small groups of families were responsible for each other's behavior, and punishment was collective—if one member of a group broke a law, all members of the group were blamed (Morris, 1910). In the cities, on the other hand, a group of night watchmen were responsible for keeping an eye on the city after dark, ensuring that there were no disturbances, including keeping a close watch for fires, as the wooden buildings could easily light up. For small-scale, rural villages, an informal, largely passive system that largely left people to themselves was sufficient for the most part.

In the 18th century, changes took place that profoundly affected the social structures of England, ultimately leading to the breakdown of feudalism and the creation of what we now recognize as a modern police force. The most significant of these was what we now know as the *Industrial Revolution*. The development of machinery, steam engines, and factories dramatically increased the ability of England to produce manufactured goods—most notably cloth. Previously, these goods were made in small batches in workshops and were expensive commodities—but industrialization massively increased output through the construction of large factories run by private owners. This change led to a decrease in the price of manufactured goods, made England an economic and political powerhouse, and in turn had dramatic consequences for all levels of British society.

One of the most important consequences of the industrial revolution was *urbanization*—the movement of people from farms and villages into cities. The new factories that began sprouting up to produce manufactured goods required lots of people to work in them—a population that had to live in one place simply so that they could get to work on time. In preindustrial England, there were few cities because they weren't necessary: Much of the economy was agricultural, and people were needed on farms and in villages to grow and harvest crops. But with the creation and spread of the factory as a means for producing goods,

Frankpledge system: Policing system in medieval Europe that relied on locals to police each other.

people needed to come together in large numbers to work the textile mills. As a result, people began leaving farms to find employment in cities like London and Manchester, hoping to find a better life for themselves and their families. Almost overnight, cities began growing at a massive rate, creating a host of new problems for British society (see Figure 5.1).

Urbanization generates a host of problems for a society. Many of these problems boil down to a decline in *social solidarity*. That is, people in smaller communities tend to feel closer to those around them, meaning that they are less likely to harm their neighbors (Durkheim, 1893/1973). Even if they don't feel loyal to their neighbors, it is difficult to get away with hurting somebody or stealing their property when everybody knows who you are and where you live. On the other hand, the anonymity of urban life often means that people often feel less sympathy or concern for those around them. Further, you are much more likely to get away with robbery, theft, or even murder when you can simply melt back into an anonymous crowd. This lack of social solidarity made crime significantly more appealing to the new urban dwellers of the Industrial Revolution.

There are plenty of other ways that urbanization led to an increase in the English crime rate in the 18th century. Urbanization led to a new mass of poor Londoners who were desperate to feed themselves. Different ethnic groups from different backgrounds crammed into crowded tenements and neighborhoods created the potential for social

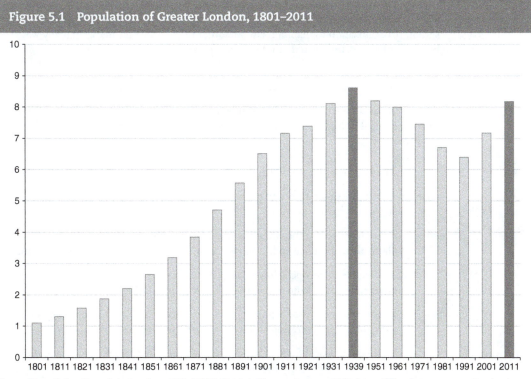

Figure 5.1 Population of Greater London, 1801–2011

Source: "Population Growth in London, 1939–2015," GLA Intelligence, January 2015, https://files.datapress.com/london/dataset/population-change-1939-2015/historical%20population%201939-2015.pdf.

friction and violence, as did the proximity between the rich and the desperately poor that exists in many cities. Some historians point to the invention of gin, a cheap, strong drink that was easily available on the streets of London, as a cause of social unrest (Abel, 2001). This gin epidemic led to mass public drunkenness and crime in many British cities. In short, urbanization made the city a tinderbox for urban crime, and city officials struggled to keep up with these new circumstances and preserve the social order. The old system, designed for a much smaller city, was inadequate to the problems that were created by these new urban societies.

The British government made several attempts to address the crime problem in English cities during the 18th century—all of which proved inadequate to the task. The *Thief Takers* were a group of street-smart men with connections to the underworld who would solve petty crimes and return stolen goods to their owners for a fee. On occasion, they would apprehend a wanted criminal for a reward offered by the court. In the middle of the 18th century, the novelist Henry Fielding and his brother John formed The Bow Street Runners, a group employed by the London courts to apprehend criminals. Finally, a police unit was set up along the Thames River that was specifically tasked with stopping smugglers who tried to illegally unload goods as well as to apprehend crooks seeking to steal cargo. These marked important developments in British policing, but none proved adequate to handle the ballooning crime problems that were overwhelming the city.

In 1829, the British parliament passed the London Metropolitan Police Act at the urging of the British home secretary Robert Peel. The **Peel Act**, as it became commonly known, established a civilian-run police force for the city of London as a permanent, qua-similitary organization to maintain law and order in the city. This marks in many ways the birth of policing in the form that we now recognize it.

Sir Robert Peel's Nine Points of Policing

The novel developments of the London police were summed up in Peel's "Nine Points" that were meant to highlight how this new police force was to be organized and how they were to operate:

1. The basic mission for which the police exist is to prevent crime and disorder.

2. The ability of the police to perform their duties is dependent upon public approval of police actions.

3. Police must secure the willing co-operation of the public in voluntary observance of the law to be able to secure and maintain the respect of the public.

4. The degree of co-operation of the public that can be secured diminishes proportionately to the necessity of the use of physical force.

5. Police seek and preserve public favor not by catering to public opinion but by constantly demonstrating absolute impartial service to the law.

Peel Act: The British law that created the London Metropolitan Police in 1829.

6. Police use physical force to the extent necessary to secure observance of the law or to restore order only when the exercise of persuasion, advice and warning is found to be insufficient.

7. Police, at all times, should maintain a relationship with the public that gives reality to the historic tradition that the police are the public and the public are the police; the police being only members of the public who are paid to give full-time attention to duties which are incumbent on every citizen in the interests of community welfare and existence.

8. Police should always direct their action strictly towards their functions and never appear to usurp the powers of the judiciary.

9. The test of police efficiency is the absence of crime and disorder, not the visible evidence of police action in dealing with it. ("Sir Robert Peel's nine principles of policing," 2017)

Even though Peel's idea for a uniformed police force seems obvious to us today, the London police were deeply unpopular in their own time. Nicknamed "Peel's Raw Lobsters" because of their blue coats (the British military, the "redcoats," were known as "the lobsters"), their creation was met with protests from the people of London. The killer of Joseph Grantham, the first officer to fall in the line of duty, was exonerated on a defense of justifiable homicide because the police were so reviled by the jurors. (It probably didn't help that many officers were intoxicated while on duty in these early years.) Whatever their necessity for 19th-century London, a permanent, uniformed police force was widely viewed as a threat to stability and democracy and the sign of a creeping police state. As one scholar puts it, for the English,

> The idea of a bureaucratic central force offended against a tradition which held that social control should be a private, local and voluntary matter, best left to the master of the household, the parish beadle [local official], and the [justice of the peace]. (Ignatieff, 1979, p. 443)

They were considered a threat even though, unlike American police officers, the London police have never carried guns while on patrol. Regardless of the feeling of the people of London, the new police force, which become known as "Bobbies" after Robert Peel, was taken as a role model for other police forces around the English-speaking world in general and the United States in particular.

Policing on the Continent: The Case of France

American policing is deeply indebted to the institutions and ideals of the English model. But there are many other policing traditions in the world worth looking at, if only for comparison. One of the most influential of these is the French. American and English police have seen themselves first and foremost as public servants, helping people with various problems that they encounter in their lives, including crime problems. The French police have traditionally held their loyalty to the government first and been public servants second. This attitude traces its origins back to the early French police forces under King Louis XIV who created the force to protect his regime. As one historian put it,

> The [French] policeman was, quite explicitly, a functionary of the regime who was separated from the people by his duties. . . . The French police was first and

foremost a control force . . . a paramilitary political (force) . . . designed . . . to crush opposition and dissidence from whatever source it emanated. (Bowden, 1978, pp. 143–144)

While the French police engaged in various forms of what they call "low policing" (that is, law enforcement, firefighting, safety inspections, and street cleaning), this was distinct from "high policing," which consisted in protecting the monarchy from internal and external threats. While French policing has become less political over time, this philosophical difference marks it apart from the "policing by consent" model that developed in the UK.

Along with these philosophical differences between Anglo-American and French policing, there is a significant organizational difference between the two approaches. There are two (and only two) different police forces operating within France: The National Police (*Police Nationale* in French) and the *Gendarmerie* or Military Police (military in the sense that they are a part of the military). There are also metropolitan police forces in many cities, but these organizations have no legal authority and are not really police as we recognize them in the United States. The National Police enforce law in cities and towns with a population over 10,000, while the Gendarmerie deal with law enforcement in the rest of the country. Policing authority is split between different ministries in the national government: National Police operate under the Ministry of the Interior, and the Gendarmerie is under the authority of the Ministry of Defense. Since it serves largely under the Ministry of Defense for most of its functions, it makes sense that the Gendarmerie is a much more "militaristic" police force than is the *Police Nationale* and is organized along military lines.

The policing tradition in France has been as influential around the globe as the British model developed by Lord Peel. Whereas the British saw the police first and foremost as public servants, the French police were servants of the state. Where the British saw civilian control as essential to policing, the French put large swaths of the police under the authority of the military. Many other countries have placed the police under the authority of the military, for example. Whereas the British saw a decentralized police force specific to a city, the French found centralizing the police to be a better way to ensure professionalism and stability. Neither approach is necessarily correct, but both reflect their respective histories as well as broader philosophies of how government should be structured and how best to maintain order.

POLICING IN AMERICA: THE EARLY YEARS

Learning Objective 5.2—Trace the early history of policing in the United States.

While modern American policing owes a great deal to the Peel Act, there were many other aspects of America that shaped policing here. One important factor was simply the relative sizes of the two countries: America is big, and much of it is sparsely populated, whereas England is small and relatively densely populated, with a few major cities dominating its economy and society. This means that a significant police presence in parts of the United States would not have been practical in the 19th century. States like Texas, Arizona, Utah, and North Dakota are so large (and largely empty) that they could not be regularly policed, and the cities there were too small to require much of a police presence. Outside of the Northeast, there was very low population density in much of America before the 20th century.

Further, the U.S. government is a federal system. This means that there are separate independent state governments within the United States. Each state is largely responsible for enforcing the laws within its own borders and can create and organize police forces in any way it feels is most appropriate. The federal government can provide funds, guidance, and in some cases regulation, but generally speaking, the states are independent. Within the 50 states, there are cities and counties and other bodies that have developed their own, largely independent law enforcement organizations. (Perhaps your campus has its own police force.) This is different from the French and British approaches, in which more centralized political systems with a great deal of power sit with the central governments in Paris and London. There is no single way to organize the police, and American policing has developed in a lot of different ways in different parts of the country. This makes it difficult to speak generally about "American policing."

The third force that shaped policing in the United States was the racism that has permeated the society in general, and the presence of slavery in the South in particular. Many early police organizations were created specifically to monitor and oppress both free and enslaved blacks. Many southerners feared a slave revolt that could erupt at any time, or they feared losing their valuable slaves if they were able to escape. Therefore, they used their police forces to keep African Americans from freedom. A significant portion of early policing in the South consisted in slave patrols—organized groups of whites whose primary job was to find and capture runaway slaves (Reichel, 1988). As Potter describes these groups,

> Slave patrols had three primary functions: (1) to chase down, apprehend, and return to their owners, runaway slaves; (2) to provide a form of organized terror to deter slave revolts; and (3) to maintain a form of discipline for slave-workers who were subject to summary justice, outside of the law, if they violated any plantation rules. (Potter, 2013, p. 3)

Although the slave patrols no longer operated after the Civil War, their members formed vigilante groups and local police forces that helped suppress the now freed black slaves and enforced the laws that kept black people poor and alienated for over a century after emancipation. This legacy is one of the many factors that have troubled relations between black Americans and the police in America that carry on until today.

Until the middle of the 19th century, much of the policing in America was informal and passive. Sheriffs, often an elected official responsible for law enforcement duties, operated in much of the country. If it became necessary, they could invoke the power of *posse comitatus* to conscript civilians into the police force. In Texas, Stephen Austin formed the famous Rangers in 1823 to capture criminals and to fight off attacks from Native Americans. Vigilance committees, groups of civilians who took it upon themselves to handle real or imagined lawbreakers, formed in the West on an ad hoc basis. They did not have a permanent presence but came together when a problem arose, and in practice they were often indistinguishable from lynch mobs. Finally, the famous Pinkerton Detective Agency developed in the 19th century as a private security force that helped serve as guards

Slave patrols: Organized groups of whites in the antebellum South whose primary job was to find and capture runaway slaves.

and investigators, but also helped factory owners fight against organized labor. Each of these developments over the course of the 19th century served to pave the way for the major developments of modern American policing, which took place in the major cities.

Alongside these developments in the American west, the cities were growing rapidly and required police forces tailored to their needs. Many of the cities in the United States had crime problems like those in England. The urban forces in the United States, following the London model of Robert Peel, began sprouting up in the few major cities that existed in the United States before the 20th century. The first was in Boston in 1837. After this, New York (1844) and Philadelphia (1854). Like London, they included an emphasis on public patrols and prevention, that is, active policing, and included uniforms and other trappings of the London Metropolitan Police. States also began to develop their own police forces to deal with their own problems, including protests from organized labor members who sought better working conditions in the mines and factories. Among the first of these was the Pennsylvania State Police, who were created in response to labor unrest and strikes in the Pennsylvania coal mines. The infamous Coal and Iron Police were created by the Pennsylvania state legislature but were funded and controlled by the mining companies, which used them to mercilessly attack miners who sought better wages and better working conditions (Couch, 1981). Along with these organizations, sheriffs, vigilance committees and other organizations still operated out in the countryside and in smaller towns through much of the 19th century.

THE ERA OF CRONYISM AND PATRONAGE

Learning Objective 5.3—Describe how cronyism and patronage shaped American policing in the 19th century.

Early policing in the United States was a highly political affair. While America is a democracy, powerful people have often manipulated state and local government through bribery and intimidation to hold on to their positions and to make themselves wealthy. As mayors and other city officials become entrenched in their positions over the 19th century, they used both their political power and other techniques of persuasion such as bribes, kickbacks, and the promise of cushy government jobs, along with outright intimidation and violence, to achieve their goals. Some of these goals served the public good, but many did not, and politicians often used their power to enrich themselves and their supporters. In New York City, for example, the political organization known as Tammany Hall ran the city for much of the 19th and early 20th centuries with the help of the immigrant community and Tammany's charismatic leader, Mayor William "Boss" Tweed. These kinds of cushy arrangements between political powerbrokers and the institutions of city government became known as *machine politics*.

The police were caught up in the machine politics of the 19th century, and police departments in many cities actively served the interests of the political bosses. The mayor or other city officials appointed the chief of police and the officers that served under him in a system that is known as *patronage*. A lucrative job was often given to a political supporter of the mayor as part of the spoils of the mayor's new political power. This meant that police officers would owe their jobs to the politicians who hired them, and if the politicians lost their jobs, so would the officers.

This collusion between officers and city politicians, sometimes known as cronyism, is obviously susceptible to abuse. Politicians often used police forces for overtly political purposes, either harassing their political opponents or enforcing laws selectively in ways that were advantageous for them. This meant ignoring the crimes that benefitted city bosses and ruthlessly prosecuting their opponents. Many early police forces had tasks that we don't think of as policing nowadays; for example, they often helped feed the poor, which in turn helped the political leadership gain the support of voters. On the other hand, because of their close links with city government, police officers could engage in corrupt dealings with little consequence—there was nobody who could stop them from soliciting bribes or engaging in their own criminal activities if they were hiding behind a badge. As a result, the police forces in many cities became known for being corrupt, inept, and politically tainted through much of the 19th century.

While there was a movement against cronyism building at the end of the 19th century, the issue came to a head in the period between the two world wars. With the onset of Prohibition—the banning of the manufacture and sale of alcoholic beverages in the United States, a culture of widespread lawbreaking took hold. While there was a good deal of support for banning alcohol, many opposed the law and felt no obligation to obey it. *Bootleggers* brewed alcohol in secret or smuggled it into the United States from Europe, Canada, South America, or the Caribbean, often with the express help of the police forces who received a cut of the profits. City bosses ran the bootlegging rackets in many cities, and the police served as their muscle. As a result, many people lost respect for local police forces. Further, many other political scandals put a spotlight on machine politics and crusading politicians like Franklin Roosevelt (who was the governor of New York in the 1920s) attacked them. Eventually many cities and states were tired of cronyism and its politics, and a series of reforms were put forward to change government, including changes in policing.

PROFESSIONALIZATION

Learning Objective 5.4—Examine how policing became a profession at the beginning of the 20th century.

During the early 20th century, under the influence of Theodore Roosevelt, the *progressive movement* began to shape American politics. The progressives argued, among other things, that the most qualified candidates should be appointed to government positions, not just those with political connections. Because of this new philosophy of government, politicians began to reexamine U.S. law enforcement—focusing on the types of persons who served as officers. This movement became stronger when Prohibition magnified police corruption and incompetence in many cities. The Wickersham Commission, formally known as the National Commission on Law Observance and Enforcement, was convened by President Herbert Hoover in 1929 to address problems that had arisen from bootlegging and to suggest ways to improve American law enforcement (National Commission on Law Observance and Enforcement, 1931). Among the commission's most significant recommendations was that governments sever the links between politicians and the police and that independent police institutions give officers a measure of political independence.

Many of these reforms were implemented by August Vollmer, the police chief in Berkeley, California. Vollmer, a member of the commission, sought to modernize American

Cronyism: A system in which politicians give government jobs, including policing jobs, to their political allies.

Professionalization: The movement in the early 20th century to make policing a more "serious" career. Involved education and training for officers.

policing by turning it into a *profession*. A profession is paid work, but it is more than that—professionals are respected members of society who are endowed with a certain social status. Doctors and lawyers, for example are often seen as professionals, whereas factory workers and janitors have jobs. Professionals not only make money from their work, but they usually have an official or unofficial code of conduct that shapes how they operate. Professions aren't just jobs—they are higher callings and are seen as serving a greater purpose. They require education and training as well as organizations that set standards for membership and shape the values and practices of the profession. Doctors have the American Medical Association, and lawyers have the American Bar Association, organizations that help develop professional standards and regulate the activities of those who practice it. Changing policing into a profession in the early 20th century was a clear effort to raise the profile of the police as well as to improve the quality of police work that was being done.

Professions usually require a certain amount of formal education and training. For Vollmer, the police would be no different. The need for a higher quality of policing meant that officers would require skills and training that their predecessors lacked. A college degree shows a level of ability, maturity, and intellectual skill that is essential to the modern police officer and, during this period, educational standards were established by many police departments. Many police departments began to demand some education from their officers, and senior officers and detectives were often required to have a college degree. In response, universities developed criminology and criminal justice programs, which became very popular majors, and Vollmer himself was the first chair of a department of criminology at the University of California at Berkeley. Many states today don't require a college degree to become an officer, though they often recommend it, but they still expect candidates to at least have a high school diploma or a GED.

Among the new developments that came about with the rise of professionalized policing was *scientific policing*. Among the new disciplines that were developing at that time was *forensics*, the use of scientific techniques to examine evidence. Blood typing, fingerprints, and similar techniques were popularized in the early part of the 20th century as means of investigating crimes. Along with forensics, sophisticated forms of record-keeping developed in criminal justice, including the acquisition of *biometric data* regarding criminal suspects. The process of gathering information about criminal suspects—including photographs of them as well as their height, weight, age, and fingerprints—was initially developed in France in the 19th century but became an essential part of American criminal justice during this era. These sophisticated techniques of crime detection and investigation required a new kind of officer, one with the intellectual skills and training to handle the new world of policing techniques.

FEDERAL POLICING

Learning Objective 5.5—Describe the role of federal law enforcement in American policing.

As American society changed, so did crime and, as a result, so did the efforts to prevent crime and catch criminals. For the first 125 years or so, American policing was almost entirely a state and local issue. Policing could be handled by states, counties, and cities, because there was little need to address crime at the national level. Crime was for the most part a local matter, simply because it was hard for criminals to get very far from the scene of the crime on foot or on horseback, so local policing was sufficient for the most part. The end of the 19th century and the early 20th century saw the rise of several different factors that made it necessary for the federal government to play a larger role in law enforcement than it had in the past. As technology advanced, the decentralized structure that had been such an important part of American policing since the colonial period was no longer tenable. This meant that in the early 20th century, the federal government became a bigger part of American policing.

One of the most significant factors in the rise of federal policing was the creation of a national transportation infrastructure. Without cars and decent roads, getting around is difficult, and leaving a state takes a lot of time and effort, whether you are a criminal or a law-abiding citizen. Cars didn't come into existence until the early part of the 20th century, and it took some time for roads to be build that could carry these machines over long distances. But by the 1930s, cars had completely supplanted horses, and smooth, concrete roads stretched across the country. Though the modern freeway system would not come into being until after the Second World War, by the early part of the 20th century, it had become much easier to get from one city to another than it had ever been before.

Criminals were quick to adapt to this new technology. A car allowed for a hasty getaway and made it easier to elude local law enforcement. In many places, a short trip can get you out of the state and beyond the reach of local police forces. A person could rob a bank in Philadelphia at noon and by sundown be three states away with little chance of being caught by the police. In the early 1930s, Bonnie Parker and Clyde Barrow, the famous "Bonnie and Clyde," robbed and killed throughout the Great Plains states, including Iowa, Missouri, Texas, and Colorado, continually eluding or killing local law enforcement officers. Lester Joseph Gillis, a.k.a. "Babyface Nelson," similarly robbed banks all over the country, escaping from prison and hiding out on the West Coast. NASCAR originated during Prohibition, as smugglers designed cars that were fast enough to elude law enforcement. New inventions opened new worlds for industrious crooks who could take advantage of the new technologies, while law enforcement remained stuck in a 19th-century political system.

A second factor that led to federalization in policing was the growing importance of the mass media. Since the invention of the telegraph in the 19th century, information was being quickly shared among large numbers of people in different parts of the country at an ever-expanding rate. News could be sent out to a wide audience that a century before would not have been able to learn about events that happened in the next town, much less on the other side of the country. Newspapers could pass along news (relatively) quickly, and they used scandalous and exciting stories from around the country to sell papers to a public that was increasingly literate and hungry for interesting reading. This meant that many criminals and many crimes received national attention in a way that they never would have had before. Figures like Bonnie and Clyde, Nelson, and the infamous John Dillinger became both national celebrities and "public enemies" around the country, as their exploits achieved notoriety in the press. This created a public relations challenge for law enforcement officials: High-profile national criminals needed high-profile national police.

The broad social and political forces that led to the creation of federal laws required new government agencies to implement and enforce these laws. The Federal Bureau of Investigation, or FBI (originally known as the Bureau of Investigation or BOI) was

CRIMINAL (IN)JUSTICE

The Mann Act

Because of the developments of the late 19th and early 20th centuries, Congress began to pass a series of laws in the 20th century that created federal crimes that could apply across the nation, rather than only in the separate states. One of the earliest of these was the Mann Act (also known as the White-Slave Traffic Act). Passed in 1910, the Mann Act made it a crime to transport across state lines "any woman or girl for the purpose of prostitution or debauchery, or for any other immoral purpose." While the law was billed as a tool to fight prostitution, it was used primarily to target black men who had relationships with white women. One of the first targets of the law was the famous boxer Jack Johnson, who was prosecuted for transporting his girlfriend and future wife Lucille Cameron. Other high-profile targets of the Mann Act have been Chuck Berry (the inventor of rock 'n' roll), Charlie Chaplin, and the architect Frank Lloyd Wright.

Not only was this law used as a tool to imprison black men, but it also reflected widespread fears of female sexuality. At the beginning of the 20th century, women were just beginning to enter the workforce and gain some economic and social independence. Conservatives feared this and sought to use the federal government's powers to "defend" these women. As one journalist put it,

With these changes came concerns about the country's moral underpinnings. By 1907, a full-fledged moral panic set in. There were rumors, taken as truth, that women were being forced into prostitution and shuttled around the country by vast networks controlled by immigrants, who were arriving in the U.S. by the millions. . . . Muckraking journalists fueled the hysteria with sensationalized stories of innocent girls kidnapped off the streets by foreigners, drugged, smuggled across the country and forced to work in brothels. (Weiner, 2008)

Protecting the "moral purity" of women from men, and in particular black men, became a central force for the expansion of federal law enforcement in the 20th century.

The act has been updated from its racist origins, and the language regarding immoral purposes was removed in favor of criminalizing transportation of minors across state lines for "any sexual activity for which any person can be charged with a criminal offense." Nonetheless there remains a great deal of anxiety in our culture around women's economic, political, and even sexual independence, and many still believe that women need protection from predatory men.

Should federal law seek to legislate morality in the way that the Mann Act originally did? Do you think that such a law could be enforced in a way that's fair to people of all races?

Mann Act: The federal law that made it a federal crime to transport women across state lines for "immoral purposes." Often used to target minorities.

first created in 1908 by President Theodore Roosevelt and his attorney general, Charles Bonaparte. Initially, Roosevelt faced resistance to the organization from Congress, which feared the creation of a secret police that would serve the interests of the President. In these early years there were few federal crimes that required investigation, and the bureau focused primarily on financial crimes. When the Mann Act was passed, the FBI became famous for its "G-men" and ultimately found its raison d'etre—enforcing a raft of new laws

WHERE DO I FIT IN?

BECOMING AN FBI AGENT

One of the most common ambitions for criminal justice majors is to become a federal law enforcement officer, and specifically an FBI agent. Special agent positions are very competitive, and very few applicants are accepted into the agency's training program, but if you make it through, it can be a very rewarding career.

To become an FBI agent, applicants must be between the ages of 23 and 36½ years old and have a college degree. Applicants must have three years of work experience, be able to pass a physical fitness test, and successfully undergo a series of background checks, including interviews with former employers and teachers. You can apply through your local FBI field office (listed on http://www.fbi.gov).

There are many skills that the FBI searches for in agents that are more important than weapons training or forensic work, though some military experience can be helpful. The FBI is always looking for applicants with foreign language skills (especially Arabic and other languages associated with the Muslim world), computer skills, and accounting abilities, including passing a certified public accountant (CPA) exam. Here is the list of professions sought by the agency:

- Science, technology, engineering, and math (STEM) specialists
- Foreign language specialists
- Lawyers
- Emergency medicine specialists
- Certified public accountants (CPAs)
- Attorneys
- Engineers
- Detectives
- Military experts (specifically those in Special Forces, explosives, WMD, and intelligence)
- Scientists (lab experience)
- Pilots (helicopter, fixed-wing)

These skills are often better suited to the day-to-day investigations into cybercrime, financial crime, and terrorism than the flashy, dramatic work that is showcased on the TV.

Once selected, recruits go through a rigorous training process that lasts for approximately 21 weeks. This includes 12 weeks of academic work and 9 of tactical training. Once candidates have graduated from their training, they are assigned to one of the 56 field offices around the country, though there are some foreign offices located in U.S. embassies abroad. Special agents usually have no real say in where they are placed, at least at the beginning of their careers. Like employees in most other federal jobs, agents are paid on the federal government's pay scale (called the general schedule or GS), which is adjusted for the cost of living where the agents are assigned. Salaries can run from about $45,000 for trainees to over $100,000 per year for experienced agents. Like other jobs in law enforcement, FBI work can be rewarding and exciting, but it can also be boring and bureaucratic.

While the FBI is the most well-known federal law enforcement body, many other parts of the federal government also include law enforcement divisions. The Department of Homeland Security includes the Immigration and Customs Enforcement bureau (ICE), the Treasury Department has several different types of agents, including IRS agents investigating criminal tax fraud, and even the Department of Health and Human Services includes an Office of the Inspector General (OIG) that investigates health care fraud. There are a great number of federal law enforcement jobs beyond the FBI that can offer exciting and rewarding careers, though they are not frequently highlighted on prime-time TV.

that Congress was passing to protect the American people from large-scale, nationwide crime problems. (Other federal law enforcement agencies, such as the Bureau of Alcohol, Tobacco, and Firearms, also came into existence around the same time, as did the Secret Service, though its roots go back further.)

The most important figure in the history of the FBI was J. Edgar Hoover, the director who shaped it into the powerful organization that it is now. From his very first years at the bureau, Hoover worked tirelessly to promote the interests of the FBI, both in the public and within the halls of the federal government. He used sophisticated public relations tools to boost the bureau's profile in the national consciousness, and carefully crafted the image of his organization as a group of tough, no-nonsense crime fighters, an image that persists today. In 1950, Hoover began compiling a "Ten Most Wanted" list of criminals sought by the FBI, not because the list meant anything, but it served as a useful publicity tool for the organization (Blakemore, 2015). As a result of Hoover's efforts, service in FBI is one of the top ambitions for criminal justice majors.

While Hoover used his organization to fight bootleggers, bank thieves, and mobsters, his control over and protection of the organization had a dark side. It was part of the FBI's mandate to uncover threats to the U.S. government, and he had a very broad interpretation of what constituted such a threat. A rabid anticommunist, Hoover went after political figures whose views he believed to be un-American, including those who had broken no laws, using agents to disrupt their operations. Along with crooks, spies, and terrorists, Hoover targeted politicians that he considered a threat to his organization, and even tried to get Martin Luther King Jr. to commit suicide by threatening to expose his extramarital affairs. Those who had initially feared that the FBI would become a secret police force were in some ways correct—most politicians (even presidents) hesitated to take on Hoover because of his power and political support. Hoover's collection of secret files that he kept on both friends and enemies allowed him to remain in power through both Republican and Democratic administrations until his death in 1972 (K. Ackerman, 2011).

TROUBLES OF THE 1960s AND 1970s

Learning Objective 5.6—Explain the cause of tensions between the police and the public in the 1960s and 1970s.

The 1960s and 1970s brought new challenges to policing in the United States. On one hand, all indicators point to a rise in crime in the 1960s—in particular, cities became more dangerous places to live, as crime and violence increased there. This placed pressure on police forces to be tougher and made them less available to the urban public.

Just as important as the change in crime, a new counterculture began to arise and shape public attitudes toward all authority figures, including the police. Starting with the assassination of President John F. Kennedy in 1963, many baby boomers, that is, people who were born after the end of the Second World War, became skeptical toward the U.S. government. Much of this distrust revolved around the American intervention in Vietnam, which many considered both immoral and ill-advised. This skepticism was further strengthened by the rise of the black consciousness movement—as many African Americans began to question the legitimacy of the U.S. government and challenge its authority over black people. Groups like the Nation of Islam with its acolyte, the charismatic and insightful Malcolm X, and the Black Panther Party argued that the U.S. government did not represent the interests of black people. As the most public face of government authority, police officers bore the brunt of this hostility, and they were on the front line of protests and were often the target of the protesters' anger.

The relations between the police and the public, particularly young people and minorities, deteriorated at the end of the 1960s and early 1970s. Police officers were sometimes labeled "pigs" by radicals, and they became hated targets for Black Nationalism and other radical movements. This hostility sometimes led to violence. On October 28, 1967, Oakland, California, police officer John Frey was killed by members of the Black Panther Party, and in the 1970s the Black Liberation Army carried out a series of bombings and killings in San Francisco and New York. In 1970, an antiwar terrorist organization known as the Weather Underground exploded a nail bomb outside of a San Francisco police office, killing one officer and wounding several others. While there were terrorist

SOME STATISTICS . . .

Police Fatalities and Injuries

The National Law Enforcement Memorial Fund keeps tabs on the numbers of police fatalities in the United States, including some very interesting historical data. As you can see in Figure 5.2, the

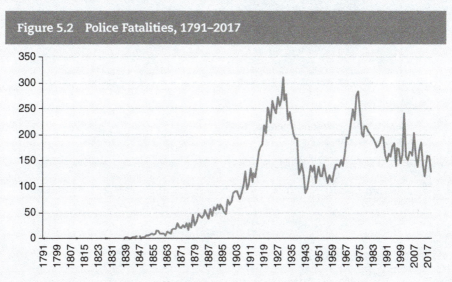

Figure 5.2 Police Fatalities, 1791–2017

Source: National Law Enforcement Officer's Memorial Fund (http://www.nleomf.org), 2018.

(Continued)

(Continued)

most dangerous eras for police officers were the 1920s, the Prohibition era, and the 1970s, the chaotic period where police public relations broke down. (The spike in fatalities in the early 2000s includes the 60 police officers killed in the September 11 attacks on the Pentagon and the World Trade Center.)

The Bureau of Labor Statistics keeps track of fatal and nonfatal injuries among police officers. As Figure 5.3 shows, while violent encounters are dangerous for officers, there are a host of more mundane harms that can befall them, including slips, overexertion, and toxic environments.

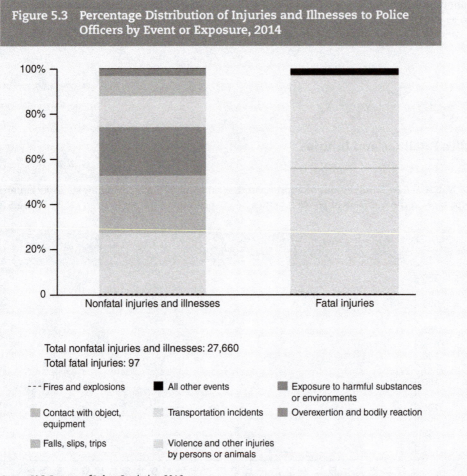

Figure 5.3 Percentage Distribution of Injuries and Illnesses to Police Officers by Event or Exposure, 2014

Total nonfatal injuries and illnesses: 27,660
Total fatal injuries: 97

- - - Fires and explosions

■ All other events

▦ Exposure to harmful substances or environments

▦ Contact with object, equipment

▦ Transportation incidents

▦ Overexertion and bodily reaction

▦ Falls, slips, trips

▦ Violence and other injuries by persons or animals

Source: U.S. Bureau of Labor Statistics, 2016.

attacks against many other symbols of government authority—such as judges, business leaders, and the military—as the starkest symbol of government power, the police were a choice target for many of these radicals. The terrorist attacks were just the most extreme examples of the antiauthority and antipolice attitudes that were dominant in much of the youth counterculture during this era. (It bears noting that many people constituted what President Nixon described in 1969 as the Silent Majority, who still stood by the police and other trusted traditional institutions of authority, and that police officers had dispensed their own share of violence against the antiwar movement.)

THE DRUG WAR

Learning Objective 5.7—Demonstrate the impact of United States drug policy on American policing.

One key factor that shaped policing in the second half of the 20th century was the war on drugs. While both drugs and alcohol have been regulated in the United States since the beginning of the 20th century, other than during the Prohibition era, there was never any serious effort to prevent the selling and distribution of illegal drugs until the 1970s. Drugs were largely considered a public health problem, not a crime problem by authorities.

In 1971, President Nixon declared "an all-out global war on the drug menace" that was meant to increase his political support in the white suburbs for the 1972 election. This declaration ratcheted up law enforcement's efforts to deal with illegal drugs and turned mainstream America against efforts to treat drugs as a public health issue. There were numerous reasons for the change in U.S. policy toward marijuana, cocaine, and other drugs, but the two primary factors were the prevalence of drug abuse in the American counterculture (including increased heroin use among returning Vietnam veterans) and the political interests of President Richard Nixon. While there were movements to decriminalize drugs and treat drug addicts in the latter half of the 1970s, by the time of the election of Ronald Reagan in 1980, the path of legalization and treatment was largely closed off, and the fight against drugs became almost entirely a matter for the criminal justice system for several more decades.

Drug traffickers and drug dealers were now targeted by police, while new legal and tactical weapons were developed to stop the flow of drugs from Asia and South America. In 1973, the Drug Enforcement Agency (DEA) was created to unify the federal government's enforcement of drug laws, and it began to work with foreign governments in South America to stop cocaine production at its source. At the same time, funding for drug treatment centers was cut in favor of a get-tough campaign against drug abusers. Laws were passed that made it easier for drug money to be seized and made it harder for drug traffickers to conduct their activities and hide their profits. In short, the war on drugs in the 1970s, but in particular the 1980s and 1990s, created a huge shift in how policing was done and where police operations were focused.

While the war on drugs affected almost every aspect of American policing, it also had a massive impact on the public. More aggressive antidrug operations targeted African Americans in particular, as the 1980s also marked the beginning of the "crack epidemic," as the use of crack cocaine rapidly increased in American cities. Aggressive policing and tougher sentencing laws only furthered the distrust that existed between the police and the black community in much of America, a distrust that predates the Civil War (Alexander, 2012). Some argued that the drug problem was worst in the black community and that law enforcement was meant to help African Americans and protect them from the damage caused by drugs, but few black Americans were convinced—they saw it as a continuation of the slave patrols and Jim Crow more than as a genuine effort to help their communities.

War on drugs: The effort, begun in the 1970s, to treat illegal drugs primarily as an issue for law enforcement and not as a public health problem.

One of the most enduring figures in policing is the detective. She is the most important part of the police force—at least on TV. On shows like *CSI, Law & Order,* and *True Detective,* diligent investigators examine blood splatter patterns at homicide sites, study ballistics reports, dust weapons for fingerprints, and carefully comb through crime scenes for clues to the identity of the criminal. The truth is that detective work as we know it from popular culture (using forensics to determine the cause of death of a murder victim) is rarely a part of policing. For one thing, few crimes are committed in such a way that the perpetrator is unknown. Most homicides happen in front of witnesses or with overwhelming evidence regarding the identity of the murderer. This means that "detective work" in the sense of investigating crimes where the perpetrator is unknown are rare.

A 1977 study by the RAND Corporation of detective work remains the most important look into what police detectives do daily—and much of it is unglamorous and bound to be disappointing to television viewers. Most criminals are caught shortly after the crime has been committed by the responding officers. Others are found shortly thereafter when they are identified by witnesses, or they are found by the police when they are arrested for other offenses. Only a small proportion (approximately 3%) of offenders are caught using detective work. As the report put it,

> Our data consistently reveal that an investigator's time is largely consumed in reviewing reports, documenting files, and attempting to locate and interview victims on cases that experience shows will not be solved. For cases that are solved (i.e., a suspect is identified), an investigator spends more time in postclearance processing than he does in identifying the perpetrator. (Cordner, 2016, p. 394)

Most detectives spend a lot of time on very basic work, including filling out reports rather than examining blood splatter patterns or comparing shoe imprints in mud.

COMMUNITY POLICING AND BROKEN WINDOWS

Learning Objective 5.8—Identify the strengths and weaknesses of community policing.

Community policing: Attempts to break down barriers between the community and the police.

While the war on drugs was raging and shaping relations between the police and American society, a very different process was simultaneously underway in policing. Frustrated with their deteriorating public standing since the 1960s, many American police departments sought to change the ways that the police relate to the communities they policed. One solution that was put forward in the 1980s was called community policing. Community policing is an approach to police-public relations that seeks to break down the barriers between police officers and the broader public. One study described this as "a collaboration between the police and the community that identifies and solves community problems" (Bureau of Justice Assistance, 1994, p. vii). The idea behind community policing is that the police cannot do their job effectively without the support of the public, and this support can only exist if the people are comfortable with officers. This requires that police departments engage with the communities that they are supposed to protect.

While community policing is in many ways a buzzword in modern police studies, the idea was first developed as a response to a number of different social forces (Cordner, 2014). Among the early progenitors of this idea were the Japanese through what is known as the *kōban* system. In Japan, police departments set up small community service offices where the public can ask for help on a wide variety of issues. Some of these are law enforcement problems, but many are not. People can go to the *kōbans* to ask for directions and to seek change for parking meters, among other things. Similar small police stations were set up in many cities in the United States to help break down the barriers between the public and the police.

Community policing was implemented in a variety of ways. Foot patrols were instituted in cities that had abandoned the approach when automobiles had become common—having officers encounter citizens in a face-to-face manner on a regular basis, it was believed, would increase trust and understanding between the two groups. Cities set up police-community commissions that allowed for the public to express their frustrations with crime and with the police. Public meetings were held in many communities, not only to address grievances with the police, but also to allow the public to discuss broader crime concerns in their neighborhoods. Oftentimes, persistent crime problems can be addressed by simply changing the environment—lighting dark corners, removing concealing shrubs, or boarding up abandoned buildings. Efforts were made by police departments to keep officers in the same community for extended periods to develop a rapport with the public and increase trust between the two. While these changes may seem small, they were part of a much broader attempt to change the attitudes of the police toward the public and vice versa, one which sought to counteract the problems that had been generated by the war on drugs.

A further development in law enforcement in this period was the development of *broken windows policing*. Through research, a group of criminologists discovered that if a neighborhood looked neglected, the appearance was likely to inspire more crime. Criminologists argued that small-scale social problems—such as broken windows, litter, graffiti, and panhandling—sent a signal that the people in an area did not care about their community, and as a result crime in that neighborhood went up (Kelling & Coles, 1998). Following this, policymakers reasoned that one way to reduce crime was to prevent such small-scale social disorder as a way to prevent other, more serious crimes (drug trafficking, gang violence). Under Mayor Rudy Giuliani, cities like New York began to crack down on these social problems, and many believe that this helped reduce crime in that city. While these reforms are credited by some with helping lower the crime rate in New York in the 1990s, many critics suggest that broken windows policing often alienated minority residents, who bore the brunt of these policies (Fagan, Geller, Davies, & West, 2010). They argue that broken windows policing led to a policy that targeted and harassed minorities and undermined their trust in the police (Childress, 2016).

THE HOMELAND SECURITY ERA

Learning Objective 5.9—Summarize the impact of the September 11 attacks on American law enforcement.

September 11, 2001, was a momentous moment in history, and it affected almost every aspect of American life. Shortly after the attacks on the Pentagon and the World Trade Center, President Bush declared a global war on terror to fight against Al Qaeda and affiliated terrorist organizations—a war that in many ways continues today. This was a very different war than those that Americans had fought in the past: Much of the fighting was not going to be done on a battlefield by soldiers (though there would be plenty of that); it would instead be fought by spies, intelligence analysts, diplomats, and, of course, police forces of all kinds. The battlefield was not just in the cities and deserts of Asia and the Middle East, but also in London, New York, and Houston. Given the hidden nature of the terrorist threat, it is no surprise that the commencement of the global war on terror marked the beginning of new forms of policing, forms that influenced far more than how the police dealt with Al Qaeda (Oliver, 2006).

Al Qaeda and affiliated terrorist organizations such as the so-called Islamic State were not traditional military enemies—they were networks that operate underground within Muslim and non-Muslim societies alike, including within the United States. In many ways, this made these organizations much more similar to the mafia than to a traditional military enemy like Nazi Germany or the Iraqi Army. On top of that, a number of terrorists were so-called lone wolves, that is, individuals who were not a part of any organized terrorist network but were instead independently inspired by Osama Bin Laden and his allies to kill innocent Americans. As a result, much of the fight against terrorism required police departments and other law enforcement agencies to uncover these networks and arrest would-be terrorists. While the fight against terrorism was not a war in the traditional sense, it was also not law enforcement in the traditional sense, either. Terrorists were not interested in any of the goals of traditional criminal organizations: They wanted to kill innocent Americans to change U.S. foreign policy and to spread their faith. Thus, the war against terrorism was neither a war in the normal sense, nor was it a fight against crime as conventionally understood.

After the 9/11 attacks, Congress created the Department of Homeland Security or DHS. This new department brought several different federal law enforcement bodies together and put them under the control of the secretary of Homeland Security, who answered directly to the president. Some of these organizations are the Secret Service, the two bodies that enforce immigration law (ICE—Immigration and Customs Enforcement and CBP—Customs and Border Protection), the Coast Guard, and FEMA (the Federal Emergency Management Agency). The hope was that combining these government units together could make them more effective in dealing with the threats to the United States that came from groups like Al Qaeda. Centralization allowed for these law enforcement units to share information and act together in order to streamline their activities and thereby make them more effective.

The federal government also passed new laws that increased the government's ability to conduct surveillance operations over suspected terrorists both on U.S. soil and abroad. Traditionally, the rules that applied to counterintelligence activities were different from those that applied to law enforcement operations. Seeking to discover whether a diplomat from a foreign embassy was paying for information from a U.S. government employee was very different from attempting to learn whether a suspect was embezzling money from his employer or selling drugs out of her van. These lines became blurry as the government passed a series of laws that allowed police agencies expanded power to conduct surveillance operations related to antiterrorism operations. The most well known of these was the Uniting and Strengthening America by Providing Appropriate Tools Required to Intercept and Obstruct Terrorism Act of 2001 (a.k.a. the USA PATRIOT Act). This law loosened some of the restrictions on the government's ability to search peoples' homes in antiterrorist activities and made it easier for the police to conduct wiretaps and other surveillance operations against terrorists.

Along with the creation of this new federal body and the use of enhanced surveillance techniques, there have been several other significant changes in post 9/11 policing. Since September 11, 2001, state and local police forces have become *militarized* (Balko, 2006). The police have begun using weapons, tools, and tactics associated with the military, including heavy weapons (M-16s) and armored vehicles more than before. The use of special, heavy-weapons teams (such as SWAT groups) has been expanded in ways that they never had been in the past, and many American police departments have begun to resemble the heavily armed units that the opponents of Robert Peel feared. There are a lot of complicated reasons why the police have become so militarized, but a great deal of the funding for the heavy equipment that police forces have obtained came from the DHS (S. Ackerman, 2014). Police forces are given powerful weaponry that it is highly unlikely that they would need. But to justify owning such weaponry, police forces must find excuses to use it, leading critics to see a massive overreaction on the part of the police to low-level disturbances (Bouie, 2014).

The rhetoric of antiterrorism has spread beyond the fight against Al Qaeda and its allies. Given the power of terrorism over the public imagination, many politicians have sought to frame other issues as matters of homeland security regardless of whether they really are. One notable example of this is immigration: Historically, immigration has been viewed as an economic issue (Will the immigrants take away jobs from natives?) or a crime issue (Will immigrants commit crimes while here or smuggle drugs?). After September 11, politicians began describing immigration as a problem of homeland security and linking immigration to security. (The term *border security* was created to highlight this point.) As Texas Governor Rick Perry put it,

> My citizens' safety is what is foremost here. And it hasn't got anything to do with anything other than those numbers of individuals who are coming across the border. And when you think about the idea that some of them are from countries that have substantial terrorist ties, whether it's Pakistan or Afghanistan or Syria, we are at historic record highs with individuals being apprehended from those countries. (as quoted in Caroll, 2014)

Given the public's fear of terrorism, it makes sense for politicians to present a whole array of problems as related to it. Expanding the role of the state and local police under the banner of homeland security is one of the ways that antiterrorist efforts have shaped American policing and have influenced broader debates about immigration, race, and the rights of individual states to control their territories (Bigo, 2002; McDonald, 2008).

WHAT WOULD YOU DO?

Terrorism and Trolls

Your friend and roommate Mark has always been something of an extreme guy. He likes to provoke and to shock people, but you've always found him to be a nice person on a one-to-one basis. Online he's a classic "troll"—he likes to say things to get people worked up and angry. Some of his posts are racist and sexist, but he says that they're all meant as a joke. "I just like to see people get worked up. They need to stop taking things online so seriously," he says.

You come back from class one day and find his computer open on the kitchen table. There, blinking on the screen is a recent post that he put anonymously on a chatgroup. He is threatening to blow up a local police station because "Cops deserve to die!" Several respondents are very angry with his post and are threatening to attack him, but there are also several other posters who are sympathetic with Mark's post. Mark has engaged in discussions with these people on the forum: discussing tactics for causing the most harm to the police department and killing the most officers. They even discuss the types of explosive materials that Mark could use and what times and targets would be the most effective.

You suspect that Mark is just messing around, but the details are being discussed very thoroughly on the website. He's never done anything like this before and would undoubtedly deny planning an attack if you asked him. Telling law enforcement about his postings could easily put him in prison and potentially ruin his life, but then again, doing nothing just might lead to officers being killed.

Do you confront Mark? Do you call the police? Do you ignore the posting? Why?

AFTER HOMELAND SECURITY?

Learning Objective 5.10—Discuss possible changes in modern policing.

It's very difficult to break history down into tidy periods, especially when we're talking about recent history. We don't know what the final outcomes of these developments will be—some event that seems important at the time could turn out to be a blip. Some event that seems trivial at the time could mark the beginning of a tremendous change. There may be some indication that we've entered a new phase of policing in the United States over the last few years, particularly in response to several high-profile cases of police abuse. Cases like the killings of black men like Trayvon Martin, Michael Brown, and Eric Garner and the rise of movements like #blacklivesmatter and Copwatch could mark the beginning of a new era. This could mark the beginning of a rolling back of the policing that has composed the homeland security era, or it could mean a change to an entirely new model of policing.

The rise of portable technology, namely cell phones with cameras, has made it possible for bystanders to document police misconduct, and social networks like Twitter and Facebook have provided a means for distributing this material. While there have been accounts of police brutality in the past, very few of them were caught on camera, and so

Homeland security era: The transformation of policing after the September 11, 2001, attacks. Included a greater emphasis on fighting terrorism and a militarization of local police forces.

they could be easily dismissed as anomalies by a public that is eager to support the police. This new visibility of the police makes misconduct harder to deny (Goldsmith, 2010). Further, changing public attitudes toward soft drugs, marijuana in particular, have made a lot of the police's antidrug efforts seem excessive. Finally, the rise in concern for civil liberties in response to the government's spying and surveillance operations (some of which were leaked to the public by the whistle blower Edward Snowden) has fueled a distrust in government policing from both the left and the right ends of the political spectrum. The initial fear of domestic terrorism that seized America in 2001 has dissipated over time, making the public less willing than it once was to trade in civil liberties for the sake of personal security.

These movements have led to a backlash against the aggressive forms of policing that have been deployed over the last few years. Aspects of the USA PATRIOT Act have been revised to (slightly) limit the government's ability to search "bulk data" (that is, records of phone calls from millions of people). Federal and local prosecutors have begun to investigate and prosecute (some) police officers who are accused of blatant misconduct. And in May 2015 the Obama administration announced that it would restrict the use of military-style equipment by police forces in the country, as the use of such gear "can alienate and intimidate local residents, and send the wrong message" (Davis & Shear, 2015). All of these efforts amount to dialing back many of the policing tools that have developed since the war on drugs and especially since the September 11 attacks.

The #blacklivesmatter movement has done a very effective job of mobilizing against police violence and the killing of unarmed African Americans by police officers. Formed by three black women after the killing of Trayvon Martin in Florida, the group has organized protests against police violence and has sought to make the broader culture aware of the risks that African Americans face when they interact with the police (Guynn, 2015). Since that killing, the organization has confronted politicians about their views regarding police violence, mobilized the support of public figures, and conducted protests in cities around the country. They have become a very important part of the fight against police violence, though they have aroused the anger of many conservatives, including Donald Trump, who has accused the movement of aiding in the murder of police officers.

These developments have been very recent and may not change the overall direction of contemporary policing. In fact, a big shift in the opposite direction occurred with the election of Donald Trump and his appointment of Jeff Sessions as his first attorney general. The Trump campaign leaned heavily on a propolice, law-and-order platform, and Sessions sought to implement policies that are reminiscent of police practices from three decades in the past. During a July 2017 speech before police officers in New York, Trump appeared to advocate using excessive force against suspects (Rosenthal, 2017). The Department of Homeland Security has used armed agents to aggressively pursue undocumented immigrants for deportation. The Trump administration allowed police officers to apply for military weapons again in the fall of 2017. These reverses may not be permanent or even logical, but they have galvanized opposition to Trump's policies from leftist activists (Legaspi, 2017). Whether the election of Trump and his police-friendly policies marks a permanent return to earlier forms of policing or is merely a momentary step back from current changes remains to be seen.

CHAPTER SUMMARY

This chapter has been a summary of the rise of modern policing. At the time that Britain adopted the Peel Act in the 19th century, America began adopting and adapting the British model for its own needs. Over the last two centuries, the police developed from a rough and ready system of posses and slave patrols to a wide network of municipal, state, and federal institutions. As American society's attitudes toward government, crime, and of course, race relations has changed, American policing has responded.

When we talk about history, much of the time we are telling a story: fitting facts together in a way that makes sense and allows us to get a grasp on events of the past and how they shape our contemporary world. *Actual* events usually don't fit into neat periods or categories, and the truth is often far messier than we'd like to admit. There are always details that must be overlooked or put aside to make sense of it all, and there are inevitably several different possible interpretations of historical events. There are plenty of other ways to break down the history of policing that would also fit the facts, and historians of policing disagree about what is important and what isn't. The point of this chapter is to give you one interpretation of the history of police in America—an interpretation that fits with the overall critical approach of this book.

One of the most exciting things about studying history is that you learn about how the current world came to be and see how unpredictable it all really was. In the case of modern policing, we take it for granted that the police wear uniforms, carry guns, and are empowered to stop us in our daily activities if they suspect us of wrongdoing, but the history here shows that it was not always so. We also take for granted that our police are professional, independent, and largely honest—again, the product of history and not a necessary consequence of it. It took a lot of historical events, and many accidents, for our modern police forces to look the way that they do. New developments, new social changes, and new historical accidents can still change the future course of policing in America in ways that we cannot predict.

In the next chapter, we will turn away from history and toward the modern police that stand as the culmination of the historical process that we discussed here: seeing what the modern police do on a daily basis and how these activities connect with our lives in both big and small ways.

REVIEW/DISCUSSION QUESTIONS

1. How have attitudes toward the police changed in your lifetime? What do you think has caused these changes? Are these changes continuous with history, or are they new?

2. What could be done to improve relations between the police and the public?

3. Which social forces and technological changes had the greatest impact on policing?

4. Do you think that the Trump administration's policing policies are going to permanently shape policing in America? Will these changes be a good thing? Why or why not?

KEY TERMS

#blacklivesmatter 110
Community policing 130
Cronyism 121
Frankpledge system 114

Homeland security era 134
Mann Act 124
Peel Act 116
Professionalization 121

Slave patrols 119
War on drugs 129

$SAGE edge™

Get the tools you need to sharpen your study skills. SAGE edge offers a robust online environment featuring an impressive array of free tools and resources.

Access practice quizzes, eFlashcards, video, and multimedia at edge.sagepub.com/fichtelberg

Sarah Yeh

The police play a lot of different roles in our society beyond enforcing the law. Where do you see the police most often in your daily life? Are they usually enforcing laws when you see them?

CHAPTER SIX

MODERN POLICING

In the last chapter, we saw the turns and twists in the historical road that lead us to what we now recognize as policing. In this chapter, we will discuss different aspects of contemporary policing. We will focus on the structure of police organizations throughout the country, discussing the differences between sheriffs, police officers, Marshals, detectives, and other law enforcement bodies. We will also examine some of the common things the police do in their average work day—if there is indeed such a thing for officers who work on the street. Afterward we will discuss some commonly held myths about policing before we turn to the legal restrictions that police face when interacting with citizens. This final section will include some practical advice on how to deal with police officers when you encounter them. Once this is done, we will turn to police misconduct and police deviance in the next chapter.

WHAT WOULD YOU DO?

Who Should Be a Police Officer?

Your roommate, Terrence, has wanted to be a police officer for as long as you've known him. He takes every criminal justice course he can, even though he's about to graduate and has all the criminal justice credits that he needs. He reads books about crime on his spare time and researches prominent cold cases as a hobby. Almost every weekend he goes on ride-alongs with local police departments seeing how they work and taking careful notes about their operations. His father was an officer. His brother is an officer. All he wants to do is follow in their footsteps and put on a badge.

While he obviously wants to serve very badly, he would make a terrible officer in your view. He is emotionally volatile, viciously attacking people who he thinks have insulted him. You've had to drag him out of more than one party when he's started fights with innocent people who

he says "disrespected him" or "looked at him funny." He's sexist and treats all the women he dates terribly. His short fuse and violent temper are at times frightening, but he's never been aggressive directly toward you.

Terrence is currently in the process of applying to be an officer for the state police department. You are contacted by the department conducting Terrence's background check and they want to ask you some confidential questions. After a few routine questions about the history of your friendship with Terrence, the investigator asks, "Is there anything you think I should know about Terrence that would affect his ability to do his job?"

How do you answer this question? Do you ignore your concerns about Terrence or do you express them? Why?

THE ORGANIZATION OF POLICING

Learning Objective 6.1—List the five main types of police officers in the United States.

The American government is organized as a federation of 50 separate states, with a single federal government standing above them. Just as each state has its own constitution, its own laws, and its own court system, each state has its own array of police forces with a distinct organizational system. This means that there is no single uniform structure to American policing: Within each state, different police systems have overlapping jobs and jurisdictions, many of which operate independently of the others. There are over 17,000 separate law enforcement agencies in the United States, each of which is given different tasks and works in different ways with other federal, state, and local police forces (Banks, Hendrix, Hickman, & Kyckelhahn, 2016). Here we will discuss some of the different organizations and different types of police officers currently operating in the United States. Bear in mind that this list is not exhaustive, and it simplifies the very complicated system of policing that exists in many states.

State and Local Policing

Sheriffs and Police

Most states distinguish between sheriffs and police officers. Police departments usually work in cities, towns, and other population centers and do much of the everyday policing. They are usually created by the city and answer to a city commission on public safety or a police commission of some kind. Usually these bodies answer to the city's mayor or to its board of supervisors. Some police systems are created by smaller bodies like university campuses.

Despite their organizational differences, most states have the same general requirement for different kinds of policing. Usually officers must complete the same training course at an academy, which is usually about a five- to six-month training period. Officers must also meet the Peace Officer Standards and Training (POST) criteria that are set out by the different state governments and include an exam that candidates must pass. These state regulations describe the requirements that candidates must fulfill to become sworn law enforcement officers, regardless of what jurisdiction they serve under.

Sheriffs on the other hand are a part of county government and usually have a wider jurisdiction, often including over unincorporated lands (that is, lands that don't belong to any city). They are created by the state government and serve as the top law enforcement officer for the county. Most sheriffs are elected by the people rather than selected by a government body. In some smaller cities, they partner with local law enforcement to help provide 24-hour coverage. Beyond this, county sheriffs use their resources to support local law enforcement on issues that may be too big for the municipal police to handle. They can also deal with civil issues such as court protection along with serving warrants and evictions—services that other police agencies typically do not handle. Often sheriff's departments have a county coroner's office whose job is to certify deaths and to determine whose deaths merit police investigation.

State Police and Highway Patrol

In most states, there are state police or "state troopers." Depending on the state, these officers usually have jurisdiction over two areas. First, they usually patrol interstate highways, handling traffic and speeding violations as well as catching criminal activity on the highway system. Second, they help coordinate investigations of offenses that cross city or county lines, serving as a statewide resource for city, county, and local police forces. Hawaii is the only state that does not have a statewide police force.

Within each police organization, there are several different types of officers.

Investigators (Detectives)

Investigators are officers who gather evidence and seek to determine who committed a crime. They often work with prosecutors and others both to determine who committed a crime and to gather evidence against the alleged criminals for prosecution. This includes interviewing witnesses, searching crime scenes, conducting surveillance, and interrogating suspects. Larger police departments will have different detective units that specialize in different types of crime such as homicide and sex crimes.

Most detectives spend several years as a regular uniformed officer before becoming a detective. Once they get there, however, many complain that detective work is boring and far removed from the action. Much of their time is absorbed by filling out reports and interviewing witnesses. According to one study of detective work, "Almost half of a typical investigator's time is devoted to such activities as administrative work or general surveillance which are not directly related to casework and are unlikely to produce arrests" (Greenwood, 1979). According to the FBI, the overall *clearance rate*, that is the number of offenses that lead to arrests, is low. While violent crimes had an overall clearance rate of 45.6% in 2016 (and homicide a rate of 59.4%), the rate for property crimes was only about 18.3%, and for burglary it was 13.1% (U.S. Department of Justice, 2017).

Special Weapons Officers

Special weapons units (sometimes known as SWAT units—short for special weapons and tactics) exist to deal with dangerous situations that are beyond the capacity of traditional police forces. Often, they wield military grade equipment, including automatic rifles, and intervene in hostage situations, terror attacks, and other high-security situations. They were originally formulated as a response to terrorist attacks in the 1960s and 1970s and have since been used in raids on drug houses and similar highly dangerous operations (Balko, 2013). Many larger metropolitan police departments have dedicated SWAT units, while smaller forces have traditional officers that are on call and serve a special weapons role should the need arise. Otherwise, these officers serve a traditional policing role.

To become members of a SWAT team, candidates must first usually serve as a traditional officer for a length of time and prove their competence and their ability to function effectively in high-pressure situations. Afterward, officers must undergo rigorous testing and training in the weapons and tactics that the police deploy in hostage situations or terrorist attacks.

Other Specialty Officers

Along with the traditional forms of policing, there are many different specialty officers, particularly in larger police forces. The NYPD for example is the largest municipal police department in the United States and includes a SCUBA team and harbor unit, an aviation unit, an organized crime unit, and a mounted police unit. Most police forces have internal affairs units that investigate claims of police misconduct (we will discuss these in more depth in the next chapter) as well as training units and many other support personnel that help officers in a variety of ways.

SOME STATISTICS...

Police Demographics

DataUSA is a joint enterprise between academic and private research institutions that seeks to make different sorts of data available and comprehensible to the public. They combine and present a lot of useful information about the makeup of the modern American police.

There are about 744,600 police officers in the United States. About 79% of officers are white, which is slightly more than the 76% in America more generally (U.S. Census Bureau, n.d.). There are about the same percentage of black officers as black Americans (13%) (see Figure 6.1).

They are also disproportionately male. About 86.7% of the police force is male (as opposed to 49.2% of the general population).

The Pew Center has done polling of police officers, asking them about their feelings regarding their job. Their report, *Behind the Badge*, collates their feelings about the work they do and the public that they interact with (Morin, Stepler, & Mercer, 2017). For example, only 8% of officers see their job primarily as enforcers, and a significantly larger majority see themselves as protectors of the public. Paradoxically, many officers believe that tough and aggressive policing tactics are sometimes necessary (see Figure 6.2).

On the other hand, many officers feel that they are not well understood by the public (see Figure 6.3).

Despite these challenges, many officers like their job. The Pew Center reports that about 74% of officers report being at least somewhat satisfied with their workplace (Morin et al., 2017).

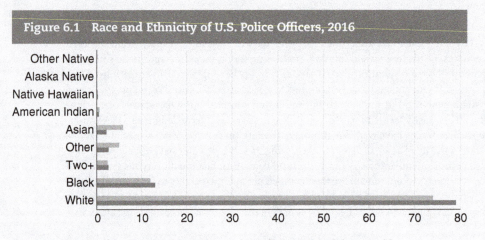

Figure 6.1   Race and Ethnicity of U.S. Police Officers, 2016

Source: Based on data from DataUSA, https://datausa.io/profile/soc/333050/#demographics.

Figure 6.2   Officer Opinions on Aggressive Police Tactics, 2016

Some officers say tough, aggressive tactics are needed with some people and in some neighborhoods

% of officers saying they_with each of the following statements

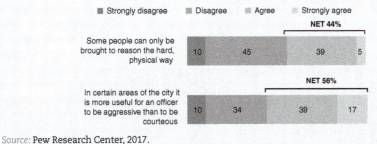

■ Strongly disagree   ■ Disagree   ■ Agree   ■ Strongly agree

	Strongly disagree	Disagree	Agree	Strongly agree
Some people can only be brought to reason the hard, physical way (NET 44%)	10	45	39	5
In certain areas of the city it is more useful for an officer to be aggressive than to be courteous (NET 56%)	10	34	39	17

Source: Pew Research Center, 2017.

Note: No answer category not shown.

Figure 6.3   Public Perceptions of the Police, 2016

Do Americans understand the challenges police face on the job?

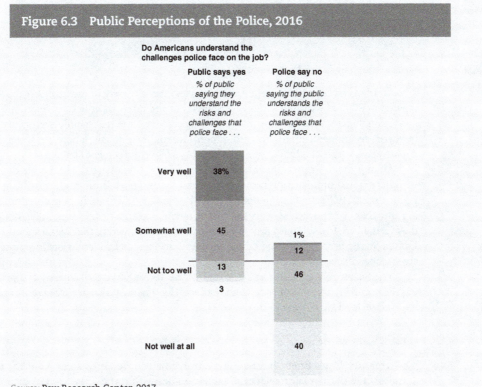

	Public says yes	Police say no
	% of public saying they understand the risks and challenges that police face . . .	*% of public saying the public understands the risks and challenges that police face . . .*
Very well	38%	
Somewhat well	45	1%
Not too well	13	12
	3	46
Not well at all		40

Source: Pew Research Center, 2017.

Note: No answer category not shown.

Federal Policing

Over the last century there has been a dramatic rise in the number and type of federal police officers in service, and they are spread across government. The federal government is composed of many different departments, all of which answer to a cabinet secretary and ultimately to the president. Along with these are numerous independent entities like the Central Intelligence Agency that have their own chains of command. Here are some of the most prominent arms of federal law enforcement.

Department of Justice

The most prominent federal law enforcement body is the Department of Justice (DOJ). Headed by the attorney general, the DOJ handles most federal law enforcement issues and includes the Federal Bureau of Investigation; the Bureau of Alcohol, Tobacco, Firearms and Explosives (ATF); the Drug Enforcement Administration (DEA); the Federal Bureau of Prisons (BOP); as well as other related agencies. Each of these sections has its own set of highly trained federal law enforcement officers that handle issues that fall under its jurisdiction, though they often combine for certain types of cases, and there can be competition between them, too (Grossman, 2014).

Within the Justice Department are the *U.S. Marshals*. Marshals are officers tasked with a wide array of different duties, including apprehending fugitives from federal custody, protecting federal courts and judicial officials, transporting federal prisoners, and confiscating assets for the court.

Department of Homeland Security

The DHS oversees protecting the United States from a variety of external threats. It was created in 2003 as part of a series of responses to the terrorist attacks of September 11, 2001. It includes several high-profile law enforcement bodies that handle everything from terrorism to immigration to protecting high-level public officials. There are seven major departments within the DHS, each of which has a law enforcement element.

Among the most prominent of the DHS policing bodies are the two units that deal with border and immigration protection. The United States Immigration and Customs Enforcement (ICE) and Customs and Border Protection (CBP) are both in charge of making sure that everything and everyone that enters U.S. territory does so legally. Alongside these is the U.S. Coast Guard, which is responsible for protecting the coastal waters of the United States, preventing smuggling, preventing foreign attacks, and rescuing those who are stranded in coastal waters.

The Secret Service is also a part of DHS. The Secret Service's primary job is protecting the president, the vice president, and other VIPs. They are also in charge of investigating counterfeit U.S. currency.

Department of the Treasury

The Treasury Department has had law enforcement officials of some kind for many decades. One of the major law enforcement bodies within the Treasury Department is the Internal Revenue Service (IRS), which has investigators who search out tax fraud. The Office of the Inspector General is responsible for investigating criminal activity within the government's economic institutions as well as investigating certain financial crimes such as bank fraud. Many high-profile criminals have been imprisoned for financial crimes—including Al Capone, who was ultimately convicted of tax fraud, and many high-profile offenders such as celebrities who have gone to jail after failing to pay their taxes.

While these are the most significant forms of federal law enforcement, almost all departments have some sort of law enforcement component to them. For example, the Department of Health and Human Services regulates insurance markets to ensure that they fit federal health care regulations, the Department of Agriculture has a U.S. Forest Service Law Enforcement & Investigations organization, and the State Department has the Diplomatic Security Service. The Defense Department has military police (MPs) that enforce military law, and the Department of the Interior has National Park Service rangers who oversee law enforcement on federal lands. While some of these are higher profile than others, each plays a role in preserving law and order, particularly regarding crimes that occur outside of the jurisdiction of individual states as well as crimes that spill across state borders.

REALITY CHECK

Policing

Police officers probably have the most mythologized job in America. Between TV, novels, and movies, most of the public has a very clear and often very false conception of what policing is like. Just like their fascination with lawyers and doctors, the public fascination with the police is often based on a misunderstanding about what officers do on a day-to-day basis and is the product of stories that are meant to attract viewers rather than reflect reality. Here we'll dispel a few myths about American policing.

If you believed everything that you saw on TV, you would think that police officers are constantly drawing their weapons and chasing "perps" down dark alleys, grabbing murderers and slamming them onto the hood of their cars, and saving the lives of innocent people from dangerous predators. In reality, discharging firearms is not a common part of policing at all. Less than 1% of encounters between the police and the public require that officers use force, and only a small percentage of situations where the officer uses force require the use of lethal force (see section "The Use of Force" that follows).

According to the Bureau of Justice Statistics, "Among persons who had contact with police in 2008, an estimated 1.4% had force used or threatened against them during their most recent contact" (Eith & Durose, 2011).

There is surprisingly little good data available on police shootings. Critics have charged that police departments have withheld this information to prevent criticism or lawsuits (Balko, 2012). Despite resistance, the International Association of Chiefs of Police (IACP) produced a report in 2001 showing that very few officers ever discharge a firearm in the line of duty (International Association of Chiefs of Police, 2001). The private, crowd-sourced website Fatal Encounters (http://www.fatalencounters.org/) that records public information about officer homicides shows approximately 7,100 individuals killed by officers. Although this data is rough, the site shows that approximately 6,100 of these fatalities were from a gunshot. While this may initially seem like a lot, officers across the United States interact with *millions* of people daily, and more people

(Continued)

die in the United States in traffic accidents every 2 days than died in 15 years from police shootings. In a recent development, the Justice Department announced in October 2016 that they will begin collecting nationwide data on the use of force by police, though they face many challenges in collecting quality data from local departments.

Policing is a very important job, and officers do a great deal of good for the communities they serve. But it is far less glamorous than it is portrayed. Officers spend a great deal of their time involved in mundane activities: dealing with public nuisances, noise complaints and other issues involving neighbors who can't get along, along with never-ending stacks of paperwork rather than high-speed chases or pursuing mysterious serial killers. TV shows about policing are exciting, but many officers often report that the most realistic depiction of policing on TV is *Barney Miller*, a 1970s sitcom based in a Manhattan precinct where officers spend most of their time at their desk chatting, drinking coffee, and filling out paperwork, and little drama happens. And every officer will tell you that paperwork—filling out reports for their superiors—sucks up far more of their time than does anything particularly exciting.

A Typical Police Officer's Day

Most officers will tell you that there is no "typical day" for an officer of any rank or on any duty, and much of their activity depends on what happens on the streets as it were. Nonetheless, there is a sort of routine in their professional lives. Officers show up before their shift begins and usually change into their uniforms and check through their equipment. Usually, most shifts begin with a short briefing at the police department; here officers are informed about police news as well as any APBs ("all points bulletins") or BOLOs ("be on the lookouts"). Further, any new policy regulations for the police may be discussed, so that officers are aware of the latest regulations that they must adhere to. In addition, any relevant events that the officers will have to deal with during their shift such as sporting events or other public gatherings are discussed.

Then the officers do their work. This can include vehicular patrol, where officers drive around a prescribed area in the city. Unless they are responding to a specific call, they are usually driving around, searching for drivers who break laws or things that JDLR, that is "just don't look right," and require further investigation. Some officers may be put on special assignment, attached to an investigation or a sting operation or some other special event. Through their shift, most patrol officers drive around waiting for a service call to which they can respond.

One thing all officers will tell you is that the only consistent part of daily police work is the paperwork that must be filled out. All police stops and arrests must be carefully documented. If a police officer is required to use force to subdue a suspect, this can trigger a mountain of paperwork, and shootings set off a complex set of procedures where different groups investigate the shooting and take a series of statements from everybody involved. More mundane activities like gasoline purchases and daily activity logs must also be completed by officers. Officers often complain that paperwork absorbs much of the time that could be spent for "real policing."

CRIMINAL (IN)JUSTICE

Female Officers

Feminists have always argued that in a patriarchal society, women are treated unequally because of their gender. Women's concerns are dismissed, and their contributions are not taken seriously by a male dominated culture. One of the places that this is most obvious in criminal justice is in the treatment of female officers. Law enforcement institutions, their (male) fellow officers, and the public at large often denigrate female officers, and they must struggle to be taken seriously. Historically, men considered women to be too physically or emotionally weak to be effective officers, though there has been notable progress in this area (Leger, 1997). On the other hand, some men may feel their masculinity threatened when they are forced to submit to the orders of a female officer. Regardless, when they have been allowed to serve, women have excelled in policing and provided benefits that most male officers cannot.

Women make up more than 50% of the U.S. population, but they are only a small part of American policing. The first female officer was hired by the police department in Portland, Oregon, in 1905, but she was restricted to social work and protecting women and children as part of what was known as the Women's Protection Division. Many cities followed suit, hiring women to handle issues that were considered "unmanly." Slowly over the last century, with the rise of feminist activists, more women were hired and began to take on less stereotypically feminine policing tasks. Currently, approximately 12% of officers in the United States are women (Reaves, 2015).

There are a lot of things that female officers bring to the law enforcement table that men don't. While there is some disagreement on the subject, research has suggested that female officers tend to handle encounters with the public in a fashion different from men. They are less likely to resort to physical force, finding ways to defuse a situation without violence. Moreover, female officers are more likely to take the claims of rape victims seriously—and prioritize the investigation and prosecution of rapists who would otherwise go free. Female officers are also better at dealing with cases of domestic violence—often saving the lives of women who would die if left solely in the hands of male officers (Miller & Segal, 2016). As a former police chief in Madison, Wisconsin put it,

> Women in policing make a difference—a big difference—they make for a better police department. Haven't you wondered why women police are not the ones involved in recent officer involved shootings? After all, they are usually smaller, somewhat weaker in physical strength, and yet they don't appear to shoot suspects as often. (Spillar, 2015)

Clearly female officers provide a great deal of resources for a police force that can be useful in a variety of situations, and given the fact that physical force is only a small part of policing, whatever physical shortcomings some women may have (though certainly many do not) are balanced by these advantages (Archbold & Schulz, 2012).

Even though female officers can make a valuable contribution to policing, they often face resistance. Many female officers and their supporters complain that hiring women is not a priority in police departments, despite efforts to diversify police departments (Asquith, 2016). Women are still often associated with nurturing and caring, values that run contrary to those of most male officers, and thus some believe they are better suited toward social work or childcare. Female officers are sometimes viewed as interlopers in a macho policing culture. Many

(Continued)

(Continued)

female officers report harassment from their male colleagues and sometimes from the public. Though studies have found different results, it is widely agreed that sexual harassment is a pervasive problem for women who serve (Lonsway, Paynich, & Hall, 2013). This can include sexually suggestive comments, showing pornography in the office, unwanted sexual advances, and other actions that make female officers feel uncomfortable. Despite these behaviors, many female officers do not complain for fear of looking weak or out of fear that a reputation for complaining will harm their chances of advancing in the force (Lonsway et al., 2013).

What do you think are the main differences between how women and men deal with conflict? What are their relative strengths and weaknesses? How would these approaches translate into police-work? Would you respond differently to orders given by a female officer? Why or why not?

THE USE OF FORCE

Learning Objective 6.2—Explain levels of the use-of-force continuum and legal restrictions on the use of force.

Even though it is not a common part of the police's job, their ability to use force is in some sense the essence of policing—it is what distinguishes the police from any other part of the government. Without this power, the police would be a toothless regulatory body with no ability to make the unwilling to submit to their authority. The importance of the use of force to policing explains why it can be so controversial when it is used and why it is sometimes highly restricted and closely monitored. There are some guides that are meant to regulate how force is applied in the line of duty, but in practice, particularly when nobody is looking, they can be skirted or ignored outright.

The use of force by the police is commonly regulated by what is known as the use-of-force continuum. There are guidelines regarding the kinds and levels of force that an officer may use against a suspect should it be necessary. Though she may have some discretion in how she uses force on the job, too much force can get an officer into trouble. Officers charged with using *excessive force* (discussed in the next chapter) can face disciplinary actions from their department, can be sued by the victim, or can even be prosecuted themselves.

The use-of-force continuum starts at the "lightest" end of the spectrum with verbal commands from the officer to the suspect, and ends with the most extreme force available: lethal force. (You can see the entire continuum in Figure 6.4.) Though continuums can break down in different ways, the Department of Justice breaks officer force down in this way (adapted from National Institute of Justice, 2009):

Officer Presence—In this situation, the officers simply resolve the problem without using any force at all. This is considered the best way to resolve a situation.

Verbalization—The officers give commands, starting with a calm, nonconfrontational approach, but slowly increasing in tone and volume.

Empty-Hand Control—In empty-hand force, the officers use bodily force to gain control over the situation. These usually start with "soft hands"—the use of open hands (including grabbing and holding) and continue to "hard hands" (punching and kicking) to gain control of a suspect.

Use-of-force continuum: The rough guidelines that determine how much force an officer should use in dealing with a suspect.

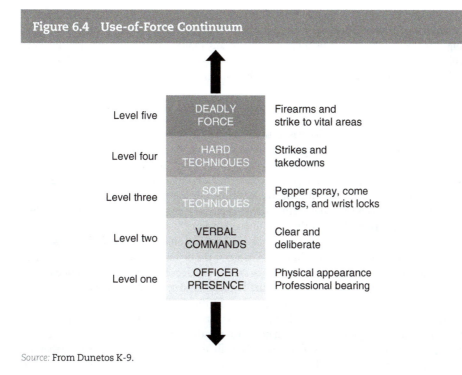

Figure 6.4   Use-of-Force Continuum

Level five	DEADLY FORCE	Firearms and strike to vital areas
Level four	HARD TECHNIQUES	Strikes and takedowns
Level three	SOFT TECHNIQUES	Pepper spray, come alongs, and wrist locks
Level two	VERBAL COMMANDS	Clear and deliberate
Level one	OFFICER PRESENCE	Physical appearance Professional bearing

Source: From Dunetos K-9.

Nonlethal Force—In these cases, officers use a wide variety of less-than-lethal methods to subdue a suspect. These can include chemical sprays like OC (oleoresin capsicum) or pepper spray, tear gas, or a conducted electrical weapon (sometimes known by the brand name Taser).

Lethal Force—Obviously, the most significant use of force is the use of lethal weapons. Most often this force is done with firearms, but other forms of lethal force can be used when necessary.

It is important to note two things about this continuum. First, the officer determines the appropriate amount of force to use, which in turn is shaped by the behavior of the suspect. If a suspect does not respond to a lower level of force (say, verbal commands), the officer is significantly more likely to ratchet up the amount of force she uses in the situation. This is known as the "one plus one" approach—an officer is supposed to go one level higher on the continuum than the suspect (The Police Policy Studies Council, n.d.). This means that, to a great degree, *the individual interacting with the officer has a good deal of control over how much force is used against her.* Second, the categories are not hard categories: "soft hands" can easily become lethal force if the officer uses a chokehold to strangle a suspect. Similarly, nonlethal force (such as a police baton) can easily be lethal if the blow strikes a suspect in the wrong place or with too much force. While the use-of-force continuum can be a useful guide for officers using force, in practice, once fists are flying, it is easy for the violence to escape the control of both the officer and the suspect.

Finally, it is key to remember that this continuum is a model for officers. In practice, officers sometimes violate the prescriptions of the continuum. While many officers are highly professional, there is no guarantee that in any individual case the officer will stick to this model for force when an encounter get sticky. As with many other aspects of policing, officers have a great deal of discretion in when and how they use force.

Legal Restrictions on Lethal Force

The use of force by police officers is restricted by the Constitution, and the Supreme Court has issued numerous rulings regarding the appropriate use of force in general and lethal force in particular. In the case of *Tennessee v. Garner* (1985), officers in Memphis shot and killed a man who they suspected had just committed a burglary. Edward Garner, the alleged burglar, was unarmed at the time of the shooting, but was nonetheless killed by officers while fleeing the scene. Garner's father sued the city, arguing that the Memphis police had violated his son's rights by shooting him unnecessarily.

Under Tennessee law at the time, the killing was considered lawful. Tennessee law stated that "if, after notice of the intention to arrest the defendant, he either flee or forcibly resist, the officer may use all the necessary means to effect the arrest." This reflected the traditional *fleeing felon rule*, which stipulated that an officer may do whatever is necessary to stop a felon who is fleeing from the police. In the *Garner* case, the court ruled that Tennessee law was unconstitutional and violated Garner's rights: "Where the suspect poses no immediate threat to the officer and no threat to others, the harm resulting from failing to apprehend him does not justify the use of deadly force to do so." The only time that the use of deadly force is allowed, according to the court, is "where the officer has probable cause to believe that the suspect poses a threat of serious physical harm, either to the officer or to others." These restrictions on police force remain in place, though as we will see in the next chapter, they are often very difficult to enforce in practice.

THE CONSTITUTION AND THE POLICE: THE FOURTH AMENDMENT

Learning Objective 6.3—Describe the different legal restrictions regarding police searches and arrests.

Policing is regulated by many different sets of rules, including state law, municipal codes, and departmental policies and regulations. The most important restrictions on policing activities come from the U.S. Constitution and the Bill of Rights. Since police officers are agents of the state, they are restricted by the Constitution just like all other parts of the government. While almost all the amendments in the Bill of Rights limit the powers of the criminal justice system, the most important of these for the purposes of policing is the Fourth Amendment. The Fourth Amendment restricts the right of government officials both to search and detain individuals, and since these are two of the police's central jobs, knowing it is essential for understanding how policing works. The Amendment reads in full:

Amendment IV

The right of the people to be secure in their persons, houses, papers, and effects, against unreasonable searches and seizures, shall not be violated, and no warrants shall issue, but upon probable cause, supported by oath or affirmation, and particularly describing the place to be searched, and the persons or things to be seized.

This amendment limits the rights of the police to either stop or search suspects in certain circumstances and restricts the ability of police officers to arrest a suspect. Effectively, it says that without a warrant, the police cannot search anybody or take something that belongs to her.

While the Fourth Amendment restricts the police, it does not give citizens a blanket protection from warrantless police searches. The courts have had to keep several competing factors in mind in interpreting the amendment. They must balance the needs of officers to catch lawbreakers and to keep themselves safe on the job with the right of individuals to be free from unreasonable government interference. Not only is understanding the limits of the Fourth Amendment important for understanding the way that the police work, but it can have very practical consequences for you: Many of you will have an encounter with the police where they suspect you of breaking the law (perhaps they've been called to break up your party, perhaps you've been pulled over by an officer, perhaps you've been stopped outside of a bar late at night), and the Fourth Amendment is your shield. It's important that you understand your rights, as there is a possibility that they may be seeking to trick you into consenting to a search that you don't have to consent to.

In most cases the police need to obtain a warrant to conduct a search. A search warrant is an official document signed by a judge that details the areas where the police can search and the times that the search can be conducted. To get the judge to sign a warrant, the police must show the judge that they have probable cause. Probable cause is usually defined as "a reasonable ground to suspect that a person has committed or is committing a crime or that a place contains specific items connected with a crime" (Garner, 2004, p. 1239). This means that the officers cannot simply harbor suspicions about the individual or have a hunch that the person is up to something. They must have clear reasons for suspecting that the individual has been involved in a specific crime and present these reasons to a judge, and if she concurs with the officer, she signs the warrant.

An important corollary to the Fourth Amendment is the *exclusionary rule*. This states that any evidence that the police discover because of an unlawful search cannot be used at trial *no matter how important that evidence is to the prosecutor's case*. Even further, under the legal principle called fruit of the poisonous tree, any further evidence that is gathered because of the tainted evidence cannot be used in court. Thus, if the police conduct an illegal search of a murder suspect (say, they enter her house without a warrant) and find a written confession along with clues that lead them to the murder weapon buried in a field a mile away, neither the clues nor the weapon can be used during a trial. The defense attorney would ask the judge *to suppress* this evidence at trial and thereby prevent the jury from learning about it. Effectively, any unlawfully obtained evidence is useless, and so the police have no incentive to violate the suspect's rights by being overaggressive in their searches.

Even though it may sound like an oxymoron, not everything that we normally think of as a "search" is considered such under the Fourth Amendment. There are many different circumstances where the police may stop you, pat you down, or look through your things without obtaining a warrant or without having probable cause. The Fourth Amendment only prescribes specific things ("persons, houses, papers, and effects") as being subject to protection from unreasonable searches and seizures. When we're not in a place or circumstances where we have a reasonable expectation of privacy, we do not necessarily have a constitutional protection from unreasonable searches. Our actions in public, for example, are not private, and so the police are not "searching" you when they see you act in public.

Probable cause: The standard of evidence needed to obtain a search warrant or search a car. Probable cause involves a reasonable belief based on evidence that a crime has occurred.

Fruit of the poisonous tree: The principle that, if evidence is gathered unlawfully, then any evidence that is gathered as a result of this evidence is not admissible in court.

Reasonable expectation of privacy: Places where individuals have a right to be protected from police searches.

Photo 6.1   A Sample Search Warrant

AO 106 (Rev. 04/10) Application for a Search Warrant

UNITED STATES DISTRICT COURT

for the

District of Alaska

In the Matter of the Search of	)
(Briefly describe the property to be searched or identify the person by name and address)	))
	)
In RE Application for a Warrant Under Rule 41 of the Federal Rules of Criminal Procedure to Disrupt the Kelihos Botnet	)))

Case No. 3:17-mj-00 135-DMS

APPLICATION FOR A SEARCH WARRANT

I, a federal law enforcement officer or an attorney for the government, request a search warrant and state under penalty of perjury that I have reason to believe that on the following person or property *(identify the person or describe the property to be searched and give its location):*

See Attachment A, incorporated here by reference.

located in the _____ District of _____ Alaska _____ , there is now concealed *(identify the person or describe the property to be seized):*

See Attachment B, incorporated here by reference.

The basis for the search under Fed. R. Crim. P. 41(c) is *(check one or more):*

☑ evidence of a crime;

☐ contraband, fruits of crime, or other items illegally possessed;

☐ property designed for use, intended for use, or used in committing a crime;

☐ a person to be arrested or a person who is unlawfully restrained.

The search is related to a violation of:

Code Section	*Offense Description*
18 USC §§ 1030, 1343, and 2511.	Fraud and related activity in connection with computers, wire fraud, and illegal wiretapping.

The application is based on these facts:

See attached Affidavit in Support of Search Warrant.

☑ Continued on the attached sheet.

☑ Delayed notice of __7__ days (give exact ending date if more than 30 days: _____) is requested under 18 U.S.C. § 3103a, the basis of which is set forth on the attached sheet.

Signature Redacted _____

_____
Applicant's signature

_____
Elliot Peterson, Special Agent, FBI
Printed name and title

Sworn to before me and signed in my presence.

Date: ___4/5/17___

/S/ DEBORAH M. SMITH
CHIEF U.S. MAGISTRATE JUDGE
SIGNATURE REDACTED
Judge's signature

City and state: __Anchorage, Alaska__

Hon. Deborah M. Smith, United States Magistrate Judge
Printed name and title

Source: U.S. Department of Justice.

Determining what is or is not a search and what are the exact requirements that police must meet for conducting kinds of searches is an immensely complicated and confusing area of the law.

There are a few types of searches where the police do not need a warrant to conduct a search but nonetheless need to have probable cause. The most significant of these are searches that take place while on the road. The police do not need a warrant to search your car—they only need probable cause. This principle, known as the automobile exception to the Fourth Amendment, allows the police to search a car if they have probable cause to believe a crime has been committed, but they need not have to get an actual warrant to conduct the search. This rule, known as the Carroll Doctrine (from the 1925 Supreme Court case *Carroll v. United States* that established it) exists because a suspect could easily drive off before the officer could get a warrant from a judge. If it turns out that the officer did not have probable cause, but thought she did, then it is likely that the evidence she obtained could not be used against you in court.

There are even fewer restrictions on the ability of the police to conduct what are known as special needs searches. In these searches, the typical Fourth Amendment rules don't apply, and officers can search anybody without probable cause. Special needs searches exist because there are a few places where there are good reasons to want to search everybody. At the airport, for example, TSA officials do not need a warrant to open your suitcase to see if you are carrying illegal or dangerous substances. You may be searched entering a prison. Similarly, when crossing the border into the United States from Canada or Mexico, officers may look through your car without warrants. Any evidence gathered during such searches is valid in court despite the lack of a warrant.

Another type of search that can be done without a warrant is a search that takes place when an officer makes an arrest. When arresting an individual, a police officer may search anything within the suspect's *immediate area*. Under a rule known as the *Chimel Rule*, named from the case *Chimel v. California* (1969), the police may search your body and anything that you could conceivably access (the so-called "grabbable area") when they arrest you. This rule exists because arresting an individual can be very dangerous for an officer, as the suspect could have weapons hidden nearby or have attempted to destroy any evidence nearby.

There are several other types of searches that do not require officers to obtain a warrant. If police officers see something criminal in plain view, even if it is on your property, then they may use it to arrest you. This can include things like a bong or open containers of alcohol inside a house if the door or windows are open. It could also include drugs or a gun that is in the seat of your car or on the floor of the car during a routine stop. Sometimes officers will use a flashlight to get a better view of what is inside the car so that more things are in "plain view." If the officer can see something without moving anything (moving things inside your car or in your house makes it a search), then that evidence is admissible. Similarly, if officers fly over an open field and see marijuana plants or other obviously illegal activity, even if they would not see this evidence if they were on the ground, the open fields doctrine allows this evidence to be admitted at trial or used as the basis for getting a search warrant.

Another obvious way that officers can gain access to evidence is through *consent*. If you allow officers to search your car/house/backpack, they can use any evidence that they find. This does not mean that they may turn the place upside down to search for evidence, but they may perform a quick protective sweep of the residence to make sure that they are safe and that there's nobody hiding somewhere to ambush them. They must ask for further permission to search the entirety of your home.

Automobile exception: The rule that officers do not need a warrant to search a car but only need probable cause.

Special needs searches: Searches that can be conducted without probable cause or a warrant. Include border searches and airport security searches.

Plain view doctrine: The principle that officers do not need a warrant to search what is in plain view.

Open fields doctrine: The principle that officers do not need a warrant to search what is in an open field.

Protective sweep: A search by the police in order to ensure their safety.

Technology and the Fourth Amendment

The modern world has many technologies that have increased the ability of the police to detect illegal activity—mostly drugs and explosives. Many of these innovations have challenged the protections envisioned by the authors of the Fourth Amendment, which, after all, was written for a world where horses were the primary mode of transportation and communication took place largely with a quill and paper. Over the last half century or so, courts have struggled to determine the limits of privacy in a world of cell phones, the internet, and high-tech surveillance technology. Each invention requires the courts to figure out exactly which searches are permissible and which are not, usually making their decisions on a case-by-case basis. This makes the court's interpretations of the Fourth Amendment one of the most interesting fields of constitutional law, one that is constantly evolving over time.

The simplest of these enhanced searches are canine searches. Officers often use "K-9 units" to find drugs in places where they could not be detectible by humans. While they are not using technology per se to discover drugs, dogs have a sense of smell that is thousands of times stronger than a human's and can pick up tiny traces of substances that no human could. They can sniff out marijuana, cocaine, and explosives even when they are carefully concealed. In 2004 in *Illinois v. Caballes*, the court ruled that a routine canine sniff was not a search under the Fourth Amendment and did not require probable cause. Later, in the 2015 case of *Rodriguez v. United States*, the Court ruled that although canine searches can be conducted, an officer cannot hold an individual simply to wait for a canine unit to arrive to the scene. If there happens to be a dog with the officer and it smells drugs, the officer can use this as the basis for a search, but the officer cannot call in a canine unit, make the suspect wait for it to arrive, and then have the dog sniff for drugs if the officer does not have other legal bases to hold the suspect.

The use of heat-detecting or thermal cameras has also been addressed by the Supreme Court. Previously, officers had mounted these cameras into helicopters and flown over neighborhoods to find the locations of "grow rooms"—marijuana growers use high powered lamps to grow the plants indoors away from the eyes of law enforcement. Then, they would use suspicious thermal readings as grounds for obtaining a warrant to search the house. In the 2001 case *Kyllo v. United States*, the Supreme Court ruled that even though the thermal camera did not go through the walls, but detected heat emanating from the exterior of the house, such searches violated an individual's privacy and therefore violated the Fourth Amendment.

Like pretty much everybody else, criminals carry cell phones. Also, like everybody else's phones, criminals' phones contain a great deal of useful information about the offenders' lives. In *Riley v. California* (2014), the court found that an officer could look at a phone if he found it while searching a suspect, but could not look through the data on the phone without a warrant:

> Digital data stored on a cell phone cannot itself be used as a weapon to harm an arresting officer or to effectuate the arrestee's escape. Law enforcement officers remain free to examine the physical aspects of a phone to ensure that it will not be used as a weapon—say, to determine whether there is a razor blade hidden between the phone and its case. Once an officer has secured a phone and eliminated any potential physical threats, however, data on the phone can endanger no one.

Given the importance of modern smart phones to our private lives, it makes sense that the court would restrict the ability of officers to search these devices during an arrest. Think of all the personal material, incriminating or otherwise, that somebody could find if she examined your phone.

These are only a small slice of the cases setting out the limits of police searches, and the courts will undoubtedly face novel questions as new technologies arise. Nobody can predict what new innovations will challenge law enforcement and force the police (and criminals) to adapt. One recent development in discussions of privacy and the Fourth Amendment is the use of remote searches to gather data from the computers of alleged criminals, as well as hacking e-mails, texts, and cell phone conversations. At this point, the courts have clearly struggled to determine what can be done in a search with no clear geographic boundaries—such as with the internet. While it's comforting to think, as some legal experts do, that we should stick to the original intent of the founding fathers, it's difficult to see what Alexander Hamilton would say about cell phones, GPS technology, drones, or remote searches over the internet.

Seizures

The Fourth Amendment not only regulates the right of the police to search you, your home, or your car, it also includes restrictions on the government's right to *seize* your property. "Seizure" has been interpreted by the courts to include not only your stuff, but also your body. When the police stop you, either through a traffic stop, a search, or an arrest, their activities are constrained by the restrictions set out in the Fourth Amendment.

There are different rules for seizures than for searches for several reasons. When the officer stops a person, the officer's safety may be jeopardized in a way that it isn't in a simple search. A police officer who suspects that an individual may be armed cannot afford to wait for probable cause to stop her. Second, arresting a suspect is limiting her freedom in a dramatic way, something that the courts are often very concerned about. The law should protect citizens from undue police interference, and holding a person unlawfully, or harming her without proper justification, are very serious forms of such interference. Thus, the Fourth Amendment's restriction on police seizures is among the most important parts of the Constitution.

On Halloween 1963, Officer Martin McFadden, a Cleveland Police detective, spotted two individuals, John Terry and Richard Chilton, standing on a street corner in downtown Cleveland. Though he could not provide an explanation as to why he was concerned about the men, he had spent many years in the area, and he declared, "When I looked over, they didn't look right to me at the time." In its opinion, the Supreme Court described the defendant's suspicious activities:

> He saw one of the men leave the other one and walk southwest on Huron Road, past some stores. The man paused for a moment and looked in a store window, then walked on a short distance, turned around and walked back toward the corner, pausing once again to look in the same store window. He rejoined his companion at the corner, and the two conferred briefly. Then the second man went through the same series of motions, strolling down Huron Road, looking in the same window, walking on a short distance, turning back, peering in the store window again, and returning to confer with the first man at the corner. The two men repeated this ritual alternately between five and six times apiece—in all, roughly a dozen trips.

Upon seeing this, McFadden stopped the two men, patted them down, and discovered that both were armed with handguns concealed underneath their jackets. The defendants complained that the officer did not have probable cause to search them, and therefore the weapons should not have been admitted at the trial.

In its opinion on the case, *Terry v. Ohio* (1968), the Supreme Court said that McFadden's stop was lawful, even though it was conducted without probable cause. Unlike an ordinary search, which does require probable cause, a stop on the street is not just about finding evidence that might be used to arrest an individual. Such stops can be necessary to protect both the officer herself as well as the public.

Reasonable suspicion: A lower standard of proof than probable cause. Requires a suspicion based on facts.

> We cannot blind ourselves to the need for law enforcement officers to protect themselves and other prospective victims of violence in situations where they may lack probable cause for an arrest. When an officer is justified in believing that the individual whose suspicious behavior he is investigating at close range is armed and presently dangerous to the officer or to others, it would appear to be clearly unreasonable to deny the officer the power to take necessary measures to determine whether the person is, in fact, carrying a weapon and to neutralize the threat of physical harm.

Terry stop: A brief detention where an officer stops and frisks a suspect. Requires a reasonable suspicion that an individual is involved in criminal activity.

Thus, officers do not need probable cause to stop and frisk an individual that they suspect might be armed. Rather, they may do so if they have a reasonable suspicion that the suspect is carrying a weapon, a much lower standard to meet. A reasonable suspicion must be based on "specific and articulable facts" rather than based on a mere hunch, but is still less than probable cause. Such a stop, now known as a Terry stop, is a common practice in modern policing, though critics believe that they are disproportionately used to target minorities.

WHERE DO I FIT IN?

HANDLING POLICE SEARCHES

The simplest piece of advice regarding police searches is to avoid engaging in any illegal activity and to obey all traffic rules while driving. Nevertheless, if you are a driver, you will probably be pulled over by the police or have the police knock on your front door some time in your life. You may even be pulled over while carrying something that could get you into trouble with the law or have the police come to your door with illegal substances around. Even if you are "driving clean," somebody else in your car may be carrying drugs or some other illegal substances and not have told you. While there is no need to be provocative toward the police, you have rights, and it is not wrong for you to assert these rights when confronting the police. Here are a few tips about how to protect yourself and your rights during this encounter and at the same time make sure that the officer does not make your life any more difficult than it needs to be. These are taken from a variety of sources, including the American Civil Liberties Union, a group of lawyers dedicated to protecting the constitutional rights of citizens.

1. Being polite and respectful is going to make your interaction with the police much easier.

   Always call the officer "sir"/ "ma'am" or "officer" when you are talking with her. Remain polite and calm and speak with a clear voice. If you are not going to answer a question from the officer, say, "I'm sorry officer, but I don't wish to answer that question." If you don't wish to allow the officer to search your car, say, "I'm sorry officer, I know you're just doing your job, but I don't consent to this search." Being obnoxious or aggressive to the officer is going to make the officer more antagonistic toward you and less willing to cut you a break should the need arise. If the officer asks you to do something and it's not obviously illegal, it's probably best to do it.

2. You don't have to consent to a search by the police.

   You have the right to refuse if the police ask if they may search your car. If they ask for permission to search your car, this means that they most likely don't have probable cause. Don't let them intimidate you into consenting and don't let them trick you into casually consenting. *Failing to consent to a search does not give officers probable cause for a search.* They may still look at what is in plain view, but they may not search further without either probable cause or your permission.

3. Be mindful of your movements.

   Keep your hands in clear view the whole time you are interacting with the officer. Do not make any sudden movements. If you're the driver, keep your hands on the steering wheel as much as possible. If it is night time, turn on the dome light so the officer can see your movements better. If you must get something out of your glove compartment, clearly explain to the officer what you are doing and get her permission to do it. "I am reaching into my glove compartment to get my identification. Is this okay officer?" This will prevent any terrible misunderstandings. Do not try to slyly hide something from the officer by subtly tossing it aside. Most likely the officer will see you do it and it will make your situation worse.

4. "Am I free to go?"

   Some officers will count on the fact that you are scared to leave when a police officer has stopped you. But there are some important limits on how long an officer may hold you without probable cause. The officer may not keep you for any longer than it takes for her to finish whatever she is doing. If she is just asking you a few questions, then when she's done, she should let you go. If she is writing a ticket, there is only a short period of time she can detain you, but she may be expecting you to be too intimidated to assert your right to leave. Asking if you are free to go establishes that the officer either has or doesn't have a reason to hold you.

5. During a routine stop, officers can insist that you get out of a car if they believe that there is a potential threat to their safety.

   If they ask you to get out of your car, do it slowly and carefully, keeping your hands clearly visible. Officers have a right to tell drivers and passengers to step out of a car.

6. You do not need to let officers into your house if you do not wish to.

   Unless they have a warrant or have a legal basis for entering your house, they cannot come inside without your permission. You may go outside to talk with the officers or you may open the door only slightly, but you need not let them in your house. If they smell marijuana or see young people drinking in your apartment, they will use that as grounds for a warrant.

Photo 6.2   A Sample Arrest Warrant

AO 442 (Rev. 11/11) Arrest Warrant

UNITED STATES DISTRICT COURT

for the

_____

United States of America

v.

)
)
)
)
)
)

Case No.

_____
Defendant

ARREST WARRANT

To: Any authorized law enforcement officer

　　　　YOU ARE COMMANDED to arrest and bring before a United States magistrate judge without unnecessary delay
(name of person to be arrested) _____ ,
who is accused of an offense or violation based on the following document filed with the court:

❑ Indictment   ❑ Superseding Indictment   ❑ Information   ❑ Superseding Information   ❑ Complaint

❑ Probation Violation Petition   ❑ Supervised Release Violation Petition   ❑ Violation Notice   ❑ Order of the Court

This offense is briefly described as follows:

Date: _____

City and state: _____

_____
Issuing officer's signature

_____
Printed name and title

Return
This warrant was received on *(date)* _____ , and the person was arrested on *(date)* _____ at *(city and state)* _____ .
Date: _____   _____ *Arresting officer's signature*   _____ *Printed name and title*

Source: U.S. Courts.

Arrests

Stopping a person is a rather low-level form of seizure, as it usually has no long-term consequences. If there are no problems, the person can soon leave. A more serious form of seizure takes place when officers arrest a suspect, that is, when she is placed in police custody. An arrest is not the same as being charged with an offense—this happens later after the prosecutor has become involved in the process. At this point, the officer is simply placing the individual under her authority and preventing her from leaving at will. The police can only hold a suspect for a short time (24–72 hours) without charging her with an offense.

There are several ways for officers to make an arrest. The simplest grounds for arrest is when the officer herself witnessed the suspect commit a crime. If this happens, the officer can immediately arrest the individual without providing any further justification. The second basis for arresting a suspect is if the officer has probable cause for arresting her: if the defendant matches the description of a suspect in a crime that was recently reported, for example. Finally, an officer may arrest an individual if she is executing an *arrest warrant*. An arrest warrant is a document signed by a judge that authorizes officers to take a person into custody. These can specify the time that the individual is to be arrested and sometimes include the bail that is to be asked of the defendant.

Once an individual is arrested by an officer, the suspect is read her rights before she is questioned. This Miranda Warning (taken from the 1966 case *Miranda v. Arizona*; see Figure 6.5) informs suspects of their basic rights after arrest, including the right to remain silent and the right to an attorney (including the right to an attorney, even if they cannot afford one on their own). This warning is essential, because persons charged with a crime can claim that any confessions that they made after arrest were invalid if they were not informed of their rights.

After arrest, the suspect is taken to the police station, where she is *booked*. Booking involves gathering information about the suspect, including fingerprints, a mug shot, and a full body search to make sure that the suspect does not have any contraband on her.

Miranda Warning: The rights that are read to individuals when they are arrested.

Figure 6.5   Miranda Warning

1. YOU HAVE THE RIGHT TO REMAIN SILENT.
2. Anything you say can and will be used against you in a court of law.
3. You have the right to talk to a lawyer and have him present with you while you are being questioned.
4. If you cannot afford to hire a lawyer, one will be appointed to represent you before any questioning if you wish.
5. You can answer at any time to exercise these rights and not answer any questions or make any statements.

Waiver

Do you understand each of these rights I have explained to you? Having these rights in mind, do you wish to talk to us now?

Source: MirandaWarning.org.

Usually, suspects are given a free phone call that they can use to contact a family member, loved one, or their attorney before they are taken to their cell. The suspect is then placed into a holding cell or local jail to await her initial appearance in court and for the court to determine bail.

Most states allow for nonofficers to carry out a so-called citizen's arrest under some circumstances if they believe an individual has committed an offense. For example, the so-called shopkeepers' privilege allows for stores to detain suspected thieves against their will. While this right is recognized in the United States, a civilian who seeks to arrest another civilian under a false pretext or based on a mistaken identity may face serious legal consequences. Be careful: *You make a citizen's arrest at your own risk!*

Shopkeepers' privilege: A common law legal principle that allows store owners to detain individuals suspected of shoplifting.

WHERE DO I FIT IN?

GETTING ARRESTED

If you are arrested, there are a few things to keep in mind. Much of this is common sense, but often when the police arrive on the scene, adrenaline is high, and some people aren't thinking rationally. This can escalate things and make it very dangerous for you and for the officers. Often, suspects are intoxicated when they are arrested, which only makes it more difficult to remain calm and collected when the officer pulls out the cuffs. Here are a few tips for getting through your arrest:

1. Remain polite.

   Even though you're mad and may feel bullied by the officers, being hostile toward the police will not improve your situation—it will only make things worse for you. You're most likely going to jail regardless, and the only possibility you have of not going to jail and being let off with a warning will happen if you are polite to the officer. Call the officer "sir," "ma'am," or more neutrally, "officer," and be polite, which is not the same as answering all their questions (see #3).

2. Don't resist the officers.

   Nothing good will come from this. As we've already seen, the officer's use of force is usually a response to the suspect's conduct. If you struggle against the officers, you are likely to get treated more roughly. Again, you're going to jail regardless of how much you struggle, so there's no point in making it worse for yourself simply because you're angry. Resisting arrest is often a misdemeanor and will make your situation worse. Assaulting a police officer lawfully carrying out her duties is a felony.

3. Shut up.

   Often suspects believe that their arrest is simply a misunderstanding and that they can convince officers to let them go. Usually they are wrong. Particularly if you are charged with a serious offense, it is far more likely that you will give the police and prosecutors information that they will use against you than you will be able to talk yourself free. Statements, even casual comments, can be used against you later, so beyond basic identifying information, it's best to say as little as possible. (But remember to say it politely!) You do not have to answer questions the police ask you.

4. Contact an attorney.

   As we will see in the next chapter, your attorney (particularly if you are paying her) is most likely the only person in this process who is in your corner. Before you even consider talking to the police, get a lawyer, consult with her, and have her present whenever you are questioned by the

POLICE DISCRETION

Learning Objective 6.4—List the various factors that impact police discretion.

One essential aspect of policing that is often left unmentioned in criminal justice textbooks is police discretion. *Police discretion* refers to the freedom that officers have in their interactions with the public. They can choose to be harsh, or they can choose to be lenient. When pulling over a driver who has broken traffic laws, an officer may choose to let the driver off with a warning, she may decide to give the driver a ticket, or she may choose to escalate the encounter further, treating the individual more harshly. This power is in the hands of the individual officer and is largely unregulated by the police department. This means that at the point of contact between officers and the public, a great deal of power is in the hands of the individual officer.

Discretion is necessary for policing because of the simple fact that officers cannot enforce every law all the time. A trained officer can find infractions virtually anywhere, and she must choose which infractions matter and which ones are best left ignored or handled informally. Moreover, in particularly complicated situations, arresting an individual may do more harm than good. The criminal justice system would be clogged with cases and overwhelmed if officers chose to pursue every legal infraction fully. In addition, officers on the ground are best suited to making an informed judgment about how to deal with a situation—commanders often are far away and do not have sufficient information to make a decision. Giving officers a free hand in how they handle suspected lawbreakers, particularly people who commit less serious offenses, can save everybody a great deal of trouble.

Given that officers have this sort of discretion and use it every day, what sort of factors shape how officers respond to a situation? What are the factors that make officers more likely to treat an individual harshly, and what factors are most likely to make an officer be lenient? Obviously, serious offenses are far more likely to lead to arrests—no officer is going to let a person suspected of murder get away with a warning. Beyond this, one of the most significant factors is, unsurprisingly, the attitude of the individuals toward the officer. If suspects are rude or disrespectful toward the officer, they are more likely to be treated harshly, while deference and respect is likely to result in more lenient treatment (Black, 1970; Schafer & Mastrofski, 2005). Another significant factor is the wishes of other people involved in the situation—if a victim wishes to see the individual arrested, the officers are more likely to arrest the suspect. A study of drunk driving stops showed that "officers in the two larger, bureaucratized departments were much less likely to arrest than those in the smaller departments" (Mastrofski, Ritti, & Hoffmaster, 1987). The decision officers make in the moment can be shaped by a great number of factors, some of which are under the control of the suspect herself, but many of which are not.

One particularly difficult challenge for police officers is handling domestic violence. One of the most common issues that officers must deal with on the job is responding to a conflict between partners or other family relations. These are often very difficult situations for officers to navigate for a variety of reasons. While the weaker individual may want her partner to stop threatening or harming her, she may not want him arrested and can even turn on the police when they threaten to do so. She might depend on her spouse for financial support that would be lost if he were in jail, or she might not want to see her child in prison, even if he is hurting her. She may fear retaliation when her partner is released from jail, particularly if prosecutors elect not to press charges against the suspect. All of this means that officers face a very delicate task when dealing with domestic situations and must use their discretion carefully.

The **Minneapolis Domestic Violence Experiment** was an attempt to understand the effects that different approaches to police discretion had in domestic violence situations (Sherman & Berk, 1984). From 1981 to 1982, officers in Minneapolis tried three different approaches to handling domestic violence calls, based on a random assignment. Some of the suspects were arrested, some were sent away from the scene for eight hours to cool down, and others were given counseling by the officers. The results showed that arresting a suspected abuser was the most effective of the three ways for preventing future violence. As a result, many states began a mandatory arrest policy in domestic violence cases, but this too can create problems, as battered spouses may hesitate to call the police if they fear that their partner will go to prison if they call. Ironically, then, restricting the discretion in domestic violence cases forces victims of this kind of violence to use their own discretion in deciding whether to call the police.

Another problem surrounding police discretion is *favoritism*. Giving officers wide discretion presents them with the temptation to use it in ways that we might not find appropriate. Anecdotal evidence shows that some officers, particularly male officers, show a predisposition to be lenient toward young, attractive women who they pull over, particularly if they respond emotionally to the stop (though there is no hard evidence for this.) Some drivers put stickers on their cars that declare that they support police organizations in the hope that officers will give them a break if they are pulled over. Many small businesses provide a discount to officers or give them free food in the hope that they will receive preferential treatment by officers should problems arise. While we may not find these uses of discretion to be corrupt, they can certainly damage the general public's perception of the police as fair-minded agents of the law.

Minneapolis Domestic Violence Experiment:
A study that investigated the impact of police discretion on domestic violence.

Discretion cannot be taken out of policing; it is an essential part of how officers function and allows them to do their job more effectively. Even when it is restricted by police departments, there is probably no way to fully prevent officers from fudging the books—they can hide the fact that they ever showed up to a scene or conceal the exact nature of what happened in a case. Regulating police officers' behavior to prevent the use of discretion is probably impossible and is probably undesirable. Nonetheless, when officers use discretion, and how they use it, is fascinating and reveals a lot about how we use the police to regulate and control people in the modern world.

CIVIL FORFEITURE

Learning Objective 6.5—Describe the laws governing the confiscation of property by law enforcement.

One of the most controversial aspects of modern policing is the practice of civil asset forfeiture. Civil forfeiture allows officers to confiscate property that they suspect was involved in criminal activity, such as vehicles used for transporting drugs or cash profits from drug transactions. They can do this without charging any person with a crime. (Criminal forfeiture occurs when material is seized by the police as part of an arrest.) The police forces then either sell or keep the property and use a portion of it to fund their operations, often without having to prove in court that the goods were associated with any explicit crime. Many critics have charged the police with abusing civil forfeiture to steal money from innocent people, while some defenders have claimed that it is an essential practice for removing some of the rewards of criminal activity (ACLU, n.d.; Ford, 2017; Snead, 2014).

This controversial practice dates back to medieval England but was first used extensively during Prohibition, when police departments confiscated and auctioned bootlegging equipment and vehicles used to smuggle illegal liquor into the United States (Mellor, 2011; Mihm, 2017). The material was often confiscated after the criminals fled the scene, meaning that nobody claimed it, but the materials were nonetheless implicated in illegal activities. It was modernized during the war on drugs and in the Controlled Substances Act in 1970, which allowed government officers to seize property if they suspected that it was related to drug trafficking. The only way for the individual to have her assets returned to her is to go to court and fight for them. Effectively, owners must prove that the confiscated goods were gained legally to get them back. This can be a very expensive proposition, and, in many states, especially so for drivers who are just passing through the territory and are unlikely to come back or to be able to afford the legal expertise required to have their materials returned (Friedersdorf, 2015; Sallah, O'Harrow, Rich, & Silverman, 2014). Those whose goods are confiscated must travel back to the jurisdiction where the goods were taken and prove that they have a legal right to possess them, an effort that would often cost more than the confiscated goods are worth.

When it is used against drug traffickers, civil forfeiture is a powerful tool for fighting crime, depriving the traffickers of vital funding and resources—after all, what drug trafficker is going to come forward to claim her goods in a court of law? Some departments have abused the practice and taken large amounts of cash or other valuable goods from completely innocent people, or people whose offenses are minor. To use one example, William Barton Davis and John Newmerzhycky were driving through Iowa on their way to gamble in Las Vegas. They reported being "stalked" by a police officer, and when they were

Civil forfeiture: The police practice of seizing goods that they believe are associated with criminal activity.

pulled over, officers stalled and delayed the two as they tried to leave until a canine unit showed up and gave the officers probable cause to search the car. In the trunk of the car, police found a marijuana grinder and $100,000 that the two had planned to use to gamble. The officers confiscated the money and let them go with a minor citation. In another case, a man in Washington, D.C., had $11,000, 5 years of savings, taken on the grounds that the police smelled marijuana in his bag. He had booked a one way ticket on Amtrak, and had no documentation for his money—none of which is crime (Ingraham, 2015).

As these and similar abuses of civil forfeiture have come before the public, several politicians on both the right and left ends of the political spectrum have sought to curb the power of the police to seize suspected drug assets, but at present seizure remains a common way to deal with drug traffickers as well as a way for police departments to boost their own revenue. The last attorney general, Jeff Sessions, has spoken highly of the practice, calling it a "key tool that helps law enforcement defund organized crime, take back ill-gotten gains, and prevent new crimes from being committed" (Ford, 2017). In early 2019, the Supreme Court found some uses of civil forfeiture to be unconstitutional (*Timbs v. Indiana*, 2019), but as of this writing it is not clear whether the practice will be curtailed by the recent ruling.

CHAPTER SUMMARY

This chapter has been a catchall chapter dealing with various aspects of modern policing. Policing is a complicated activity with a lot of dimensions to it: Police are the "muscle" of government, enforcing the laws that the government passes, but they're also social workers, crisis responders, and marriage counselors, and they perform a million other jobs. For an officer on the street, every day is different, and every day brings new challenges and new frustrations. The job is diverse and complex, which is probably why so many people find it so appealing. Undoubtedly, your university's criminal justice program has at least one course that focuses exclusively on policing, and if you are interested in the subject, this course is well worth your time. Many police departments have ride-along programs that allow civilians to spend a day traveling with officers to get a taste of what it's like being an officer, which is a great way to learn more about life in law enforcement.

In the next chapter, we will look more closely at some of the darker sides of law enforcement. While most police officers are conscientious professionals, seeking to do the best job that they can, the unique powers, the unique pressures, and the unique temptations of police work create opportunities for some officers to stray from the principles of good policing. In the next chapter, we will look at some of the ways that policing can go wrong, ways that police officers can become dangerous or outright harmful to the people that they are supposed to protect.

REVIEW/DISCUSSION QUESTIONS

1. Have you ever been arrested or searched by the police? What was the experience like?

2. How much discretion should officers have on the job? What are the dangers of too much and too little discretion?

3. Should law enforcement be able to confiscate property that they believe is related to criminal activity without charging anybody with a crime? Why or why not?

KEY TERMS

Automobile exception 153
Civil forfeiture 163
Fruit of the poisonous tree 151
Minneapolis Domestic Violence
    Experiment 162
Miranda Warning 159

Open fields doctrine 153
Plain view doctrine 153
Probable cause 151
Protective sweep 153
Reasonable expectation of
    privacy 151

Reasonable suspicion 156
Shopkeepers' privilege 160
Special needs searches 153
Terry stop 156
Use-of-force continuum 148

$SAGE edge™

Get the tools you need to sharpen your study skills. SAGE edge offers a robust online environment featuring an impressive array of free tools and resources.

Access practice quizzes, eFlashcards, video, and multimedia at edge.sagepub.com/fichtelberg

Sarah Yeh

Police officers are often unwilling to criticize other officers. Where does this loyalty come from? Is it helpful?

CHAPTER SEVEN

POLICE DEVIANCE

Police officers are human beings, and, as with all human beings, there are good ones and bad ones, honest ones and corrupt ones. But the power and authority that the police have over the rest of us makes police misconduct unique and uniquely dangerous. Sometimes they misbehave for what they believe are good reasons, and sometimes they misbehave for selfish reasons. Often it's somewhere in between the two. Sometimes they are responding to pressure from other officers, sometimes they are acting on their own initiative, and sometimes they are simply caught up in much bigger social forces that are beyond everyone's control. But because they have power over us and because most Americans place a great deal of trust in the police, the misconduct of officers can be a very big problem—if a society is rotten, it is often the police that are the core of the problem.

In this chapter, we will discuss **police deviance**. We will look at all forms of police misbehavior or police misconduct that are committed by officers in their professional capacity. If a police officer steps out of line in her private life, this is certainly a form of deviance, but it is not police deviance—the abuse of the unique powers of an officer are what we will discuss here. Police deviance includes *corruption*, that is, the abuse of police authority for personal gain—usually for money but sometimes for favors, including sexual favors. But police deviance can also involve things like *excessive force*, *police brutality*, and *racial profiling*—misconduct that is committed because officers believe that it is necessary for them to do their jobs, rather than being committed out of self-interest. While corruption and excessive force are very different forms of deviance in many respects, in each case, the police officers violate their own codes of professional behavior, and so they become a danger to the people that they have sworn to protect.

We will first look at the overall problem of police deviance, that is, we will examine why police deviance presents unique problems for society. Then we will turn to the various forms of misconduct: First we will look at the problems that result from what I will call *overenthusiastic* policing. By this I mean crime-fighting efforts by police officers that cross the line of legitimate police conduct. Then we will turn to outright corruption, examining its forms and causes. Then, we will look at the causes of these behaviors and examine some of the ways that have been used to control police deviance.

Through all this discussion, a few things should be kept in mind. First, while American policing has its problems, it is a remarkably effective institution and a remarkably ethical one, particularly when compared with the police in many other countries. While there are *plenty* of problems with American policing, the most surprising thing is that it is not very corrupt, at least when compared to other police forces around the world. In some countries, policing is considered a for-profit job—it is expected that officers are to

Police deviance: Misconduct or misbehavior on the part of officers while operating in their official capacity.

167

be bribed, and police corruption and government corruption more generally is considered a fact of ordinary life. Also, in many other countries, particularly in dictatorships, the loyalty of the police is first and foremost to the state, not to the people, and officers can show remarkably little regard for the well-being of the public. Modern American policing is more effective and ethical now than at any other time in our history. When placed on a scale and weighed against other police forces, the modern American police force is among the best in the world, and among the best of all time. This does not mean its problems are acceptable—it simply means that they should be seen in their appropriate context.

POLICE DEVIANCE IN CONTEXT

Learning Objective 7.1—Explain why the topic of police deviance is important to the study of American policing.

The reality is that society needs some type of agency to maintain order, and this requires that officers have the authority to use force over those who will not obey the law. Once they have control over us, it is very tempting for police officers to abuse this power, because it's extremely difficult for anybody to stop them. There are no real political or social counterweights to the police with the authority to use force, so if officers "go rogue," there is little that can be done to stop them. While armed citizens might be able to stop an unjust police force, this is extremely unlikely, as officers are highly trained and heavily armed. Even if such a group did stop the police from hurting the public, this new group would simply replace the police and the same problem would return. All societies need force to keep the public in check, but this is extremely difficult to do without inviting those who wield force to abuse it.

Many officers look at their job in "us versus them" terms—seeing nonofficers as outsiders who cannot understand the pressures and demands of police work. After dealing with countless people who are dishonest or disrespectful toward them, officers can become cynical about the public. Officers must often interact with the public in situations where nobody is happy to see them and where people are belligerent and rude to them, causing officers to develop strong bonds with each other and show hostility to nonofficers. This has led to the creation of what some officers call a blue wall of silence—a strongly held belief among officers that policing problems are not to be shared with outsiders (that is, non–police officers), and any officer who openly discusses police problems is not to be trusted. This wall makes it extremely difficult for outsiders, that is politicians and those who study the police, to get a good grasp on the nature and scope of police deviance, much less find ways to effectively reform police departments.

Many people are reluctant to second-guess the behavior of officers and are inclined to take their side when they are under attack. Most of us want to believe in the police and think that they are usually doing the right thing—even when officers are clearly involved in wrongdoing. This is particularly the case when those complaining about police behavior are "others," that is, people who do not look or act like us. If those complaining about the police appear different and the police officers look like us, we're naturally inclined to be biased in favor of the police. Psychologists describe this difference in how we evaluate others as *ingroup* versus *outgroup* attitudes (Hewstone, Rubin, & Willis, 2002). We are far more likely to be sympathetic to people who look like us (our ingroup) and skeptical about

Blue wall of silence: The informal code among police officers that prevents them from reporting on abusive behaviors from their fellow officers.

people who look different (the outgroup), which, in turn, shapes how we look at many policing problems. A white person is more likely to trust the police, particularly when those complaining about the police are not white and the officers that are the subject of the complaints are white (Morin & Stepler, 2016). Even in the face of numerous high-profile police shootings, overall support for police officers has not changed from historical averages of about 57% (Norman, 2017). For whites, the percentage is 61%, for blacks it is 30%. When largely white groups chant "Blue Lives Matter" in response to the #blacklivesmatter movement, they are reflecting these attitudes.

All of this means that police deviance is different from other kind of deviance we encounter, such as acts of deviance committed by crooks or corrupt politicians. When police officers break the rules, it takes place in very different circumstances than when other types of people misbehave. The police have a form of power that ordinary people do not, and they have the respect and good will of much of the public. Many of these issues have come to the public's attention over the last few years with many high-profile cases of police violence. In Ferguson, Missouri; Staten Island, New York; and Baltimore, Maryland, unarmed black men have been killed by (usually white) police officers, and some of these incidents have been caught on video camera by bystanders. This has led to protests and even riots from angry citizens. On the other hand, many other citizens have shown unwavering support for officers, closely examining the evidence for any hint that that officer's actions may have been the right ones. There have been reports of work stoppages by police departments who have refused to accept criticism from the public and from politicians (Celona, Golding, & Cohen, 2014). Many voters supported Donald Trump because of his vocal support of police officers, which they compared favorably to President Obama's mild criticisms of police violence. Like many conflicts in American society, the debate over police violence is both racialized and political—those who support the police in Ferguson, New York, and Baltimore tend to be white and conservative; those who are protesting police violence tend to be black and/or liberal.

In short, American society is having a difficult argument about the role of the police in society. This argument reflects deeper social divides and has been brought on largely by responses to overaggressive policing and excessive violence on the part of officers. As we saw when we looked at the history of policing in Chapter 5, the police have always played a role in racial and economic conflicts in the United States, so it should be unsurprising that on the subject of police deviance, those on the bottom of the social ladder have it worst. When the police step out of line, it is usually those already on the bottom who feel it most.

OVERENTHUSIASTIC POLICING

Learning Objective 7.2—Describe the major forms of excessive force and racial profiling.

A lot of police deviance does not stem from selfish motives. Rather, sometimes police officers break the rules because they believe that doing so is necessary to protect the public and to do their job more effectively. In these situations, officers believe that their professional duty requires that they break the laws that they are supposed to uphold, and that at times they must consider the greater good rather than the rights of the defendant. There is a great deal of pressure on the police to stop criminals and protect the public, and there is a certain amount of public support for using aggressive tactics against suspected criminals. Television often lauds officers who are not afraid to get their hands dirty if it helps save innocent lives. Shows like *24* show heroic officials resorting to torture to save lives, and the detective who will break the rules to catch criminals is a staple of TV dramas. The police scholar Carl Klockars describes this as the **Dirty Harry problem** (named after the famous movie detective "Dirty" Harry Callahan who, in a string of movies in the 1970s and 1980s, broke laws to catch criminals). As Klockars asks, "When and to what extent does the morally good warrant or justify [the use of] ethically, politically, or legally dangerous means to its achievement?" (Klockars, 1980, p. 35). Overenthusiastic policing is simply policing that goes beyond the bounds of appropriate law enforcement to achieve the goals of law enforcement.

The two examples of overenthusiastic policing we will discuss here are *excessive force* and *racial profiling*.

Excessive Force

One common form of overenthusiastic policing is the use of **excessive force** against suspects. Either officers use force when there is no need to do so, or in other cases they use more force than is necessary—they go too high or too fast on the use of force continuum discussed in the last chapter. Most often, the excessive force used is nonlethal, such as physical pushing and punching, the use of batons, et cetera. While nonlethal force may be better than guns, supposedly nonlethal force can cause death, and even nonlethal force when used unnecessarily is a violation of an individual's civil rights. Violence can profoundly damage a person, not only causing physical harm, but also leading to long-lasting psychological and emotional damage.

One aspect of excessive force is the phenomenon of **net widening**. Officers sometimes use nonlethal weapons (pepper spray, tear gas, etc.), when there may not be cause to do so, simply because it's a relatively easy way to subdue a suspect. This fact that technologies like pepper spray have made it easier for the police to avoid using their fists or their firearms to handle dangerous situations has not led to a decrease in the use of force, but rather has led to an overall increase in it—only the force being used is often nonlethal. Officers sometimes conclude that it is easier and safer to subdue a suspect who is not cooperative and potentially hostile than to risk escalating the situation to the point where it could get out of hand (Amnesty International, 2004). Handling a person who is uncooperative is difficult and frustrating, and could potentially lead to a dangerous confrontation. It's sometimes better and safer (for the officer) to simply subdue the suspect with a Taser or pepper spray and sort out the situation afterward. The relative safety of nonlethal weapons makes them a tempting tool for officers to use in situations where it may not be necessary.

Of course, the most serious form of excessive force is the unnecessary use of lethal force. Officers do sometimes kill suspects when it is unnecessary. Sometimes, this is simply a result of bad judgment on the part of the officer—either a rookie officer is scared and escalates the violence unnecessarily, or an officer uses too much force without knowingly doing so. Officers must make split-second decisions based on the evaluation of a threat under high pressure. Other times officers use force against an individual and do not intend to kill their victim. The line between lethal and nonlethal force can be fuzzy when officers use controversial tactics like a chokehold, which essentially involves using a forearm across a suspect's windpipe to prevent the flow of oxygen and thereby subdues the suspect. Many police departments ban the use of the chokeholds because they are considered too dangerous. In these cases, nonlethal force gets out of hand, and a suspect is killed as a result.

Dirty Harry problem: The problem that the public often wants police officers to catch criminals and often approves of illegal means for doing so.

Excessive force: The use of too much force by the police or the use of force unnecessarily.

Net widening: In this context, the use of nonlethal force by officers in situations where they may not otherwise resort to force.

In the adrenaline-soaked context of physical conflicts with the public, it is not surprising that unnecessary lethal violence occurs, even when the officers are highly trained. This, of course, does not mean that it is acceptable.

Two high-profile examples of police killings help illustrate how excessive force can happen. One example of supposedly nonlethal force suddenly turning lethal was in Staten Island, New York, on July 17, 2014, where Officer Daniel Pantaleo killed Eric Garner, 43, by holding him in a chokehold. The killing was captured on video by a bystander. Police officers who had been patrolling the area stopped Garner and accused him of illegally selling cigarettes. Garner angrily rejected the officers' charges against him, declaring, "I didn't do shit." Officers moved in on Garner who stated, "Don't touch me please." Officer Pantaleo applied a chokehold on Garner, placing his forearm across the victim's throat, and pulled him down to the ground. Officer Pantaleo continued to choke Garner until the other officers handcuffed him. As he was being choked, Garner repeatedly stated, "I can't breathe! I can't breathe!" While Officer Pantaleo claimed that he never used a chokehold against Garner, the New York City Medical Examiner's Office declared that Garner died from "compression of neck (chokehold), compression of chest and prone positioning during physical restraint by police."

On August 9, 2014, Michael Brown, an 18-year-old black teenager, was shot and killed by Officer Darren Wilson in the city of Ferguson Missouri, just outside of St. Louis. Wilson, a 28-year-old city police officer who had been working in law enforcement for five years was responding to a call that a suspect wearing a red Cardinals hat and a white shirt had stolen cigarettes from a nearby liquor store. The altercation was short, and the details are disputed. According to reports, Brown, who was unarmed at the time, reached into Officer Wilson's police SUV, and the two struggled over Wilson's gun. Wilson fired two shots, slightly wounding Brown, who reportedly then ran from Wilson. At this point, Wilson claims that Brown turned and charged him, at which point Wilson fired 10 shots at Brown, killing him. Some witnesses claim Brown didn't move toward Wilson; others that he had his hands up. The coroner's report largely backs up Wilson's claims about Brown's behavior. After a grand jury refused to indict Wilson for shooting Brown, several days of riots began in Ferguson, which in turn led to what many people charged was an excessive police response. The Justice Department later issued a scathing report on the widespread civil rights violations of the Ferguson Police Department that ultimately led to the riots, though it largely absolved Wilson in the killing.

These, of course, are only a two of the recent police killings that have been in the public eye over the last few years. Other police homicides in South Carolina, Ohio, and Texas have brought to light the large number of unjustified killings of civilians by officers that occur in the United States. The fact that these victims have all been black men and they all have been unarmed at the time that they were killed has not gone unnoticed by the public. The riots have also brought to light the excessively militarized police forces that are operating in much of America that were discussed in Chapter 5.

Racial Profiling

Another example of overenthusiastic policing is the targeting of individuals for stops, searches, or even arrests based on their race, religion, or ethnicity. Often profiling takes place when young black men are targeted as suspected criminals, but racial profiling can occur in many other circumstances. Many Arabs and Muslims (and those who "look Muslim" with darker skin and beards) report being excessively stopped and searched, especially

Racial profiling: Targeting an individual for searches or arrests based on her race.

SOME STATISTICS...

Excessive Force

Police encounters have a lot of grey areas in them, and it is often hard to sift out which uses of force are truly excessive. Along with this, officers are often unwilling to snitch on each other, and victims are sometimes not believed. Police departments are not eager to make this information public, and some states pass laws that make it unlawful to share data regarding police misconduct (Fischer-Baum, 2014; Stock, Carrol, Nious, & Pham, 2014). This means that we don't have a very clear view about how much excessive force is used by the police.

One of the few sources for comprehensive data on police misconduct is the National Police Misconduct Reporting Project (NPMRP), a research program conducted by the conservative-leaning Cato Institute. In their 2010 report, they found that excessive force was the most frequent form of police misconduct (see Figure 7.1).

Another useful set of statistics regarding police criminality has been compiled by a pair of criminologists at Bowling Green State University in Ohio. Their database, "The Henry A. Wallace Police Crime Database," can be found at https://policecrime.bgsu.edu/. It allows for searches based on location and the type of crime committed by the officer. It also includes a helpful map of where police crime is committed most frequently. Figure 7.2 is a map of crimes committed by officers around the country (based on crimes per 100,000 residents).

The most populated states clearly have the highest number of cases of police misconduct. While this information is very informative, the problems with gathering data regarding police misconduct means that these conclusions can only be partial.

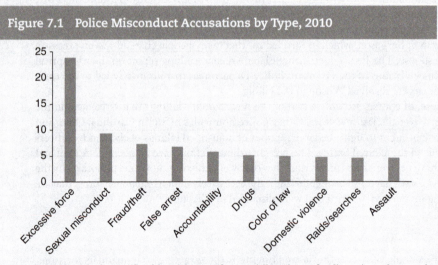

Figure 7.1 Police Misconduct Accusations by Type, 2010

Sources: FiveThirtyEight, https://fivethirtyeight.com/features/allegations-of-police-misconduct-rarely-result-in-charges/. Data from the National Police Misconduct Reporting Project.

Note: 6,613 officers were accused of misconduct in 2010. Latest data available.

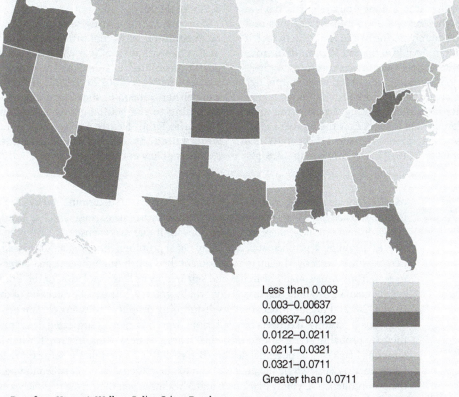

Figure 7.2   Heat Map of Crimes Committed by Nonfederal Sworn Law Enforcement Officers, 2005–2013

Less than 0.003
0.003–0.00637
0.00637–0.0122
0.0122–0.0211
0.0211–0.0321
0.0321–0.0711
Greater than 0.0711

Source: Data from Henry A. Wallace Police Crime Database.

when flying (Baker, 2002; Bennett, 2006). Police officers often possess the same prejudices as the rest of society and are as inclined to assume that young black men are up to no good as most of the rest of America is. The only difference is that most of us have little power to act on these prejudices in the way that police officers do.

It might seem to make sense to target groups that are considered likely to engage in criminal activity. If most people who conduct terrorist attacks at airports are Muslims, it seems logical to subject such people to extra scrutiny, particularly in sensitive places like airports or federal buildings. It would be a waste of resources to treat an 80-year-old grandmother as a potential drug trafficker while ignoring a group of young men hanging out on a corner dressed and acting like they are in a street gang. The police evaluate suspects

One of the most common myths about policing is that it is a dangerous job. It is not—at least when compared to many other jobs that are commonly performed in America. In fact, it doesn't make it into the top 10 most dangerous professions according to most rankings. Agricultural jobs (farming), construction work (roofing), and transportation work (driving) have higher fatality rates than policing. Probably the most dangerous field to work in is the lumber industry, where accidents claimed 135.9 per 100,000 workers in 2016. This compares to 14.6 per 100,000 workers for the police (Stebbins, Comen, & Stockdale, 2018).

Further, while getting shot is one of the most common ways that officers can die, it is just as likely that an officer will die in a transportation-related accident as be killed by a suspect. Between 2007 and 2016, 549 officers were either stabbed or shot in the line of duty, according to the National Law Enforcement Memorial Fund. Nearly an identical amount were killed by transportation accidents ("Causes of law enforcement deaths," 2018).

based on a wide array of criteria—age, dress, behavior—to determine if they are involved in unlawful activity. Why shouldn't race or ethnicity be one of these criteria? While many critics dismiss profiling, there may be reasons for it that make sense.

All profiling is problematic, especially racial profiling. Stopping an individual simply because she is black or Muslim is a violation of the Fourth Amendment's guarantee of protection from unreasonable searches and seizures, as well as a violation of the Fourteenth Amendment's guarantee that everybody will be granted "the equal protection of the laws" (Feder, 2012). Further, it becomes a self-fulfilling prophecy to select certain groups for heightened scrutiny. If officers target African American men as suspected drug traffickers, they are probably going to find more black drug dealers. This, in turn, further justifies targeting black men as potential dealers (Banks, 2003). As a result, the sense that a group is being unfairly targeted by the police is sure to affect the relations between the police and the group, alienating young black men and Muslims, when their trust in police is essential to fighting both crime and terrorism. Being repeatedly stopped by police officers for little or no reason is going to make an individual less likely to trust officers and go to them when there is a real problem (Tyler, 2005).

Finally, targeting individuals based on their race or their religion just seems un-American: A country that declares that all are "created equal" and guarantees that people have a right to "equal treatment" before the law should not discriminate between different groups based solely on issues of race or religion. As we saw in Chapter 5, American policing has had a very troubled history in its relations with the black community, and regardless of whether it could be justified, racial profiling feels like a continuation of segregation, Jim Crow, and other racist policies that were propped up by police forces. Racial profiling, whether it could be justified in some ways or not, probably does a good deal more harm that it does good.

Some have suggested that there are other, better criteria for profiling individuals that are more sophisticated and less morally questionable than racial profiling (Fredrickson & Siljander, 2002). One suggestion is not to treat people suspiciously based on their race but rather to keep an eye out for behaviors that indicate that a person is involved in suspicious activity. Terrorists and drug traffickers know that officers are looking for a type of person and therefore often seek to use people who don't look like the type to carry out their criminal activities. Many Muslims look white, and many drug traffickers seek out people who seem clean, respectable (and white) to help move their merchandise. But there are often behaviors that are better guides to a person's likelihood for being criminal than the bare fact that she is black or Arab. For example, a terrorist might book a ticket in a certain way (such as booking a one-way ticket or following a suspicious pattern of travel), or a drug dealer may be standing in a suspicious place or dress in a way that indicates a likelihood of engaging in criminal activity. So, rather than focusing on the color of individuals' skin, their facial hair, or their race; focusing on what they do and how they act may ultimately produce better results than racial profiling.

Racial profiling can take place in a lot of different ways, not all of which are overtly illegal. The most extreme version of racial profiling is sometimes referred to as pulling a person over for DWB (driving while black) or stopping a person at the airport for FWM (flying while Muslim). In each case, the officers pick an individual and stop, search, or arrest her *exclusively* because of her race or religion. While this undoubtedly happens and is clearly illegal, this is not the only form of racial profiling that is carried out by the police, and though it is outrageous, it is certainly not the most common.

More common than overt cases of profiling like DWB are pretextual stops of minority drivers. A pretextual stop involves pulling an individual over for a minor infraction as an excuse to find out other information about the individual or scan for incriminating evidence. The police use the initial stop as an excuse to look inside the individual's car, check the driver for any outstanding arrest warrants, or find an excuse to search the car. A driver who an officer suspects of being a drug trafficker makes a turn without using the turn signal. Ordinarily an officer would ignore such a small infraction, but instead she pulls the driver over, expecting that doing so will probably lead to an arrest. This belief is often based on the race of the driver or other similar circumstances. Sometimes officers will give the driver a minor citation during this stop with the expectation that the driver won't pay the ticket, which could give the next officer an excuse to arrest and search the driver. There are so many regulations that govern driving that a shrewd officer could easily find an excuse to pull over anybody at virtually any time—and if necessary the officer can invent an error that the driver would be helpless to defend herself against. Since it is the job of the police to enforce the law, it should come as no surprise that most of this is legal.

While there are some cases where officers openly express a bias against certain groups and use their powers to persecute minorities, often this is not the case. There are far more complicated facts that shape how officers interact with black suspects, many of which are far subtler than any overt racial biases held by individual officers. A surprising number of officers who have been involved in incidents of excessive force have not been white. For example, the New Orleans Police Department is among the most diverse in the country but nonetheless has problems with bias (Craven, 2015). Different forms of bias work together to show that minorities and black men have a very different relationship with the police than other groups in the United States. White Americans are significantly more likely to trust the police than African Americans and are significantly more likely to give officers the benefit of the doubt in cases like that of Freddie Gray, Eric Garner, or Walter Scott (Ekins, 2016).

Overt racism and unconscious bias are different from what is sometimes called *systemic racism* or *institutional racism* in criminal justice. Systemic racism refers to a wide array of

Driving while black (DWB): A slang term that refers to the racial profiling of African American drivers.

Flying while Muslim (FWM): A slang term that refers to the profiling of people who appear to be Muslims at airports.

Pretextual stop: A practice where officers find an excuse, usually a minor infraction, to stop a driver so officers can look inside the individual's car or check to see if the driver is intoxicated or has outstanding warrants.

WHERE DO I FIT IN?

UNCONSCIOUS BIAS

While there are plenty of cases of overt racial profiling, one of the subtlest types of racial bias in policing is one that the officer isn't even aware of. These biases, sometimes called unconscious biases or implicit biases, do not depend on the officer holding racist views or racist suspicions about black people or other minorities. Rather, implicit bias studies show that sudden reactions, such as when an officer is faced with an attacker, can reveal secret prejudices that the officer holds. In timed tests with subjects who were expected to react as quickly as possible, giving them no time to reflect on their attitudes, psychologists have shown that officers are quicker to assume that black people are armed and dangerous than are white people (Correll et al., 2007).

Unconscious or implicit biases take over in these situations, and officers unknowingly decide that a black person is threatening and not a white person. Equally important, these biases are not unique to police officers. We all have some unconscious biases that shape how we interact with others, especially other people who are from different racial backgrounds. In a country like America, where there is a great deal of racial segregation and cultural stereotypes in the media, it only makes sense that many of us hold racial prejudices that we're unaware of, regardless of how "un-racist" we might like to think we are. While it's not clear what the significance of this data is for understanding the nature of racial profiling, it is powerful data that shows how complicated and deeply rooted racial prejudice is in policing and across America more broadly.

While it is not a "trigger-based" study, you can take an online test of your own unconscious racial biases at http://www.understanding prejudice.org/ and see how you compare to others.

How did you do on this test? Does it make you think differently about your own assumptions about race? Do you think that there might be ways to address such unconscious biases?

disadvantages that affect the lives of African Americans and shapes their relations to the police—none of which has anything to do with the mentalities of officers. Poorer cities tend to be blacker cities. This poverty leads to a higher crime rate, which in turns leads to more policing and a deterioration of relations between the police and the public. Black people are treated differently by the police because the poverty that African Americans face has made it nearly impossible for black people to live within the law. According to those who perceive institutional racism in American policing, the attitudes of officers toward African Americans is irrelevant—what matters is that there are a wide range of social forces at work to ensure that African Americans will constantly be under the thumb of the police. From a critical perspective, the only way to fix racism in policing is to address the institutional problems of law, education, economics, health care, and work such that blacks are equal to whites.

As we've seen throughout our discussion of policing, the toxic relationship between the police and the African American community has a history stretching back to the fugitive slave patrols of the early 19th century, if not earlier. More recently, many black Americans are hostile toward the police simply because they have experiences of being unfairly stopped, harassed, and mistreated by the police. Few white people have had these experiences and have instead been taught to respect the police and to believe that officers are on their side. This has led many to be either confused or dismissive of black complaints about policing. When rappers performed songs like "F- tha Police" and "Cop Killer" in the 1980s and 1990s, they were denounced by many police organizations, conservative political groups, and both the president and the vice president of the United States, who called for a boycott of the company that released these songs. Almost nobody in mainstream white culture bothered to take seriously what these people said, and nobody inquired about what kind of experiences of the police the rappers had had, much less why such attitudes would resonate in the African American community. With recent revelations, largely using camera phones and dashboard video cameras, the rest of America has been given a glimpse (and in fact only a small glimpse) into what black Americans have known about the police since slavery. Maybe for once their anger won't be dismissed.

CORRUPTION

Learning Objective 7.3—List the major forms of police corruption.

Police corruption is in many ways far less complicated than overenthusiastic policing. There is nobody who is willing to publicly defend officers caught taking bribes or participating in other types of overtly criminal activity. The explanations are less complicated, and the politics of police corruption are much more straightforward than with overenthusiastic policing. This doesn't mean that there aren't problems with understanding police corruption—some grey areas as it were—but corruption generates a lot less hand wringing: It's wrong and we all know it.

Among these grey areas in police corruption are the small-scale benefits that officers get in the line of duty. In the 1970s, the Chicago Police Department listed 10 different types of corruption that officers engage in. At the bottom level was **mooching**, defined as "receiving gratuities (such as free meals) sometimes in exchange for favoritism." Many restaurants and stores offer discounts to officers in part as a measure of support for their efforts and in part to curry favor with officers. After all, a place that is known as a police hangout is unlikely to be robbed. Often these gifts may come with invisible strings attached. Those businesses who give them out often expect special treatment from officers: Perhaps the officers will look the other way when the owner is pulled over, or perhaps they will come a little more quickly if the store is robbed. Even if the gift does not come with such strings attached, it looks fishy to the public, and many officers are told to avoid even the appearance of impropriety, and so they are not allowed to accept free gifts from businesses.

Beyond mooching, there are much larger and more serious forms of corruption. In some cases, officers work in collusion with existing criminal elements, either working alongside criminals or accepting bribes to look the other way when they encounter their criminal activities. This is what is known as **quid pro quo** ("this for that") corruption—money or services are given explicitly in exchange for preferential treatment by the police. In 1999, for example, two NYPD officers were indicted for accepting cash payments and sexual favors from the staff of a Manhattan brothel in exchange for warning the owners of the establishment of upcoming police raids (Barstow, 1999). The police have cooperated with drug traffickers and other criminals for as long as there has been policing, as officers have sought to supplement their meager income by taking advantage of the much higher incomes found in much of the underworld. Other times, officers have been criminal entrepreneurs, seeking to make money on their own volition by either engaging in their own

Police corruption: The abuse of police authority for personal gain.

Mooching: The act of taking small-scale gifts offered by citizens to officers.

Quid pro quo: Literally "this for that." The form of corruption where officers explicitly trade favors for goods or services.

Mooching and Corruption

You are a new officer who has just begun your career in a small-town police department. On your very first day on the job you decide to walk into a local convenience store to buy yourself a drink. You pick up a soda and wait in line behind three other people. The cashier looks at you in the back of the line and waves you forward. "You want the soda? Police get drinks for free! They've been a great help for us in preventing robberies. Thank you for your service!"

You look around and there are about 10 people in the store who saw all of this happen. On one hand, you are happy to get the drink for free, but clearly some of the people there aren't happy about it. On the other hand, the cashier seems genuinely grateful and you're afraid that he might be offended if you refuse his offer.

What would you do in this situation? If you refuse the drink, how would you explain it to the cashier?

criminal activity, for example selling drugs that have been confiscated from criminals, or by forcibly extracting money from known criminals—also known as a shakedown.

Frank Serpico and the Knapp Commission

Shakedown: Threats from officers to arrest suspected lawbreakers unless they pay the officers a bribe.

Knapp Commission: An investigative body created in the wake of Frank Serpico's revelations regarding corruption in the NYPD.

Grass eaters: Corrupt officers who accept bribes if they are offered to them but do not actively seek bribes.

Meat eaters: Officers who actively seek money or other bribes while on duty.

The most famous example of overt police corruption in American history was probably the widespread misconduct in the NYPD in the 1970s that was exposed by Detective Frank Serpico. In part, this case is famous because it kicked off the most influential study on police corruption (at least since the Wickersham Commission), and in part it is famous because Detective Serpico's story became the basis for a hit 1973 movie starring Al Pacino entitled *Serpico*. Detective Serpico was an officer in the NYPD in the 1960s who refused to take the bribes that were taken by his fellow officers and had been shared throughout the precinct. He began to make complaints to officers higher upon in the chain of command and to the local press. Because of his whistleblowing activities, several NYPD officials set Serpico up to be killed, sending him into an apartment against an armed suspect but neglecting to provide him with appropriate backup. Serpico was shot but ultimately survived to talk about his experiences.

The commission that was convened after this case broke was known as the Knapp Commission, after its chair, Whitman Knapp. The commission explored the nature of corruption in the NYPD but also provided some general guides for thinking about and countering police corruption. In its report, the commission described two different forms of corrupt officer: grass eaters and meat eaters. Grass eaters are officers who accept bribes when they are offered to them on the job (say, when they arrest an individual), but they do not actively seek out the money. Meat eaters, on the other hand, are officers who engage in police activity for the sake of their own profit. For example, an officer might shake down a prostitute or a bookie, a person who runs an illegal gambling operation. If the officer in need of money seeks out these people and threatens them with arrest if they don't pay a bribe, then the officer is engaged in meat eating.

The Knapp Commission's report was highly influential in how departments think about and confront police corruption. After another high-profile corruption case in 1992 where several officers were arrested for selling narcotics (including one officer with 15 different outstanding corruption allegations—none of which were investigated by the NYPD), the City of New York convened a second commission known as the *Mollen Commission*. This body revised much of the city's thinking about corruption (Rosoff & Pontell, n.d.) The commission found many officers were involved in drug trafficking, which often entailed killing other traffickers and stealing their drugs. This marked a change from the days of the Knapp Commission; now officers were active participants in the drug trade, along with all the violence that accompanied it. As a result, the commission suggested that a permanent civilian commission, known as the *Commission to Combat Police Corruption*, be formed to oversee police corruption complaints in the city.

THE CAUSES OF POLICE DEVIANCE

Learning Objective 7.4—Describe the different significant causes of police deviance.

Why do police officers become deviant? Very few people become police officers with the intention of being corrupt or abusive, so what is it that makes them lose their way? There are many different possible explanations for police misconduct, and in any individual case they can all work together. Different groups like to emphasize certain causes of corruption for their own purposes—if you don't like the police, you're going to be inclined toward explanations that make the police seem like bad people. If you harbor positive feelings toward the police, you're likely to gravitate toward explanations that blame a few bad apples but put the rest of the police in a positive light. There is no single explanation of police deviance, but each of several partial explanations have compelling points to make.

Sometimes, it is possible to look at the personalities of individual officers to understand why they misbehave—they have a need to dominate others and use their authority as officers to do so, even to the point of abusing their powers. Psychologists refer to these officers as possessing authoritarian personalities. Authoritarian personalities belong to individuals whose identity is based on ensuring the submission of everybody else they encounter, and they feel a need to dominate anybody who fails to respect their authority. Authoritarians not only expect others to submit to their will but are also inclined to consider any person who does not fit in with the mainstream values that the officers support to be a threat. People who do not conform to social norms are singled out for abuse by authoritarians. Authoritarians are usually very intolerant and very conservative and often need to be in charge of those around them, interpreting the behavior of anybody who does not submit to their will as a threat of some kind.

It is understandable why many people with authoritarian personalities would be attracted to policing—anecdotal evidence suggests officers tend to be socially conservative individuals who believe strongly in law and order. As we suggested at the opening of this section of the book, police officers often protect the status quo, for good or ill, and authoritarian personalities tend to be hostile to anybody who is different. Authoritarian officers not only enforce laws but are hostile to anybody who is perceived as different or who challenges the status quo, whether it is civil rights activists, homosexuals, or those who too aggressively promote their civil rights. The stereotype of the mustachioed bully-cop who brutalizes anybody who

Bad apples: The theory that only a few deviant police officers cause the rest of American police to get a bad reputation.

Authoritarian personalities: Individuals whose identity is based on ensuring the obedience and submission of everybody else they encounter, who feel a need to dominate anybody who fails to respect their authority.

is different comes from these authoritarian officers. Again, not all officers are authoritarians, but some, particularly those who are overly aggressive in how they enforce the law, may have authoritarian personalities that are the root of their deviance.

Another possible explanation for police corruption looks at the stresses of being an officer—asserting that there is something about the job that can lead an officer to misbehave. Even if an individual officer has every desire to be a good cop at the start of her career, the pressures of the job can lead her to misbehave. The power that officers have can be very tempting to abuse, and it is unsurprising that some officers slowly become more comfortable with misconduct over the course of their careers. Small acts can snowball into big ones over years as an officer becomes more comfortable with the power she has in her job. After enough time on the job, she just may not care any more about what happens.

One example of this is *police burnout*. When officers must repeatedly deal with the stresses of confronting a public that is sometimes distrusting or openly hostile toward them, it is often the case that this can shape their attitudes toward the public. It can make them uncaring and unsympathetic to those they interact with and cynical about the motives of the public. This can easily lead officers either to reject their traditional role as a protector of the public and instead begin to prey on the public, or to become jaded about the everyday abuses of authority that they experience on the job. Burned out officers are likely to be tempted into corruption or to become abusive as they lose their sympathy toward the public.

On the other hand, looking at the psychology or experiences of individual officers may be too simplistic a way to examine police deviance. Many police departments like to suggest that corruption is only the work of a few officers that somehow made it into police departments where they could thrive in secret. The rest of the officers, they maintain, are good people who conscientiously do their work enforcing the law and protecting the public. Others have suggested that corruption and overenthusiastic policing are the result of broader forces that are inherent in the job. In this view, more officers will become deviant over time because the nature of the job tends to push otherwise good officers in that direction.

The frustrations of the job can sometimes push an officer toward deviance. In fighting drug trafficking, officers are exposed to large amounts of money, more money than they would ever make in their own jobs. They are expected to enforce laws that many see as futile or stupid: No matter how many people are sent to prison, drugs remain on the street and are popular with many people. This is bound to create a sense that much police work is largely a waste of time. Since drugs and prostitution have not disappeared and probably never will, some officers figure that profiting from these crimes makes no overall difference in the grand scheme of things. It is unsurprising that a great deal of police corruption revolves around drug trafficking and other reportedly victimless crimes, as there is a great deal of money in these trades, and there is little evidence that enforcing these laws does anything to prevent crime. According to these observers, it is not the makeup of the individual officer that leads to corruption or deviance, but rather that misconduct is in some sense a natural consequence of police work.

Other researchers look at *organizational explanations* for police deviance. These researchers focus on aspects of the police department—its culture, its leadership, its organization—for clues as to why officers go bad. These features can include poor management and poor leadership as causes of misconduct. If there is a sense that corruption is normal or not a big deal in a police department, it is likely to spread among officers. As one Washington, D.C., police officer put it, "The major cause in the lack of integrity in American police officers is mediocrity" (Parks, 2000, p. i). On the other hand, tightly knit organizations can also shield officers who break the rules, providing them with effective cover and allowing bad apples

CRIMINAL (IN)JUSTICE

Flaking

Lasou Kuyateh was pulled over in Staten Island on February 28, 2018, with several of his friends, all of whom were young African American men. Officers Kyle Erickson and Elmer Pastran pulled over Kuyateh's BMW for having excessively tinted windows and for turning without using his signals. After they pulled the car over, Officer Pastran told the men that he smelled marijuana on the men ("I don't appreciate being lied to. I know there's marijuana in the car; I can smell it," he said.) and used this as grounds for searching the car. During the search, Officer Erickson's body camera mysteriously and inexplicably shut off. It turned back on just as he declared that he found a lit joint on the floor of the back seat of the car. Kuyateh was arrested and charged with possession, among other things, and spent two days in jail.

There were plenty of aspects about the search that were fishy. Beyond the suspicious timing of the camera's deactivation, other body cameras that recorded the car's interior prior to the discovery do not show a joint where the officer claims he found it. Equally suspicious, the officer's camera turns on just before he finds the joint and not later. All of these concerns created legal problems for the case, and the prosecutor abruptly dropped the charge during the officer's testimony at a pretrial hearing. When Kuyateh's lawyers tried to raise objections to the police's tactics, the judge ended the case and declared, "What I'm not going to allow [to] happen is [for] my courtroom to become a political place where these things are brought up" (Goldstein, 2018). There have been several cases similar to this that have arisen in the era of body cams. In April 2017,

a Los Angeles police officer accidentally video-recorded himself planting cocaine in the wallet of a hit and run suspect. The camera the officer was using saves video from 30 seconds before the audio begins, meaning that the officer in question probably did not realize the camera had already started recording when he allegedly planted the drugs (CBS News, 2017). In July of that same year, a Baltimore officer similarly video-recorded himself planting cocaine on a suspect, also not realizing that his camera was already recording before he switched it on (Fortin, 2018).

As with other aspects of police deviance, it is difficult to know how often police officers plant evidence on suspects. Officers and their departments don't disclose this type of information, for obvious reasons. An internal NYPD investigation found no evidence of misconduct on Officer Erickson's part, but the other two officers faced disciplinary action, including criminal prosecution for the Baltimore officer. While we don't know how often it happens, it is common enough that there are slang terms for it. Officers call it *flaking* when an officer plants evidence on a suspect. *Padding*, on the other hand, consists in adding additional evidence to suspects to put them in greater legal jeopardy (Punch, 1985). One New York City detective described these practices as a routine part of policing: "It's almost like you have no emotion with it . . . they're going to be out of jail tomorrow anyway; nothing is going to happen to them anyway" (Lee, 2011).

Do you think that flaking is an ordinary part of policing? If so, how could it be prevented?

to operate without consequences. In this view, "Punishing individual cops will not cure the problem of police violence, if systemic features of the police organization permit, sanction, or even encourage the officers' violent behavior" (Armacost, 2003, p. 456). To reform the police it is not enough to change officers' behavior or to recruit better officers: The entire structure of a police department needs to be reformed.

HANDLING POLICE DEVIANCE

Learning Objective 7.5—Examine the different strategies police forces and the public have used to prevent corruption and overenthusiastic policing.

There are many ways that police forces and other groups have tried to address police misconduct over the years. Some seek to change police forces from the inside, using the officers themselves as the primary motor of change, while others seek to force change on police forces from outside as it were. While police deviance is an ongoing problem, there are many difficulties that prevent politicians and prosecutors from getting a handle on police misconduct, even in cases where it is flagrant, and the public is aware of it.

Politicians are often very hesitant to take on police misconduct. There is always a great deal of public support for the police, and politicians are hesitant to challenge them out of a fear of being perceived as soft on crime or insufficiently supportive of "police heroes." Prosecutors have close working relationships with police departments, so they may not be inclined to investigate police deviance too carefully for fear of alienating their professional allies. Finally, most police departments are part of a union that is there to protect the interests of officers. These unions often strongly resist efforts to investigate and prosecute officers for alleged misbehavior, and they provide free legal assistance to officers facing misconduct charges. They also can block efforts to reform the police if these efforts are not seen as benefitting the officers themselves (Kupfer, 2018). The blue wall of silence that keeps officers from reporting their fellow officers further protects them from scrutiny and prosecution. All these forces arrayed together make it very challenging to arrest and prosecute officers who abuse their authority (Kindy & Kelly, 2015).

Not only are prosecutors skittish about prosecuting officers, but juries are often unwilling to convict officers of even the most blatant misconduct. In April 2015, Michael Slager, a white police officer, shot and killed Walter Scott, an unarmed African American man, in the town of North Charleston, South Carolina. Slager had pulled Scott over for a broken tail light, and when Scott fled because he had outstanding warrants, Slager shot him in the back eight times from approximately 15 feet away. The whole incident was caught on a video by a bystander, and Slager was charged with murder. Despite the seemingly damning evidence, a jury of eleven white jurors and one black juror was unable to come to agreement, and a mistrial was declared. Slager ultimately pled guilty to the federal crime of denying Scott his civil rights and was sentenced to 20 years in prison. Even in cases where violence is captured on video and prosecutors seek convictions for officers, they are often difficult to obtain.

Despite these difficulties, investigating and sanctioning officers who misbehave can be an effective way to handle police deviance. Almost all police forces have internal affairs (IA) units that are responsible for investigating police officers who misbehave. They make sure that ordinary police officers do not overstep their authority or engage in corruption. All officers have records, and bad reports regarding their conduct can harm their chances of moving up in the police ranks. Because they attempt to break through the blue wall of silence, IA officers sometimes report skepticism and mistrust from other officers. While ordinary officers understand that the police need some sort of oversight, they nonetheless often see the IA division as an unwelcome intrusion on their work.

In their reports, the Knapp and the Mollen commissions made several recommendations to help prevent future corruption at the NYPD. The Knapp Commission recommended a permanent prosecutor tasked exclusively with investigating corruption in the criminal justice process (including, but not exclusively, in the police force). Among the Mollen Commission's many recommendations was the creation of a permanent outside body designed to root out corruption with a subpoena power over police officers and the ability to independently investigate allegations against police officers.

Other approaches to addressing police deviance include training officers differently so that they are better able to de-escalate confrontations with the public. Some departments have been experimenting with reorganizing the way that officers work, allowing the officers who work the graveyard shift (working late at night) an opportunity to work the same neighborhoods in the daytime so that they do not exclusively interact with the underworld. People who encounter the police late at night tend to be more troublesome than those who they would meet in a daytime shift, who may be more polite, respectful, and appreciative of officers when they arrive. This sort of schedule can give officers a more sympathetic relationship with the public and help prevent officer burnout.

There has been a serious effort to recruit African American police officers to help improve relationships between the police and the black community. This has proven difficult for several reasons. The history of distrust between the police and African Americans means that black officers are sometimes viewed as traitors by other African Americans. Organizations like the National Black Police Association have sought to change perceptions about black officers and change how the African American community thinks about the police, but they have only had limited success. Ironically, the desire for a more diverse work force in the business world has made it hard for police departments to compete with private companies for the top black college graduates. They can make more money in business without the stigma of being perceived as betraying their people. Even though police departments have actively sought out black candidates, and even though police work is relatively high-paying work that provides many of the benefits that one looks for in a job (health insurance, a retirement program, and job security), few African Americans are willing to seriously consider becoming police officers. The NYPD has reported a decline in the number of black candidates attending their police academy of nearly 50% over the last 10 years (Swarns, 2015).

Along with these internal approaches to addressing police deviance are external approaches, where reformers have worked outside of the departments to create change. Many cities have civilian review boards that are tasked with keeping an eye on police behavior and handling complaints from the public. These boards are usually appointed by city officials and often work with IA units to investigate complaints about police misconduct. If an individual believes she has been mistreated by the police, she can bring her case to the board, which can investigate and make recommendations about what should be done. While some police officials consider such boards to be an unnecessary and unwelcome intrusion into police activities, believing that they are too susceptible to the whims of public opinion, they can help maintain the delicate balance that officers must maintain between being considered legitimate by the public and retaining their ability to effectively maintain order (Hudson, 1971).

Other times, the federal government can investigate a police department and report on the department's failings in protecting the civil rights of citizens. One such investigation took place in Ferguson, Missouri, prompted by the riots following the death of Michael Brown. The Justice Department report on Ferguson was damning toward the entire police department and the broader city government that supported it. They found that the police department was targeting poor minorities living in the city for citations and arbitrary arrests

Civilian review boards: Government committees that are tasked with keeping an eye on police behavior and handling complaints from the public.

primarily as a means for raising funds for the city government. Poor, minority citizens have little ability to pay fines issued by the courts, and a failure to pay guaranteed that the fines would then increase until the person would be forced to find some way to pay the fine or go to jail. The city's black citizens became a "cash machine" for the city, and by the time of the riots, nearly a quarter of the city's budget came from police fines. The report recommended deep changes in the way the police department and the courts operated in the city, including implementing an "ability to pay" system to make fines more realistic for poor offenders.

Another common way to get the police to change their behavior is through civil suits. The police are often sued by individuals or groups who are not only seeking compensation for the harms that the police have caused (say, through excessive force), but also trying to get the police to change how they behave in the future. These are usually called *civil rights lawsuits* and usually argue that an individual's or a group's constitutional rights have been violated by the officers or by entire police departments. Some of these suits seek monetary compensation, but often they simply want the police to change their policies. While suing police departments can be effective, lawsuits face many hurdles in court, because officers have what is known as *qualified immunity*. That is, they have a protection from many lawsuits to prevent them from being harassed by a hostile public. Sometimes, the suits won't result in a reward for the plaintiff, but nonetheless there will be a court-structured plan to change how the police operate. These judicial orders are known as *consent decrees*; they usually do not require the police department to pay compensation but instead force it to change its practices. Several cities, including New Orleans, Oakland, and Los Angeles have signed consent decrees.

Looking at it from the perspective of a critical criminologist, we can see that none of these reforms will probably be enough to truly address the problems of police deviance and improve police relations with the public. While they may improve things regarding racial profiling or corruption, these reforms overlook the deeper, structural problems that create police deviance. As you may recall, critical criminology argues that the deep economic and racial inequalities in a society are reflected throughout the criminal justice system—including in the police. Police practices only reflect these deeper problems. The police have race problems because society has race problems and addressing one without addressing the other will ultimately be inadequate. Of course, changing the dynamics of race in American society so that race does not have such a deep impact on how people are treated and their success or failure in life is a much bigger project. Undoing nearly 500 years of white domination and the subordination of black people through slavery, segregation, and Jim Crow (not to mention the economic and social inequalities that these institutions have created) is an effort that will take generations. As long as society remains unequal and unfair, there will be no ultimate solution to the problem of police deviance.

CHAPTER SUMMARY

This chapter has been an overview of all the ways that police can go bad. These include some forms of misconduct where officers misbehave in ways that align with the traditional goals of policing, such as deviance control. Others, such as corruption, result from officers turning away from their role as the guardians of society and turn toward outright criminality. They both are problems unique to policing, and both can share similar root causes in the personality of police officers, the nature of police work, or the structures of police institutions. Approaches from both inside and outside of the police system have worked to address these problems through reforms, better screening and hiring practices, and lawsuits.

Police deviance is a complicated and troubling problem. Because officers have so much power over our lives, their misconduct can be very dangerous. All humans have flaws and all humans have prejudices, but when these basic human weaknesses are present in a person who is both armed and possesses a great deal of authority over us, they can become very dangerous. Few of us have the power to act violently on our prejudices, much less do we have the power to use lethal force against our fellow citizens under the cover of law. The power and authority that officers possess over us magnifies their all-too-human flaws and can allow them to do great harm.

As was mentioned at the opening of this chapter, it should be remembered that the American police system is far from the worst police force in the world. Many countries, particularly in the developing world, have police forces that are known primarily for their brutality, incompetence, and corruption. In the United States, police misconduct still shocks the public and still makes the news. When videos surface showcasing police abuses, it creates public outcry, protests, and even riots. In many parts of the world, bribing the police and facing abuse from officers is an everyday occurrence that wouldn't generate more than an exasperated sigh—and very rarely a protest. In other parts of the world, police abuse and police corruption is the norm; in much of America it remains an exception. Despite all the problems discussed here, there is much to be grateful for in American policing.

REVIEW/DISCUSSION QUESTIONS

1. What do you believe is the best way to deal with corruption? Is it possible to completely stamp it out, or will officers always be tempted to abuse their powers for personal gain?

2. Overenthusiastic policing in general, and racial profiling in particular, have become major elements of public debate in America. Why do you think that is? Are defenders and critics of police departments biased? If so, how?

3. This chapter examines several different causes of police deviance as well as different ways to address and prevent it. Are these connected? That is, what do you believe are the most significant causes of police deviance, and based on this, what are the best strategies for preventing it?

KEY TERMS

Authoritarian personalities 179
Bad apples 179
Blue wall of silence 168
Civilian review boards 183
Dirty Harry problem 170
Driving while black
 (DWB) 175

Excessive force 170
Flying while Muslim
 (FWM) 175
Grass eaters 178
Knapp Commission 178
Meat eaters 178
Mooching 177

Net widening 170
Police corruption 177
Police deviance 167
Pretextual stop 175
Quid pro quo 177
Racial profiling 171
Shakedown 178

$SAGE edge™

Get the tools you need to sharpen your study skills. SAGE edge offers a robust online environment featuring an impressive array of free tools and resources.

Access practice quizzes, eFlashcards, video, and multimedia at edge.sagepub.com/fichtelberg

Sarah Yeh

One of the main goals of a criminal trial is to uncover the truth. How does it work to do this? Are there aspects of criminal trials that get in the way of this goal?

COURTS AND TRIALS

In this third section of the book we will be discussing criminal courts and trials. This will take us from the moment when the suspect is charged with an offense through conviction and appeal. It will include three main components: Pretrial processes (everything up to the commencement of the trial), the trial itself (the presentation of evidence before the court), and the posttrial process, including appeals. It will include a discussion of the most significant procedures in a criminal trial as well as a discussion of the most important actors both inside and outside of the courtroom. Before we get into the details of courts and trials, it is perhaps a good idea to talk a little bit about what trials are *for*.

The most obvious reason for a trial is to figure out what happened in an individual case—the court exists to determine the truth. An individual has been charged with an offense, and she disputes the charge. The trial is there to determine whether the person had committed the crimes. We can call this the *epistemological function* of a trial (*epistemology* is a term to describe the different ways that we can seek to discover the truth). The American legal system is based on the belief that the best way to determine this truth is to have two sides, a prosecutor and a defense, argue with each other in front of a neutral jury. From this argument, the truth will be revealed. This is called the *adversarial process*. The theory is that through the two sides "fighting" each other, the truth will ultimately shine through.

To be a little technical about this, we can't say that the courtroom determines THE TRUTH in a case, because in the real world, "truth" is a complicated thing. Courts only deal with a single, narrow question: the guilt of a defendant. If Sarah is charged with a murder and put on trial, it may be the case that Mike committed the crime. At trial, the court cannot decide that Mike is guilty, it can only decide whether or not Sarah is guilty—a separate trial with Mike as a defendant would be required to convict him for the crime. Further, it may come up at trial that Sarah committed armed robbery but did not commit the murder. Sarah could not be convicted of robbery in her murder trial unless the robbery was part of the indictment against her. The court is only there to determine whether an individual or group is guilty of a specific set of offenses. This means that the truth that the trial uncovers is a very limited one and does not often consider the bigger picture surrounding the crime, including who else was involved in the offense and what broader forces might have pushed the offender down the path to criminal activity.

Uncovering the truth is not the only function of a trial. It also serves a *punitive* function. The trial affixes blame and determines the *sanction*, that is, the punishment, that should be given to the person convicted of the offense. Was the crime particularly heinous, and therefore the perpetrator deserves serious punishment? Was the killing so cold hearted that the criminal should be punished severely? Were there factors that should be considered that make the offender less responsible for what she did and therefore deserving less punishment? Determining how much punishment should be given to a person found guilty of a crime is an important part of a criminal trial.

For decades, the country of South Africa was organized according to a racist system known as *apartheid*. Under the apartheid government, black South Africans were kept in desperate poverty and denied any say in how their country was run. The white South African government tortured and murdered many black South Africans who tried to change the system. This went on for decades until the nation's black majority were ultimately successful in toppling the apartheid system in 1994. Many of the leaders of the apartheid regime as well as the police officers that served the racist government were clearly guilty of serious crimes against black South Africans. Though their work was done in the name of protecting the political system that they had sworn to serve, they were now considered criminals by the new political order.

Rather than prosecute many of these offenders, the new government under President Nelson Mandela set up a body known as the *Truth and Reconciliation Commission* or TRC. The TRC made an offer to the old apartheid leaders: If you went before the tribunal and admitted the crimes that you committed in defense of apartheid, telling the whole truth about your actions and apologizing for what you did, they would let you go without serious punishment. The new government concluded that this was the only way to get the society to move beyond the pain caused by apartheid. What resulted was some of the most riveting testimony imaginable, as people described the tortures and murders they committed and asked for forgiveness from the families of those they killed. The families of many victims were angry, as they believed that the TRC was allowing murderers to escape punishment. The truth is that black South Africans never would have learned about the fates of their loved ones if their killers had refused to speak out of fear of punishment. Those accused of crimes would have hired lawyers and refused to cooperate with any investigations into apartheid. They would never admit responsibility if such an admission led to imprisonment. While forgiveness was a high price to pay for learning the truth, many believed that knowing the whole truth about what happened under apartheid was necessary for South Africa to move beyond a history of racial oppression.

The case of the TRC reveals two things: First, it shows that the epistemological and punitive functions of trials can be at odds with each other. Threatening to punish somebody is a good way to get her to lie about what she did or to clam up entirely. A child who fears being grounded by her parents for getting bad grades is more likely to hide her report card than is one who doesn't. Second, it shows that there are other things beyond punishment at stake at a trial: Some victims aren't interested in seeing their attackers punished as much as they are interested in healing the trauma they feel after being attacked. Knowing that your attacker is being punished may be enough for some, but for others this is not what they need to move forward. Finding out the truth about a crime and punishing the perpetrator aren't always compatible goals.

Beyond its epistemological and punitive functions, there is an additional function of the criminal trial: its *symbolic function*. Courts are weird places if you think about it. Though they are governmental institutions, they are not like any other government body: Judges wear robes, sit in a raised chair, bang a gavel, and are addressed as "your honor." You don't see that at the DMV or at the Social Security office. Nowhere else in the modern world do these medieval formalities still exist, and a court feels more like a church or a royal court in many ways than it does a government institution. Everything from the architecture to the dress code to the language used in a courtroom is strange.

There are many reasons why the court is such an unusual place, and such unusual codes of behavior apply there. The modern court has inherited many traditions that stretch back hundreds of years from its origins in England, where judges and lawyers still wear wigs in court. But one of the most important reasons for these features is a symbolic one: The features are meant to communicate to the public. Symbols are simply ways that institutions subtly or not so subtly communicate messages to the public. A cross in a church is a symbol that is meant to announce the presence of God, whereas more mundanely, a red traffic light symbolizes "stop." Courts are no different; they are full of very subtle and overt symbols that are meant to communicate many things about the law, the government, and the authority of the state.

When courts communicate to the public, they are sending their audience several different messages. On one hand, they are telling the audience that the courts are to be respected, even when we disagree with them. They are serious, sober places where important people make important decisions. Judges are not flighty people who are going to make decisions for arbitrary or superficial reasons. The courtroom and its actors are also symbolizing fairness: The judges are not like ordinary people who are going to be prejudiced by their own interests but rather are presented as higher beings who are only concerned with what is right or fair. None of this means that they really behave in this way, but rather the court is meant to communicate the fact that they deserve respect.

Equally, the courts are symbolically communicating the power that the state holds over all of us. The fact that one must call the judge "your honor" and stand when she enters the courtroom is meant to symbolize that the state has supreme authority. The state has the power to prosecute, judge, and punish us. The state can send people to jail. The state even has the power to execute those convicted of the most serious crimes. The authority of the law and the authority of the government as the body empowered to enforce the law are symbolized in the courtroom, and just as we are supposed to submit to the will of the judge, we are expected to submit to the will of the state. Whether we like it or not, we must submit to the rulings of the court.

The image of "lady justice" as a blindfolded woman holding a scale in one hand and a sword in another nicely encapsulates the symbolism of the courtroom (see Chapter 2, page 28).

The scale represents justice, the blindfold represents a fair and unbiased system, and the sword symbolizes the power standing behind the court's judgements. The law and the courts are supposed to be fair and just, and they have the power to dispense this justice by force. As we will see in the next few chapters, this image is appealing but often inaccurate in practice. The law can be blind and fair, but in practice it often is anything but.

Sarah Yeh

A criminal trial is designed to be a "fight" between the two sides. What are the strengths and weaknesses of this approach to determining guilt?

CHAPTER EIGHT

COURTS

Alongside the police, the courts are among the most mythologized parts of American criminal justice. Images of tough prosecutors grilling witnesses on the stand or idealistic defense attorneys protecting innocent defendants with every ounce of energy are everywhere on TV and in the movies. High-profile criminal trials are a staple of American television, be they trials for celebrities, for alleged terrorists, or for whatever shocking crime captures the public imagination. Celebrity attorneys in expensive suits are hired by television networks to provide their expertise and comment on every piece of evidence and every bit of witness testimony that appears in these trials. When verdicts are finally reached, they are breathlessly covered by the media with dramatic flair, as juries shakily read out verdicts in front of crying or celebrating defendants, and journalists breathlessly narrate the outcome. The trial is barely over before reporters begin the hunt for the next shocking case to fill airtime and attract viewers.

In reality, high-profile trials are better seen as reality entertainment, where prosecutors, defense attorneys, and even judges understand that they are playing roles in a drama. They are performing for the media and often providing a parody of criminal justice—often so that they can cash in on the public attention with lucrative book contracts and television gigs when the trial is over. Very few ordinary cases ever go to trial, and when they do, it is usually a tedious and technical proceeding. There are few opportunities for courtroom theatrics and high drama in an actual trial. Most commonly, the court process consists in a quick negotiation between prosecutors and defense attorneys on the terms of a plea bargain before the parties move on to the next case. The courtroom hearing itself is for the most part a perfunctory exercise with little to no drama. In this chapter, we will attempt to peel back some of the myths about criminal trials and examine how they really work in the real world.

As with most aspects of criminal justice, there are two different ways to look at how courts operate: the official version of how trials work and the realities of how the system functions for most offenders. The first version involves prosecutors and defense attorneys fighting over the guilt or innocence of a defendant; the second is something far less confrontational and far more cooperative. Therefore, before we get into the roles of the different actors in the courtroom, we must look at these two models of American criminal courts: the adversarial system, and what is commonly referred to as the courtroom workgroup (Eisenstein & Jacob, 1977). These different models operate at the same time in most courts, and they define the roles of judges, prosecutors, and defense attorneys.

ADVERSARIAL JUSTICE

Learning Objective 8.1—Define the roles of prosecutors, defense attorneys, and judges in the adversarial system.

American justice is based on what is known as the adversarial model of justice—an approach we share with most other English-speaking countries because of its origins in the English legal system. Adversarial systems believe that the best way to determine the truth in a case is to have two sides fight it out, metaphorically speaking. One side, the prosecution, represents the state, and its goal is to get the accused convicted. The other side of the trial is the defense, which seeks to get the defendant either acquitted or, barring that, to get as light a punishment as possible. The judge serves as an umpire of sorts, making sure that both sides are following the proper rules and procedures before and during the hearing. The judge is expected to remain neutral about whether the defendant is guilty—only ensuring that the participants on both sides obey the rules. (We sometimes describe her role as the finder of law.) The jury is neutral too, only determining at the end of the trial which side "won" by voting to convict or acquit the defendant. (We sometimes call this role the finder of fact.) In American criminal trials, justice is set up like a sporting event with referees, winners, and losers.

This system is so ingrained in Americans' understanding of criminal justice that it is sometimes hard to imagine an alternative way to run a trial. But most countries in Europe have a very different approach to trials, called the *inquisitorial* system (Deffains & Demougin, 2008). In these courts, judges play a much more active role. There are often several judges in any case, one of whom (called the *investigating judge*) examines the evidence to determine whether there is enough to proceed with a trial. This judge gathers evidence and presents it to the court in a *dossier*, determining what charges the defendant will face. While prosecutors and defense attorneys may question witnesses during the trial and have a role to play in the proceedings, the judges are also questioning witnesses—they do not sit by passively while the lawyers for both sides do all the talking. Thus, unlike the adversarial system, the inquisitorial system sees the courtroom as a place where a neutral investigator finds the truth, rather than a battlefield for victory between two different sides (van Caenegem, 1999).

In the adversarial system, the lone individual accused of a crime stands opposed to THE STATE, that is the prosecutor, the police, and all their funding, staff, and support. The state has so much more power than defendants that without some serious protections, it would be very easy for the government to convict innocent people, simply because defendants lack the resources and experience to match their opponents in the prosecutor's office. To compensate for this power imbalance, the American system gives defendants certain legal protections: The rules of criminal trials are tilted in many ways that are meant to favor the defendant, making it less likely that an innocent person will be convicted. These handicaps placed on the state are intended to compensate for the power imbalance between the defendant and the state and make the procedures fairer than they would otherwise be.

One way that the courtroom is tilted in favor of the defendants is through the burden of proof. The criminal defendant is considered innocent until she is proven guilty. This means that the prosecutor must show that the defendant committed a crime. The defendant does not need to prove that she is innocent, only that the prosecutor didn't prove that she is guilty. This is the reason why an acquitted defendant is declared "not guilty" rather

Adversarial model: The criminal procedure in the Anglo-American system.

Finder of law: The person at the trial who is officially authorized to determine what the law says.

Finder of fact: The person or group that determines the guilt or innocence of a defendant. Usually the jury.

Burden of proof: The principle that a defendant is innocent until proven guilty.

than "innocent" in a trial—the court says that the prosecution failed to prove the defendant was guilty. The jury is not saying that the defendant truly is innocent. Bearing the burden of proof means that the state's job at trial is significantly harder than the defendant's, who only needs to play defense.

A second way the adversarial system handicaps the state is through the standard of evidence that the prosecutor must meet to get a conviction. The state must show "beyond a reasonable doubt" that the defendant is guilty. This is a high bar to clear: It is defined as a situation where, "No other logical explanation can be derived from the facts except that the defendant committed the crime." This is a higher standard than is found in civil lawsuits, where a "preponderance of the evidence standard" applies. This lower standard suggests that it is more likely than not that the defendant is responsible. Other legal standards that apply in different contexts include "clear and convincing evidence," "substantial evidence," and as we discussed in earlier chapters "probable cause." By requiring a very high standard of proof in criminal cases, the legal system tries to make it hard for the government to convict innocent individuals. All of this is done to prevent it from being too easy to convict an accused criminal and prevent the abuse of the criminal justice system by unscrupulous prosecutors.

There are several other important elements of the adversarial process that aid the defendant at trial. The **Brady rule** requires that prosecutors share **exculpatory evidence** (that is, evidence that helps the defendant) with the defense, but the defense is not required to share evidence that aids the prosecutor's case for the most part (*Brady v. Maryland*, 1963). The rule against **double jeopardy** prevents prosecutors from prosecuting the same defendant twice, regardless of whether new incriminating evidence has come to light. The Fifth Amendment's famous rule against *self-incrimination*, that is, the rule that states that a defendant need not testify in her trial, is there to help the defendant present her case and to make it harder for the prosecution to conduct its case. These rules are woven throughout the trial process and are meant to protect the defendant from unfair prosecutions and to limit the power of the government during a criminal trial. Effectively the government must go to trial with one hand tied behind its back to prevent it from abusing its authority.

Despite these rules, the court system is massively weighted against most criminal defendants—particularly poor ones. The reality is that few of these rights are given to most defendants, because almost all of them only apply in actual criminal trials and very few cases get that far. If a defendant can afford a private attorney and continue paying her over the course of a criminal trial, then it is likely that she will have many of these rights, but in practice most poorer defendants face a great deal of pressure to take a plea bargain and avoid a trial outright. This means that if a prosecutor wishes to go after a defendant and convict her of an offense, it is often very difficult for her to avoid criminal punishment. Rather than the adversarial system advertised by TV dramas, most criminal defendants face a very different reality when they are charged with a crime.

PLEA BARGAINS AND THE COURTROOM WORKGROUP

Learning Objective 8.2—Examine how the prosecutor, defense attorney, and judge cooperate in the courtroom workgroup.

The adversarial system is the philosophical model that animates American criminal courts, and in some situations the system approaches this ideal. In most cases, however, it looks

Brady rule: The rule that prosecutors must share exculpatory evidence with defendants.

Exculpatory evidence: Evidence that tends to show that the defendant is not guilty.

Double jeopardy: Putting somebody on trial twice for the same crime. It is not allowed in American criminal justice.

quite different. In ordinary cases, whatever their differences, the various parties of the adversarial process actually work together to achieve a larger goal—getting through the huge stack of cases that is in front of them. The fact that they all fear getting overwhelmed by their caseload forces them to cooperate much of the time. Legal scholars call this *the courtroom workgroup*. In their famous study of courts, James Eisenstein and Herbert Jacob argued that

> incentives and shared goals motivate the persons in a courtroom workgroup. . . . [Workgroup members] operate in a common task environment, which provides common constraints on their actions. The defendant does not encounter single persons or agencies as his case is processed; rather he confronts an organized network of relationships, in which each person who acts on his case is reacting to or anticipating the acts of others. (1977, p. 10)

Although prosecutors, defense attorneys, and judges represent different sides of a case, they have a loyalty to their coworkers in the court that can take precedence over the adversarial process.

Most people accused of crimes face a great deal of pressure to take a **plea bargain** offered by the prosecutor: Prosecutors offer the defendant a chance to plead guilty to a less serious charge in exchange for waiving her right to a trial. If the defendant refuses to accept the plea and insists on going to trial, she faces a threat of more serious charges, will probably spend a great deal of money on her legal defense, and may spend time in jail while awaiting trial. For example, a defendant could be charged with a very serious offense (say, attempted murder), but the prosecutor is willing to only charge her with battery (a less serious offense) with a lenient sentencing recommendation (say, one year in prison) if the defendant pleads guilty to the crime without a trial. The prosecutor avoids a costly, time-consuming process, while the defendant does not have to take the risk of spending many years behind bars for attempted murder if she is convicted. Plea bargains save the government, the courts, and the client money and time. On the other hand, they create a pressure for defendants, including those who are innocent, to accept the plea and go to jail. While the adversarial system is designed to protect defendants at trial, *less than 5% of cases actually go to trial—more than 95% of criminal cases end in a plea bargain* (Devers, 2011, p. 1).

All members of the courtroom workgroup benefit from a plea agreement. The prosecutor gains a relatively painless conviction with a plea bargain. The judges and most defense attorneys do too, because they too have cleared one more case from their workload. They all have an enormous number of cases to get through during their workday and do not have the time or resources to fight them all out in a full-blown trial. Even if you hire an attorney to defend you, she is better off in many ways if you accept a plea bargain—she avoids risking failure at trial and getting you sentenced to a long time in prison, and she maintains a good relationship with the court, one which will benefit her in a future case. Your private attorney wants to get you the best deal, and she may be convinced that a plea is a better offer than an unsuccessful trial. Judges too have long lists of cases to get through and cannot afford to get bogged down with long criminal trials, particularly for minor offenses. The reality is that nobody in the courtroom has time for actual criminal trials in most cases—nobody except an innocent defendant.

Plea bargain:
An agreement that a defendant makes with the prosecutor to plead guilty to a lesser offense to avoid prosecution (and possible conviction) for a more serious charge.

While many people find plea bargaining troubling, it is an essential part of the way that modern criminal justice operates. If every individual who was accused of a crime demanded a trial, the court system would crash very quickly under a massive backlog of cases. This means that the actors must convince the accused that the plea is a good deal. As one author put it,

> The system of mass incarceration depends almost entirely on the cooperation of those it seeks to control. If everyone charged with crimes suddenly exercised his constitutional rights, there would not be enough judges, lawyers or prison cells to deal with the ensuing tsunami of litigation. (Alexander, 2012)

Plea bargains make the current criminal justice system possible, but they put a great deal of pressure on the defendant. If she accepts a deal, she will probably spend less time in prison than she would if she were convicted of a crime at trial. If she asserts her right and loses, she is punished worse than if she waives her constitutional right to a trial. This means that the defendant is effectively being punished more severely for exercising her rights if she is convicted after a trial. A guilty defendant benefits from a plea bargain in most cases, but an innocent defendant must make a terrible choice: admit guilt for a crime she didn't commit or risk serving serious prison time if the case goes to trial.

The courtroom workgroup and the adversarial process are two aspects of criminal courts, and they often operate alongside each other. Sometimes the system is more adversarial and there is a great deal of fighting between the different sides; on the other hand, it often operates in a manner closer to the cooperative workgroup. Given this enormous pressure on defendants to accept guilty pleas offered by prosecutors, it is unusual for the process to resemble a purely adversarial system. Most often, the system becomes more adversarial when an accused individual has hired a private attorney, something that can cost a great deal of money. In these cases, the attorney has no loyalty to the other members of the courtroom workgroup and therefore may be more willing to aggressively protect her client. The point here is both that going to trial is unusual, and that when a case goes to trial, there are usually reasons that have little to do with the guilt or innocence of the defendant.

There is such a strong incentive to find a plea bargain that when cases do go to trial, it is usually for a specific set of reasons. In most of these cases, somebody wants to go to trial. In some instances, the defendant doesn't wish to accept a plea agreement and instructs her lawyer to reject any offers from the prosecutor. She may refuse to accept a plea because she believes that she is innocent or believes that she can win her case at trial. A defendant's attorney is not allowed to accept a plea without the consent of her client, and if she doesn't agree with her client's refusal of the plea offer, her only recourse is to withdraw from the case and tell her client to find a new attorney. On the other hand, the prosecutor may want a trial, either because she is unwilling to compromise in a plea bargain or because she wants the publicity benefits of an actual trial. One exception to this is **capital cases**, cases where the prosecutor seeks the death penalty for the defendant—in these cases there is no chance to plea bargain because there is no room to bargain. A trial is not the normal process of dealing with accused criminals—rather it is the result of a breakdown in the normal state of things: a plea bargain where everybody avoids the risks of a criminal trial.

In the remainder of this chapter we will examine the various members of the courtroom workgroup, looking at the different pressures that each faces when trying to fulfill the different

Capital case: A case where the defendant could receive the death sentence if convicted.

SOME STATISTICS...

Plea Bargains and Conviction Rates

There are many pressures on the courtroom workgroup to reach a plea agreement in lieu of going to trial. Money and time are in short supply, and so the court seeks to reach an agreement for a guilty plea whenever possible. According to research, over 95% of cases result in a plea bargain of some kind, a number that has increased over the last three decades (see Figure 8.1).

There are some cases where courts do not come to an agreement and, as a result, a full trial is conducted. Unsurprisingly, more serious crimes, most notably murder, are less likely to result in a plea bargain. In 2006, the Bureau of Justice Statistics reported that 61% of murder convictions were the result of a guilty plea and 39% were the result of a trial. A failure to plead guilty is likely to lead to a harsher sentence in a murder case (see Table 8.1).

Going to trial is a risky situation in many cases. If you are acquitted, you can go free, but if you are convicted, you are far more likely to face a stiffer punishment than would have resulted from a plea agreement. Defendants are given the choice of accepting responsibility or taking a great risk in a trial.

Figure 8.1   Percentage of Guilty Pleas Among Convictions in U.S. District Courts, 1965–2010

Source: "Understanding guilty pleas," n.d.

Note: Latest data available.

Table 8.1 Types of Sentences Imposed on Felons Convicted				
Type of Conviction	Total	Life	Death	Other*
Total	100%	23	2	75
Trial	100%	41	6	53
Jury	100	41	7	52
Bench	100	22	0	78
Guilty Plea	100	12	1	87

Source: **Rosenmerkel, Durose, & Farole, 2009.**

Note: **Latest data available.**

and sometimes contradictory roles of the adversarial process and the courtroom workgroup. We will start with the prosecutor's different jobs and her different loyalties. We will then turn to defense attorneys, both private defense attorneys and public defenders. Then, we will look at judges, both elected judges and appointed judges. Finally, we will look at related staff, including experts, bailiffs, court reporters, and other personnel who help the court function. Once we've set up these *dramatis personae* (the characters in the drama), we will watch them in action in the next chapter when we discuss criminal procedure and criminal trials.

Prosecutors

While judges probably have the highest status of any actor in the criminal justice system, prosecutors are unquestionably the most powerful. The main source of this power is their prosecutorial discretion. Like police officers, prosecutors have a great deal of freedom in how they handle criminal cases and experience very little supervision. They can charge a suspect with an offense, or they can opt not to. If they decide to charge a defendant, they can charge her with a serious offense or with a less serious one. It is almost entirely up to them. If the prosecutor wishes to pursue the death penalty, she can, but she doesn't have to. A thoughtful prosecutor will listen to several people including the victims, as well as carefully analyze the facts, but the ultimate decision regarding how to pursue a case is hers. As we will see in the next chapter, the prosecutor must be able to convince a grand jury to indict a defendant, but beyond this low bar, there is little holding a prosecutor back. In the criminal trial, it is the prosecutor, not the judge, who holds many of the cards—the judge can only deal with a case that has been presented to her by the prosecutor.

Prosecutorial discretion: The authority that officers have to charge or not charge a person with a crime and to determine what the precise charges against a defendant will be.

As with other parts of the criminal justice system, there are many important differences between prosecutors at the federal level and those at the state level, and there is some variation among the states. Federal prosecutors, more accurately called U.S. attorneys, serve under the Justice Department—meaning that they are often part of a federal bureaucratic hierarchy and answer to the head of the Justice Department, the attorney general (AG). The attorney general serves "at the pleasure of the president," meaning that the president can fire the AG at will.[1] State and local prosecutors are often elected officials and must answer to the voters, though this varies from state to state. Many prosecutors, though certainly not all, see the job as a stepping stone to a bigger career in politics and are keeping an eye on the next rung of the political ladder when they make decisions about who to prosecute. (Among the current group of national politicians who were once prosecutors are Kamala Harris, Chris Christie, Ted Cruz, and Rudy Giuliani, but many others use their prosecutor job as a first step to higher office.) Developing a reputation as a tough crime fighter is perceived as a good way to get people to support you for bigger things, and therefore the prosecutor's office is appealing to many politicians (Sawyer & Clark, 2017).

Clearly, prosecutorial discretion is an important power—we want prosecutors to determine which cases are best to pursue and which are best left behind. This decision can be based on the severity of the crime and the likelihood that the prosecutor can get a conviction but also by other factors (Frederick & Stemen, 2012). In their survey of prosecutors, two researchers found that "most participants described justice as a balance between the community's public safety concerns and the imperative to treat defendants fairly. In considering that balance, survey respondents overwhelmingly considered fair treatment to be more important than public protection" (Frederick & Stemen, 2012, p. 4). Further, researchers suggested that cost and other considerations affected their decisions, as "shortages of courtrooms, judges, clerks, court reporters, and scheduled court hours—and especially unscheduled reductions in court hours—often forced prosecutors to undercharge, reevaluate and change plea offers, or dismiss cases" (Frederick & Stemen, 2012, p. 4). There are a host of factors that can affect a prosecutor's decision whether to pursue a case and how exactly to pursue it.

In August 2013 President Obama's attorney general Eric Holder sent a memo to all federal prosecutors telling them that in most cases, they should not prosecute individuals who are involved in the marijuana trade in states where pot has been legalized (Perez, 2013). This meant that, even though Congress has passed laws criminalizing marijuana, prosecutors were told not to pursue drug traffickers if their activities were legal under state law. It would have been too difficult and expensive to take on these cases without the help of local law enforcement. Similarly, in 2014, President Obama issued an executive order telling federal officials to not enforce immigration laws and not deport many undocumented aliens. There was never enough money to deport even a fraction of the 11 million

---

[1] Though the president can fire attorneys general at will, this can be a politically dangerous thing for presidents to do. In October 1973 President Richard Nixon directed his attorney general to fire a special prosecutor investigating a break-in at the Watergate Hotel that was conducted by Nixon's staffers. The attorney general (Elliot Richardson) refused and resigned in protest. The resulting outcry forced President Nixon to appoint a new special prosecutor and contributed substantially to the pressures on Nixon to resign the presidency less than a year later. While the attorney general answers to the president, in many ways her obligation to uphold the law is higher than her duty to the president in office.

plus undocumented workers regardless; Obama just made the policy official. President Trump then overturned this order in 2017. Both cases were very controversial and created anger among Obama's critics; they show the power of prosecutorial discretion. With a few exceptions prosecutors and their political leaders have an incredible ability to determine who goes to jail and who does not.

In their work, prosecutors often face three different pressures: *politics*, *justice*, and *prosecution*, and sometimes these can conflict with each other. By *politics*, I mean that prosecutors are in some ways politicians who must deal with demands either from voters if they are elected or from their political superiors if they are appointed. This can put pressure on prosecutors to pursue or ignore cases under certain circumstances. Further, by *justice*, I mean the prosecutor faces pressure from her duty to uphold the law—meaning that she must make sure that the law is enforced in a fair and impartial manner. This can include making sure that innocent people are not prosecuted, and that people are not punished too harshly by the courts. Finally, prosecutors face a duty to *prosecute*. In the adversarial process, prosecutors are expected to convict defendants either through plea bargains or actual trials, and they are often judged by the number of convictions they get. This means that modern prosecutors must participate in a sort of balancing act as they seek to make the public happy and fulfill their obligations to uphold the law and simultaneously to get convictions.

These three forces can pull a prosecutor in different directions in some situations. If a prosecutor genuinely believes that prosecuting a suspect would be unpopular and hurt her career (say, a police officer accused of lying under oath to get a conviction), she may choose not to prosecute the suspect even if the suspect is likely to be guilty (Bloch, 2018). Similarly, she may choose not to prosecute somebody because she fears that she might not get a conviction, which could hurt her career. Or, in extreme cases, a prosecutor may be tempted to charge an individual simply for political benefit. This could be a person whose offenses are not serious but who is widely disliked by the public or a person who is particularly flagrant in her offenses, even if the offenses were not serious in nature. It can also lead a prosecutor to "push the boundaries" to get convictions. As one journalist put it,

> Prosecutors get no credit for cases they decide not to bring, either because of a lack of evidence or because pressing charges wouldn't be in the interest of justice. They're only rewarded for winning convictions. That's what gets them promoted, or re-elected, or gives them the elevated profile to run for higher office. Every incentive points toward winning convictions. And particularly with prosecutors, there's really no penalty at all for going too far to get a guilty verdict. ("Prosecutor or politician?" 2010)

There are a vast number of reasons why a prosecutor may choose to use her prosecutorial discretion to advance her career or to pursue some other goal that may not necessarily be a noble one. While these cases may be rare, they are important (Davis, 2005).

Once a trial is underway, the prosecutor can face a great deal of pressure to convict a defendant. In the adversarial system, it is the prosecutor's job to get a conviction. A failure to convict would be a black mark on the prosecutor's record—giving the prosecutor an incentive to get a conviction regardless of the quality of the case. In March 2014, Debra Milke was released from death row in Georgia. The charges against Milke were thrown out, and she was freed from prison after serving 22 years for allegedly murdering her son.

Prosecutorial Discretion and Mandatory Minimums

Over the years, many people have been unhappy about sentencing practices in the United States. Some have complained about *sentencing disparities*, that is, very large differences in the sentences given to offenders who commit similar crimes. Also, they have been unhappy about early-release programs such as parole. If an offender is sentenced to 20 years in prison, she should serve all 20 of those years. Allowing judges to choose a sentence leaves too much to the biases of individual judges, critics have charged. So-called truth-in-sentencing laws, that is, laws that require a judge to sentence an offender to a certain length of time and prevent early release, were created at both the federal and state levels to prevent judges from holding too much power over sentencing. While some states consider these guidelines to be only suggestions, some states make sentencing requirements mandatory.

While these laws may have taken sentencing discretion out of the hands of judges, they passed this discretion directly into the hands of the prosecutor. Truth-in-sentencing laws require that judges give a predetermined sentence to an offender; what they don't do is require that the prosecutor charge the offender with a crime. She can charge the defendant with a lesser offense or a greater one depending on what she feels is appropriate and what she believes will give her the best chance of a plea bargain or a conviction at trial. She now has a great deal more power over the fate of criminal defendants, and observers noted that these laws led to higher incarceration rates (Rosich & Kane, 2005).

In places where judges have a great deal of discretion, this power of prosecutors is limited—they can charge a defendant with a serious offense, but ultimately the judge gets to determine the punishment (Boerner, 1994). If the prosecutor charged a defendant with a serious offense, the judge can still offer a lighter punishment if she believes that the defendant does not deserve a harsh sentence. With truth-in-sentencing laws, that power is largely taken away from the judge. Her hands are tied.

Such sentencing laws empower prosecutors to use their discretion in ways that can distort the adversarial process (Bowman, 2005). They can use this power to threaten alleged criminals, which can be useful when trying to get them to testify against others. Also, these laws give prosecutors a much stronger hand in sentencing, because they can effectively dictate the amount of time the offender would spend in prison. Keep in mind that only one of the three jobs that prosecutors have is to uphold principles of justice—they also have their own political interests and their role in the adversarial process to consider when charging an offender. Prosecutors then have a strong incentive to seek long sentences for offenders. While prosecutorial discretion is important, it is a power that could easily be abused, and sentencing requirements increase the already enormous powers of prosecutors in the adversarial system.

As a result of some of these concerns, many truth-in-sentencing laws have been either overruled or watered down by courts and transformed into simple suggestions that judges aren't obliged to follow. The Supreme Court watered down such a law in the 2005 case *United States v. Booker* (Reitz, 2005).

The "confession" that was central to the case was not recorded, but a detective stated under oath that Milke confessed to murdering her son for insurance money. The prosecutor covered up the fact that the detective had a long history of lying under oath and had many ethical lapses (Ahmed & Botelho, 2015). Clearly the prosecutor wanted to convict the

CRIMINAL (IN)JUSTICE

The Case of Michael Nifong

Sometimes political pressure can lead prosecutors to make grossly unethical decisions that get them in a great deal of trouble. Perhaps the most well-known example of this is the case of Michael Nifong. In March 2006, the lacrosse team for Duke University held a party where the boys called a service to have a group of strippers "entertain" them. When the strippers arrived, they had an altercation with the boys. (They had requested white dancers, and when the dancers arrived, they reportedly referred to the dancers with racist slurs.) After leaving the party, one of the dancers, who went under the name "Crystal Magnum," reported that she had been sexually assaulted by several of the boys at the party.

Michael Nifong was the prosecutor for Durham County, where Duke University is located. Like many other prosecutors, Nifong was an elected official who needed the votes of his largely liberal and African American constituents. Given that Duke University has a student body that is very white and perceived as very privileged by much of the population, he must have seen this case as a great opportunity to get the political support of his constituents and bolster his political career. He aggressively pursued the case and frequently attacked the students in public statements. "The circumstances of the rape indicated a deep racial motivation for some of the things that were done," Nifong said, making it "a crime that is by its nature one of the most offensive and invasive even more so" ("Report," 2006). Demonstrators from the community protested against the team and the university leadership over the case. Three members of the team were arrested and charged with first degree forcible rape.

Unfortunately for Nifong, the case quickly began to unravel as important pieces of evidence that pointed to the innocence of the Duke students were uncovered. Most important, genetic material taken from Magnum was not linked with any member of the Duke lacrosse team. Rather than share this important evidence with the defendants' attorneys, as he was required to do by law, Nifong concealed it and continued with the prosecution. More evidence revealed later further pointed to the innocence of the students, and investigators found inconsistencies in the testimony of the alleged victim. The charges against the men were soon dropped, and Nifong himself became the subject of an investigation. As one of the defense attorneys stated against Nifong, "It is the ethical duty of a district attorney not to win a case, not to prosecute all cases, but to see that justice is done." ("Rape Charges Dropped," 2006). Ultimately Nifong was punished for his misconduct: He was forced to resign from his position as district attorney, was disbarred, and ultimately sent to prison for one day.

Nifong's case is an important lesson for understanding how prosecutors can easily overstep their bounds and do serious harm. It is important to note that Nifong is very much an exceptional case: Most DAs who commit acts of misconduct are not severely sanctioned. As one former prosecutor put it, "You have rogue prosecutors all over the country who have engaged in far, far more egregious misconduct [than Nifong's], and in a pattern of cases. And nothing happens" (Liptak, 2007). Alan Gell was sentenced to death in North Carolina after prosecutors withheld key eyewitness evidence that showed that Gell could not have been the murderer. When the evidence was discovered, the defendant was ultimately released. Gell's prosecutors were reprimanded for their misconduct but received no real punishment. Perhaps it was because of the high-profile nature of the case, or perhaps because the Duke students were privileged (and white), but regardless, Nifong's treatment in the aftermath of the Duke lacrosse case is very much an exception, not a rule.

How could lawmakers prevent prosecutorial abuses like those committed by Nifong? Would any reforms make it more difficult for prosecutors to fight crime? Would they make us less safe?

defendant regardless of the evidence. He may have genuinely believed Milke was guilty, but attempts to cover up exculpatory evidence are illegal (see "The Case of Michael Nifong" that follows) and are examples of what is known as *prosecutorial misconduct*—the abuse of the prosecutor's authority. The Marshall Project (https://www.themarshallproject.org), a nonprofit journalism organization, monitors and tracks cases of alleged prosecutorial conduct that can be very enlightening. Many prosecutors conduct their work ethically and thoughtfully, but there are sometimes intense political and professional pressure on them that can lead to such damaging misconduct.

Defense

The prosecutor is beholden to the people in some form or another—it is her job to represent the people at trial and make sure that justice is impartially and fairly carried out. The defense attorney has no similar obligation to uphold justice. She is simply in charge of defending her client within the bounds of the law and the codes of legal ethics. The technical term for the defense attorney's job is this: She is to provide a *zealous defense* for her client. For her professional responsibilities, the guilt or innocence of the defendant is irrelevant; she must fight for the best interests of her client either way. She only cares about how she can best represent her clients' interests. That may mean convincing the defendant to accept a plea deal or fighting for her client at trial. In the adversarial system, the defense attorney's only job is to make sure that her client gets the best outcome that she can get for her.

Again, this idea of the defense attorney is only partially true in practice. Many poor clients are represented by a public defender of some sort—a person whose interests may diverge from those of her client. The Sixth Amendment to the Constitution states that, "In all criminal prosecutions, the accused shall enjoy the right to . . . have the assistance of counsel for his defense." In the case of *Gideon v. Wainwright* (1963), the Supreme Court determined that this right entails that individuals who cannot afford an attorney of their own have a right to an attorney paid for by the state. As the court stated, "In our adversary system of criminal justice, any person hauled into court, who is too poor to hire a lawyer, cannot be assured a fair trial unless counsel is provided for him." This is only for cases where there is the chance of incarceration—if there is no chance the defendant will go to prison, there is no right to counsel. Similarly, *Gideon* determined that "indigent defendants" have the right to counsel, but "indigence" is often difficult to prove. Children or defendants with intellectual disabilities are usually given an attorney regardless.

There are several different means by which the court can appoint an attorney to defend an indigent client. The most common way for this to happen is through a regular public defender—a person employed directly by the court to defend the indigent. While many public defenders are idealistic, hardworking attorneys, they are often saddled with *hundreds* of cases to handle at one time and cannot possibly provide each client with the attention necessary for a strong defense.

This is not the only way that the government can provide counsel for indigent defendants. One way for the court to get an attorney for a defendant who cannot afford one is through pro bono legal work. Pro bono means "for the common good," and though criminal defense is not the only type of pro bono work lawyers can do, this can nonetheless be a valuable resource for the court to find legal counsel. Lawyers are often expected to do a certain amount of pro bono work to maintain their ability to practice law and as it is

Pro bono: Legal work that is done without charge.

meant to be part of the professional responsibility of attorneys, this work is unpaid. A third way is through contracts with lawyers or private law firms where the attorneys receive a set fee per case.

While these different approaches may be valuable tools for providing counsel for criminal defendants, each has problems. As we've discussed, as a permanent part of the court, the public defender is part of the courtroom workgroup. She must maintain good relations with the other members of this group. This means that she develops a working relationship with the other members of the court and can negotiate with them. Further, given the budget constraints placed on her job, she cannot provide a completely zealous defense for every individual who is charged by the court, as there is neither the time nor the money for it. This means that public defenders often have an incentive to convince a criminal defendant to accept a plea bargain to avoid the expense of a full criminal trial.

While the other forms of public defense may avoid some of these problems, they too have their share of problems. Attorneys sometimes do not wish to do pro bono work, as it is not paid, and therefore they may not be inclined to zealously defend their client's interests. Private attorneys who are paid by the court through a contract may see their referrals decline if they get a reputation for being too difficult for the rest of the workgroup. Private attorneys can often provide a better defense than public defenders, but there are many stories of attorneys bilking money out of defendants who are terrified of going to jail. By dragging out cases through the appeals process, an attorney can make more money than she might through a shorter trial. Also, if a defendant does not have a great deal of money, her attorney may be inclined to accept a plea before it runs out.

Criminal defense attorneys have a bad public reputation as unscrupulous characters who would defend anyone for a buck. While there are criminal attorneys who are ethically challenged (and some who have been involved in outright criminal activities), many criminal defense attorneys are passionate about defending their clients and making sure that they get a fair shake from the criminal justice system. High-profile cases pay a great deal of money, but criminal law is not a particularly lucrative field, and criminal lawyers typically make less than lawyers working in corporate law or tax law. Only high-profile criminal lawyers and those who work in fields like white collar criminal defense (defending executives and bankers) make a significant income. Further, many criminal lawyers reportedly leave the field because they find the people that they must interact with to be difficult or distasteful. Those criminal defense lawyers who go the distance and stay in the field are often deeply committed to helping defendants who are in a tight spot. (Over the years I've had many students who were skeptical about the ethics of criminal defense lawyers be grateful for their help when they were charged with an offense.)

The type of attorney that an accused individual has can have a tremendous impact on the outcomes of her case. A study conducted by the RAND Corporation of over 3,000 murder cases in Philadelphia from 1994 to 2005 concluded that a public defender was likely to produce much better outcomes for defendants than would a private attorney appointed by the court (Anderson & Heaton, 2011). On the other hand, some evidence suggests that an attorney hired by the client is much more likely to be helpful for the defendant than would either a public defender or a court-appointed attorney (Hoffman, Rubin, & Shepherd, 2005). Private lawyers paid by the defendant are willing to fight hard for their clients and, as a result, are often able to produce better outcomes for the accused. On the other hand, some researchers have argued that the working

WHAT WOULD YOU DO?

Hiding Exculpatory Evidence

You have received your dream internship in the local city prosecutor's office. Even better, the prosecutors are giving you real work to do, not just fetching coffee or making photocopies but helping to prepare evidence for important cases. They've brought you in to help prosecute a grisly, high-profile murder. The defendant, Jared Sylvester, is accused of murdering both of his parents to inherit their fortune. Sylvester is currently awaiting trial, and the prosecutors are seeking the death penalty, so there's a lot of media coverage and a lot of excitement in the office.

You've been assigned the job or sorting through the evidence found in Sylvester's home, noting precisely where it was found and entering this information into a database the prosecutor is using to keep track of it all. While looking through the material, you find Sylvester's journal, some of which marks out the plan to kill his parents. It looks damning, but he claims that the journal was just a bunch of fantasies and that he is innocent.

When you look at the journal and where it was discovered, you realize that it was found outside of the area described by the search warrant the judge signed. Specifically, the judge allowed the police to search the property at the Sylvester house. The book was found at a small garage that Sylvester rented that belonged to Sylvester's next-door neighbor. The police should have gotten a separate warrant to search

that property, but probably didn't even realize that the garage wasn't on Sylvester's grounds—there is no way that you'd know it wasn't on his property if you just looked at it. You mention this problem to your supervisor, the head prosecutor in the case. She looks you in the eye and says, "You didn't see this, ok?" and then tears up the note about where it was found. She opens the database and enters information that the evidence was found in Sylvester's house and not the garage.

You know that the journal is important to the prosecutor's case. They can still convict Sylvester without it, but their case would be much harder. It might also affect the prosecutor's ability to get a death sentence for Sylvester, as the journal seems to show that the murder was carefully thought through, and it would be harder to prove that without the journal. On the other hand, if it turned out later that the journal was used at the trial but should not have been, the entire case could be thrown out of court and the prosecutor could get in trouble. Further, if you leaked the information to the defense counsel, the prosecutors will know that it was you, as you are the only person other than your supervisor who knows that the journal should not be allowed.

What do you do? Do you contact the defense attorney and let her know about the evidence? Why or why not?

relationship between a public defender and the prosecutor's office can compensate for this (Hartley, Miller, & Spohn, 2010; Wolf-Harlow, 2000). Of course, private attorneys are very expensive, and most poor defendants could never afford one, regardless of whether it would help their case.

Judges

Like the two other main players in the criminal courts, the judge faces many competing pressures on the job. Within the adversarial process, her primary task is to make legal decisions during the trial—for example, she[2] is responsible for determining whether evidence should be admitted to the jury or should be excluded (a subject for the next chapter). Along with this role, she is also in charge of the administration of the courtroom, making sure that it runs efficiently and stays on budget. Like the other people we've discussed in this chapter, judges are beholden to the demands of the courtroom workgroup—they must work together to process the large number of cases that appear on their docket. That means that judges are often a part of the plea-bargaining process, as they ultimately determine a sentence—which may turn out to be different from the sentence that the prosecutor and the defendant agreed to. A judge can also put pressure on both sides to come to a plea agreement if she believes that going to trial would not be a good idea for one or both parties.

Like prosecutors, some judges are elected, and others are appointed. Federal judges are appointed by the president with the approval of the Senate, but many state and local judges are elected by the people in their state, county, or city. Once federal judges are appointed, they serve for life, and the only way to remove them is by impeachment. (**Impeachment** is the process by which public officials are removed from office by Congress or state legislators for improper conduct.) Historically, the election of judges has been a nonpartisan process that didn't raise many concerns. Recently some judicial elections have been hotly contested, and judges have been voted out of office for controversial decisions. In 2012, three Iowa Supreme Court judges were removed from office by Iowa voters largely because they had issued an opinion in favor of legalizing gay marriage. Both unelected judges appointed for life and judges who can be voted out of office for making unpopular decisions present problems for the criminal justice system.

The election of judges can take place in a wide variety of ways and varies a great deal among the different states. Many states have elections that are no different from traditional partisan elections, but many have nonpartisan elections, where political parties don't participate, and the judges cannot list any party affiliations on their ballots. Other states allow voters to re-elect or reject a judge but do not allow another candidate to run against a sitting judge. Some states mix it up—electing different judges in different ways for higher courts and lower courts.

The fact that some judges must face the voters through an election creates many different issues for judges. In criminal cases, judges often feel that they must look tough on crime to keep their jobs. Studies have shown that elected judges offer harsher sentences than nonelected judges, including more death sentences when they are facing an election (Bright & Keenan, 1995). Any hint that a judge is soft on criminals is potentially devastating in a close election with a well-funded opponent. While many of these campaigns center on the issue of criminal justice, a lot of judges' work involves noncriminal matters, and many business groups contribute to probusiness judges who they expect to rule in their favor.

While appointed judges avoid some of these problems, they too have come under criticism. In recent years the judicial appointment process has been politicized, as different groups such as corporations have sought to shape the courts that might hear their cases. Rather than picking judges based on their experience and ability, many politicians have

Impeachment: The process where public officials are removed from office by Congress or state legislators for improper conduct.

---

[2] In both state and federal courts, approximately 33% of judges are women (National Association of Women Judges, 2018).

chosen judges with an eye toward shaping the future of American society. A judge who is on your side of a political divide is not likely to overrule your laws and is more likely to overrule laws passed by your political opponents—making the ability to influence the makeup of courts an incredibly important power. While judges aren't supposed to be political, partisan political observers often talk about "liberal judges" and "conservative judges" because they believe that many judges are politically biased. Conservative judges tend to make decisions that support Republican policies, and liberals tend to do the same for Democrats. The term judicial activism has been used to describe judges who use their power to promote a political agenda, and in recent years judges have been chosen by presidents and by governors more often for their political loyalties than for their legal expertise or their skills as a judge.

OTHER COURTROOM STAFF

Learning Objective 8.3—Name the ancillary courtroom staff.

Along with the three main figures in the courtroom workgroup, there are numerous people who help the court run on a day-to-day basis. Some of these are employed by the court full-time, while others are brought in for specific situations. For example, the court might need a social worker or psychologist to help with children involved in a case, or an interpreter can be brought in if a witness does not speak English.

Bailiff

In most states, the bailiff is the law enforcement officer of the court. It is her job to maintain order within the courtroom, including arresting people who misbehave, escorting defendants, and even using force in the courtroom when necessary. Some states use different terms for bailiffs—such as *court officer* or *marshal*. Some of these figures are sworn law enforcement officers who happen to be assigned to work in the courtroom, while others are officers who have law enforcement powers exclusively within the court buildings.

Clerk

The clerk is the head administrator for the court. She keeps records for the court (including informing attorneys, defendants, and witnesses about important trial dates), handles schedules for trials, deals with personnel issues, and often administers the oath to witnesses.

Court Reporter

Judicial activism: A term used to criticize judges who are believed to make legal decisions based on their political views rather than on the law.

The court reporter's job is to write down the testimony during the trial. She uses a special typing machine called a *stenotype* that is designed so that the reporter can quickly write down what is said during the trial. The court uses these human recorders rather than tapes or digital recorders so that important testimony is not missed because of noises in the courtroom (such as a cough or a phone ringing).

Social Workers

Social workers, psychologists, and other professionals participate in criminal trials in different ways. They can be appointed by the court to interview criminal defendants or witnesses and provide recommendations for the court.

Juris doctorate (JD): The official name for a law degree.

WHERE DO I FIT IN?

BECOMING AN ATTORNEY

The key figures in criminal courts are all lawyers, and becoming an attorney is an ambition of many college students. All prosecutors, defense attorneys, and judges are lawyers. The job provides an opportunity to make a great deal of money (if you're particularly talented and hard working) as well as challenging and interesting work (if you're lucky). Becoming a lawyer is a long and difficult road, and only a few practicing attorneys opt to focus on criminal law.

To get into law school, you need to take the Law School Aptitude Test (LSAT) and get letters of recommendation from professors or other people in your life. Most universities and colleges have prelaw advisors who can help you through this process. Once you are admitted, law school is a grueling three-year process toward a juris doctorate (JD) degree. Usually the first year of law school is the hardest, as the workload is demanding, and law students can be very competitive. By the third year, many students have begun to transition out of the school and have begun working in firms as interns. After you graduate, you must pass the difficult bar exam for the state where you wish to practice. This test certifies that you have the requisite knowledge to practice law there. Once you pass the bar exam, you then begin the often-unglamorous work of a young lawyer, which can include preparing legal briefs, sifting through material for a case, or reading contracts for more senior attorneys.

Law school can be quite expensive, as most schools anticipate that you will make back the money spent on tuition over the course of your legal career. Law school can easily cost $150,000 in tuition alone (not including living expenses), though most schools have scholarships or grants for particularly promising students. In short, law school is not something to do simply because it sounds interesting or because you're not ready to leave school and face the real world.

One more thing to keep in mind is this student loan debt needs to be repaid, which can mean that new graduates are saddled with up to $2000/month loan payment on top of other living expenses like mortgages and car insurance. This can affect a young lawyer's career choices and helps explain why few newly minted JDs go into criminal law—it rarely pays a lot of money, at least when compared to more lucrative fields like corporate or tax law. At the beginning of their careers, public defenders and prosecutors make about $47,500, which is a pittance compared to other legal careers (National Association for Law Placement, 2010). There are some programs that can help young lawyers who go into parts of the law that benefit society pay back their loans, but these can be competitive. Private criminal defense attorneys can make a lot more, but this often depends on finding clients, which can be a lot of work.

CHAPTER SUMMARY

In this chapter, we have looked at the cast of characters that make up American criminal courts, including the prosecutor, the defense attorney, and the judge. While there is often an overlap with other courts (such as civil courts, family courts, and appellate courts), criminal courts have their own distinct modes of operation. There is no prosecutor or defense attorney in civil court, there are no witnesses during appeals, and courts that handle juvenile offenders are not aimed at punishing criminals but rather helping delinquent juveniles get their life on track. Remember that while prosecutors, defense attorneys, and judges are part of the adversarial process, they are also aspects of a much broader courtroom structure (the courtroom workgroup) and are also part of bigger governmental bureaucracies that can sometimes shape their decisions.

In the next chapter, we will see how these different actors function when the courtroom workgroup's process breaks down and there is no plea agreement. Then, the process becomes much more adversarial, and the two sides "fight it out" throughout a series of complex courtroom proceedings that compose the criminal trial.

REVIEW/DISCUSSION QUESTIONS

1. Why do American courts run on two different "systems" (the adversarial model and the courtroom workgroup)? How are they similar? How are they different?

2. The prosecutor is a conflicted position. She must balance a lot of different goals, some of which can conflict with each other. What are these conflicts, and how do you think an ethical prosecutor might resolve them in her work?

3. What are some of the ways that criminal courts protect the rights of defendants? Do you think these are sufficient? If so, why? If not, how might they be improved?

KEY TERMS

Adversarial model 192
Brady rule 193
Burden of proof 192
Capital case 195
Double jeopardy 193

Exculpatory evidence 193
Finder of fact 192
Finder of law 192
Impeachment 205
Judicial activism 206

Juris doctorate (JD) 207
Plea bargain 194
Pro bono 202
Prosecutorial discretion 197

$SAGE edge™

Get the tools you need to sharpen your study skills. SAGE edge offers a robust online environment featuring an impressive array of free tools and resources.

Access practice quizzes, eFlashcards, video, and multimedia at edge.sagepub.com/fichtelberg

Sarah Yeh

Studies show that jurors of different race sometimes reach different conclusions in a case. Do you think you could be objective as a juror?

CHAPTER NINE

CRIMINAL TRIALS

In this chapter we're going to look at what happens after a suspect is arrested by the police, following her through the courts and up to the prison gate. This means that we will start with *pretrial procedures*, what happens before a trial begins, and then look at the *trial* itself, including laws governing interrogating witnesses and presenting evidence. Then we will turn to the appeals process—what happens when a defendant is convicted of a crime but seeks to have her conviction overturned by a higher court. As with policing, each of the 50 states conducts its criminal procedures in slightly different ways, and so we will only be able to discuss these processes in a broad fashion, hitting some of the features of criminal courts that are found in almost every state. You should do some careful research on your own state's court system, preferably with the guidance of an attorney, if you are faced with the possibility of a criminal trial.

PRETRIAL

Learning Objective 9.1—List the major aspects of the initial appearance, jury selection, and pretrial motions.

Once the suspect has been arrested and informed of her rights, she is then taken to the police station for *booking*. Booking is the process of gathering technical information about the suspect such as name, age, height, et cetera. Usually mug shot photos will be taken. The suspect will then be placed in a *holding cell* to await the next stage of an *initial appearance*. Here, the defendant is informed of the charges against her and asked about whether she needs to hire an attorney, and the judge sets bail. The purpose of the initial appearance is to ensure that the defendant is not being held without proper justification and to further inform the defendant about her rights. If the arrest happened without a warrant, the judge must determine whether there are sufficient grounds to hold the suspect. The evidence that is used to establish probable cause here is minimal—the police must swear that the evidence against the suspect is valid. The defendant need not have an attorney present and witnesses are not called.

The initial appearance is usually different from an *arraignment*. During an arraignment the defendant is informed of the official charges against her and can enter a plea to the court. Defendants can plead guilty, not guilty, or **nolo contendere** or "nolo." A nolo plea means that the defendant does not accept guilt for the charges against her but declines her right to defend herself. She is not contesting the charges against her. This is effectively

Nolo contendere: A plea where a defendant does not admit guilt but also does not contest the charges against her.

the same thing as a guilty plea, since the defendant is punished as though she were guilty, but because the defendant does not accept legal responsibility for her acts, she cannot automatically be found liable in a civil suit. Most of the time, defendants will initially plead not guilty and later change their plea to guilty after a plea bargain is negotiated among the members of the courtroom workgroup. If you plead guilty, you give up any future negotiating power with the prosecutor. Along with the defendant entering a plea, the judge usually sets bail during an arraignment.

Municipal Courts and the Right to Counsel

In October 2017, the American Civil Liberties Union sued the City of Beaufort and the Town of Bluffton, both located in coastal South Carolina just across the border from Savannah, Georgia. The suit alleges that these towns use municipal courts to try, convict, and sentence offenders without providing defendants any legal counsel, in violation of the Sixth Amendment. Municipal courts are courts that are set up by local governments to handle small-scale criminal cases. Most of the judges in these courts are lawyers who work part-time as municipal court judges ("Order and Opinion," 2018, p. 3). The ACLU charge that these courts unlawfully deprive citizens of their constitutional right to a fair trial and adequate representation (*Bairefoot v. City of Beaufort et al.*, 2017).

Many of the people arrested by the Beaufort police are low-level offenders who have committed only minor offenses but wind up serving long stretches of prison because they lack the ability and resources to defend themselves. Many of these defendants, such as Tina Bairefoot, the plaintiff in the case, are mentally ill and are picked up for petty crimes like shoplifting or trespassing. According to a *New York Times* report on the case, one mentally ill resident of Beaufort has been arrested 270 times for minor offenses (Williams, 2017). This person suffered a head trauma when he was younger and lives on disability payments, which are halted when he is imprisoned. As a result, when he gets out, he has no money and is quickly picked up again for some minor infraction.

Providing attorneys for these small-time offenders would be a huge financial drain on any city. Municipal courts were created largely to provide a quick and inexpensive response to these kinds of small-scale infractions. They often prioritize expedience over justice, as defendants are encouraged to accept a quick resolution to the conflict or face extensive waiting periods before a trial. Poor defendants who cannot afford bail are particularly under threat, as they will be forced to await their trials in a jail cell.

Bail and Bail Bondsmen

Bail is a sum of money put forward by the defendant to guarantee that she will appear for her trial and not skip town. The court will usually calculate the defendant's bail based on several factors that are likely to affect whether the defendant will show up for her trial. This can include the defendant's ties to the community (Does she have family nearby? Does she own a home?) and the working situation of the defendant (Does she have a job?) as well as the seriousness of the offense. The more serious the offense, the more likely it is that the defendant poses a flight risk—that is, that she will skip bail and go into hiding to avoid going to prison. With these factors in mind, the court determines how much money is appropriate to ask from the defendant to let her go free until her court date. Defendants who are considered trustworthy and likely to show up for the court date can be released "ROR"—released on their own recognizance (effectively allowed to leave with a promise that she will return). If the defendant is considered a particularly bad risk, that is, if the court concludes that she is highly likely to flee, the court will not allow her to post bail, and she will be held in jail until her trial. All others are asked to give the court money to guarantee that they return for trial. If a defendant presents the court with the money (posts bail), she is allowed to go free. If she shows up for the trial, she gets (most of) it back, but if she does not show up for her trial—she "skips out on bail"—the money is usually forfeit, and a warrant is issued for the defendant's arrest.

Private *bail bondsmen* are licensed to front the money for an individual defendant's bail, so she can go free until her trial even if she hasn't got the money for her bail. Usually, bail bondsmen take a fee of about 10% of the bond from the defendant or her friends and family to post bail for the defendant. Then, the bail bondsman is liable to the court for the money if the defendant flees, unless she can retrieve the defendant herself, often with the help of a *bounty hunter*—an agent empowered to arrest and return a fleeing defendant.

Some states have recently passed laws that are designed to reduce or eliminate cash bail from their criminal justice systems. The Bail Reform and Speedy Trial Act in New Jersey replaces cash bond with a point system based on facts of a case and information about the accused. These points then allow the judge to determine whether the defendant can go free until her trial or should be kept in custody. Advocates of the bill argue that requiring defendants to put up cash or linger in jail until their trial commences places an unfair burden on the poor, who often lack necessary funds. Reviews from law enforcement have been mixed, and one sex offender was caught soliciting sex from a minor on release (DeRosier, 2017). On the other hand, there has been a 20% drop in people in jail awaiting trial since the law was put into effect—though critics say that this is unrelated (Ibarra, 2018). The billion-dollar bail industry, which will be destroyed by the new laws, has sued in court to force New Jersey to reinstate the old system.

Grand Juries and Preliminary Hearings

In many states a *grand jury* must review evidence against an individual before the suspect can be officially charged with a crime. A grand jury (as opposed to a *petit jury*, the jury that sits through the trial) is a group of about 20 individuals, though the numbers vary, that is charged with hearing the evidence against a suspect to determine whether there is sufficient evidence to charge her with an offense. Criminal charges are serious things that can damage a person's reputation and will ultimately cost her a great deal of money even if she is acquitted. To prevent abuse, the Fifth Amendment declares that "no person shall be held to answer for a capital, or otherwise infamous crime, unless on a presentment or indictment of a grand jury, except in cases arising in the land or naval forces, or in the militia, when in actual service in time of war or public danger." Essentially, the grand jury is intended to protect suspects from malicious prosecutions based on flimsy evidence.

The procedures of a grand jury are very different from those of an actual trial. The proceedings are conducted in secret, and the defense counsel is not allowed to question or challenge the evidence against her client. This means that the procedures are *very* biased

Grand jury proceedings are so biased in favor of the prosecutors that observers are often suspicious about cases where a prosecutor fails to get an indictment—particularly in cases where police officers are accused of killing civilians. Critics allege that prosecutors do not wish to pursue officers because they work so closely with the police, and prosecuting officers are often unpopular with the community. The prosecutor in Staten Island, Dan Donovan, could not get an indictment for the officers who killed Eric Garner, a black man who was choked to death by officers for (allegedly) resisting arrest. Many white residents supported the officers, and Donovan soon successfully ran for Congress as a Republican. Prosecutors in Ferguson, Missouri, were unable to secure a grand jury indictment for Darren Morris, the officer who shot Michael Brown. These cases map onto much bigger trends in which officers are not indicted by juries despite the odds being stacked in the prosecutor's favor.

A grand jury indictment does not mean that an offender is guilty, only that there is reason to believe that she has committed a crime. But the odds are stacked so heavily in the prosecutor's favor during the grand jury process that it's hard to see whether this system really prevents prosecutors pursuing whichever cases they wish and gives them a way to avoid pursuing cases that they do not wish to pursue. Equally important, a failure to indict is such a rarity (except in cases of police violence) that a no bill is somewhat suspicious. As one law professor observed, "The prosecutor doesn't have to a say [sic] 'I charged it or I didn't charge it,' but rather [she] sent a case to a jury of peers" (Nelson, 2018). That is, grand juries give prosecutors an easy way to avoid indicting an officer who kills an innocent person.

Do you think that such cases are suspicious? Should there be different rules for indicting officers accused of misconduct? How should grand juries be changed to prevent abuse?

in favor of the prosecutor. It is a cliché of court observers that with a grand jury, a prosecutor could "indict a ham sandwich" if she so desired. Once they have heard the evidence, the grand jury must decide whether there is probable cause to believe that the suspect has committed a crime. They can either return a "no bill," also known as "a bill of ignoramus," which means that the evidence is insufficient for indictment, or return a "true bill," meaning that there is enough evidence to indict. Even if the grand jury does return a no bill, the prosecutor can always bring new evidence against the defendant—it doesn't violate principles of double jeopardy, because the suspect has not yet been put into jeopardy by being charged with a criminal offense.

States that don't use grand juries usually hold *preliminary hearings* to evaluate the evidence against a defendant. This is an adversarial process before a judge who determines whether there is probable cause to charge the defendant. In preliminary hearings, defendants can question witnesses and review the evidence against them. The rules of a preliminary hearing are somewhat laxer than those for a full-blown criminal trial, as some evidence that would not be allowed at a trial can be used in this hearing. As with the grand jury, a decision by the judge to allow the charges does not entail guilt, only that there is sufficient reason to believe that the defendant might be guilty.

Pretrial Motions

During the pretrial process, the prosecutor and defense can enter motions (the legal term for requests) to the court. These motions are in some ways strategic in that they are intended to put both sides in a strong position for the oncoming trial, or they can be used for leverage during plea bargaining. Here are some common pretrial motions:

Change of Venue. A motion for a change of venue is a motion to move the site of the trial from one location, usually in the jurisdiction where the crime happened, to another location in the same state. Defense attorneys sometimes argue that in cases where either the defendant is well known or the crime has received a great deal of publicity, it would be impossible for the defendant to receive a fair hearing in the court where the trial is scheduled. Usually this is because it would be impossible to find a jury that was not biased against the defendant. Dzhokhar Tsarnaev, the accused Boston Marathon bomber, asked for a change of venue because of the high publicity that the bombing and the ensuing man-hunt received. His lawyers stated,

> The nature and extent of the impact of the Marathon bombings and related events and the pretrial publicity engendered by those events require a change of venue if Mr. Tsarnaev is to receive the fair trial by a panel of impartial, indifferent jurors guaranteed by the United States Constitution.

The petition was denied, and Tsarnaev was convicted and sentenced to death in May 2015.

Suppression. A motion to suppress is a request to exclude certain evidence against a defendant before a criminal trial has begun. Often this is because the evidence was gathered in an illegal fashion.

Discovery. In a motion for discovery, a defense attorney requests access to evidence held by the prosecutor that she believes will benefit her client.

Motion to Dismiss. In some cases, due to a new situation such as the suppression or discovery of key evidence, the defense can then move to dismiss the charges against the defendant. If this motion is granted by the judge, the charges are dropped, and the case ends.

Voir Dire

While pretrial motions are being filed with the court, the process of jury selection is usually underway. Most criminal trials have a jury, particularly all felony cases—though a defendant may opt to waive her right to a jury and instead opt for a bench trial. In a bench trial the judge not only determines legal questions during the trial but also determines whether the defendant is guilty. Bench trials are often preferred in cases where the defendant is extremely unlikeable, or the facts of the case are very complex. Judges are perceived as less likely to be swayed by emotional factors and are often better at dealing with technical subjects than are conventional juries.

The process for jury selection is known as voir dire. The point of voir dire is to examine prospective jurors to make sure that they will be unbiased when they hear the evidence

Change of venue: A motion to move the location of a trial.

Suppress: A motion to prevent evidence from being entered during a trial.

Discovery: Efforts by defendants to see material held by the prosecutor.

Bench trial: A trial where the judge is both the finder of law and the finder of fact.

Voir dire: The process of selecting juries to serve during a trial.

at trial. In reality neither side really wants an impartial jury in our adversarial system. Each side wants a jury that will be biased in their favor: A defendant wants a jury sympathetic to her, and a prosecutor wants people who are more likely to convict somebody. Sometimes, both sides will hire consultants whose job it is to examine the potential jurors for signs indicating that they will be inclined to rule for or against their client. The two sides are both trying to manipulate the jury selection process toward their own ends, and, according to the idea of the adversarial process, an impartial jury is supposed to come out.

Voir dire begins with a jury pool, known formally as a *venire*. The venire is a group of randomly selected individuals who are brought to the courthouse as potential jurors. Usually this list is taken either from registered voters or from individuals who have driver's licenses in a state. Individuals are then selected at random and brought before the judge and the lawyers for both the defense and the prosecution, who ask them questions. These questions are meant to tease out whether they either know somebody involved in the case or have experiences that might make them biased in one direction or the other. These can relate to the experiences of the juror ("Have you ever been robbed?" "Do you have any money at the First National Bank?"). They can also relate to the feelings of the juror about topics ("What are your views on the right to bear arms?" "What do you think about the legalization of drugs?"). Once these questions have been asked, the prospective juror will be asked to leave, and the prosecutor and defense will decide whether they will allow her to serve as a juror on the case.

Both sides of the case can object to a prospective juror and have her removed from consideration. These objections, called challenges, can take two different forms: A challenge for cause, sometimes called a strike for cause, removes a prospective juror because there is clear reason to believe that she cannot or would not be impartial during the trial. If a defendant knows somebody involved in the case, has experienced a situation similar to that in the case (say, an individual lost a loved one in a murder similar to the one allegedly committed by the defendant), or has a manifest prejudice against the defendant or against the victim, the prosecutor or defense attorney can enter a challenge for cause. There is no limit to the number of such challenges that attorneys can make during voir dire.

Alternatively, the defense or prosecution can eliminate a prospective juror without providing a justification, simply objecting to the juror and ending it there. This is called a peremptory challenge. While the attorney does not need to justify a peremptory challenge, there are some limitations to these challenges. First, both sides have a limited number of such challenges. (In a federal felony case, for example, the U.S. attorney has six peremptory challenges, while the defendant has ten.) Further, the Supreme Court has ruled that peremptory challenges cannot be used to exclude prospective jurors on the basis of their race (*Batson v. Kentucky*, 1986) or gender (*J. E. B. v. Alabama*, 1993), and the Ninth Circuit Court of Appeals made a similar ruling in regard to sexual orientation (*SmithKline Beecham (SKB) v. Abbott Laboratories*, 2014).

Usually a jury consists of 12 people along with several alternates. Once a jury has been *impaneled*, that is, the final list of jurors has been agreed upon, either the jurors elect or the judge selects a *foreperson*, that is, the person who speaks for the jury. In cases where the jury could be subject to publicity (say, being exposed to an important piece of evidence that has been excluded from the trial) or is in danger of being tampered with, the judge can order that the jury be *sequestered*, meaning that they are shielded from the world, usually kept in hotel rooms and denied access to the outside world over the course of the trial. Once the jury is sworn in, the trial itself begins.

Challenge for cause: When one side objects to a prospective juror on account of a bias.

Peremptory challenge: When one party at a trial objects to a potential juror without providing a reason.

THE TRIAL

The trial itself typically goes through five basic stages:

1. Opening statements

2. Case in chief

3. Defense case

4. Closing statements

5. Jury instructions/verdict

In the first phase of the trial, the prosecution and the defense each make an opening statement to the jury. This statement is meant to frame the evidence that the jury will later hear, as well as to capture the jury's attention and elicit their sympathy by providing information about the crime, the victims, or the defendant. Through the opening statements, which can go on for days, each side seeks to create a context for the evidence that will be presented later, a frame that is meant to explain the facts that will be put before the jury later. Sometimes this narrative is known as a **theory of the case**—what both the prosecutor and the defense believe really happened in the case.

The trial procedures are intended to be biased in favor of the defendant, and it is harder to get a conviction than it is an acquittal. The *burden of proof* is on the state, not on the defendant. The defendant does not need to prove that she is innocent, only that the prosecution failed to show that she is guilty. The jury determines only whether the state has proven its case, not who committed a crime. All the defendant's attorney does at trial is refute the claims of the prosecution: Sometimes this is done by attacking the prosecutor's evidence, but it is often done by presenting an alternative theory of the case that is meant to create doubt in the minds of the jury. For example, a defendant may claim that another person committed the crime—a claim she doesn't need to prove but instead only needs to use to undermine the prosecution's case and introduce doubt in the minds of the jurors.

Further, to convict somebody, the prosecutor must show that the defendant is guilty *beyond a reasonable doubt*. Though this standard is not the same as an absolute certainty, it is often a very high bar to clear. By requiring the prosecution to meet this high standard, the court has attempted to make it difficult for the prosecution to convict an innocent person at trial.

PRESENTING EVIDENCE

The trial is where evidence is presented to the jury, so they can determine whether the defendant is guilty of the crimes in the indictment. Both the prosecution and the defense get to present their own evidence to the court, each in turn. Any evidence not brought before the jury, or before the judge in the case of a bench trial, cannot be considered by the jury, *regardless*

Theory of the case: What both the prosecutor and the defense believe really happened in the case.

of how relevant it is. This means that jurors cannot allow themselves to be persuaded by news reports or other material that they see on their own time. If a jury doesn't see it in the courtroom, it doesn't count. It is then up to the jurors to evaluate the evidence presented before them and determine which evidence they like and which evidence they don't find compelling.

After the opening statements, the prosecution presents the state's case. This is sometimes called the *case in chief* and can include the testimony of witnesses, documents, expert testimony—anything that points to the guilt of the accused. The defense attorney can cross-examine, that is, question, all the prosecutor's witnesses and vice versa. Once the state has concluded or rested its case, the defense then presents its evidence, the aim of which is to show that there is reasonable doubt about whether the defendant is guilty. After the defense has rested, there may be further evidence presented on both sides before the trial comes to an end, and the jury is tasked with evaluating the evidence and rendering a decision.

Witnesses

Witnesses are sworn in by the bailiff and then asked questions by the attorneys. If the witness is providing evidence for the prosecution's case (a "witness for the prosecution"), the prosecutor will first ask her questions. If the witness is testifying for the defense (a "witness for the defense"), the defendant's attorney asks questions first. This first set of questions is known as a *direct* examination, and during this examination, the witness is considered *friendly*. That is, the witness is on that attorney's side. Once these questions have been asked, the other side is given an opportunity to question the witness in what is known as a cross-examination. During cross-examination, the witness is called a hostile witness.

There are different rules regarding the kinds of questions that may be asked of friendly and hostile witnesses. Friendly witnesses may not be asked *leading questions*, while hostile witnesses may. A leading question is a question that points to or hints at the answer within the question itself. For example, a question such as, "Why were you going to the store that day; was it to get some medicine for your mother?" is leading, because the attorney is clearly telling the witness what the appropriate answer to the question is. Because a hostile witness is not on the side of the attorney asking her questions, it can be presumed that the witness will not be cooperative and answer the questions the way that the questioning attorney wishes. If an ostensibly friendly witness is not being cooperative, the defense attorney may make a motion to treat the witness as hostile, which would allow her to ask leading questions of the witness, but in general it is not allowed.

The Fifth Amendment of the Constitution states that "no person . . . shall be compelled in any criminal case to be a witness against himself." A criminal defendant may decline to take the stand in her own defense, or when on the stand, she may refuse to answer questions that would require her to admit or deny guilt for the crime. Legally, the jury is not supposed to conclude from a defendant's refusal to take the stand or to answer questions as an admission of guilt. In practice, juries sometimes do report that a defendant's refusal to testify makes jurors suspicious about her guilt during the trial. ("After all, if the defendant were innocent, why wouldn't she take the stand and defend herself?" jurors might ask themselves.) Regardless, testifying in criminal cases is complex business, and defendants can be tricked or misled by clever attorneys while on the stand, and therefore it may be smart for a defendant to avoid testifying in her own defense. Nevertheless, refusing to testify can come at a cost for the defendant.

Cross-examination:
The examination of a witness from the opposing side during a trial.

Hostile witness:
A witness for the opposition in a trial.

Evidence is a somewhat technical term in criminal law, it's not the same as clues or proof. All material presented to the jury is evidence in some form or another. Testimony is evidence. So are bullet casings, fingerprints, videos, or incriminating documents. There are different ways to "break down" evidence:

Exculpatory Versus Inculpatory Evidence

Evidence that tends to show that a defendant is innocent is known as exculpatory evidence, whereas inculpatory evidence points to her guilt. As we discussed in the previous chapter under the Brady Rule, the prosecutor is obliged to share all exculpatory evidence with the defense, but the defense need not show inculpatory evidence to the prosecutor.

Direct Versus Circumstantial Evidence

Direct evidence is evidence that requires little to no interpretation. For example, an eye-witness account of a defendant robbing a store is direct evidence. So is a video of the crime that shows the defendant in the act of the offense. Circumstantial evidence requires interpretation by the jury and does not immediately point to the guilt or innocence of the defendant. For example, the fact that the defendant had bought a ski mask shortly before a robbery whose perpetrator wore a ski mask is circumstantial. It doesn't *prove* that the defendant committed the crime, but it points in the direction of guilt. Often cases will be based entirely on circumstantial evidence because there are no eyewitnesses or other forms of direct evidence available to the prosecutor.

Probative and Prejudicial Evidence

Evidence that is relevant to proving the case of one side or the other has probative value. That is, it helps prove an important part of the prosecutor's or defendant's case. To have probative value, evidence must be relevant to proving a *material fact* of the trial—that is, it must relate to a significant issue in the defendant's guilt or innocence.

Some evidence may be valuable to help prove a point but can also affect juries in ways that are unfair to the defendant. This evidence is described as *prejudicial* evidence and is often excluded during the trial if either the prosecutor or defense attorney objects to it. For example, a defendant who is on trial for robbery may have been arrested a few years earlier for domestic violence. If the jurors learned about this previous arrest, they may be inclined to convict the defendant regardless of whether they believe that she committed the robbery. They may hate her and simply want to convict her because of her past abusive behavior. At a minimum, the jury will find it harder to be fair minded when they examine the case. If this earlier arrest has nothing to do with the current charges that the defendant is facing, then it is important that it be withheld from the jurors to keep them objective.

Testimony Versus Physical Evidence

Most of the evidence in a criminal trial comes before the jury as testimony—that is, verbal or written statements presented to the court made while under oath. Some of the evidence is physical evidence, material objects that show guilt or innocence. Physical evidence can

Circumstantial evidence: Evidence that requires interpretation.

Probative value: The value of evidence that is relevant to proving the guilt or innocence of a defendant.

be from the crime scene (tire tracks, bloody clothes, weapons with fingerprints, etc.) or supporting evidence (recorded conversations, wills, etc.). Even physical evidence must usually be entered into the court using a witness who explains what the evidence means. Thus, a police detective can explain where a weapon believed to be used in a murder was found, and how detectives linked the weapon to the victim and to the defendant.

OBJECTIONS

Learning Objective 9.4—Define the eight most common objections presented at trial.

It is common for both sides to object to evidence being presented to the jury by the other side. Most often, one side objects to the evidence because it weakens the opponent's case. There are other reasons to object: First, an objection can be used to disrupt the other side's "flow"—that is, trial attorneys can use objections tactically during the trial. Defense attorneys will object to a piece of evidence because it is significantly more difficult to appeal a piece of evidence if they did not object to it during the trial. If a defendant does not object to a piece of evidence, she cannot say the trial judge erred by allowing it after the trial has concluded. The technical way to put this is to say that the defense must object to a piece of evidence to claim that the trial judge made a *reversible error*. There are a lot of good reasons to object as much as possible during a trial, though too many objections can anger the judge and lead to her admonishing the attorneys.

There are any number of grounds for objecting to a piece of evidence, and there is no strict rule about how and why an attorney may object. The most common objections given at trial are described in the paragraphs that follow, and you've probably seen a number of these used in courtroom dramas:

Hearsay

Hearsay evidence is second-hand testimony. An individual is testifying as to what another person told her. For example, Wilson testifies, "George told me that he saw Sarah attack the victim." This kind of evidence violates the right of a defendant to confront her accuser. If George saw the attack, then George, not Wilson, should testify about what he saw. Then, Sarah's attorneys could question George about what exactly he saw—maybe he was joking or jumped to an unwarranted conclusion. Without George's presence in court, it is impossible to know what George saw and to subject George's statement to scrutiny.

Narrative

Most witnesses may only testify to what they saw and what they did. If they try to fit other material into a story, it can distort their testimony.

Scope

Hearsay: Evidence that a person overhead from another person.

In cross-examinations, witnesses may not go beyond what they initially testified about. Anything beyond this should not be admitted.

Badgering the Witness

Badgering the witness involves asking a question in a hostile manner intended to upset the witness and throw her off. The attorney can ask a question and not allow the witness to answer it, or she can ask a question in a mocking, sarcastic way. Throwing a witness off is sometimes a strategy for getting witnesses to make mistakes and say things that can damage a case.

Speculation

Witnesses may not speculate about what they think *might* have happened—only what they themselves saw or heard.

Asked and Answered

This term refers to when an attorney asks the same question multiple times in one examination. Attorneys can do this to trip up a witness, getting her to contradict herself on some small detail of her testimony, and thereby call everything she says into question.

There are two motions that attorneys may make during a trial that do not pertain to the evidence but seek to end the trial early, before a jury has had an opportunity to hear all the evidence and render a verdict. These are motions for a *directed verdict* and for the judge to declare a *mistrial*.

OTHER MOTIONS AT TRIAL

Directed Verdict

The defense sometimes makes a motion for a directed verdict just after the prosecution has rested its case. At this point in the trial, the prosecution's case is at its high point and is not going to get any stronger. The defense attorney is only going to weaken the prosecution's argument when she presents her case, and it is very unlikely that any of the defense's case would help the prosecution. With a motion for a directed verdict, the defense attorney is telling the judge that, even at this strongest point, the prosecutor has not proven that the defendant is guilty beyond a reasonable doubt, and it would be a waste of the court's time to keep going. If the judge agrees with the motion and finds that no reasonable jury could convict the defendant at this point, the trial ends with an acquittal.

Mistrial

A mistrial is a trial that is declared invalid because of something that has happened in the courtroom. If an event happens during the trial that "taints" the jury, that is, influences the jury in ways that damage the entire proceedings (for example, if a witness or a member of the public physically attacks the defendant, or the judge calls an attorney a liar), the judge will declare a mistrial. The judge concludes that there is simply no way that the jury can be impartial after what they have been exposed to. The judge can also declare a mistrial if she concludes that, despite what was previously believed, the court does not have jurisdiction over the case.

Directed verdict: A motion to end a trial after the prosecution has presented its case.

Mistrial: A trial that is ended by the judge prematurely.

If a mistrial is declared, the defendant is neither acquitted nor convicted. It is as though the trial never happened, and everybody goes back to square one. The prosecutor can choose to start over from the very beginning with a new voir dire process and a new jury, or she can drop the charges completely if she doesn't think she'll get a better result next time. Alternatively, the prosecutor and defendant can negotiate a new plea agreement before another trial commences.

Perjury and "Testilying"

Lying in the context of a criminal investigation or criminal trial is often, though not always a crime. Perjury consists of knowingly giving a false statement while under oath, and it is a crime. On the other hand, lying to police officers in the context of a criminal investigation, even if it is not under oath, can also be a crime. The Federal Criminal Code, 18 U.S.C. §1001, makes it a criminal offense to "make . . . any false, fictitious or fraudulent statements or representations" to federal officials. *Suborning perjury*, that is, attempting to get an individual to commit perjury, is likewise a criminal offense.

While lying under oath is a crime, many critics have argued that it is very common for police officers to lie under oath to help secure a conviction. So-called *testilying* is widespread, as some officers believe that they must lie to courts or fabricate evidence to put criminals in prison. A 2014 report by the NYPD's Civilian Review Board noted a dramatic rise in false statements by officers over the preceding four years (2014). Many of these statements were later disproven by videos or audio recordings or by other witnesses on the scene at the time. The *New York Times* reported the case of Detective Kevin Desormeau, a decorated officer who was accused of lying in several cases, throwing in doubt all testimony he gave in other cases. They reported that "on more than 25 occasions since January 2015, judges or prosecutors determined that a key aspect of a New York City police officer's testimony was probably untrue" (Goldstein, 2018). Such false statements by officers undermine the credibility of the police officers more generally and undermine the trust between the police and the public, and many prosecutors seek to conceal the evidence of perjury from the public by "sealing" the transcript of the case.

Closing Statements

Once all the evidence has been presented to the jury from both the prosecution and the defense, both sides are allowed an opportunity to make a final appeal to the jury in their closing statements. Here, the attorneys for both sides summarize the facts to the jury and put a final spin on the evidence to help the jury make sense of what they have heard. These can go on for some period before the jury is read its instructions and allowed to leave the courtroom and go into its deliberations.

JURY INSTRUCTIONS, DELIBERATION, AND VERDICT

Learning Objective 9.5—Identify the options facing juries when rendering a verdict.

Perjury: Knowingly giving a false statement while under oath; this is a crime.

Once the closing statements have been completed, the jury is read its instructions. The language in these instructions is very important, because they contain the precise legal definitions of the different offenses. The instructions tell the jury what they must believe the defendant did for the act to be a crime. For example, instructions might read, "In order to find the defendant guilty of first-degree murder, you must find beyond a reasonable doubt that the defendant killed the victim and that the killing was premeditated." The instructions could then define "premeditated" as "conscious or deliberate" for the jurors. Both sides of the case will sometimes quarrel over the exact wording of these instructions, trying to give the jury directions that are friendlier to their side, and the language of the instructions can become the basis for an appeal if the defendant is convicted.

After the instructions are read out, the jurors go into a closed room and begin discussing whether the state has proven beyond a reasonable doubt that the defendant is guilty. How the juries make this decision is usually up to the jurors themselves. Often, they will make a quick first vote to see if there is already agreement on the charges. If there isn't unanimity, they will begin deliberating the points upon which they disagree. While the play *12 Angry Men* is in many ways exaggerated, it is a decent representation of how juries go about making decisions. If they need more guidance about the law, the jury can ask the judge for guidance about her instructions, and they can refer to the evidence presented at trial and look over the transcripts made by the court reporter.

Most but not all states require that the jury be unanimous when they reach a verdict. Often the jury is not given a simple choice between "guilty" or "not guilty"—the jury can be presented with a set of options. A jury can conclude that the defendant is guilty of second-degree murder and not first-degree murder as the prosecution wished. The jury could believe that the defendant killed the victim but did not do it in a way that would constitute first-degree murder. For example, in some states first-degree murder must be committed with "malice aforethought," and if the jury finds that the defendant did not have such malice when she killed her victim, they can refuse to convict her of this crime. In this case, the jury would find the defendant guilty of what is known as the lesser offense of second-degree murder. Further, a defendant could face multiple charges in a single trial—she can face charges of robbery and aggravated battery for example—and the jury may convict the defendant of one of these offenses but not another. Thus, the jury's deliberations can be more complicated than simply deciding whether the defendant "did it."

Nullification

Jury nullification refers to the power of juries to acquit a defendant even if they believe she really is guilty. It originated in the English legal system, when jurors refused to convict a person when they believed that the law was unjust. Among the earliest cases of jury nullification was the trial of William Penn and William Mead in 1670—the two were charged with belonging to the Quaker religious sect. During the trial, the two effectively admitted to breaking the law but had claimed the law was unjust and should not have been obeyed. After the jury refused to convict them, the judge threatened to jail the jurors but eventually relented. American juries have similarly refused to convict publishers who criticized governors in violation of sedition laws and abolitionists who had helped slaves escape the South.

Nullification is a highly controversial aspect of American criminal justice and has generated a great deal of angry debate. Some find nullification to be a danger to American law. After all, if the jury could acquit a defendant on a whim, who could trust the system at all? Jurors take an oath to base their verdict on the evidence before them, and those who advocate nullification are asking for jurors to violate this oath. Christians could refuse to convict individuals who kill doctors who provide abortions, or racists could refuse to convict defendants who hurt minorities. Some have argued that the 1995 acquittal of O. J. Simpson for murdering his wife was an example of jury nullification—a response to what they perceived as a racist Los Angeles Police Department (Fukurai, 1998). In 2010, Julian Heicklen, a retired professor and political activist, was arrested outside of a New York City courthouse for handing out literature that advocated nullification. Heicklen was charged with jury tampering, but a judge ultimately rejected the case, arguing that jury tampering only involves seeking to influence a specific case, not shaping the opinions of all jurors (Weiser, 2012).

Some critical race scholars have argued that African Americans should use the power of nullification against what they believe to be a racist criminal justice system. In his article, "Racially Based Jury Nullification: Black Power in the Criminal Justice System" (Butler, 1995), the controversial legal scholar (and former prosecutor) Paul Butler argued that black jurors should refuse to render a guilty verdict in nonviolent drug cases where the defendant is African American. As he put it,

> [the] black community is better off when some nonviolent lawbreakers remain in the community rather than go to prison. The decision as to what kind of conduct by African-Americans ought to be punished is better made by African-Americans themselves, based on the costs and benefits to their community, than by the traditional criminal justice process, which is controlled by white lawmakers and white law enforcers. (Butler, 1995, p. 195)

This view was unsurprisingly scandalous, and many critics responded that people like Butler undermine the belief that African Americans can be credible jurors in criminal cases. Behind this controversy, it is important to bear in mind that very few criminal cases go to trial, and so Butler's ideas would probably have very little impact beyond generating some controversy.

Once the jury members have reached their verdict, they notify the judge. The judge then calls the parties back into the court, where the jury foreperson reads the jury's findings out to the courtroom. If the jury acquits the defendant, then the trial ends, and the defendant is free to go and cannot be prosecuted again for the same offense. The rule banning *double jeopardy* set out in the Fifth Amendment states that an individual cannot be tried for the same crime twice, even if compelling new evidence is discovered. This means that a defendant could openly declare her guilt after acquittal and still walk free, though doing so would not be wise, as the defendant could open herself up to civil suits and a host of other legal problems. An acquittal means the end of the criminal case and the defendant is free to go, though she could still face civil action or other sanctions in a noncriminal court.

If the defendant is convicted, then in most cases the judge thanks the jury for their time and dismisses them. She then begins to determine the appropriate sentence for the defendant, who is now a convicted criminal, the subject of the next section of the book. This may mean an entire new period in which the appropriate sentence is deliberated, and a series of experts are called in to determine what punishment is best for the now convicted criminal. As we will see in a later chapter, *capital cases*, that is, cases in which the defendant faces the death penalty, differ on this point, as a capital jury begins to deliberate whether they should recommend that the defendant be executed.

SOME STATISTICS...

Race and Juries

The Sixth Amendment to the Constitution requires that all criminal defendants be judged by an impartial jury. What it means to be impartial is difficult to determine. It is clear from the evidence that the racial and gender composition of a jury affects their decisions. Research has shown that placing minorities and women on a jury shapes the outcome of a trial, even if only to a small degree. Whether that makes these juries more or less "partial" is an open question.

In an important study of the impact of African Americans on juries that focused on the state of Florida over the course of about 10 years, a group of economists found that even having black jurors in the jury pool and not necessarily serving on an actual jury shaped the outcomes of trials (Anwar, Bayer, & Hjalmarsson, 2012). Juries selected from jury pools that included African Americans were less likely to convict African American defendants but were *more* likely to convict whites (see Figure 9.1).

Studies regarding the inclusion of women on juries show equally significant findings. While the evidence is somewhat murky, most reports suggest that the presence of women in juries for most criminal cases, particularly those cases involving male-on-male violence, does not have an impact on conviction rates. But in a novel historical study of the inclusion of women on juries in London, England, researchers discovered that juries that included women were more likely to convict defendants in sexual assault cases (Figure 9.2).

Perhaps it is because female jurors were more sympathetic to female victims or because male jurors were less likely to take sexual assault allegations seriously, but regardless, who is on a jury has a clear impact on the outcomes of trials.

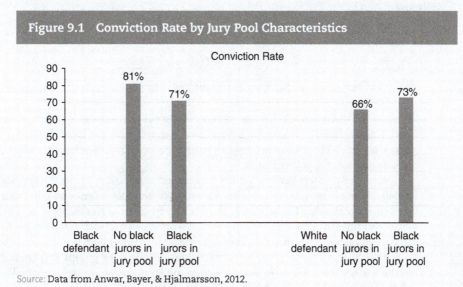

Figure 9.1   Conviction Rate by Jury Pool Characteristics

Source: Data from Anwar, Bayer, & Hjalmarsson, 2012.

(Continued)

(Continued)

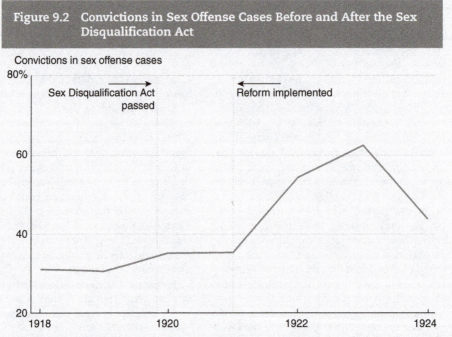

Figure 9.2 Convictions in Sex Offense Cases Before and After the Sex Disqualification Act

Convictions in sex offense cases

Sex Disqualification Act passed

Reform implemented

Sources: Jay Fitzgerald, "The Impact of Early Female Jurors on Criminal Cases." NBER Digest, April 2016. Retrieved from https://www.nber.org/digest/apr16/w21960.html. Data from Anwar, Bayer, & Hjalmarsson, 2016.

APPEALS AND APPELLATE COURTS

Learning Objective 9.6—Summarize the difference between appellate hearings and trials.

A convicted defendant still has one more way to avoid punishment: appealing the conviction. If this appeal is successful, the conviction is overturned, and the defendant probably gets a new trial. The appeals process can go on for a long time, decades even, as it winds its way up a series of appellate courts.

An appellate court looks very different from a criminal court. Physically, appeals courts usually do not have witness stands but instead have multiple judges sitting in front of the lawyers for both sides. These point to the fact that appellate judges do not look at evidence during an appellate hearing but simply look at written material such as transcripts from the trial as well as written statements, known as *briefs*, provided by both the prosecutor and the defense. Other documents may be submitted by individuals or groups who are not a part of the trial who have a stake in the case—these are known as *amicus curiae* briefs. These are all the materials that the court will use to make their decision.

During the appeals hearing there are no witnesses and no evidence. The appeals hearing, sometimes called oral arguments, are relatively brief and formal proceedings. The attorneys representing one side of the case present their arguments before the judges, who ask both critical and helpful questions. After a certain period, the first attorney steps down and the other attorney takes her place to present her side, and they are subjected to the same scrutiny by the judges. Once these different sides have presented their cases before the panel of judges, the judges retire to their chambers and, over the course of weeks or months, they look at the written briefs and oral arguments, discussing with each other the merits of the case. After a while, they reconvene and present their findings, including points where the judges agree and points where they disagree, in sometimes lengthy written opinions. The opinion that gets the support of the most judges determines the outcome and becomes law, while those who oppose these majority opinions can write out their own dissenting opinions in the hope of influencing the views of future judges.

Appellate courts are incredibly important, and not only for criminal cases. They have played a role in pretty much every major social issue over the last century. They were a part of ending segregation, expanding gay rights, defining women's rights, ensuring access to abortion, clarifying election law, ensuring free speech, and a host of other issues. Regardless of how you feel about any of these issues, the courts have been at their center. We often say that cases like *Roe v. Wade* "legalized abortion" and that *Brown v. Board of Education* "ended segregation"—these statements are technically untrue, because appeals courts do not make law, but only interpret it. Regardless, such cases show how much of our lives are shaped by the appellate courts. While we will focus here on appeals of criminal cases, there are a lot of ways that appellate courts shape our lives far beyond criminal law.

The reason appellate hearings are so different from criminal trials is because they only deal with legal questions: Was the law applied properly during the trial? Did the trial judge misinterpret the law? If the judge made a mistake during the trial, was it so serious that it invalidates the verdict? Whether or not the defendant is guilty is not the issue in the appeals hearing—only the legal decisions of the judge who conducted it. If you recall, during a criminal trial the judge is the finder of law, meaning that she is the official legal expert in the room—and the appeals court is simply checking to make sure that she applied the law correctly. It is not the defendant who is on trial during the appeals hearing. Rather, it is the decisions of the trial judge that are under scrutiny.

An appeals court has several options answering an appeal. It may conclude that the lower court was correct and therefore deny the appeal. It may conclude that the trial court made a mistake, but it was a *harmless error* that did not impact the outcome of the trial. On the other hand, it could conclude that the trial court made a *reversible error* that throws the outcome of the trial into doubt. If the trial court made a reversible error, the conviction is overturned (or "vacated"). This does not mean that the appellant is free to go. Rather, the entire trial process begins again—a new jury is selected, and new cases are presented by both sides, unless the prosecutor decides to abandon the case or seek a new plea bargain.

APPELLATE COURT SYSTEMS

Learning Objective 9.7—Identify the differences between state and federal appeals courts.

Different states have different ways of structuring their appellate processes. In smaller states, there are usually trial courts that handle all traditional cases, and a state supreme court that handles all appeals in the state. Usually criminal cases, particularly felonies, are conducted in a superior court that is equipped to handle them. Many states have different types of lower courts that address specific types of issues, such as a family court to handle custody and divorce cases, and small claims or common pleas courts that deal with small civil disputes. Some larger states have midlevel appellate courts that handle most appeals from the trial courts. Every state is slightly different, and their court systems are more or less complicated depending on the legal system in the state as well as upon the decisions of the policymakers there. Figures 9.3 and 9.4 show two states' justice systems.

Federal Appeals

The court systems in the 50 states deal with most criminal cases simply because almost all ordinary crimes are violations of state law. Despite this, federal courts are very important in criminal appeals for a number of reasons. First, there are federal trials for federal crimes—crimes defined by the federal criminal code. Federal criminal cases are often cases that involve civil rights issues, murder of federal officers such as FBI agents, and smuggling across state lines or across international borders. If a defendant is convicted of a federal crime and wants to appeal it, the appeal then goes through the federal appeals courts.

Criminal cases can also be appealed to federal appeals courts if they involve an issue of federal or constitutional law. This is particularly the case if the appeal involves the Bill of Rights. If a defendant believes that the courts misapplied the Fourth Amendment at trial (say, by allowing evidence that should have been excluded), the appeal may go through the federal appeals system. Often, appellants must go through their state appeals process before they can go to federal courts, but these federal courts remain an option if defendants can't get a satisfactory result in state court. (A fuller description of the appeals process can be seen in Figure 9.5.) If a federal appeals court makes a ruling, all lower courts under its jurisdiction, including state courts, are obliged to follow its precedent.

Bill of Rights: The first ten amendments to the Constitution, spelling out the limits of the federal government's authority.

Figure 9.3 Commonwealth of Pennsylvania's Unified Justice System

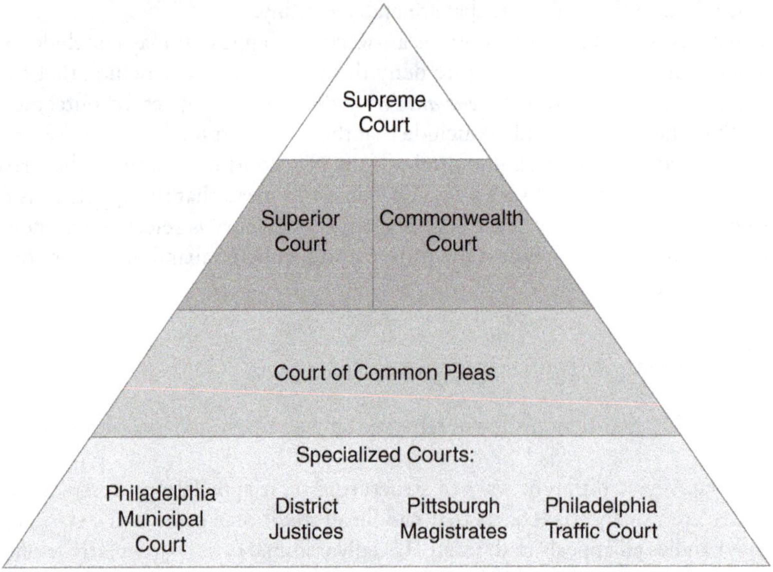

Supreme Court

Superior Court   Commonwealth Court

Court of Common Pleas

Specialized Courts:

Philadelphia Municipal Court   District Justices   Pittsburgh Magistrates   Philadelphia Traffic Court

Source: Adapted from The Unified Juridical Court System of Pennsylvania, http://www.pacourts.us/learn.

Figure 9.4   Oregon Judicial Department Court Jurisdiction Structure

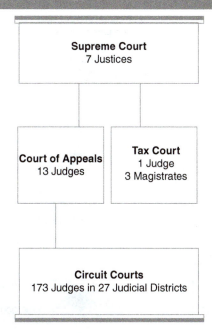

Source: Oregon Judicial Branch.

WHERE DO I FIT IN?

INNOCENCE PROJECTS

Getting an appeal is often an expensive, time-consuming effort, and few convicted offenders have the expertise, ability, or resources to pursue appeals, even when they've been convicted for crimes that they didn't commit. *Innocence projects* have been formed around the country to help convicted criminals who maintain their innocence fight for their freedom in the courts. Innocence projects are organizations, usually operated in law schools, that help convicted criminals prepare legal cases to contest their convictions. They prepare legal cases, argue in court, and provide other forms of support to the wrongfully convicted . . . and they're often looking for interns and volunteers.

While many of these organizations need trained lawyers or full-time law students, they are often looking for other kinds of support such as office assistance, fundraising, or other forms of legal activism. You can help draw attention to wrongful convictions, meet with convicted offenders to help their cases, help reform the criminal justice system, and participate in other activities that can help free the wrongfully convicted and improve the criminal justice system.

To get involved, do some internet searching for innocence projects in your area and contact them. A good place to start is the nationwide Innocence Project, which serves as a network for independent innocence projects around the country. Its website is https://www.innocenceproject.org/.

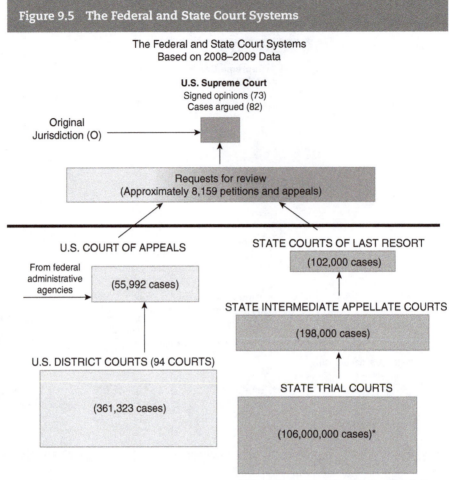

Figure 9.5   The Federal and State Court Systems

**The Federal and State Court Systems
Based on 2008–2009 Data**

U.S. Supreme Court
Signed opinions (73)
Cases argued (82)

Original Jurisdiction (O)

Requests for review
(Approximately 8,159 petitions and appeals)

U.S. COURT OF APPEALS

From federal administrative agencies

(55,992 cases)

STATE COURTS OF LAST RESORT
(102,000 cases)

STATE INTERMEDIATE APPELLATE COURTS
(198,000 cases)

U.S. DISTRICT COURTS (94 COURTS)
(361,323 cases)

STATE TRIAL COURTS
(106,000,000 cases)*

*Note: If this box were shown in proportion to the other boxes below the blue line, the actual size would be approximately 3 feet wide x 1 foot high.

The federal courts have three tiers: district courts, courts of appeals, and the Supreme Court. The Supreme Court was created by the Constitution; all other federal courts were created by Congress. State courts dwarf federal courts, at least in terms of case load. There are more than 100 state cases for every federal case filed. The structure of state courts varies from state to state; usually, there are minor trial courts for less serious cases, major trial courts for more serious cases, intermediate appellate courts, and the supreme courts. State courts were created by state constitutions.

Source: From Janda/Berry/Goldman/Schildkraut. *The Challenge of Democracy* (with Aplia Printed Access Card), 12E. © 2014 South-Western, a part of Cengage, Inc. Reproduced by permission. www.cengage .com/permissions.

Note: Latest data available.

Not every appeal that involves criminal justice issues must be a criminal case. Civil cases can have implications for the police, the courts, or for prisoners. A prisoner can sue the prison administration claiming that her treatment violates the Constitution, and further demand that they change their prison policies. A suspect who was shot by a police officer can sue the department claiming that the police should not have used force when they did. A group of people can sue a city if they believe that its police practices are unconstitutional in some other fashion. If these civil suits get to the appellate level, the judges there must look at the legal and constitutional issues surrounding these policies and practices and make rulings that can shape how prisons and police officers can operate going forward. For example, in 2017, New York City residents sued the NYPD over their stop-and-frisk tactics, demanding that the police change their practices because they violated the Constitution (Mueller, 2017). This was a civil suit, not a criminal case, but it had huge implications for how the NYPD operated. Many civil suits have had a more profound impact on how the criminal justice system is run than do the criminal cases.

The reason federal appellate courts have so much power over both state and federal criminal cases is simply because federal laws and the Constitution are considered superior to state laws. If a state law contradicts federal law, the state law has no authority. This legal principle is spelled out in the **Supremacy Clause** of the U.S. Constitution. Article Six of the Constitution says,

> This Constitution, and the Laws of the United States which shall be made in pursuance thereof; and all treaties made, or which shall be made, under the authority of the United States, shall be the supreme law of the land; and the judges in every state shall be bound thereby, anything in the constitution or laws of any state to the contrary notwithstanding.

This clause effectively sets up a hierarchy in the American legal system. At the top of the pile is the U.S. Constitution. Under this are federal laws and the treaties that are ratified by Congress. Below these are the laws passed by the state legislatures, and at the bottom of the pile are the ordinances passed by cities and other substate political bodies (like towns or counties) (see Figure 9.6). Because federal courts deal with cases involving the U.S. Constitution and U.S. federal law, they are superior to all state-level courts.

Like the systems in the different states, the federal court system is broken into different levels. At the lowest levels are the federal trial courts, called *district courts*, which in turn are divided up based on the different subjects that the courts deal with. For example, there are military courts that deal with issues involving the various armed forces. There are courts that deal with federal bankruptcies and federal courts that handle issues in international trade. Most federal criminal trials are conducted by the U.S. district courts. Above the district courts are the federal appeals courts, also known as *circuit courts of appeal*. There are 13 of these courts, 12 of them for different parts of the country, and a federal circuit just for Washington, D.C. The term *circuit* comes from the fact that, historically, Supreme Court judges would travel to different parts of the country—riding circuit—to hear appellate cases. Each of the circuits deals with all federal appeals from within its jurisdiction, and they can disagree with each other on legal issues. Some of these courts have a reputation for being very progressive in how they interpret the law, others for being more conservative, which can lead to variation in how the Constitution is interpreted around the country. When their disagreements become severe enough, the Supreme Court steps in to resolve the issue.

Supremacy Clause: The section of the Constitution that makes the Constitution the supreme law of the land.

Figure 9.6 Hierarchy of United States Law

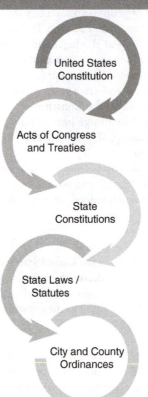

United States
Constitution

Acts of Congress
and Treaties

State
Constitutions

State Laws /
Statutes

City and County
Ordinances

Source: Adapted from http://www.civiceducationva.org/federalism3.php.

THE SUPREME COURT

Learning Objective 9.8—Examine the key elements of the U.S. Supreme Court.

At the top of the legal heap in the American court system is the appropriately titled Supreme Court (see Figure 9.7). The Supreme Court has several different tasks under the Constitution. First, and most important, it is the duty of the Supreme Court to determine the meaning of the Constitution, including the appropriate way to interpret the Bill of Rights. While the Constitution lays out the rights we have, they are described very broadly, and it is not easy to figure out how these rights can be applied in every case. For example, the Eighth Amendment states, "Excessive bail shall not be required, nor excessive fines imposed, nor cruel and unusual punishments inflicted." What makes bail "excessive"? How do we determine which punishments are considered "cruel and unusual"? Should we use modern ideas of excessiveness and cruelty, or should we rely on the understandings of these terms that were predominant in 1787 when the Constitution was written? It is one of the most important jobs of the Supreme Court to figure out the meanings of these vague words in a modern context.

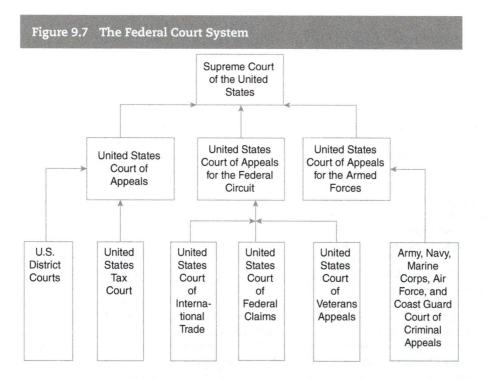

Figure 9.7 The Federal Court System

There are nine members of the Supreme Court, all of whom are appointed by the president with the approval of the Senate. The chief justice oversees the court, though the justices may vote whatever way they choose and may write whatever they want in their opinions. Different periods of the history of the Supreme Court are often referred to by the name of the chief justice at the time—thus the Warren Court ran from 1953 until 1969 when Earl Warren was chief justice. The current court, the Roberts court, began in 2005 when John Roberts was appointed by President George W. Bush. It takes four Supreme Court justices to vote to hear a case, but a majority of five is required to decide the final ruling one way or another. Sometimes several judges will agree with one side but will do so for different reasons, meaning that they will write separate opinions, known as *concurring opinions*. The opinion that has the most votes behind it is then taken to be the law of the land and must be applied by all lower courts.

In Supreme Court cases and almost all appellate cases, the judges will often write lengthy opinions explaining the reasons behind their vote. There they will pick out the legal issues in the case that they consider most relevant and explain that they believe that their interpretation of the law is the correct one. These may be technical issues that seem pretty far removed from the guilt or innocence of the defendant: Was evidence obtained lawfully? Were police procedures followed correctly? Is the law written clearly? Was the courtroom run in the proper way? Did the lawyer for the defendant do her job properly? Often justices will criticize the views of their colleagues in the case, and their written opinions are full of references to previous court opinions to back up their points. All of this can make Supreme Court opinions difficult to completely understand without a law degree. Sometimes judges will only briefly discuss the facts of the case before getting into the technical legal question, another reason why these opinions often make dry reading.

CRIMINAL (IN)JUSTICE

"Get Me a Lawyer, Dog"

The Sixth Amendment to the Constitution guarantees people charged with a serious crime the right to an attorney. When a suspect asks to see a lawyer, the police are supposed to stop questioning the suspect until her lawyer is present—a precedent set out in the case of *Edwards v. Arizona* (1981). In October 2015, Warren Demesme was questioned by New Orleans detectives for allegedly raping two 15-year-old girls. (He maintains his innocence.) As he was being questioned, Demesme grew frustrated and declared, "This is how I feel; if y'all think I did it, I know that I didn't do it so why don't you just give me a lawyer, dog, 'cause this is not what's up."

Despite this statement, officers continued to interrogate Demesme, charging him with first-degree rape and indecent behavior with a juvenile. Demesme's lawyers sought to have his statements suppressed before his trial, citing the Supreme Court's *Edwards* decision. The case was appealed to the Louisiana Supreme Court, which refused to hear the case. In justifying its decision, one of the justices asserted, "In my view, the defendant's ambiguous and equivocal reference to a 'lawyer dog' does not constitute an invocation of counsel that warrants termination of the interview and does not violate *Edwards v. Arizona*."

It's possible that the officers did not understand the meaning of what Demesme was asking for, particularly if they were uninformed about slang. It's also possible that Demesme was asking for an actual dog with a law degree. Most likely, officers wanted to convict Demesme and therefore ignored his requests.

Should Demesme's conviction be overturned? Was the refusal of the Louisiana Court to hear the case unfair? Is this an example of racial bias?

THE POLITICS OF APPELLATE JURISPRUDENCE

Learning Objective 9.9—Identify the central political issues around appointing appellate judges.

Appeals courts claim to simply be checking to see that the presiding judge applied the law correctly during the trial. In fact, reality is much more complicated than this. The law is often ambiguous and does not necessarily provide a single right answer in a case. One of the best examples of this is the Fourth Amendment—which, if you recall, protects us from "unreasonable searches and seizures." When they wrote the Bill of Rights in the 18th century, the founding fathers had no idea what the future would look like. There was no such thing as a telegram, much less a phone or a smart phone, so there's no obvious way to interpret whether the police have the right to read the contents of a person's cell phone as a part of a search. To say that the appeals courts are simply applying the Fourth Amendment in a case where the police conduct a search using, say, drone technology, is dishonest. Though appeals courts claim to be simply interpreting or applying the law, they are often in fact making new laws.

All of this can make appellate jurisprudence, the legal decisions of appellate courts, very challenging and at times very political. The opinions of appellate judges allow for the laws to change in ways that were never imagined by the legislatures that originally passed the laws. They can even interpret the law in ways that legislatures do not wish them to.

The political views of appellate judges can shape how they interpret laws, giving them very different meanings than were originally intended. These interpretations are often shaped by the political and legal views of the judges—a conservative judge is likely going to interpret the law in the ways that conservatives like, while a liberal judge is likely to interpret it in a way that liberals like. Given that politicians appoint judges and the laws are interpreted by judges, it makes sense that politicians have a huge interest in who is on the appeals courts.

Another important aspect of appellate courts that tends to make them political is that they have a great deal of influence over how the law is applied in trials. Appellate rulings have a lot of influence, because these courts shape the way lower courts apply the law. If a higher court makes a ruling about the correct interpretation of a law, the courts below it must follow this interpretation or risk have their rulings overturned on appeal. Unless an even higher court overrules the findings of the appellate court, a rare phenomenon, or the appellate court changes its mind on an issue, the appellate court's rulings can shape hundreds if not thousands of cases going forward. In short, appellate courts are very influential and shape the lives of a great many people through their power over the lower, trial courts.

These powers mean that there is a lot of political fighting over the appointment of these judges. Both conservative and liberal politicians want to control who sits on the appellate courts, because they believe that liberal judges are likely to support liberal causes and conservatives will help conservative ones. Both liberals and conservatives accuse judges from the other side of being influenced by political considerations rather than deciding cases in a purely legal matter. Since the 1980s, there have been many ugly political battles in the U.S. Senate over who gets to be a federal appeals court judge, and these fights only get uglier each time a vacancy becomes available. Perhaps the biggest of these took place in the spring of 2016, when the U.S. Senate refused to allow President Obama to appoint a liberal justice named Merrick Garland to replace a Republican judge, Antonin Scalia, who died while in office, even though appointing justices is one of the president's powers under the Constitution. After Donald Trump was elected to office, Garland's nomination was withdrawn, and conservative judge Neil Gorsuch was appointed to replace Scalia.

THEORIES OF CONSTITUTIONAL INTERPRETATION

Learning Objective 9.10—Differentiate between the main schools of constitutional interpretation.

There are no clear rules regarding how to interpret the Constitution, and different judges have different philosophies on the issue. Nonetheless, among the judges in the Supreme Court, as well as among those who study and follow the Court, there are many different philosophies about how to interpret laws. Some judges, most notably the late conservative judge Antonin Scalia, are what are known as *textualists*. Textualists believe that the best way to interpret the Constitution is to determine what the law meant at the time it was passed: Punishments are "cruel and unusual" if people in 1788 would have thought that they were cruel and unusual, not if we think so now. Scalia sometimes pointed to the use of whipping posts as a legitimate form of punishment because it was widely practiced when the Constitution was passed.

Others have taken different approaches. Some judges are more practical, looking at the real-world consequences of an interpretation of the law rather than the meaning of the

Interpreting the Constitution

You are an appellate judge hearing the case of a woman, Lauren, who is accused of drug trafficking. The primary evidence against her was gathered using drone technology. The police, without a warrant, used unmanned aerial drones to follow her for several days, circling her home or any building she was in until she came outside. She was effectively under 24-hour surveillance. Eventually, the drone spotted her in her backyard exchanging amphetamines for money with a customer, and she was arrested.

The Fourth Amendment protects individuals from "unreasonable searches and seizures." In the case of *California v. Ciraolo* (1986), the Supreme Court ruled that surveillance from an airplane flying over 1,000 feet is not a search, and therefore does not require a warrant. Lauren's attorneys argued that the level and intensity of the surveillance that their client endured was much more intrusive than merely flying over her house. She was followed around all day and night without a warrant, though she was only seen on camera while she was out in public. This, they argue, was unreasonable, and therefore, they claim, the evidence against her should be thrown out of court.

How would you rule in this case? How would you go about interpreting the Fourth Amendment? Does California v. Ciraolo *help you determine the answer, or is Lauren's lawyer correct that unmanned drones are different from traditional, manned aircraft?*

words on the paper alone. Regardless of whether the words on paper have a clear meaning, if that interpretation would be disastrous, judges should interpret the law in a different way, they argue. Some judges maintain that we should seek to understand the original intent of Congress when it passed a law—what did Congress *mean* when it wrote a statute? This can be tricky, because Congress consists of over 400 people who may each have intended different things when they wrote the law. Still others argue that judges should interpret concepts like "cruel and unusual" according to contemporary standards, not the original ones—what is cruel and unusual to us might not be cruel to a person of 1788. Each approach has defenders, and there are good reasons in favor of each approach—though conservatives tend to be textualists and liberals more open to modern interpretations of laws. Once the Supreme Court has offered its interpretation of the Constitution or of the law in a case, lower courts are expected to follow its lead and not to contradict it. Only rarely does the Supreme Court change its mind about an issue and overrule a previous judgment.

While the actual criminal defendant and the actual victim are not closely connected to the appellate process, appeals are incredibly important for criminal justice. American courts are designed to address legal issues through individual cases—there is no other way to determine that a law or a practice is unconstitutional other than to have an individual case go before the court and have judges or Supreme Court justices make rulings. These judgments can have a significant impact on future cases across the country and even around the world, as many foreign judges look up to the American legal system. Important decisions can have a lasting positive or negative impact. Though it is far from the streets, the Supreme Court has influence that shapes every part of American criminal justice as well as every other part of American life.

CHAPTER SUMMARY

This chapter has summarized all the courtroom activities, from right after a suspect is arrested through her trial and her appeals, if she tries to have her conviction overturned. Keep in mind that very rarely does a defendant have a full-blown trial where evidence is presented to a jury that renders a verdict. Rather, the pressure to arrive at a plea bargain is so strong and the expense of a trial so great that it is only in rare circumstances that a defendant gets an actual trial. It's the same for appeals—the expertise required to appeal a case is far beyond the reach of most offenders, and appellate lawyers are very expensive to hire.

Further, there are far more defendants seeking to appeal their convictions than there are resources to handle all of these appeals. This means that few appeals are ever heard by a higher court. In short, trials are rare, and appeals are even rarer.

Once a defendant has been convicted or pled guilty, she enters the next stage of the process—sentencing and ultimately some sort of punishment. In the next section we will turn to the legally, politically, and morally complex world of criminal punishment and criminal corrections.

REVIEW/DISCUSSION QUESTIONS

1. When do you think a bench trial would be a better choice than a jury trial?

2. Do you think that the system of cash bail should be kept, or should it be replaced by a system that does not require an accused criminal to put forward money to be freed before trial?

3. Should juries be allowed to nullify a case when they believe that the defendant is guilty but the crime in question should not exist?

4. Which objections during trial do you think are the most significant? Why?

5. Do you think that the way that a trial is organized is balanced? Does it make conviction too hard? Too easy? Which elements of the trial process lead you to your conclusions?

KEY TERMS

Bench trial 215
Bill of Rights 228
Challenge for cause 216
Change of venue 215
Circumstantial evidence 219
Cross-examination 218
Directed verdict 221

Discovery 215
Hearsay 220
Hostile witness 218
Mistrial 221
Nolo contendere 211
Peremptory challenge 216
Perjury 222

Probative value 219
Suppress 215
Supremacy Clause 231
Theory of the case 217
Voir dire 215

$SAGE edge™

Get the tools you need to sharpen your study skills. SAGE edge offers a robust online environment featuring an impressive array of free tools and resources.

Access practice quizzes, eFlashcards, video, and multimedia at edge.sagepub.com/fichtelberg

Sarah Yeh

Fighting boredom is one of the biggest challenges of prison life. Do you think you would handle prison well?

CORRECTIONS AND SPECIAL TOPICS

In this section of the book we will be examining the subject of punishment/corrections. Already, in this first sentence; we can begin to see a problem: In our society we are confused about what we are supposed to be doing to people who have been convicted of serious crimes. We often speak as though prison, probation, and parole were aimed at correcting the criminal (such as when we call prisons "correctional institutions") or somehow benefitting society, but in fact, many people simply want to see a criminal suffer for the harm she caused. This confusion over whether we want to punish offenders or rehabilitate them lurks at the heart of the American penal system. As we have seen in earlier chapters, many parts of the criminal justice system are not as they appear; this is even more so as we discuss punishment. To put it plainly, this part of the criminal justice system is the most screwed up of all parts of American criminal justice—and this is really saying something.

Before we examine America's penal system in depth, we should first seek to understand why we punish offenders in the first place. *Something* must be done to individuals who commit a crime, particularly those who are guilty of serious offenses. But when we seek to understand the rationale for punishment, that is, when we ask why we should punish offenders, people quickly begin to disagree. Some want to punish the offender out of righteous anger; some wish to help the offender find a better life. Some just want the criminal element off the streets so she won't hurt any more innocent people. Some want a combination of these.

Not only do we disagree about *why* we punish offenders, but we also often disagree about *how* we should punish them. Prison, home confinement, parole, probation, psychological counseling, and even execution are all forms of punishment intended to serve a purpose. And the two questions are linked: Our *penal practices* and our *penal policies* (the actual types of punishment that we impose) are shaped in part by the goals of punishment, what we want punishment to achieve (though as we will see, there are other influences on our penal practices). The effectiveness of the forms of punishment we impose can be measured by the goals we set for them, and these goals in turn are shaped by the rationales or reasons we punish. In short, why we punish an offender shapes how we punish her.

One common reason for punishing an offender is to send a message that criminal behavior will not be tolerated by society. Criminals are punished as a warning to would-be lawbreakers, letting them know that society's rules must be respected and obeyed. Punishment prevents crime by showing that the rewards of criminal activity are not worth the harm that offenders will endure if they are caught. This is known as *deterrence* and is rooted in the theories of Bentham and Beccaria that we discussed in Chapter 3. Potential offenders will not commit crimes if they fear the consequences of being caught—at least in theory.

Deterrence breaks down further into two different types: *Specific deterrence* and *general deterrence*. Specific deterrence is aimed at an individual offender and seeks to prevent her from committing crimes in the future. If a student is caught cheating and is given an F grade and has her name given to the university's conduct board, this could serve as a specific deterrent. She is less likely to cheat in the future (again, in theory). Nobody else needs to know about this punishment for it to work as a specific deterrent. On the other hand, if the cheater is brought before the class and publicly shamed for cheating, this might serve as a general deterrent. She is being punished so that *others* will not be tempted to cheat in the future. She may not be affected by this shaming, but others will get the message. Specific deterrence seeks to prevent individual offenders from offending again in the future, whereas general deterrence seeks to send a message to society that breaking the law isn't worth the consequences.

If we really wanted to focus our penal system on deterrence, we would probably have to make some changes in how we do things. To deter a would-be offender, we should probably make the punishment much harsher than the potential benefits that the criminal would receive if she got away with the crime. If the punishment is less severe than the potential rewards of the crime itself, it would be very unlikely to deter. Further, if the punishment is meant to have a general deterrent effect, it should probably be done in public for all to see. Whatever its other problems, hanging a criminal in a public square would maximize its deterrent effect by making it clear to as many people as possible that there are serious consequences for lawbreaking. If we want punishment to deter, we should design our punishments to maximize their deterrent effect.

A second rationale for punishment is *incapacitation*. Like deterrence, incapacitation seeks to prevent an offender from committing more crimes, but it does this by making it extremely difficult for the individual to reoffend. Putting an offender behind bars to keep her off the streets is a form of incapacitation. A sentence of a life imprisonment without parole incapacitates the offender—she is no longer a threat to society. The death penalty could serve as a type of incapacitation, since it permanently prevents a criminal from reoffending. Even if an offender wants to keep breaking the law, incapacitation makes it extremely difficult for the criminal to harm anybody again.

Along with deterrence and incapacitation is *rehabilitation*. When we rehabilitate an offender, we are "fixing" her: We are trying to make the offender change her behavior so that she will be unlikely to commit crimes in the future. For advocates of rehabilitation, criminals are not bad people, but rather are "broken" or "sick" and need to be healed or repaired so that they can eventually return to society. Psychologists working in prisons seek to help offenders return to the public without reoffending. Prisons are often referred to as "correctional institutes" because of their efforts (at least on paper) to rehabilitate offenders.

Deterrence, incapacitation, and rehabilitation all share several common features. First, they are all *future-oriented*: All three approaches use punishment to prevent crimes in the future, either by convincing the offender to not offend again, or by making it difficult for her to commit more crimes. Punishment in this view is required because punishing offenders makes society safer than it would be if we did not punish offenders. In addition, these approaches are all targeting the offender (or potential offender), and not the crime that the offender committed. This is to say that they all base their punishment on how the offender herself or the general public is likely to react to the punishment rather than the severity of the crime itself. If it took a long time to rehabilitate an individual who committed a relatively minor crime, rehabilitation theory would say that she should probably be kept incarcerated for as long as it takes to fix her. For deterrence, punishment should be determined by its potential deterrent effect, not by crime itself. For each of these theories, the punishment does not fit the crime, but rather the punishment fits the criminal.

The final common justification for punishment is substantially different from the three we've already discussed. This justification seeks to punish the offender because she committed a crime, independent of whether the punishment benefits society. *Retributivism* maintains that the reason why we punish somebody has little to do with whether it prevents crime in the future, but rather we punish an offender because she chose to commit a crime. Retributivists argue that the only reason why we should punish an offender is simply because *she deserves it*.

While retributivism as a theory of punishment is as old as punishment itself, it probably found its best defender in the 18th-century German philosopher Immanuel Kant. Kant asserted that human beings are distinguished from all other living creatures by the fact that we possess reason and free will. According to Kant, rehabilitation, incapacitation, and deterrence are good reasons to punish animals—not humans. An animal needs to be rehabilitated or deterred because it is a creature of instinct, but human beings are not; we can choose to commit or crime or we can choose to obey the law. A person who commits a crime is not a victim of society or of her baser instincts, but instead chooses to harm people, and so society must punish her. Kant argued that our reason and our free will make it possible for humans to be either good or evil and therefore serve as the primary reasons why we punish people who break the law.

As with the other justifications for punishment, retributivists also have suggestions for *how* we should punish lawbreakers. Kant's version of this is known as *the categorical imperative*. Roughly speaking, the categorical imperative is an inverted version of "the golden rule." While the golden rule ("do unto others as you would have them do unto you") is meant as a guide for how to treat people, the categorical imperative says that society can treat you how you have treated others. Thus, like the principle of *lex talionis* ("an eye for an eye"), retributivists believe that the punishment should fit the crime and not the criminal. A person who commits murder should be killed because, by her own actions, she has determined that it is acceptable to kill another person. Therefore, she cannot complain when her actions are turned back on her. All punishers do when they carry out a sentence is take the offender's acts and apply them back onto the offender. Thus, for retributivists, the criminal herself chooses the form and severity of her own punishment by choosing to commit the crime.

Deterrence, incapacitation, rehabilitation, and retribution are not just philosophical theories. They are all used by prosecutors to determine how to charge criminals and by judges to determine appropriate sentences. Further, each of them can justify the same kinds of punishments but in different ways. Retribution, deterrence, and incapacitation can all be used to explain why we incarcerate people, for example, and many of the punishments (with the exception, perhaps, of rehabilitation and specific deterrence) can be used to justify the death penalty. The death penalty "fits the crime" for murderers but it also incapacitates offenders, and under certain circumstances, could deter others. Each rationale shapes the nature of the punishments that are carried out in different ways: Rehabilitation does not need punishment to be particularly unpleasant, while deterrence wants punishment to be unpleasant enough that it makes future criminal conduct unappealing. Nonetheless, in modern American punishment these different rationales are combined in different ways.

Critical criminologists have a very different view about all of this, of course. Critical criminologists do not believe that criminal punishment is intended to benefit society or help the offender, but rather they see it as serving the broader inequalities that are shot through our society. Imprisonment is another tool to maintain social, economic, and racial inequalities in our society, and it is no surprise that marginalized groups such as the poor and minorities are disproportionately imprisoned. The American penal system is a tool of broader injustices, containing and oppressing groups of people who are already on the bottom of the social ladder. Like the police and the courts, the system works to disadvantage the poor and minorities and benefits the wealthy and the white.

In this section I will argue that when it comes to punishment, the American criminal justice system is deeply confused about what it is doing. We often speak about prisons as though they were guided by principles of rehabilitation, but very little energy and few resources are invested in turning the offenders into law-abiding citizens. Many crimes probably can't be deterred (such as those committed by the mentally ill), but we act as though they can. Rather, much of the public wants to see offenders suffer for their crimes— we take satisfaction in knowing that she got "what was coming to her" (Finckenauer, 1988). This means that we are often fixated on retribution as a society, despite what we say about the goals of punishment. This confusion about the aims and goals of modern punishment helps explain the troubling nature of modern criminal punishment.

At the end of this section, we will turn to one special subset of American criminal justice: juvenile justice. There, we will sketch out the criminal justice system as it applies to people under the age of 18. Because they are young and are usually considered too immature to be held fully responsible for their actions, the system looks very different for juveniles. The topic fits nicely with the chapters on punishment, because juvenile justice is rooted in a rehabilitative approach to punishment, what is sometimes called the *therapeutic model*. In many ways, young offenders are treated far more leniently than adults because of their age and immaturity. Rather than punishing young people, the juvenile justice system seeks to help juveniles avoid transitioning into adult criminality. This is all on paper of course. In reality, the juvenile system often recapitulates the problems and injustices that we saw in earlier chapters—it is often racially biased and provides very different outcomes for privileged juveniles than for their poorer peers.

Sarah Yeh

Humiliation has often been a part of punishment. Do you think it's helpful to humiliate offenders?

CHAPTER TEN

THE HISTORY OF PUNISHMENT

Perhaps the oddest thing about the history of punishment is that the most frequently used form of punishment today was among the least common in earlier periods. *Incarceration*, that is, confining criminals to prison for a predetermined period, is now the standard punishment for serious offenders in Western societies, whereas in earlier periods it was almost never practiced. Moreover, while many people now consider punishments like torture and execution to be barbaric, some earlier societies would have considered incarceration to be inhumane and would have considered execution to be far kinder. In this chapter we will examine the history of punishment in its broad outlines and ask the question: How did we get to the point where incarceration is our go-to punishment for serious offenders?

Keep in mind that there are a lot of reasons why incarceration is not an ideal form of punishment, particularly in less developed societies. First, prisons take up a lot of resources and produce little benefit for society overall. Prisoners must be housed, fed, and guarded—clearly an expensive proposition. (According to the *Federal Register*, it costs about $36,000 per year to incarcerate a federal prisoner, not including salaries for guards and construction costs [Federal Bureau of Prisons, 2018, April 30].) Second, earlier societies rarely considered rehabilitation to be a goal of punishment. Even if they did seek to "fix" criminals, the idea of confining the offender to a building and supervising an intensive process of rehabilitation was not around until the modern era. The modern prison or "correctional institution" could only exist in a society that had the resources for such an institution as well as a belief that offenders could, and should, be rehabilitated. None of this really existed before the Enlightenment period of the 18th century.

The history of punishment is not necessarily a history of things getting better. Western history is often portrayed as a story where we were once barbaric, violent, and superstitious and are now civilized, rational, and enlightened. It is easy to look at the history of punishment this way—we once used gruesome, bloody, and bizarre punishments like torture and beheading and have since become more humane and more rational. This is not necessarily the case. In his landmark historical study of prisons, *Discipline & Punish* (1995), Michel Foucault pointed out that just because punishment is less violent does not necessarily make it better. Despite looking more humane on the surface, modern punishment has its own subtle forms of cruelty. Seeking to shape and control the thoughts and behaviors of prisoners in order to rehabilitate them can be a form of "thought control" that is in its own way far more brutal than the violence of preceding forms of punishment. Prisoners are subject to all sorts of "micro controls," such as how they may walk, talk, eat, and dress, that not only seek to change their behavior but in some sense shape their souls—almost every aspect of a prisoner's life is under the thumb of prison officials. Foucault pointed out that prison is far more invasive and ruthless in its own way than the violent tortures of the past: Now the target for punishment is not the prisoner's body, but her spirit: "Less violent" does not necessarily mean "better."

PREMODERN FORMS OF PUNISHMENT

Learning Objective 10.1—List the six main forms of punishment that were used prior to the rise of incarceration.

Just as they are in the modern era, earlier forms of punishment were meant to serve the purposes of rehabilitation, incapacitation, deterrence, and retribution. These punishments met these goals in different ways than do modern punishments, but nonetheless they all sought to control crime and punish offenders, and so in some ways they still make sense to us.

Execution. Though we will discuss the history of the death penalty in greater depth in a later chapter, execution has been one of the most common forms of punishment in human history. At least in terms of incapacitation, execution is effective, and compared to incarceration and other ways of dealing with offenders, it is cheap to carry out. While many modern people recoil at the idea of executing thieves and petty criminals, in societies where executions were more common than now, this was not as serious a concern.

Exile. Rather than being directly punished, sometimes offenders were kicked out of a community and never allowed to return. While this may sound like a relatively mild punishment, the consequences could be quite severe. Many societies placed a great deal of emphasis on being in a community, tribe, or clan, and so being kicked out of these groups could be considered a fate worse than death. More practically, it was often difficult to live outside of your community if you did not have resources to feed and protect yourself. In earlier societies, outsiders were feared and shunned, and you could not expect much help or support if you were forced to survive in a strange land. Exiles were often left to wither away in a remote spot without any loved ones or any social support. Exile was not execution, but to many who endured it, it led to the same result.

While it is no longer practiced as a form of criminal punishment, there are many examples of **exile** from relatively recent history. In the 18th and 19th centuries, convicts from the United Kingdom were sent to convict colonies in Australia so that they would not be able to cause trouble in England. The French government also established colonies for convicted criminals in French Guyana, a colony in South America. Known as "Devil's Island," the colony was notorious for its brutality and held many infamous French prisoners. In 1980, Cuban dictator Fidel Castro allowed

Exile: Punishing offenders by kicking them out of society.

125,000 people to leave Cuba for the United States in the Mariel Boatlift. Only after they arrived on U.S. soil was it discovered that many of these "refugees" were in fact violent criminals. Heroin addicts in parts of the United States have been given one-way tickets to another state with vague promises of treatment (Cardona-Maguigad, 2015). Offenders who are noncitizens are sometimes deported to their home country as opposed to being punished. While getting rid of undesirables, including criminals, is appealing for almost every country, in a world where it is very hard to send somebody abroad without a passport, visa, and other documentation, it can be very hard to get a criminal out of the country.

Corporal Punishment. **Corporal punishments** are aimed at the offender's body, using physical pain to punish. Such punishments can include *flogging* (that is, public whipping), burning, branding, or any other way one can imagine causing pain. Offenders in some societies can be blinded or have their tongues ripped out. For many, seeing the offender suffer intense physical agony for a short period is more satisfying than a long imprisonment. For others, seeing the victim scream in agony might be an effective general deterrent, making crime less appealing. While we cringe at the idea of "barbaric" punishments like these, they are cheap (again, compared to a lengthy incarceration) and often over quickly, both saving money and allowing offenders to get on with their lives.

Disfigurement. Permanently marking criminals so that their criminal past is recognizable to those around them has been a form of punishment in most societies. Under traditional *sharia* (Islamic law), the punishment for theft is to amputate the offender's hand in a ritualistic fashion. Many societies branded criminals for all to see their crimes and to shame the offenders. During the Civil War both sides branded deserters with a capital *D* on their foreheads to make everyone aware of their alleged cowardice. Cutting off the ears and noses of criminals has been done in many different times and places. These punishments not only cause pain but also mark the offender as an immoral person for the rest of the community. This allows everybody to know about their crimes and treat them accordingly, but it also reminds others about the consequences for breaking the law.

Enslavement. Many offenders in history have been sentenced to some form of slavery, being forced to toil in dangerous or tedious labor until either they died, or they had completed their sentence. As we will see, there has almost always been a labor component to punishment, and there is a close connection between slavery and punishment in the United States (particularly in the South).

Humiliation. Humiliating a criminal by forcing the offender to behave in mortifying ways in public has been a popular approach to punishing offenders in a variety of civilizations. Many societies have placed convicts into stocks or pillories (wooden slats that held their head and arms still and made them immobile), which allowed the community to publicly ridicule and shame them. The colonial period in America revived the practice of "tarring and feathering" representatives of the English government and "running them out of town

Corporal punishment: Punishment that causes physical pain.

on a rail"—these victims were covered in pine tar and feathers and forced to sit on a fence rail as they were paraded out of town to a jeering audience. In the famous novel *The Scarlet Letter*, Hester Prynne is punished for adultery by being forced to wear a bright red *A* on her chest to shame her. After the Second World War, French and Dutch women who had relationships with German soldiers had their heads shaved in public so that they could be shamed and marked out for later abuse by an angry public. Seeing a criminal publicly degraded can satisfy the public's demands for justice as well as serve the various goals that punishment is meant to achieve.

Humiliation is still a common if unspoken part of modern punishment in the United States. Being labeled a criminal and suffering indignities as a result is an important part of punishment for many—we want, even expect, criminals to be ashamed of their actions. Forcing offenders to clean public spaces (such as the side of the highway) is undeniably a humiliating experience, regardless of its other merits. While the courts have argued repeatedly that an offender may not be punished simply to humiliate her, they have allowed shaming as a form of punishment in a variety of circumstances. Shawn Gementera was convicted of stealing mail and was sentenced to spending a day outside of a post office with a sign stating, "I stole mail. This is my punishment," a sentence that was upheld by the courts (*United States v. Gementera*, 2004). Many other cases of shaming and humiliation have been used by courts to tailor the punishment to fit the crime and use the public as a tool for getting an offender to change her ways. As labeling theory (Chapter 3) showed, criminality always has a social dimension, and facing the disapproving eyes of the public is (in theory) a way to get offenders to change their behaviors.

Many punishments practiced in earlier periods combined these different types of punishment. The punishment for being a gossip in medieval England was what is known as a "scold's bridle." This was a mask that the offender was forced to wear that forced a metal spike in the mouth that would cut her tongue if she tried to speak or eat. Wearing this in public was obviously humiliating (sometimes the mask had a bell on it to alert the public of the offender's presence), but equally important, it created a great deal of physical suffering for the offender. Similarly, disfigurement by scarring or dismemberment is a way of both hurting and shaming the offender—she is marked forever as a criminal and must endure the suffering of being physically maimed. Corporal punishment and humiliation were both piled on top of the offender in many punishments.

While some of these early punishments may seem barbaric to modern ears, there may be some good reasons to prefer them to the expensive and often counterproductive practice of putting offenders in prison. While corporal punishment is ugly and violent, given a choice between short-term physical suffering and an extended period (perhaps years) of incarceration, which would you prefer? Which one is likely to prevent you from straying from the straight and narrow? We don't have to agree with the use of humiliation or corporal punishments as means for dealing with criminals, but we should not dismiss them outright simply because they seem strange or cruel to us. Much of the world still clings to these older practices and has lower crime rates than our own. On the other hand, many Americans would probably love to see our most serious offenders tortured in lieu of being put in prison.

WHAT WOULD YOU DO?

Alternative Punishments

You have been caught red-handed stealing alcohol from a liquor store. The other day you grabbed a case of beer and tried to make a run for it. In trying to escape, however, you knocked over a clerk and caused him to break his leg. There's no denying that you are responsible. There's also no denying that this is your third offense—you've gotten into a bit of trouble over the last couple of years.

You come to the courthouse to meet with your lawyer, where she sits you down. "I'm not going to lie," she says. "There is a chance you could do some real time for this. I'm going to meet with the prosecutor to discuss your case, but I can't promise you good results. I suspect that you will probably spend about a year in prison for this."

Your attorney goes into a meeting with the prosecutor, and after a few minutes she calls you in. They're trying a new approach to dealing with offenders like you, she says. You can avoid prison

if you agree to pay for the clerk's injuries and lost work time. Also, however, you must wear a t-shirt that says, "I am a thief—I cannot be trusted not to steal from you," with the logo of the Department of Corrections and a police contact number, every day for 10 years. You must wear it outside of your clothes, so it is always visible, and every time you walk into a store you must speak to the cashier and show her your shirt. The Department of Corrections will randomly monitor your compliance with this order, and a failure to wear the shirt or talk to store employees will lead to a five-year prison sentence.

Your attorney says that this is very unusual, but it is your only option to avoid prison. She leaves it up to you, however.

Do you take the deal? Why or why not? Do you think this punishment would serve any of the goals for punishment discussed in the introduction to this section (that is, deterrence, incapacitation, rehabilitation, or retribution)?

THE RISE OF THE PRISON

Learning Objective 10.2—Describe the characteristics of early prisons in Europe and the United States.

For the most part, these early gruesome forms of punishment have disappeared from modern criminal justice in the West. Some non-Western societies still use some of them, though most violate international human rights laws. What we've seen, over the last several hundred years in Europe and the United States, is a narrowing down of punishments toward a far more limited set of options, for good or ill. For serious offenders, only one form of punishment has been taken as the norm by American society: incarceration.

While prisons were not a primary form of punishment in the West before the 18th century, there were nonetheless many prisons in existence. England had the Tower of London, where many enemies of the king were held before they were ultimately executed. France had the Bastille, an infamous prison that held enemies of the king until it was famously attacked and torn down by the Paris mob during the early days of the French Revolution. In Venice, Italy, convicted criminals were led from the courthouse over the famous Bridge of Sighs to the prison next door, where they were placed in dark, cramped cells for many years. However, aside from the fact that these prisons were big buildings that held lawbreakers inside, they did not resemble the modern prison in any serious way. They were not aimed at rehabilitating prisoners, nor were the prison terms organized in a way that was humane. Often, convicted offenders were tossed in a dark room and occasionally fed (though wealthier inmates could often arrange for significantly better accommodations for a price) until they were forgotten about, died, or eventually were released. These prisons are nothing like what we see now—the product of nearly two and a half centuries of social, political, and even economic change. Early prisons were prisons, not "penitentiaries" or "correctional institutions." These latter institutions are decidedly modern creations.

Early Philadelphia Prisons

The prison as we know it began in Philadelphia in the late 18th century with a group of Quaker reformists. Quakerism is an offshoot of Protestant Christianity that flourished in that area at the time. (William Penn, the founder of the state of Pennsylvania, was a Quaker himself.) Its religious tenets emphasize pacifism and the importance of internal reflection, usually in silence, as the ultimate path to God. With this theological perspective, the Quakers began to design a prison that would facilitate the reform of offenders by encouraging them to quietly seek God and thereby become rehabilitated. This approach became known as the separate and silent system and was first put into effect in Eastern State Penitentiary and in a modified form in the nearby Walnut Street Jail. (Walnut Street is gone, but Eastern State is open as a museum, and its creepy, run-down structure serves as an excellent site for an annual Halloween haunted house [https://www.easternstate.org].)

The religious elements of these prisons were key to their design and operations. Eastern State was called a penitentiary and not a prison because it was intended to produce penitence and religious transformation in the heart of the criminal, not punishment or suffering. There was a strict ban on talking among the prisoners, and they were not allowed to see others during their incarceration. At Eastern State, prisoners spent all day locked in their cell, food was given to them through a small slot in the door, and each cell had a small courtyard attached to it where they were allowed access to fresh air and sunshine. When they held religious services, curtains were arranged so that prisoners could see the minister conducting the services but could not look at each other. Total isolation was deemed necessary to keep the prisoners from corrupting each other and to allow them maximum time to reflect on their misbehavior and turn toward God. As the famous French writer Alexis de Tocqueville described this system,

Separate and silent system: A model in which prisoners were not allowed to have contact with each other.

Penitentiary: A model of prison that focuses on spiritual and personal rehabilitation.

> Thrown into solitude [the prisoner] reflects. Placed alone, in view of his crime, he learns to hate it; and if his soul be not yet surfeited with crime, and thus have lost all taste for anything better, it is in solitude, where remorse will come to assail him. . . . Can there be a combination more powerful for reformation than that of a prison which hands over the prisoner to all the trials of solitude, leads him through reflection to remorse, through religion to hope; makes him industrious by the burden of idleness? (de Tocqueville & de Beaumont, 1833, pp. 22, 51)

By isolating the prisoner, the separate and silent system leaves the offender to her own conscience and to the voice of God. In this relationship the Quakers believed, perhaps naively, the offender will turn naturally toward mending her ways.

The separate and silent system was in place for a short time in Eastern State but had to be dropped for several reasons. First, it was very expensive: Building an individual cell for each prisoner with its own yard took up a lot of space and keeping them truly separate from each other took great effort, as prisoners constantly found new ways to communicate secretly with each other to escape the loneliness. Further, even though it was meant to gently help prisoners reform, many observers found the system to be cruel. Among these critics was Charles Dickens, who toured the prison in 1842 and wrote,

> I hold this slow and daily tampering with the mysteries of the brain to be immeasurably worse than any torture of the body; and because its ghastly signs and tokens are not so palpable to the eye . . . and it extorts few cries that human ears can hear; therefore the more I denounce it, as a secret punishment in which slumbering humanity is not roused up to stay. (Dickens, 1842/2009, p. 186)

The costs and difficulty of running such an elaborate system eventually led the managers of Eastern State to abandon it and to adopt a more communal living environment for the prisoners. Eastern State operated as a more conventional prison until it was shut down in 1970.

At Auburn Prison in upstate New York, officials developed a second model alongside the Pennsylvania system. Here, prisoners were kept isolated at night but could congregate together in silence and under strict supervision during the day while laboring in the prison workshops. The Auburn system is described as the "congregate and silent" system in contrast to Pennsylvania's system. Throughout the prison, strict, military-style discipline was maintained, and prisoners were required to march in formation with one hand on the shoulder of the person in front of them whenever they moved around the prison. Offenders had their heads shaved, were denied all access to the outside world, and were forced to wear the traditional black and white striped pajamas associated with historical incarceration. Failure to follow orders was met with beatings. While the Pennsylvania and Auburn models were similar, the Auburn system was considered a cheaper and more efficient way to achieve the same results. Both viewed crime as a disease that could only be treated by preventing offenders from being "infected" by other criminals.

PRISON LABOR AND INDETERMINATE SENTENCING

Learning Objective 10.3—Summarize the key aspects of parole, probation, and prison labor.

In the latter half of the 19th century and the beginning of the 20th century, two other developments defined prisons in the Western world. The first was the development of indeterminate sentencing. Rather than sentencing an offender to prison for a set length of time, punishment experts concluded that it would better suit the goals of rehabilitation to allow prison officials a certain amount of leeway in how long prisoners were incarcerated. This policy, initially developed in New York in the early 19th century, was formally adopted by the National Prison System in 1870 as part of a much broader culturally progressive movement that sought to humanize and reform prison. (For a history of indeterminate sentencing around the world, see Lindsey, 1925.) By making prison times indefinite, officials thought that prisoners would have an incentive to behave while in prison and thereby to reform themselves.

Indeterminate sentencing: Prison sentences that do not have a definite end date or can be ended early for good behavior.

Along with the imposition of indeterminate sentences, prison officials began implementing *parole* and *probation* programs. Parole refers to the supervised release of a prisoner who has shown that she has been reformed and can become a law-abiding member of society. Probation is a deferred sentence that is given to individuals who are convicted of crimes: Instead of spending their sentence in prison, offenders may go free if they don't violate the law and if they submit to supervision (including random drug tests) over the course of their sentences. This allows the prisoners to behave. While the two are often confused, the best way to keep them straight is to remember it is the phrase: "Parole after, probation instead."

By holding out the possibility of early release, indeterminate sentences gave prisoners an incentive to behave while incarcerated as well as a motivation for self-improvement. If they could show prison officials that they had learned their lesson while inside, prisoners could be released early. Or stay longer if they misbehaved. While this makes good sense from a rehabilitative perspective, the practice also creates some significant problems. First, it gives prison officials and the parole board a great deal of power over the prisoner: They can mark prisoners down for misconduct and make it significantly harder for them to qualify for an early release. This can be unfair to prisoners who, for whatever reason, are treated harshly by parole boards or by prison officials—they are at the mercy of the prison staff who might be inclined to treat them unfairly for whatever reason. In the latter part of the 20th century, prisoners begin to be given the right to contest disciplinary procedures in prison, but prior to this development, prisoners were at the mercy of prison officials who could extend the prisoner's stay almost at will.

While indeterminate sentences were an important development of the 19th century, the 20th century saw a politically powerful movement against it. Critics argued that indeterminate sentences were too lenient and made it too easy for offenders to get out of prison early. It seemed wrong that an offender sentenced to 20 years in prison should only spend 10 or so years behind bars. They also argued that the public had a right to know how long those convicted of a crime would be punished and this decision should not be made by a parole board out of the public eye. In response, *truth-in-sentencing laws* were passed in many states, which made it far more difficult for prisoners to obtain early release and made probation far more difficult to achieve. As one influential study showed, however, the restrictions on flexibility in punishment made other parts of the system more lenient toward criminal punishment so as not to overburden the penal system (Savelsberg, 1992). The accused would sometimes simply be charged with a lesser offense, more appropriate to the offender's guilt.

Along with indeterminate sentencing, a second development in 19th-century American prisons was the use of *prison labor*. Prisoners have always worked. Whether it was breaking rocks, making shoes in their cells, working in the prison facilities (cafeteria, laundry, etc.) or helping clean the side of the road, prisoners have been expected to engage in physical labor as a part of their punishment. Prison labor can have a lot of benefits. It can help to offset the costs of incarceration: The prisoner either reduces the labor needed to run the prison (by, say, working as a librarian) or produces goods that the prison can then sell on the market to offset its costs. Further, labor gives prisoners something to occupy their time while in prison, allowing the time to pass with less boredom. Labor can sometimes teach a prisoner some valuable skills to use once on the outside. Finally, many Americans subscribe to what is known as the Protestant work ethic, that is, the belief that

Parole: The practice of releasing incarcerated offenders early.

Probation: Allowing a convicted offender to avoid imprisonment and remain free under close supervision.

labor is an inherent moral good and that not working is a sign of sloth and sin (Pierson, Price, & Coleman, 2014). The idea of making prisoners work fits the modern penal system as well as many aspects of the American view of life.

CRIMINAL (IN)JUSTICE

The Thirteenth Amendment

We are told in school that slavery was abolished in the United States during the Civil War with the passage of the Thirteenth Amendment. This is not completely true. The Thirteenth Amendment ended slavery in general but left one important exception that unscrupulous racists used to re-enslave many southern blacks after emancipation. The amendment reads, "Neither slavery nor involuntary servitude, *except as a punishment for crime* whereof the party shall have been duly convicted, shall exist within the United States, or any place subject to their jurisdiction" (emphasis added). During the post–Civil War years, southern states took advantage of this punishment loophole to return many blacks to a form of slavery, this time under the guise of criminal justice. In this system, known as the *convict lease system*, the criminal justice system colluded with plantation owners and legislators to effectively return freed slaves back to their prewar state.

After the war, many African Americans were arrested on false charges or prosecuted for vague offenses and then given lengthy prison sentences. The passage of black codes, pig laws, and other racist criminal statutes allowed the police to round up and prosecute liberated blacks almost at will and charge them with serious crimes. Pig laws made it a felony to "steal" livestock and other private property but were used by white landowners to prevent blacks from claiming property that rightfully belonged to them. Antivagrancy laws in effect allowed the police to arrest blacks for doing anything that could be construed as not working. These convicts were then put to work doing the same labor that they would have been forced to do as slaves prior to emancipation. Effectively, prison became a new sort of slavery, and the criminal justice system became part of a constellation of forces working to prevent African Americans from living as free and equal members of society.

Felon disenfranchisement has likewise prevented millions of offenders from participating in democracy by denying them the vote. Though the Constitution bans racial discrimination in voting, it does not guarantee all American citizens the right to vote. After the Civil War, southern states used felon disenfranchisement as a tool to restrict the voting rights of their black populations (Bazelon, 2018). Disenfranchisement was used along with tactics like poll taxes and literacy tests to keep blacks from holding any political power in much of the former Confederacy. Not only were black codes a tool for keeping African Americans in prison, they have kept many blacks out of the voting pool. Though many states have eliminated such disenfranchisement (in the 2018 election, Florida voters opted to abandon it), it remains on the books in two states, and many others don't allow citizens in prison or on probation to vote (Brennan Center for Justice, 2018).

Criminal justice institutions (police, prisons) were, and remain in many cases, integrated into a bigger political system that keeps black people in general, and black men in particular, in poverty and in prison. Criminal laws and the prison system have been used to effectively continue slavery by other means—a continuation of a long trend that we discussed in Chapter 5 when we discussed the history of American policing.

Prison labor became less important with the stock market crash and the onset of the Great Depression in 1929. The crash caused a massive rise in unemployment across the United States, and manufacturing jobs were scarce until the beginning of the Second World War. Because inmates did not work by choice and were not paid, prisons were often able to undercut paid labor, making it difficult for nonprison labor to compete for contracts. Many politicians and labor leaders did not want to see work that could be done by free men go to people who had broken the law. In response, politicians created laws such as the Hawes-Cooper Convict Labor Act that restricted the sale and purchase of products manufactured by prisoners. Prison labor still exists and is an important part of modern prisons (it is mandatory in many places), but laws restrict who can buy the goods that the prisoners produce. UNICOR, for example, is a company owned by the federal government that sells products manufactured by federal prisoners, though they are only allowed to sell to other parts of the federal government and not to private parties.

REHABILITATION

Learning Objective 10.4—Analyze the rise of rehabilitation as a goal of incarceration.

Another major element of the 20th-century prison was a new emphasis on rehabilitation as a goal of incarceration. While rehabilitation has been a part of the prison system since the days of the Walnut Street and Eastern State penitentiaries, with the rise of modern psychology and criminology as tools to understand and change human behavior, rehabilitation took on new dimensions in the American prison system. As a result prisons began to take on what is sometimes called a "therapeutic" approach to punishment—using psychotherapy and other modern tools to treat offenders, rather than thinking of prisoners as bad people who deserve punishment.

The 1970s saw several challenges to the idea that prisons were akin to hospitals for sick people. One of the most significant was the charge by political activists that prisoners were not ill or damaged, but rather were victims of an unjust social order. Among the most influential of these was the *black power movement*, which saw society as enmeshed in a struggle between racial groups. The mass incarceration of African Americans, they argued, was the product of a racist society, not a product of a prisoner's illness—and rehabilitation turned the genuine dissatisfaction of black offenders into a kind of illness. Pointing to the history of the prison system and to society's inequalities, they argued that the prison was a natural extension of broad social injustices. As one critic put it, "The prison is similar to the ghetto in that in both places those outside have the power to control and to define those inside. The appeal of Black separatists is to offer to those inside the alternative of determining their own fate and their own values" (Johnson, 1975). As African Americans became dissatisfied with the social order, they challenged the view that prisoners were somehow damaged people who needed help.

Alongside black power, movements like the *antipsychiatry movement* argued that a therapeutic approach to dealing with prisoners could be far more invasive and far more intrusive than would ordinary incarceration. Finally, many conservatives pushed for a more retributive approach to punishment and were skeptical about the value of reform as a goal for incarceration. While many prisons still call themselves "correctional institutions," there has been less enthusiasm for rehabilitation overall (Allen, 1981).

MASS INCARCERATION

What is most shocking about the last quarter of the 20th century is the sharp rise in incarceration rates throughout the United States. Many more people went to prison in this period than in any other period in human history. During this time, the United States became the country with the largest prison population per capita in the world. Most of these were African Americans and Hispanics, and it almost goes without saying that almost all of them were men. All of this was happening while the crime rate was decreasing. As we discussed in the first chapter, the crime rate went down dramatically in the 1990s, a phenomenon referred to as *the crime drop*. Fewer crimes were being committed, but simultaneously more people were going to prison. This period, from about the mid-1970s until the 21st century, marks a change in the history of prisons.

There were several different social forces that came together to massively increase the prison population. Among the most significant of these was the *war on drugs*. While drugs and other substances have been a problem for American society and have been regulated since the beginning of the 20th century, it wasn't until the 1970s that drugs were viewed primarily as a problem that needed to be addressed through law enforcement, courts, and prisons. The consensus before the war on drugs was that the best way to prevent drug abuse was to lower the demand for drugs by public education and by treating abusers (similar to how we treat alcohol abuse today), not to spend a great deal of energy arresting drug traffickers. This changed during the 1970s, when conservative politicians began exploiting stereotypes about drug users and drug traffickers to get support among white voters. This emphasis on punishing drug abusers meant that many more people were arrested on drug charges than in the past, and therefore more prisons were constructed to house these new offenders.

A second force that led to the increase in the prison population was the reduction of mental health services. In the 1980s, the federal government drastically cut public spending on a variety of social services, including those helping the mentally ill. In his first federal budget, Ronald Reagan slashed federal mental health funding by 30% and gave block grants to states so that they could address the issues on their own (if they chose to) (Pan, 2013). This meant that many people who were once living in facilities where they were cared for and monitored were now on the street in one form or another. A person with serious mental illness, when forced to live without supervision or medication, is far more likely either to self-medicate (seeking to treat her mental health problems through drugs and alcohol) or violate the law because she is incapable of obeying the law. In both cases, she is very likely to wind up in prison and return to prison if she is let out. Because of this, the prisons become de facto hospitals for the mentally ill, and more than half of all prisoners have mental health issues according to some studies (Khazan, 2015). (Ironically, it probably costs more to keep the mentally ill in prisons than it would to treat them in a mental hospital.)

The rise of a get-tough mentality toward crime also helped fuel the rise in incarceration rates. Few if any politicians wanted to appear soft on crime and therefore were willing to promote a "lock 'em up" mentality that led to longer sentences for offenders. Presidential candidate Michael Dukakis, for example, was perceived as being soft on crime when he supported a program that allowed prisoners to work out in the world. (A black man named Willie Horton raped a white woman and stabbed her fiancée while on furlough, a fact that helped doom Dukakis's candidacy.) President Bill Clinton signed a tough crime bill, the "Violent Crime Control and Law Enforcement Act," that further expanded the powers of the federal and state governments to arrest people and sentence them to longer prison terms. Truth in sentencing laws prevented or restricted plea bargains and restricted the ability of prisons to release an individual early regardless of whether she was deemed rehabilitated. There were a lot of political and cultural forces that pushed to put more people in prison for longer times and to make it harder to let people out.

THE PRISON-INDUSTRIAL COMPLEX

Learning Objective 10.6—Identify how interest groups have profited from mass incarceration.

Critical criminologists have pointed to the rise of what they call the prison-industrial complex to help explain the rise of mass incarceration. They point to several overlapping economic and political interests that have fueled the massive rise in incarceration rates. Many prisons are built in areas that are poor and have high levels of unemployment. Constructing, guarding, and maintaining prisons provides many good, well-paying, and secure jobs to people in these communities, who would have fewer employment options if the prison wasn't there. These guards are often members of labor unions that can have a great deal of influence on government officials—and more prisoners means more guards, and therefore more members for the unions. This creates an economic incentive for these groups to have more prisoners and more prisons. To use one example: The California Prison Guard's Union has been an active supporter of "three strikes" laws, which require certain felons to be automatically sentenced to life imprisonment (Knafo, 2013). These groups have a strong interest in having prisons constructed and staffed—all at the taxpayers' expense—and mass imprisonment is a result of these different forces coming together.

Further, the politicians who make criminal laws, including those involving the length of sentences, have their own incentives. Lawmakers who represent regions where prisons exist (or areas that want a prison built) have an interest in increasing the number of prisoners to increase the number of prisons and prison personnel. The money that the government provides for prisons and their staff can help them win support in their home districts by creating construction and prison staff jobs. Thus, there is a political benefit to sentencing prisoners to longer and longer periods of prison for many politicians.

Politicians have another reason to increase the sentences for criminals: By promoting tougher sentences for convicted criminals, politicians get to look tough. It's a well-worn truth that the public likes politicians that are perceived as "tough." This usually means that they are tough on criminals (as well as on "welfare cheats" and "illegal immigrants"), and an easy way to show their toughness is by supporting longer sentences for convicted criminals. It is very unlikely that an American politician would lose an election for being too tough on crime, and supporting tougher laws on criminals is often an easy vote-getter. Therefore, politicians can benefit from passing tougher crime laws with longer prison sentences.

Under the prison-industrial complex, politicians and the public have a strong set of interlocking incentives to give offenders longer sentences. The only people who suffer in this model are the prisoners themselves and those who love and support them. Most prisoners are poor and are members of minority groups, people who already have very little economic and political influence, so there are few incentives for politicians to help them

Prison-industrial complex: The historical collusion between politicians and private businesses to boost the prison population for financial and political gain.

by reforming the law. Further, African Americans vote in lesser numbers than do white Americans, and their votes are often concentrated in a few areas, giving them comparatively little influence. And of course, offenders and exoffenders can't vote in many states. Almost everybody gains from mass incarceration, and the only people who suffer from it are comparatively powerless.

Another aspect of the incarceration boom in the United States is the role of prosecutors. As we discussed in Chapter 3, prosecutors have a great deal of influence over who is charged with offenses. Many of these prosecutors use their position as a stepping stone to higher offices, and sending offenders to prison is a way to bolster their reputation for toughness. This means that prosecutors have an incentive to send more people to prison than may be necessary and are sometimes inclined to charge offenders with more serious offenses than they might otherwise. This tough attitude, coupled with the fact that prosecutors are not responsible for funding the prisons that house the people they've convicted, means that there is little incentive for prosecutors to avoid seeking long prison sentences for offenders. As a result, incarceration rates have skyrocketed over the last three decades (Pfaff, 2012).

REALITY CHECK

Race and Sentencing

As we've already seen, the prison system has been used against African Americans in many ways, going back at least until the years after the Civil War. However, more recent studies have shown that the American penal system remains stacked against black Americans even after the black codes, pig laws, and Jim Crow were dismantled. Many different studies have shown that African Americans still get longer sentences than do white offenders.

Although critical criminologists have been studying this issue for years, determining racial bias in sentencing is a complicated matter. There are a lot of different factors that shape a criminal sentence: the crimes the offender is charged with, any aggravating circumstances surrounding the crime, the quality of legal representation that a defendant receives, the jurisdiction where the crime is committed, et cetera. There is no simple way to compare cases, and criminologists fear equating apples with oranges when looking at criminal sentences.

Too glibly attributing sentencing disparities to race would overlook a lot of important factors.

In one study, a pair of researchers did their best to account for the differences between cases to determine just how much difference race made in an offender's criminal sentence. Focusing on federal cases, they used a statistical model to counteract many of the other differences among offenders, such as where the crime was committed and the different pretrial decisions made by the courtroom workgroup. After analyzing the data, they concluded that, "On average, blacks receive almost 10% longer sentences than comparable whites arrested for the same crimes" (Rehavi & Starr, 2012) (see Figure 10.1).

Regardless of how they study this question, there is near unanimity that the race of the offender impacts criminal sentences and that black offenders receive longer sentences than do similar white ones. A *meta-analysis* of studies of this issue, that is, a study of other studies of racial differences in criminal sentences,

(Continued)

(Continued)

concluded that "unwarranted racial disparities persist" and that "African-Americans generally are sentenced more harshly than whites" (Mitchell, 2005). This of course does not include racially biased decisions that take place earlier on in the criminal justice system, such as racial profiling by the police and racially biased criminal laws that subject African Americans to additional scrutiny. While the matter is more complex than simple slogans, all the research suggests that, all things being equal, blacks are given longer sentences than whites by judges.

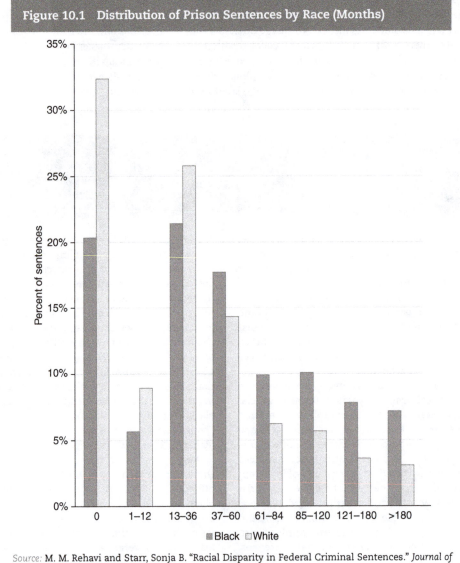

Figure 10.1   Distribution of Prison Sentences by Race (Months)

Source: M. M. Rehavi and Starr, Sonja B. "Racial Disparity in Federal Criminal Sentences." *Journal of Political Economy* 122, no. 6 (2014): 1320–54. Reprinted with permission.

SOME STATISTICS...

Incarceration Rates

Even a passing glance at incarceration rates in modern America shows a stunning increase in imprisonment rates in the United States since the 1970s (see Figure 10.2).

This statistic is particularly striking when we separate the incarceration rates by race (see Figure 10.3). Clearly, much of the increase of incarceration has been the result of the arrest of African Americans that began in the early 1980s.

One particularly hopeful note is that the incarceration rate for African Americans has been decreasing over recent years. There are a lot of possible explanations for this: The drug war has shifted away from drugs associated with the African American community, such as crack cocaine, and toward "white drugs" (drugs associated with white people), such as methamphetamine and heroin; criminal justice reform in urban areas, et cetera (Hager, 2017). Observers have noted that the switch to a focus on white drug abuse has resulted in greater sympathy for drug addicts among public figures and less talk about tough punishments than when drug abusers where stereotypically black or Latino (Lopez, 2017).

Compared to the rest of the world, the United States has the highest number of

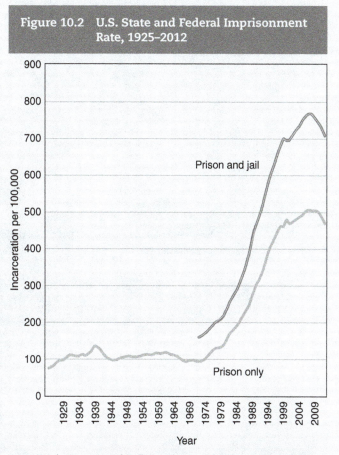

Figure 10.2 U.S. State and Federal Imprisonment Rate, 1925–2012

Source: Travis, Western, and Redburn, 2014, p. 35. Reprinted with permission.
Note: Latest data available.

prisoners *by far* (see Table 10.1). According to the research institute Prison World, the United States has a half million more prisoners than the second most incarcerated nation (China, which has nearly four times the population of the United States).

(Continued)

(Continued)

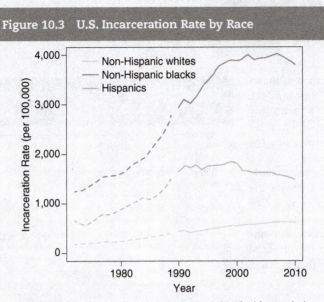

Figure 10.3 U.S. Incarceration Rate by Race

Source: Travis, Western, and Redburn, 2014, p. 63. Reprinted with permission.

Note: Latest data available.

Table 10.1 Countries With the Largest Numbers of Prisoners, as of July 2018

1	United States of America	2,121,600
2	China	1,649,804
3	Brazil	682,901
4	Russian Federation	592,467
5	India	419,623
6	Thailand	349,804
7	Indonesia	249,419
8	Turkey	232,179
9	Iran	230,000
10	Mexico	204,749
11	Philippines	178,661

Source: World Prison Brief, Institute for Criminal Policy Research.

Similarly, the United States has the highest number of prisoners as a percentage of the population (655 per 100,000 people) (see Table 10.2).

Finally, the United States spends *a lot of* money on prisons, prisoners, and related services (Figure 10.4). According to The Hamilton Project, an independent research organization, the United States spends about $80 billion on incarceration. This is a result of both spending more per prisoner and having a higher number of offenders.

Table 10.2	Number of Prisoners per 100,000 People, by Country	
1	United States of America	655
2	El Salvador	609
3	Turkmenistan	552
4	Virgin Islands (United States)	542
5	Cuba	510
6	Thailand	506
7	Maldives	499
8	Northern Mariana Islands (United States)	482
9	Virgin Islands (United Kingdom)	470
10	Rwanda	464

Source: World Prison Brief, Institute for Criminal Policy Research.

Figure 10.4 Total Corrections Expenditures by Level of Government and Per Capita Expenditures

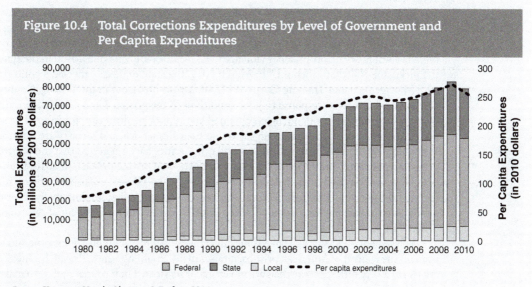

Source: Kearney, Harris, Jácome, & Parker, 2014.

Private Prisons

A further element of the incarceration boom is the rise of private prisons. These prisons are not run by the federal or state governments but instead are staffed and managed by private companies, which contract with state governments. Private prisons are based on the philosophy of *neoliberalism*, the belief that most services are best left to private companies that are contracted by the state, rather than being provided directly by the government. (Similar approaches are taken in many other aspects of the government, which has contracted with private contractors for services like military support and legal work for indigent criminal defendants.) Neoliberals argue that companies can run prisons more efficiently than the government could, providing better outcomes and saving the government money. This is the view held by most American conservatives about many services that the government ordinarily provides—and indeed private prisons only came into existence in the United States in the1980s under President Ronald Reagan, a leader famous for supporting a limited government.

There are hundreds of juvenile and adult prisons in the United States. Approximately 6% of all prisoners and 20% of federal prisoners are in private facilities (Carson, 2015; "Private prisons," n.d.). The Corrections Corporation of America (CCA) is the largest private prison company in America, and it manages 65 different prisons in the United States—most of which are federal prisons. CCA designs and builds the prisons and staffs them with guards and other prison personnel. CCA also has reentry programs that are designed to help former prisoners return to society. Not only do these companies profit from government contracts, they also profit directly from prisoners by running in-prison commissaries and selling other services to prisoners such as snacks and phone cards. Prisons are a nearly $70 billion industry, and most of these companies are traded on the New York Stock Exchange.

The private prison system has faced a great deal of criticism. There have been several high-profile cases of abuse in private facilities, often linked with poorly provided services. In 2013, the state of Idaho canceled its contracts with the CCA after reports of high levels of prisoner-on-prisoner violence in CCA prisons, giving one prison in the state the nickname "Gladiator School." In March 2015, the state of Texas canceled a contract with Management and Training Corp (MTC) after riots broke out in the Willacy County Correctional Center in response to poor conditions in the prison. The prisoners, most of whom were nonviolent offenders, complained about poor medical care for injured prisoners. A number of studies have suggested that the care, service, and security are inferior at privately run correctional institutions, and other critics have suggested that the private prison corporations misrepresent the cost effectiveness of private prisons. In 2016, President Obama declared that the federal government would no longer use private prisons for federal prisoners, but President Trump largely reversed this policy, sending many federal prisoners to private facilities, some of which donated to the Trump presidential campaign (Gill, 2018).

While neoliberalism may have some advantages over private industry in some situations, in the context of American prisons, it raises many troubling issues. Private businesses are run in a very different way than are government services: Their primary job is to make a profit. This gives private prisons a strong incentive to cut corners and provide inferior services to prisoners. In most industries, if a company provides an inferior product, their

Private prisons: Prisons not run by the government but by private corporations.

customers can opt to go somewhere else, but prisoners have no options; they are being held against their will. State or federal governments could choose to stop working with private companies that provide inferior services to prisoners, but suggesting that the government should spend more of its tax dollars to provide care for convicted criminals is unlikely to be a popular view. Even those states that canceled contracts with the CCA were simply looking for other corporations to run their prisons.

Equally perverse, these industries profit from incarceration and so have an incentive to lobby legislatures to increase criminal sanctions. Many of the contracts that these companies sign with state governments "lock in" occupancy rates—meaning that the state promises to keep the prisons full *regardless of the crime rate* (Johnson, 2012). While neoliberalism may be a useful approach to handling some services, there is a great deal of evidence that injecting profit motives into the prison system can distort how the corrections system works.

AFTER INCARCERATION?

Learning Objective 10.7—Analyze the present and future of incarceration as a form of punishment.

Over the last few years, many different forces have come together to question how we punish offenders in the United States. Historically, prison reform has been largely a progressive cause, but recently many conservatives have taken up the cause. In some ways this makes sense: If conservatives worry about the overreach of government power, then they should worry about the overuse of prisons. The cliché that politics makes strange bedfellows applies here, as both conservatives and liberals have questioned the wisdom of locking up so many people.

One reason for this skepticism regarding prison is the costs that high rates of imprisonment impose on the government. Even though there are obvious economic benefits for communities where prisons are located as well as the private companies that run many of the prisons, it often strains state and federal budgets to house, clothe, and guard convicted offenders. This means that some of those conservatives who worry about excessive government waste are trying to find alternatives to prison (Bauer, 2014). Others worry about its impact on civil rights. As 2016 Republican presidential candidate and Kentucky senator Rand Paul stated,

> I also think it's a problem to lock people up for 10 and 15 and 20 years for youthful mistakes. If you look at the War on Drugs, three out of four people in prison are black or brown. White kids are doing it too. In fact, if you look at all the surveys, white kids do it just as much as black and brown kids—but the prisons are full of black and brown kids because they don't get a good attorney, they live in poverty, it's easier to arrest them than to go to the suburbs. There's a lot of reasons. (Ashtan, 2014)

Lowering the number of people in prison means saving money and protecting people from the abuse of government power. The legal scholar Hadar Aviram has referred to this as humonetarianism: "a value-free, superficial, cost-centered approach to correctional

Humonetarianism: Limiting the number of people imprisoned because it's too expensive for the government, not because it is morally right.

initiatives and institutions, which are assessed by their contribution to the state's deficit rather than on their actual or even perceived merits" (Aviram, 2010).

There have been several attempts to reduce the number of people in prisons in the United States. The Supreme Court has issued rulings that have restricted the sentences that both states and the federal government may give an offender. In 2012, the court ruled that it was unconstitutional to sentence juvenile offenders to life imprisonment without parole (*Miller v. Alabama*). A few other cases have limited the ability of courts to impose so-called mandatory minimums (that is, minimum sentences) for some offenses (*Alleyne v. United States*, 2013; *Johnson v. United States*, 2015). The Fair Sentencing Act of 2010 eliminated the minimum five-year prison term for possessing crack cocaine and helped reduce some drug-related mandatory sentences. In October 2015, the Obama administration backed the Sentencing Reform and Corrections Act of 2015, a bipartisan bill in the U.S. Senate that aimed to reduce the prison sentences for nonviolent drug offenders. While it isn't surprising that a Democratic president would support such a bill, it is remarkable that the law has received support from conservative Republicans along with congressional Democrats (Jalonick, 2015). While America remains the country with the highest incarceration rate in the world, politicians on both the left and the right have begun to question the wisdom of a system that puts so many of its people behind bars.

During his presidential campaign, Donald Trump proudly declared that he would "liberate our citizens from the crime and terrorism and lawlessness that threatens their communities" and that "the crime and violence that today afflicts our nation will soon, and I mean very soon, come to an end." Many believe that he will reverse this trend of decriminalization and that the number of prisoners will again rise. After he won the election, the stock values of private prison corporations rose dramatically—not only because investors believe that the incarceration rate will increase, but further they believe that these companies will play a large role in holding and deporting the 11 million undocumented immigrants that Trump has promised to remove from the country (Surowiecki, 2016). On the other hand, one of the most significant legislative achievements of the first two years of the Trump administration was the First Step Act, which allowed many federal prisoners to apply for early release and reduced sentences for a variety of nonviolent offenders (Wagner, 2018). It is difficult to know whether or not President Trump's threats will come to pass, but if so, this movement away from mass incarceration will have turned into a brief respite in a half-century-long march to imprisoning ever greater numbers of people.

WHERE DO I FIT IN?

WORKING THE PRISON (GUARDS AND VOLUNTEERS)

There are a lot of different ways, both paid and unpaid, to work in a prison. Being a guard is the most obvious career inside the prison system; but you could also work in administration, medical care, psychological counseling, or teaching; or you could volunteer. Becoming a corrections officer is a lot like becoming a police officer: One usually must be over the age of 21, possess a high school diploma or GED, and have no convictions for violent crimes or domestic violence. Guards are required to undergo training at a correctional officer academy, where they learn everything from communication strategies and suicide prevention to riot control. The work can be demanding, as the prisons need to be constantly manned—there is little flexibility for holidays. It can also be stressful, as inmates present a constant threat of violence—even if actual violence itself is rare. Like police officers, correctional officers face an increased risk of job burnout as well as alcoholism and PTSD (Schaufeli & Peeters, 2000).

There are a lot of different ways to serve as a volunteer in a prison, even while you are still in college. You can teach, you can work in parenting workshops for prisoners with children, or you can teach a variety of skills to inmates, helping them obtain personal or professional skills that can benefit them after they are released or while they are still inside. For example, the California Department of Corrections has a prison education program (http://www.prisoneducationproject.org) that provides educational programming in a dozen state correctional institutions, using student volunteers to help inmates work toward a GED or a bachelor's degree, among other things. To volunteer in the prison system, you must apply, usually to your state department of corrections, undergo a background check to ensure that you are not a security concern, and attend training sessions to navigate the prison environment safely.

CHAPTER SUMMARY

This chapter has tracked the history of punishment/corrections from the ancient world to today. We started with earlier forms of punishment and then tracked the rise of the prison over the last two hundred years. The first thing to keep in mind is how rare incarceration was as a form of punishment until the late 18th century. It really wasn't until rehabilitation became the primary reason for punishment that the prison took on a defining role in the criminal justice system. If your goals are retribution, deterrence, or incapacitation, then holding people in a cell for years (feeding, clothing, and housing them) seems wasteful. It's only when the primary goal of prison is rehabilitation that isolating offenders and controlling their behavior 24 hours a day makes sense. Thus, the rise of the prison is a consequence of the rise of rehabilitation as the primary ideology of criminal punishment.

Despite the primacy of rehabilitation as the central goal of modern punishment, the other reasons for punishing offenders have not disappeared. Incapacitation is still a reason given for modern punishment (hence, some offenders are sentenced to life imprisonment without parole), as is deterrence. Most important, however, retribution and its ally revenge have remained in our penal toolbox. While society gives lip service to the idea that prisons are "correctional institutes," few politicians have the stomach for giving prisons the resources necessary to truly reform prisoners. In other countries, most notably those in much of Western Europe and Scandinavia, rehabilitation is a central goal of punishment, and as a result prisons are much nicer places to spend time, and prisoners are given far more resources to help them turn their lives around. These countries also spend a lot more on their prisons, and citizens often pay much higher taxes. The point is that we often speak about rehabilitating prisoners but fail to put our money where our mouth is.

In the next chapter we will turn to the modern prisons themselves, discussing different aspects of contemporary prison life. Then we will turn to alternative forms of punishing offenders in the last chapter of this section.

REVIEW/DISCUSSION QUESTIONS

1. How has punishment changed over the last 300 years, and what social forces have caused these changes?

2. How important do you think incarceration is for punishing offenders? Would other punishments better serve justice?

3. Where do you think punishment/corrections will go in the future? Do you think prison will always be a central part of criminal justice?

KEY TERMS

Corporal punishment 247
Exile 246
Humonetarianism 263
Indeterminate sentencing 251

Parole 252
Penitentiary 250
Prison-industrial
    complex 256

Private prisons 262
Probation 252
Separate and silent
    system 250

$SAGE edge™

Get the tools you need to sharpen your study skills. SAGE edge offers a robust online environment featuring an impressive array of free tools and resources.

Access practice quizzes, eFlashcards, video, and multimedia at edge.sagepub.com/fichtelberg

Sara Yeh

Prisons are required to provide sufficient nutrition and calories to inmates, but many choose to make their own food in their cells if possible.

CHAPTER ELEVEN

PRISON LIFE

Shows like *Oz* and *Orange Is the New Black* and movies like the ubiquitous *Shawshank Redemption* portray prison as a hothouse of violence, especially sexual violence, perpetrated by an array of terrifying and colorful personalities. It is, according to mythology, a place of intense brutality, where the tiniest slip makes a person vulnerable to assault, rape, or even murder. "The yard," the cafeteria, the showers, and every other corner of the prison is full of gangs hunting for their next victim, and any show of weakness from a prisoner is an open invitation for a beat down. Every step, every wrong move on the part of a prisoner makes her vulnerable to exploitation, attack, and even death.

Of course, by this point in the book you've probably figured out that this popular image of prison life has only the faintest resemblance to what goes on inside America's correctional institutions. Most of prison is extremely boring and prisoners often report that keeping themselves occupied, not the threat of violence from guards or their fellow prisoners, is the hardest part of prison life. Sitting in your cell for hours on end with little to look forward to but meals or whatever distractions are presented (movies, library) is a soul-crushing way to spend years of your life. Violence is real, especially at higher-security institutions, but it is relatively rare, particularly if the prison is well run. Time is the greatest enemy in prison, not the other prisoners. In this chapter we will seek to get beyond the hype and fear about prison life and look at American correctional institutions as they really are.

In this chapter we will look at some key aspects of modern prison life. We will discuss the types of institutions that currently operate in the United States as well as some of the most important features of life on the inside. This will include some of the daily activities of prisoners as well as some of the more notorious features of prison life (gangs, sex, etc.). Like other parts of the book, this section will include some tips to keep in mind should you be unfortunate enough to spend time in prison. Finally, at the end of the chapter we will look at issues regarding prisoner rights—that is, we will discuss the legal tools that are available for prisoners to challenge aspects of their incarceration. Once we have done this, we will then turn to discussing forms of punishment beyond incarceration, the subject of the next two chapters.

Just as there are state-level differences in policing and in courts, there are different prison systems for each state as well as 122 federal institutions. The federal system is run by the Bureau of Prisons (BOP), a part of the Department of Justice. There is also a

269

military prison system under the Department of Defense, which is also responsible for the special prison set up for suspected terrorists in Guantanamo Bay, Cuba. Finally, many counties have a separate jail for people awaiting trial or for convicts serving shorter sentences. Each state has its own department overseeing its prisons, though many states are willing to take prisoners from other states for a fee. Privately run prisons make a substantial profit from housing and guarding prisoners from out of state (Equal Justice Initiative, 2018). While this arrangement may be necessary given current prison conditions, it also means that many prisoners are sometimes housed thousands of miles away from family and friends (not to mention their attorney), reducing the ability of these loved ones to visit them and further increasing their isolation.

We should be careful about overgeneralizing about prison life. Different institutions have different cultures, that is, different spoken and unspoken rules about how to behave while inside. What might be standard practice in a maximum-security prison in Texas is very different from what might be done at a medium-security institution in Maine. When a prisoner transfers from one institution to another, she must adjust to a new order—new rules, new ways of doing things, new guards, and of course, new prisoners. Some prisons allow behavior that would never be allowed in other institutions. In short, we can only speak about prison life in a broad way—prisoners must figure out the specifics when they get there.

Sociologists often describe prisons as total institutions (Goffman, 1961). Total institutions are unique social spaces that seek to shape people by isolating them from the outside world and controlling even the tiniest aspects of their existence, including how they dress, eat, walk, and talk. Such a life is almost completely unrecognizable when compared to the one the prisoner left behind. The only other institutions in the modern world that compare to prisons in this way are military organizations, psychiatric hospitals, and perhaps extreme religious institutions such as cults or monasteries. The goal is to control the individual's behavior at the most minute level, so that officials can both manage them more effectively and change them. Imprisonment can have dramatic effects on how people act, and prisoners behave very differently in prison than they might in the outside world. When they leave they are often very different persons than when they went in, which is part of the goal of prison but also can make things difficult when prisoners return to the outside world.

Total institutions: Institutions like prisons, mental hospitals, and the military where virtually every aspect of an individual's life is controlled.

GOING TO PRISON

Learning Objective 11.1—List the procedures that take place after conviction leading to incarceration.

Presentence investigation report: An analysis of a convicted offender provided to the court by a probation officer that examines the background of the offender.

Once a defendant is convicted at trial or has pled guilty in court, the sentencing process begins. If the case is not a capital one (that is, one where the death penalty is being considered), the jury's work is done when they vote to convict or acquit a defendant. The judge is the one who decides the appropriate punishment, usually within limits set out by the laws of the state. To help her decide, the judge will often receive a report from a probation officer known as a presentence investigation report (PSIR) that examines the background of the defendant and includes details about the crime and the victim.

Also, during the sentencing hearing both the prosecution and defense can argue for or against a serious punishment, and the victim(s) can sometimes provide a victim impact statement, explaining how the crime has affected their lives. Then, the judge will render her sentence.

Then, in most states, offenders are evaluated by prison officials to determine what their incarceration should look like. After sentencing, prisoners are sent to a reception center where they are evaluated by a classification team—that is, a group of experts who are going to determine what the prisoners' time in prison will look like. Among the things that the team wants to learn about new prisoners are facts about their backgrounds—their history, skills, mental and physical health, et cetera. Other criteria evaluated include age, gender, the offender's history of violence, gang membership, and disciplinary history (Austin, 2003). The team will also make a security assessment of new prisoners, determining exactly how dangerous they are likely to be to guards and to their fellow prisoners. (Later, if a prisoner's behavior merits it, she can be reclassified and given a different placement at either a higher- or lower-security facility.) All this material will be worked into a file on the criminal that will be used to assign her to a prison, though practical concerns like the availability of bed space also play a significant role.

Victim impact statement: Testimony from a victim provided at sentencing, where she explains the effect that the crime had on her.

Reception center: A location where newly incarcerated offenders are processed.

Classification team: A group of experts who evaluate newly incarcerated prisoners.

WHERE DO I FIT IN?

GOING TO PRISON

There are a lot of different lessons that "fish," slang for new prisoners, need to learn when they arrive in prison. Many former prisoners have written guides for surviving in prison for the benefit of newly convicted offenders. Every prison is different, with different rules and even different slang, so you must be careful about the official and unofficial rules of the institution that you are in. Here are a few pieces of advice that ex-cons give.

Avoid gifts and debts.

In prison, owing people favors, money, or anything else can get you into a lot of trouble. Even if something is given to an inmate "freely," there are usually strings attached. Accepting a gift from the wrong person can get you in trouble.

Don't gossip about others behind their back.

A lot of prisoner drama comes from gossip or "shit talking" among prisoners. Minding your own business is very important to successfully navigating prison.

Don't talk about offenses with other prisoners.

Many offenders don't like to be defined by their offenses and will only share this information after time has passed and trust has developed. Also, offenders convicted of certain crimes (such as child abuse) can face danger while inside, and so they will not easily share information about their crimes. ("Short timers"—people who will soon leave prison—are also advised to be quiet about that fact.)

(Continued)

THE PRISON POPULATION

Learning Objective 11.2—Identify the makeup of the American prison system.

The United States has the highest rate of prisoners per capita in the world (that is, the highest percentage of the population is imprisoned) as well as the most prisoners overall ("Countries With," 2019). The Bureau of Justice Statistics (BJS) has a national prison statistics program that tracks both state and federal prison populations and puts out an annual report. The statistics here are based on the 2014 BJS report, which counted populations in the previous year, supplemented with some related research.

At the end of 2013, there were over 1.5 million prisoners in state and federal prisons (along with another 5+ million on either probation or parole) out of a population of approximately 325 million people (see Figure 11.1). Most prisoners are in state prisons, with Louisiana, Oklahoma, Mississippi, and Alabama having the most prisoners, and Maine and Minnesota having the fewest. Many prisoners are also held in jails rather than prisons because of overcrowding—which means that convicted criminals are being held in facilities with people who have yet to be convicted of any offense and who may in fact be innocent. Over 700 people per 100,000 Americans are currently incarcerated in the United States. These numbers place us at the top of the per capita prison population—Russia is second, and the Ukraine is third (Figure 11.2).

Unsurprisingly, given what we've seen in earlier chapters, the prison population skews disproportionately toward men and African Americans. Of the 1.5 million people in U.S. prisons, only about 92,000 of them were women (approximately 16%). Of the total prison population, 526,000 were African American (about 35%), 314,000 were Hispanic (about 20%), and 454,000 were white (30%). Compare this to the general population of the United States, which is about 12% African American, 63% white, and 16% Hispanic. A disproportionate percentage of the prison population is young, under the age of 40, and across age brackets the highest number of prisoners are African American.

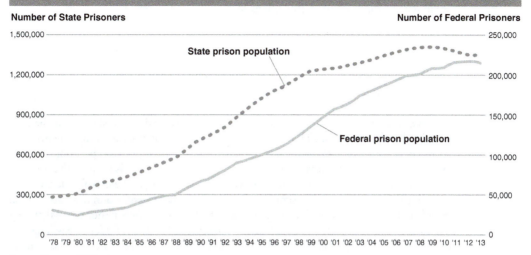

Figure 11.1   Total State and Federal Prison Populations, 1978–2013

Source: Carson, 2014.

Note: Counts based on all prisoners under the jurisdiction of state and federal correctional authorities.

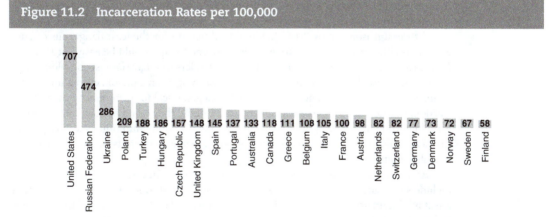

Figure 11.2   Incarceration Rates per 100,000

Source: Data from the American Psychological Association, 2014. http://www.apa.org/monitor/2014/10/incarceration .aspx.

Violent felonies and drug felonies are the most frequent reasons why offenders are incarcerated. At the state level, violent offenders make up just over half of the prison population, while at the federal level, less than 10% of all federal prisoners are in prison for violent crimes. Offenders convicted of federal crimes go to federal prisons, while people who break state laws go to state prisons. Most conventional violent crimes such as murder and assault are violations of state law, and such crimes only become federal offenses in special circumstances (such as when a federal officer is killed). On the other hand, nearly half of federal prisoners are locked up for drug offenses, while less than 20% of offenders are in state prison because of drug offenses.

TYPES OF PRISONS

Learning Objective 11.3—Differentiate between the types of prisons and identify the professionals who work in correctional facilities.

As is well known, there are several different types of prison distinguished by the level of security that they maintain. These levels are based largely on the threat that the prisoner represents to others as well as the likelihood that she will attempt to escape. Some of these facilities do not resemble prisons at all—there are no bars or guards keeping the prisoner in the facility, while others have barbed wire, armed guards, and electrified fences surrounding them. A prisoner is assigned to her facility by her classification team and can be transferred to less-secure facilities or to facilities with better services if they prove that they are not a threat or an escape risk while in higher-security institutions. Here we will discuss the different types of prison, using the security levels of the federal prison system as a guide. Keep in mind that many prison facilities have more than one type of prison within their walls. Thus, a single facility could include a minimum-security prison and a high-security prison, though the prisoners are usually kept separate from each other for the most part. This allows states to pool their resources and save money and allows correctional officers to be exposed to different varieties of prisoners while on duty.

At the lowest level are *minimum-security institutions*, which at the federal level are called federal prison camps (FPCs). These facilities are for the least dangerous offenders and usually have dormitory-style living quarters. Escape would be easy, but it is rare. Most prisoners are either nonviolent felons or offenders who have almost completed their sentences, giving them little incentive to flee. Escaping from a prison, even a minimum-security facility, is a crime, and therefore there is a great deal for prisoners on the verge of freedom to lose if they try to escape. If they are caught, they could be sent back to prison for a long time. Further, by allowing inmates more freedom, minimum security prisons can help some prisoners prepare themselves for re-entering the outside world when they complete their sentences.

Above minimum-security are *low-security* facilities. They are usually fenced in and include some safety measures—prisoners are not allowed to leave in the way that they are at minimum-security facilities. The prison is guarded and patrolled, and though some facilities use dormitory-style facilities, much of the living is communal.

Above these are *medium-security* prisons. Medium-security facilities look closer to what we think of as "prison." They are usually surrounded by razor wire and patrolled regularly by guards. In medium-security facilities, prisoners usually live in dormitory environments, not cells.

Finally, there are *high-security* facilities (some states refer to these as *maximum-security prisons*) that handle the most dangerous prisoners. These prisons are surrounded by intense security, razor wire, electrified fences, and armed guards. Prisoners are usually in individual cells where they spend 23 hours per day, with one hour on the exercise grounds.

Perhaps the *most* secure prison in the United States, if not the entire world, is ADX Florence, a supermax prison in Colorado. ADX holds what are purportedly the most dangerous federal criminals. Among those incarcerated at ADX Florence are the "Unabomber," Ted Kaczynski; Zacharias Moussaoui, the alleged "20th hijacker" of the September 11, 2001, attacks; Terry Nichols, one of the architects of the 1995 Oklahoma City bombing; and Robert Hanssen, a federal intelligence officer who sold secrets to the Russians; as well as a number of high-profile drug traffickers and murderers and a few who escaped from less secure facilities. Prisoners at ADX spend 23 hours each day alone in a concrete cell and have no access to natural sunlight. As a *New York Times* article described the prison,

> Since opening in 1994, the ADX has remained not just the only federal super-max but also the apogee of a particular strain of the American penal system, wherein abstract dreams of rehabilitation have been entirely superseded by the architecture of control. (Binelli, 2015)

Holding "the worst of the worst" in some of the most distressing circumstances represents the most extreme form of punishment available in the United States.

Other Types of Prisons (Jails Versus Prisons)

Along with the traditional security-level prisons, there are other institutions that hold people convicted of crimes. Some of these are within the larger prisons, and some of these are kept separate. All prisons have hospitals that are designed to treat prisoners for a variety of illnesses, both short and long term. Though many report that the health care provided is substandard, the advantage is that it is free or cheap for prisoners (leading some to opt to stay in prison longer than they must, rejecting parole, so that they can continue receiving lifesaving care). Prisoners may be charged a copay for their health care out of their commissary accounts but cannot be denied it completely (Andrews, 2015).

Within prisons there is often a protective custody unit or PCU. These "prisons within a prison" are set up for inmates who are in danger of being harmed by other inmates. These can include prisoners who have been labelled as a snitch by other prisoners or prisoners who have been targeted in a gang conflict. While prisoners are discouraged from disclosing the reasons for their incarceration, those who are suspected of having "short eyes" (prison slang for being a pedophile) are often targeted for abuse from their fellow prisoners (James, 2003; Kerbs & Jolley, 2007). Others who get placed in protective custody include prisoners who could be targeted because they testified in high-profile cases or celebrity inmates who could be attacked by another prisoner seeking notoriety. Finally, former police officers who are in prison could be placed in a PCU if they fear retaliation from other prisoners.

Those convicted of lesser offenses often serve their time in *jails*. Jails are intended to hold people who are awaiting trial or for those who are serving short sentences. These jails are usually run by local governments and are not intended for long-term incarceration, as they usually offer minimal resources and services to inmates.

Supermax: The highest security level of incarceration.

Protective custody unit (PCU): A section of a prison where offenders who need to be separated from other inmates are held.

Guards and Abuse

There are good reasons for prison bureaus to be concerned about the people that they hire to guard prisons. There is a long history of research that suggests that abusing prisoners is not an aberration or the consequences of a few bad apples but is a constant temptation for anybody who has spent enough time in a prison. The most famous of these is the Stanford Prison Experiment. In this experiment, psychologists at Stanford University set up a mock prison in the basement of a campus building and had a group of students act as guards and another group as prisoners. After a short period of time, the students stopped treating the experiment as a joke, and tensions between the "prisoners" and their "guards" became serious, and the student guards began to abuse some of the prisoners. The experimenters stopped the experiment early, fearing that the situation could escalate, but they concluded that if even the "good kids" of Stanford could easily become abusive guards in such a situation, then it is easy to imagine ordinary guards turning bad very quickly. The point of the experiment is that the abuse of prisoners is not a result of bad guards but instead is inherent to the prison environment.[1]

Along with the dangers of abuse, there is the constant temptation for guards to take advantage of prisoners in different ways. Some guards have been known to abet criminal activities among prisoners for their own gain. By employing guards to smuggle in contraband, prisoners can acquire drugs, alcohol, and cell phones, and the guards who allow or assist in the smuggling can profit. Officers can get money, assistance, sexual favors, or simple cooperation from the prisoners. Some guards have used access to contraband as a means for keeping order within the prison, doling it out as a reward to cooperative prisoners (Kalinich & Stojkovic, 1985). Other guards, most commonly female guards, have sometimes developed romantic relationships with inmates that have sometimes had disastrous consequences (Marquart, Barnhill, & Balshaw-Biddle, 2001). In 2015, Joyce Mitchell, a prison employee, pled guilty to helping two murderers escape from Clinton Correctional Institute in upstate New York after she reportedly fell in love with one of them. One of the escaped prisoners was killed, while the other was arrested. Mitchell was sentenced to seven years in prison.

Other Correctional Professionals

Stanford Prison Experiment: A psychological study conducted on college students that examined how the prison structure of guards and inmates affects human behavior.

Prisons are run by a specialized group of individuals who oversee the prisoners as well as the other services that the prison provides. Among these are chaplains to address the spiritual needs of the prisoners and psychologists to help with emotional issues that prisoners face while serving their time. There are teachers to help students pursue educational goals and support personnel to organize the correctional personnel. Doctors and nurses also staff large prisons attending to the medical needs of the prisoners. Large prisons have employees and volunteers working in a wide variety of jobs.

---

[1] It is important to note that the Stanford Prison Experiment has undergone a great deal of scrutiny and criticism in recent years (Resnick, 2018).

SOME STATISTICS...

Prison Populations

The Federal Bureau of Prisons (BOP) provides a wide array of statistical information on the federal prison population. As one would expect given what we've discussed so far in this book, African Americans represent a disproportionate percentage of the prison population (see Figure 11.3).

Similar numbers exist in state prisons (see Table 11.1).

Figure 11.3   Inmate Race as of October 2018

Statistics based on prior month's data
Last updated: Saturday, November 24, 2018

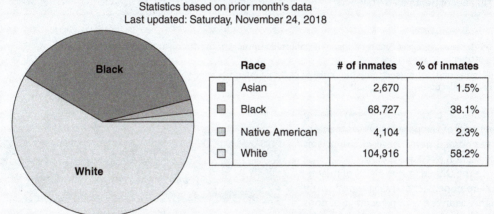

Race	# of inmates	% of inmates
Asian	2,670	1.5%
Black	68,727	38.1%
Native American	4,104	2.3%
White	104,916	58.2%

Source: Federal Bureau of Prisons, 2018.

Table 11.1   Percentage of Sentenced Prisoners in State Correctional Institutions by Race, 2016

Race/Hispanic Origin	Male NPS[a]	SPI[b]	Female NPS[a]	SPI[b]
Total	100%	100%	100%	100%
White	39.0	30.6	61.0	47.5
Black	41.3	34.9	23.9	19.8
Hispanic	16.6	21.1	10.6	16.2

(Continued)

Table 11.1   (Continued)

American Indian or Alaska Native	1.3	2.6	2.0	1.4
Asian	0.6	0.8	0.6	0.4
Native Hawaiian or Other Pacific Islander	0.2	0.4	0.4	0.3
Two or More Races	0.0	10.9	0.1	13.8
Other	0.7	0.0	0.5	0.0
Unknown	0.2	0.0	0.2	0.0
Number of Sentenced Prisoners	1,193,760	1,160,096	94,291	89,208

Source: Carson, 2018.

[a]NPS data are aggregate counts of prisoners collected annually from administrative databases in state departments of corrections.

[b]SPI is a periodic in-person computer-assisted personal interview survey of state prisoners conducted by data collection agents on behalf of BJS.

On the other hand, despite being over half of the population, women are a very small percentage of the prison population (see Figure 11.4).

In the United States, 18.7% of prisoners are noncitizens; this is significantly higher than the total percentage of noncitizens in the general population of the United States, which is about 7%.

While the statistics can easily be misleading, many offenders who are released from prison return for a variety of reasons. According to a 2014 report from the Bureau of Justice Statistics, 71% of all former inmates were rearrested within three years of release. And more than a third (36.8%) of these were rearrested within six months of their release, and over 50% were rearrested within the first year—though a large number of these were for parole violations or other technical offenses (Durose, Cooper, & Snyder, 2005). We will discuss parole and probation, including some of the injustices in the parole system, in the next chapter.

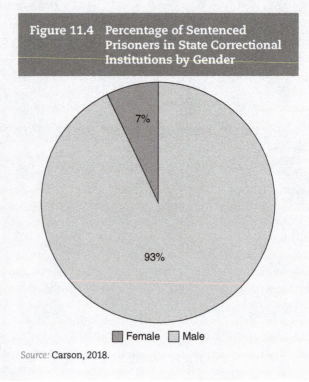

Figure 11.4   Percentage of Sentenced Prisoners in State Correctional Institutions by Gender

7%

93%

■ Female   □ Male

Source: Carson, 2018.

LIFE IN PRISON, THE INMATE CODE

Learning Objective 11.4—Describe the day-to-day life of a prisoner.

Most days in prison follow roughly the same schedule, as inmates shuffle between classes (for those lucky enough to have access to education), work, exercise, and meals. Here is a rundown of the daily routine of one prisoner at San Quentin State Prison in California:

> 5:30–6:30 AM: Breakfast, a.k.a. "chow time," and the start of most guys' day. The breakfast isn't good, so I skip it and sleep in during that hour, which is much needed as you will see.
>
> 6:30–7:15 AM: Start day with a morning prayer and devotional reading.
>
> 7:15–8:00 AM: Breakfast in my cell and prepare for work. My breakfast usually consists of a bowl of oatmeal or a Danish and a cup of coffee, all of which are sold from the prison's commissary, a.k.a. inmate canteen.
>
> 8:00 AM–2:00 PM: Work. I work in the prison's general maintenance shop as a metal-fabricator/welder. I make 32 cents an hour. Yep, you read it right, a whopping 32 cents per hour.
>
> 2:00–3:00 PM: Shower grab a bite to eat and prepare for either a self-help group or college class.
>
> 3:00–5:00 PM: Self-help group or college class.
>
> 5:00–6:00 PM: Dinner. It tends to be better than the breakfast so I go.
>
> 6:00–8:00 PM: Another self-help group or college class.
>
> 8:00–9:00 PM: Socialize with friends or use the prison phone to talk to my loved ones.
>
> 9:00 PM: All inmates are locked in their cells or dorm until breakfast. There is no lights out policy.
>
> 9:00–11:00 PM: Watch T.V., listen to music or write a letter, and fix something to eat.
>
> 11 PM-12:30 AM: Homework, including play-writing for chapel.
>
> 12:30–6:30 AM: Sleep
>
> *Source:* Cavett, 2017. Reprinted with permission.

While this represents one prisoner's experience, it's worth noting that not every prisoner has the opportunities of a San Quentin inmate. San Quentin is well known as a prison that provides unique opportunities for inmates not available elsewhere, and many prisoners in other institutions seek placement there for this reason. (There is a podcast produced by San Quentin inmates—*Ear Hustle*—that provides interesting insights on life in that unique facility.)

Most prisoners—and those who study prisons—report the existence of an unspoken code among prisoners. The criminologist Gresham Sykes examined prisons for decades and unpacked the basic principles guiding how prisoners are expected to interact with each other while inside—which he described as the inmate code. They are as follows:

1. *Don't Interfere with Inmate Interests.* Never rat on an inmate and don't be nosy.

2. *Don't Fight with Other Inmates.* Do your own time.

3. *Don't Exploit Inmates.* If you make a promise, keep it, don't steal from inmates, don't sell favors, and don't go back on bets.

4. *Maintain Yourself.* Don't: weaken, whine, cop out. Be a man and be tough.

5. *Don't Trust Guards or The Things They Stand For.* Don't be a sucker, the officials are wrong, and the prisoners are right.

Source: Sykes & Messinger, 1960.

All prisoners are expected to abide by these rules, and prisoners who do not follow them are likely to be shunned by their fellow inmates or face retaliation. Minding your own business and "hanging tough" are the basic rules of being a prisoner in the United States, though the rules vary a great deal from place to place.

Prison Gangs

As is well known, there are many gangs operating in American prisons. Some of these are simply a branch of street gangs from the outside world, though they can often take on a life of their own within the prison system. Among the largest of these gangs at present are the Nuestra Familia, the Mexican Mafia, the Aryan Brotherhood, the Black Guerrilla Family, the Northern Structure, and the Nazi Lowriders. As the names indicate, many of these gangs are based on the racial identifications of their members, and they can exacerbate racial tensions among prisoners.

Some criminologists have argued that, rather than being a problem for prison officials, the gangs themselves represent a source of prison discipline. When everybody follows the rules of gang life, these gangs can help reduce the amount of violence, though they can prey on nonmembers once they've established sufficient order (Skarbek, 2012). According to this account, the informal inmate code doesn't hold the power that it once did given the increasing numbers of people locked up since the beginning of the era of mass incarceration. There are simply too many people in prison for an informal ethical system like the code to hold much sway. Instead, the gangs police the conduct of their own members, and as long as there is a power balance among the prison gangs and an understanding between their respective leaders, there is peace for the most part (Skarbek, 2014). While prison gangs are involved in a great deal of prison misconduct such as violence, drug use, and contraband smuggling, they can also provide stability and discipline among a population of unruly prisoners.

Inmate code: The informal social rules governing prisoner conduct.

Institutionalization

As total institutions, prisons can have a profound impact on the minds of their occupants—particularly if they have served lengthy sentences. The regulated and highly controlled nature of prison life leaves a mark on inmates that can make it difficult to adjust to life outside of prison. After a person serves many years in prison, the freedoms of the outside world are confusing and at times terrifying for former prisoners. Being used to a strict schedule, limited options, and direction from authorities for much of your day can have a lasting impact on a person's thinking. If you are used to one brand of toothpaste for years, a shelf with dozens of brands in a typical drugstore is paralyzing.

Institutionalization (sometimes called *prisonization*) refers to the slow eroding of the prisoner's ability to function outside of the context of the prison. Haney (2002) points to seven different ways that institutionalization can affect prisoners and hamper their ability to function in the free world:

1. A dependence on institutional structure and contingencies.

   Prisoners get used to the prison system and can feel lost without it.

2. Hypervigilance, interpersonal distrust, and suspicion.

   Prisoners learn to be on guard while in prison and find it difficult to trust people on the outside.

3. Emotional overcontrol, alienation, and psychological distancing.

   Prisoners can develop a "prison mask," hiding their emotions so they don't appear vulnerable. This can hinder emotional relations on the outside.

4. Social withdrawal and isolation.

   In extreme cases, the isolation of prison can lead to clinical depression, even when the offender is freed.

5. Incorporation of exploitative norms of prison culture.

   Former offenders are sometimes unable to trust others and express vulnerability.

6. Diminished sense of self-worth and personal value.

7. Posttraumatic stress reactions to the pains of imprisonment.

The dangers and stress of prison life can cause prisoners to suffer the effects of posttraumatic stress disorder (PTSD), which can include a host of emotional and physical problems that can make it extremely difficult to function in a relationship, family, or workplace.

The highly structured life of a prisoner and the dangers of prison life can impair her ability to function in the modern world, and the prisoner can have a great deal of trouble functioning outside of it.

Institutionalization: The effect of long-term incarceration that leaves inmates unable to function outside of the prison's structure.

Institutionalization can have a dramatic impact on the ability of former prisoners to adjust to the outside world—particularly when offenders are simply cut loose from the prison with few or no resources to help them adapt to their new environment. An inability to adjust to the demands of life on the outside—failure to find a job, a supportive social environment, and a general sense of personal security—can lead to *recidivism*, or reoffending. Many offenders commit new crimes because they are unable to adjust to life outside of prison (Thomas, 1977). As a result, support organizations have been created (many by exconvicts) to facilitate prisoners' reentry into the world. Not only do they help with the primary needs of exconvicts, such as finding shelter and work, but they also can provide emotional support and guidance through what many former offenders find to be a bewildering set of choices and a daunting set of challenges.

Conjugal visits: Unsupervised visits between prisoners and their spouses.

REALITY CHECK

Prison Sex/Prison Rape

Being raped in prison is a common fear among those facing prison time. Incoming prisoners often list a fear of sexual assault as one of the greatest sources of anxiety upon entering the correctional system. In 2003, Congress passed the Prison Rape Elimination Act, which mandated the development of guidelines for eliminating rape in adult and juvenile facilities and funded research to that end. According to all existing research, nonconsensual sex is relatively rare—a study of prisoners in 2011 and 2012 showed that approximately 4% of prisoners reported some unwanted sexual contact, but only about 1.2% of prisoners reported nonconsensual sexual acts (Beck, Berzofsky, Caspar, & Krebs, 2013). This number is significantly lower than that for female college students—approximately 6.1% of female students report being sexually assaulted (Sinozich & Langton, 2014).

It should be said that consensual homosexual relations among prisoners (particularly men in prison) are not uncommon, though again, they are not as common as you'd expect. Some men who identify as straight while on the outside engage in homosexual relations while in prison because they are the only available sexual release outside of masturbation. As one prisoner put it, "I'm completely straight; what happened then was just about having my sexual needs met, in a particular time and place, where I couldn't get [heterosexual] sex" (Preece, 2015). Open homosexuality is highly stigmatized, and a prisoner who presents himself as gay will often face abuse. Many prisons do not allow prisoners to engage in consensual sexual intercourse with each other, and condoms can be difficult to get (which increases the risk of HIV and AIDS among prisoners). Masturbation is not allowed in most prisons, a rule that is about as effective as you'd expect it to be. Some states allow conjugal visits (time where prisoners can be alone with members of their family), and this can include an opportunity to have sex with a spouse. Being denied an ordinary and fulfilling sex life is one of the great deprivations that defines prison life for many inmates.

WOMEN IN PRISON

Learning Objective 11.5—Compare and contrast the experiences of female prisoners to their male counterparts.

There are nearly 10 times the number of men incarcerated as women, but the number of female prisoners has been steadily increasing, particularly at the state level (see Figure 11.5). The reasons for this disparity are complicated and not well understood. One suspected cause is the expansion of the war on drugs. As law enforcement efforts to deal with drug trafficking began to focus on lower-level drug offenses, women were more likely to face more serious charges for drug-related activity that might have been ignored or lightly punished in the past. As a result, women are swept up by law enforcement at increasing rates (Swavola, Riley, & Subramanian, 2016, p. 23). Other researchers suggest that many efforts to lower incarceration rates have primarily been aimed at male prisoners and have not helped female prisoners, leading to more recidivism among female offenders and extending their sentences. As a researcher for the Prison Policy Initiative put it, "In many states, treating women's incarceration as an afterthought has, in effect, held back efforts to decarcerate" (Sawyer, 2018). As with other issues involving crime and incarceration rates, the data is inconclusive, but the rising incarceration rate for women in the United States adds urgency to the need to examine the important differences between men and women in prison.

While the demographics of female prisoners are similar to those of their male counterparts—they tend to be young, undereducated, underemployed, and disproportionately from minority groups—there are many significant differences between the two (Zaitzow & Thomas, 2003). Women tend to be imprisoned less for violent offenses

Figure 11.5 Women's State Prison Populations Have Grown Faster Than Men's

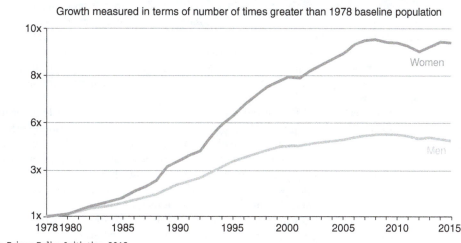

Growth measured in terms of number of times greater than 1978 baseline population

Source: Prison Policy Initiative, 2018.

than for property crimes. Over half of male prisoners have been incarcerated for violent crimes, but only about a third of women are convicted for some kind violence (murder, manslaughter, assault). On the other hand, a greater percentage of women are incarcerated for property crimes, and they are over four times more likely to be imprisoned for fraud (Belknap, 2014, p. 228).

Perhaps most troubling, incarcerated women are far more likely than incarcerated men to have been victims of sexual or physical abuse from male partners or family members. According to a 1999 Bureau of Justice Statistics report, "Forty-four percent of women under correctional authority reported that they were physically or sexually assaulted at some time during their lives. Sixty-nine percent of women reporting an assault said that it had occurred before age 18" (Greenfeld & Snell, 1999). Psychologists researching the issue suggest that drug abuse, one of the common factors behind women's criminal conduct, is often the result of an attempt to self-medicate—women are traumatized by the abuse that they suffered and turn to drugs to cope (Ney, Ramirez, & Van Dieten, 2012). As one criminologist put it,

> The picture that emerges of the female inmate is troubling. Female criminal behavior in society at large appears to be the product of continuing personal and social problems—the impact of physical and emotional abuse and extreme disadvantage exacerbated by economic problems as well as drug and alcohol abuse. (Zaitzow, 2003, p. 23)

When they are in prison, female offenders are often treated differently by the prison institutions. Prison discipline is much stricter for women then for men. They often face more severe punishments for smaller infractions than their male counterparts. As one study of Texas prisons observed, "Women are more often cited for rule violations than men; most citations received by women are less than serious, but women are punished more severely; and certain rules are scrupulously enforced in women's institutions but ignored in men's" (McClellan, 1994, p. 71). In California, between 2016 and 2018, women had a total of 1,483 years added to their sentences for conduct citations, and time was added at a higher rate for women than it was for male prisoners (Shapiro, 2018). There are also fewer opportunities for female inmates to improve themselves while inside: Studies have consistently shown that there are far fewer educational and vocational opportunities in women's prisons than there are for their male counterparts. What educational opportunities are available for women are often sexist. "Men are offered programs such as construction carpentry, electrical technology, and advanced industrial design. Meanwhile, women are offered office administration and culinary arts" (Harris, 2018).

There is a very different culture in women's prisons than in male institutions. Researchers in women's prisons have reported that the rules that apply among male prisoners don't necessarily apply in women's prisons. According to experts, there are several reasons for this. Women tend to be more social with each other and are less likely to see the guards as the enemy. This means that they are less likely to do their own time and are more likely to cooperate with authorities (Pollock, 2002). Social interactions between female prisoners are much less predatory and often include supporting relationships, but female prisoners are more inclined to manipulate other inmates or officials to achieve their own ends. These relations can morph into romantic relationships over time, and sexual assault rates among female prisoners are even lower than they are among male prisoners (Struckman-Johnson & Struckman-Johnson, 2006).

One key distinction between women and men in prison involves parenting. According to the Bureau of Justice Statistics, about 80% of women in prison under the age of 34 have children who are minors, while this figure is only 63% for men (Glaze & Maruschak, 2008). The close bond that many female prisoners have with their children has a tremendous impact on these women. It can magnify the pains of imprisonment but also provide a strong motivation for mothers to behave in prison to get released as early as possible. On the other hand, children of incarcerated mothers often suffer serious emotional stress that can have a long-term impact.

Between 5% and 10% of women go into prison or jail while pregnant, and about 2,000 babies are born in prison every year (Clarke & Simon, 2013). This can create a lot of different problems for prison officials and is very difficult for the new mothers (Glaze & Maruschak, 2008). Usually, after giving birth, new mothers are given a short time to spend with their child before the baby is handed off to family members to raise outside of prison. With the increase in the female inmate population, some prisons have experimented with onsite nurseries, where mothers and children live together segregated from the prison's general population. Recently, the federal government passed the "First Step Act," which reformed some important aspects of federal prison, including a ban on the shackling of women giving birth. It also required federal prisons to provide tampons and sanitary napkins for prisoners at no charge (Samant, 2018). While women in prison have the right to terminate their pregnancies, it is often difficult for them to obtain an abortion due to prison bureaucracy or the personal convictions of prison officials (Grant, 2017).

Women in prison face other challenges that male prisoners don't. They are more likely to suffer abuse from guards, particularly sexual assault. A 2013 report from the *Wilmington News Journal* regarding prisoners at Baylor Women's Correctional Institute in Delaware found high levels of sexual misconduct in the prison, including rape, harassment, and trading sexual favors for contraband. The security chief for the prison was even arrested for having sex with an inmate in his office (Barrish & Horn, 2015). While the situation at Baylor is notably bad, sexual abuse is a constant threat in a situation where male guards have an immense amount of power over female inmates and not a great deal of accountability. Amnesty International reported a total of 2,298 allegations of staff sexual misconduct against both male and female inmates in 2004, and over half of these involved women as victims, despite the fact that they are only a fraction of the total prison population (Summer, 2008).

Obviously, this short discussion here doesn't do justice to the issues facing women in prison. If the incarceration rate for women continues to increase in the coming years, researchers will have to learn a good deal more about how to deal with women in prison in a way that doesn't just assume that they're just like men.

PRISONER RIGHTS

Learning Objective 11.6—Describe the history of prisoner rights and the legal restrictions on prisoners' rights.

One aspect of prison life that has undergone a great deal of change over time is the rights that are afforded to prisoners. Until the later part of the 20th century, prisoners were sometimes described as slaves of the state—not a great label, given the high number of black Americans that are incarcerated in American prisons. The Thirteenth Amendment to the Constitution (ratified in 1865) declares that slavery is illegal in the United States

General population ("genpop" or GP): The main part of the prison where most offenders are kept.

Slaves of the state: The legal status of prisoners until the 1960s.

"except as a punishment for crime whereof the party shall have been duly convicted," and historically, courts took this to mean that prisoners have the same rights as slaves did prior to the Civil War. In the 1871 case of *Ruffin v. Commonwealth*, the Virginia Supreme Court ruled that a prisoner effectively had no rights, as the prisoner "has, as a consequence of his crime, not only forfeited his liberty, but all his personal rights except those which the law in its humanity accords to him. He is for the time being the slave of the state." Judges are not experts in prison management and so were hesitant to insert themselves into issues involving prisons and prisoner management. This meant that short of the right to not be murdered, prisoners could do little about abuses in prison and were at the mercy of the warden, the guards, and others who had control over their lives.

The hands-off doctrine lasted until the 1960s, when a more activist Supreme Court began to revisit the question of a prisoner's rights. The Supreme Court Chief Justice Earl Warren was known for taking progressive/liberal stands on a variety of criminal justice issues, including those involving the treatment of prisoners. In *Wolff v. McDonnell* (1974), the court overturned the hands-off doctrine and ruled that prisoners may challenge administrative punishments that occur in a prison, and, "though prison disciplinary proceedings do not implicate the full panoply of rights due a defendant in a criminal prosecution, such proceedings must be governed by a mutual accommodation between institutional needs and generally applicable constitutional requirements." In effect, the court concluded that although prisoners do not have all the rights that a free individual possesses, they do not lose all their constitutional protections at the prison gate. The constitutional rights of prisoners must be balanced with the needs of prison officials to maintain a safe and well-ordered prison.

Unlike individuals accused of crimes, prisoners are not usually put through a formal trial when they are punished or sanctioned by prison officials. For example, if guards discover contraband in a prisoner's cell, an inmate may be disciplined by the prison administration (say, denied privileges or sent into solitary confinement) without the benefit of a trial. Similarly, a prisoner who is accused of misbehaving (say, fighting with another prisoner) could have this fight included on her record without providing her an opportunity to refute the charges. This could then be used against her when she goes up for parole—used by the parole board to prevent her from being released early. These punishments are known as *administrative punishments* because they are handled by the prison administration, not the formal criminal justice system. Because they are not criminal punishments, different rules apply to disciplinary measures that are taken by prison officials.

Due Process

In *Wolff v. McDonnell* (1974) the court granted due process rights to prisoners, that is, it gave prisoners the right to not be punished by prison officials without a fair, impartial hearing. While this doesn't amount to a full-blown criminal trial as discussed in Chapter 9, prisoners can still contest the disciplinary measures taken against them. For example, the prison must provide the prisoner with written notice regarding the charges against the prisoner and the evidence that was used as grounds for punishment. Further, the prisoner must be allowed to provide her own exculpatory evidence, though the inmate doesn't have the right to cross-examine hostile witnesses. Further, the prisoner has the right to counsel as well as the right to private correspondence with her attorney. Again, this is not "the full panoply of rights due a defendant in a criminal prosecution," but it does still provide the inmate with some procedural protections.

Hands-off doctrine: The (now abandoned) legal doctrine that believed that courts should let prison officials run prisons in whatever way these officials deemed appropriate.

Freedom of Speech

Prisoners do not possess the same free speech rights as free people. Prisoners must be respectful of prison officials and not mouth off to them when they feel like it. Further, some speech that would be lawful outside of prison could undermine the safety of prisoners or prison employees, such as discussions about security protocols within the prison. Moreover, many prisoners hold controversial political views and are often vocal about them. When Mumia Abu-Jamal, a journalist and political activist convicted of murdering an FBI officer (he claims he is innocent), was asked to give a commencement speech at his alma mater, Goddard College, his victim's family protested. In response, Pennsylvania passed a law allowing crime victims the right to sue an institution if the prisoner's statements caused "a temporary or permanent state of mental anguish," a law that has made many critics concerned, particularly given the fact that Abu-Jamal considers himself a political prisoner.

Despite these restrictions, prisoners have the right to freedom of speech and cannot be punished simply for holding or expressing controversial political ideas. Provided their speech does not undermine safety or security in the prison, prisoners can speak freely without fear of reprisal. Incoming and outgoing correspondence can be censored by prison officials if such censorship is necessary to protect the safety of the prisoners and prison officials. Correspondence between a prisoner and her attorney is privileged.

Freedom of Religion

As we saw in the last chapter, American penitentiaries were rooted in different branches of Christianity. Given that the American public skews heavily Christian, it is no surprise that there has been an immense pressure for prisoners to be Christian and that prisoners from other faiths have sometimes faced discrimination. In many prisons, historically, the only reading available to prisoners was the Bible, and only Christian services were provided in prisons. All prisoners may practice their faiths, and prisons are required to make reasonable accommodations for prisoners, provided that these religious beliefs are sincerely held by the prisoner (and not, say, a way for a prisoner to get extra perks for herself). If the inmate's faith is sincere, the prison must seek to accommodate her needs.

A prisoner's right to practice her religious faith has several restrictions. First, limitations on prisoners' religious practices are allowed if the restrictions are neutral (that is, they apply to everybody and are not intended to discriminate against a particular faith) and serve "legitimate penological interests" (that is, the restrictions are in place for purposes of prisoner safety and prison security). For example, a prison would have a good reason to restrict Sikh prisoners from carrying ceremonial daggers known as *kirpan,* as these represent a danger to guards and other prisoners, and such a restriction is in accord with a general ban on weapons in prison.

Further, prisons should seek to allow prisoners alternative means by which to practice their faiths, provided the prisoners' needs can be met by prison officials without too much effort, and if the alternative means do not endanger prisoners or prison employees. For example, many religions have special restrictions on how meat is prepared (halal, kosher). If it is too difficult to meet these dietary restrictions, the prison can offer a vegetarian option at meal time, which would meet these dietary requirements. While prisoners may prefer meat, a healthy vegetarian option meets the requirements of their faith and so accommodates the prisoner's religious freedom.

A recent case addressed by the Supreme Court involved restrictions on beards worn by Muslims. According to most interpretations of their religion, Muslim men are expected to wear beards as part of their faith, but many prisons require that prisoners be clean shaven, as beards can be used to hide weapons or contraband. One prisoner, Gregory Holt, a convert to Islam, sued the Arkansas Department of Corrections for the right to grow a beard as part of his new faith. In *Holt v. Hobbs* (2015), the Supreme Court found in his favor, arguing that wearing a short beard is not different from wearing clothing: "The Department already searches prisoners' hair and clothing, and it presumably examines the 1/4-inch beards of inmates with dermatological conditions. It has offered no sound reason why hair, clothing, and 1/4-inch beards can be searched but 1/2-inch beards cannot." In short, the prison is not justified in restricting the rights of Muslim prisoners to grow (short) beards as an expression of their faith. As with other parts of the law, the court has continually had to develop new rulings to accommodate different religious faiths in prison.

Administrative segregation ("AdSeg"): Separating offenders from the general population of the prison. Often in solitary confinement.

CRIMINAL (IN)JUSTICE

Solitary Confinement

Sometimes known as "the box," "the SHU" (Special Housing Unit), or simply "the hole," solitary confinement involves separating a prisoner from the rest of the prisoners; putting her in a small, usually windowless room; and depriving her of almost all human contact. Prisoners in solitary confinement are often let out of the cell for only one hour each day and have some access to books and other distractions, though they are usually not let out of their cell for library or meal time. (Outside contact is usually given as a reward for good behavior on the part of the prisoner.) Usually prisoners are placed in solitary for misconduct ("disciplinary segregation") or because they are believed to be a threat to the safety of other prisoners or to prison officials (administrative segregation, or AdSeg) and such isolation can last for months or even years.

Such prolonged periods of seclusion can be horribly damaging to the mental health of offenders. One examination of the current state of research on the subject stated that "solitary confinement produces a higher rate of psychiatric and psychological health problems than 'normal' imprisonment" (Smith, 2006). Further, many prisoners who are placed in solitary confinement are often emotionally and mentally disturbed to begin with, lacking the psychological resilience necessary to help them endure the solitude. Many critics of solitary confinement have even begun to call it a form of "torture" to leave prisoners in isolation for a long

period of time. In his concurring opinion in *Davis v. Ayala* (2015), Justice Kennedy wrote,

Of course, prison officials must have discretion to decide that in some instances temporary, solitary confinement is a useful or necessary means to impose discipline and to protect prison employees and other inmates. But research still confirms what this Court suggested over a century ago: Years on end of near-total isolation exact a terrible price. . . . (common side-effects of solitary confinement include anxiety, panic, withdrawal, hallucinations, self-mutilation, and suicidal thoughts and behaviors). In a case that presented the issue, the judiciary may be required, within its proper jurisdiction and authority, to determine whether workable alternative systems for long-term confinement exist, and, if so, whether a correctional system should be required to adopt them.

While this opinion was not a part of the majority opinion in the case, and so it does not have the authority of law, many observers have begun to suggest that the court may soon find that the extended use of solitary confinement is cruel and unusual punishment and therefore a violation of the Eighth Amendment. Like all parts of the criminal justice system, the techniques of imprisonment are being reevaluated as the Constitution is reinterpreted by the court.

CHAPTER SUMMARY

This chapter has focused on the primary form of punishment in America today: incarceration. We've looked at the different types of prisons as well as some of the formal and informal rules and institutions that shape prison life. As we've discussed, prison is one of the most expensive and probably least effective ways to deal with prisoners. There is little evidence that prisons deter or rehabilitate offenders and staffing and guarding these prisons is an expensive proposition for any government. In addition, incarceration has damaging effects beyond those felt by the prisoner herself: Her family may depend on her to provide food and shelter, and without the primary breadwinner, they will undoubtedly suffer. In the next chapter we will explore a set of alternative punishments that seek to rehabilitate or punish offenders without the burdens of housing, feeding, and guarding convicted offenders, but that instead keep them in their jobs and with their loved ones. These punishments are generally placed under the heading of *community corrections*.

REVIEW/DISCUSSION QUESTIONS

1. Which aspects of prison life do you think help serve the purposes of rehabilitation and deterrence, and which don't?

2. How could prison be improved to better serve the aims of punishment?

3. How do you think you would do in prison? What aspects of prison life do you think would cause you the most trouble? Why?

KEY TERMS

Administrative segregation 288
Classification team 271
Conjugal visits 282
General population 285
Hands-off doctrine 286
Inmate code 280

Institutionalization 281
Presentence investigation report 270
Protective custody unit 275
Reception center 271
Slaves of the state 285

Stanford Prison Experiment 276
Supermax 275
Total institutions 270
Victim impact statement 271

$SAGE edge™

Get the tools you need to sharpen your study skills. SAGE edge offers a robust online environment featuring an impressive array of free tools and resources.

Access practice quizzes, eFlashcards, video, and multimedia at edge.sagepub.com/fichtelberg

Sarah Yeh

Some victims and offenders benefit from a face-to-face
encounter where both sides can talk about the crime.
Why do you think this might make a difference?

CHAPTER TWELVE

ALTERNATIVES TO PRISON

Prison is the primary tool for punishing people in the United States. However, only a relatively small percentage of convicted criminals are sent to prison, and some people who are incarcerated have not been convicted of any crime. Instead, courts around the country have used a variety of tools other than imprisonment to deal with offenders. Many of these approaches are aimed at producing better results more cheaply and mitigating some of the damage that incarceration does to both the offender and to her community. Others seek to imprison people who either haven't committed an explicit crime or who have served their sentence but are still considered dangerous. Here, we will critically discuss some of these alternatives to traditional prison.

In this chapter, we will examine several ways that the criminal justice system punishes convicted offenders other than incarceration—though some will look a lot like imprisonment on the surface. We will look at these punishments in increasing severity, starting with the least harsh forms, under the title community corrections. These include community service programs, diversion programs, and house arrest regimes as well as both *probation* and *parole*. On the other end of the spectrum we will look at noncriminal forms of incarceration, such as civil commitment and the detention of illegal immigrants. While these punishments may look a lot like prison, they operate by a very different set of rules and are intended to serve different purposes. Finally, at the end of the chapter we will look at the *restorative justice* movement, an approach to criminal justice that seeks to radically change how we think about crime, punishment, and the roles of victims and perpetrators after conviction. In short, this chapter will be a grab bag of different approaches to punishment, all of which seek to avoid the downsides of the modern prison we discussed in the last chapter.

Community corrections: Forms of criminal punishment that seek to keep the offender in society rather than locking her away.

THE COLLATERAL EFFECTS OF INCARCERATION

Learning Objective 12.1—List the impact of incarceration on victims, their families, and their communities.

Community corrections seek to keep the offender out of the prison system. Many advocates of these approaches believe that keeping the offender in the community is not only a cheaper way to deal with her, but in addition, it limits the collateral consequences that can result from incarceration. Collateral consequences are the indirect harms that imprisonment causes for the people who surround and depend on the offender. If the offender is

Collateral consequences (of incarceration): The effects of imprisonment that go beyond the imprisonment itself on the families of the incarcerated offender.

a parent, children often suffer from her absence, losing her daily guidance and support. Her partner or other family members must now shoulder the burden of raising the children and paying the bills alone—otherwise the child must go into foster care, which requires further support from the federal government and can have damaging consequences for these children. (Over half of all prisoners have children who are still minors [Glaze & Maruschak, 2008].) Parents of offenders can also lose the vital assistance that the offender provides. Even though they have caused harm, criminals are part of a community, and taking them out of that community can have a serious impact on many of the people around them.

There is a great deal of research showing that incarceration harms those who both love and rely on the offender. Partners who are not in prison must handle the financial and emotional burdens of family alone, which can put a great deal of stress on marriages (Siennick, Stewart, & Staff, 2014). Further, the children of incarcerated offenders often are more likely to break the law than others. (See Figure 12.1 for an estimation of the number of parents in prison.) As one report put it, "Children's delinquent behavior, according to parent reports, was predicted by a history of parental incarceration. Family victimization and sibling delinquency was also predicted by a history of parental incarceration" (Aaron & Dallaire, 2010, pp. 1479–1480). One economic study argued that the total cost of incarceration, including lost revenue to communities, amounts to about one trillion dollars, or 6% of the nation's gross domestic product, significantly higher than the $80 billion spent annually by the government on corrections (McLaughlin, Pettus-Davis, Brown, Veeh, & Renn, 2016).

Even after incarceration, the stress of prison and the challenges of living as an ex-con affect those surrounding the former inmate. The stresses of re-entering society and a web of legal restrictions dictating where an exoffender may live and what she may do make postprison life very difficult for exprisoners. (The Justice Center, a nonpartisan research

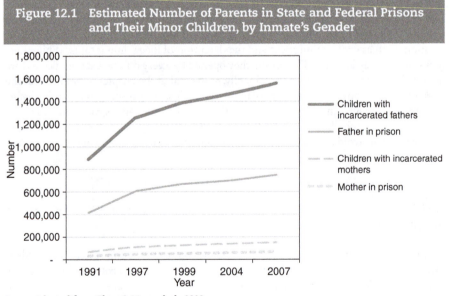

Figure 12.1 Estimated Number of Parents in State and Federal Prisons and Their Minor Children, by Inmate's Gender

Source: Adapted from Glaze & Maruschak, 2008.

Note: Latest data available.

institution dealing with criminal justice issues, has an online map of the different laws applying to exoffenders in different states. You can see it at https://niccc.csgjusticecenter.org/map/.) Many employers require felons to disclose their criminal past on an application, often leading employers to reject their applications (Stoll & Bushway, 2008). All of this means that there are good reasons to keep offenders out of prison if possible and to keep the offender in the community, hopefully serving as a productive, engaged member of society.

In part to reduce some of these collateral consequences, states, counties, and the federal government have developed a variety of alternative approaches to punishment, keeping offenders out of prison. These approaches are usually tailored to the individual offender and can be flexible if the offender proves able to function in society without sliding into recidivism. The most violent, dangerous offenders are almost always sent to prison, but if a convicted offender is not considered a danger, often the court can find better ways to punish her. Although these approaches don't eliminate all these collateral consequences, they can help an offender limit the damage done by a criminal conviction.

COMMUNITY CORRECTIONS

Learning Objective 12.2—Identify the five main types of community corrections.

One common alternative for dealing with offenders is through *community corrections*. The idea motivating this approach is that a better way to deal with offenders who aren't a danger to anybody is to keep them within their community—in their homes, among their families and friends—but still punish them. While in some ways, this may seem counterintuitive— after all, many offenders are parts of communities where crime is rampant—advocates believe that an offender can often be better rehabilitated without bars. With proper supervision and guidance, an offender can be handled while avoiding the unnecessary suffering that prison usually entails. Equally important, community corrections programs can produce satisfactory results without the high costs of incarceration, freeing up the money for other purposes (Vera Institute of Justice, 2013). Keep in mind that behind all the alternatives stands the threat of prison—if offenders do not live up to the sometimes-demanding expectations of community corrections, the courts can always send them to prison to finish out their sentences. Community corrections have a much softer touch than prison, but if offenders do not behave appropriately on the outside, they can quickly face much rougher consequences.

Community Service

It is very common for courts to sentence low-level offenders to community service, sometimes known as *community restitution*, for a predetermined number of hours. This can include working in a community center, "volunteering" at a charity organization, or cleaning trash from public places such as roads or parks. Corrections departments usually supervise this work, and the court often ties the form of service to the crime that the individual committed. The court may sentence a litterer to cleaning the side of the road, a person charged with a DUI may be required to give speeches to schools on the dangers of alcohol abuse, or people charged with spraying graffiti will be sentenced to cleaning graffiti from public places. (Some jurisdictions allow the offender herself to propose the terms of her community service.) Many groups complain that offenders make terrible volunteers, as they are only there

(Continued on page 296)

SOME STATISTICS...

Probation and Parole

As you can see in Table 12.1 and Figure 12.2, many people convicted of crimes are not currently in prison, though many are incarcerated in other places. According to the Bureau of Justice Statistics, 3,789,800 people were on probation in 2015, and 870,500 were on parole. This doesn't account for the large number of people incarcerated but not held in a prison. Jails, for example, hold over 10% of the incarcerated population. Jails are not prisons and are usually designed to hold offenders for a much shorter period, usually while awaiting trial—though in some cases individuals can spend years in jails for a variety of reasons. On the other hand, nearly two thirds of individuals within the criminal justice system are on probation or parole, meaning that they are not imprisoned at all.

Table 12.1	Rates of U.S. Adult Residents on Community Supervision, Probation, and Parole					
	Number per 100,000 U.S. Adult Residents			U.S. Adult Residents on—		
Year	Community Supervision*	Probation	Parole	Community Supervision*	Probation	Parole
2000	2,162	1,818	344	1 in 46	1 in 53	1 in 285
2005	2,215	1,864	351	1 in 45	1 in 54	1 in 285
2010	2,067	1,715	356	1 in 48	1 in 58	1 in 281
2011	2,017	1,663	358	1 in 50	1 in 60	1 in 279
2012	1,984	1,634	356	1 in 50	1 in 61	1 in 281
2013	1,946	1,603	348	1 in 51	1 in 62	1 in 287
2014	1,911	1,568	348	1 in 52	1 in 64	1 in 288
2015	1,872	1,526	350	1 in 53	1 in 66	1 in 285
2016	1,811	1,467	349	1 in 55	1 in 68	1 in 287

Source: Kaeble, 2018, Table 2.

*Includes adults on probation and parole.

Further, the probation and parole populations have followed the broader trends in incarceration, including a large jump and a leveling off over the last decade (see Figure 12.3).

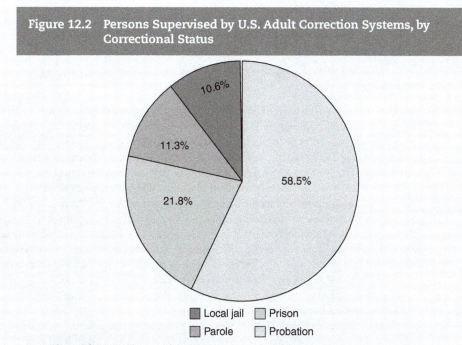

Figure 12.2   Persons Supervised by U.S. Adult Correction Systems, by Correctional Status

10.6%

11.3%

21.8%

58.5%

■ Local jail   ☐ Prison
■ Parole   ☐ Probation

Source: Adapted from Kaeble & Cowhig, 2018.

Note: Counts are rounded to the nearest 100 and include estimates for nonresponding jurisdictions. Detail may not sum to total due to rounding and because offenders with dual correctional statuses were excluded from the total correctional population but included in individual populations.

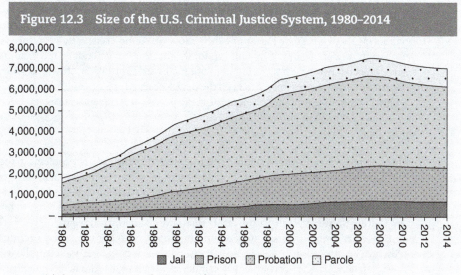

Figure 12.3   Size of the U.S. Criminal Justice System, 1980–2014

■ Jail   ▨ Prison   ▨ Probation   ⸬ Parole

Sources: Friedman, 2016. Sources by Bureau of Justice Statistics; Courtesy of Brennan Center for Justice.

(Continued from page 293)

grudgingly and have no real wish to help. Nonetheless, community service seeks to allow the offender to make up for her misdeeds by helping serve the community and thereby to become reintegrated in it—whether it works or not is an entirely different matter.

Home Confinement

Another option for convicted offenders is to let them serve out their sentences in their own homes. In this option, usually called *house arrest* or *home confinement*, offenders are restricted to their house and property during certain hours of the day or over certain periods. Offenders typically wear an electronic monitor around their ankle to enforce the terms of their confinement. Most of these monitors are designed to ensure that the offender stays at home by detecting when she leaves a certain area, while others use GPS tracking to monitor the offender's movements. (Many states require the offenders to pay for maintaining the monitoring device.) Still others can monitor an offender's alcohol and drug use, either by continuously monitoring the offender's blood alcohol content or by requiring random check-ins. The offender is often allowed out of the house at very specific times for very specific reasons—work, shopping, Alcoholics Anonymous meetings, and other activities, but these trips out must occur according to a very restricted schedule. Offenders who have a drug problem may be further required to wear a patch that monitors their sweat to ensure that they remain drug free. Often, courts require that offenders pay for their own monitoring.

There are many ways to enforce home confinement, and offenders can often negotiate the rules of their sentence with the court. (A lawyer can often help with this process.) Traditionally, there are three levels of home confinement: *curfew* (offenders must be home at certain times but otherwise are generally free), *home detention* (allows offenders to leave during prescribed times for specific reasons), and *home incarceration* (offenders are on 24-hour "lockdown" at home and may only leave for court dates or emergencies). Sometimes, offenders can arrange to work outside of the home during the day, provided they clear their schedules with the court, but many people under house arrest complain that it is difficult to find a job while wearing a monitoring anklet and that meeting the requirements of a regular job can be difficult while being constantly monitored. Often, probation officers will stop by and randomly check in on offenders and examine their ankle bracelet. Any attempts to tamper with the bracelet or take it off will usually lead to imprisonment—as can a failure to keep the device charged. Thus, while home confinement is clearly preferable to imprisonment for many people, it is not a vacation.

Diversion

Many people who are imprisoned are there because they have other problems in their lives that led them to commit a crime. Some of these problems are emotional—they cannot manage their aggression toward others or suffer from some other form of mental illness. Others are dealing with crippling drug and alcohol problems that lead them to break the law. Putting these people in prison, rather than addressing the root causes of their criminality, makes little sense from a purely practical perspective. If her crime was a result of drug addiction, an offender is far less likely to reoffend if she is no longer addicted; she will probably reoffend when she gets out of prison if the addiction isn't addressed. Mentally troubled offenders are far less likely to reoffend if they get needed psychological help. Rather than punishing an offender by sending her off to prison, addressing underlying causes of her criminality makes sense. This is what diversion programs seek to do—address the roots of criminal behavior rather than simply make the offender suffer.

Diversion programs also try to prevent the stigma that often results from the label "criminal" and all the collateral consequences that result from a criminal record. As was discussed in Chapter 3, labeling theory argues that the labels that attach to an individual can shape her future behavior—if society labels a person as a "crook" or a "scumbag," that person is far more likely to behave like a crook or a scumbag in the future. This labeling can happen officially through a criminal record or unofficially when peers label an offender after learning about the crime. By diverting an individual away from the criminal justice system and finding ways to avoid the negative labels associated with criminality, diversion programs seek to prevent recidivism and to give the offender a better shot at a future.

One common form of diversion program is drug court. These courts are set up to deal with offenders who commit crimes to fuel this addiction. Unlike most traditional courts, they are not set up to punish lawbreakers but instead to help addicted offenders find treatment and become productive members of society. They are run by a judge (who may also deal with more conventional criminal cases), but she is assisted by a variety of actors, including prosecutors, defense attorneys, social workers, probation officers, and drug and alcohol treatment providers. Together, this team monitors the offender for a period of about a year to 18 months. During this time, the offender submits to a series of random drug tests and checks in regularly with the judge. The court monitors the offender's progress, praising the offender for her successes and monitoring her failures, including seeking treatment, staying sober, and finding housing and work. If the offender completes her course of monitoring and treatment, the court expunges her crimes, and she can go on with her life without the stigma of a criminal conviction.

Another type of diversion program is mental health courts. These courts process mentally ill offenders and keep them from going to a regular prison, where they are unlikely to receive the services that they need. Like drug courts, judges and staff who are experts in mental health issues run these courts. These courts can sentence offenders to mental health treatment and observe their behavior over time. If they continue to observe the requirements of the court, the court will expunge their record.

Drug courts and mental health courts are part of a broader movement to create so-called *problem-solving courts*. These courts seek to think outside the box when handling certain kinds of offenders in ways that avoid the harms of imprisonment. Some states have experimented with other specialized courts, including a gambling court (to assist people whose crimes stem from gambling addiction), gun court, truancy court (for juveniles who miss too much school), homeless court, and domestic violence court. All these courts share a common belief that, for certain kinds of offenders, criminal punishments in general and imprisonment in particular should be a last resort, applied only after other, less punitive approaches have been tried. A group of trained experts can intervene and get to the root problems without the damage done by more traditional punishments. Further, many addicted or mentally ill offenders would not seek help on their own and need the threat of incarceration to get them the treatment and help that they need. The threat of punishment is a way to force these people to get help.

Diversion: Programs that attempt to keep offenders out of prison by providing services and guidance.

Drug court: Courts that are set up to deal with nonviolent offenders with drug problems, offering counseling and monitoring instead of punishment.

Mental health courts: Problem-solving courts that are experts in handling offenders with mental health problems.

Diversion programs too have faced some criticism. Often, offenders must pay a host of extra fees to participate in them, fees that poorer offenders would not be able to afford. Moreover, some critics argue that the intense monitoring of drug users in these courts constitutes an excessive form of surveillance over people who may not necessarily deserve it. One critic of drug courts described them as "invasive behavior modification" (Miller, 2004). On the other hand, research shows that offenders who go through these programs are far less likely to reoffend than those who are put through more conventional criminal proceedings. (See for example Spohn, Piper, Martin, & Frenzel, 2001.) As one study put it, "Drug courts outperform virtually all other strategies that have been attempted for drug-involved offenders" (Marlow, DeMatteo, & Festinger, 2003). While diversion programs are not perfect, they represent a serious attempt to address criminality beyond simply punishing those people who break the law.

Probation

Probation is given to convicted offenders as a substitute for serving actual prison time. Probationers consent to be monitored and agree to check in with their probation officer for a set period instead of serving time behind bars. This monitoring can include unannounced house visits by probation officers, random drug tests, and regular meetings with a probation officer, along with other forms of supervision. Probationers are expected to avoid criminal activity, stay off drugs and (sometimes) alcohol, and be an otherwise upstanding member of society. Often probationers also face travel restrictions, limiting their ability to leave the jurisdiction of the court. Usually, there are varying degrees of supervision for offenders who are placed under probation: At the least severe end is a probation with little or no supervision, sometimes called *banked caseload probation*—effectively there is no supervision and, provided that the probationer does not get in any legal trouble, she may carry on mostly as normal. At the other extreme is *intensive supervision probation (ISP)*, which involves regular, unannounced checks on probationers.

The practice of granting probation to offenders began with the Bostonian John Augustus in 1841. Augustus owned a successful boot-making factory and was an advocate of abstinence from alcohol. He attended criminal courts in the city and offered to take in "drunkards" from the court and help them to sober up and find work. Over his life, he took in nearly two thousand offenders as a volunteer, helping many of them straighten up their lives and earning him the title of "the father of probation." After his death, a law was passed in Massachusetts that formalized Augustus's approach to rehabilitating offenders, and it became commonplace throughout the United States, and there are currently over 4.5 million people on probation (Kaeble, 2018).

Violating probation can be a very serious problem with very serious consequences. If an individual violates the terms of her probation, say by failing to meet with her probation officer at the scheduled time, failing a drug test, or "catching a new case"—that is, by getting involved in another crime, she can have her probation revoked and be sent to prison. Usually the probationer must appear before a judge who will consider a variety of factors in determining whether to revoke her probation and send her back to prison. While awaiting her fate, the probationer is often reincarcerated in a process sometimes called a *detainer*.

Parole

Parole is slightly different from probation. If an offender has spent some time in prison, she can qualify for early release under parole programs. Parole can be used as an incentive for prisoners—they are more likely to behave if they believe that it will help them to earn an early release date. It also allows governments to save money by releasing prisoners who no longer need to be detained and rewarding prisoners who have made progress in their rehabilitation. According to the Bureau of Justice Statistics, over 800,000 people are currently on parole, about one in every 291 adults in the United States (Herberman & Bonczar, 2013).

Prisoners can seek parole by petitioning a parole board once they have served a certain portion of time and reached what is known as a *parole eligibility date*. Often, this date is determined based on the total sentence with time subtracted for good behavior and other considerations. Each state organizes its parole boards differently, but they are usually appointed by governors. Offenders go before parole boards, who weigh a variety of factors in determining whether the individual can leave the prison. This can include the nature of the offense, the prisoner's conduct while incarcerated, and the ability of the offender to understand the gravity of the offense. They can also weigh the likelihood that the offender will commit another crime after they are released. (Prisoners who maintain their innocence are usually denied parole.) In some cases, victims and their families can attend these hearings and oppose or support parole for the offenders. Usually parole is subject to conditions similar to those of probation—the parolee is expected to avoid criminal activities, submit to random drug tests, and meet with a parole officer regularly. Failure to meet these expectations can lead to revocation of parole and a return to prison.

Congress eliminated conventional parole for the federal penal system when it passed the Sentencing Reform Act of 1984. Essentially, Congress was worried about offenders getting out early and hurting innocent people. In lieu of parole, federal prisoners can get *supervised release*. The primary difference between the two is that parolees are offenders who can serve some of their sentence "free" under certain conditions. Under the federal system, offenders are sentenced to a certain amount of time, but some of that sentence is stipulated as supervised release at sentencing. That is, a federal offender can be sentenced to a fixed time in prison plus an additional time under supervised release. If the offender fails to live up to the conditions of her release, she can then be returned to federal prison. Offenders in federal prisons can still get early release for good behavior or under a few other circumstances (such as "compassionate release" for very sick prisoners), but these are much rarer than they are in the state prison systems.

It is not entirely clear how effective parole boards are in determining who is likely to reoffend after release. In part, this is because parole decisions and recidivism rates vary widely among states, and there are so many factors that can cause an exoffender to commit a new crime. A 2011 study by the Pew Center showed that nearly 44% of all paroled offenders return to prison within three years of release, but in many states, nearly half of these were for parole violations, not for committing a new offense (Pew Center on the States, 2011). The age of the parolee matters a great deal—older parolees are less likely to reoffend than younger ones. Similarly, the quality of the services provided to the parolee matter: Substance abuse counseling and family support can also help (Bahr, Harris, Fisher, & Armstrong, 2010). Predicting whether a prisoner is likely to commit new crimes after release is in many ways a very difficult job, and the results are never certain.

Truth-in-sentencing laws: Laws that require offenders to serve their entire sentence rather than being released early.

Parole has been controversial since its inception, and many states have acted to limit it by introducing truth-in-sentencing laws. These laws severely restrict the ability of parole boards to release offenders early and often limit the flexibility judges have in determining how they sentence an offender. Often, these laws require that offenders serve about 85% of their sentence in prison before being eligible for early release.

CRIMINAL (IN) JUSTICE

Punitive Probation

Probation and parole were both designed to help rehabilitate convicted criminals. However, both have come under fire by critics who charge that they have become unnecessarily harsh. They argue that the constant and strict monitoring of probationers amounts to a new form of punishment rather than a genuine effort to reform offenders. Further, they charge that a for-profit probation industry has sucked needed cash away from impoverished offenders. Courts can string an offender's probation out for decades and threaten to send the probationers back to prison for even the slightest infraction, introducing stress and uncertainty to probationers' lives. Private companies can demand fees from probationers and threaten them with a return to prison if they don't pay up. Probation has become a new form of prison, and even extortion, according to these critics.

Like so many other parts of the criminal justice system, probation has begun to be turned into a capitalist enterprise that is organized and run by private companies, often to the detriment of the probationers themselves. "Offender-funded probation" is the business model used by companies like Judicial Correction Services, Inc. (JCS), one of the largest of the private probation firms. Under this model, companies agree to monitor probationers at no cost to the state itself. Instead, probationers are charged fees for their supervision, which they must pay or risk being locked up. These fees can add up to thousands of dollars and can be very difficult for poor offenders to pay. As one offender put it after struggling to pay the company,

> These people at JCS don't want to hear it. . . .They gonna tell you, you got to come up with that money one way or another or you going to jail. They don't want to hear why you can't pay. I know if I go to court they are going to carry me off to jail, so I don't go. (Human Rights Watch, 2014)

Observers charge that these private companies operate with little oversight and a great deal of power over offenders, often making it very difficult for probationers to get their lives on track. The state is happy to avoid having to pay the costs of supervising offenders, but the offenders are significantly worse off as a result.

Unsurprisingly, critics also charge that black and white offenders are treated differently by the probation system, and that black probationers face very different consequences for violating probation than do their white counterparts. A study by the Urban Institute (a research center based in Washington, D.C.) examined probation practices in Iowa, Oregon, and New York City and found that black probationers were far more likely to have their probation revoked than were whites and Hispanics. While there are several complicated reasons why this is the case—the police target African Americans more, meaning that they are more likely to face charges that can lead to their probation being revoked, and black offenders face a host of challenges that can lead them to reoffend at

higher rates—these troubling facts aren't the only explanation. Factoring out these issues still reveals a racial bias in probation: "Revocation rates for black probationers were higher than for white and Hispanic probationers in every study site. The greater odds of revocation remained statistically significant after controlling for differences in probationer characteristics across the three groups" (Jannetta, Breaux, Ho, & Porter, 2014, pp. 8–9). As is the case in many other parts of the criminal justice system, black and white probationers are not treated the same.

When the rapper Meek Mill was imprisoned in 2017 for parole violations relating to a minor drug offense that he had committed over a decade earlier, many critics, including his celebrity friends, spoke up in his defense. They charged that his probation was stretched out unfairly and that his case was just one example of what probationers face every day. As the rapper Jay-Z put it in a *New York Times* editorial on Mill,

> What's happening to Meek Mill is just one example of how our criminal justice system entraps and harasses hundreds of thousands of black people every day. . . . Instead of a second chance, probation ends up being a land mine, with a random misstep bringing consequences greater than the crime. A person on probation can end up in jail over a technical violation like missing a curfew. (Jay-Z, 2017)

Because probation is cheaper than incarceration, the criminal justice system has taken advantage of this system and turned it into a new way to monitor, control, and punish offenders, one that falls disproportionately on African Americans. Rather than being a route to escape prison, probation has become another kind of prison—one without bars.

Are there ways that probation could be reformed to avoid becoming excessively punitive? What changes could criminal justice systems make to help rehabilitate offenders while still imposing meaningful controls on offenders?

SEX OFFENDERS

Learning Objective 12.3—List the restrictions placed on convicted sex offenders.

Sex offenders of all kinds are singled out for particularly harsh sentences, both in and out of the prison system. In part this is because we consider sex crimes to be particularly loathsome, and our society considers rape to be (in the words of Supreme Court Justice Byron White) the "ultimate violation of self." Further, we tend to think that sex offenders are often unreformable. That is, we believe that they cannot be changed on a deep level and will always be a danger to society. Pedophiles in particular are considered incorrigible by the public—if a person is sexually attracted to children, she will always be sexually attracted to children and will remain a danger after her sentence has been completed. (The evidence for this latter belief is in fact quite weak. [West, 2000].) For many reasons, sex offenders are hated by much of society, and the criminal justice system follows suit, creating a host of alternative ways to deal with sex criminals.

Under federal law, individuals convicted of crimes that are considered "sex offenses" are required to register with a federal sex offender registry. The Office of Sex Offender Sentencing, Monitoring, Apprehending, Registering, and Tracking (SMART) was created by the Adam Walsh Child Protection and Safety Act of 2006. Placed under the Department of Justice, SMART registers and monitors individuals convicted of sex crimes against children around the country. Offenders must register their home, their place of work, and where they attend school. Sex offenses vary from state to state and at the federal level but usually include a variety of crimes, including child pornography, sex with a minor, rape, indecent exposure, sexual assault, statutory rape, and soliciting prostitution.

There are also residency restrictions placed on convicted sex offenders that vary from state to state. Usually, they may not live near schools or other places where children are often found. In some states, neighbors receive written notification that a sex offender lives in the neighborhood, leading wealthier neighborhoods to fight to have these people removed. Along with these restrictions, many property owners will not rent to sex offenders, and sex offenders face great challenges finding and keeping work (Tewksbury, 2005). This has led to a chronic problem of homeless sex offenders in many areas as well as sex offenders being forced into impoverished, high-crime neighborhoods (Mustaine & Tewksbury, 2011). Research has shown that life stress and a feeling that they have nothing to lose is a leading cause for sex offenders to reoffend, meaning that, in many cases, these laws can be self-defeating in preventing sex crimes. A study by the Minnesota Department of Corrections found,

> [T]here were no examples that residential proximity to a park or school was a contributing factor in any of the sexual reoffenses. . . . Enhanced safety due to proximity restrictions may be a comfort factor for the general public, but it does not have any basis in fact. (Minnesota Department of Corrections, 2003)

REALITY CHECK

Sex Offenders and Megan's Law

All states incorporate a version of what is known as Megan's Law into their criminal justice systems. Named after a young girl who was raped and murdered by her neighbor in 1994, Megan's Law requires that the names and addresses of sex offenders be made public to allow the public to monitor their activities. This information is posted online by state governments and will often contain information about the whereabouts and activities of sex offenders. The hope is that residents of a neighborhood can use the database to find those people who are a threat to their children and take appropriate action to keep their families safe.

While it may seem a good idea to publicize the identities and whereabouts of sex offenders, research shows that these registries are not very effective, and there is little evidence that these laws protect the public from predators. This is in part because the public often relies on false stereotypes about sex offenders in general, and those who prey on children in particular. As a Human Rights Watch report on sexual offender registries put it,

> Sex offender laws are based on preventing the horrific crimes that inspired them-but the abduction, rape, and murder of a child by a stranger who is a previously convicted sex offender is a rare event. The laws offer scant protection for children from the serious risk of sexual abuse that they face from family members or acquaintances. Indeed, people children know and trust are responsible for over 90 percent of sex crimes against them. ("No Easy Answers," 2007)

Most sexual predators of children target family members or others with whom they have developed a trusted relationship. They rarely grab a child off the street (Children's Bureau, 2011). Even those sex offenders who randomly target children unrelated to them do not necessarily seek out children near where they live— they will simply travel to a place where they are unknown and commit their crimes there. In short, Megan's Laws may give neighbors comfort in knowing who the known sexual predators are in their neighborhood, but there is little evidence that they stop these offenders (Zgoba, Witt, Dalessandro, & Veysey, 2008).

One recent victim of the excessive punishment for a sex offender was Zachery Anderson. A 19-year old Indiana native, Anderson hooked up with a girl he met on a website called "Hot or Not" in 2014. After they had sex, she revealed that she had been lying about her age (she said she was 17 but was really 14 at the time). Her parents learned about their encounter and went to the police. Anderson pled guilty to fourth-degree sexual assault ("sexual conduct with a person between the ages of fourteen and sixteen when the offender was under the age of 21") and spent 75 days in prison. He was forced to register and has been suffering the consequences ever since (Bosman, 2015). Originally, he was not allowed to talk to anybody under the age of 17, had to be home at 8:00 PM, and was not allowed to own a smartphone or use the internet. Eventually he was able to get some of these restrictions lifted, but regardless, it's hard to see how forcing Anderson to register and restrict his freedom so strictly would either facilitate his rehabilitation or protect children from dangerous sexual predators.

(Continued)

Megan's Law:
A federal law that requires sex offenders to register with a federal database.

(Continued)

Anybody with a conscience is horrified by sexual predators. Critics, however, have argued that registries, housing restrictions, and civil commitment are all ineffective and can unfairly target people who may not deserve such treatment. Not every sexual offender is a hard-core, lifelong sexual predator, and being forced to register as one can cripple an individual and prevent an offender from working or getting an education. Civil commitment, based on the assumption that a child abuser is never going to change, can be a way of denying these people basic rights for the rest of their life. Under some state laws, an arrest for urinating in public can lead to being considered a registered sex offender (Sethi, 2014). While child abuse is a terrible thing, a one-size-fits-all response to sexual offenders can cause a great deal of harm to people who may be innocent of the serious offenses that we consider to be sex crimes. Just as significant, these approaches may lure us into a false sense of security regarding who is truly a danger to America's children.

ALTERNATIVE INCARCERATIONS

Learning Objective 12.4—Classify the ways that offenders and others can be held in custody outside of traditional incarceration.

The Fifth Amendment to the Constitution declares that a person cannot "be deprived of life, liberty, or property, without due process of law." This means that the government cannot take away your freedom without meeting certain legal requirements. However, the government does not need to convict you of a crime to incarcerate you. They just need to provide "due process" before doing it. They must follow the appropriate procedures, but they do not need to convict you of any actual offense before locking you up. There are many people held by the government against their will—sometimes for years—who have committed no crimes, or if they did commit one, they were never convicted of it. Almost all these people have been committed *civilly* rather than criminally incarcerated. This can happen for a variety of reasons, most often because the individual is mentally ill or is in the United States unlawfully. Given that the detainment of noncriminal immigrants and others has become an important part of contemporary politics, it's a good idea to discuss some of these noncriminal forms of incarceration, including how they operate and the legal restrictions upon them.

Civil Commitment

Civil commitment involves placing a person in custody and denying her freedom without convicting her of a crime first. The most common form of civil commitment is the detention of an individual who is mentally ill and considered by the court to be a danger to herself or to others. This can happen if an individual has been found not guilty by reason of insanity and thus, instead of being punished by imprisonment, she is committed to a mental health care facility. Her time in a mental health institution can even be much longer than it would be were she sentenced to prison. It is important to note that a person can be civilly committed without a criminal charge if a qualified expert (such as a doctor or psychiatrist) believes the person is a danger—for example, if the expert fears the person will commit suicide. While so committed, the individual must undergo regular evaluations by psychologists to determine whether she will continue to be a danger if released. Only after she is deemed safe will the person be allowed back into the community.

Civil commitment: Holding a person who has not been convicted of a crime (or who has already served her sentence) because experts believe that she is a danger to herself or to the public.

Some people convicted of sex crimes can face civil commitment even after they have completed their sentence, amounting to a "second sentence" that can last decades. The Marshall Project, a nonprofit that studies criminal justice, estimates that there are over five thousand people being held in civil commitment programs because they are considered sex offenders (Steptoe & Goldet, 2016). Judges and parole boards are sometimes hesitant to release sex offenders because of the perception that they are incapable of reform (Hood, Shute, Feilzer, & Wilcox, 2002). This means that these offenders can face a long time behind bars even after they have served their sentence.

The other group that can be held against their will are undocumented immigrants, that is, people who are in the United States unlawfully. Immigrants are detained by the Immigration and Customs Enforcement (ICE) of the Department of Homeland Security and are held until they are either allowed to stay or are returned to their home country. (The Criminal Alien Program or CAP is the division of ICE that deals with unlawful aliens who have committed crimes.) Many of these aliens undergo what are called ERO arrests. ERO stands for "Enforcement and Removal Operations," and according to the ICE over 158,000 individuals were arrested in ERO in 2018 fiscal year (U.S. Immigration and Customs Enforcement, 2018). At the end of 2017, 58,776 people were held in detention as illegal aliens (Department of Homeland Security, 2017). Most of these aliens are being held in prisons or privately run detention facilities, where some have alleged that they are forced to work without compensation (Mitchell, 2017). The Center for Migration Studies reported that over 45,000 migrants were being detained in immigration centers in the 2018 fiscal year, including about 10,000 children (Reyes, 2018).

While those held by the government outside of the regular criminal justice system have some rights, they do not have all of those provided to those accused of crimes. They all have the right to contest their commitment if they believe that they are not a danger to society—what is known as a *habeas corpus* petition. On the other hand, they often do not have the right to a court-appointed attorney if they cannot afford one on their own, nor do they have the right to a trial by jury to contest their detention. If they are charged with a felony, they can be provided representation, but if the government doesn't prosecute them but simply wants to remove them from the country, they usually aren't given a lawyer (Frazee, 2018). In short, many people in America are locked up without having committed any sort of crime and with significantly fewer protections than those given to accused criminals.

Holding Suspected Terrorists in Guantanamo Bay

Perhaps the most famous "nonprison" on Earth is located at a U.S. military base in Guantanamo Bay, Cuba. The detention facility was created after the September 11, 2001, attacks on New York City and Washington, D.C., to hold suspected members of the Al Qaeda terrorist organization as well as members of the Afghan Taliban. These prisoners were picked up by the U.S. military overseas and held without trial in Cuba, sometimes for decades. The U.S. government has maintained that these people are too dangerous to be allowed onto U.S. soil, but the evidence against them may not be good enough to stand up in a regular criminal trial. (Evidence gathered under torture is inadmissible in U.S. courts, for example.) The Supreme Court has ruled that, even though they are not on U.S. soil and aren't American citizens, suspected terrorists still have some rights (*Rasul v. Bush*, 2004). For example, they can challenge the fact that they are being held before a review board.

You have been living in your home with your partner and kids for several years when a new neighbor, Martin, moves in next door. You start to hear rumors from neighbors about some mysteries in his past that lead you to do some research into Martin and his background. Doing some investigation work online, you discover that 20 years ago, he was convicted of unlawful sexual contact with a minor. He has since served his time and completed his probation.

Of course, you march right over to his house to demand an explanation. He invites you into his house. (He is single with no kids.) He confesses to the arrest and explains that he did have a sexual relationship with a young girl. She was 15 at the time, and he was 28. They met online playing video games and had a brief sexual relationship. He explains that he never forced himself on her and that he was only arrested after the child's mother discovered evidence of their relationship. He says that he hasn't done anything similar since then and would never do it again. Since his arrest, he has had a completely clean record and has even given up video games. Martin explains that he is willing to do whatever is necessary to make you feel comfortable with his presence, but he bought the house lawfully and he will not move.

How would you respond to Martin? What, if anything, could Martin do to make you feel comfortable as his neighbor? Would it matter if you had daughters that were in their early teens?

Currently, there are about 55 people held in "Gitmo," significantly down from the over 700 that were there over a decade ago. While he was president, Obama tried to shut down the prison but was unsuccessful, and President Trump has called for expanding the prison and has sought to allow the use of torture on suspected terrorists.

RESTORATIVE JUSTICE

Learning Objective 12.5—Summarize the differences between restorative justice and traditional criminal punishment.

While community corrections programs represent an approach to criminal justice that diverges from simple punishment, in recent years reformers have begun advocating for an even more radical approach known as restorative justice. Rather than seeing punishment as a harm done to an offender for something that the offender did, restorative justice tries to think of the crime as a harm done both to a victim and to the perpetrator and views the criminal justice system as only a secondary actor in the process. Advocates argue that instead of punishing the offender, the criminal justice system should instead bring the offender and her victim together to "heal" and hopefully find peace. This approach to criminal punishment (if it can even be called "punishment") is rooted in non-Western cultures such as traditional African and Native American philosophies as well as in Japan, each of which emphasizes reintegrating offenders into the community rather than harming or ostracizing them. Restorative justice does not punish the offender as much as it seeks to repair the emotional damage done by a crime—damage both to the victim and to the offender herself.

Restorative justice: An approach to justice that seeks to heal the victim rather than punish the offender by bringing the offender and her victim together.

In practice, restorative justice approaches bring offenders and their victims together, usually in a face-to-face meeting so that they can understand each other better and thereby commit to a process of reconciliation and forgiveness. One common form of restorative justice is victim-offender mediation—offenders and victims are brought together to talk about the crime and how it affected their lives. This usually takes place in a supervised space where a victim can meet the offender, explain to the offender how the crimes affected her and those around her and ask questions about the offender's conduct. The offender then may express regret and remorse while explaining the actions that led to the crime and answering any lingering questions from the victim or her survivors.

Many victims report that seeing the offender punished for her actions is a secondary consideration in their lives and that finding closure is much more important to them. Humanizing the attacker, and at times forgiving her, allows a victim to lift the burden that comes from being victimized and to ultimately find peace. Studies have shown that victims are often satisfied with the outcomes of restorative justice processes (Umbreit, Bradshaw, & Coates, 1999). Further, research has shown that restorative justice can reduce recidivism rates, as it gives offenders an opportunity to redeem themselves and rebuild their sense of self (Latimer, Dowden, & Muise, 2005). As one study of restorative justice practices in the UK observed, "Offenders in [restorative justice programs] are many times more likely to admit that they breached their moral obligations, and by apologizing reaffirm their commitment to those obligations, than similar, willing, offenders who are not allowed to engage in [restorative justice]" (Sherman et al., 2005).

Restorative justice practices have begun to influence criminal justice practices throughout the United States. Though it does not replace criminal punishment, an agreement to participate in restorative justice can help both sides move past the harms done. Offenders can sometimes receive a more lenient sentence for agreeing to participate in restorative justice practices and may benefit themselves from the outcome. Outside of criminal justice, restorative justice models have been used for a variety of purposes, including the handling of sexual assault on college campuses. Some universities have begun to facilitate interactions between students who committed sexual assault and their victims so that both sides may move past the crime (Koss, Wilgus, & Williamsen, 2014). Restorative justice has become one of the most exciting aspects of modern criminal justice, and if it continues to spread, it could lead to an entirely new culture of crime and punishment in the country.

Victim-offender mediation: The process of bringing a victim together with the person who harmed her in a supervised environment so that they can discuss the crime and its impact.

CHAPTER SUMMARY

This chapter has focused on different ways to deal with offenders apart from imprisonment. Some of these have meant a reexamination of the nature and purpose of criminal punishment. Community corrections, civil commitment, and restorative justice each try to handle offenders in ways that experts believe are more effective and more humane (not to mention cheaper) than simply "locking them up." Just as with incarceration, there are some notable downsides to these alternative approaches.

Community corrections, for example, seek to address punishing offenders but to avoid a lot of the negative collateral effects of incarceration, both on the offender and her family. There are a lot of positive aspects of community corrections—they are cheap and often more effective at preventing recidivism than simply locking up criminal offenders. In addition, they can help keep families and communities together and prevent younger generations from growing up without parents—a common cause of many social problems. Probation and parole can effectively promote rehabilitation without the downsides. Diversion can help offenders without stigmatizing them and crippling their future.

On the other hand, as time has gone on, some of these innovations have become less about helping offenders rehabilitate and more about controlling their behavior and reducing the risk that offenders might present to society. Politicians and policymakers have become stricter with and more controlling of lawbreakers out of a fear that offenders on probation or parole could reoffend and harm others. This can lead to a blowback against politicians who advocate for offenders. A "better safe than sorry" mentality means that probation, parole, and diversion have become increasingly strict as policymakers seek to prevent offenders from committing future crimes. These alternatives can make it easier to convict and sentence people for behavior that may not otherwise merit punishment—creating a net widening effect (Mainprize, 1992). Further, technological developments have made is easier to monitor and control offenders when they are out of prison, extending the reach of the criminal justice system far beyond the prison walls. As we saw in our discussion of the history of prisons, punishments that seem less harsh are not necessarily better or more humane in practice and the same principle applies to corrections outside of the prison.

The need to control offenders who are not in prison is part of a broader movement to reduce the risk that offenders and ex-offenders present to politicians and policymakers. On the other hand, some researchers have pointed to a "Willie Horton effect" as judges act tough on crime and keeping offenders behind bars longer than may be necessary out of fear that they will be criticized by the public. After Arkansas parolee Darrell Dennis committed a murder in 2013, that state's corrections department dramatically reduced the number of offenders let out on parole, causing a 17% increase in the state's prison population (Pfaff, 2017). When released, it is undeniable that some will reoffend and some of these offenses may be violent. In a free society there is no way to reduce the risk of violence to zero. Rather than continuing the harms of mass incarceration, it might be helpful to rethink how ex-offenders are brought back into the community as well as the support and resources that they receive once they are out.

In the next chapter, we will turn away from the "lighter" punishments of community corrections and restorative justice and turn to the most serious form of punishment available: The Death Penalty.

REVIEW/DISCUSSION QUESTIONS

1. How is restorative justice different from other forms of criminal punishment? If you had been attacked by an offender, would you want to meet the person who hurt you? What would you want to say to her or hear from her?

2. How do you feel about holding sex offenders in civil confinement indefinitely? Do you think this is a good way to handle these people? Would it be better to lengthen their prison sentences instead?

3. Both parole and probation seek to rehabilitate the offender without imprisoning her. What are their relative strengths and weaknesses?

KEY TERMS

Civil commitment 304

Collateral consequences 291

Community corrections 291

Diversion 297

Drug courts 297

Megan's Law 303

Mental health courts 297

Restorative justice 306

Truth-in-sentencing laws 300

Victim-offender mediation 307

$SAGE edge™

Get the tools you need to sharpen your study skills. SAGE edge offers a robust online environment featuring an impressive array of free tools and resources.

Access practice quizzes, eFlashcards, video, and multimedia at edge.sagepub.com/fichtelberg

Sarah Yeh

Lethal injection is designed to "sanitize" executions. Is it a good idea to make executions clean and painless? Why or why not?

CHAPTER THIRTEEN

THE DEATH PENALTY

The death penalty, or more technically *capital punishment*, is the ultimate expression of government power: When the state executes an individual, it does not kill her in a situation of immediacy, emergency, or self-defense. It does so in a deliberate, calculated, and highly ritualized way. It is by ending the life of one of its own citizens that the government shows exactly how powerful it is and is displaying its authority in the most dramatic way possible. Simply put, there is nothing like it in the criminal justice system.

Because of the unique nature of the death penalty, it is often said by criminal justice professionals that "death is different." Many of the rules of criminal justice change in important ways when dealing with capital cases. (*Capital* in this context means cases that involve execution, originating from Latin where *capital* meant head, and in the ancient world capital punishment was often decapitation.) There are two reasons why death is different: First, as a form of punishment, the death penalty is particularly severe—it is not just "more punishment," it is a kind of punishment that is completely unlike all others. Second, the death penalty, once carried out, is irrevocable. The severity and irrevocability of the death penalty, along with changing cultural values about the subject, have made capital punishment a unique and uniquely controversial part of criminal justice. Opponents often find it barbaric, while supporters can't imagine why society wouldn't want to kill "the worst of the worst."

Here we will briefly touch on the history of capital punishment as well as some contemporary legal and practical issues with it. While the forms of execution have undergone serious changes over time, and the scope of its application has been reduced by the courts, there are a number of reasons to believe that it is unlikely to go away any time soon. Too many Americans want to see convicted murderers executed to support a nationwide ban on the death penalty. There are few practical reasons for keeping the death penalty around, but its popularity nonetheless remains strong. According to the Gallup polling company, at only one time over the last 80 years (during the mid-1960s) has opposition to the death penalty been greater than support in America (Gallup, 2017). Nonetheless, the use of the death penalty has been restricted in many significant ways in recent years, and execution looks very different now than it did centuries ago.

The death penalty provokes very strong feelings among both supporters and defenders. Opponents of the death penalty point to its failure to deter criminals, its arbitrariness, its irrevocability, and ultimately, its cruelty. Defenders usually appeal to retributivist ideas about justice—that executing criminals, particularly the worst criminals, is ultimately reasonable and justified. Even within the Christian faith, there is disagreement about the death penalty: The Catholic Church sees banning the death penalty as an expression of the value of God's gift of life (Meixler, 2017) while the Southern Baptist Convention declared its "support [for] the fair and equitable use of capital punishment by civil magistrates as a legitimate form of punishment for those guilty of murder or treasonous acts that result in death" (Southern Baptist Convention, 2000).

CRIMINAL (IN)JUSTICE

Executions of the Innocent

How many innocent people have been executed by the U.S. criminal justice system? It's hard to know for sure, as there are many cases where the evidence is murky, and experts disagree about whether or not the executed criminal was truly guilty. If it were possible to know with 100% certainty that a defendant was innocent, we wouldn't need to worry about the problem in the first place. A 2014 study of death-penalty and death-row exonerations argues that about 4% of those sentenced to death were actually innocent (Gross, O'Brien, Hu, & Kennedy, 2014). According to the Death Penalty Information Center, 164 people on death row have ultimately been found to be innocent (Death Penalty Information Center, 2018b). Further, 35% of those offenders who were initially sentenced to death had their executions overturned later by courts—which does not necessarily mean that the defendants were innocent but does raise troubling questions.

The high rate of exonerations can be explained by several factors, but perhaps the most important of these is the intense scrutiny that death-penalty cases face. Lawyers and detectives look over these cases with a much more careful eye than they would a noncapital case, meaning that it is much more likely that new exculpatory evidence will emerge. Kirk Bloodsworth was sentenced to be executed in Maryland for the rape and murder of a nine-year old-girl. Only later, when semen stains in the girl's underwear were tested for a DNA match, experts discovered that the semen had

belonged to another man, Kimberly Ruffner, who had already been convicted of a different rape. Bloodsworth was the first death-row inmate to be exonerated on account of DNA evidence, and he was given $300,000 for having spent 10 years on death row. According to the American Civil Liberties Union, as of 2011, 17 people have been released from death row because of DNA evidence (American Civil Liberties Union, 2011).

Beyond DNA evidence, the history of executions in the United States shows a number of cases where executed people were shown to be innocent or whose conviction was later proven to be highly dubious. Willie McGee, an African American man, was executed by the state of Mississippi in 1951 for allegedly raping a white neighbor. McGee's case became an international cause as anti-death-penalty organizations and others protested his sentence. Shortly before he was to be executed, McGee reportedly shared with the sheriff (who could not do anything to help McGee even if he believed him innocent) that McGee had had sex with the alleged victim but that she wanted it as much as he did ("Willie McGee," 2017). His final statement to his family was,

> Tell the people the real reason they are going to take my life is to keep the Negro down. . . . They can't do this if you and the children keep on fighting. Never forget to tell them why they killed their daddy. I know you won't fail me. Tell the people to keep on fighting.

Jesse Tafero was executed in 1990 for murdering two highway patrol officers—only to have an associate, Walter Rhodes, confess to the killings. While there are others that may have been innocent, without a new trial (which is impossible once the sentence has been carried out), it is pretty hard to know for sure whether or not these convicted offenders were in fact innocent. The Death Penalty Information Center keeps a list at https://deathpenaltyinfo.org/executed-possibly-innocent.

Do cases where innocents have been executed raise questions in your mind about the legitimacy of capital punishment? Are there ways to avoid wrongful executions? Given what you've studied so far, what improvements do you think would be helpful?

THE HISTORY OF THE DEATH PENALTY

Learning Objective 13.1—List the major transformations in the death penalty from antiquity to the 20th century.

As we discussed in Chapter 10, execution has been a common means for dealing with offenders throughout most of human history. It is inexpensive and quick, and it is believed to serve the ends of incapacitation, deterrence, and retribution, if not rehabilitation. In societies that lack the resources to build and run prisons, execution is a cost-effective way to handle the criminal element. Further, historically, in many societies life was considered to be a pretty cheap commodity, so killing people wasn't considered that big of a deal. Life was short and violent regardless, so why be particularly merciful when dealing with undesirables?

While execution has been a staple of criminal punishment for millennia, the way that capital punishment has been carried out has changed drastically over time. Modern capital punishment is in many ways the antithesis of its historical predecessors. That is, many of the aspects of capital punishment that were considered central to it in the past are now believed to be downsides to execution that should be avoided whenever possible. Until the 19th century, in much of the western world at least, capital punishment had several features that distinguish it from its contemporary counterparts:

Historically speaking, capital punishment was often supposed to be both violent and painful. Getting killed is never pleasant, but it need not necessarily be painful. Many historical forms of execution were not just designed to cause death but were calculated to maximize the offender's suffering before she died. They were intended to be slow, gruesome, terrifying, and usually excruciating. Often, the actual killing took place at the end of a long series of tortures and humiliations, or were the result of deprivation and starvation. Crucifixion, for example, was a particularly slow and painful death. Crucified criminals usually died of exposure to the elements, starvation, or asphyxiation as their windpipe was slowly cut off by their sinking body. (While Jesus Christ is the most famous victim of crucifixion, tens of thousands were crucified in the Roman Empire.) Fortunate victims had their arms broken while on the cross so that death would be quicker. Other painful forms of execution have included sawing a living person in half, peeling a person's flesh while she is alive ("flaying"), being cooked alive, or having a victim's ribs cut and her ribcage opened to stand as wings (the Vikings' infamous "blood eagle"). Historically, pain and suffering were an essential ingredient of executions through most of human history.

Second, capital punishment was often intended to be symbolic. Execution was not just about killing the defendant; the death had to be brought about in a symbolically loaded fashion. The form of execution was meant to communicate something about the nature of the offense. For example, in ancient Rome, the offense of *parricide* (killing a parent) was punished with what was known as *poena cullei*. This punishment consisted first in beating the offender with red-colored rods and covering her head with the skin of a wolf. Then, the offender was sewn up in a sack with a dog, a rooster, a snake, and an ape, and the sack was thrown into a river. Each of the animals symbolized something about the offender's crime in Roman culture, and the *poena cullei* was in many ways as much a religious ritual as a punishment. In many other places, offenders were killed in ways that were meant to connote the crime that they had committed—some were even executed with the weapon that they had used to slay their victim, for example. In many societies, the symbolism of capital punishment was meant to communicate right and wrong to the public.

Just as the form of execution was often tailored to the nature of the crime, it also often varied widely based on the social status of the offender. The wealthy, powerful, and privileged often had a very different fate than the poor or common criminal. Anne Boleyn, the former queen of England (the first unfortunate wife of Henry VIII), was executed with a painless and nimble stroke of a sword by the famous "Sword of Calais," while lesser criminals would face a simple axe or a burning at the stake. Soldiers were shot dead by a firing squad, while civilians were hanged by a rope. In societies where one's position on the social ladder mattered tremendously, it makes sense that even the method of execution would reflect the status of the condemned.

Many of the social and political changes of the Enlightenment began to affect the death penalty in a variety of ways. As we discussed in Chapter 3, the Enlightenment was the broad intellectual, social, and political movement in Europe that emphasized the use of reason and science to solve human problems. The use of reason and science in the 18th century marked the beginning of a transformation in both the methods of execution and its frequency. Execution became, for lack of a better word, *humanized*. Western societies became more concerned about the suffering of the condemned prisoner than ever before, and pain and blood slowly became anathema to capital punishment. Because the desire to see the criminal suffer seemed unhealthy according to the advocates of the Enlightenment, the practice of execution needed to be made more "civilized." The use of the infamous Catherine Wheel (or "breaking wheel"), which required that the condemned's limbs be broken and woven between the spokes of a wooden wheel prior to execution, was changed in the 18th century, when many offenders were secretly strangled before they were "broken" (Ward, 2015). Further, the Enlightenment advocated democracy and equality for citizens—different punishments for different groups just didn't make sense in an egalitarian society.

Perhaps the most significant development in the humanization of execution was the invention of the guillotine. The guillotine was the creation of a French surgeon named Antoine Louis but was later popularized by another French doctor, Joseph-Ignace Guillotin, from which the device gets its name. By dropping a heavy, sharp blade down on an immobilized victim whose head is held in place by a constraint, the guillotine guaranteed a quick, certain, and relatively painless death. While we commonly associate the guillotine with the darkest days of the French Revolution, in many ways, the device was

Guillotine: A device created in France to ensure a quick beheading.

a mark of progress over traditional forms of beheading. An axe swung by a person can miss its target or fail to completely sever its victim's head, leading to a great deal of gore and unnecessary suffering. By ensuring a quick cut, the guillotine made death swift and certain. Moreover, the fact that every person executed died in the exact same way made the guillotine a very democratic punishment—King Louis XVI was executed in the same manner as a common criminal.

The guillotine was not the only form of punishment intended to humanize executions developed in the Enlightenment period. A second technique was the so-called long drop. While hanging has always been a common method for executions, historically most victims were hanged only a small distance from the ground. When a box was kicked out from underneath a person who has a noose tied around her neck (or a horse she was sitting on was taken away), the condemned would dangle from the rope and ultimately suffocate. The long drop was designed to end this unnecessary suffering by using the force of gravity to snap the condemned prisoner's neck and ensuring a quick death. As with the guillotine, the long drop was meant to be kind to the condemned, even as, paradoxically enough, she was killed.

The 20th century saw several different developments in the methods of execution, all of which were intended to ensure that the condemned suffered a certain, quick, and (relatively) painless death—the exact opposite of what was expected from earlier forms of execution. One of the first to be developed was the electric chair. The chair was designed to pump a series of shocks of approximately 2,000 volts of electricity into a person who is strapped into a wooden chair. The surge of electricity causes the condemned's muscles to contract and her heart to stop, usually causing a quick death, though the process can be repeated if a preliminary examination shows that the prisoner is not yet dead. The method was originally promoted as a modern, technological solution to execution that was developed by employees of Thomas Edison's company and promoted by Edison himself. It remains a legal form of execution in many states as of this writing, and the most recent person to be executed by electrocution was Robert Gleason in Virginia in 2013.

The electric chair developed as a result of the harnessing of electricity in the 19th century; in the 20th century, people began to understand the potential of gas as a tool for killing humans. Following in the footsteps of the First World War, where mustard gas and other chemicals were used on the battlefield to kill or disable enemy troops, the gas chamber was created as another, modernized means for executing condemned criminals. Locked in an airtight tank, an offender is either asphyxiated (that is, suffocated) or poisoned by exposure to either hydrogen cyanide or carbon monoxide. This method of killing is less popular than electrocution simply because it has proven to be less certain and less "humane" than the others. The United States is the only nation that has used the gas chamber as a form of criminal punishment, though Nazi Germany infamously used gas to kill millions of Jews and others in the Holocaust.

In 1977, lethal injection, currently the preferred means of execution in the United States, was first proposed, and it was used five years later to execute Charles Brooks in Texas. Lethal injections involve administering a deadly cocktail of drugs to an offender who has been strapped onto a gurney. Usually, the first injection is designed to induce unconsciousness, and the later injections induce paralysis and stop the heart. Often these injections are not performed by doctors, as they are unwilling to assist in the killing of

Long drop: A method for hanging convicted criminals that ensures a quick death by breaking the neck of the condemned.

patients (though some do). Moreover, getting the drugs from manufacturers can be difficult, as some companies (particularly in Europe) are averse to playing any role in killing people (Eckholm, 2016). According to the Death Penalty Information Center, seven states have imposed a moratorium on executions, largely because of concerns about the accessibility of drugs (Death Penalty Information Center, 2007).

In sum, the history of execution is a very strange one. What was once an intentionally symbolic, painful, and gruesome form of punishment has slowly been sapped of almost all its defining features. Modern executions are conducted far from the public eye under antiseptic conditions—the needles used in lethal injections are sterile to avoid the possibility of infection. Further, the Supreme Court has been forced to debate whether or not the most "humane" form of execution remains too painful to be used, given the Eighth Amendment's ban on "cruel and unusual punishment." All executed criminals are given the same few forms of execution that are available, rather than the tailored and symbolically loaded executions of antiquity. There are probably a number of complex historical and sociological reasons as to why the means we have for executing criminals has been so radically transformed (and they probably have little to do with society becoming more "humane"), but suffice it to say that over the last 250 years, there has been a tremendous transformation in how we kill off "the worst of the worst."

THE DEATH PENALTY AND THE CONSTITUTION

Learning Objective 13.2—Name the major Supreme Court cases that have shaped the death penalty in modern America.

Though the Supreme Court has ruled that the death penalty is constitutional, not every state in the United States has the death penalty, and among those states that do allow convicted criminals to be executed, not every state actually uses it. In some states, governors have decided to prevent the execution of offenders in what is known as a *moratorium*. For example, shortly before leaving office in 2000, Illinois governor George Ryan declared, "I have grave concerns about our state's shameful record of convicting innocent people and putting them on death row" before commuting every death sentence in the state ("A timeout," 2000). The states that have executed the most offenders are Texas (which has executed 548 people since the death penalty was reimposed in 1976), Virginia (113 executions) and Oklahoma (112 executions), and overall the Southern states execute far more convicted offenders than states in other parts of the country. Fifteen states have not executed anybody since the Supreme Court reinstated the death penalty in its 1976 decision in *Greg v. Georgia* (Death Penalty Information Center, 2018a). See Figure 13.1 for a map of states that use the death penalty.

While the United States has the highest ratio of prisoners per capita in the world, we are not the country that uses the death penalty most frequently. In fact, we are relatively low on the list. Even though it doesn't make its data public, China is widely believed to be the country that executes the most offenders (Death Penalty Information Center," n.d.a).

As we discussed in Chapter 9, there are many different ways to interpret the sometimes vague language in the Constitution, and each judge has different ideas about how to do it. One of the places where this issue generates a great deal of controversy surrounds the death penalty.

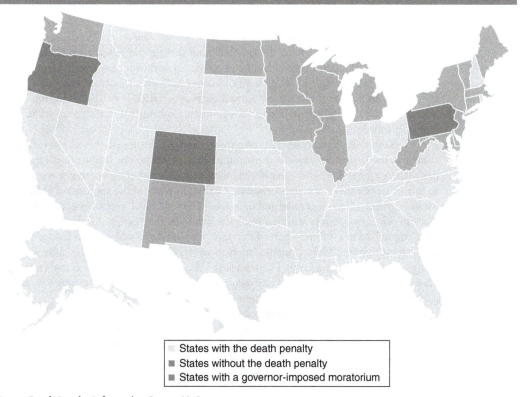

Figure 13.1   States With and Without the Death Penalty, as of October 2018

- States with the death penalty
- States without the death penalty
- States with a governor-imposed moratorium

Source: Death Penalty Information Center, 2018a.

The **Eighth Amendment** bans "cruel and unusual punishment." The Constitution itself does not clearly state how the courts are supposed to figure out which punishments are "cruel and unusual" and which aren't. This has led to a long history of cases where the judges have had to argue about whether the court should use 18th-century ideas about cruelty or instead rely on more modern standards. The 18th century was a much rougher time, and the public was willing to put up with a lot more cruelty—especially when this cruelty was inflicted on a convicted criminal.

Given the ambiguous language in the Eighth Amendment, it makes sense that the courts would revise their attitude toward the death penalty over time. While there are several different ways that the Supreme Court has intervened in executions, here we will focus only on two aspects of the court's views. The first is the brief period in the early 1970s when the court ruled that the death penalty was unconstitutional and only brought it back after a series of reforms in how capital cases were handled by the courts. The second consists in a series of cases where the court restricted the types of defendants and cases that could be eligible for execution. These *limiting cases* have slowly constricted the right of states and the federal government to execute convicted criminals over the last three decades.

Eighth Amendment: The constitutional amendment that bans "cruel and unusual punishment" (among other things).

In 1972, the Supreme Court ruled that the death penalty as it was used in the United States at the time was unconstitutional. In the case of *Furman v. Georgia*, the court did not say that the death penalty *as such* was unconstitutional, but rather that the rules that governed which criminals were executed violated the Eighth Amendment's ban on cruel and unusual punishment as well as the Fourteenth Amendment's requirement that all have equal protection under the law (meaning that people deserve equal treatment). The defendant William Furman had been convicted of murdering a man during a burglary that he had committed along with two other individuals. Furman claimed that the killing was an accident, but he was nonetheless prosecuted for the murder under the felony-murder rule, which states that any homicide committed during a felony is automatically murder.

In its opinion on the case, the court argued that the death penalty was too erratically applied in the United States to be constitutionally acceptable. The problem with the death penalty, they argued, was not that it was inherently wrong, but rather that it was applied so inconsistently that it was unacceptable. The randomness of the application of the punishment effectively made it cruel and unusual—if an individual were convicted of a particular offense in one county within a state, she would be executed, but if that same offense were committed in a different part of the state, she would probably not. As Justice Stewart put it in his opinion, "These death sentences are cruel and unusual in the same way that being struck by lightning is cruel and unusual." Without some sort of clear and consistent lines for determining who would be executed and who would not, capital punishment was constitutionally unacceptable to the court.

Many states quickly responded, searching for a way to make the death penalty acceptable to the court. Initially some states sought to make it more predictable by making it mandatory for certain offenses. When this failed (the Supreme Court rejected this approach in *Woodson v. North Carolina* in 1976), the states took several steps to ensure that the death penalty was applied in a more evenhanded way. After several attempts, the Supreme Court ruled four years after *Furman* in *Gregg v. Georgia* that the state had sufficiently reformed its death penalty practices so that they were now constitutional. These reforms included the following:

Bifurcated Trials. As we discussed in Chapter 9, in most traditional criminal trials it is the responsibility of the jury to determine whether the defendant is guilty. Once they have completed that process, they have completed their work, and the judge then determines the appropriate punishment. In post-*Furman* death-penalty cases, the jury participates in a second round of hearings (a penalty phase), where evidence is heard as to whether or not the convicted criminal deserves to die. At this point, the convicted individual can present mitigating evidence, that is, evidence that is meant to show that the defendant does not deserve to die for her crimes. There is no restriction on the type of evidence that is considered mitigating. It can include evidence that the defendant was mentally ill, was addicted to drugs, was a generally good person before committing the crime, et cetera. During the 2015 trial of the "Boston Marathon Bomber," Dzhokhar Tsarnaev, Tsarnaev's cousin mentioned that the defendant cried while watching the movie *The Lion King* as mitigating evidence (O'Neill & McLaughlin, 2015). Anything that the defense's legal team believes will make the jury less likely to sentence the defendant to death can be brought up at this point of the trial.

Furman v. Georgia: A 1972 Supreme Court ruling that argued that the death penalty (as it was then practiced) was too arbitrary to be constitutional.

Gregg v. Georgia: A 1976 Supreme Court ruling that reinstated the death penalty in the United States.

Bifurcated trials: Trials that are split between a guilt phase (when the defendant is either convicted or acquitted) and a penalty phase when the jury decides whether or not to recommend the death penalty.

Mitigating evidence: Evidence presented to a jury that attempts to limit the perceived severity of the crime.

WHAT WOULD YOU DO?

Could You Be an Executioner?

Could you kill somebody who was convicted of a crime? The psychology of executions is a complicated issue. While many people like to talk tough about being able to kill a person, particularly a bad person, in reality, it is an emotional issue and a difficult issue for people who are asked to do it. Firing squads have often loaded one dummy cartridge in one of the executioners' guns prior to executing the convicted criminal. Known as a "conscience bullet," this blank was meant to allow every member of the squad to console themselves with the knowledge that they may not have killed the prisoner. Clearly killing can produce a great deal of trauma in people, even when their target has been convicted by a court of law.

Many people who commit executions find the experience very difficult and later regret participating. One report suggests that 31% of all corrections officers involved with the death penalty suffer from some form of posttraumatic stress disorder (Bushman, 2014). Jerry Givens, a Missouri executioner who quit his job after performing 62 executions said,

If I had known what I'd have to go through as an executioner, I wouldn't have done it. It took a lot out of me to do it. You can't tell me I can take the life of people and go home and be normal. (Nelson, 2015)

Of course, other executioners do not have such ambivalence or regret about their job. A police officer in Utah who participated in the firing squad that killed John Albert Taylor for murder declared coolly, "I haven't lost three seconds of sleep over it," adding, "It's true justice" (Hayes, 2010).

It is easy to say that one could kill another person. The reality is that executing a person, even a person who is guilty of a terrible crime, is much more difficult than you'd think, and its ultimate effects on the person who does it can be deep and long lasting.

Would you be willing to serve as an executioner? Why or why not? What if you were certain that the offender was guilty? Would that make a difference to you?

On the other hand, at this point of the trial the prosecution can also bring in aggravating evidence—that is, evidence that is meant to show that the defendant deserves to die. Aggravating evidence is usually restricted to specific aspects of the case. That is, the jury (or judge) must find that there were specific factors at play during the crime for a factor to be aggravating.[1] These aggravating factors can include things like the killing of a law enforcement officer in the line of duty, the use of explosives or poison, the targeting of a victim for racial reasons, or the killing of the victim(s) in a particularly cruel fashion.

Aggravating evidence: Evidence presented to a jury that makes a crime seem more severe. Juries can use this evidence to determine whether to recommend execution.

---

[1] It should be noted that in some states, the jury does not impose the death penalty; it only recommends that the defendant be executed. The final decision is up to the judge in these states. In other states the judge makes the determination alone, and in some it is solely up to the jury (Death Penalty Information Center, n.d.b).

Automatic Appeals. A second reform that was implemented by states that wished to keep the death penalty after *Furman* was the use of automatic appeals in any case where the trial court recommends death. This is meant to ensure that capital punishment is handed out in an evenhanded way across a state, preventing capital punishment being imposed at the whim of particular judges or local prosecutors in a particular region.

Voir Dire. Many states have expanded the voir dire process for death penalty cases. (If you recall, voir dire is the process by which attorneys for both sides ask questions of prospective jurors to determine if they should serve on the jury.) In these states, both sides have significantly more peremptory challenges of prospective jurors in death penalty cases than in other types of cases. For example, in ordinary federal felony cases, both sides have six peremptory challenges, while in death penalty cases, both sides have twenty peremptory challenges. (See Rule 24 of Federal Rules of Criminal Procedure.) This expanded voir dire process usually makes the pre-trial phase of death penalty cases much longer than normal, but it (in theory) allows for a better jury than a shorter process would allow. Prospective jurors are screened by the prosecution to weed out anybody that would never be willing to apply the death penalty. A jury composed of individuals who are willing to at least consider executing a defendant is known as a death-qualified jury. While such a jury makes sense in capital cases, it might look very different from a jury drawn from the community where the trial takes place, and research suggests that death-qualified juries may be more likely to convict a defendant than would a jury that had not undergone this process (Haney, 1984).

Limiting Cases

Since the court reinstated the death penalty in 1976, it has created a series of constraints on the use of the death penalty, rather than eliminating it altogether. Limiting cases are cases in which the court has restricted the ability of states to impose the death penalty without banning it outright. While the court in each case presents different reasons for restricting capital punishment, many of them rely on changing notions of what constitutes cruel and unusual punishment under the Eighth Amendment. In doing so, justices point to what they describe as "evolving standards of decency," arguing that most states (and more controversially, many foreign countries) have decided not to execute certain classes of people, indicating a broader change in attitudes on the subject. Because society has "evolved" on the subject of the death penalty, the court argues in these cases, the Eighth Amendment must be reinterpreted for modern times. Here are a few of these limiting cases:

Death-qualified jury: A jury that could impose the death penalty if they found it appropriate.

Limiting cases: Supreme Court cases that restrict the types of cases in which the death penalty can be applied.

Coker v. Georgia (1977). In *Coker*, the Court held that the only crime for which a person could be executed was murder. In this case, the defendant, who was already serving a life sentence in prison for various crimes (including murder), escaped from prison and during his escape raped a woman before he was ultimately recaptured. Here the court ruled that, while rape is a terrible crime, it was insufficient for execution. As the majority opinion in the case put it,

> Rape is without doubt deserving of serious punishment; but in terms of moral depravity and of the injury to the person and to the public, it does not compare

with murder, which does involve the unjustified taking of human life. . . . The murderer kills; the rapist, if no more than that, does not. Life is over for the victim of the murderer; for the rape victim, life may not be nearly so happy as it was, but it is not over, and normally is not beyond repair.

(It is worth noting that in *Kennedy v. Louisiana* [2008], the court upheld *Coker* in relation to the rape of a child.)

Atkins v. Virginia (2002). In 1996, two men abducted an airman, named Eric Nesbitt, from a convenience store at gunpoint. After they took their victim to an ATM machine to withdraw $200, they drove him to a remote location where they shot him dead. The two were quickly caught and arrested. One of the two defendants, Daryl Atkins, was determined to be the triggerman in the killing and put on trial for capital murder. During the trial, the defense presented evidence that Atkins was "mildly mentally retarded," having an IQ of 59 (the average IQ is about 100). The defense's lawyers argued that it was a violation of the Eighth Amendment to execute a person with an intellectual disability.

In its opinion, the court agreed, arguing that American society had changed, and acknowledged that executing offenders with intellectual disabilities was now considered to be cruel and unusual. Executing such people served none of the traditional aims of punishment: It does not serve deterrence, as their limited capacities "make it less likely that they can process the information of the possibility of execution as a penalty and, as a result, control their conduct based upon that information." Similarly, executing persons with intellectually disabilities does not serve the interest in retribution as, in retribution, "only the most deserving of execution are put to death, [and therefore] an exclusion for the mentally retarded is appropriate." The court concluded that there was no constitutional basis for executing people like Atkins, and he was sentenced to life imprisonment.

Roper v. Simmons (2005). *Roper* addressed a related question about the execution of a minor. In this case, the defendant was convicted of participating in a gruesome murder— as part of a thought-out, deliberate plan, Simmons and a friend kidnapped a woman named Shirley Crook, tied up her arms and legs and dropped her off of a bridge into a Missouri river in September 1993. Simmons, who was 17 years old when he committed the killing, bragged about his crime and was quickly apprehended and charged with capital murder. (During the trial, it was shown that as a child Simmons was the victim of brutal beatings and neglect by his parents, was a drug addict, and may have suffered from mental illness.)

In arguing that the Eighth Amendment prohibited the execution of offenders who are minors at the time of the crime, the court cited several different factors. First, there was a "national consensus against the death penalty for juveniles" that made it unconstitutional. Further, the court ruled that juveniles are not fully capable of being aware of their actions, and so they cannot be classified as the "worst offenders," regardless of the character of their crimes. "Once the diminished culpability of juveniles is recognized, it is evident that the penological justifications for the death penalty apply to them with lesser force than to adults." Thus, executing a minor is now cruel and unusual, though it was once widely accepted.

SOME STATISTICS...

Who Gets Executed

The United States is one of about 55 countries that still have the death penalty, and we are the only Western state that executes criminals. Many of the countries have the death penalty "on the books" but do not apply it. (The European Union considers it a violation of human rights.) However, in terms of executions carried out, the United States is nowhere near the top: China executes a great deal more than we do in the West, but they do not release their execution data to the public. Most of the other states that execute criminals are Islamic governments (see Figure 13.2).

At present, there are about 2,800 people on death row in the United States. The highest number of condemned prisoners (740) are in California, which last executed an offender in 2006. See Table 13.1 for other top states.

These numbers reflect a steep drop in death sentences in the United States over the last two decades (see Figure 13.3).

There is a racial disparity in the death penalty, but it is more complex than it would initially appear. According to the Legal Defense Fund of the NAACP, the percentage of African Americans

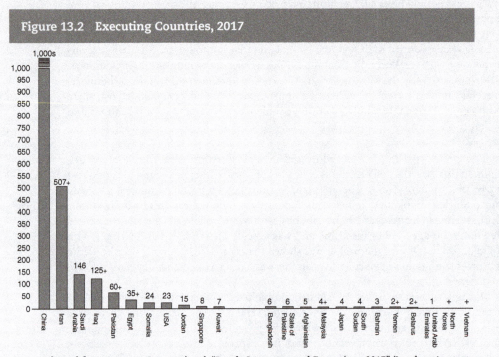

Figure 13.2   Executing Countries, 2017

Source: Adapted from Amnesty International, "Death Sentences and Executions 2017" (London: Amnesty international, 2018). Reprinted with permission.

Note: + indicates that the figure that Amnesty International has calculated is a minimum. Where + is not preceded by a number, this means Amnesty International is confident that there was more than one execution, but it was not possible to establish a figure. Judicial executions may have taken place in Libya and Syria, although Amnesty International was unable to confirm any figures.

Table 13.1　Death Row Inmates by State, as of July 2018

State	Number of Prisoners
California	740
Florida	353
Texas	232
Alabama	185
Pennsylvania	160
North Carolina	144
Ohio	144
Arizona	121
Nevada	75
Louisiana	71
Tennessee	62
U.S. Federal Government	63
Georgia	56
Oklahoma	49
Mississippi	47
South Carolina	39
Kentucky	32
Oregon	33
Arkansas	31
Missouri	25
Indiana	12
Nebraska	12
Kansas	10
Utah	9
Idaho	9
Washington	8
U.S. Military	5
Colorado	3
South Dakota	3
Virginia	3
Montana	2
New Mexico*	2
New Hampshire	1
Wyoming	1

Source: **Death Penalty Information Center, 2018a.**

Notes: **The Delaware Supreme Court declared the state's death penalty statute unconstitutional in 2016. The state's 17 former death-row prisoners have been resentenced to life without parole.**

* New Mexico repealed the death penalty in March 2009, but the law was not made retroactive. Two remain on death row.

on death row (out of all inmates on death row) is greater than the percentage of African Americans in the total prison population (See Table 13.2).

The most interesting facts about racial disparities in the death penalty don't focus on the race of the offender, but rather the race of the victim (see Figures 13.4 and 13.5). It is clear from death penalty data that those who kill black people are less likely receive the death penalty than those who kill white people.

(Continued)

(Continued)

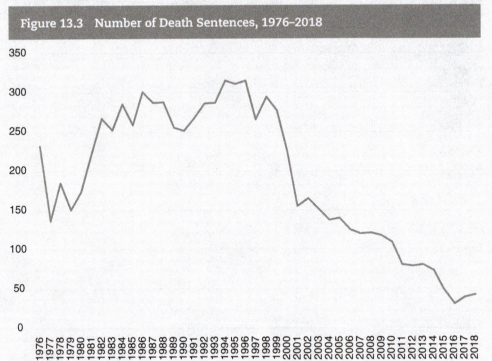

Figure 13.3   Number of Death Sentences, 1976–2018

Source: Data from Death Penalty Information Center, 2019.

Table 13.2   Number of Death Row Inmates Known to the NAACP Legal Defense Fund, July 2018

Race of Defendant		
White	1,196	42.46%
Black	1,168	41.46%
Latino/Latina	373	13.24%
Native American	26	0.92%
Asian	53	1.88%
Unknown	1	0.04%
Gender of Defendant		
Male	2,764	98.12%
Female	53	1.88%

Source: Fins, 2018.

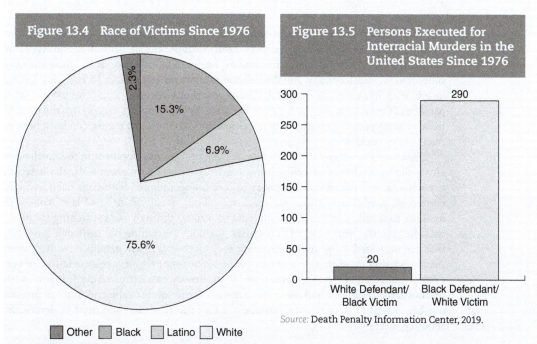

Figure 13.4 Race of Victims Since 1976

2.3%

15.3%

6.9%

75.6%

■ Other ■ Black □ Latino □ White

Source: Death Penalty Information Center, 2019.

Figure 13.5 Persons Executed for Interracial Murders in the United States Since 1976

290

20

White Defendant/ Black Victim   Black Defendant/ White Victim

Source: Death Penalty Information Center, 2019.

Killings with white victims make up more than 75% of capital cases despite the fact that only about 50% of all killings involve white victims. Criminologists have shown that where two murders are virtually identical, a black offender killing a white victim will more often get the death penalty (van den Haag, 1984).

OTHER DEVELOPMENTS IN THE DEATH PENALTY

Learning Objective 13.3—Describe the practical and financial issues in carrying out the death penalty in the United States today.

Since these limiting cases were decided by the Supreme Court, there have been several important developments in death-penalty law and practice. First, states have faced problems obtaining the combination of drugs that are necessary for administering a lethal injection. While different states use a different mixture of drugs to kill a prisoner, they are all surprisingly difficult to obtain and administer correctly. Some of the pharmaceutical companies that manufacture the drugs have refused to sell them to prisons, because they have a moral objection to the death penalty. As the spokesperson for Pfizer, a major pharmaceutical company stated, "Pfizer makes its products solely to enhance and save the lives of the patients we serve. We strongly object to the use of any of our products in the lethal injection process for capital punishment" (Berman, 2016). Companies who are known for producing goods that help people are not eager to be associated with executions.

Some state governments have likewise reduced or eliminated capital punishment. The state legislature in Nebraska voted to end the death penalty in 2015 after one legislator made the case that it was ineffective and expensive. The populace at the time strongly supported the death penalty, and the ban was overturned a year later. In 2003, just before he left office in a corruption scandal, Illinois governor George Ryan commuted the death penalties of everybody on death row in the state. While these are exceptions, the general trend in death penalty practice in the states has been to reduce the number of death penalty cases, not increase them.

Innocence Projects and DNA Evidence. Another recent development in the death penalty is the formation of so-called innocence projects. These groups, usually based in law schools, seek out cases where they believe innocent individuals have been wrongly convicted, particularly those on death row. They usually consist of law professors working alongside a group of law students who comb through cases searching for proof that the case was mismanaged. This often includes examining old evidence for DNA that can be tested using more contemporary methods. These groups have had some success getting questionable convictions and innocent prisoners released. To cite one example, in 2014, Henry McCollum and Leon Brown, two African American men with intellectual disabilities, had their 30-year-old conviction for rape and murder thrown out because of DNA evidence found on the victim that matched neither defendant (Possley, 2015).

Innocence projects: Groups that research criminal convictions that they believe are wrong and should be overturned.

REALITY CHECK

The Death Penalty and Deterrence

One of the main justifications for punishing an offender is *deterrence*—to show that the law must be respected and that breaking the law has consequences. Executions were once public spectacles in part to teach young people the importance of obeying the law. Killing offenders is sometimes portrayed as a tool to save the lives of innocent people. But most of the evidence suggests that the death penalty has no impact on criminal behavior. A historical analysis of homicides showed that there was no distinct difference in the homicide rates between those states with the death penalty and those without it, and "most of the variation in homicide rates is driven by factors that are common to both death penalty and non-death-penalty states" (Donohue & Wolfers, 2006) (see Figure 13.6). The states with the highest murder rates are also states where the death penalty is most frequently applied (Death Penalty Information Center, 2018a). In 2007 the American Society of Criminology, the nation's leading association of crime researchers, adopted this official position:

> Be it resolved that because social science research has demonstrated the death penalty to be racist in application and social science research has found no consistent evidence of crime deterrence through execution,

The American Society of Criminology publicly condemns this form of punishment, and urges its members to use their professional skills in legislatures and courts to seek a speedy abolition of this form of punishment. (American Society of Criminology, 1989)

In short, the death penalty has no discernable impact on homicide rates—there are simply too many other factors that affect these rates for the death penalty to have any measurable effect.

The fact that the death penalty does not save lives does not mean that it is necessarily wrong, of course. Execution could be justified as a form of incapacitation for serious offenders or as a tool of retribution against the worst offenders, but as a tool for saving lives or preventing murders, it serves no purpose.

If the death penalty doesn't deter killers, does that matter to you? Why or why not? Is it possible for capital punishment as it is practiced in the United States to be changed so that it could have a deterrent effect? If so, how?

Figure 13.6   Death Penalty Laws and Homicide Rates in the United States

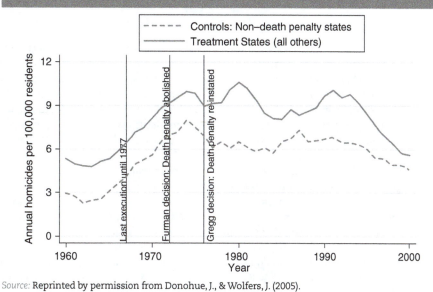

Source: Reprinted by permission from Donohue, J., & Wolfers, J. (2005).

Costs

In many cases, the costs of life imprisonment are significantly less than the costs of executing a prisoner. As we've already seen, the trial process for capital cases is significantly lengthier and more involved than for noncapital cases, which itself generates a great deal of the expense for the government. The judges and attorneys must devote their time to the extended voir dire procedures, the lengthy bifurcated trial, and the often very lengthy appeals process. Given that these convicted offenders are fighting for their lives, it's understandable that they would seek every possible grounds to appeal their sentence. This means that many offenders often spend decades on death row before execution. According to the

Death Penalty Information Center, the average time between sentencing and execution is nearly 16 years (Death Penalty Information Center, 2013). Studies by various states have shown that capital cases are up to 70% more expensive than noncapital murder cases (Amnesty International, n.d.).

Further, while offenders are undergoing appeals, they must be kept on *death row*, a special section of a prison that is designed to hold offenders awaiting execution. Death row is a particularly isolated place, where prisoners are often kept in their cells for 22–23 hours per day and in many states are given little access to family or the outside world. Regardless of whether or not these conditions are warranted or even humane, they are very expensive. Further, the cost of carrying out the execution can be quite high— obtaining the necessary drugs to administer a lethal injection is often difficult and costly. According to a report from the *Sacramento Bee*, it costs approximately $15 million per execution, whereas life imprisonment costs only a fraction of that (Magagnini, 1988). All for executing one offender with little chance that this will have any deterrent effect on future potential murderers.

American Culture and the Death Penalty

Even though it makes little economic sense and has no discernible effect on the overall crime rate, there is nonetheless lasting support for executing serious offenders in the United States. There are many good reasons for this. Clearly, the death penalty seems to be deeply rooted in American culture, perhaps from the "Old West" days when executions were common. When the Nebraska legislature banned the death penalty in 2015, a group of citizens banded together, signing petitions and forcing the government to reinstate capital punishment in the state a year later, despite the fact that nobody has been executed in the state since 1997. Even if it is not used, even if it is costly, and even if it doesn't deter would-be killers, many Americans support the death penalty—some 55% of Americans support it currently, according to polling (Gallup, 2017).

One feature of American society that might help explain the persistence of support for the death penalty is American individualism. Americans are individualists in the sense that many of us believe that your ultimate success or failure in life is up to you. If you work hard you are likely to be successful; if you are lazy you will fail. If you commit a crime, it is your fault and you should be punished, regardless of any other factors that might have affected your choices (Pew Research Center, 2015). Few Americans are sympathetic to people who believe that their bad acts aren't their fault, and only a small group accept the claim that society is to blame for our inability to get ahead. Studies have supported this: Countries with a high degree of individualist beliefs tend to support tougher punishments more than those without such beliefs (Kornhauser, 2015).

Sociologists and political scientists also find a strong link between racial hostility and support for capital punishment. It is commonly observed that white people are far more inclined to support capital punishment than other ethnic groups, in particular, African Americans (see Figure 13.7).

Equally important, feelings of hostility toward minorities or a fear of minorities correspond to support for capital punishment. Negative feelings toward African Americans are linked to support for the death penalty (Soss, Langbein, & Metelko, 2003). According to one writer, "Consistent with conflict theory, white support of the

American individualism: The common belief that people are responsible for their own conduct, independent of external circumstances.

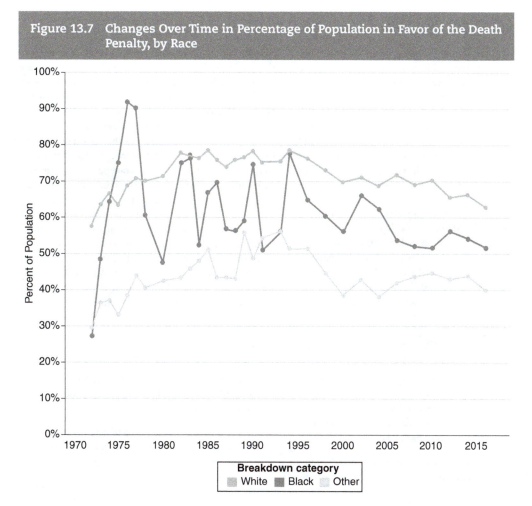

Figure 13.7 Changes Over Time in Percentage of Population in Favor of the Death Penalty, by Race

Breakdown category
White Black Other

Source: Smith, Davern, Freese, & Hout, 2018.

death penalty is likely based on the perceived 'social threat' posed by racial, ethnic, and immigrant groups" (Unnever, Cullen, & Jonson, 2008). On the other hand, African Americans' failure to support the death penalty is strongly rooted in the history of lynch mob justice as well as their reasonable belief that the criminal justice system is biased against them (Unnever & Cullen, 2007). None of this is helped by the fact that the vast majority of executions take place in states that were part of the old Confederacy and have a history connected with the oppression of blacks (Love, 2012). American feelings about the death penalty are heavily racial, whether or not death penalty supporters believe that it is.

CHAPTER SUMMARY

This chapter has been a discussion of the ultimate form of punishment the criminal justice system has to offer: the execution of criminals. We have followed the history of execution from its bloody, symbolic origins to its modern, sanitized form. We have looked at the Supreme Court's efforts to restrict and regulate execution through changing crucial aspects of criminal procedure in capital cases, and we have examined features of modern capital punishment that might point to a future when capital punishment has been significantly reduced or completely eliminated.

Execution is the only situation where the state is legally entitled to end the life of somebody in its custody and, as a result, execution gets special treatment throughout the criminal justice system. Trials, in particular, but also appeals, look very different when the offender is looking at the possibility of execution. Execution is both incredibly severe and irreversible; hence "death is different."

Equally important, the death penalty is symbolic in a way that other punishments are not. Executions incorporate a society's beliefs about human responsibility, the potential for redemption, and the appropriate use of violence. Gruesome executions weren't just designed to kill the offender; they were meant to communicate to the public the unacceptability of crime and the importance of justice and order. Later, more "humane" forms of execution sought to express our views about democratic equality and unnecessary suffering as well as the ability of technological innovations such as electricity (the electric chair), chemistry (the gas chamber), pharmacology (lethal injections) and even physics (the long drop) to solve the thorny problem regarding the best way to dispense with evil. The symbolism behind the death penalty helps explain why it remains so important to many Americans and why we are willing to expend such a great amount of resources on it, even if it is of little value for reducing crime.

REVIEW/DISCUSSION QUESTIONS

1. Do you think the death penalty is worth maintaining in American criminal justice? Why? Which justifications for punishment that were discussed in earlier chapters make sense or don't make sense to you when thinking about capital punishment?

2. Are there ways that the death penalty as practiced in the United States can be fairer? How? Are there ways that the death penalty should been restricted or regulated beyond those suggested by the Supreme Court?

3. Why do you think the forms of execution have changed so dramatically through history?

KEY TERMS

Aggravating evidence 319
American individualism 328
Bifurcated trials 318
Death-qualified jury 320

Eighth Amendment 317
Furman v. Georgia 318
Gregg v. Georgia 318
Guillotine 314

Innocence projects 326
Limiting cases 320
Long drop 315
Mitigating evidence 318

⑤SAGE edge™

Get the tools you need to sharpen your study skills. SAGE edge offers a robust online environment featuring an impressive array of free tools and resources.

Access practice quizzes, eFlashcards, video, and multimedia at edge.sagepub.com/fichtelberg

Sarah Yeh

Social workers and others work to prevent juveniles from become adult criminals. What are some effective ways to do this?

CHAPTER FOURTEEN

JUVENILE JUSTICE

Crimes committed by minors (that is people under the "age of majority"—18 years old in most states) are treated differently at almost every level of the criminal justice system. Juvenile justice is distinct for a host of reasons, but primarily it is because young people are believed to lack the capacity to truly control their behavior or to understand the consequences of their actions. If they're not wholly responsible for their conduct, the thinking goes, then they should not be fully blamed for their misdeeds or be punished like adult offenders. This benefits young offenders because their punishments are often lighter than those faced by adults, but it can also work against them, as juveniles often have fewer rights and privileges in our society. Juveniles cannot buy alcohol if they are under 21 or drive a car if they are under 16, and a whole host of other behaviors are off limits for young people. Because of the youth of the offenders, juvenile justice is very different from adult criminal justice, and this affects everything from how children are policed to how they are prosecuted in court to how they are punished: Overall, the system is much more interested in correcting and helping juveniles than punishing them (at least in theory).

To reflect the philosophical differences of juvenile justice, experts use entirely different terminology to talk about juvenile offenders and the juvenile justice system. For example, juveniles are not called criminals, they are **delinquents**, and rather than having been found guilty of a crime, they are "adjudged a delinquent minor." A delinquent act usually would be a crime if it were committed by somebody over the age of 18, but there are crimes that only juveniles can commit, too. The juvenile corrections system refers to juvenile detention centers or juvenile hall and even sometimes calls detention centers "schools." Although juvenile crime is investigated by the police like any other crime, the sentence is usually more focused on rehabilitation and is referred to as a **disposition**. The entire model is premised around the idea that the system should help juveniles rather than punish them.

Similarly, most juvenile offenders are typically handled by a set of institutions separate from those for adults. Juveniles are often under the care of social services departments rather than a department of justice. When juvenile justice matters are handled within a criminal justice system, they are usually under a division of juvenile justice that is separate from the adult department. For example, the Oregon Youth Authority is an independent body that works with several different criminal justice and social services departments within the state government to handle juvenile offenders (see Figure 14.1).

Just as with capital punishment, there is an entirely different track for cases involving juveniles—and just as death is different, so are kids.

Delinquent:
A juvenile who is found responsible for an offense.

Disposition:
A "sentence" in a juvenile case.

Figure 14.1   Oregon's Juvenile Justice System

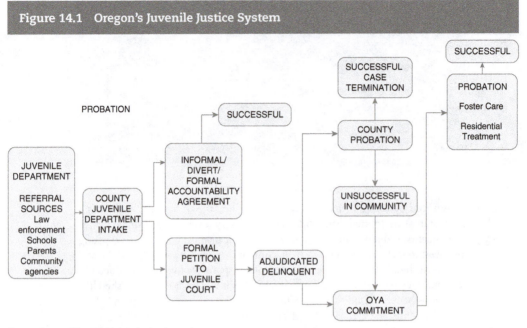

Source: State of Oregon Youth Authority, n.d.

Young people who commit crimes are unlikely to become adults who commit crime. As we saw in the discussion of life course criminology in Chapter 2, criminal behavior committed early in an individual's life does not often lead to a lifetime of criminality. Many criminals stop their antisocial behavior as they transition to adults—usually in the latter half of their 20s (see Figure 14.2).

Young people in general, and young men in particular, often engage in aggressive, destructive, and frankly stupid behavior in their youth that they find to be highly embarrassing or troubling when they become adults. Now social media means that stupid things that young people say or do online can hang over their heads for the rest of their lives—ruining their educational opportunities and their career ambitions. As they age, experience more of the world, build more ties to those around them (career, marriage, family, home ownership, etc.), they are far less likely to engage in lawbreaking or otherwise dangerous activities. They have matured and often have a lot more to lose. The juvenile justice system seeks to prevent youth from harming themselves or from continuing on a path that leads to an adult criminal career.

Critics have identified a **school-to-prison pipeline** that effectively funnels young people, particularly minorities, into the criminal justice system. Not only do social factors such as poverty and family instability incline young people to become criminals, but the way that young people are treated by schools, the police, and other authority figures effectively prepares them for a life of crime. As one study put it,

> Many [young people] will be taught by unqualified teachers, tested on material they never reviewed, held back a grade, placed in restrictive special education programs, repeatedly suspended, and banished to alternative out-placements

School-to-prison pipeline: The view that schools prepare some students for criminality through excessive rules, unfair treatment, and unnecessarily harsh discipline.

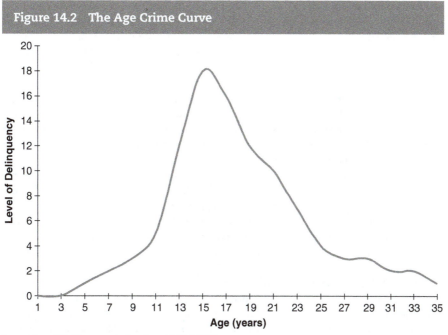

Figure 14.2 The Age Crime Curve

Source: Reprinted by permission from DeLisi, 2015.

before dropping or getting pushed out of school altogether. Without a safety net, the likelihood that these same youths will wind up arrested and incarcerated increases sharply. (Wald & Losen, 2003, p. 11)

School discipline practices such as metal detectors, zero tolerance policies, suspensions, and detentions correlate with later criminality and in fact can cause young people to become more likely to engage in crime (Hirschfield, 2009, p. 40). Students effectively learn that they are criminals because they are treated like criminals by their educational institutions. While schools and other institutions are intended to promote success for young people, they can make it more difficult for poor and minority students and even push them toward a life of crime.

THE HISTORY OF CHILDHOOD CRIME

Learning Objective 14.1—Explain the historical context leading up to the modern juvenile justice system.

The idea that young people should be treated differently from adults is a relatively modern idea—until the 18th century, the two were treated the same for the most part. Early experts believed that from infancy to the age of seven, children could not be punished criminally for alleged crimes, but between the ages of seven and fourteen, it was thought that children were capable of a certain amount of moral choice and thus could be subject to criminal punishment. As one 14th-century English legal expert put it, in this period *malitia supplet aetatem*: "Malice supplies the age." That is, if the evidence against juvenile offenders supported the belief that they were both cunning and aware of the nature of their acts (such as by hiding evidence or lying to authorities), then they could be held liable for their misdeeds, even to the point of execution (Kean, 1937). Without this sort of evidence, they would most likely not be prosecuted.

There were several changes in the 19th century that led to the creation of the juvenile justice system. Social reformers believed the harsh punishments given to young people were cruel, and they organized for social change. The Child Savers were a loose movement of largely female activists who stressed redemption and the prevention or delinquency through early identification and intervention, training, and education (Platt, 1977). In New York, the Society for the Prevention of Juvenile Delinquency began to push for the creation of a distinct juvenile justice system to deal with children, separating these offenders from the more dangerous adults and promoting juvenile reform. The first juvenile courts were used in 1899 in Cook County, Illinois (American Bar Association Division for Public Education, n.d.). Slowly, new institutions developed to reflect a belief that children were not the same as adults and that even those who break the law deserve assistance and support of some kind rather than simple punishment.

In the 19th century, it became common to send convicted juvenile offenders to houses of refuge where they would be put to work. Later, when educating children became mandatory, juvenile offenders were placed in *reform schools*, many of which were run by private philanthropic organizations. The House of Refuge in New York (1824) and the Chicago Reform School (1855) were early examples. They sought to provide delinquent children with an opportunity to lead a productive life, running on a strict program of discipline enforced by corporal punishment:

> At sunrise, the children are warned, by the ringing of a bell, to rise from their beds. Each child makes his own bed, and steps forth, on a signal, into the Hall. They then proceed, in perfect order, to the Wash Room. Thence, they are marched to parade in the yard, and undergo an examination as to their dress and cleanliness; after which they attend morning prayer. (Bremner, 1971, p. 688)

While they may have been created with the best of intentions, these institutions developed a reputation for being overcrowded, dirty, and abusive toward the children they held. Nonetheless modern juvenile corrections institutions (a.k.a. "juvenile hall" or "juvie") were developed from these earlier institutions.

These early efforts to distinguish between adults and children did not have the benefit of modern neuroscience and developmental psychology. In more recent history, researchers have learned a great deal about the differences between the brains of young people (even college-aged people) and those belonging to adults, much of which can help us to understand juvenile delinquency. While the brain is an immensely complicated organ, experts believe that young people are neurologically prone to emotional responses to situations, because adolescent brains have not completely developed. "Differential development of brain regions can lead to an imbalance in their activity, with greater reliance on emotional regions than on prefrontal control regions during adolescence as compared to both childhood and adulthood" (Cohen & Casey, 2014). Further, psychologists believe that

Malitia supplet aetatem: "Malice supplies the age"— An approach used in earlier periods; juveniles could be convicted of crimes if their acts showed that they understood what they were doing.

Houses of refuge: Early forms of juvenile incarceration.

young people are particularly prone to the influence of their peers—making risky behavior more likely (Steinberg & Monahan, 2007). While these neurological and psychological differences don't explain everything about juvenile delinquency, they help us understand why people are more prone to criminal activity when they are young and why many abandon it as they mature.

Our new understandings regarding the developmental differences between adolescents and adults have been reflected in modern law in different ways. While executing juveniles was never very common in American history, it has been practiced at various times. In 1652, Thomas Graunger was executed in Plymouth, Massachusetts, at the age of 16—he was the first juvenile executed in the American colonies. George Stinney, a 14-year-old African American boy, was executed by electrocution in 1944 for the murder of two white girls after a one-day trial. (His conviction was vacated 70 years later.) In 2005, the Supreme Court ruled in *Roper v. Simmons* that only those who were over 18 when they committed their crimes could be executed, and in the 2012 case *Miller v. Alabama*, the court ruled, "Mandatory life without parole for a juvenile precludes consideration of his chronological age and its hallmark features—among them, immaturity, impetuosity, and failure to appreciate risks and consequences," and therefore violates the Eighth Amendment's ban on cruel and unusual punishment. As our knowledge regarding the cognitive and sociological differences between juveniles and adults develops, the criminal justice system responds.

JUVENILE JUSTICE

Learning Objective 14.2—List the legal, law enforcement, and courtroom aspects of juvenile justice.

Juveniles can commit all the same crimes that adults can: Robbery, murder, rape, et cetera. In addition, there is an entirely separate set of offenses that *only* apply to minors. These crimes belong to a legal category known as **status offenses**. Status offenses are crimes that can only be committed by certain types of people. Most status offenses for adults—such as the status offense of being a gang member or being a drug addict—are unconstitutional, but the same rules don't apply for minors. For juveniles, the most common status offenses are these:

1. Truancy—Missing school repeatedly without an appropriate excuse.

2. Consuming alcohol while under 21.

3. Violating curfew—Staying out past a designated time without a guardian.

4. Runaways—Leaving home without permission for an extended period.

5. Incorrigibility—Children are required to obey their legal guardians. If they fail to do so repeatedly and act in dangerous and disobedient ways, the court can find them **incorrigible** and recommend intervention.

While few of these would lead to any kind of detention or incarceration, they are still offenses that only juveniles can commit.

Status offenses: Acts that would otherwise be legal except for the type of person who is committing them (examples: juveniles drinking while under age or being out past a curfew).

Incorrigible: Juveniles who are considered by a juvenile court to be nonreformable.

Policing Juveniles and Early Intervention

As it does with other parts of the criminal justice system, law enforcement deals with juveniles quite differently than it does adult offenders. Specialized juvenile units, staffed largely by female officers, were created in the professionalism era to help address juvenile problems. Some of the first female officers ("police matrons") oversaw juveniles. Later, during the era of community policing, police departments participated in a variety of community engagement programs, such as police athletic leagues, to help connect with youth. Also, officers were encouraged to play a more active role regarding children in the community, working with social services departments to help handle youth who misbehave.

On the streets, officers generally have a great deal of discretion in how they handle juvenile offenders. Often, if the misconduct isn't serious, officers will simply return children to their guardians, saving formal criminal justice procedures for the most serious offenses. The police are often the first people on the scene when children are abandoned, endangered, or abused by their parents, leaving them with some difficult decisions. Experts have pointed to a few factors that influence police discretion toward juveniles, including the attitude of the juvenile herself, the nature of the violation, the preferences of the individuals who called the police, and the perceived ability of the parents to deal with the situation appropriately (Cox, Allen, & Hanser, 2017).

In the 1985 case of *New Jersey v. T. L. O.*, the Supreme Court addressed the question of whether schools have a right to search students without probable cause as required by the Fourth Amendment. In this case, two high school students were suspected by their vice principal of smoking cigarettes in the restroom. The principal searched the purse belonging to one of them and found marijuana, a pipe, and indications that the student had been involved in drug dealing. The court ruled that schools are different from other contexts, and therefore administrators or law enforcement officers do not need probable cause to conduct a search of a student. Rather, they only need to show that there "are reasonable grounds for suspecting that the search will turn up evidence that the student has violated or is violating either the law or the rules of the school." Thus, the search of the student's purse was constitutional even though the vice principal lacked probable case.

One way that law enforcement bodies have sought to address juvenile delinquency is through *early intervention*. Intervention programs seek to disrupt the track that some juveniles follow from juvenile delinquency to adult criminality. Intervention programs are designed to address both problem behavior among juveniles and the root causes of delinquent behavior. These programs can include classroom behavior management programs, mentoring for youth, antibullying programs, and conflict resolution programs (Loeber, Farrington, & Petechuk, 2003). By providing positive role models, structured and supervised activities, and opportunities to spot potentially troubled children, these programs can catch problem behaviors before they rise to the level of criminality (Burns et al., 2003). Much of this work is not carried out by traditional law enforcement officers, but rather by departments of family services and social workers of various kinds. It is usually only when delinquent behavior becomes serious that law enforcement steps in directly.

There have been several law enforcement programs designed to address juvenile delinquency and misbehavior. One well-known one is the DARE (Drug Abuse Resistance Education) program. DARE is an antidrug curriculum taught in elementary and high schools around the country that is led by police officers. Begun in the 1980s by the Los Angeles Police Department, DARE puts officers in schools to explain the dangers of drug

New Jersey v. T. L. O.: A Supreme Court decision that juveniles may be searched if officials have a reasonable belief that they are involved in illegal activity.

use and to help students resist the peer pressure that leads some to use drugs. Critics have argued that it is, for the most part, a waste of millions of dollars, as it has no discernible impact on drug use among young people (Cima, 2015).

One trend that has emerged over the last few decades has been putting police officers in schools to help handle student misbehavior. These programs developed in part because of a fear that students were becoming increasingly violent, and in part because of a fear of violent school shootings, such as the shootings in Columbine, Colorado, in 1999 that killed 15 students. Placing officers in schools would keep students safe from dangers both inside and outside the school. These officers, known as *student resource officers* (SROs) receive special training to deal with juveniles and spend much of the day patrolling the halls or dealing with student conflicts.

School discipline is incredibly difficult to maintain, and there is a great deal of public fear surrounding school shootings. On the other hand, critics have argued that SROs create a "police state" atmosphere in schools that are already replete with locked doors, security cameras, and metal detectors, while defenders have suggested that if used appropriately they can help build trust between young people and police officers. Even though SROs are usually given additional training to help them work with young people, they have been accused of treating behavior that would otherwise be treated as a simple matter of school discipline as a crime (Theriot, 2009). That is, at one time a fight between students was a problem for a principal to address, but with the deployment of police officers in schools, it is far more likely to be treated as a crime, which can have long-term effects for kids who have made a mistake typical of their age (Kupchik, 2012). This is particularly the case with minority students, who often perceive these officers as unfair or biased (Kupchik & Ellis, 2008). The fact that there was an SRO on duty during the 2018 Stoneman Douglas High School shooting in Parkland, Florida, that killed 17 who was unable to do anything to stop the killing has only fueled this skepticism.

WHERE DO I FIT IN?

JUVENILE CASE MANAGERS

There are many ways that college graduates can work in the juvenile justice system, ranging from social work to juvenile probation to police and corrections. Each of these jobs can provide a rewarding experience helping young people avoid serious trouble. Perhaps the most significant of these is the juvenile case manager.

Juvenile case managers are professionals who work with juvenile offenders and their families in a variety of ways during different phases of the juvenile justice process. In many ways the title is a general term for social workers who work with juveniles who are involved in the criminal justice system. Sometimes they serve as a liaison between the court, the juvenile, and her family, helping the family understand the procedures that their child is facing and communicating the court's decisions to the family. Other times they help juveniles find the necessary services to help them get their lives back on track, including school counseling, psychological services, and drug/alcohol dependency treatment. Managers can work in juvenile detention centers, helping

(Continued)

Juvenile Courts

In most states, juveniles are prosecuted in special juvenile courts, separate from the adult system. In superficial ways they resemble the adult model. They have judges, prosecutors, and defense attorneys. There are arraignments, hearings, examinations, cross-examinations, and either a disposition/conviction or an acquittal, but the underlying approach is very different. Juvenile courts rely on a **therapeutic model** of justice aimed at helping the juvenile rather than convicting and punishing her. As a result, social workers and other actors such as court-appointed special advocates (CASAs—volunteers who represent the child's interests at trial) are more heavily involved in the court than they would be in adult criminal cases. Trials are held behind closed doors and usually much quicker than adult trials, and judges are often granted a great deal more discretion in determining the appropriate way to deal with a juvenile.

Again, there is different terminology to describe the phases of a juvenile case. Charges are filed through a *petition*—the juvenile equivalent of a criminal complaint or indictment. Then, rather than a trial, there is an **adjudicatory hearing**, where the charges are examined by the judge to determine whether the juvenile should be adjudicated delinquent (found guilty). In its ruling *In re Gault* (1967), the Supreme Court determined that juveniles charged with a crime had many, though not all, of the same rights that an adult defendant would have—those due process rights set out in the Fourteenth Amendment. This includes a right to an attorney as well as a right to confront witnesses. While they don't have all of the traditional rights given to adults (because technically they are not facing criminal punishment), they nonetheless have many of them. For example, juveniles do not have the right to a jury, though some states may allow jury trials for juveniles under certain circumstances.

The penal phase of a juvenile trial also resembles that phase of the adult system in many significant respects. What would be a sentencing hearing in adult court is referred to as a *disposition hearing* in juvenile court, and the judge decides the appropriate response to the juvenile offenders, including probation, community service, fines, treatment, or incarceration. Often a juvenile will be expected to explain to the court why her acts were wrong and how she will change her behavior going forward. Judges in juvenile cases typically have significantly more discretion than do judges in adult cases, and a judge can sentence the juvenile to probation, a detention center, or whatever sentence she believes will best help the juvenile rehabilitate.

Figure 14.3 is an example of one state's (Pennsylvania's) juvenile justice process from arrest through incarceration.

Therapeutic model: The approach of most juvenile justice institutions, emphasizing rehabilitating rather than punishing juvenile offenders.

Adjudicatory hearing: A "trial" for juveniles to determine whether they are responsible for an offense.

In re Gault: A Supreme Court case that gave juveniles due process rights during a hearing.

Figure 14.3 Pennsylvania's Juvenile Justice Flowchart

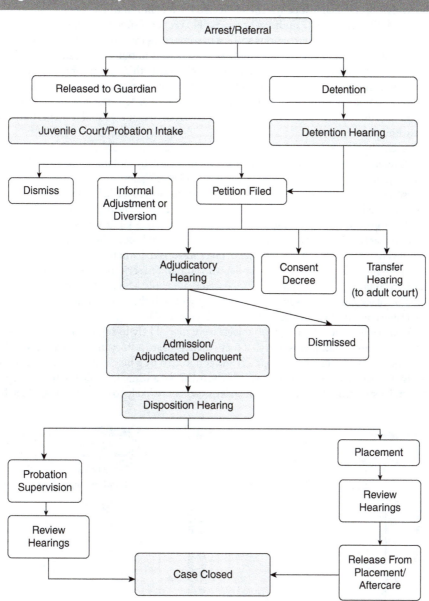

Source: Pennsylvania Council of Chief Juvenile Probation Officers, 2012.

Note: A consent decree in this context is an agreement regarding probation between the prosecutor and the juvenile.

Who Gets to Be a Child? Race and Juvenile Justice

The American criminal justice system has decided that children who break the law should be treated differently than adult lawbreakers. This reflects society's belief that children are less accountable for their actions and are in some ways innocent, and therefore harsh punishments are inappropriate for young offenders. But in our society, sharply divided along racial and ethnic lines like it is, not every child gets this benefit of the doubt, and not every child gets to be innocent. Or more accurately, not every juvenile gets the benefits of being considered a child by much of the public. As is the case in many other aspects of criminal justice, African American children are not treated as generously as their white peers.

Psychological research has shown that Americans tend to evaluate the behavior of white juveniles differently than they do black juveniles, usually looking at black youth more negatively. In one experiment in which two groups of participants were given an account of a gruesome crime committed by a minor, participants showed a marked racial bias in how they responded (Rattan, Levine, Dweck, & Eberhardt, 2012). The only difference between the subject groups was that some were told that the juvenile killer was black, and others were told that the offender was white. Then, they were asked about their feelings regarding harsh juvenile sentences more generally: They were asked whether they supported the sentence of life without parole for juveniles who committed serious crimes. (Psychologists call this technique *priming*.) The results showed that people who read about a crime committed by black juveniles responded more harshly overall than those who read about the same crime committed by white children (see Figure 14.4).

After reading these stories, the subjects were more likely to support harsher punishments for juvenile delinquents overall if they had first heard a story involving a black child. That is, subjects who had read about a crime committed by a black juvenile became more punitive toward all children than those who heard about a white juvenile offender. A separate, similar study showed that black juveniles were "more likely to be mistaken as older, be

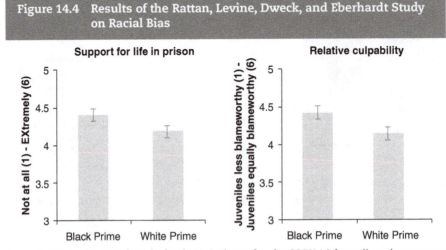

Figure 14.4 Results of the Rattan, Levine, Dweck, and Eberhardt Study on Racial Bias

Source: Rattan, Levine, Dweck, & Eberhardt, 2012. Licensed under CC BY 4.0, https://creativecommons.org/licenses/by/4.0/.

perceived as guilty and face police violence if accused of a crime" (Goff, 2014). When we see black juveniles commit crimes, we respond harshly and are less likely to write off the incident as a youthful mistake.

Given this pervasive prejudice against African American youth and the social and economic disadvantages facing many black families, it is unsurprising that African American juvenile offenders are treated more harshly throughout the criminal justice system and are overly represented in juvenile corrections. The Sentencing Project, a nonprofit research institute, sorted through years of Justice Department crime data to show that throughout the criminal justice system, African American children are treated more harshly than whites (The Sentencing Project, 2017). Even though African Americans are about 16% of the total juvenile population, they are 38% of the population of juvenile detention facilities across the United States (National Council on Crime and Delinquency, 2007). The systemic bias against African Americans in the criminal justice system is deeply rooted and even works against black children.

SOME STATISTICS...

Juvenile Delinquency

As with adult crimes, there has been a marked decline in juvenile crimes overall over the last few decades (see Figure 14.5). The high point of juvenile crime was 1996, and then there was a 70% decline over the next two decades.

The most common offenses committed by juveniles are assault and theft, though property crimes are the largest general category (see Figure 14.6). Drug offenses are a surprisingly small number of offenses committed by juveniles.

On the other hand, the majority of offenses were committed by boys, and of those, white boys were the largest racial group (see Figure 14.7).

Detention is relatively rare in the world of juvenile justice (see Figure 14.8). Most juveniles

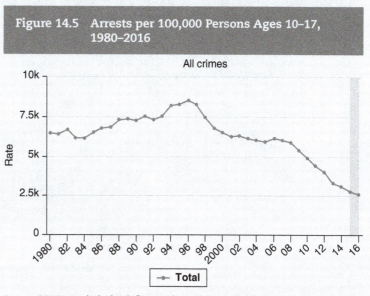

Figure 14.5   Arrests per 100,000 Persons Ages 10–17, 1980–2016

All crimes

Source: OJJDP Statistical Briefing Book. Online. Available: http://www.ojjdp.gov/ojstatbb/crime/JAR_Display.asp?ID=qa05201. December 06, 2017.

(Continued)

found delinquent are given probation or community corrections of some kind. Only about a quarter receive some form of incarceration. This makes sense given the generally therapeutic approach to juvenile justice discussed above.

Figure 14.6   Delinquency Cases by Category, 2016

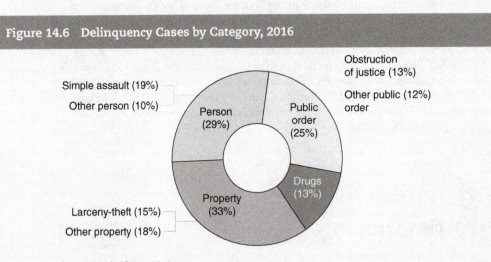

Source: Puzzanchera & Hockenberry, 2018.

Figure 14.7   Delinquency Caseload by Age, Race, and Ethnicity, 2016

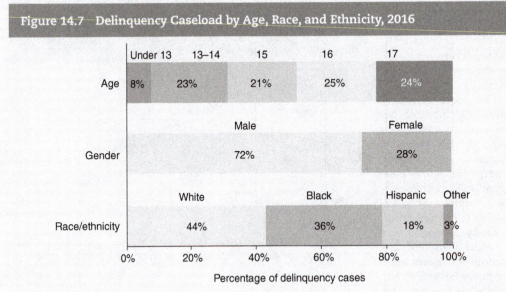

Source: Puzzanchera & Hockenberry, 2018.

Notes: Other race includes American Indian/Alaskan Natives, Asian/Pacific Islanders, and youth of unknown race. Numbers may not sum to total due to rounding.

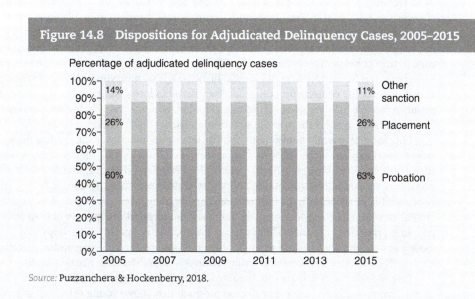

Figure 14.8   Dispositions for Adjudicated Delinquency Cases, 2005–2015

Percentage of adjudicated delinquency cases

Source: **Puzzanchera & Hockenberry, 2018.**

JUVENILE CORRECTIONS

Learning Objective 14.3—Identify the different forms of juvenile corrections.

Juveniles are rarely placed in prison with adult offenders, though they can be transferred to an adult facility after they become adults (or sometimes a few years later). Juvenile correctional institutions or youth detention centers are in some ways similar to adult correctional institutions, though there is usually a good deal more emphasis on rehabilitation. Almost all juvenile offenders are incarcerated in state- or county-level correctional institutions, where almost all juveniles are prosecuted. One study reported that in 2016 there were only 26 juveniles in federal custody (Schwartzapfel, 2016). This is in part because of the types of crimes that are federal offenses are limited to adult offenders and, as a result, the only juvenile offenses that fall under federal jurisdiction are those committed on Native American tribal lands and in Washington, D.C. (Schwartzapfel, 2016). As we saw earlier in this chapter, most juveniles are placed in some form of community corrections after they are adjudicated delinquent.

There are different types of juvenile detention facilities, and they vary from state to state. Juvenile detention centers run the gamut from supervised group homes to full-scale prison-like conditions for the most serious and violent offenders. For example, the state of Kansas has 11 different juvenile detention facilities located in different parts of the state, all of which are run by county governments and hold juveniles for a short term, up to 31 days. Like all youth and childcare facilities, they are licensed by the Kansas Department of Health and Environment. The statewide juvenile detention facility, the Kansas Juvenile Correctional Complex, and the affiliated girls' institution, are run by the state's Department of Corrections Juvenile Services Division. When juveniles arrive there, they are held in a classification unit (RDU—"reception and diagnostic unit") until they are placed within the general juvenile population. Through weekly evaluations with a case manager, privileges can be either granted or revoked. There are also several privately run group homes in the state to help nonviolent juvenile offenders. Similarly, California has several different types of facilities run by the Division of Juvenile Justice (DJJ) with varying degrees of intensity as well as a wildlife conservation camp for low-risk offenders. County police departments maintain juvenile halls for lesser offenders and for kids awaiting trial. Each state is different, but they all seek to tailor the juvenile system to a variety of different offenders.

One form of juvenile punishment that has become popular over the last few decades is *boot camp* (also known as intensive incarceration programs). These programs were first developed in the tough-on-crime era of the 1980s, and they are modeled on traditional military camps, often including military-style uniforms, ranks, and strict disciplinary systems. (There are adult boot camps, too.) Further, they often use vigorous exercise to rehabilitate juvenile offenders in the belief that strict physical discipline will help young people get their lives in order. These approaches are often popular with groups who promote a get-tough policy toward juvenile offenders—but research has suggested that they are largely ineffective at reducing juvenile recidivism rates (Meade & Steiner, 2010).

Juvenile offenders can also participate in a variety of community corrections programs. Every state has a juvenile probation program that allows young offenders to avoid incarceration by submitting to regular supervision, including drug tests, school visits, and electronic monitoring. The programs can be of varying intensity, and while most juvenile probation officers are unarmed, they can work with either local police or special probation agents trained to deal with more difficult juvenile offenders. Many juvenile probation officers find their jobs a rewarding way to help at-risk youth and prevent these kids from a life in and out of the adult criminal justice system.

There are some important restrictions on sentencing juvenile offenders—particularly around JLWOP (juvenile life without parole).[1] In 2003, 16-year-old Terrence Jamar Graham was convicted of participating in a series of armed robberies while on parole from an earlier conviction for armed burglary and assault. (He had been charged as an adult for the earlier offense.) As the judge explained at his sentencing hearing,

> If I can't do anything to help you, if I can't do anything to get you back on the right path, then I have to start focusing on the community and trying to protect the community from your actions. And, unfortunately, that is where we are today is [sic] I don't see where I can do anything to help you any further. You've evidently decided this is the direction you're going to take in life, and it's unfortunate that you made that choice.

Graham was thereby sentenced to life imprisonment without the possibility of parole. However, the Supreme Court overturned the conviction, and in *Graham v. Florida* (2010) ruled that juveniles cannot be sentenced to life imprisonment without the possibility of parole. As Justice Kennedy put it in his opinion,

Intensive incarceration programs: "Boot camp" programs for juvenile and adult offenders.

JLWOP: Juvenile life without parole.

---

[1] As we discussed in the previous chapter, the Supreme Court ruled in *Roper v. Simmons* that juveniles could not be given the death penalty.

A State is not required to guarantee eventual freedom to a juvenile offender convicted of a nonhomicide crime. What the State must do, however, is give defendants like Graham some meaningful opportunity to obtain release based on demonstrated maturity and rehabilitation.

The case of *Miller v. Alabama* (2012) expanded the ruling in *Graham* to include a ban on *mandatory* life without parole for juveniles who kill. However, as of this writing, it is still constitutional to sentence a juvenile to life in prison without parole, provided the judge is given adequate discretion when giving a sentence. By banning mandatory JLWOP sentences, *Miller* allows judges to consider the age and unique experiences of juvenile offenders, many of whom come from troubled homes. One report from The Sentencing Project found that 79% of these juveniles reported witnessing violence at home, and 46.9% experienced physical abuse, including 79.5% of girls (Nellis, 2012). At present there are approximately 2,100 juveniles serving life sentences in the United States, 42% of whom are African American despite being only 23% of juveniles arrested for homicide.

WHAT WOULD YOU DO?

Helping a Young Offender

You are a teacher teaching 10th grade. One student in your class, Megan, has recently given you cause for concern. You know that she comes from a family that struggles to make ends meet—she often skips meals and has confided to you that her family has been homeless several times in her life, living in shelters or with friends. Despite these challenges, she's generally been a good student who is respectful, works hard, and receives good grades. You like Megan and believe that she has a great deal of potential in the future. You could see her overcoming her background and succeeding in college and beyond.

All of that has seemed to change lately. Megan has been coming to school with a new phone, new clothes, and a very different attitude. Her grades are still good, but she seems very distracted in the classroom. Her phone is always going off, and she's suddenly become very popular among her fellow students, who are constantly trying to get her attention before, after, and sometimes during class.

You're almost certain that Megan has been selling drugs. She's denied it to you, but all the signs are there. Students have made vague comments in coded language about getting or buying things from her after school. In class, you saw her looking through a list of what you think are code names with dollar amounts next to them. You thought you saw a glimpse of a small glass pipe for smoking pot in her bag as she was putting her books away.

Your school has a zero-tolerance policy toward drugs on campus, and the principal has become suspicious about Megan. The principal has told you that she will be searching Megan's locker soon with the police, and if there are indications that she is involved in drug trafficking, she will probably be expelled and charged by the police. Arrest could lead to some serious trouble for her, derail her academic career, and possibly affect her family life. On the other hand, it might benefit her to get arrested by getting her some help. Who knows?

What would you do? Would you try to warn Megan about the search? Would you let the police search her locker and hope for the best? Given what you've read, what do you think would happen? How do you think Megan's race would affect the outcome in this situation?

SPECIAL CASES

Learning Objective 14.4—Discuss the subjects of infancy, transfer, and parental liability.

Very Young Offenders

In many states there is also a rule of infancy, which prevents very young children from being charged for criminal activity. The age is set by the states, though not all states choose to set one. The lowest age of responsibility is six in North Carolina, while several states set the bar at eleven years old. Thirty-three states have no lower age limit for prosecutions and so could (conceivably) charge an infant with a crime—though that is very unlikely (Juvenile Justice, Geography, Policy, Practice & Statistics, n.d.).

Transfer to Adult Court

Some juvenile offenders can be tried as adults rather than as juveniles and are processed through the criminal justice system as described in the previous chapters. The technical way to put this is to say that their cases are **transferred** to an adult court. Some states have laws that require certain juvenile cases to be transferred to an adult court; in other cases prosecutors may request it for specific reasons. This is usually for particularly violent offenses or if the offender is over the age of 16 when she commits the crime. In many states, prosecutors have a great deal of freedom in determining whether to transfer juvenile offenders to adult courts. Some states even allow juvenile court judges to sentence young offenders to juvenile incarceration followed by an adult sentence (Podkopacz & Feld, 2001). This is often done through a **waiver**, that is, a document that certifies that the offender is to be tried as an adult.

Offenders can fight these transfers to adult court if they wish—but they may not always want to, as there are some advantages to being tried as an adult. Juvenile offenders have fewer rights in a juvenile court (for example, few states allow for juries in juvenile courts), and young people may face more sympathetic judges and juries in an adult court. On the other hand, the stakes are much higher in adult court, and if offenders are convicted there, they will probably face more serious punishment. Juvenile cases are not public, while adult cases are. Further, it is usually much more difficult to have an adult criminal record expunged. If the juvenile offender is sentenced as an adult, she will spend much of her time up to her 23rd birthday in a juvenile facility (though states vary regarding the transfer age) in what is called a **blended sentence**. At that point, she will be transferred to an adult facility to finish her sentence among adult offenders.

The Liability of Parents

Many times, when a juvenile misbehaves, our first instinct is the blame the parents. "They should have done something to prevent the kid from hurting others!" and "If the parents had been more involved, this would never have happened," are common refrains when a young person breaks the law. Though public opinion is somewhat more nuanced on the subjects, these complaints are often caught up in broader debates about parenting and the role of women in society—as conservatives often charge that moves away from

Transfer: When a juvenile case is tried in an adult court.

Waiver: A document that certifies that an offender is to be tried as an adult.

Blended sentence: A sentence imposed by a juvenile court that begins as a juvenile sentence but becomes an adult sentence after the juvenile becomes an adult.

the traditional family (two parents of different genders, with the father working and the mother staying at home to take care of the kids) has shaped crime rates (Brank & Haby, 2011; Moore, 1999; Pickett, 2017). The legal principle of *parens patriae* ("the nation as parent") was developed to justify the incarceration of juveniles whose parents were unable or unwilling to raise their children themselves.

In some cases, the law has taken this view to the extreme, holding parents legally responsible for the misconduct of their children. Most states have parental liability laws in some form that allow a court to fine parents if their kids do damage. Delaware, for example, allows parents (as well as persons who loan cars to juveniles) to be liable for damages done by a child who is driving a motor vehicle negligently, and it makes parents responsible for up to $10,000 if a child intentionally or recklessly destroys property. Some states allow parents to be criminally prosecuted if their child breaks the law, often under charges like "contributing to the delinquency of a minor." California declares that "a parent or legal guardian to any person under the age of 18 years shall have the duty to exercise reasonable care, supervision, protection, and control over their minor child." If they fail to do this, they can be sentenced to up to a year in prison. Texas has laws that make a parent criminally liable if a minor gets access to the parents' firearms and "discharges the firearm and causes death or serious bodily injury to himself or another person" (again, a misdemeanor). While these are relatively light punishments, they underline the idea that parents are to blame when children misbehave.

Blaming parents for the misdeeds of their children is common in many cultures, but this desire to make parents responsible for their children's crimes overlooks a lot about parenting—particularly in the modern world. Psychologists have cautioned that the causes of juvenile misconduct are often far more complex than just "bad parenting" or "neglectful parenting."

> Psychology research and practice has certainly demonstrated the importance of the parent-child relationship. We know that different parenting styles and attachment are related to various outcomes. But, no matter how much we know about the role parents play, we know that research cannot perfectly predict outcomes because of the innumerable other factors that influence children. And we do not know if punishing the parents would have the intended effect of reducing juvenile crime. (Brank & Haby, 2011)

Childhood and adolescence are simply too complicated to point to only one or two factors in the brain, in the family, or in society when things don't go well.

Even the most engaged and well-intentioned parents don't know what their children are up to all the time, and young people can be very skillful at concealing their activities from their parents. (Did your parents know what you were up to when you were a teenager?) After her son Dylan helped kill 12 students at Columbine High School, Susan Klebold and her husband were blamed by much of the public and by Colorado politicians for their son's crimes. She defended herself, saying that she believed her son was a typical, if introverted, young person:

> These thoughts may seem foolish in light of what we now know, but they reflect what we believed to be true about Dylan. Yes, he had filled notebook

Parens patriae ("the nation as parent"): The idea that the government may step in to take care of somebody whose family is unable or unwilling to take responsibility for her.

Parental liability laws: Laws that can make a parent civilly or criminally responsible for the misbehavior of their child.

pages with his private thoughts and feelings, repeatedly expressing profound alienation. But we'd never seen those notebooks. And yes, he'd written a school paper about a man in a black trenchcoat who brutally murders nine students. But we'd never seen that paper. . . . We didn't see the paper, or Dylan's other writings, until the police showed them to us six months after the tragedy. (Klebold, 2011)

There certainly are parents who seriously neglect their children, and this can be linked to delinquent behavior, but many parents (especially single parents) are caught up in the struggle to feed their families and put a roof over their heads.

CRIMINAL (IN)JUSTICE

The Kids for Cash Scandal

The growth of private prisons is not only a feature of the adult criminal justice system—it has also begun to influence juvenile justice too. Many juvenile services, ranging from probation services to drug rehabilitation programs to juvenile corrections, have been contracted out to private groups that operate for a profit. In Florida, for example, all 60 juvenile residential detention facilities were run by private companies under contract with the state government as of 2013 (Flannery, 2017). The money flowing to these businesses from families, insurance companies, and the government have had a profound impact on how juvenile justice is handled by the criminal justice system, causing concern among many observers.

Perhaps the worst example of the dangers regarding the privatization of juvenile justice was in Luzerne County, Pennsylvania. There, two judges, Mark Ciavarella and Michael Conahan, were convicted of receiving kickbacks for sending juvenile offenders to a privately run juvenile detention facility. In what was known as the "Kids for Cash" scandal, the judges were secretly given millions of dollars by the company to sentence juveniles to their facilities (Urbina, 2009). Many of these kids had been responsible for only minor offenses, such as stealing change from unlocked cars or shoplifting, but because the judges gained personally, they handed down lengthy sentences without mercy. One first-time offender, 17-year-old Edward Kenzakoski, committed suicide after being sentenced by one of the judges. (Sadly, Kenzakoski was innocent—his father had framed him, believing that Judge Ciavarella would straighten him out, not knowing that the judge would send him to prison to line his own pockets [Janoski, 2011].) The two judges were eventually exposed, and both received lengthy prison sentences, as did two people associated with the private correctional company, though some of these charges were recently overturned on appeal (Bohman, 2018). The state of Pennsylvania created a special commission to investigate the judges' convictions, and their victims have received millions of dollars in compensation.

In your view, is it possible to privatize juvenile corrections without the risk of cases like the Kids for Cash scandal? How could this be done? What steps could policymakers take to protect juveniles in such a system?

CHAPTER SUMMARY

This chapter has been an examination of the parallel criminal justice system that exists for young people who break the law. An entire system exists that matches the adult system in many ways, but because of the unique features of its offenders, it has some important differences. There is a much stronger emphasis on rehabilitation in lieu of punishment, and juvenile justice activities sometimes blur the line between criminal justice and social work. Given that young people often cease criminal activity when they enter adulthood (or at least by their mid- to late 20s), and there are very few career criminals who commit crimes later in life, in some ways it makes sense to focus on helping juveniles avoid the bad choices and behavioral habits that can lead to serious offenses that place them in the adult system.

Nonetheless, despite its more humane approach, we still see a lot of the same problems in the juvenile system that we saw in its adult version. Minority juveniles are disproportionately targeted just like their adult peers, leading to a racial disparity in juvenile justice that echoes into the adult system. The desire to use the police as the primary way to handle crime, here through SROs, remains, as does the idea that getting tough with lawbreakers is the best way to deal with them. Juvenile offenders may become adult offenders, or delinquency may just be a phase that some young people go through before growing up and becoming responsible adults. Finally, the profit motive can warp criminal justice responses to juveniles, placing incentives on criminal justice professionals to treat kids with inappropriate harshness. It is doubtful that, except for the most extreme cases, getting tough and cracking down on these kids is going to improve their situation in the long term.

REVIEW/DISCUSSION QUESTIONS

1. Why do young people commit more offenses than adults in your view? Is the answer social? Is it psychological? Biological?

2. Do you know people who broke the law when they were young? Why did they do it? How are they doing now? If they did change, why?

3. In what cases do you think it is acceptable to treat juveniles like adults in criminal justice? Does the type of crime matter? The way it was carried out? The age of the juvenile?

4. Is a therapeutic approach to juvenile justice the best way to handle young offenders in your opinion? Why or why not?

KEY TERMS

Adjudicatory hearing 340
Blended sentence 348
Delinquent 333
Disposition 333
Houses of refuge 336
In re Gault 340

Incorrigible 337
Intensive incarceration programs 346
JLWOP 346
Malitia supplet aetatem 336
New Jersey v. T. L. O. 338
Parens patriae 349

Parental liability laws 349
School-to-prison pipeline 334
Status offenses 337
Therapeutic model 340
Transfer 348
Waiver 348

$SAGE edge™

Get the tools you need to sharpen your study skills. SAGE edge offers a robust online environment featuring an impressive array of free tools and resources.

Access practice quizzes, eFlashcards, video, and multimedia at edge.sagepub.com/fichtelberg

GLOSSARY

Actus reus—"The bad act"—The action that constitutes the offense.

Adjudicatory hearing—A "trial" for juveniles to determine whether they are responsible for an offense.

Administrative segregation ("AdSeg")—Separating offenders from the general population of the prison. Often in solitary confinement.

Adversarial model—The criminal procedure in the Anglo-American system.

Aggravating evidence—Evidence presented to a jury that makes a crime seem more severe. Juries can use this evidence to determine whether to recommend execution.

American individualism—The common belief that people are responsible for their own conduct, independent of external circumstances.

Atavism theory—The criminological theory that sees criminal behavior as a result of holdovers from earlier, primitive forms of human life.

Authoritarian personalities—Individuals whose identity is based on ensuring the obedience and submission of everybody else they encounter, who feel a need to dominate anybody who fails to respect their authority.

Automobile exception—The rule that officers do not need a warrant to search a car but only need probable cause.

Bad apples—The theory that only a few deviant police officers cause the rest of American police to get a bad reputation.

Behavioral theory—The psychological theory that argues that criminal behavior is learned through a series of rewards and punishments.

Bench trial—A trial where the judge is both the finder of law and the finder of fact.

Bifurcated trials—Trials that are split between a guilt phase (when the defendant is either convicted or acquitted) and a penalty phase when the jury decides whether or not to recommend the death penalty.

Bill of Rights—The first ten amendments to the Constitution, spelling out the limits of the federal government's authority.

#blacklivesmatter—The movement that seeks to criticize the excessive use of force against African Americans.

Blended sentence—A sentence imposed by a juvenile court that begins as a juvenile sentence but becomes an adult sentence after the juvenile becomes an adult.

Blue wall of silence—The informal code among police officers that prevents them from reporting on abusive behaviors from their fellow officers.

Brady rule—The rule that prosecutors must share exculpatory evidence with defendants.

Burden of proof—The principle that a defendant is innocent until proven guilty.

Capital case—A case where the defendant could receive the death sentence if convicted.

Capital offenses—Offenses that merit the death penalty.

Carceral feminism—The feminist theory that the best response to crimes against women is to aggressively push for harsher punishments against those who commit these crimes.

Challenge for cause—When one side objects to a prospective juror on account of a bias.

Change of venue—A motion to move the location of a trial.

Circumstantial evidence—Evidence that requires interpretation.

Civil commitment—Holding a person who has not been convicted of a crime (or who has already served her sentence) because experts believe that she is a danger to herself or to the public.

Civil forfeiture—The police practice of seizing goods that they believe are associated with criminal activity.

Civilian review boards—Government committees that are tasked with keeping an eye on police behavior and handling complaints from the public.

Class struggle—The Marxist theory that human history is shaped by the fight for power between different economic groups (classes).

Classical criminology—Criminological theories of the enlightenment era that sought to use reason to explain and prevent criminal behavior.

Classification team—A group of experts who evaluate newly incarcerated prisoners.

Collateral consequences (of incarceration)—The effects of imprisonment that go beyond the imprisonment itself on the families of the incarcerated offender.

Common law—The legal tradition in England and the United States where courts determine the meanings of laws through a series of opinions or precedents that are binding.

Community corrections—Forms of criminal punishment that seek to keep the offender in society rather than locking her away.

Community policing—Attempts to break down barriers between the community and the police.

Conjugal visits—Unsupervised visits between prisoners and their spouses.

Corporal punishment—Punishment that causes physical pain.

Corporate crimes—Crimes committed for a company's profits (example: price fixing).

Crimes against persons—Crimes where a victim is physically harmed (examples: murder, assault, rape).

Crimes against property—Crimes that cause financial or economic harm (examples: theft, embezzlement).

Crimes against public order—Crimes that undermine society's stability and make it a less pleasant place to live (examples: loitering, public drunkenness).

Crimes against the state—Crimes that hurt a government (examples: espionage, treason).

Criminal justice policies—Ways that societies seek to prevent crime through laws, policing, and other programs.

Criminal justice system—The various organizations that respond to criminal behavior: courts, judges, police, et cetera, whose purpose is to fight crime.

Critical race theory—The view that American society is structurally unequal and that minorities are targeted by the government in general and by the criminal justice system in particular.

Cronyism—A system in which politicians give government jobs, including policing jobs, to their political allies.

Cross-examination—The examination of a witness from the opposing side during a trial.

Dark figure of crime—Crime that does not show up in traditional crime research.

Death-qualified jury—A jury that could impose the death penalty if they found it appropriate.

Delinquent—A juvenile who is found responsible for an offense.

Differential association theory—The criminological theory that argues that criminal behaviors and outlooks are determined by those that we spend time with.

Directed verdict—A motion to end a trial after the prosecution has presented its case.

Dirty Harry problem—The problem that the public often wants police officers to catch criminals and often approves of illegal means for doing so.

Discovery—Efforts by defendants to see material held by the prosecutor.

Disposition—A "sentence" in a juvenile case.

Diversion—Programs that attempt to keep offenders out of prison by providing services and guidance.

Double jeopardy—Putting somebody on trial twice for the same crime. It is not allowed in American criminal justice.

Driving while black (DWB)—A slang term that refers to the racial profiling of African American drivers.

Drug court—Courts that are set up to deal with nonviolent offenders with drug problems, offering counseling and monitoring instead of punishment.

Eighth Amendment—The constitutional amendment that bans "cruel and unusual punishment" among other things.

Excessive force—The use of too much force by the police or the use of force unnecessarily.

Exculpatory evidence—Evidence that tends to show that the defendant is not guilty.

Exile—Punishing offenders by kicking them out of society.

Felony—Serious offenses, usually punished by over one year of incarceration.

Feminist criminology—The criminological theory rooted in the view that women are treated unjustly in society and that these inequalities are reflected in criminal justice.

Finder of fact—The person or group that determines the guilt or innocence of a defendant. Usually the jury.

Finder of law—The person at the trial who is officially authorized to determine what the law says.

Flying while Muslim (FWM)—A slang term that refers to the profiling of people who appear to be Muslims at airports.

Frankpledge system—Policing system in medieval Europe that relied on locals to police each other.

Fruit of the poisonous tree—The principle that, if evidence is gathered unlawfully, then any evidence that is gathered as a result of this evidence is not admissible in court.

Furman v. Georgia—A 1972 Supreme Court ruling that argued that the death penalty (as it was then practiced) was too arbitrary to be constitutional.

General population ("genpop" or GP)—The main part of the prison where most offenders are kept.

Grass eaters—Corrupt officers who accept bribes if they are offered to them but do not actively seek bribes.

Green criminology—The field of criminology that studies environmental crimes.

Gregg v. Georgia—A 1976 Supreme Court ruling that reinstated the death penalty in the United States.

Guillotine—A device created in France to ensure a quick beheading.

Hands-off doctrine—The (now abandoned) legal doctrine that believed that courts should let prison officials run prisons in whatever way these officials deemed appropriate.

Hate crimes—Crimes motivated by antipathy toward a group (example: gay bashing).

Hearsay—Evidence that a person overheard from another person.

Hierarchy rule—The practice of the Uniform Crime Report of only counting the most serious crime in its measures.

Homeland security era—The transformation of policing after the September 11, 2001, attacks. Included a greater emphasis on fighting terrorism and a militarization of local police forces.

Hostile witness—A witness for the opposition in a trial.

Houses of refuge—Early forms of juvenile incarceration.

Humonetarianism—Limiting the number of people imprisoned because it's too expensive for the government, not because it is morally right.

Ideology—In Marxism, the view that the beliefs and values of a society reflect the interests of the dominant class.

Impeachment—The process where public officials are removed from office by Congress or state legislators for improper conduct.

In re Gault—A Supreme Court case that gave juveniles due process rights during a hearing.

Inchoate crimes—Crimes that have yet to lead to any real harm, such as attempt, solicitation, and conspiracy.

Incorrigible—Juveniles who are considered by a juvenile court to be nonreformable.

Indeterminate sentencing—Prison sentences that do not have a definite end date or can be ended early for good behavior.

Inmate code—The informal social rules governing prisoner conduct.

Innocence projects—Groups that research criminal convictions that they believe are wrong and should be overturned.

Institutionalization—The effect of long-term incarceration that leaves inmates unable to function outside of the prison's structure.

Intensive incarceration programs—"Boot camp" programs for juvenile and adult offenders.

Intersectionality—The critical approach that seeks to understand how different inequalities (race, class, gender) interact.

JLWOP—Juvenile life without parole.

Judicial activism—A term used to criticize judges who are believed to make legal decisions based on their political views rather than on the law.

Juris doctorate (JD)—The official name for a law degree.

Knapp Commission—An investigative body created in the wake of Frank Serpico's revelations regarding corruption in the NYPD.

Labeling theory—The theory that says that criminal behavior is often a result of society labelling individuals as criminals.

Learning theory—The belief that our behavior is learned from observing others.

Limiting cases—Supreme Court cases that restrict the types of cases in which the death penalty can be applied.

Long drop—A method for hanging convicted criminals that ensures a quick death by breaking the neck of the condemned.

Malitia supplet aetatem—("malice supplies the age")—An approach used in earlier periods; juveniles could be convicted of crimes if their acts showed that they understood what they were doing.

Mann Act—The federal law that made it a federal crime to transport women across state lines for "immoral purposes." Often used to target minorities.

Marxism—The social theory formulated by Karl Marx that views society as structured by conflicts between economic groups or classes.

Meat eaters—Officers who actively seek money or other bribes while on duty.

Megan's Law—A federal law that requires sex offenders to register with a federal database.

Mens rea—"The bad mind"—The psychological state that must accompany the *actus reus* of the offense.

Mental health courts—Problem-solving courts that are experts in handling offenders with mental health problems.

Minneapolis Domestic Violence Experiment—A study that investigated the impact of police discretion on domestic violence.

Miranda Warning—The rights that are read to individuals when they are arrested.

Misdemeanors—Relatively minor infractions, often punished by under one year of imprisonment.

Mistrial—A trial that is ended by the judge prematurely.

Mitigating evidence—Evidence presented to a jury that attempts to limit the perceived severity of the crime.

Mooching—The act of taking small-scale gifts offered by citizens to officers.

National Crime Victim Survey (NCVS)—A survey of crime that involves calling a random selection of homes and asking about crimes that they have experienced.

Net widening—In this context, the use of nonlethal force by officers in situations where they may not otherwise resort to force.

New Jersey v. T. L. O.—A Supreme Court decision that juveniles may be searched if officials have a reasonable belief that they are involved in illegal activity.

Nolo contendere—A plea where a defendant does not admit guilt but also does not contest the charges against her.

Open fields doctrine—The principle that officers do not need a warrant to search what is in an open field.

Paradigms—Underlying assumptions about the nature of reality that shape scientific theories.

Parens patriae ("the nation as parent")—The idea that the government may step in to take care of somebody whose family is unable or unwilling to take responsibility for her.

Parental liability laws—Laws that can make a parent civilly or criminally responsible for the misbehavior of their child.

Parole—The practice of allowing an offender to leave prison under supervision before serving her entire sentence.

Patriarchy—The feminist view of society that argues that social power is in the hands of men and serves male interests.

Peel Act—The British law that created the London Metropolitan Police in 1829.

Penitentiary—A model of prison that focuses on spiritual and personal rehabilitation.

Peremptory challenge—When one party at a trial objects to a potential juror without providing a reason.

Perjury—Knowingly giving a false statement while under oath; this is a crime.

Perpetrator Self-Report Studies—A means of measuring crime where individuals are (usually anonymously) asked about the crimes they have committed.

Phrenology—The (now debunked) theory that a person's personality and propensity for crime can be determined by studying the shape of her skull.

Plain view doctrine—The principle that officers do not need a warrant to search what is in plain view.

Plea bargain—An agreement that a defendant makes with the prosecutor to plead guilty to a lesser offense to avoid prosecution (and possible conviction) for a more serious charge.

Police corruption—The abuse of police authority for personal gain.

Police deviance—Misconduct or misbehavior on the part of officers while operating in their official capacity.

Postmodernism—A collection of social theories that question both conservative and leftist criminology theories and reject the idea that there is a right way to organize a society.

Presentence investigation report—An analysis of a convicted offender provided to the court by a probation officer that examines the background of the offender.

Pretextual stop—A practice where officers find an excuse, usually a minor infraction, to stop a driver so officers can look inside the individual's car or check to see if the driver is intoxicated or has outstanding warrants.

Prison-industrial complex—The historical collusion between politicians and private businesses to boost the prison population for financial and political gain.

Private prisons—Prisons not run by the government but by private corporations.

Pro bono—Legal work that is done without charge.

Probable cause—The standard of evidence needed to obtain a search warrant or search a car. Probable cause involves a reasonable belief based on evidence that a crime has occurred.

Probation—Allowing a convicted offender to avoid imprisonment and remain free under close supervision.

Probative value—The value of evidence that is relevant to proving the guilt or innocence of a defendant.

Professionalization—The movement in the early 20th century to make policing a more "serious" career. Involved education and training for officers.

Prosecutorial discretion—The authority that officers have to charge or not charge a person with a crime and to determine what the precise charges against a defendant will be.

Protective custody unit (PCU)—A section of a prison where offenders who need to be separated from other inmates are held.

Protective sweep—A search by the police in order to ensure their safety.

Psychoanalysis—The psychological theory that people are motivated by unconscious drives or desires.

Queer criminology—The field of criminology that examines crime and justice issues that impact lesbian, gay, transgendered, bisexual, and queer people.

Quid pro quo—Literally "this for that." The form of corruption where officers explicitly trade favors for goods or services.

Racial profiling—Targeting an individual for searches or arrests based on her race.

Racial threat theory—The theory that white Americans see African Americans as a threat to their power, wealth, and security, and as such must be controlled.

Rape shields—Laws that prevent defense lawyers from interrogating the sexual history of rape victims.

Rational egoism—The theory that individuals rationally seek to promote their own interests.

Reasonable expectation of privacy—Places where individuals have a right to be protected from police searches.

Reasonable suspicion—A lower standard of proof than probable cause. Requires a suspicion based on facts.

Reception center—A location where newly incarcerated offenders are processed.

Restorative justice—An approach to justice that seeks to heal the victim rather than punish the offender by bringing the offender and her victim together.

School-to-prison pipeline—The view schools prepare some students for a criminality through excessive rules, unfair treatment, and unnecessarily harsh discipline.

Separate and silent system—A model in which prisoners were not allowed to have contact with each other.

Shakedown—Threats from officers to arrest suspected lawbreakers unless they pay the officers a bribe.

Shopkeepers' privilege—A common law legal principle that allows store owners to detain individuals suspected of shoplifting.

Slave patrols—Organized groups of whites in the antebellum South whose primary job was to find and capture runaway slaves.

Slaves of the state—The legal status of prisoners until the 1960s.

Social control theory—An approach that seeks out the roots of law-abiding behavior, rather than the sources of criminal behavior.

Social disorganization theory—The belief that crime is often a result of a lack of certain social factors, such as stable families.

Sociobiology—The belief that much of our social behavior is determined by our biological makeup.

Special needs searches—Searches that can be conducted without probable cause or a warrant. Include border searches and airport security searches.

Stand-your-ground-laws—Laws that make it easier for individuals to use force in self-defense.

Stanford Prison Experiment—A psychological study conducted on college students that examined how the prison structure of guards and inmates affects human behavior.

Status offenses—Acts that would otherwise be legal except for the type of person who is committing them (examples: juveniles drinking while under age or being out past a curfew).

Strain theory—Criminological theory that believes that crime often results from the inability of people to realize socially prescribed goals by socially prescribed means.

Strict liability offenses—Crimes that do not require a *mens rea*.

Supermax—The highest security level of incarceration.

Suppress—A motion to prevent evidence from being entered during a trial.

Supremacy Clause—The section of the Constitution that makes the Constitution the supreme law of the land.

Terry stop—A brief detention where an officer stops and frisks a suspect. Requires a reasonable suspicion that an individual is involved in criminal activity.

Theory of the case—What both the prosecutor and the defense believe really happened in the case.

Therapeutic model—The approach of most juvenile justice institutions, emphasizing rehabilitating rather than punishing juvenile offenders.

Total institutions—Institutions like prisons, mental hospitals, and the military where virtually every aspect of an individual's life is controlled.

Transfer—When a juvenile case is tried in an adult court.

Transitional neighborhoods—Neighborhoods with a large number of immigrants.

Truth-in-sentencing laws—Laws that require offenders to serve their entire sentence rather than being released early.

Uniform Crime Report (UCR)—A federally run measure of crime based largely on police reports.

Use-of-force continuum—The rough guidelines that determine how much force an officer should use in dealing with a suspect.

Victim impact statement—Testimony from a victim provided at sentencing, where she explains the effect that the crime had on her.

Victimization surveys—A means of measuring crime by asking people whether they have been the victim of a crime.

Victim-offender mediation—The process of bringing a victim together with the person who harmed her in a supervised environment so that they can discuss the crime and its impact.

Voir dire—The process of selecting juries to serve during a trial.

Waiver—A document that certifies that an offender is to be tried as an adult.

War on drugs—The effort, begun in the 1970s, to treat illegal drugs primarily as an issue for law enforcement and not as a public health problem.

White collar crime—Crime that occurs in a professional context (example: stealing from your employer).

REFERENCES

A timeout on the death penalty. (2000, February 1). *The New York Times*. Retrieved from https://www.nytimes.com

Aaron, L., & Dallaire, D. H. (2010). Parental incarceration and multiple risk experiences: Effects on family dynamics and children's delinquency. *Journal of Youth and Adolescence, 39*(12), 1471–1484.

Abel, E. L. (2001). The gin epidemic: Much ado about what? *Alcohol and Alcoholism, 36*(5), 401–405.

Ackerman, K. (2011, November 9). Five myths about J. Edgar Hoover. *The Washington Post*. Retrieved from https://www.washingtonpost.com

Ackerman, S. (2014, August 20). US police given billions from Homeland Security for "tactical" equipment. *The Guardian*. Retrieved from https://www.theguardian.com

Ackermann, N., Goodman, M. S., Gilbert, K., Arroyo-Johnson, C., & Pagano, M. (2015). Race, law, and health: Examination of 'stand your ground' and defendant convictions in Florida. *Social Science & Medicine, 142*, 194–201.

ACLU. (n.d.). *Asset forfeiture abuse*. Retrieved March 2, 2019, from https://www.aclu.org/issues/criminal-law-reform/reforming-police-practices/asset-forfeiture-abuse

Ahmed, S., & Botelho, G. (2015, March 24). *Debra Milke, who spent 22 years on death row, has murder case tossed.* Retrieved from https://www.cnn.com/2015/03/24/justice/arizona-debra-milke-death-sentence/index.html

Alexander, M. (2012). *The new Jim Crow: Mass incarceration in the age of colorblindness.* New York: The New Press.

Alexander, M. (2012, March 10). Go to trial: Crash the justice system. *The New York Times*. Retrieved from https://www.nytimes.com

Allen, F. A. (1981). *The decline of the rehabilitative ideal: Penal policy and social purpose.* New Haven, CT: Yale University Press.

American Bar Association Division for Public Education. (n.d.). *The history of juvenile justice*. Retrieved from https://www.americanbar.org/content/dam/aba/migrated/publiced/features/DYJpart1.authcheckdam.pdf

American Civil Liberties Union. (2011). DNA testing and the death penalty. Retrieved from https://www.aclu.org/other/dna-testing-and-death-penalty

American Psychological Association. (2014). *Incarceration nation*. Retrieved from https://www.apa.org/monitor/2014/10/incarceration.aspx

American Society of Criminology. (1989). *Official policy position of the American Society of Criminology with respect to the death penalty*. Retrieved from https://www.asc41.com/policies/policyPositions.html

Amnesty International. (2004). *Excessive and lethal force? Amnesty International's concerns about deaths and ill-treatment involving police use of Tasers*. London, UK: Author.

Amnesty International. (2018). *Death sentences and executions: 2017*. Retrieved from https://www.amnesty.org/en/latest/news/2018/04/death-penalty-sentences-and-executions-2017/

Amnesty International. (n.d.). *Death penalty cost*. Retrieved from https://www.amnestyusa.org/issues/death-penalty/death-penalty-facts/death-penalty-cost/

Anderson, J. M., & Heaton, P. (2011). *How much difference does the lawyer make?* [Working paper]. RAND Corporation. Retrieved from https://www.rand.org/pubs/working_papers/WR870.html

Andrews, M. (2015, September 30). *Even in prison, health care often comes with a copay*. NPR. Retrieved from https://www.npr.org/sections/health-shots/2015/09/30/444451967/even-in-prison-health-care-often-comes-with-a-copay

Anwar, S., Bayer, P., & Hjalmarsson, R. (2012). The impact of jury race in criminal trials. *The Quarterly Journal of Economics, 127*(2), 1017–1055.

Anwar, S., Bayer, P., & Hjalmarsson, R. (2016). *A jury of her peers: The impact of the first female jurors on criminal convictions* [Working paper no. 21960]. Cambridge, MA: National Bureau of Economic Research.

Archbold, C., & Schulz, D. (2012). Research on women in policing: A look at the past, present and future. *Sociology Compass, 6*(9), 694–706.

Archer, J. (1994). Testosterone and aggression. *Journal of Offender Rehabilitation, 21*(3–4), 3–25.

Armacost, B. E. (2003). Organizational culture and police misconduct. *George Washington Law Review, 72*, 453–546.

Ashtan, S. (2014, June 17). Rand Paul tackles prisons "full of black and brown kids" amid GOP reach for minority votes. *Huffington Post.* Retrieved from https://www.huffingtonpost.com/2014/06/17/rand-paul-racist-drug-laws_n_5504062.html

Asquith, C. (2016, August 30). Recruiting more women could help solve many of the problems with American policing. *The Atlantic.* Retrieved from https://www.theatlantic.com/politics/archive/2017/07/sessions-forfeiture-justice-department-civil/534168/

Atkins v. Virginia, 536 U.S. 304 (2002).

Austin, J. (2003). *Findings in prison classification and risk assessment.* National Institute of Corrections. Retrieved from https://nicic.gov/findings-prison-classification-and-risk-assessment

Aviram, H. (2010). Humonetarianism: The new correctional discourse of scarcity. *Hastings Race & Poverty Law Journal, 7*(1), 1–52.

Bahr, S. J., Harris, L., Fisher, J. K., & Armstrong, A. H. (2010). Successful reentry: What differentiates successful and unsuccessful parolees? *International Journal of Offender Therapy and Comparative Criminology, 54*(5), 667–692.

Bairefoot v. City of Beaufort et al., Complaint (2017, October 12). Retrieved March 5, 2019, from https://www.aclu.org/cases/bairefoot-v-city-beaufort-et-al

Baker, E. (2002). Flying while Arab: Racial profiling and air travel security. Comment. *Journal of Air Law and Commerce, 67*, 1375–1406.

Balko, R. (2006, July 17). *Overkill: The rise of paramilitary police raids in America* [White paper]. Retrieved from the The Cato Institute website: https://www.cato.org/white-paper/overkill-rise-paramilitary-police-raids-america

Balko, R. (2012, December 11). Why are there no good data on police use of force? *Huffington Post.* Retrieved from https://www.huffingtonpost.com/radley-balko/why-is-there-no-good-data_b_2278013.html

Balko, R. (2013). *Rise of the warrior cop: The militarization of America's police forces.* New York: Public Affairs.

Banks, D., Hendrix, J., Hickman, M., & Kyckelhahn, T. (2016, October 4). *National sources of law enforcement employment data.* Washington, DC: Bureau of Justice Statistics. Retrieved from https://www.bjs.gov/content/pub/pdf/nsleed.pdf

Banks, R. R. (2003). Beyond profiling: Race, policing, and the drug war. *Stanford Law Review, 56*(3), 571–603.

Baron, R. A., & Bell, P. A. (1976). Aggression and heat: The influence of ambient temperature, negative affect, and a cooling drink on physical aggression. *Journal of Personality and Social Psychology, 33*(3), 245–255.

Barrish, C., & Horn, B. (2015, July 7). *Baylor security boss arrested for sex with female inmate.* Retrieved from https://www.delawareonline.com/story/news/local/2015/07/07/prison-security-boss-suspended-inmate-sex-probe/29817969/

Barstow, D. (1999, April 28). Police officers charged with taking bribes from brothel. *The New York Times.* Retrieved from https://www.nytimes.com

Batson v. Kentucky, 476 U.S. 79 (1986).

Bauer, S. (2014, March/April). How conservatives learned to love prison reform. *Mother Jones.* Retrieved from https://www.motherjones.com/politics/2014/02/conservatives-prison-reform-right-on-crime/

Bazelon, E. (2018, September 26). Will Florida's ex-felons finally regain the right to vote? *The New York Times.* Retrieved from https://www.nytimes.com

Beccaria, C. (1872). *An essay on crimes and punishments.* Albany, NY: W. C. Little. (Original work published 1764)

Beck, A., Berzofsky, M., Caspar, R., & Krebs, C. (2013). *Sexual victimization in prisons and jails reported by inmates, 2011–12.* Washington, DC: Bureau of Justice Statistics.

Becker, H. S. (1997). *Outsiders: Studies in the sociology of deviance.* New York: Free Press.

Beckett, K., Nyrop, K., & Pfingst, L. (2006). Race, drugs, and policing: Understanding disparities in drug delivery arrests. *Criminology, 44*(1), 105–137.

Belknap, J. (2014). *The invisible woman: Gender, crime, and justice* (4th ed.). Stamford, CT: Cengage Learning.

Bennett, J. (2006, November 21). "Flying while Muslim": Religious profiling? *Newsweek*. Retrieved from https://www.newsweek.com

Bentham, J. (1879). *The principles of morals and legislation*. Oxford, UK: Oxford at the Clarendon Press. (Original work published 1823)

Berman, M. (2016, May 13). Pfizer tightens restrictions to keep drugs from being used in executions. *The Washington Post*. Retrieved from https://www.washingtonpost.com

Bernstein, D., & Isackson, N. (2014, April 7). The truth about Chicago's crime rates. *Chicago Magazine*. Retrieved from https://www.chicagomag.com

Bertrand, M., & Mullainathan, S. (2004). Are Emily and Greg more employable than Lakisha and Jamal? A field experiment on labor market discrimination. *American Economic Review*, *94*(4), 991–1013.

Bigo, D. (2002). Security and immigration: Toward a Critique of the Governmentality of Unease. *Alternatives: Global, Local, Political*, *27*(1 suppl.), 63–92.

Binelli, M. (2015, March 26). Inside America's toughest federal prison. *The New York Times*. Retrieved from https://www.nytimes.com

Bjork-James, S. (2019, January 4). Many hate crimes never make it into the FBI's database. *The San Francisco Chronicle*. Retrieved from https://www.sfchronicle.com

Black, D. J. (1970). The social organization of arrest. *Stanford Law Review*, *23*, 1087.

Blackmon, D. (2009). *Slavery by another name: The re-enslavement of black Americans from the Civil War to World War II* (Reprint ed.). New York: Anchor.

Blakemore, E. (2015, March 13). "Most wanted": The long history of the FBI's top ten list. *Time*. Retrieved from http://time.com/3742696/history-fbi-top-ten-list/

Blalock, H. M. (1967). *Toward a theory of minority-group relations*. New York: John Wiley & Sons.

Bloch, M. (2018, February 22). When cops lie under oath, prosecutors must take some blame. *USA Today*. Retrieved from https://www.usatoday.com/story/opinion/policing/2018/02/22/when-cops-lie-under-oath-prosecutors-must-take-some-blame/360414002/

Boerner, D. (1994). Sentencing guidelines and prosecutorial discretion. *Judicature*, *78*, 196–201.

Bohman, D. (2018, January 8). *Some convictions against former judge Ciavarella vacated*. WNEP. Retrieved from https://wnep.com/2018/01/08/some-charges-against-former-judge-ciavarella-vacated/

Borkenhagen, C. (1975). The legal bias against rape victims (The rape of Mr. Smith). *American Bar Association Journal*, *61*, 464.

Bosman, J. (2015, July 4). Teenager's jailing brings a call to fix sex offender registries. *The New York Times*. Retrieved from https://www.nytimes.com

Bouie, J. (2014, August 13). The militarization of the police. *Slate*. Retrieved from https://slate.com/news-and-politics/2014/08/police-in-ferguson-military-weapons-threaten-protesters.html

Bowden, T. (1978). *Beyond the limits of the law: Comparative study of the police in crisis politics*. Harmondsworth, UK, and New York: Penguin Books.

Bowman, F. O. I. (2005). The failure of the federal sentencing system: A structural analysis. *Columbia Law Review*, *105*, 1315–1350.

Bradley, R., Schwartz, A. C., & Kaslow, N. J. (2005). Posttraumatic stress disorder symptoms among low-income, African American women with a history of intimate partner violence and suicidal behaviors: Self-esteem, social support, and religious coping. *Journal of Traumatic Stress*, *18*(6), 685–696.

Brady v. Maryland, 373 U.S. 83 (1963).

Brank, E., & Haby, J. (2011). Why not blame the parents? *Monitor on Psychology*, *42*(10), 28.

Bremner, R. H. (1971). *Children and youth in America: A documentary history* (Vol. 2: 1866–1932, Parts 7–8). Cambridge, MA: Harvard University Press.

Brennan Center for Justice. (2018, December 7). *Criminal disenfranchisement laws across the United States*. New York: Brennan Center for Justice.

Bright, S. B., & Keenan, P. J. (1995). Judges and the politics of death: Deciding between the Bill of Rights and the next election in capital cases. *Boston University Law Review*, *75*, 759.

Bureau of Justice Assistance. (1994). *Understanding community policing: A framework for action*. Washington, DC: Author.

Bureau of Justice Statistics. (2011). *Crime in the US, 1960–2004*. Retrieved from http://bjsdata.ojp.usdoj.gov/dataonline/Search/Crime/State/StateCrime.cfm

Bureau of Labor Statistics. (2016, August). *Injuries, illnesses, and fatalities*. Retrieved from https://www.bls.gov/iif/oshwc/cfoi/police-officers-2014-chart5-data.htm

Burns, B. J., Howell, J. C., Wiig, J. K., Augimeri, L. K., Welsh, B. C., Loeber, R. (2003, March). *Treatment, services, and intervention programs for child delinquents* [Child delinquency series]. Washington, DC: Office of Juvenile Justice and Delinquency Prevention, U.S. Department of Justice. Retrieved from https://www.ncjrs.gov/pdffiles1/ojjdp/193410.pdf

Bushman, B. (2014, January 19). It's time to kill the death penalty. *Psychology Today*. Retrieved from http://www.psychologytoday.com/blog/get-psyched/201401/it-s-time-kill-the-death-penalty

Butke, P., & Sheridan, S. (2010). An analysis of the relationship between weather and aggressive crime in Cleveland, Ohio. *Weather, Climate, and Society, 2*, 127–139.

Butler, P. (1995). Racially based jury nullification: Black power in the criminal justice system. *The Yale Law Journal, 105*(3), 677–725.

California v. Ciraolo, 476 U.S. 207 (1986).

Callahan, L. A., McGreevy, M. A., Cirincione, C., & Steadman, H. J. (1992). Measuring the effects of the guilty but mentally ill (GBMI) verdict: Georgia's 1982 GBMI reform. *Law and Human Behavior, 16*(4), 447–462.

Callahan, L. A., Steadman, H. J., McGreevy, M. A., & Robbins, P. C. (1991). The volume and characteristics of insanity defense pleas: An eight-state study. *The Bulletin of the American Academy of Psychiatry and the Law, 19*(4), 331–338.

Cannon, A. (2016). *Aiming at students: The college gun violence epidemic*. New York: Citizens Crime Commission of New York City.

Caollai, E. O. (2010, January 30). Man arrested in connection with €7.6m bank robbery in Dublin. *The Irish Times*. Retrieved from https://www.irishtimes.com

Cardona-Maguigad, A. (2015, April 10). *Puerto Rico exports its drug addicts to Chicago*. Retrieved from https://www.wbez.org/shows/wbez-news/puerto-rico-exports-its-drug-addicts-to-chicago/ee2c2bc5-8410-4dfa-b2fd-5a5f4aa119ee.

Caroll, L. (2014, August 3). *Rick Perry: "Historic record highs" of people from terrorist states being apprehended at border*. Retrieved from http://www.politifact.com/truth-o-meter/statements/2014/aug/03/rick-perry/rick-perry-historic-record-highs-people-terrorists/

Carroll v. United States, 267 U.S. 132 (1925).

Carson, E. A. (2014). *Prisoners in 2013* [No. NCJ 247282]. Washington, DC: Bureau of Justice Statistics.

Carson, E. A. (2015). *Prisoners in 2014*. Washington, DC: Bureau of Justice Statistics.

Carson, E. A. (2018). *Prisoners in 2016* [No. NCJ 251149]. Washington, DC: Bureau of Justice Statistics.

Causes of law enforcement deaths, 2008–2017. (2018, March 15). National Law Enforcement Officers Memorial Fund. Retrieved from https://nleomf.org/facts-figures/causes-of-law-enforcement-deaths

Cavett, J. (2017, December 6). What is a typical inmate day like in San Quentin? What's the schedule? *Huffington Post*. Retrieved from https://www.huffingtonpost.com/quora/what-is-a-typical-inmate_b_1315012.html

CBS News. (2017, November 15). *LAPD officer pulled from field after apparent drug planting caught on body cam*. Retrieved from https://www.cbsnews.com/news/lapd-officer-pulled-from-field-after-apparent-drug-planting-caught-on-body-cam/

Celona, L., Golding, B., & Cohen, S. (2014, December 30). Arrests plummet 66% with NYPD in virtual work stoppage. *The New York Post*. Retrieved from https://nypost.com

Chandler, R. (1946). *Red wind: A collection of short stories*. Cleveland, OH: World.

Chesney-Lind, M., & Pasko, L. (2013). *The female offender: Girls, women, and crime*. Thousand Oaks, CA: Sage.

Children's Bureau, U.S. Department of Health & Human Services. (2011). *Child maltreatment 2011* [Annual report]. Washington, DC: Author.

Childress, S. (2016, June 2). *The problem with "broken windows" policing*. Retrieved from https://www.pbs.org/wgbh/frontline/article/the-problem-with-broken-windows-policing/

Chimel v. California, 395 U.S. 752 (1969).

Cima, R. (2015, October 1). *DARE: The anti-drug program that never actually worked*. Retrieved from http://priceonomics.com/dare-the-anti-drug-program-that-never-actually/

Clark v. Arizona, 548 U.S. 735 (2006).

Clarke, J. G., & Simon, R. E. (2013). Shackling and separation: Motherhood in prison. *AMA Journal of Ethics, 15*(9), 779–785.

Cohen, A. O., & Casey, B. J. (2014). Rewiring juvenile justice: The intersection of developmental neuroscience and legal policy. *Trends in Cognitive Sciences, 18*(2), 63–65.

Coker v. Georgia, 433 U.S. 584 (1977).

Collins, P. H. (2008). *Black feminist thought: Knowledge, consciousness, and the politics of empowerment.* New York: Routledge.

Commonwealth of Virginia Department of Education. (2019). *Civics education: Federalism.* Retrieved from http://www.civiceducationva.org/federalism3.php

Cordner, G. (2014). Community Policing. In M. D. Reisig & R. J. Kane, Eds., *The Oxford Handbook of Police and Policing* (pp. 148–171). Oxford, UK: Oxford University Press.

Cordner, G. W. (2016). *Police administration* (9th ed.). London: Routledge.

Correll, J., Park, B., Judd, C. M., Wittenbrink, B., Sadler, M. S., & Keesee, T. (2007). Across the thin blue line: Police officers and racial bias in the decision to shoot. *Journal of Personality and Social Psychology, 92*(6), 1006–1023.

Couch, S. R. (1981). Selling and reclaiming state sovereignty: The case of coal and iron police. *Insurgent Sociologist, 11*(1), 85–91.

Countries with the largest number of prisoners per 100,000 of the national population, as of July 2018. (2019). Retrieved from https://www.statista.com/statistics/262962/countries-with-the-most-prisoners-per-100-000-inhabitants/

Cox, S. M., Allen, J. M., & Hanser, R. D. (2017). *Juvenile justice: A guide to theory, policy, and practice.* Thousand Oaks, CA: Sage.

Craven, J. (2015, June 2). Black cops aren't better for black communities just because they have the same skin color. *Huffington Post.* Retrieved from https://www.huffingtonpost.com/2015/06/02/community-policing_n_7486576.html

Crenshaw, K. (1991). Mapping the margins: Intersectionality, identity politics, and violence against women of color. *Stanford Law Review, 43*(6), 1241–1299.

Daly, K. (2005). Feminist thinking about crime and criminal justice. In S. Henry & M. Lanier (Eds.), *The essential criminology reader* (pp. 205–213). Boulder, CO: Westview Press.

Daly, K., & Stephens, D. (1995). The "dark figure" of criminology: Towards a Black and multi-ethnic feminist agenda for theory and research. In N. H. Rafter & F. Heidensohn (Eds.), *International feminist perspectives in criminology: Engendering a discipline* (pp. 189–215). Buckingham, UK, and Philadelphia, PA: Open University Press.

Davis v. Ayala, 576 U.S. ___ (2015).

Davis, A. J. (2005). The power and discretion of the American prosecutor. *Droit et Cultures. Revue Internationale Interdisciplinaire, 49,* 55–66.

Davis, J. H., & Shear, M. D. (2015, May 18). Obama puts focus on police success in struggling city in New Jersey. *The New York Times.* Retrieved from https://www.nytimes.com

de Tocqueville, A., & de Beaumont, G. (1833). *On the penitentiary system in the United States and its application in France* (F. Lieber, Trans.). Philadelphia, PA: Carey, Lea & Blanchard.

Death Penalty Information Center. (2007). *Death penalty in flux.* Retrieved from https://deathpenaltyinfo.org/death-penalty-flux

Death Penalty Information Center. (2013). *Time on death row.* Retrieved January 4, 2019, from https://deathpenaltyinfo.org/time-death-row

Death Penalty Information Center. (2018a). *Facts about the death penalty.* Retrieved from https://deathpenaltyinfo.org/documents/FactSheet.pdf

Death Penalty Information Center. (2018b, November 5). *Innocence: List of those freed from death row.* Retrieved from https://deathpenaltyinfo.org/innocence-list-those-freed-death-row

Death Penalty Information Center. (n.d.a). *The death penalty: An international perspective.* Retrieved March 10, 2019, from https://deathpenaltyinfo.org/death-penalty-international-perspective

Death Penalty Information Center. (n.d.b). *Supreme Court declares defendants have a right to jury determination of eligibility for death sentence.* Retrieved March 10, 2019, from http://www.deathpenaltyinfo.org/us-supreme-court-ring-v-arizona

Deffains, B., & Demougin, D. (2008). The inquisitorial and the adversarial procedure in a criminal court setting. *Journal of Institutional and Theoretical Economics (JITE) / Zeitschrift für die Gesamte Staatswissenschaft, 164*(1), 31–43.

DeKalb Co. crime stats questioned in federal audit. (2014, October 30). *The Covington News.* Retrieved from https://www.covnews.com.

DeLisi, M. (2015). Age–crime curve and criminal career patterns. In J. Morizot & L. Kazemian (Eds.), *The development of criminal and antisocial behavior* (pp. 51–63). Berlin, Germany: Springer.

Department of Homeland Security. (2017, December 21). *Departments of Justice and Homeland Security release data on incarcerated aliens—94 percent of all confirmed aliens in DOJ custody are unlawfully present* [Press release]. Retrieved from https://www.dhs.gov/news/2017/12/21/departments-homeland-security-and-justice-release-data-incarcerated-aliens-94

Dern, H., Dern, C., Horn, A., & Horn, U. (2009). The fire behind the smoke: A reply to Snook and colleagues. *Criminal Justice and Behavior, 36*(10), 1085–1090.

DeRosier, J. (2017, March 30). Is New Jersey's new bail reform system actually working? *The Press of Atlantic City.* Retrieved from https://www.pressofatlanticcity.com

Devers, L. (2011). *Plea and charge bargaining.* Bureau of Justice Assistance.

Dickens, C. (2009). *American notes: For general circulation.* Auckland, NZ: The Floating Press. (Original work published 1842)

Dijk, J., Van Kesteren, J., & Smit, P. (2007). *Criminal victimisation in international perspective. Key findings from the 2004–2005 ICVS and EU ICS.* The Hague, Netherlands: Boom Juridische Uitgevers.

Dionne, E. J. (2012, April 15). Why the NRA pushes "Stand Your Ground." *The Washington Post.* Retrieved from https://www.washingtonpost.com/pb/opinions/why-the-nra-pushesstand-your-ground/2012/04/15/gIQAL458JT_story.html

Dollar, C. B. (2014). Racial threat theory: Assessing the evidence, requesting redesign. *Journal of Criminology, 2014,* e983026.

Donohue, J., & Wolfers, J. (2006). *Uses and abuses of empirical evidence in the death penalty debate. Stanford Law Review 58,* 791–846.

Doris J., & Glaze, L. (2006). *Mental health problems of prison and jail inmates.* Washington, DC: Bureau of Justice Statistics.

Drake, B. (2015, April 28). *Divide between blacks and whites on police runs deep.* Retrieved from http://www.pewresearch.org/fact-tank/2015/04/28/blacks-whites-police/

Dressler, J., & Garvey, S. (2015). *Cases and materials on criminal law* (7th ed.). St. Paul, MN: West Academic.

Drum, K. (2016, February 11). Lead: America's real criminal element. *Mother Jones.* Retrieved from https://www.motherjones.com

Durkheim, É. (1973). *The division of labor in society.* New York: Free Press. (Original work published 1893)

Durkheim, É. (1997). *Suicide.* New York: Free Press. (Original work published 1897)

Durkheim, É., & Halls, W. D. (1997). *The division of labor in society.* New York: Simon & Schuster.

Durose, M., Cooper, A., & Snyder, H. (2005). *Recidivism of prisoners released in 30 states in 2005: Patterns from 2005 to 2010.* Washington, DC: Bureau of Justice Statistics.

Eckholm, E. (2016, May 13). Pfizer blocks the use of its drugs in executions. *The New York Times.* Retrieved from https://nytimes.com

Edwards v. Arizona, 451 U.S. 477 (1981).

Eisenstein, J., & Jacob, H. (1977). *Felony justice: An organizational analysis of criminal courts.* Boston: Little, Brown.

Eith, C., & Durose, M. R. (2011, October). *Contacts between police and the public, 2008.* Washington, DC: Bureau of Justice Statistics. Retrieved from https://www.bjs.gov/content/pub/pdf/cpp08.pdf

Ekins, E. (2016, December 7). *Policing in America: Understanding public attitudes toward the police* [Survey report]. Retrieved from the Cato Institute website: https://www.cato.org/survey-reports/policing-america

Equal Justice Initiative. (2018, August 8). *Private prison population skyrockets.* Retrieved from https://eji.org/news/private-prison-population-skyrockets

Evidence of rape ignored [Editorial]. (2013, January 20). *The New York Times.* Retrieved from https://www.nytimes.com

Fagan, J., Geller, A., Davies, G., & West, V. (2010). Street stops and broken windows revisited. In S. K. Rice & M. D. White (Eds.), *Race, ethnicity, and policing: New and essential readings* (pp. 309–348). New York: NYU Press.

Farrell, G., Tilley, N., & Tseloni, A. (2014). Why the crime drop? *Crime and Justice, 43*(1), 421–490.

Farrington, D. P., & Murray, J. (2013). *Labeling theory: Empirical tests.* London: Routledge.

Feder, J. (2012). *Racial profiling: Legal and constitutional issues.* Washington, DC: Congressional Research Service.

Federal Bureau of Investigation (FBI). (2017). *Arrests by race and ethnicity, 2016 (UCR).* Retrieved from https://ucr.fbi.gov/crime-in-the-u.s/2016/crime-in-the-u.s.-2016/tables/table-21

Federal Bureau of Prisons. (2018). *Inmate race*. Retrieved from https://www.bop.gov/about/statistics/statistics_inmate_race.jsp)

Federal Bureau of Prisons. (2018, April 30). Annual determination of average cost of incarceration. *Federal Register*. Retrieved from https://www.federalregister.gov/documents/2016/07/19/2016-17040/annual-determination-of-average-cost-of-incarceration

Ferraro, K. J., & Moe, A. M. (2003). Mothering, crime, and incarceration. *Journal of Contemporary Ethnography*, *32*(1), 9–40.

Finckenauer, J. O. (1988). Public support for the death penalty: Retribution as just deserts or retribution as revenge? *Justice Quarterly*, *5*, 81–100.

Finneran, C., & Stephenson, R. (2013). Gay and Bisexual men's perceptions of police helpfulness in response to male-male intimate partner violence. *Western Journal of Emergency Medicine*, *14*(4), 354–362.

Fins, D. (2018). *Death row U.S.A.* Baltimore, MD: NAACP Legal Defense and Educational Fund. Retrieved from https://deathpenaltyinfo.org/documents/DRUSASummer2018.pdf

Fischer-Baum, R. (2014, November 25). Allegations of police misconduct rarely result in charges. *FiveThirtyEight*. Retrieved from https://fivethirtyeight.com/features/allegations-of-police-misconduct-rarely-result-in-charges/

Flannery, M. E. (2017, November 14). *Follow the money: The school-to-(privatized)-prison pipeline*. Retrieved from http://neatoday.org/2017/11/14/school-to-privatized-prison-pipeline/

Ford, M. (2017, July 19). The bipartisan opposition to Sessions's new civil-forfeiture rules. *The Atlantic*. Retrieved from https://www.theatlantic.com/politics/archive/2017/07/sessions-forfeiture-justice-department-civil/534168/

Fortin, J. (2018, January 25). Baltimore police officer charged with fabricating evidence in drug case. *The New York Times*. Retrieved from https://www.nytimes.com

Foucault, M. (1995). *Discipline & punish: The birth of the prison* (2nd ed.) (A. Sheridan, Trans.). New York: Vintage Books.

Foucault, M., & Sheridan, A. (1995). *Discipline & punish: The birth of the prison*. New York: Random House.

Franklin, T. W. (2013). Sentencing Native Americans in US federal courts: An examination of disparity. *Justice Quarterly*, *30*(2), 310–339.

Frazee, G. (2018, June 25). *What constitutional rights do undocumented immigrants have?* PBS.org. Retrieved from https://www.pbs.org/newshour/politics/what-constitutional-rights-do-undocumented-immigrants-have

Frederick, B., & Stemen, D. (2012). *The anatomy of discretion: An analysis of prosecutorial decision making* [Technical report]. National Institute of Justice. Retrieved from https://www.ncjrs.gov/pdffiles1/nij/grants/240334.pdf

Fredrickson, D. D., & Siljander, R. P. (2002). *Racial profiling: Eliminating the confusion between racial and criminal profiling and clarifying what constitutes unfair discrimination and persecution*. Springfield, IL: Charles C Thomas.

Friedersdorf, C. (2015, May 12). The injustice of civil-asset forfeiture. *The Atlantic*. Retrieved from https://www.theatlantic.com/politics/archive/2015/05/the-glaring-injustice-of-civil-asset-forfeiture/392999/

Friedman, M. (2016, March 29). *Just facts: The probation nation*. Brennan Center for Justice. Retrieved from https://www.brennancenter.org/blog/probation-nation

Fukurai, H. (1998). *Is O. J. Simpson verdict an example of jury nullification? Jury verdicts, legal concepts, and jury performance in a racially sensitive criminal case* [SSRN scholarly paper no. 2584168]. Rochester, NY: Social Science Research Network.

Furman v. Georgia, 408 U.S. 238 (1972).

Gallup. (2017). *Death penalty*. Retrieved from http://news.gallup.com/poll/1606/Death-Penalty.aspx

Garner, B. A. (Ed.). (2004). *Black's law dictionary* (8th ed.). St. Paul, MN: Thomson West.

Garner, B. A. (2009). *Black's law dictionary, standard ninth edition*. Eagen, MN: West.

Gideon v. Wainwright, 372 U.S. 335 (1963).

Gill, L. (2018, January 30). The Trump administration is pumping up private prison campaign donors, leaked memo shows. *Newsweek*. Retrieved from https://www.newsweek.com/trump-private-prison-campaign-donors-leaked-memo-795681

Gladwell, M. (2007, November 12). Dangerous minds: Criminal profiling made easy. *The New Yorker*. Retrieved from https://www.newyorker.com

Glaze, L., & Maruschak, L. (2008). *Parents in prison and their minor children* [Special report no. NCJ 222984]. Washington, DC: Bureau of Justice Statistics.

Glaze, L., & Maruschak, L. (2008). *Parents in prison and their minor children*. Washington, DC: Bureau of Justice Statistics.

Goff, P. (2014, March 6). *Black boys viewed as older, less innocent than whites, research finds*. Retrieved from https://www.apa.org/news/press/releases/2014/03/black-boys-older

Goffman, E. (1959). *The presentation of self in everyday life*. New York: Anchor.

Goffman, E. (1961). *Asylums: Essays on the social situation of mental patients and other inmates*. New York: Anchor Books/Doubleday.

Goldsmith, A. J. (2010). Policing's new visibility. *The British Journal of Criminology, 50*(5), 914–934.

Goldstein, D. (2014, November 24). *10 (not entirely crazy) theories explaining the great crime decline*. Retrieved from The Marshall Project website: https://www.themarshallproject.org/2014/11/24/10-not-entirely-crazy-theories-explaining-the-great-crime-decline

Goldstein, J. (2018, November 20). Teenager claims body cams show the police framed him. What do you see? *The New York Times*. Retrieved from http://www.nytimes.com

Goldstein, J. (2018, March 18). "Testilying" by police: A stubborn problem. *The New York Times*. Retrieved from https://www.nytimes.com/2018/03/18/nyregion/testilying-police-perjury-new-york.html

Graham v. Florida, 560 U.S. 48 (2010).

Grant, R. (2017, March 16). *Abortion behind bars: What it's like to terminate a pregnancy in prison*. Retrieved from https://news.vice.com/en_us/article/3kp9b5/abortion-behind-bars-terminating-a-pregnancy-in-prison-can-be-next-to-impossible

Greenfeld, L., & Snell, T. (1999). *Women offenders* [Special report no. NCJ 175688]. Washington, DC: Bureau of Justice Statistics.

Greenwood, P. (1979). *The Rand criminal investigation study: Its findings and impacts to date*. Santa Monica, CA: The Rand Corporation.

Gregg v. Georgia, 428 U.S. 153 (1976).

Gross, S. R., O'Brien, B., Hu, C., & Kennedy, E. H. (2014). Rate of false conviction of criminal defendants who are sentenced to death. *Proceedings of the National Academy of Sciences, 111*(20), 7230–7235.

Grossman, A. (2014, August 26). FBI agents say rivals encroach on their turf. *Wall Street Journal*. Retrieved from https://www.wsj.com

Grundetjern, H. (2018). Negotiating motherhood: Variations of maternal identities among women in the illegal drug economy. *Gender & Society, 32*(3), 395–416.

Guynn, J. (2015, March 4). Meet the woman who coined #BlackLivesMatter. *USA Today*. Retrieved from https://www.usatoday.com/story/tech/2015/03/04/alicia-garza-black-lives-matter/24341593/

Hager, E. (2017, December 15). *A mass incarceration mystery*. Retrieved from The Marshall Project website: https://www.themarshallproject.org/2017/12/15/a-mass-incarceration-mystery

Hale, M. (1847). *Historia placitorum coronae: The history of the pleas of the crown* (Vol. 1). Philadelphia, PA: Robert H. Small. (Original work published 1736)

Hall, D. E. (2008). *Criminal law and procedure* (5th ed.). Clifton Park, NY: Cengage.

Haney, C. (1984). On the selection of capital juries: The biasing effects of the death-qualification process. *Law and Human Behavior, 8*(1–2), 121–132.

Haney, C. (2002). *The psychological impact of incarceration: Implications for post-prison adjustment*. Urban Institute. Retrieved from http://webarchive.urban.org/publications/410624.html

Hans, V., & Slater, D. (1983). *John Hinckley, Jr. and the insanity defense: The public's verdict*. Ithaca, NY: Cornell Law Faculty Publications.

Hari, J. (2015, January 17). The hunting of Billie Holiday. *Politico*. Retrieved from https://www.politico.com/magazine/story/2015/01/drug-war-the-hunting-of-billie-holiday-114298

Harrell, E., Langton, L., Berzofsky, M., Couzens, L., & Smiley-McDonald, H. (2014). *Household poverty and nonfatal violent victimization, 2008–2012* (p. 18). Washington, DC: Bureau of Justice Statistics.

Harris, A. (2018, April 30). Women in prison take home economics, while men take carpentry. *The Atlantic*. Retrieved from https://www.theatlantic.com/education/archive/2018/04/the-continuing-disparity-in-womens-prison-education/559274/

Hartley, R. D., Miller, H. V., & Spohn, C. (2010). Do you get what you pay for? Type of counsel and its effect on criminal court outcomes. *Journal of Criminal Justice, 38*(5), 1063–1070.

Hauser, C. (2018, November 28). Florida police chief gets 3 years for plot to frame black people for crimes. *The New York Times.* Retrieved from https://www.nytimes.com/2018/11/28/us/florida-police-chief-frame-black-people.html

Hayes, A. (2010, June 10). Executioner: Death by firing squad is "100 percent justice." Retrieved from http://www.cnn.com/2010/CRIME/06/09/utah.firing.squad/index.html

Herberman, E., & Bonczar, T. (2013). *Probation and parole in the United States, 2013.* Washington, DC: Bureau of Justice Statistics.

Hermann, W. (2011, January 26). Phoenix's crime stats audited by Feds after claim. *The Arizona Republic.* Retrieved from https://www.azcentral.com/community/phoenix/articles/2011/01/26/20110126phoenix-crime-stats-federal-audit.html

Hewstone, M., Rubin, M., & Willis, H. (2002). Intergroup bias. *Annual Review of Psychology, 53*(1), 575–604.

Hirschfield, P. (2009). School surveillance in America: Disparate and unequal. In T. Monahan & R. Torres (Eds.), *Schools under surveillance: Cultures of control in public education* (pp. 38–54). Piscataway, NJ: Rutgers University Press.

Hirschi, T. (2001). *Causes of delinquency.* New Brunswick, NJ: Routledge. (Original work published 1969)

Hirschi, T., & Stark, R. (1969). Hellfire and delinquency. *Social Problems, 17*(2), 202–213.

Hoffman, M. B., Rubin, P. H., & Shepherd, J. M. (2005). An empirical study of public defender effectiveness: Self-selection by the marginally indigent commentaries. *Ohio State Journal of Criminal Law, 3*, 223–256.

Holt v. Hobbs, 574 U.S. ___ (2015).

Hood, R., Shute, S., Feilzer, M., & Wilcox, A. (2002). Sex offenders emerging from long-term imprisonment: A study of their long-term reconviction rates and of parole board members' judgements of their risk. *The British Journal of Criminology, 42*(2), 371–394.

Hopper, J. (2018, April 3). Freezing during sexual assault and harassment. *Psychology Today.* Retrieved from https://www.psychologytoday.com/blog/sexual-assault-and-the-brain/201804/freezing-during-sexual-assault-and-harassment

Hudson, J. R. (1971). Police review boards and police accountability. *Law and Contemporary Problems, 36*(4), 515–538.

Human Rights Watch. (2007, September 11). *No easy answers: Sex offender laws in the U.S.* Retrieved from https://www.hrw.org/report/2007/09/11/no-easy-answers/sex-offender-laws-us

Human Rights Watch. (2014). *Profiting from probation: America's "offender-funded" probation industry.* Retrieved from https://www.hrw.org/report/2014/02/05/profiting-probation/americas-offender-funded-probation-industry

Hunter, A. D. (1985). Private, parochial and public social orders: The problem of crime and incivility in urban communities. In G. D. Suttles & M. N. Zald (Eds.), *The challenge of social control: Institution building and systemic constraint* (pp. 230–242). Santa Barbara, CA: Praeger.

Ibarra, R. (2018, July 9). *New Jersey's bail reform law gets court victory.* WNYC. Retrieved from https://www.wnyc.org/story/new-jerseys-bail-reform-law-gets-court-victory/

iyarah. (2007, December 11). *The complete Joe Horn 9-11 call* [Video file]. Retrieved from https://www.youtube.com/watch?v=LLtKCC7z0yc

Ignatieff, M. (1979). Police and people: The birth of Mr. Peel's blue locusts. *New Society, 49*(30), 443–445.

Illinois v. Caballes, 543 U.S. 405 (2005).

In re Gault, 387 U.S. 1 (1967).

Ingraham, C. (2015, June 30). Drug cops took a college kid's savings and now 13 police departments want a cut. *The Washington Post.* Retrieved from https://www.washingtonpost.com/blogs/wonkblog/wp/2015/06/30/drug-cops-took-a-college-kids-life-savings-and-now-13-police-departments-want-a-cut/

International Association of Chiefs of Police. (2001). *Police use of force in America.* Alexandria, VA: Author.

J. E. B. v. Alabama, 511 U.S. 127 (1993).

Jacob, B., Lefgren, L., & Moretti, E. (2007). The dynamics of criminal behavior evidence from weather shocks. *Journal of Human Resources, 42*(3), 489–527.

Jacobs, B. (2017, July 19). Gary girl, 15, charged as adult in mother's February death. *The Chicago Tribune.* Retrieved from https://www.chicagotribune.com

Jalonick, M. C. (2015, October 19). Obama administration backs bill to reduce prison time. *The New York Times.* Retrieved from https://www.nytimes.com

James, M. (2003, August 6). *Prison is "living hell" for pedophiles.* Retrieved from https://abcnews.go.com/U.S./prison-living-hell-pedophiles/story?id=90004

Janda, K., Berry, J., & Goldman, J. (2008). *The challenge of democracy* (9th ed.). Boston: Houghton-Mifflin.

Jannetta, J., Breaux, J., Ho, H., & Porter, J. (2014). *Examining racial and ethnic disparities in probation revocation: Summary findings and implications from a multisite study.* Washington, DC: The Urban Institute.

Janoski, D. (2011, February 23). Father of suicidal man in kids-for-cash case: "I basically framed him." *The Times-Tribune.* Retrieved from https://www.citizensvoice.com/news/father-of-suicidal-man-in-kids-for-cash-case-i-basically-framed-him-1.1109065

Jay-Z. (2017, November 17). The criminal justice system stalks black people like Meek Mill. *The New York Times.* Retrieved from https://www.nytimes.com/2017/11/17/opinion/jay-z-meek-mill-probation.html

Johnson v. United States, 576 U.S. ___ (2015).

Johnson, B. R., Larson, D. B., & Pitts, T. C. (1997). Religious programs, institutional adjustment, and recidivism among former inmates in prison fellowship programs. *Justice Quarterly, 14*(1), 145–166.

Johnson, K. (2012, March 8). Private purchasing of prisons locks in occupancy rates. *USA Today.* Retrieved from https://usatoday30.usatoday.com/news/nation/story/2012-03-01/buying-prisons-require-high-occupancy/53402894/1?AID=4992781

Johnson, R. A. (1975). The prison birth of black power. *Journal of Black Studies, 5*(4), 395–414.

Juvenile Justice, Geography, Policy, Practice & Statistics. (n.d.). *Jurisdictional boundaries.* Retrieved January 7, 2019, from http://www.jjgps.org/jurisdictional-boundaries#delinquency-age-boundaries

Kaeble, D. (2018). *Probation and parole in the United States, 2016* [No. NCJ 251148]. Retrieved from https://www.bjs.gov/content/pub/pdf/ppus16.pdf

Kaeble, D., & Cowhig, M. (2018). *Correctional populations in the United States* [NCJ 251211]. Retrieved from https://www.bjs.gov/content/pub/pdf/cpus16.pdf

Kalinich, D. B., & Stojkovic, S. (1985). Contraband: The basis for legitimate power in a prison social system. *Criminal Justice and Behavior, 12*(4), 435–451.

Kansal, T., & Mauer, M. (2005). *Racial disparity in sentencing: A review of the literature.* Washington, DC: The Sentencing Project.

Kean, A. W. G. (1937). The history of the criminal liability of children. *Law Quarterly Review, 53,* 364–370.

Kearney, M. S., Harris, B. H., Jácome, E., & Parker, L. (2014). *Ten economic facts about crime and incarceration in the United States.* Washington, DC: The Hamilton Project.

Keedy, E. (1949). History of the Pennsylvania statute creating degrees of murder. *University of Pennsylvania Law Review, 97*(6), 759–777.

Keeler v. Superior Court, 470 P. 2d 617, Supreme Court (1970).

Kelling, G. L., & Coles, C. M. (1998). *Fixing broken windows: Restoring order and reducing crime in our communities.* New York: Free Press.

Kennedy v. Louisiana, 554 U.S. 407 (2008).

Kerbs, J. J., & Jolley, J. M. (2007). Inmate-on-inmate victimization among older male prisoners. *Crime & Delinquency, 53*(2), 187–218.

Khazan, O. (2015, April 7). Most prisoners are mentally ill. *The Atlantic.* Retrieved from https://www.theatlantic.com/health/archive/2015/04/more-than-half-of-prisoners-are-mentally-ill/389682/

Kibbe v. Henderson, 534 F. 2d 493, 2nd Circuit (1976).

Kindy, K., & Kelly, K. (2015, April 11). Thousands dead, few prosecuted. *The Washington Post.* Retrieved from https://www.washingtonpost.com/sf/investigative/2015/04/11/thousands-dead-few-prosecuted/?utm_term=.e00b1f12fc3a.

Klebold, S. (2011, November). I will never know why. *Oprah Magazine.* Retrieved from http://www.oprah.com/omagazine/susan-klebolds-o-magazine-essay-i-will-never-know-why

Klockars, C. B. (1980). The Dirty Harry problem. *The Annals of the American Academy of Political and Social Science, 452*(1), 33–47.

Knafo, S. (2013, September 9). California prison guards union pushes for prison expansion. *Huffington Post.* Retrieved from https://www.huffingtonpost.com/2013/09/09/california-prison-guards_n_3894490.html

Knowles, J., Persico, N., & Todd, P. (1999). *Racial bias in motor vehicle searches: Theory and evidence* [Working paper no. 7449]. Cambridge, MA: National Bureau of Economic Research. Retrieved from http://www.nber.org/papers/w7449

Kochel, T. R., Wilson, D. B., & Mastrofski, S. D. (2011). Effect of suspect race on officers' arrest decisions. *Criminology, 49*(2), 473–512.

Kornhauser, R. (2015). Economic individualism and punitive attitudes: A cross-national analysis. *Punishment & Society, 17*(1), 27–53.

Koss, M. P., Wilgus, J. K., & Williamsen, K. M. (2014). Campus sexual misconduct: Restorative justice approaches to enhance compliance with Title IX guidance. *Trauma, Violence, & Abuse, 15*(3), 242–257.

Kubrin, C. E., & Weitzer, R. (2003). New directions in social disorganization theory. *Journal of Research in Crime and Delinquency, 40*(4), 374–402.

Kuhn, T. S. (1996). *The structure of scientific revolutions* (3rd ed.). Chicago, IL: University of Chicago Press.

Kupchik, A. (2012). *Homeroom security: School discipline in an age of fear* (Reprint ed.). New York: NYU Press.

Kupchik, A., & Ellis, N. (2008). School discipline and security: Fair for all students? *Youth & Society, 39*(4), 549–574.

Kupfer, T. (2018, February 2). Law-enforcement unions have too much power. *National Review.* Retrieved from https://www.nationalreview.com/2018/02/law-enforcement-unions-powerful-obstacle-criminal-justice-reform-fiscal-responsibility/.

Kyllo v. United States, 533 U.S. 27 (2001).

Latimer, J., Dowden, C., & Muise, D. (2005). The effectiveness of restorative justice practices: A meta-analysis. *The Prison Journal, 85*(2), 127–144.

Lee, M. (2007). *Inventing fear of crime: Criminology and the politics of anxiety.* Cullompton, UK, and Portland, OR: Willan.

Lee, T. (2011, October 13). Stephen Anderson, Ex NYPD cop: We planted evidence, framed innocent people to reach quotas. *Huffington Post.* Retrieved from https://www.huffingtonpost.com/2011/10/13/ex-nypd-cop-we-planted-ev_n_1009754.html

Legaspi, A. (2017, July 12). Attorney General Jeff Sessions wants to revive D.A.R.E. *Rolling Stone.* Retrieved from https://www.rollingstone.com/culture/culture-news/attorney-general-jeff-sessions-wants-to-revive-d-a-r-e-program-205620/

Leger, K. (1997). Public perceptions of female police officers on patrol. *American Journal of Criminal Justice, 21*(2), 231–249.

Lehmann, P. S., Chiricos, T., & Bales, W. D. (2017). Sentencing transferred juveniles in the adult criminal court: The direct and interactive effects of race and ethnicity. *Youth Violence and Juvenile Justice, 15*(2), 172–190.

Lemert, E. M. (1951). *Social pathology: A systematic approach to the theory of sociopathic behavior.* Whitefish, MT: Literary Licensing.

Levitt, S., & Dubner, S. (2009). *Freakonomics: A rogue economist explores the hidden side of everything.* New York: William Morrow.

Liebler, C. M. (2010). Me(di)a culpa? The "missing white woman syndrome" and media self-critique. *Communication, Culture & Critique, 3*(4), 549–565.

Lindsey, E. (1925). Historical sketch of the indeterminate sentence and parole system. *Journal of Criminal Law and Criminology, 16*(1), 9–69.

Liptak, A. (2007, June 24). Prosecutor becomes prosecuted. *The New York Times.* Retrieved from https://www.nytimes.com

Liptak, A. (2007, December 4). Serving life for providing car to killers. *The New York Times.* Retrieved from https://www.nytimes.com

Lisak, D., Gardinier, L., Nicksa, S. C., & Cote, A. M. (2010). False allegations of sexual assault: An analysis of ten years of reported cases. *Violence Against Women, 16*(12), 1318–1334.

Loeber, R., Farrington, D. P., & Petechuk, D. (2003, May). *Child delinquency: Early intervention and prevention* [Child delinquency series]. Washington, DC: Office of Juvenile Justice and Delinquency Prevention, U.S. Department of Justice. Retrieved from https://www.ncjrs.gov/pdffiles1/ojjdp/186162.pdf

Lonsway, K. A., Paynich, R., & Hall, J. N. (2013). Sexual harassment in law enforcement: Incidence, impact, and perception. *Police Quarterly, 16*(2), 177–210.

Lopez, G. (2017, April 4). *When a drug epidemic's victims are white.* Retrieved from https://www.vox.com/identities/2017/4/4/15098746/opioid-heroin-epidemic-race

Love, D. A. (2012, January 3). The racial bias of the US death penalty. *The Guardian.* Retrieved from https://www.theguardian.com/commentisfree/cifamerica/2012/jan/03/racial-bias-us-death-penalty

Lundman, R. J. (1980). *Police and policing: An introduction.* New York: Holt McDougal.

Lymburner, J., & Roesch, R. (1999). The insanity defense: Five years of research (1993–1997) (Vol. 22). *International Journal of Law and Psychiatry, 22*(3–4), 213–240.

Macartney, S., & Bishaw, K. (2013). *Poverty rates for selected detailed race and Hispanic groups by state and place:*

2007–2011. Washington, DC: U.S. Department of Commerce, Economics and Statistics Administration, U.S. Census Bureau.

Magagnini, S. (1988, March 28). Closing death row would save state $90 million a year. *The Sacramento Bee,* p. 1.

Mainprize, S. (1992). Electronic monitoring in corrections: Assessing cost effectiveness and the potential for widening the net of social control. *Canadian Journal of Criminology, 34,* 161–180.

Makalani, M. (2016, October 15). The many costs of campus carry. *The New Yorker.* Retrieved from https://www.newyorker.com

Marijuana arrests by the numbers. (n.d.). Retrieved July 24, 2017, from https://www.aclu.org/gallery/marijuana-arrests-numbers

Marlow, D., DeMatteo, D., & Festinger, D. (2003). A sober assessment of drug courts. *Federal Sentencing Reporter, 16*(2), 153–157.

Marquart, J. W., Barnhill, M. B., & Balshaw-Biddle, K. (2001). Fatal attraction: An analysis of employee boundary violations in a southern prison system, 1995–1998. *Justice Quarterly, 18*(4), 877–910.

Marx, K., Engels, F., & Tucker, R. (1978). *The Marx-Engels reader.* New York: W. W. Norton.

Mastrofski, S. D., Ritti, R. R., & Hoffmaster, D. (1987). Organizational determinants of police discretion: The case of drinking-driving. *Journal of Criminal Justice, 15*(5), 387–402.

Masucci, M., & Langton, L. (2017). *Hate crime victimization, 2004–2015.* Washington, DC: Bureau of Justice Statistics.

McCarthy, J. (2016, August 8). One in eight U.S. adults say they smoke marijuana. *Gallup News.* Retrieved from https://news.gallup.com/poll/194195/adults-say-smoke-marijuana.aspx

McCarthy, N. (2016, March 31). America's most prestigious professions in 2016 [Infographic]. *Forbes.* Retrieved from https://www.forbes.com/sites/niallmccarthy/2016/03/31/americas-most-prestigious-professions-in-2016-infographic/

McClellan, D. S. (1994). Disparity in the discipline of male and female inmates in Texas prisons. *Women & Criminal Justice, 5*(2), 71–97.

McDonald, M. (2008). Securitization and the construction of security. *European Journal of International Relations, 14*(4), 563–587.

McLaughlin, M., Pettus-Davis, C., Brown, D., Veeh, C., & Renn, T. (2016). *The economic burden of incarceration in the U.S.* [Working paper #CI072016]. St. Louis, MO: Concordance Institute for Advancing Social Justice. Retrieved from https://joinnia.com/wp-content/uploads/2017/02/The-Economic-Burden-of-Incarceration-in-the-US-2016.pdf

Meade, B., & Steiner, B. (2010). The total effects of boot camps that house juveniles: A systematic review of the evidence. *Journal of Criminal Justice, 38*(5), 841–853.

Meehan, A. J., & Ponder, M. C. (2002). Race and place: The ecology of racial profiling African American motorists. *Justice Quarterly, 19*(3), 399–430.

Meixler, E. (2017, October 13). Pope Francis condemns death penalty as "inhumane." *Time.* Retrieved from http://time.com/4980984/pope-francis-death-penalty-catholic-church/

Mellor, C. (2011, June 8). Civil forfeiture laws and the continued assault on private property. *Forbes.* Retrieved from https://www.forbes.com/2011/06/08/property-civil-forfeiture.html#7a74d42d39fa

Merton, R. (1938). Social structure and anomie. *American Sociological Review, 3,* 672–682.

Mihm, S. (2017, August 7). Civil forfeiture came from a strange place. *Bloomberg Opinion.* Retrieved from https://www.bloomberg.com/view/articles/2017-08-07/civil-asset-forfeiture-history-in-the-united-states

Miller v. Alabama, 567 U.S. 460 (2012).

Miller, A. R., & Segal, C. (2016). *Do female officers improve law enforcement quality? Effects on crime reporting and domestic violence* [SSRN scholarly paper no. 2335990]. Rochester, NY: Social Science Research Network.

Miller, E. J. (2004). Embracing addiction: Drug courts and the false promise of judicial interventionism. *Ohio State Law Journal, 65,* 1479–1576.

Minnesota Department of Corrections. (2003). *Level three sex offenders residential placement issues—2003 legislative report.* St. Paul, MN: Author.

Miranda v. Arizona, 384 U.S. 436 (1966).

Mitchell, K. (2017, March 2). Class action suit: Immigrants held in Aurora required to work for $1 a day, threatened with solitary if refused. *The Denver Post*. Retrieved from https://www.denverpost.com/2017/03/02/class-action-ice-detention-aurora-immigration/

Mitchell, O. (2005). A meta-analysis of race and sentencing research: Explaining the inconsistencies. *Journal of Quantitative Criminology, 21*(4), 439–466.

Moore, D. (1999, December 10). Public divided over blaming parents for their children's crimes. *Gallup News Service*. Retrieved from https://news.gallup.com/poll/3418/public-divided-over-blaming-parents-their-childrens-crimes.aspx

Morgan, R., & Kena, G. (2018). *Criminal victimization, 2016: Revised* [No. NCJ 252121]. Washington, DC: Bureau of Justice Statistics.

Morgan, R. E., & Truman, J. L. (2018). *Criminal victimization, 2017*. Washington, DC: Bureau of Justice Statistics. Retrieved from https://www.bjs.gov/content/pub/pdf/cv17.pdf

Morin, R., & Stepler, R. (2016, September 29). *The racial confidence gap in police performance*. Washington, DC: Pew Research Center. Retrieved from http://www.pewsocialtrends.org/2016/09/29/the-racial-confidence-gap-in-police-performance/

Morin, R., Stepler, R., & Mercer, A. (2017). *Behind the badge*. Washington, DC: Pew Research Center.

Morris, W. A. (1910). *The frankpledge system*. New York: Longmans, Green.

Mueller, B. (2017, December 22). New York Police Dept. agrees to curb stop-and-frisk tactics. *The New York Times*. Retrieved from https://www.nytimes.com

Mustaine, E. E., & Tewksbury, R. (2011). Residential relegation of registered sex offenders. *American Journal of Criminal Justice, 36*(1), 44–57.

National Association for Law Placement. (2010, September). *New findings on salaries for public interest attorneys*. Retrieved from https://www.nalp.org/sept2010pubintsal

National Association of Women Judges. (2018). *Statistics*. Retrieved January 5, 2019, from https://www.nawj.org/statistics

National Association of Women Judges. (2018). *US state court women judges*. Retrieved from https://www.nawj.org/statistics/2018-us-state-court-women-judges

National Commission on Law Observance and Enforcement. (1931). *Report on the enforcement of the prohibition laws of the United States*. Washington, DC: U.S. Department of Justice.

National Council on Crime and Delinquency. (2007). *And justice for some: Differential treatment of youth of color in the justice system*. Madison, WI: Author. Retrieved from https://www.nccdglobal.org/sites/default/files/publication_pdf/justice-for-some.pdf

National Institute of Justice. (2009, August 4). *The use-of-force continuum*. Retrieved from http://www.nij.gov/topics/law-enforcement/officer-safety/use-of-force/Pages/continuum.aspx

National Research Council. (2014). *The growth of incarceration in the United States: Exploring causes and consequences*. Washington, DC: The National Academies Press.

Nellis, A. (2012). *The lives of juvenile lifers: Findings from a national survey*. Washington, DC: The Sentencing Project.

Nellis, A. (2016). *The color of justice: Racial and ethnic disparity in state prison*. Washington, DC: The Sentencing Project.

Nelson, C. (2018, January 4). *Grand juries, explained*. Minneapolis Public Radio. Retrieved from https://www.mprnews.org/story/2018/01/24/grand-jury-explain

Nelson, S. (2015, October 8). "I executed 62 people. I'm sorry": An executioner turned death-penalty opponent tells all. *Salon*. Retrieved from https://www.salon.com/2015/10/08/i_executed_62_people_im_sorry_an_executioner_turned_death_penalty_opponent_tells_all/

New Jersey v. T. L. O., 469 U.S. 325 (1985).

New York City Civilian Complaint Review Board. (2014). *Annual report*. Retrieved from http://www.nyc.gov/html/ccrb/downloads/pdf/Annual%20Report%202014-Rev2Final.pdf

Ney, B., Ramirez, R., & Van Dieten, M. (2012). *Ten truths that matter when working with justice involved women*. Washington, DC: National Resource Center on Justice Involved Women.

Norman, J. (2017, July 10). Confidence in police back at historical average. *Gallup*. Retrieved from https://news.gallup.com/poll/213869/confidence-police-back-historical-average.aspx

NPR/Robert Wood Johnson Foundation/Harvard T. H. Chan School of Public Health. (2017). *Discrimination in America: Experiences and views of African Americans*. Retrieved from https://www.npr.org/assets/img/2017/10/23/discriminationpoll-african-americans.pdf

Office of Juvenile Justice and Delinquency Prevention. (2018, October 22). *Statistical briefing book*. Retrieved from https://www.ojjdp.gov/ojstatbb/crime/JAR_Display.asp?ID=qa05200

Oliver, W. M. (2006). The fourth era of policing: Homeland security. *International Review of Law, Computers & Technology, 20*(1–2), 49–62.

O'Neill, A., & McLaughlin, E. (2015, May 5). *Cousin: Dzhokhar Tsarnaev cried during "The Lion King."* Retrieved from https://www.cnn.com/2015/05/04/us/boston-bombing-tsarnaev-sentencing/index.html

Order and opinion denying defendants' motion to dismiss. (2018, May 16). Retrieved from ACLU website: https://www.aclu.org/legal-document/order-and-opinion-denying-defendants-motion-dismiss

Oxfam International. (2015, January 8). *Richest 1% will own more than all the rest by 2016.* Retrieved from http://www.oxfamamerica.org/press/richest-1-will-own-more-than-all-the-rest-by-2016/

Pan, D. (2013, April 29). Timeline: Deinstitutionalization and its consequences. *Mother Jones.* Retrieved from https://www.motherjones.com/politics/2013/04/timeline-mental-health-america

Panfil, V. R. (2018). Young and unafraid: Queer criminology's unbounded potential. *Palgrave Communications, 4*(1), 110.

Papachristou v. City of Jacksonville, 405 U.S. 156 (1972).

Parks, B. (2000). *Board of inquiry into the rampart area corruption incident.* Los Angeles, CA: Los Angeles Police Department.

Paternoster, R., & Iovanni, L. (1989). The labeling perspective and delinquency: An elaboration of the theory and an assessment of the evidence criminological theory. *Justice Quarterly, 6,* 359–394.

Pattillo, M. E. (1998). Sweet mothers and gangbangers: Managing crime in a black middle-class neighborhood. *Social Forces, 76*(3), 747–774.

Pennsylvania Council of Chief Juvenile Probation Officers. (2012). *A family guide to Pennsylvania's juvenile justice system.* West Chester, PA: Author.

People v. Anderson, Supreme Court of California, 28 Cal. 4th (1965).

Perez, E. (2013, August 30). *No federal challenge to pot legalization in 2 states.* Retrieved from http://www.cnn.com/2013/08/29/politics/holder-marijuana-laws/index.html

Pew Center on the States. (2011). *State of recidivism: The revolving door of America's prisons.* Washington, DC: Author.

Pew Research Center. (2015, February 18). Does hard work lead to success? Retrieved from http://www.pewresearch.org/fact-tank/2015/02/19/are-americans-ready-for-obamas-middle-class-populism/2-18-2015-5-22-10-pm/

Pew Research Center. (2016). *On views of race and inequality, blacks and whites are worlds apart.* Retrieved from http://www.pewsocialtrends.org/2016/06/27/1-demographic-trends-and-economic-well-being/

Pew Research Center. (2018, January 31). *Public perception of crime rate at odds with reality.* Retrieved from http://www.pewresearch.org/fact-tank/2016/11/16/voters-perceptions-of-crime-continue-to-conflict-with-reality/ft_16-11-16_crime_trend-2/

Pfaff, J. (2017, May 14). The never-ending "Willie Horton effect" is keeping prisons too full for America's good. *Los Angeles Times.* Retrieved from https://www.latimes.com/opinion/op-ed/la-oe-pfaff-why-prison-reform-isnt-working-20170514-story.html

Pfaff, J. F. (2012). *The micro and macro causes of prison growth* [SSRN scholarly paper no. 2181062]. Rochester, NY: Social Science Research Network.

Pickett, J. T. (2017). Blame their mothers: Public opinion about maternal employment as a cause of juvenile delinquency. *Feminist Criminology, 12*(4), 361–383.

Pierson, A., Price, K., & Coleman, S. (2014). Prison labor. *Politics, Bureaucracy, and Justice, 4*(1), 12–23.

Platt, A. M. (1977). *The child savers: The invention of delinquency.* Chicago: University of Chicago Press.

Podkopacz, M. R., & Feld, B. C. (2001). The back-door to prison: Waiver reform, "blended sentencing," and the law of unintended consequences. *The Journal of Criminal Law and Criminology, 91*(4), 997.

Police. (n.d.). *Oxford English Dictionary.* Oxford, UK: Oxford University Press.

The Police Policy Studies Council. (n.d.). *Policy model: Police & procedures for police use of force.* Retrieved from http://www.theppsc.org/Archives/Police-Policy/Force_policy_model.htm

Pollock, J. M. (2002). *Women, prison, and crime.* Boston, MA: Wadsworth Thomson Learning.

Possley, M. (2015, September 2). *Henry McCollum.* National Registry of Exonerations. Retrieved from https://www.law.umich.edu/special/exoneration/Pages/casedetail.aspx?caseid=4492

Potter, G. (2013). *The history of policing in the United States*. Eastern Kentucky University Police Studies Online. Retrieved from https://plsonline.eku.edu/insidelook/history-policing-united-states-part-1.

Preece, R. (2015, March 17). *Former prisoners share their experiences of sex in prison*. Retrieved from https://howardleague.org/news/prisonersexperiencesofsexinprison/

Press, A. (2014, May 6). Chinese human rights lawyer detained before Tiananmen anniversary. *The Guardian*. Retrieved from https://www.theguardian.com

Private prisons. (n.d.). Retrieved from the American Civil Liberties Union website: https://www.aclu.org/issues/mass-incarceration/privatization-criminal-justice/private-prisons

Prosecutor or politician? (2010, January 13). *The Economist*. Retrieved from https://www.economist.com/democracy-in-america/2010/01/13/prosecutor-or-politician.

Punch, M. (1985). *Conduct unbecoming: The social construction of police deviance and control*. London, UK, and New York, NY: Tavistock.

Puzzanchera, C., & Hockenberry, S. (2018). *Characteristics of delinquency cases handled in juvenile court in 2015*. Washington, DC: Office of Juvenile Justice and Delinquency Prevention. Retrieved from https://www.ojjdp.gov/ojstatbb/snapshots/DataSnapshot_JCS2015.pdf

Rape charges dropped in Duke lacrosse case. (2006, December 23). ESPN.com. Retrieved from http://sports.espn.go.com/ncaa/news/story?id=2706267

Rape, Abuse & Incest National Network. (n.d.). *Victims of sexual violence: Statistics*. Retrieved March 12, 2019, from https://www.rainn.org/statistics/victims-sexual-violence

Rattan, A., Levine, C. S., Dweck, C. S., & Eberhardt, J. L. (2012). Race and the fragility of the legal distinction between juveniles and adults. *PLOS ONE*, 7(5).

Reaves, B. (2015). *Local police departments, 2013: Personnel, policies, and practices*. Washington, DC: Bureau of Justice Statistics.

Rehavi, M. M., & Starr, S. B. (2012). *Racial disparity in federal criminal charging and its sentencing consequences* (SSRN scholarly paper 1985377). Rochester, NY: Social Science Research Network.

Reichel, P. L. (1988). Southern slave patrols as a transitional police type. *American Journal of Police*, 7, 51–78.

Reitz, K. R. (2005). Structure: The enforceability of sentencing guidelines. *Stanford Law Review*, 58, 155–174.

Rennison, C. M., & Dodge, M. (2017). *Introduction to criminal justice* (2nd ed.). Thousand Oaks, CA: Sage.

Report: Duke lacrosse players charged before. (2006, March 31). Retrieved from http://sports.espn.go.com/ncaa/news/story?id=2387151

Resnick, B. (2018, June 13). Stanford Prison Experiment: Why famous psychology studies are now being torn apart. *Vox*. Retrieved from https://www.vox.com/2018/6/13/17449118/stanford-prison-experiment-fraud-psychology-replication

Reyes, J. R. (2018). *Immigration detention: Recent trends and scholarship*. New York: Center for Migration Studies. Retrieved from https://cmsny.org/publications/virtualbrief-detention/

Riley v. California, 573 U.S. ___ (2014).

Roberts, D. E. (1998). Race, vagueness, and the social meaning of order-maintenance policing. *Journal of Criminal Law and Criminology*, 89, 775–836.

Robinson, M. (2016, January 4). The united nations of London: Map reveals the areas where 50% of residents are born abroad as capital's population hits record 8.6 million. *The Daily Mail*. Retrieved from https://www.dailymail.co.uk/news/article-2950401/How-one-three-Londoners-born-abroad-areas-live-in.html.

Rodriguez v. United States, 575 U.S. ___ (2015).

Romer, D., Jamieson, K. H., & Aday, S. (2003). Television news and the cultivation of fear of crime. *Journal of Communication*, 53(1), 88–104.

Roper v. Simmons, 543 U.S. 551 (2005).

Rosenmerkel, S., Durose, M., & Farole, D., Jr. (2009). *Felony sentences in state courts, 2006*. Washington, DC: Bureau of Justice Statistics.

Rosenthal, B. M. (2017, July 29). Police criticize Trump for urging officers not to be "too nice" with suspects. *The New York Times*. Retrieved from https://www.nytimes.com

Rosich, K., & Kane, K. (2005). Truth in sentencing and state sentencing practices. *National Institute of Justice*, 252.

Rosoff, S., & Pontell, H. N. (n.d.). *Encyclopedia Britannica*. Retrieved March 3, 2019, from http://www.britannica.com/topic/Mollen-Commission

Rousseau, J.-J. (1992). *Discourse on the origin of inequality* (D. Cress, Trans.). Indianapolis, IN: Hackett. (Original work published 1755)

Rubenstein, J. M. (2016). *Contemporary human geography* (3rd ed.). Hoboken, NJ: Pearson.

Ruffin v. Commonwealth, 62 Va. 790 (1871).

Sallah, M., O'Harrow, R., Jr., Rich, S., & Silverman, G. (2014, September 6). Aggressive police take hundreds of millions of dollars from motorists not charged with crimes. *The Washington Post*. Retrieved from https://www.washingtonpost.com

Samant, A. (2018, December 27). *The First Step Act is a small step for incarcerated women*. ACLU. Retrieved from https://www.aclu.org/blog/prisoners-rights/women-prison/first-step-act-small-step-incarcerated-women

Savelsberg, J. J. (1992). Law that does not fit society: Sentencing guidelines as a neoclassical reaction to the dilemmas of substantivized law. *American Journal of Sociology*, 97(5), 1346–1381.

Sawyer, W. (2018, January 9). *The gender divide: Tracking women's state prison growth*. Retrieved from the Prison Policy Initiative website: https://www.prisonpolicy.org/reports/women_overtime.html

Sawyer, W., & Clark, A. (2017, July 13). *New data: The rise of the "prosecutor politician."* Prison Policy Initiative. Retrieved from https://www.prisonpolicy.org/blog/2017/07/13/prosecutors/

Schafer, J. A., & Mastrofski, S. D. (2005). Police leniency in traffic enforcement encounters: Exploratory findings from observations and interviews. *Journal of Criminal Justice*, 33(3), 225–238.

Schaufeli, W. B., & Peeters, M. C. W. (2000). Job stress and burnout among correctional officers: A literature review. *International Journal of Stress Management*, 7(1), 19–48.

Schwartz, S. S. (2008). Is there a common law necessity defense in federal criminal law? Comment. *University of Chicago Law Review*, 75, 1259–1294.

Schwartzapfel, B. (2016, January 27). *There are practically no juveniles in federal prison—Here's why*. Retrieved from The Marshall Project website: https://www.themarshallproject.org/2016/01/27/there-are-practically-no-juveniles-in-federal-prison-here-s-why

The Sentencing Project. (2013, August). *Report of The Sentencing Project to the United Nations Human Rights Committee regarding racial disparities in the United States criminal justice system*. Washington, DC: Author.

The Sentencing Project. (2014, July). *Fewer prisoners, less crime: A tale of three states*. Washington, DC: Author.

The Sentencing Project. (2017). *Black disparities in youth incarceration*. Retrieved from https://www.sentencingproject.org/publications/black-disparities-youth-incarceration/

Sethi, C. (2014, August 12). *Three maps of laws that put people on the sex offender list for ridiculous reasons*. Retrieved from https://slate.com/news-and-politics/2014/08/mapped-sex-offender-registry-laws-on-statutory-rape-public-urination-and-prostitution.html

Sexton, J. (1998, January 11). Ideas & trends: Don't shoot; the culture of cops and guns. *The New York Times*. Retrieved from https://www.nytimes.com

Shapiro, J. (2018, October 15). *In prison, discipline comes down hardest on women*. NPR. Retrieved from https://www.npr.org/2018/10/15/647874342/in-prison-discipline-comes-down-hardest-on-women

Sherman, L. W., Strang, H., Angel, C., Woods, D., Barnes, G. C., Bennett, S., & Inkpen, N. (2005). Effects of face-to-face restorative justice on victims of crime in four randomized, controlled trials. *Journal of Experimental Criminology*, 1(3), 367–395.

Sherman, L., & Berk, R. (1984). *The Minneapolis domestic violence experiment*. Washington, DC: Police Foundation.

Siennick, S. E., Stewart, E. A., & Staff, J. (2014). Explaining the association between incarceration and divorce. *Criminology*, 52(3), 371–398.

Simon, J. (2007). *Governing through crime: How the war on crime transformed American democracy and created a culture of fear*. New York: Oxford University Press.

Simon, J. (2009). *Governing through crime: How the war on crime transformed American democracy and created a culture of fear*. Oxford, UK: Oxford University Press.

Sinozich, S., & Langton, L. (2014). *Rape and sexual assault victimization among college-age females, 1995–2013*. Washington, DC: Bureau of Justice Statistics.

Sir Robert Peel's nine principles of policing. (2017, December 20). *The New York Times*. Retrieved from https://www.nytimes.com

Skarbek, D. (2012). Prison gangs, norms, and organizations. *Journal of Economic Behavior & Organization*, 82(1), 96–109.

Skarbek, D. (2014). *The social order of the underworld: How prison gangs govern the American penal system*. Oxford, UK: Oxford University Press.

Sklansky, D. (1994). Cocaine, race, and equal protection. *Stanford Law Review, 47*, 1283–1322.

Skogan, W. G. (1995). Crime and the racial fears of white Americans. *The Annals of the American Academy of Political and Social Science, 539*, 59–71.

Smith, E., & Cooper, A. (2013). *Homicide in the U.S. known to law enforcement, 2011*. Washington, DC: Bureau of Justice Statistics.

Smith, P. S. (2006). The effects of solitary confinement on prison inmates: A brief history and review of the literature. *Crime and Justice, 34*(1), 441–528.

Smith, T., Davern, M., Freese, J., & Hout, M. (2018, August). *General Social Surveys, 1972–2016*. Chicago: National Opinion Research Center.

SmithKline Beecham (SKB) v. Abbott Laboratories, No. 11-17357 (9th Cir. 2014).

Snead, J. (2014, March 26). *Civil asset forfeiture: 7 things you should know* [Courts report]. Washington, DC: Retrieved from The Heritage Foundation website: https://www.heritage.org/research/reports/2014/03/civil-asset-forfeiture-7-things-you-should-know

Snook, B., Eastwood, J., Gendreau, P., Goggin, C., & Cullen, R. M. (2007). Taking stock of criminal profiling: A narrative review and meta-analysis. *Criminal Justice and Behavior, 34*(4), 437–453.

Soss, J., Langbein, L., & Metelko, A. R. (2003). Why do white Americans support the death penalty? *The Journal of Politics, 65*(2), 397–421.

Southern Baptist Convention. (2000). *Resolution on capital punishment*. Retrieved from http://www.sbc.net/resolutions/299

Spillar, K. (2015, July 2). How more female police officers would help stop police brutality. *The Washington Post*. Retrieved from https://www.washingtonpost.com

Spohn, C., Piper, R. K., Martin, T., & Frenzel, E. D. (2001). Drug courts and recidivism: The results of an evaluation using two comparison groups and multiple indicators of recidivism. *Journal of Drug Issues, 31*(1), 149–176.

Starr, S. B., & Rehavi M. M. (2014). Racial disparity in federal criminal charging and its sentencing consequences. *Journal of Political Economy, 122*(6), 1320–1354.

State of Oregon Youth Authority. (n.d.). *How Oregon's juvenile justice system works*. Retrieved from https://www.oregon.gov/oya/docs/juv_justice_system.ppsx

Stebbins, S., Comen, E., & Stockdale, S. (2018, January 9). Workplace fatalities: 25 most dangerous jobs in America. *USA Today*. Retrieved from https://www.usatoday.com/story/money/careers/2018/01/09/workplace-fatalities-25-most-dangerous-jobs-america/1002500001

Steinberg, L., & Monahan, K. C. (2007). Age differences in resistance to peer influence. *Developmental Psychology, 43*(6), 1531–1543.

Steptoe, G., & Goldet, A. (2016, January 27). *Why some young sex offenders are held indefinitely*. Retrieved from The Marshall Project website: https://www.themarshallproject.org/2016/01/27/why-some-young-sex-offenders-are-held-indefinitely

Stock, S., Carrol, J., Nious, K., & Pham, S. (2014, April 28). *State law hides police from scrutiny*. Retrieved from http://www.nbcbayarea.com/investigations/State-Law-Hides-Investigations-of-Police-Misconduct-from-Public-Scrutiny-257080571.html

Stoll, M. A., & Bushway, S. D. (2008). The effect of criminal background checks on hiring ex-offenders. *Criminology & Public Policy, 7*(3), 371–404.

Struckman-Johnson, C., & Struckman-Johnson, D. (2006). A comparison of sexual coercion experiences reported by men and women in prison. *Journal of Interpersonal Violence. 21*(12), 1591–1615.

Summer, N. (2008, January 15). *Powerless in prison: Sexual abuse against incarcerated women*. Just Detention. Retrieved from https://justdetention.org/powerless-in-prison-sexual-abuse-against-incarcerated-women/

Surowiecki, J. (2016, December 5). Trump sets private prisons free. *The New Yorker*. Retrieved from https://www.newyorker.com/magazine/2016/12/05/trump-sets-private-prisons-free

Sutherland, E. H. (1983). *White collar crime*. Westport, CT: Praeger.

Sutherland, E. H., Cressey, D. R., & Luckenbill, D. F. (1992). *Principles of criminology*. Lanham, MD: Rowman & Littlefield.

Swarns, R. L. (2015, July 5). A tough beat for a detective: Recruiting black police officers. *The New York Times*. Retrieved from https://www.nytimes.com

Swavola, E., Riley, K., & Subramanian, R. (2016). *Overlooked: Women and jails in an era of reform*. New York: Vera Institute of Justice.

Sweet, E. L. (2016). Carceral feminism: Linking the state, intersectional bodies, and the dichotomy of place. *Dialogues in Human Geography, 6*(2), 202–205.

Sykes, G., & Messinger, S. (1960). The inmate social system. In R. Cloward, D. Cressey, G. Grosser, R. McCleery, L. Ohlin, G. Sykes, & S. Messenger (Eds.), *Theoretical studies in social organization of the prison* (pp. 5–19). Brooklyn, NY: Social Science Research Council.

Tennessee v. Garner, 471 U.S. 1 (1985).

Terry v. Ohio, 392 U.S. 1 (1968).

Tewksbury, R. (2005). Collateral consequences of sex offender registration. *Journal of Contemporary Criminal Justice, 21*(1), 67–81.

Theriot, M. T. (2009). School resource officers and the criminalization of student behavior. *Journal of Criminal Justice, 37*(3), 280–287.

Thomas, C. W. (1977). Prisonization and its consequences: An examination of socialization in a coercive setting. *Sociological Focus, 10*(1), 53–68.

Timbs v. Indiana, 586 U.S. ___ (2019).

Travis, J., Western, B., & Redburn, S. (2014) *The growth of incarceration in the United States: Exploring causes and consequences*. Retrieved from https://www.nap.edu/read/18613/chapter/1

Tyler, T. R. (2005). Policing in black and white: Ethnic group differences in trust and confidence in the police. *Police Quarterly, 8*(3), 322–342.

Umbreit, M. S., Bradshaw, W., & Coates, R. B. (1999). Victims of severe violence meet the offender: Restorative justice through dialogue. *International Review of Victimology, 6*(4), 321–343.

Understanding guilty pleas. (n.d.). Retrieved March 3, 2019, from https://www.albany.edu/understanding-guilty-pleas/

Uniform Crime Reporting Statistics. (n.d.). Retrieved January 15, 2019, from https://www.ucrdatatool.gov/Search/Crime/State/RunCrimeStatebyState.cfm

United States v. Gementera, 379 F.3d 596 (2004).

Unnever, J. D., & Cullen, F. T. (2007). The racial divide in support for the death penalty: Does white racism matter? *Social Forces, 85*(3), 1281–1301.

Unnever, J., Cullen, F. T., & Jonson, C. (2008). Race, racism, and support for capital punishment. *Crime and Justice, 37*, 45–96. doi:10.1086/519823

Urbina, I. (2009, March 27). Despite red flags, judges ran kickback scheme for years. *The New York Times*. Retrieved from https://www.nytimes.com

U.S. Census Bureau. (2018). *QuickFacts: United States*. Retrieved from https://www.census.gov/quickfacts/fact/table/US/PST045218

U.S. Census Bureau. (n.d.). *QuickFacts: United States*. Retrieved from https://www.census.gov/quickfacts/fact/table/US/PST045217

U.S. Department of Justice. (2017). *Offences cleared (Crime in the United States, 2016)*. Washington, DC: Author.

U.S. Immigration and Customs Enforcement. (2018). *Fiscal year 2018 ICE Enforcement and Removal Operations report*. Retrieved from https://www.ice.gov/doclib/about/offices/ero/pdf/eroFY2018Report.pdf

Van Caenegem, W. (1999). Advantages and disadvantages of the adversarial system in criminal proceedings. *Law Faculty Publications*, Paper 224.

van den Haag, E. (1984). The death penalty once more. *U.C. Davis Law Review, 18*, 957–972.

Vera Institute of Justice. (2013). *The potential of community corrections to improve safety and reduce incarceration*. New York: Vera Institute of Justice.

Vieraitis, L. M., & Williams, M. R. (2002). Assessing the impact of gender inequality on female homicide victimization across U.S. cities: A racially disaggregated analysis. *Violence Against Women, 8*(1), 35–63.

Villavicencio, M. (2007, July 19). *A history of dogfighting*. NPR. Retrieved from https://www.npr.org/templates/story/story.php?storyId=12108421

Wagner, J. (2018, December 18). Senate overwhelmingly backs overhaul of criminal justice system. *The Washington Post*. Retrieved from https://www.washingtonpost.com/politics/senate-overwhelmingly-backs-overhaul-of-criminal-justice-system/2018/12/18/89efffb6-02e7-11e9-9122-82e98f91ee6f_story.html?noredirect=on

Wald, J., & Losen, D. J. (2003). Defining and redirecting a school-to-prison pipeline. *New Directions for Youth Development, 2003*(99), 9–15.

Ward, R. (2015). *A global history of execution and the criminal corpse*. Berlin, Germany: Springer.

Weiner, E. (2008, March 11). *The long, colorful history of the Mann Act*. NPR. Retrieved from http://www.npr.org/templates/story/story.php?storyId=88104308

Weiser, B. (2012, April 19). Case against jury-nullification advocate Heicklen dismissed. *The New York Times*. Retrieved from https://www.nytimes.com/2012/04/20/nyregion/indictment-against-julian-heicklen-jury-nullification-advocate-is-dismissed.html

West, D. (2000). Paedophilia: Plague or panic? *The Journal of Forensic Psychiatry*, *11*(3), 511–531.

Williams, L. S. (1984). The classic rape: When do victims report? *Social Problems*, *31*(4), 459–467.

Williams, T. (2017, October 12). Courts sidestep the law, and South Carolina's poor go to jail. *The New York Times*. Retrieved from https://www.nytimes.com/2017/10/12/us/south-carolina-jail-no-lawyer.html

Willie McGee and the traveling electric chair. (2017, August 17). Retrieved from http://www.radiodiaries.org/willie-mcgee-and-the-traveling-electric-chair/

Wolff v. McDonnell, 418 U.S. 539 (1974).

Wolf-Harlow, C. (2000). *Defense counsel in criminal cases*. Washington, DC: Bureau of Justice Statistics.

Woods, E., & Poor, N. (Producers). (2017, September 13). Episode 7: Unwritten. *Ear hustle*. Retrieved from https://www.earhustlesq.com/episodes/2017/9/13/unwritten

Yakas, B. (2011, February 17). Brooklyn's 77th precinct probed for crime stat manipulation. *Gothamist*. Retrieved from http://gothamist.com

Zaitzow, B. (2003). "Doing gender" in a women's prison. In B. Zaitzow & J. Thomas (Eds.), *Women in prison: Gender and social control* (pp. 21–38). Boulder, CO: Lynne Rienner.

Zaitzow, B. H., & Thomas, J. (2003). *Women in prison: Gender and social control*. Boulder, CO: Lynne Rienner.

Zamichow, N. (1998, July 19). The fractured life of Jeremy Strohmeyer. *Los Angeles Times*. Retrieved from https://www.latimes.com/archives/la-xpm-1998-jul-19-mn-5552-story.html

Zgoba, K., Witt, P., Dalessandro, M., & Veysey, B. (2008). *Megan's Law: Assessing the practical and monetary efficacy*. Trenton, NJ: New Jersey Department of Corrections. Retrieved from https://www.ncjrs.gov/pdffiles1/nij/grants/225370.pdf

INDEX

CPSIA information can be obtained
at www.ICGtesting.com
Printed in the USA
BVHW012202190922
647475BV00009B/234